Spanish Phrasebook
and Dictionary

Dictionary Compiled by
The Editors of Biblograf, S.A.

North American Edition Prepared by
the Editors of McGraw-Hill

McGraw·Hill

New York   Chicago   San Francisco   Lisbon   London   Madrid   Mexico City
Milan   New Delhi   San Juan   Seoul   Singapore   Sydney   Toronto

Library of Congress Cataloging-in-Publication Data

Vox Spanish phrasebook and dictionary / dictionary compiled by the editors of
Biblograf, S.A.—North American ed. / prepared by the editors of McGraw-Hill.
        p.   cm.
    ISBN 0-07-140025-7
    1. Spanish language—Dictionaries—English.   2. English
language—Dictionaries—Spanish.   3. Spanish language—Conversation
and phrase books—English.   I. Biblograf, S.A.   II. McGraw-Hill
Companies.

PC4640 .V6975   2002
463'.21—dc21   2002075339

Cover photo copyright © Neil Gilchrist/Panoramic Images, Chicago

  2 3 4 5 6 7 8 9 0   LBM/LBM   1 0 9 8 7 6 5 4 3

ISBN 0-07-140025-7

This book is printed on acid-free paper.

CONTENTS

HOW TO USE THIS BOOK

The *Vox Spanish Phrasebook and Dictionary* is designed to provide language assistance for all your travel needs.

The **Phrasebook** section presents in convenient thematic sections the Spanish words and phrases required for most typical travel situations, from arrival to shopping, from sightseeing to emergencies. Each expression and phrase in Spanish is followed by an easy-to-read transliteration. Italics indicate the syllable to be stressed in each word. On occasion, alternative expressions are provided in parentheses to reflect regional differences in Spanish. Try these alternatives if the first term has not been understood.

Where appropriate, Spanish terms are listed first: for help in reading menus (pages 32–35), filling out forms (page 85), and understanding doctor's instructions (pages 85–86). For more advanced speakers of Spanish, extended dialogs provide examples of conversations in typical travel situations. The English translation is provided on the facing page.

The **Dictionary** section includes over 15,000 terms, providing travelers with the information they need in a most manageable and concise form. The lexicon in this remarkably compact bilingual dictionary has been specially edited to include only the most frequently used words and their most common meaning in Spanish and English.

To make this book even more useful, helpful appendices are included: monetary units, weights and measures, numbers, temperature conversions, a listing of the most commonly used abbreviations in Spanish, and five detailed maps of the major Spanish-speaking countries and regions.

In every way, the *Vox Spanish Phrasebook and Dictionary* is ideal for anyone who needs a complete, comprehensive, and truly portable language aid for travel.

ARRIVAL

At the airport

Where do I check in?	**¿Dónde puedo chequear (facturar) mis boletos (billetes)?** *dondeh pwedo chekeyar (faktoorar) mees boletos (beel-yetes)?*
Where is the check-in desk for Iberia Airlines, please?	**¿Dónde está el mostrador del check-in (de facturación) de la Aerolínea Iberia, por favor?** *dondeh esta el mostrador del chek-een (deh faktooratheeyon) deh la ayeroleeneya eebereeya, por favor?*
I'd like a window/aisle seat, please.	**Quisiera un asiento junto a la ventana/al pasillo, por favor.** *keeseeyera oon aseeyento hoonto a la ventana/al pasil-yo, por favor*
Is there a weight limit for luggage?	**¿Hay límite de peso para el equipaje?** *ay leemeeteh deh peso para el ekeepaheh?*
How many carry-on items am I allowed?	**¿Cuánto equipaje de mano se permite?** *kwanto ekeepaheh deh mano se permeeteh?*
Where is gate 8B?	**¿Dónde está la sala (puerta de embarque) 8B?** *dondeh esta la sala (pwerta deh embarkeh) ocho beh?*
Why has the plane been delayed?	**¿Por qué está el avión retrasado?** *porkeh esta el aveeyon retrasado?*
Is there someone here who speaks English?	**¿Hay alguien aquí que hable inglés?** *ay algeeyen akee keh ableh eengles?*

On the plane

I'd like a vegetarian meal, please.	**Quisiera una comida vegetariana, por favor.** keeseeyera oona komeeda vehetareeyana, por favor
Is there going to be a movie?	**¿Va a haber una película?** va a aber oona peleekoola?
My seatbelt won't fasten.	**Mi cinturón no abrocha.** mee seentooron no abrocha
My headphones don't work.	**Mis audífonos (auriculares) no sirven.** mees aoodeefonos (aooreecoolares) no seerven
I feel sick. Can I have some water, please.	**Me siento mal. ¿Puedo tomar tantita (un poco de) agua, por favor?** meh seeyento mal. pwedo tomar tanteeta (oon poko deh) agwa, por favor?
What time are we scheduled to land?	**¿Para qué hora está programado el aterrizaje?** para keh ora esta programado el aterrisaheh?
I have a connection to Cuernavaca.	**Tengo una conexión a Cuernavaca.** tengo oona konekseeyon a kwernavaka

Customs & security

Do you need my passport?	**¿Necesita mi pasaporte?** neseseeta mee pasaporteh?
I'm here on vacation/business.	**Estoy aquí de vacaciones/de negocios.** estoy akee deh vakaseeyones/deh negoseeyos
I'll be here for ten days.	**Estaré aquí diez días.** estareh akee deeyes deeyas
I'll be staying at the Intercontinental Hotel.	**Me voy a quedar en el Hotel Intercontinental.** meh voy a kedar en el otel eenterkonteenental

I have nothing to declare.	**No tengo nada que declarar.** no *teng*o *nad*a keh dekla*rar*

Directions

How do you get to Plaza Santa Ana?	**¿Cómo se llega a la Plaza Santa Ana?** *kom*o seh *l*-*yeg*a a la *plas*a *sant*a *an*a?
Am I going in the right direction for…?	**¿Voy en la dirección correcta para...?** voy en la deerekee*yon* ko*rrect*a *par*a...?
I think I'm a little lost.	**Creo que ando un poco perdido.** *krey*o keh *and*o oon *pok*o per*deed*o
Could you help me with this map?	**¿Me podría ayudar con este mapa?** meh po*dree*ya a*yood*ar kon *est*eh *map*a?
north	**el norte** el *nor*teh
south	**el sur** el soor
east	**el este** el *est*eh
west	**el oeste** el *oest*eh
ahead	**derecho** de*rech*o
behind	**detrás de** de*tras* deh
next to	**junto a** *hoon*to a
across from	**enfrente de** en*frent*eh deh
Turn...	**Voltee... (Gire...)** vol*tey*eh (*heer*eh)
to the right	**a la derecha** a la de*rech*a
to the left	**a la izquierda** a la eeskee*yer*da
Follow the signs	**Siga las señales (los letreros)** *seeg*a las se*nyal*es (los *letr*eros)

Arrival

arrival	**la llegada** la l-ye*ga*da
baggage trolley	**el carrito de equipaje** el ka*rree*to deh eke*pa*heh
baggage	**el equipaje** el eke*e*paheh
baggage reclaim hall	**la sala de reclamación (recogida) de equipajes** la *sa*la deh reklama*see*yon (reko*hee*da) deh eke*e*pahes
boarding card	**el pase de abordar (la tarjeta de embarque)** el *pa*seh deh abor*dar* (la tar*he*ta deh em*bar*keh)
boarding gate	**la sala de abordar (la puerta de embarque)** la *sa*la deh abor*dar* (la *pwer*ta deh em*bar*keh)
bus station	**la estación de autobuses** la esta*see*yon deh aooto*boo*ses
check-in desks	**los mostradores de check-in (facturación)** los mostra*do*res deh chek-*een* (faktoorathee*yon*)
customs	**la aduana** la a*dwa*na
departure	**la salida** la sa*lee*da
departure lounge	**la sala de abordar (embarque)** la *sa*la deh abor*dar* (em*bar*keh)
duty free	**libre de impuestos** *lee*breh deh eem*pwes*tos
elevator	**el ascensor** el as-sen*sor*
entrance/exit	**la entrada/la salida** la en*tra*da/la sa*lee*da
escalator	**la escalera eléctrica (mecánica)** la eska*le*ra e*lek*treeka (me*ka*neeka)
flight number	**el número de vuelo** el *noo*mero deh *vwe*lo
form of identification	**la forma de identificación** la *for*ma deh eedenteefeeka*see*yon
gate	**la puerta** la *pwer*ta
gents	**caballeros** kaba*l-ye*ros
goods to declare	**algo que declarar** *al*go keh dekla*rar*
information desk	**la oficina de información** la ofee*see*na deh eenforma*see*yon
ladies	**señoras** sen*yo*ras
left baggage	**la consigna de equipaje** la kon*seg*na deh eke*e*paheh
lost baggage	**el equipaje extraviado** el eke*e*paheh ekstrave*ya*do
lost property	**los objetos perdidos** los ob*he*tos per*dee*dos

mail box	**el buzón** el boo*son*
moving walkways	**las cintas transportadoras** las *seen*tas transporta*do*ras
nothing to declare	**nada que declarar** *na*da keh dekla*rar*
passport control	**el control de pasaportes** el kon*trol* deh pasa*por*tes
personal items	**los artículos personales** los ar*tee*koolos perso*nal*es
post office	**la oficina de correos** la ofee*see*na deh ko*rre*yos
restroom	**los baños (servicios)** los *ban*yos (serbee*thee*yos)
security control	**el control de seguridad** el kon*trol* deh segoo*ree*dad
skycap	**el mozo de equipaje** el *mo*so deh ekee*pa*heh
stairs	**las escaleras** las eska*le*ras
ticket	**el boleto (billete)** el bo*le*to (bee*l-yeh*teh)
e-ticket	**el boleto (billete) electrónico** el bo*le*to (bee*l-yeh*teh) elek*tro*neeko
trolley	**el carrito** el ka*rree*to
walkway	**el pasillo** el pa*seel*-yo

On the plane

air hostess	**la azafata** la asa*fa*ta
baggage rack	**el portaequipajes** el portaekee*pa*hes
boarding card	**el pase de abordar (la tarjeta de embarque)** el *pa*seh deh abor*dar* (la tar*he*ta deh em*bar*keh)
crew	**la tripulación** la treepoolasee*yon*
emergency exit	**la salida de emergencia** la sa*lee*da deh emer*hen*seeya
fasten seat belt	**abróchense el cinturón** ab*ro*chenseh el seentoo*ron*
hand baggage	**el equipaje de mano** el ekee*pa*heh deh *ma*no
landing	**el aterrizaje** el aterree*sa*heh
life jacket/life vest	**el chaleco salvavidas** el cha*le*ko salva*vee*das
row 21 seat C	**fila 21 asiento C** *fee*la veye*en*teh-*oo*no asee*yen*to seh
seat belt	**el cinturón de seguridad** el seentoo*ron* de segoo*ree*dad
seat	**el asiento** el asee*yen*to
steward	**el sobrecargo** el sobre*kar*go
stewardess	**la sobrecargo** la sobre*kar*go
take-off	**el despegue** el des*pe*gheh

Dialog: At the airport

Hombre	¿Dónde puedo comprar revistas y periódicos?
Señorita	En el puesto (quiosco), allí a la derecha.
Señora	¿Hay alguna cafetería aquí?
Señorita	Sí, señora; a la izquierda subiendo las escaleras.
Joven	¿Para chequear los boletos (facturar los billetes)?
Señorita	Abajo, señor; enfrente de la entrada principal.
Anciana	Perdone, ¿podría decirme dónde está el mostrador de check-in (facturación) de la compañía Mexicana, por favor?
Señorita	Sí, señora; baje las escaleras eléctricas (mecánicas) y voltee (gire) a la izquierda; está justo enfrente de la entrada principal.
Jovencita	Perdone, ¿podría decirme dónde están los baños (aseos), por favor?
Señorita	Sí; enfrente de la cafetería, subiendo las escaleras.
Hombre	¿Para cambiar dinero?
Señorita	En el banco que hay nada más pasando las escaleras eléctricas (mecánicas).
Joven	¿Alquiler de coches?
Señorita	Al fondo a la izquierda.
Señora	¿Hay algún teléfono público aquí?
Señorita	Por allí a la derecha, al lado del puesto (quiosco).

Man	Where can I get magazines and newspapers?
Girl	At the bookstall over there on the right, sir.
Lady	Is there a cafeteria here?
Girl	Yes, madam; on the left at the top of the stairs.
Young man	Where do I check in?
Girl	Downstairs, sir; opposite the main entrance.
Old lady	Excuse me. Could you tell me where the check-in desk for Mexicana Airlines is, please?
Girl	Yes, madam; down the escalator, turn left and it is opposite the main entrance.
Young lady	Excuse me. Could you tell me where the toilets are, please?
Girl	Yes; opposite the cafeteria at the top of the stairs.
Man	To change money?
Girl	At the bank counter just past the escalator.
Yong man	Rent-a-car?
Girl	On the left at the far end.
Lady	Are there any public telephones here?
Girl	Over there on the right next to the bookstall.

ACCOMMODATION

Checking in

Could you recommend a good moderately-priced hotel?	**¿Podría recomendarme un buen hotel de precio moderado?** podreeya rekomendarmeh oon bwen otel deh preseeyo moderado?
We have a reservation.	**Tenemos una reservación.** tenemos oona reservaseeyon
We'll be staying for five nights.	**Nos vamos a quedar cinco noches.** nos vamos a kedar seenko noches
We'd like a double bed, not twin beds.	**Quisiéramos cama matrimonial (de matrimonio), no camas individuales.** keeseeyeramos kama matreemoneeyal (deh matreemoneeyo), no kamas eendeeveedwales
The room has air conditioning, right?	**La habitación tiene aire acondicionado, ¿no?** la abeetaseeyon teeyeneh ayreh akondeeseeyonado, no?
Could you give us a wake-up call?	**¿Nos podría hablar (llamar) para despertarnos?** nos podreeya ablar (l-yamar) para despertarnos?
How do you make an outside call?	**¿Cómo se marca para la calle?** komo seh marka para la kal-yeh?
Could someone help us with our bags?	**¿Hay alguien que nos pueda ayudar con nuestras maletas?** ay algeeyen keh nos pweda ayoodar kon nwestras malehtas?
What floor is the dining room on?	**¿En qué piso está el comedor?** en keh peeso esta el komedor?

What time does breakfast begin/end?

¿A qué hora empieza/termina el desayuno? a keh ora empeeyesa/termeena el desayoono?

Complaints

The air conditioning/heating doesn't work.

El aire acondicionado/La calefacción no funciona. al ayreh akondeeseeyonado/ la kalefakseeyon no foonseeyona

My room hasn't been cleaned.

No han limpiado mi cuarto. no han leempeeyado mee kwarto

Our neighbors are too noisy.

Nuestros vecinos son muy ruidosos. nwestros veseenos son mwee rweedosos

This charge is incorrect.

Este cargo no está correcto. esteh kargo no esta korrekto

Departure

We're ready to check out.

Estamos listos para desocupar. estamos leestos para desokoopar

Can you get my bill ready and send someone up to collect our baggage, please?

¿Puede preparar la cuenta y enviar a alguien para que baje nuestro equipaje, por favor? pwedeh preparar la kwenta ee enveeyar a algheyen para keh baheh nwestro ekeepaheh, por favor?

Can I have my bill, please?

¿Me puede dar la cuenta, por favor? me pwedeh dar la kwenta, por favor?

Could we leave our baggage here for a short time?

¿Podríamos dejar nuestro equipaje aquí un rato? podreeyamos dehar nwestro ekeepaheh akee oon rato?

Could you get me a taxi, please? **¿Me podría pedir un taxi, por favor?** me podreeya pedeer oon taksee, por favor?

Dialog: In the hotel

Recepcionista	Buenos días, señor. Buenos días, señora. ¿En qué puedo servirles?
Sr. Austen	Tenemos reservadas dos habitaciones para cinco días. El nombre es Austen.
Recepcionista	Señores Austen e hija. Sí, aquí está: una habitación doble con baño y una individual con regadera (ducha). Cinco días, desde hoy hasta el doce de abril.
Sra. Austen	¿Está cerca la habitación de nuestra hija de la nuestra?
Recepcionista	De hecho, señora, están casi pegadas. Ustedes tienen la habitación 612 y su hija la 614.
Recepcionista	¿Le importaría llenar esta forma (rellenar este impreso), señor? Ponga su nombre, dirección y número de pasaporte y firme aquí, por favor.
Sra. Austen	¿A qué hora se sirve el desayuno?
Recepcionista	El desayuno se sirve en el comedor desde las siete y media hasta las diez, señora.
Sr. Austen	¿Está correcto?
Recepcionista	Perfecto, señor, gracias. El botones tiene sus llaves. Les subirá el equipaje y les enseñará las habitaciones. Espero que tengan una estancia agradable. Si necesitan algo, les ruego que no duden en pedirlo.
Sr. Austen	Muchas gracias.

Clerk	Good morning, sir. Good morning, madam. Can I help you?
Mr. Austen	Yes. We have two rooms booked here for five days. The name is Austen.
Clerk	Mr. and Mrs. Austen and daughter. Yes, here we are, sir: one double room with bathroom en suite and one single room with shower. Five days from today till the 12th of April.
Mrs. Austen	Is our daughter's room near ours?
Clerk	As a matter of fact, madam, it's almost next door. You have room 612 and your daughter has room 614.
Clerk	Would you mind filling in this card, sir? Just your name, home address and passport number. Then sign it here.
Mrs. Austen	What time is breakfast?
Clerk	Breakfast is served in the restaurant from 7.30 to 10.00 madam.
Mr. Austen	Is this correct?
Clerk	Perfect, sir. Thank you. The porter has your keys. He will take your luggage up and show you to your rooms. I hope you have a pleasant stay. If there is anything you need, please don't hesitate to ask.
Mr. Austen	Thank you very much.

In the hotel

air conditioning	**el aire acondicionado**	el ayreh akondeeseeyonado
ashtray	**el cenicero**	el seneesero
bathroom	**el cuarto de baño**	el kwarto deh banyo
bed	**la cama**	la kama
double bed	**la cama matrimonial (de matrimonio)**	la kama matreemoneeyal (deh matreemoneeyo)
twin beds	**las camas individuales**	las kamas eendeeveedwales
bedside table	**la mesita de noche**	la meseeta de nocheh
bell	**el timbre**	el teembreh
bill	**la cuenta**	la kwenta
blanket	**la cobija (manta)**	la kobeeha (manta)
central heating	**la calefacción central**	la kalefakseeyon sentral
chambermaid	**la camarera**	la kamarera
concierge	**el conserje**	el konserheh
door	**la puerta**	la pwerta
electric socket	**el enchufe**	el enchoofeh
envelopes	**los sobres**	los sobres
faucet	**la llave (el grifo)**	la l-yaveh (el greefo)
fax machine	**la máquina de fax**	la makeena deh faks
floor	**el suelo/el piso**	el swelo/el peeso
bedroom floor	**el suelo de la habitación**	el swelo de la abeetaseeyon
second floor	**el primer piso**	el preemer peeso
full board	**la pensión completa**	la penseeyon kompleta
gymnasium	**el gimnasio**	el heemnaseeyo
hairdryer	**el secador de pelo**	el sekador deh pelo
internet connection	**la conexión para el internet**	la konekseeyon para el eenternet
lamp	**la lámpara**	la lampara
bedside lamp	**la lámpara de la mesita de noche**	la lampara deh la meseeta deh nocheh
laundry	**la lavandería**	la lavandereeya

light	**la luz**	la loos
luggage/baggage	**el equipaje/las maletas**	el ekee*pah*eh/las ma*le*tas
manager	**el gerente/el director**	el he*ren*teh/el deere*k*tor
meal	**la comida**	la ko*mee*da
pillow case	**la funda de almohada**	la *foon*da deh almo*a*da
pillow	**la almohada**	la almo*a*da
radio	**el (la) radio**	el (la) *ra*deeyo
reservation	**la reservación (reserva)**	la reservasee*yon* (re*ser*va)
room	**la habitación**	la abeetasee*yon*
single	**individual**	eendeeveedoo*al*
double	**doble**	*dob*leh
with bath	**con baño**	kon *ban*yo
with shower	**con regadera (ducha)**	kon rega*de*ra (*doo*cha)
number	**el número**	el *noo*mero
key	**la llave**	la *l-ya*veh
service	**el servicio**	el ser*vee*seeyo
shampoo	**el champú**	el cham*poo*
sheet	**la sábana**	la *sa*bana
soap	**el jabón**	el ha*bon*
swimming pool	**la alberca (piscina)**	la al*ber*ka (pees*thee*na)
telephone	**el teléfono**	el te*le*fono
television	**la televisión/la tele**	la televeesee*yon*/la *te*leh
toilet	**el escusado (wáter)**	el eskoo*sa*do (*ba*ter)
toilet paper	**el papel higiénico**	el pa*pel* eeheeye*nee*ko
towels	**las toallas**	las to*yal*-yas
hand towel	**la toalla para las manos**	la to*yal*-ya *pa*ra las *ma*nos
face towel	**la toalla para la cara**	la to*yal*-ya *pa*ra la *ka*ra
bath towel	**la toalla de baño**	la to*yal*-ya deh *ban*yo
sink	**el lavabo**	el la*va*bo
cold water	**el agua fría**	el *a*gwa *free*ya
hot water	**el agua caliente**	el *a*gwa kalee*yen*teh
window	**la ventana**	la ven*ta*na
writing paper	**el papel de escribir**	el pa*pel* deh eskree*beer*

Dialog: Checking out

Sr. Austen   ¿Me podría dar la cuenta, por favor?

Recepcionista   Naturalmente, señor. Habitaciones seiscientos doce y seiscientos catorce: una habitación doble y una individual durante cinco días; cena para tres el viernes y el domingo. Cinco llamadas de teléfono, todas a los Estados Unidos. ¿Está correcto, señor?

Sr. Austen   Sí, mi mujer llama a su madre todas las noches.

Recepcionista   Servicio de habitaciones: nada. ¿El minibar, señor?

Sr. Austen   Sí, tomé dos de esas botellas miniaturas de whisky.

Recepcionista   Gracias. Eso es todo. ¿Paga usted en efectivo o con tarjeta de crédito?

Sr. Austen   Con tarjeta de crédito, Visa.

Recepcionista   Gracias, señor. ¿Podría firmar aquí, por favor? Gracias. Su tarjeta, su comprobante y la cuenta. Gracias, señor. Espero que hayan disfrutado de su estancia.

Sr. Austen   Sí, muchísimo. ¿Podríamos dejar aquí las maletas durante media hora aproximadamente?

Recepcionista   Naturalmente, señor. ¿Son sólo esas dos maletas?

Sr. Austen   Esas dos maletas y este paquete.

Recepcionista   Estarán aquí en recepción cuando vuelvan, señor.

Sr. Austen   Gracias. Otra cosa más, ¿Podría pedirnos un taxi cuando volvamos?

Recepcionista   Sí, no hay ningún inconveniente.

Mr. Austen	Could I have the bill, please.
Receptionist	Certainly, sir. That's room 612 and 614: one double room and one single room for five days. Dinner for three on Friday and Sunday. Telephone calls five, all to the United States. Is that correct?
Mr. Austen	Yes, my wife phones her mother every night.
Receptionist	Room service: nothing. Room bar, sir?
Mr. Austen	Yes, I had two of those miniature bottles of whiskey.
Receptionist	Thank you, sir. That's all. Are you paying in cash or with a credit card, sir?
Mr. Austen	With a credit card. Visa.
Receptionist	Thank you, sir. Could you just sign here, please? Thank you. Your card, your credit card receipt, and your bill. Thank you, sir. I hope you have all enjoyed your stay here.
Mr. Austen	Yes, very much. Could we leave our baggage here for half an hour or so?
Receptionist	Certainly, sir. Is it just the two suitcases?
Mr. Austen	Two suitcases and this package.
Receptionist	They will all be here in reception when you come back, sir.
Mr. Austen	Thank you. Just one other thing. Can you a taxi when we come back?
Receptionist	Yes, no trouble at all, sir.

TRANSPORTATION

What is the best way to get to Plaza Mayor?	**¿Cuál es la mejor forma de ir a la Plaza Mayor?** kwal es la mehor forma de eer a la plasa mayor?
Have you any maps of central Santiago?	**¿Tienen mapas (planos) del centro de Santiago?** teeyenen mapas (planos)del sentro deh santeeyago?
Where can I get information about train times?	**¿Dónde puedo obtener información de los horarios de trenes?** dondeh pwedo obtener eenformaseeyon deh los orareeyos deh trenes?

Taxi

Please take us to...?	**¿Nos puede llevar a...?** nos pwedeh l-yevar a?
How much will it cost to...?	**¿Cuánto cuesta a.../al...?** kwanto kwesta a/al?
The corner ahead is fine.	**La siguiente esquina está bien.** la seegeeyenteh eskeena esta beeyen
What's the total?	**¿Cuánto es el total?** kwanto es el total?
Can you wait for two minutes?	**¿Puede esperar dos minutos?** pwedeh esperar dos meenootos?
fare	**el precio del viaje** el preseeyo del veeyaheh
for hire	**libre** leebreh
suitcase	**la maleta** la maleta
surcharge	**el suplemento** el sooplemento
taxi/cab	**el taxi** el taksee
taxi driver	**el taxista** el takseesta

taxi rank	**la parada de taxis** la parada de *tak*sees
taximeter	**el taxímetro** el tak*see*metro
tip	**la propina** la pro*pee*na

Bus

Is this the right bus for...?	**¿Éste es el camión (autobús) para...?** esteh es el kamee*yon* (aooto*boos*) para?
How often does the bus run?	**¿Cada cuándo pasa el camión (autobús)?** *kada kwando pasa* el kamee*yon* (aooto*boos*)?
bus	**el camión (autobús)** el kamee*yon* (aooto*boos*)
bus fare	**el precio del boleto (billete)** el *preseeyo* del bo*leto* (beel-*yeteh*)
bus stop	**la parada de camión (autobús)** la *parada* de kamee*yon* (aooto*boos*)
driver	**el conductor** el kondook*tor*
exact fare	**el cambio exacto** el *kambeeyo* e*sakto*
next stop	**la próxima parada** la *prokseema parada*
no standing	**prohibido estar de pie** proee*beedo* es*tar* deh pee*yeh*
ticket	**el boleto (billete)** el bo*leto* (beel-*yeteh*)

Train

Is this the platform for the train to Valparaiso?	**¿Éste es el andén para el tren de Valparaiso?** esteh es el an*den* para el tren de valpa*rayso*?
Is this seat taken?	**¿Está ocupado este asiento?** es*ta* okoo*pado* esteh asee*yento*?
What station is this?	**¿Qué estación es ésta?** keh estasee*yon* es esta?
arrival	**la llegada** la l-*yegada*
booking office	**la taquilla** la ta*keel*-ya

destination	**el destino** el de*stee*no
luggage rack	**el portaequipajes** el portaekee*pa*hes
no smoking	**prohibido fumar** proee*bee*do foo*mar*
passengers	**los pasajeros** los pasa*he*ros
platform	**el andén** el an*den*
rail station	**la estación de ferrocarril** la estasee*yon* deh ferroka*rreel*
ticket	**el boleto (billete)** el bo*le*to (bee*l*-yeteh)
one-way	**el boleto sencillo (billete de ida)** el bo*le*to sensee*l*-yo (bee*l*-yeteh deh *ee*da)
roundtrip	**el boleto (billete) de ida y vuelta** el bo*le*to (bee*l*-yeteh) deh *ee*da ee *vwel*ta
train	**el tren** el tren

Subway

Which line should I take to get to…?	**¿Qué línea debo tomar para llegar a…?** keh *lee*neya *de*bo to*mar* para l-ye*gar* a?
Is this the correct platform to go to…?	**¿Ésta es la plataforma correcta (el andén correcto) para ir a…?** esta es la plata*for*ma ko*rrek*ta (el an*den* ko*rrek*to) *para* eer a?
What's the next station?	**¿Cuál es la siguiente estación?** kwal es la seegee*yen*teh estasee*yon*?
escalator	**la escalera eléctrica (mecánica)** la eska*le*ra e*lek*treeka (me*ka*neeka)
platform	**el andén** el an*den*
station	**la estación** la estasee*yon*
subway	**el metro** el *me*tro
ticket machine	**la máquina expendedora de boletos (billetes)** la *ma*keena ekspende*do*ra deh bo*le*tos (bee*l*-yetes)
train fare	**el precio del boleto (billete)** el *pre*seeyo del bo*le*to (bee*l*-yeteh)

Car rental

We have a reservation for a compact for three days.	**Tenemos una reservación (reser** **un coche compacto para tres días.** te*nemos oona reservaseeyon (reserba) deh oon ko*cheh kom*pak*to para tres *deeyas*
What does the insurance cover?	**¿Qué cubre el seguro?** keh *koo*breh el se*goo*ro?
There will be two drivers.	**Serán dos conductores.** se*ran* dos kondook*to*res
I would like to drop the car off at the airport.	**Me gustaría entregar el coche en el aeropuerto.** meh goosta*reeya* entre*gar* el *ko*cheh en el ayro*pwer*to
Does the car take regular or diesel?	**¿Qué gasolina usa el coche?** keh gaso*lee*na *oo*sa el *ko*cheh?
How do I undo the gas cap?	**¿Cómo se quita la tapa del tanque de la gasolina?** *ko*mo seh *kee*ta la *ta*pa del *tan*keh deh la gaso*lee*na?
accident report form	**el parte de accidentes** el *par*teh deh aksee*den*tes
breakdown	**la avería** la ave*ree*ya
car rental	**la renta (el alquiler) de coches** la *ren*ta (el alkee*ler*) deh *ko*ches
collision damage waiver	**el renunciante a daños de colisión** el renoonseey*an*teh a *dan*yos deh kolee*see*yon
dent	**la abolladura** la abol-ya*doo*ra
driver's license	**la licencia de manejar (el carné de conducir)** la lee*sen*seeya deh mane*har* (el car*neh* deh condoo*theer*)
excess miles	**las millas de exceso** las *meel*-yas deh eks*eso*
insurance policy	**la póliza de seguro** la *po*leesa deh se*goo*ro
rental rate	**la tarifa de alquiler** la ta*ree*fa deh alkee*ler*

...ound

... ...as. ¿Me puede decir cuál es la mejor ... ...overse por la ciudad?

... ...es generalmente tomo el metro. Es muy ... ...nso. Lo deja a unas cuantas cuadras (manzanas) de donde quiera ir.

... Austen	¿Cada cuándo hay trenes?
Empleado	En las líneas principales, cada cinco o diez minutos. Ya en la noche, los trenes son cada quince o veinte minutos.
Sr. Austen	¿Cuál es la forma más barata de comprar boletos (billetes)? ¿Hay algún descuento por comprar más de un boleto (billete)?
Empleado	Yo le recomendaría comprar un boleto que se llama de "diez viajes". Es un boleto que se puede usar diez veces.
Sra. Austen	¿Y los camiones (autobuses)?
Empleado	Yo creo que pueden ser complicados si no está usted familiarizado con la ciudad. En primer lugar, no se alcanzan a ver los letreros de las calles desde el camión (autobús), y el conductor casi nunca anuncia los nombres de las calles.
Sr. Austen	¿Y los taxis? Me imagino que deben ser muy caros.
Empleado	Pueden llegar a serlo. Yo casi siempre evito tomar taxis excepto cuando ya es de noche.
Sr. Austen	Supongo que mejor tomamos el metro entonces. ¿Nos puede decir cómo llegamos al nuevo museo de arte?
Empleado	¡Ah! No sabía que querían ir ahí. Mire este mapa. Pueden llegar ahí caminando en menos de diez minutos.
Sra. Austen	Es un día muy bonito así que yo creo que la mejor idea es ir caminando.

Mr. Austen	Good morning. Can you tell us what's the best way to get around the city?
Hotel clerk	Well, I usually take the subway. It's really extensive. It'll take you within blocks of almost anywhere you want to go.
Mrs. Austen	How often do the trains run?
Clerk	The main lines run every five to ten minutes. Later at night the trains run every fifteen to twenty minutes.
Mr. Austen	What's the cheapest way to buy tickets? Is there some kind of discount for buying more than one?
Clerk	I'd recommend getting a ticket called "ten trips". One ticket that can be used ten times.
Mrs. Austen	What about the buses?
Clerk	I think it might be confusing if you're not familiar with the city. For one thing, you can't really see the street signs from the bus, and the driver often doesn't call out the street names.
Mr. Austen	And taxis? I imagine that they're quite expensive.
Clerk	They can be. I usually avoid taking taxis except when it's late at night.
Mr. Austen	I suppose we'll take the subway then. Could you tell us how to get to the new art museum?
Clerk	Oh, I didn't know you wanted to go there. Here, look at this map. You could walk there in less than ten minutes.
Mrs. Austen	It's a nice day too, so I think a walk is the best idea.

MAKING FRIENDS

Greetings

Hi	**Hola** *o*la
Good morning	**Buenos días** *bw*enos *dee*yas
Good afternoon	**Buenas tardes** *bw*enas *tar*des
Good evening/night	**Buenas noches** *bw*enas *no*ches
My name is John. Pleased to meet you.	**Me llamo John. Encantado de conocerlo.** meh *l*-yamo jon. enkan*ta*do deh kono*ser*lo
Sorry, I didn't catch your name.	**Perdón, no escuché su nombre.** per*don*, no eskoo*cheh* soo *nom*breh

Farewells

Goodbye	**Adiós** adee*yos*
See you later.	**Hasta luego.** *a*sta *l*wego
See you tomorrow.	**Hasta mañana.** *a*sta ma*nya*na

Arranging meetings

Let's meet at 6:30.	**Nos vemos a las seis y media.** nos *ve*mos a las *se*yees ee *me*deeya
I'll meet you at the fountain in the plaza.	**Nos vemos en la fuente de la plaza.** nos *ve*mos en la *fwen*teh deh la *pla*sa
I'll call if I'm going to be late.	**Te llamo si voy a llegar tarde.** teh *l*-yamo see voy a l-ye*gar tar*deh
What do you want to do?	**¿Qué quieres hacer?** keh kee*ye*res a*ser?*
Let's get a drink.	**Vamos a tomar algo.** *va*mos a to*mar al*go

Family

This is my wife and daughter.	**Ésta es mi mujer y mi hija.**
	esta es mee mooher ee mee eeha
How old is your daughter?	**¿Cuántos años tiene su hija?**
She is seven.	**Tiene siete años.** kwantos anyos teeyeneh
	soo eeha? teeyeneh seeyeteh anyos
Our son goes to college.	**Nuestro hijo va a la universidad.**
	nwestro eeho va a la ooneeverseedad
My daughter/son is married.	**Mi hija está casada./Mi hijo está casado.**
	mee eeha esta kasada/mee eeho esta kasado
I have one sister and two	**Tengo una hermana y dos hermanos.**
brothers.	tengo oona ermana ee dos ermanos

mother	**la madre** la madreh
father	**el padre** el padreh
sister	**la hermana** la ermana
brother	**el hermano** el ermano
aunt	**la tía** la teeya
uncle	**el tío** el teeyo
grandmother	**la abuela** la abwela
grandfather	**el abuelo** el abwelo
wife	**la mujer** la mooher
husband	**el marido** el mareedo
girlfriend	**la novia** la noveeya
boyfriend	**el novio** el noveeyo

Professions/Jobs

What area of work are you in?	**¿En qué trabaja?** en keh trabaha?
What company do you work for?	**¿Para qué compañía trabaja?**
	para keh kompanyeeya trabaha?

I'm an engineer and I work for General Motors.	**Soy ingeniero y trabajo para la General Motors.** soy eenheneeyero ee trabaho para la 'General Motors'
My girlfriend is studying to become an architect.	**Mi novia está estudiando para ser arquitecta.** mee noveeya esta estoodeeyando para ser arkeetekta
We're students but we have part-time jobs.	**Somos estudiantes pero trabajamos medio tiempo.** somos estoodeeyantes pero trabahamos medeeyo teeyempo
I'm looking forward to my retirement.	**Ya tengo ganas de retirarme.** ya tengo ganas deh reteerarmeh
accountant	**el contador/la contadora (el/la contable)** el kontador/la kontadora (kontableh)
civil servant	**el funcionario/la funcionaria** el foonseeyonareeyo/la foonseeyonareeya
dentist	**el/la dentista** el/la denteesta
doctor	**el médico/la médica** el medeeko/la medeeka
editor	**el redactor/la redactora** el redaktor/la redaktora
engineer	**el ingeniero/la ingeniera** el eenheneeyero/la eenheneeyera
housewife	**el ama de casa (pl. las amas de casa)** el ama deh kasa (las amas deh kasa)
journalist	**el/la periodista** el/la pereeyodeesta
manager	**el/la gerente** el/la herenteh
mechanic	**el mecánico/la mecánica** el mekaneeko/la mekaneeka
musician	**el músico/la música (la músico)** el mooseeko/la mooseeka (la mooseeko)
pharmacist	**el farmacéutico/la farmacéutica** el farmaseeyooteeko/la farmaseeyooteeka
physicist	**el físico/la física** el feeseeko/la feeseeka
police officer	**el/la policía** el/la poleeseeya

programmer	**el programador/la programadora**
	el programa*dor*/la programa*dora*
teacher	**el maestro/la maestra** el *may*stro/la *may*stra
salesman/woman	**el vendedor/la vendedora**
	el vende*dor*/la vende*dora*
technician	**el técnico/la técnica** el *tek*neeko/la *tek*neeka
writer	**el escritor/la escritora**
	el eskree*tor*/la eskree*tora*

Meetings and plans

Are you here with anyone?	**¿Está aquí con alguien?**
	es*ta* a*kee* kon algee*yen*?
I'm here on my own.	**Estoy aquí solo.** es*toy* a*kee* *solo*
Are you married or single?	**¿Es casado o soltero?** es ka*sado* o sol*tero*?
My boyfriend/husband and I are here on vacation.	**Mi novio/marido y yo estamos aquí de vacaciones.** mee no*veeyo*/ma*reedo* ee yo es*tamos* a*kee* deh vakasee*yones*
Can I buy you a drink?	**¿Le puedo invitar algo para tomar?**
	leh *pwedo* eenvee*tar* *algo* para to*mar*?
Would you like to meet for some coffee?	**¿Le gustaría vernos para tomar un café?**
	leh goosta*reeya* *vernos* para to*mar* oon ka*feh*?
Would you like to go for a walk in the park?	**¿Le gustaría ir a dar una vuelta al parque?** leh goosta*reeya* eer a dar *oona* *vwelta* al *parkeh*?
Let's go dancing tonight.	**Vamos a bailar hoy en la noche.**
	vamos a bay*lar* oy en la *nocheh*
Call me at my hotel.	**Llámeme a mi hotel.**
	*l-ya*memeh a mee o*tel*

Countries & languages

Where do you live?	**¿Dónde vive?** *dondeh veeveh?*
I come from...	**Soy de...** *soy deh*
I don't speak Spanish very well.	**No hablo español muy bien.** *no ablo espanyol mwee beeyen*
I'd like to practice my Spanish.	**Me gustaría practicar mi español.** *meh goostareeya prakteekar mee espanyol*
Do you speak English?	**¿Habla (usted) inglés?** *abla (oosted) eengles?*
America (U.S.)	**Estados Unidos** *estados ooneedos*
American	**estadounidense** *estado-ooneedensen*
Argentina	**Argentina** *arhenteena*
Argentinian	**argentino** *arhenteeno*
Chile	**Chile** *cheeleh*
Chilean	**chileno** *cheeleno*
Colombia	**Colombia** *kolombeeya*
Colombian	**colombiano** *kolombeeyano*
Costa Rica	**Costa Rica** *kosta reeka*
Costa Rican	**costarricense** *kostarreesensen*
Cuba	**Cuba** *kooba*
Cuban	**cubano** *koobano*
Dominican	**dominicano** *domeeneekano*
Dominican Republic	**República Dominicana** *repoobleeka domeeneekana*
Ecuador	**Ecuador** *ekwador*
Ecuadorian	**ecuatoriano** *ekwatoreeyano*
England	**Inglaterra** *eenglaterra*
English	**inglés** *eengles*
Europe	**Europa** *eyooropa*
European	**europeo** *eyoorepeyo*
France	**Francia** *franseeya*
French	**francés** *franses*

Honduran	**hondureño** ondoo*re*nyo
Honduras	**Honduras** on*doo*ras
Italy	**Italia** ee*ta*leeya
Italian	**italiano** eetalee*ya*no
Latin America	**América Latina/Latinoamérica** a*me*reeka la*tee*na/lateenoa*me*reeka
Latin American	**latinoamericano** lateenoamee*ree*kano
Mexican	**mexicano (mejicano)** meksee*ka*no (mehee*ka*no)
Mexico	**México** *mek*seeko
Nicaragua	**Nicaragua** neeka*ra*gwa
Nicaraguan	**nicaragüense** neekaragw*en*seh
North America	**América del Norte** a*me*reeka del *nor*teh
North American	**norteamericano** norteyamee*ree*kano
Paraguay	**Paraguay** para*gway*
Paraguayan	**paraguayo** para*gwa*yo
Peru	**Perú** pe*roo*
Peruvian	**peruano** pe*roo*ano
Puerto Rican	**puertorriqueño/portorriqueño** pwertorree*ke*nyo/portorree*ke*nyo
El Salvador	**El Salvador** el salva*dor*
Salvador(i)an	**salvadoreño** salvado*re*nyo
South America	**Sudamérica/América del Sur** sooda*me*reeka/a*me*reeka del *soor*
South American	**sudamericano** soodamee*ree*kano
Spain	**España** es*pa*nya
Spanish	**español** espa*nyol*
Spanish (Hispanic) America	**Hispanoamérica** eespanoa*me*reeka
Spanish (Hispanic) American	**hispanoamericano** eespanoamee*ree*kano
United States (of America)	**Estados Unidos (de América)** es*ta*dos oo*nee*dos (deh a*me*reeka)
Uruguay	**Uruguay** ooroo*gway*
Uruguayan	**uruguayo** ooroo*gwa*yo
Venezuela	**Venezuela** venes*we*la
Venezuelan	**venezolano** veneso*la*no

EATING OUT

What type of cuisine does this restaurant serve?	**¿Qué clase de cocina sirve este restaurante?** keh *kla*seh deh ko*see*na *seer*veh este restaoo*ran*teh?
Can we make a reservation?	**¿Podemos hacer una reservación (reserva)?** po*de*mos a*ser oo*na reservasee*yon* (re*ser*ba)?
A reservation for four people at 8 pm.	**Una reservación (reserva) para cuatro personas a las ocho de la noche.** *oo*na reservasee*yon* (re*ser*ba) *para kwa*tro per*so*nas a las *o*cho deh la *no*cheh
A table for two, please.	**Una mesa para dos, por favor.** *oo*na *me*sa *para* dos, por fa*vor*
Do you have a menu in English?	**¿Tiene el menú en inglés?** tee*ye*neh el me*noo* en een*gles*?
I'd like to try some typical regional cooking.	**Quisiera probar unos platos típicos de la región.** keesee*ye*ra pro*bar oo*nos *pla*tos *tee*peekos deh la rehee*yon*
What's the difference between enchiladas and tortillas?	**¿Qué diferencia hay entre las enchiladas y las tortillas?** keh deefe*ren*seeya ay *en*treh las enchee*la*das ee las tor*teel*-yas?
Can you tell me what this is?	**¿Me puede decir qué es esto?** me *pwe*deh de*seer* keh es *es*to?
Can you tell me how this is prepared?	**¿Me puede decir cómo se prepara esto?** me *pwe*deh de*seer ko*mo seh pre*para es*to?
Is the food very hot?	**¿Es muy picante la comida?** es mwee pee*kan*teh la ko*mee*da?

How would you like your steak: rare, medium, or well done?
¿Cómo quiere el filete: poco cocido, término medio (en su punto) o bien cocido (muy hecho)? *komo keeyereh el feeleteh: poko koseedo, termeeno medeeyo (en soo poonto) o beeyen koseedo (mwee echo)?*

Could you bring another glass?
¿Podría traer otro vaso? *podreeya trayer otro vaso?*

Have you any olive oil?
¿Tiene aceite de oliva? *teeyene aseyeeteh deh oleeva?*

Black or white coffee, sir?
¿Café (solo) o café con leche? *Kafeh (solo) o kafeh kon lecheh?*

Could I have the bill, please?
¿Puede traerme la cuenta, por favor? *pwedeh trayermeh la kwenta, por favor?*

Can I pay with my credit card?
¿Puedo pagar con mi tarjeta de crédito? *pwedo pagar kon mee tarheta deh kredeeto?*

What time do you close?
¿A qué hora cierran? *a keh ora seeyerran?*

Are you open on Sundays?
¿Están abiertos los domingos? *estan abeeyertos los domeengos?*

In the restaurant

Flatware/Cutlery

dessert spoon	**la cucharita (cuchara) de postre** la koochareeta (koochara) deh postreh
fork	**el tenedor** el tehnehdor
knife	**el cuchillo** el koocheel-yo
soup spoon	**la cuchara sopera** la koochara sopera
spoon	**la cuchara** la koochara
teaspoon	**la cucharita (cucharilla)** la koochareeta (koochareel-ya)

Meals

meal	**la comida** la komeeda
breakfast	**el desayuno** el desayoono
lunch	**el almuerzo (la comida)** el almuerzo (la komeeda)
dinner	**la cena** la sena

Menu

cheese	**el queso** el keso
coffee	**el café** el kafeh
white	**con leche** con lecheh
black	**solo** solo
dessert	**el postre** el postreh
fish dishes	**el pescado** el peskado
main course	**el plato principal (el segundo plato)** el plato preenseepal (el segoondo plato)
meat	**la carne** la karneh
menu	**la carta, el menú** la karta, el menoo
fixed-price meal	**el menú del día** el menoo del deeya
salad	**la ensalada** la ensalada
soups	**la sopa** la sopa
starter	**para empezar (el primer plato)** para empesar (el preemer plato)
tea	**el té** el teh

Service

wine list	**la carta de vinos** la karta de veenos
bill	**la cuenta** la kwenta
table for two	**la mesa para dos** la mesa para dos
tip	**la propina** la propeena
service charge	**el servicio** el serveeseeyo

Staff

waitress	**la mesera (la camarera)** la mesera (la kamarera)

waiter	**el mesero (el camarero)**
	el mesero (el kamarero)
chef	**el cocinero** el koseenero
manager	**el/la gerente** el/la herenteh

Tableware

cup	**la taza** la tasa
glass	**el vaso** el vaso
jug of water	**la jarra de agua** la harra de agwa
mayonnaise	**la mayonesa** la mayonesa
napkin	**la servilleta** la serveel-yeta
oil	**el aceite** el aseyeeteh
pepper	**la pimienta** la peemeeyenta
plate	**el plato** el plato
salt	**la sal** la sal
sauce	**la salsa** la salsa
saucer	**el plato para la taza**
	el plato para la tasa
seasoning	**los condimentos** los kondeementos
table cloth	**el mantel** el mantel
vinegar	**el vinagre** el veenagreh
wine glass	**la copa de vino** la kopa deh veeno

Breakfast

butter	**la mantequilla** la mantekeel-ya
cereal	**los cereales** los sereyales
coffee	**el café** el kafeh
jelly	**la mermelada** la mermelada
milk	**la leche** la lecheh
orange juice	**el jugo (zumo) de naranja**
	el hoogo (thoomo) deh naranha
sugar	**el azúcar** el asookar
toast	**el pan tostado (la tostada)**
	el pan tostado (la tostada)

Alcoholic drinks

bebida f. **alcohólica** be*bee*da al*ko*leeka	alcoholic drink
cerveza f. ser*ve*sa	beer
champán m. cham*pan*	champagne
coñac m. *ko*nyak (*ko*nyak)	brandy
ginebra f. hee*ne*bra	gin
jerez m. he*res*	sherry
oporto m. o*por*to	port
ron m. ron	rum
tequila f. te*kee*la	tequila
vino m. *vee*no	wine

Food items

aceite m. **de oliva** a*se*yeeteh deh o*lee*va	olive oil
cacao m. ka*ka*yo	cocoa
caramelos mpl. kara*me*los	candy
champiñón m./**seta** f. champee*nyon*/*se*ta	mushroom
chocolate m. choko*la*teh	chocolate
galleta f. gal-*ye*ta	cookie
gelatina f. hela*tee*na	jelly
helado m. e*la*do	ice cream
huevo m. *we*vo	egg
leche f. *le*cheh	milk
mantequilla f. mante*kee*l-ya	butter
mermelada f. merme*la*da	jam
miel f. mee*yel*	honey
nata f. *na*ta	cream
pan m. pan	bread
pastel m. pas*tel*	cake
queso m. *ke*so	cheese
salchicha f. sal*chee*cha	sausage
sopa f. *so*pa	soup

zumo m. **de naranja** *soomo deh naranha*   orange juice

Fish and shellfish

almejas fpl. *almehas*	clams
anchoas fpl. *anchoas*	anchovies
atún m. *atoon*	tuna
bacalao m. *bakalao*	cod
cangrejo m. *kangreho*	crab
gambas fpl. *gambas*	shrimp
gambas rebozadas fpl. *gambas rebosadas*	scampi
langosta f. *langosta*	lobster
lenguado m. *lengwado*	sole
mejillones mpl. *meheel-yones*	mussels
merluza f. *merloosa*	hake
ostras fpl. *ostras*	oysters
salmón m. *salmon*	salmon
trucha f. *troocha*	trout

Herbs

acedera f. *asedera*	sorrel
ají m. *ahi*	red pepper
ajo m. *aho*	garlic
canela f. *kanela*	cinnamon
estragón m. *estragon*	tarragon
menta f./**hierbabuena** f. *menta/eeyerbabwena*	mint
perejil m. *perehil*	parsley

Nuts

almendras fpl. *almendras*	almonds
avellanas fpl. *avel-yanas*	hazel nuts
cacahuetes mpl. *kakawetes*	peanuts
castañas fpl. *kastanyas*	chestnuts
nueces fpl. *nweses*	walnuts

Fruit

albaricoques fpl. albaree*k*okes	apricots
ananá(s)/piña f. anan*a*(s)/*pee*nya	pineapple
cerezas fpl. se*r*esas	cherries
ciruelas fpl. see*r*welas	plums
dátiles mpl. *d*ateeles	dates
frambuesas fpl. fram*b*we*s*as	raspberries
fresas fpl. *freh*sas	strawberries
fruta f. *f*roota	fruit
higos mpl. *ee*gos	figs
limones mpl. lee*m*ones	lemons
mango m. *man*go	mango
manzanas fpl. man*s*anas	apples
melocotones mpl. meloko*t*ones	peaches
melón m. me*lon*	melon
naranjas fpl. na*ran*has	oranges
plátanos mpl. *p*latanos	bananas
uva f. *oo*va	grapes

Meat

carne f. **de vaca/buey** *k*arneh deh *v*aka/*b*wey	beef
carne f. **de cerdo** *k*arneh deh *s*erdo	pork
carne m. *k*arneh	meat
conejo m. ko*n*eho	rabbit
cordero m. **lechal** kord*e*ro le*chal*	lamb
ganso m. *gan*so	goose
jamón m. ha*mon*	ham
pato m. *p*ato	duck
pavo m. *p*avo	turkey
pollo m. *p*ol-yo	chicken
ternera f. ter*n*era	veal
tocino/bacon m. to*seen*o/*b*aykon	bacon

Vegetables

alcachofa f. alca*chofa*	artichoke
apio m. a*peeyo*	celery
arroz m. a*rros*	rice
berenjena f. beren*hena*	eggplant
calabacín m. kalaba*seen*	zucchini
cebollas mpl. se*bol*-yas	onions
col f. kol	cabbage
espinacas fpl. espee*nakas*	spinach
guisantes mpl. gee*santes*	peas
judías fpl. hoo*deeyas*	beans
lechuga f. leh*chooga*	lettuce
lentejas fpl. len*tehas*	lentils
patatas fpl. pa*tatas*	potatoes
pepino m. peh*peeno*	cucumber
pimientos mpl. peemee*yentos*	peppers
tomates mpl. to*mates*	tomatoes
zanahorias fpl. sanao*reeyas*	carrots

Typical dishes and drinks

antojitos mpl. anto*heetos*	appetizers
arroz m. **con leche** *arros* kon *lecheh*	rice pudding
caldo m. *kaldo*	a broth-like soup
ceviche m. se*veecheh*	raw fish with lemon juice
chorizo m. cho*reeso*	a spicy sausage
cocido m. ko*seedo*	a meat and vegetable stew
gazpacho m. gas*pacho*	a cold tomato soup
paella f. pa*yel*-ya	a rice dish
mole m. *moleh*	chili cocoa, and peanut sauce
sangría f. san*greeya*	red wine, soda and fruit
tapas fpl. *tapas*	popular bar snacks (Sp)
tortilla f. tor*teel*-ya	a potato omelet (Sp); a thin pancake (Mex)

Dialog: In the restaurant

Maitre	Buenas noches, señor. Buenas noches, señora. ¿Una mesa para cenar?
Sr. Austen	Sí, por favor. Una mesa para tres. Nuestra hija está por llegar.
Sra. Austen	¿Podríamos sentarnos en aquella mesa de la esquina?
Maitre	Naturalmente, señora.
Sra. Austen	Queremos cenar algo típicamente español esta noche.
Sr. Austen	Así podremos decirles a nuestros amigos en casa lo que pensamos de la comida española.
Maitre	Creo que les gustarán los platos de nuestra carta. ¿Con qué les gustaría empezar?
Sra. Austen	Mi marido y yo tomaremos el caldo gallego y nuestra hija la ensalada.
Maitre	Gracias, señora. ¿Y como plato principal? (¿Y de segundo?)
Sr. Austen	Tengo que probar la paella.
Sra. Austen	Yo voy a probar el pollo al chilindrón; Carmen quiere el bacalao a la riojana.
Maitre	¿Qué verduras quieren usted y su hija, señora?
Sra. Austen	Yo judías verdes y Carmen tomará los chícharos (guisantes).
Maitre	Gracias, señora. El mesero (camarero) les atenderá cuando quieran pedir los postres. ¿Desea beber vino, señor?
Sr. Austen	Sí, por favor. Una botella de vino tinto.
Maitre	Gracias, señor. Espero que disfruten de la cena.

Head waiter	Good evening, sir. Good evening, madam. A table for dinner?
Mr. Austen	Yes, please. A table for three. Our daughter's just coming.
Mrs. Austen	Could we have that table over there in the corner?
Head waiter	Certainly, madam.
Mrs. Austen	We want to have something typically Spanish this evening.
Mr. Austen	Then we can tell our friends back home what we think of Spanish food.
Head waiter	I think you will like the dishes on our menu. What would you like to start with?
Mrs. Austen	My husband and I will have the caldo gallego and our daughter will have the salad.
Head waiter	Thank you, madam. And for the main course?
Mr. Austen	I must have paella.
Mrs. Austen	I'm going to try the chicken dish with red peppers and ham. Carmen wants the cod with tomatoes.
Head waiter	What vegetables would you and your daughter like, madam?
Mrs. Austen	I'll have green beans and Carmen will have peas.
Head waiter	Thank you madam. The waiter will take your order when you are ready for dessert. Would you like wine, sir?
Mr. Austen	Yes, please. A bottle of red wine.
Head waiter	Thank you, sir. I hope you enjoy your meal.

MONEY

Can I cash traveller's checks here?	**¿Puedo cambiar cheques de viajero (viaje) aquí?** *pwe*do kam*bee*yar *che*kes deh veeya*he*ro (bee*ya*he) a*kee*?
Do you charge commission?	**¿Cobran comisión?** *ko*bran komee*see*yon?
How much do you charge to cash traveller's checks?	**¿Cuánto cobran por cambiar cheques de viajero (viaje)?** *kwan*to *ko*bran por kam*bee*yar *che*kes deh veeya*he*ro (bee*ya*he)?
Can I change these pesos for pounds?	**¿Puedo cambiar estos pesos por dólares?** *pwe*do kam*bee*yar *es*tos *pe*sos por *do*lares?
Can I see your passport, please?	**¿Puedo ver su pasaporte, por favor?** *pwe*do ver soo pasa*por*teh, por fa*vor*?
How would you like the money, sir?	**¿Cómo quiere el dinero, señor?** *ko*mo kee*ye*re el dee*ne*ro, sen*yor*?
Fifty dollars in tens, forty in fives and the rest in ones, please.	**Cincuenta dólares en billetes de diez, cuarenta de cinco y el resto de un dólar, por favor.** seen*kwen*ta *do*lares en beel-*ye*tes deh dee*eyes*, kwa*ren*ta deh *seen*ko ee el *res*to deh oon *do*lar, por fa*vor*
I'd like to exchange some money please.	**Me gustaría cambiar dinero, por favor.** meh goosta*ree*ya kam*bee*yar dee*ne*ro, por fa*vor*
Can you tell me what the exchange rate for pesos/euros is?	**¿Me puede decir a cómo está el peso/euro contra el dólar?** meh *pwe*deh de*seer* a *ko*mo es*ta* el *pe*so/e*yoo*ro *kon*tra el *do*lar?
What is the fee for exchanging money?	**¿Cuánto es la comisión por cambiar dinero?** *kwan*to es la komee*see*yon por kam*bee*yar dee*ne*ro?

In the bank

automatic teller machine	**cajero automático** kahero aootomateeko
bank clerk	**el empleado de banco** el empleyado deh banko
bank manager	**el director de banco** el deerektor deh banko
bank notes	**los billetes de banco** los bil-yetes deh banko
buy/sell	**comprar/vender** komprar/vender
cash a check	**cobrar un cheque** kobrar oon chekeh
change money	**cambiar dinero** kambeeyar deenero
check	**el cheque** el chekeh
coins	**las monedas** las monedas
commission	**la comisión** la komeeseeyon
counter	**el mostrador** el mostrador
credit card	**la tarjeta de crédito** la tarheta deh kredeeto
exchange rate	**la tasa de cambio** la tasa deh kambeeyo
identification	**la identificación** la eedenteefeekaseeyon
passport number	**el número de pasaporte** el noomero deh pasaporteh
receipt	**el recibo** el reseebo
signature	**la firma** la feerma
traveller's checks	**los cheques de viajero** los chekes deh veeyahero (beeyahe)

Dialog: In the bank

Empleado	Buenos días.
Sr. Austen	Buenos días. ¿Podría cambiar unos cheques de viajero (viaje) aquí?
Empleado	Sí, naturalmente, señor. ¿Son de euros?
Sr. Austen	Sí. Quisiera cambiar cien euros.
Empleado	Estos cheques de viajero (viaje) son de otro banco.
Sr. Austen	¿No se pueden cambiar estos cheques aquí?
Empleado	Sí podemos cambiárselos señor, pero tendrá que pagar por el servicio.
Sr. Austen	¿Quiere decir una comisión?
Empleado	Sí. Cargamos un uno por ciento con un mínimo de cinco euros. Le costará cinco euros cambiar el número que desee de cheques de viajero (viaje) hasta quinientos euros. Si cambia seiscientos euros, tendrá que pagar seis euros. Si va usted directamente a su banco, se los cambiarán sin cobrarle comisión.
Sr. Austen	Ya iré la próxima vez. Hoy los cambiaré aquí y pagaré la comisión.
Empleado	¿Cómo quiere el dinero?
Sr. Austen	Ochenta en billetes de diez y el resto de cinco.
Empleado	Cien euros menos cinco euros de comisión son noventa y cinco euros. Así que serán ocho de diez y tres de cinco. Gracias, señor. ¿Le puedo dar un consejo?
Mr. Austen	¡Por supuesto!
Bank clerk	Yo que usted consideraría usar los cajeros automáticos. Dan el mejor tipo de cambio y son mucho más fáciles de usar.

Bank clerk	Good morning.
Mr. Austen	Good morning. Can I cash some traveller's checks here, please?
Bank clerk	Yes, of course, sir. Are they in euros?
Mr. Austen	Yes, they are. I want to cash 100 euros.
Bank clerk	These traveller's checks are from a different bank.
Mr. Austen	Isn't it possible to cash these checks here?
Bank clerk	We can cash them for you, sir; but you will have to pay for the service.
Mr. Austen	Commission, you mean.
Bank clerk	Yes. We charge 1% with a 5 euro minimum. It will cost you 5 euros to cash any number of travellers checks up to 500 euros. If you cash 600 euros, you pay 6 euros. If you take these checks to your own bank, they will cash them without charge.
Mr. Austen	I will next time. Today I'll cash them here and pay the commission.
Bank clerk	How would you like the money, sir?
Mr. Austen	I'll have eighty in ten-euro notes and the rest in fives.
Bank clerk	100 euros less 5-euro commission is 95 euros. That's eight tens and three fives. Thank you, sir. Can I give you some advice, sir?
Mr. Austen	Yes, please do.
Bank clerk	You might consider using an automatic teller machine. They give the best exchange rates and are much easier to use.

SHOPPING

Have you a list of shops specializing in…?	**¿Tienen una lista de tiendas especializadas en…?** teeyenen oona leesta deh teeyendas espeseeyaleesadas en?
Do you sell toys?	**¿Venden juguetes?** venden hooghetes?
Have you a doll for a girl of six?	**¿Tienen muñecas para una niña de seis años?** teeyenen moonyekas para oona neenya deh seys anyos?
How much is this?	**¿Cuánto vale esto?** kwanto valeh esto?
How much is it a meter (a kilo, etc.)?	**¿A cuánto es el metro (el kilo, etc.)?** a kwanto es el metro (el keelo, etc.)?
Could you tell me where I could find a shop selling maps?	**¿Podría decirme donde hay una tienda que venda mapas (planos)?** podreeya deseermeh dondeh ay oona teeyenda keh venda mapas (planos)?
Could you recommend a good shop for china and glass?	**¿Podría recomendarme una buena tienda de porcelana y cristalería?** podreeya rekomendarmeh oona bwena teeyenda deh porselana ee kreestalereeya?

Paying

Could you put it in a bag, please?	**¿Puede ponerlo en (darme) una bolsa, por favor?** pwedeh ponerlo en (darmeh) oona bolsa, por favor?
Can I change this for a larger one, please?	**¿Puedo cambiarlo por uno más grande, por favor?** pwedo kambeeyarlo por oono mas grandeh, por favor?
Could you wrap it up, please?	**¿Me lo puede envolver, por favor?** meh lo pwedeh envolver, por favor?

Can I pay with credit card?	**¿Puedo pagar con tarjeta de crédito?** *pwe*do pa*gar* kon tar*he*ta deh *kre*deeto?
Can I pay for it now and pick it up later?	**¿Puedo pagarlo ahora y pasar a recogerlo más tarde?** *pwe*do pa*gar*lo a*o*ra ee pa*sar* a reko*her*lo mas *tar*deh?
Can you deliver it to the hotel?	**¿Puede enviarlo al hotel?** *pwe*deh envee*yar*lo al o*tel*?
Is sales tax/VAT included?	**¿Está incluído el I.V.A. (Impuesto sobre el valor añadido)?** es*ta* eenkloo*yee*do el *ee*va (eem*pwes*to *so*breh el va*lor* anya*dee*do)?
Is there a guarantee?	**¿Tiene garantía?** tee*ye*neh garan*tee*ya?
Can I order this by Internet?	**¿Puedo encargar esto por Internet?** *pwe*do en*kar*gar *es*to por eenter*net*?

Containers

una caja de (a box/carton of):	**cerillos (cerillas)** (matches), **puros** (cigars), **chocolates (bombones)** (chocolates), **leche** (milk), **jugo (zumo) de frutas** (fruit juice), **crema (nata)** (cream)
un paquete de (a packet of):	**cigarrillos** (cigarettes), **galletas** (biscuits), **servilletas de papel** (paper napkins)
una bolsa de (a bag of):	**papas (patatas) fritas** (chips), **caramelos** (candy)
una lata de (a tin/can of):	**sopa** (soup), **pintura** (paint), **grasa** (grease), **cerveza** (beer)
un bote de (a pot of):	**jalea (mermelada)** (jelly), **mermelada de naranja** (marmalade)
una botella de (a bottle of):	**vino** (wine), **limonada** (lemonade)
un saco de (a sack of):	**papas (patatas)** (potatoes), **carbón** (coal), **madera** (wood)

Shops and stores
_____

Shops

antique shop	**el anticuario** el antee*k*wareeyo
baker's	**la panadería** la panade*ree*ya
bookstore	**la librería** la leebre*ree*ya
butcher's	**la carnicería** la karneese*ree*ya
cake shop	**la pastelería** la pastele*ree*ya
camera shop	**la tienda de fotografía** la tee*yen*da de fotogra*fee*ya
china and glass shop	**la cristalería** la kreestale*ree*ya
dress shop	**la boutique** la boo*teek*
dry cleaner's	**la tintorería** la teentore*ree*ya
fish shop	**la pescadería** la peskade*ree*ya
flower shop	**la florería (floristería)** la flore*ree*ya (floreeste*ree*ya)
furniture shop	**la tienda de muebles** la tee*yen*da deh *m*webles
greengrocer's	**la verdulería** la verdoole*ree*ya
grocer's	**el ultramarino** el ooltrama*ree*no
hair salon	**la peluquería** la pelooke*ree*ya
hardware store	**la ferretería** la ferrete*ree*ya
jewelry store	**la joyería** la hoye*ree*ya
liquor store	**la tienda de licores (la bodega)** la tee*yen*da deh lee*k*ores (la bo*d*ega)
menswear shop	**la tienda de ropa de caballero** la tee*yen*da deh ropa deh cabal-*y*ero
music store	**la tienda de discos** la tee*yen*da deh *d*eeskos
newsstand	**el puesto de periódicos (quiosco)** el *p*westo deh pereey*od*eekos (keey*os*ko)
pharmacy	**la farmacia** la far*m*aseeya
shoe store	**la zapatería** la sapate*ree*ya
stationer's	**la papelería** la papele*ree*ya

tobacco shop	**el estanquillo (estanco)** el estan*keel*-yo (es*tan*ko)
toy store	**la juguetería** la hoogete*ree*eya
travel agency	**la agencia de viajes** la a*hen*seeya deh vee*ya*jes

Other establishments

department store	**el almacén (los grandes almacenes)** el alma*sen* (los *grandes* alma*the*nes)
gas station	**la gasolinera** la gasol*ee*nera
post office	**el correo (correos)** el kor*re*yo (kor*re*yos)
supermarket	**el supermercado** el soopermer*ka*do

Camera

Can you repair this camera?	**¿Puede componer esta cámara?** *pwe*deh kompo*ner* esta *ka*mara?
Do you have film for this video camera?	**¿Tiene película para esta cámara de video (vídeo)?** tee*ye*neh pe*lee*koola para esta *ka*mara deh vee*de*yo?
camera	**la cámara** la *ka*mara
camera film	**el rollo de película** el *rrol*-yo deh pe*lee*koola
video camera	**la cámara de video (vídeo)** la *ka*mara deh vee*de*yo (vee*de*yo)
exposures	**las exposiciones (fotografías)** las eksposeesee*yo*nes (fotogra*fee*yas)
15-minute video film	**una película de video (vídeo) de quince minutos** *oo*na pe*lee*koola deh vee*de*yo (vee*de*yo) deh *keen*seh mee*no*tos

Gas station

Please fill up the tank.	**¿Me puede llenar el tanque, por favor?** meh *pwe*deh l-ye*nar* el *tan*keh, por fa*vor*?

Is this gas station self-service?	**¿Esta gasolinera es de autoservicio?** *esta gasoleenera es deh aootoserveeseeyo?*
regular/super	**regular/super** *regoolar/sooper*
unleaded/diesel	**sin plomo/diesel** *seen plomo/deesel*

Newstand

newspaper	**el periódico** *el pereeyodeeko*
magazine	**la revista** *la reveesta*
cigarettes	**los cigarrillos** *los seegarreel-yos*

Pharmacy

analgesic	**el analgésico** *el analheseeko*
aspirin	**la aspirina** *la aspeereena*
bandages	**las vendas** *las vendas*
compresses	**las compresas** *las kompresas*
condom	**el condón/el preservativo** *el kondon/el preservateevo*
cotton wool	**el algodón** *el algodon*
disinfectant	**el desinfectante** *el deseenfektanteh*
ear drops	**las gotas para los oídos** *las gotas para los oyeedos*
eye drops	**las gotas para los ojos** *las gotas para los ohos*
gauze	**la gasa** *la gasa*
insect cream	**la loción contra insectos** *la loseeyon kontra eensektos*
ointment	**la pomada** *la pomada*
for cuts	**para cortadas (cortes)** *para kortadas (kortes)*
for burns	**para quemaduras** *para kemadooras*
oxygenated water	**el agua oxigenada** *el agwa okseehenada*
plaster/bandage	**la bandita (tirita)** *la bandeeta (teereeta)*
sanitary towels	**los paños higiénicos (las compresas)** *los panyos eeheeyeneekos (las kompresas)*

sticking plaster/adhesive bandage	**la cinta adhesiva (el esparadrapo)** la *seen*ta adhe*see*va (el espara*dra*po)
suppository	**el supositorio** el soopose*to*reeyo
syrup	**el jarabe** el ha*ra*beh
thermometer	**el termómetro** el ter*mo*metro
toothpaste	**la pasta de dientes** la *pas*ta deh dee*yen*tes

Post office

How much to send a postcard to the U.S.?	**¿Cuánto cuesta mandar una postal a los Estados Unidos?** *kwan*to *kwes*ta man*dar oo*na pos*tal* a los es*ta*dos oo*nee*dos?
I want to send this parcel to Canada.	**Quiero mandar este paquete a Canadá.** kee*ye*ro man*dar* esteh pa*ke*teh a kana*da*
stamp	**la estampilla/el timbre (el sello)** la estam*peel*-ya/el *teem*breh (el *sel*-yo)
letter	**la carta** la *kar*ta
postcard	**la postal** la pos*tal*
parcel	**el paquete** el pa*ke*teh
by airmail	**por correo aéreo** por ko*rre*yo a*ye*reyo
registered mail	**correo registrado (certificado)** ko*rre*yo rehees*tra*do (therteefee*ka*do)

Souvenirs

book	**el libro** el *lee*bro
blanket	**la cobija (manta)** la ko*bee*ha (*man*ta)
castanets	**las castañuelas** las kasta*nywe*las
ceramics	**la cerámica** la se*ra*meeka
fan	**el abanico** el aba*nee*ko
guitar	**la guitarra** la ghee*ta*rra
poster	**el póster** el *pos*ter
hat	**el sombrero** el som*bre*ro
tee shirt	**la camiseta** la kamee*se*ta
textiles	**los textiles** los teks*tee*les

Dialog: Going shopping

Sra. Austen	¿Qué te parece esta tienda?
Dependiente	Tenemos una gran variedad de productos tradicionales aquí.
Sr. Austen	Que no se nos olvide que tenemos que llevarle un souvenir a mi madre.
Sra. Austen	Mira toda esta exposición de cerámica. ¿Crees que a tu madre le gustaría algo así?
Dependiente	Tengo muchos tamaños y estilos. Tenemos platos de todas las regiones del país.
Sra. Austen	Los colores son hermosísimos.Quizá le compre uno a mi tía.
Sr. Austen	No estoy seguro de que a mi madre le vaya a gustar este tipo de cosas.
Sra. Austen	Está bien. ¿Qué tal uno de estos chales?
Dependiente	¡El trabajo es increíble! ¡La tela es de lo más suave!
Sr. Austen	No estoy seguro de que jamás se lo pondría.
Sra. Austen	¿Qué tal uno de estos abanicos?
Sr. Austen	¿No tiene algo más barato?
Dependiente	Pero considere todo el trabajo que tienen. Son hechos a mano.
Sr. Austen	¿Ves algo más que le podríamos llevar a mi madre?
Dependiente	Aquí hay mucha joyería. Vamos a ver. Tenemos collares, aretes (pendientes) y pulseras.
Sr. Austen	No creo que mi madre use mucha joyería. No creo que le gustara nada de eso tampoco.
Sra. Austen	¡Yo creo que están preciosos! Me voy a comprar una pulsera para mí.
Sr. Austen	¿Pero qué va a pasar con lo que le tenemos que llevar a mi madre?
Dependiente	Yo creo que a este paso va a terminar con una esferita de cristal.

Mrs. Austen	How about this store?
Assistant	We offer lots of traditional things here.
Mr. Austen	Don't forget that we have to get a souvenir for my mother.
Mrs. Austen	Look at this pottery display. Do you think your mother would like something like this?
Assistant	I have lots of sizes and styles. We have plates from every region of the country.
Mrs. Austen	The colors are gorgeous. Maybe I'll get one for my aunt.
Mr. Austen	I'm not sure that my mother would like that kind of thing.
Mrs. Austen	Okay. How about these shawls?
Assistant:	The craftsmanship is amazing! The fabric is so soft!
Mr. Austen	I'm not sure that she'd ever wear it.
Mrs. Austen	What about one of these fans?
Mr. Austen	Do you have anything cheaper?
Assistant:	But consider all the work that went into them! They're handmade.
Mr. Austen	Do you see anything else we could get my mother?
Assistant	Over here is a lot of jewelry. Let's see. We have necklaces, earrings, and bracelets.
Mr. Austen	I don't think that my mother wears a lot of jewelry. I'm not sure that she'd like those either.
Mrs. Austen	I think they're adorable! I'm going to buy a bracelet for myself.
Mr. Austen	But what about something for my mother?
Assistant	I think at this rate that she's going to end up with a snowglobe.

Departments

Ropa de señora (ladieswear):	**vestidos** (dresses), **blusas** (blouses), **faldas** (skirts), **abrigos** (coats), **impermeables** (raincoats)
Ropa de caballero (menswear):	**trajes** (suits), **sacos (americanas)** (jackets), **pantalones** (pants/trousers), **abrigos** (overcoats), **impermeables** (raincoats), **camisas** (shirts), **corbatas** (ties), **calcetines** (socks)
Ropa de niños (childrenswear):	**chaquetas y pantalones para niños** (jackets and pants for boys), **vestidos y faldas para niñas** (dresses and skirts for girls)
Calzado (footwear):	**botas** (boots), **zapatos** (shoes), **sandalias** (sandals), **pantuflas (zapatillas)** (slippers)
Medias y calcetines (hosiery):	**medias** (stockings), **pantimedias (medias)** (tights), **calcetines** (socks)
Ropa deportiva (sportswear):	**ropa de playa** (beachwear), **ropa (de) sport** (leisurewear)
Productos de belleza: (cosmetics)	**agua de colonia** (toilet water), **jabón de tocador** (toilet soap), **polvos para la cara** (face powder), **lápiz (barra) de labios** (lipstick)
Porcelana y cristalería: (china and glassware)	**tazas** (cups), **platitos** (saucers), **platos** (plates), **platones (fuentes)** (dishes), **jarrones** (vases), **vasos/copas** (glasses)
Ropa blanca (household linen):	**sábanas** (sheets), **fundas de almohadas** (pillow cases), **cobijas (mantas)** (blankets), **manteles** (table cloths)
Utensilios de cocina: (kitchenware)	**cacerolas** (saucepans), **sartenes** (frying pans), **charolas (bandejas)** (trays)
Joyería (jewelry):	**collares** (necklaces), **anillos** (rings), **aretes (pendientes)** (earrings)

Accesorios (accessories):   **bolsos de señora** (handbags), **bufandas y pañuelos** (scarves), **guantes** (gloves), **paraguas** (umbrellas)

Mercería (fabric store):   **lana** (wool), **agujas de tejer (hacer punto)** (knitting needles), **hilo** (thread), **alfileres y agujas** (pins and needles)

Telas (dress fabrics):   **algodón** (cotton), **lana** (wool), **seda** (silk), **telas para trajes** (suitings)

Artículos de viaje:
(travel goods)   **maletas** (suitcases), **baúles** (trunks), **bolsas** (bags), **portafolios (maletines)** (brief cases)

Artículos de escritorio:
(stationery)   **papel de escribir** (writing paper), **plumas** (pens), **máquinas de escribir** (typewriters), **cuadernos** (notebooks)

Tapicería (furnishings):   **cortinas** (curtains), **alfombras** (carpets), **cojines** (cushions)

Relojería (clocks and watches):   **despertadores** (alarm clocks), **relojes de pulsera** (wrist watches)

Radio y televisión:
(radio and television)   **sistemas de estéreo** (stereo systems), **radios portátiles** (portable radios)

Electrodomésticos:
(household appliances)   **refrigeradores (frigoríficos)** (refrigerators), **hornos microondas** (microwave ovens), **aspiradoras** (vacuum cleaners)

Can you tell me where the men's clothing is?   **¿Me puede decir donde está la ropa de caballero?** meh *pwe*deh de*seer don*deh es*ta* la *ro*pa deh kabal-*yero*?

I'm looking for an umbrella.   **Estoy buscando un paraguas.** es*toy* boos*kan*do oon pa*rag*was

Do you sell cosmetics?   **¿Venden cosméticos?** *ven*den kos*me*teekos?

Can I pay for these here?   **¿Puedo pagar esto aquí?** *pwe*do pa*gar* esto a*kee*?

In the store

Building	
basement	**el sótano** el sotano
doors	**las puertas** las pwertas
elevator	**el ascensor** el as-sensor
emergency exit	**la salida de emergencia** la saleeda deh emerhenseeya
entrance/exit	**la entrada/salida** la entrada/saleeda
escalator	**la escalera eléctrica (mecánica)** la eskalera elektreeka (mekaneeka)
floors	**las plantas** las plantas
first floor	**la planta baja** la planta baha
second floor	**la primera planta** la preemera planta
third floor	**la segunda planta** la segoonda planta
main door	**la puerta principal** la pwerta preenseepal
main entrance	**la entrada principal** la entrada preenseepal
rear entrance	**la entrada trasera** la entrada trasera
side door	**la puerta lateral** la pwerta lateral
side entrance	**la entrada lateral** la entrada lateral
stairs	**las escaleras** las eskaleras
shop window	**el escaparate** el eskaparateh
Counter	
assistant	**el dependiente/la dependienta** el dependeeyenteh/la dependeeyenta
bag	**la bolsa** la bolsa
by check	**con cheque** kon chekeh
cash register	**la caja** la kaha
counter	**el mostrador** el mostrador
exchange goods	**cambiar artículos** kambeeyar arteekooloos
display	**la exposición** la eksposeeseeyon
in cash	**en efectivo** en efekteevo
to pay	**pagar** pagar

receipt	**el recibo** el re*see*bo
with credit card	**con tarjeta de crédito** kon tar*het*a deh *kred*eeto
to wrap	**envolver** envol*ver*
Departments	
childrenswear	**la ropa de niños** la *rop*a deh *neen*yos
china and glass	**la porcelana y la cristalería** la porse*lan*a ee la kreestale*ree*ya
clocks and watches	**la relojería** la relohe*ree*ya
cosmetics	**la perfumería** la perfoome*ree*ya
dress material	**las telas para ropa** las *te*las para *rop*a
fabrics	**los tejidos** los te*heed*os
footwear	**la zapatería** la sapate*ree*ya
furniture	**los muebles** los *mwe*bles
hosiery	**las medias y los calcetines** las *med*eeyas ee los kalse*teen*es
jewelry	**la joyería** la hoye*ree*ya
kitchenware	**los utensilios de cocina** los ooten*see*leeyos deh ko*seen*a
ladieswear	**la ropa de señora** la *rop*a deh se*nyor*a
menswear	**la ropa de caballero** la *rop*a deh kaba*l-yer*o
music	**los discos** los *dees*kos
pets	**los animales domésticos** los anee*mal*es do*mest*eekos
radio and television	**el (la) radio y la televisión** el (la) *rad*eeyo ee la televee*see-yon*
sports equipment	**los deportes** los de*port*es
sportswear	**la ropa de deportes** la *rop*a deh de*port*es
stationery	**la papelería** la papele*ree*ya
toys	**la juguetería** la hooghete*ree*ya
Sale	
sale	**las rebajas** las re*bah*as
discount	**el descuento** el desk*went*o

Dialog: In the department store

Sr. Austen	Perdone, ¿podría decirme dónde puedo comprar pañuelos de caballero, por favor?
Dependiente	Departamento de caballeros, segunda planta, señor.
Sra. Austen	¿Dónde puedo encontrar ropa de playa?
Dependiente	Ropa de señora, primera planta, señora.
Carmen	¿Los baños (servicios)?
Dependiente	Los baños (servicios) de señora están en la cuarta planta, señora. Puede subir en el ascensor que hay allí.
Joven	¿A qué hora cierran ustedes?
Dependiente	A las seis.
Joven	¿Todos los días?
Dependiente	No, señor; los jueves, viernes y sábados estamos abiertos hasta las ocho.
Extranjero	¿Aceptan cheques de viajero (viaje)?
Dependiente	Si son en euros, sí, señor.
Extranjero	¿Y tarjetas de crédito?
Dependiente	Sí, todas las tarjetas principales (más conocidas).
Extranjero	Muchas gracias. Ah, otra cosa; ¿tienen ustedes un departamento donde vendan piezas para rasuradoras (maquinillas de afeitar) eléctricas?
Dependiente	Tendrá que ir al departamento de electro-domésticos, en el sótano, señor. Baje por esas escaleras, voltee (gire) a la derecha y verá el mostrador a la izquierda.
Extranjero	Muchas gracias.

Mr. Austen	*Excuse me, could you tell me where I can find men's handkerchiefs, please?*
Assistant	*Men's department on the third floor, sir.*
Mrs. Austen	*Where can I find beachwear?*
Assistant	*Ladieswear, second floor, madam.*
Carmen	*The restroom?*
Assistant	*The ladies' restroom is on the fifth floor, madam. You can go up in the elevator over there.*
Young man	*What time do you close?*
Assistant	*Six o'clock.*
Young man	*Every day?*
Assistant	*No, sir; on Thursdays, Fridays and Saturdays we're open till eight.*
Foreigner	*Do you accept traveller's checks here?*
Assistant	*If they are in euros, yes, sir.*
Foreigner	*And credit cards too?*
Assistant	*Yes, all the main credit cards.*
Foreigner	*Thank you very much. Oh, one more thing: have you a department where they sell spare parts for electric shavers?*
Assistant	*That will be in electrical goods in the basement, sir. Go down those stairs over there, turn right and you'll see the counter on the left.*
Foreigner	*Thank you very much.*

CLOTHING

Where could I find a pair of boots like these?
¿Dónde podría encontrar un par de botas como éstas? *dondeh* podreeya enkon*trar* oon par deh *botas komo estas?*

Are there any shops that specialize in children's clothes?
¿Hay alguna tienda especializada en ropa de niños? ay al*goona* tee*yenda* espeseeya*leesada* en *ropa* deh *neenyos?*

The sleeves are too long.
Las mangas están (son) demasiado largas. las *mangas* es*tan* (son) demasee*yado largas*

The pockets are too small.
Los bolsillos están (son) demasiado pequeños. los bol*seel*-yos es*tan* (son) demasee*yado* pe*kenyos*

The lapels are too wide.
Las solapas están (son) demasiado anchas. las so*lapas* es*tan* (son) demasee*yado an*chas

The jacket is too big.
El saco (La chaqueta) está (es) demasiado grande. el *sako* (la cha*keta*) es*ta* (es) demasee*yado grandeh*

The trousers are too short.
Los pantalones están (son) demasiado cortos. los panta*lones* es*tan* (son) demasee*yado kortos*

Can you shorten/lengthen the sleeves?
¿Pueden acortar/alargar las mangas? *pweden* akor*tar*/alar*gar* las *mangas?*

Can you take in/let out the hem?
¿Pueden coger (meter)/sacar el dobladillo? *pweden* ko*her* (me*ter*)/sa*kar* el dobla*deel*-yo?

Can you alter the collar?	**¿Pueden cambiar el cuello?** pweden kambeeyar el kwel-yo?
Can you change the buttons?	**¿Pueden cambiar los botones?** pweden kambeeyar los botones?
Can you take in/let out the waist?	**¿Pueden coger (meter)/sacar la cintura?** pweden koher (meter)/sakar la seentoora?
Haven't you got this dress in a darker blue?	**¿Tiene este vestido en un azul más oscuro?** teeyeneh este vesteedo en oon asool mas oskooro?
Have you got this blouse in any other colors?	**¿Tiene esta blusa en otros colores?** teeyeneh esta bloosa en otros kolores?
Have you got a blouse in a larger size?	**¿Tiene una blusa en una talla más grande?** teeyeneh oona bloosa en oona tal-ya mas grandeh?
Have you got a blouse to match this skirt?	**¿Tiene una blusa que haga juego con esta falda?** teeyene oona bloosa keh aga hwego kon esta falda?
Could I change this for a size smaller?	**¿Podría cambiar éste por una talla más chica (menor)?** podreeya kambeeyar este por oona tal-ya mas cheeka (menor)?

Clothing sizes

(Shirt) What size, sir?	**¿Qué talla, señor?** keh tal-ya, senyor?
(Shoes) What size, sir?	**¿Qué número, señor?** keh noomero, senyor?
(Dress) What size, madam?	**¿Qué tamaño (talla), señora?** keh tamanyo (tal-ya), senyora?

Colors

beige	**beige** bej (beyj)
black	**negro** *ne*gro
blue	**azul** a*sool*
brown	**café (marrón)** *ka*feh (ma*rron*)
fuchsia	**fucsia** *fook*seeya
gold	**dorado** do*rado*
green	**verde** *ver*deh
grey	**gris** grees
khaki	**caqui** *ka*kee
mauve	**lila (malva)** *lee*la (*mal*va)
orange	**naranja** na*ran*ha
pink	**rosa** *ro*sa
red	**rojo** *ro*ho
silver	**plateado** plate*ya*do
white	**blanco** *blan*ko
yellow	**amarillo** ama*reel*-yo
a red pleated skirt	**una falda roja plisada** *oo*na *fal*da *ro*ha plee*sa*da
a light green silk dress	**un vestido de seda verde claro** oon ves*tee*do deh *se*da *ver*deh *kla*ro
black patent leather shoes	**unos zapatos de charol negros** *oo*nos sa*pa*tos deh cha*rol ne*gros

Materials

algodón	cotton	**hilo**	linen
ante	suede	**lana**	wool
charol	patent leather	**nilon**	nylon
cheviot	cheviot	**pana**	corduroy
crepé (crespón)	crepe	**poliéster**	polyester
cuero	leather	**popelina**	poplin
estambre	worsted	**rayón**	rayon
fieltro	felt	**satín (satén)**	satin
franela	flannel	**seda**	silk
gasa	gauze	**terciopelo**	velvet

Items of clothing

abrigo	overcoat	shorts	shorts
bata de baño (albornoz)	bathrobe	sombrero	hat
		traje de baño	trunks, swimsuit
bata	dressing gown		
blusa	blouse	traje	suit
brasier (sujetador)	bra	vestido de noche	evening dress
		vestido	dress/frock
bufanda	scarf		
calcetines	socks	Footwear	
calzoncillos	underwear (pants)	botas	boots
		de tacón alto	high heels
calzones (bragas)	panties	de tacón bajo	low heels
camisa	shirt	pantuflas (zapatillas)	slippers
camiseta	undershirt		
camisón	nightdress	sandalias	sandals
capa	cape	zapatos de deporte	sports shoes
chaleco	waistcoat		
corbata	tie	Accessories	
falda	skirt	bolsillo	pocket
guantes	gloves	botón	button
impermeable	raincoat	cinturón	belt
lencería	lingerie	cremallera	zip
medias	stockings	cuello	collar
pantalones	pants	dobladillo	hem
pantalones vaqueros	jeans	faja	sash
		forro	lining
pantimedias (medias)	tights	hebilla	buckle
		manga	sleeve
pijama	pajamas	olán (volante)	frill
ropa interior	underwear	puño	cuff
saco (americana)	jacket	solapa	lapel

Dialog: Shopping for clothes

Dependiente	Buenos días, señor. ¿En qué puedo servirle?
Sr. Austen	Quisiera ver uno de los trajes del escaparate. Es azul.
Dependiente	¿Es éste señor?
Sr. Austen	Sí, ése es.
Dependiente	¿Qué talla usa?
Sr. Austen	No estoy seguro. Cada vez que me compro un traje es distinta.
Dependiente	No se preocupe caballero. Puedo tomar sus medidas. Primero su pecho: treinta y ocho pulgadas. Ahora la cintura: treinta y ocho también. Ahora el largo de pierna: treinta y cuatro. Este traje debería de quedarle bien, señor.
Sra. Austen	Pruébate primero el saco (la chaqueta), John.
Dependiente	Las mangas le quedan un poco largas.
Sra. Austen	¿Tiene algo más claro, en gris, por ejemplo?
Dependiente	Sí, tenemos esos trajes en gris; éstos en café (marrón); y aquéllos verdes de allí. ¿Qué le parece éste?
Sr. Austen	Me gusta. La tela es muy suave.
Sra. Austen	No me gustan los bolsillos; están demasiado grandes. Los pantalones están demasiado estrechos y no tienen valenciana (vuelta).
Dependiente	Hoy en día muchos trajes tienen bolsillos grandes. Los pantalones rara vez llevan valenciana (vuelta). ¿Qué opina de este traje gris con raya, señor?
Sr. Austen	No, no me gustan los trajes con rayas. ¿Tiene sacos (americanas) de sport?
Dependiente	Los sacos (Las americanas) están en aquel departamento, señor.
Sr. Austen	Creo que voy a ir a echarles una ojeada.
Dependiente	Muy bien, señor.

Assistant	Good morning, sir. Can I help you?
Mr. Austen	I'd like to see one of the suits in the window. It's blue.
Assistant	Is it this one, sir?
Mr. Austen	Yes, it is.
Assistant	What size to you take?
Mr Austen	I'm not sure. It changes every time I buy a suit.
Assistant	Don't worry, sir. I can measure you. First your chest – thirty-eight inches. Now your waist – that's thirty-eight too. Now your trouser leg – thirty-four. This suit should fit you, sir.
Mrs Austen	Try the jacket on first, John.
Assistant	The sleeves are a little too long.
Mrs Austen	Have you anything lighter, in grey perhaps?
Assistant	Yes, we have those grey suits; these brown ones; and the green ones over there. What do you think of this one?
Mr Austen	I like it. The material is very smooth.
Mrs Austen	I don't like the pockets; they are too big. The trousers are too narrow and they have no cuffs.
Assistant	Most suits have big pockets nowadays and trousers rarely have cuffs. What do you think of this grey pin striped one, sir.
Mr Austen	No, I don't like pin striped suits. Have you any sports jackets?
Assistant	Sports jackets are in that department there, sir.
Mr Austen	I think I'll go and have a look at them.
Assistant	Certainly, sir.

ENTERTAINMENT

Where could I find the program of concerts for this month?

¿Dónde podría encontrar el programa de conciertos de este mes? *dondeh podreeya enkontrar el programa deh konseeyertos deh esteh mes?*

Is it possible to book tickets for the theater here?

¿Se pueden reservar localidades (entradas) del teatro aquí? *seh pweden reservar lokaleedades (entradas) del teyatro akee?*

Can you recommend a good movie?

¿Puede recomendarme una buena película? *pwedeh rekomendarmeh oona bwena pehleekoola?*

What's on at the Palace theater?

¿Qué dan en el teatro Palacio? *keh dan en el teyatro palaseeyo?*

Have you two good seats in the stalls?

¿Tiene dos buenas butacas en (de) platea? *teeyeneh dos bwenas bootakas en (deh) plateya?*

There are two in the middle of the fifth row – row E.

Hay dos en el centro (medio) de la quinta fila, fila E. *ay dos en el sentro (medeeyo) deh la keenta feela, feela eh*

How much are the seats in the balcony?

¿Cuánto cuestan las localidades en la galería? *kwanto kwestan las lokaleedades en la galereeya?*

Have you anything cheaper?

¿Tiene algo más barato? *teeyeneh algo mas barato?*

What time does the show begin?	**¿A qué hora empieza el espectáculo?** a keh ora empeeyesa el espektakoolo?
Where can I get a program?	**¿Dónde puedo conseguir un programa?** dondeh pwedo konsegheer oon programa?
Could I book a table for dinner after the concert?	**¿Podría reservar una mesa para cenar después del concierto?** podreeya reservar oona mesa para senar despwes del konseeyerto?
Is there any charge for admission?	**¿Hay que pagar entrada?** ay keh pagar entrada?
What sort of music do they play here?	**¿Qué tipo de música ponen aquí?** keh teepo deh mooseeka ponen akee?
Can we get a taxi after the show?	**¿Podemos coger un taxi después de la función?** podemos koher oon taksee despwes deh la foonseeyon?

Booking by phone

Can I pay for these over the phone?	**¿Puedo pagar por teléfono?** pwedo pagar por telefono?
My credit card number is…	**El número de mi tarjeta de crédito es…** el noomero deh mee tarheta deh kredeeto es
The expiry date is...	**La fecha de vencimiento (caducidad) es el…** la fecha deh venseemeeyento (kadootheedad) es el
Is there a confirmation number?	**¿Hay algún número de confirmación?** ay algoon noomero deh konfeermaseeyon?

General

box office	**la taquilla** la takeel-ya
entertainment	**los espectáculos** los espektakooloos
coatcheck	**el guardarropa** el gwardarropa
seats at the front	**las butacas delanteras** las bootakas delanteras
in the middle	**centrales** sentrales
at the back	**traseras** traseras
upstairs/downstairs	**arriba/abajo** arriba/abaho
orchestra	**orquesta** orkesta
dress circle	**la platea** a plateya
gallery	**la galería** la galereeya
row C	**la fila C** la feela seh
ticket	**la entrada** la entrada

Classical music

concert hall	**la sala de conciertos** la sala deh konseeyertos
opera house	**la ópera** la opera
orchestra	**la orquesta** la orkesta
conductor	**el director/la directora** el deerektor/la deerektora
singer	**el/la cantante** el/la kantanteh
musician	**el músico/la música (la músico)** el mooseeko/la mooseeka (la mooseeko)

Theater

intermission	**el entreacto/el descanso (el intermedio)** el entreyakto/el deskanso (el eentermedeeyo)
play	**la obra de teatro** la obra deh teyatro
program	**el programa** el programa
comedy	**la comedia** la komedeeya
drama	**el drama** el drama

Movie theater

film	**la película** la pe*lee*koola
movie theater	**el cine** el *see*neh
actor/actress	**el actor/la actriz** el ak*tor*/la ak*trees*
screen	**la pantalla** la pan*tal*-ya
subtitles	**los subtítulos** los soob*tee*toolos
dubbed	**doblada** dob*la*da

Bars, etc.

discotheque	**la discoteca** la deesko*te*ka
bar	**el bar** el bar
live music	**la música viva (en directo)** la *moo*seeka *vee*va (en dee*rek*to)
night club	**night club** "night club"
dance	**bailar** bay*lar*
identification	**identificación** eedenteefeekasee*yon*

Sport

baseball	**el béisbol** el *bey*eesbol
basketball	**el básquetbol (baloncesto)** el *bás*quetbol (balon*thes*to)
bullfight	**la corrida de toros** la ko*rree*da deh *to*ros
game	**el partido** el par*tee*do
golf	**el golf** el golf
horseback riding	**montar a caballo** mon*tar* a ka*bal*-yo
ice-skating	**el patinaje sobre hielo** el patee*na*heh *so*breh *eey*elo
skiing	**esquiar** es*kée*yar
soccer	**el fútbol** el *foot*bol
stadium	**el estadio** el es*ta*deeyo
team	**el equipo** el e*kee*po
tennis	**el tenis** el *te*nees
working out	**el ejercicio** el eher*see*seeyo

Dialog: Going out for the evening

Sr. Austen	¿Podría decirnos algo sobre las diversiones que hay aquí?
Recepcionista	Para eso les aconsejo que hablen con Ricardo. Es nuestro experto en el tema. Ric, ¿te importaría informar a estos señores acerca de las diversiones que hay aquí en la ciudad?
Sr. Austen	¿Hay algo que usted recomendaría a dos turistas norteamericanos y su hija de dieciséis años?
Ricardo	Bueno, tenemos el Auditorio Nacional, donde puede encontrar muchos espectáculos si le gustan la música clásica o el teatro.
Sr. Austen	Nos gusta la música clásica pero tenemos que excluir el teatro si está en español.
Sra. Austen	No nos importan las películas con subtítulos.
Ricardo	El cine que está en la plaza aquí cerca a menudo tiene películas con subtítulos.
Sr. Austen	¿Qué más hay aquí cerca?
Ricardo	Hay dos salas de conciertos y también hay otro lugar que es para recitales.
Sra. Austen	¿Los tres para música clásica?
Ricardo	No siempre, depende. Vamos a ver el periódico. El Ballet Nacional pone (representa) «El lago de los Cisnes» en el Festival Hall; hay un concierto de jazz de los años treinta en el Music Hall y hay un concierto de música popular (folk) en el Folkloric Center.
Sr. Austen	¿Qué más hay ahí?
Ricardo	También está el teatro pero está (es) en español . También está el museo de arte contemporáneo. Tienen dos exposiciones estos días, una del pintor y escultor Gerardo Rueda.
Sra. Austen	Vamos a la plaza, John.

Mr. Austen	*Could you give us some idea about entertainment here?*
Receptionist	*You had better ask Ricardo here about that, sir. He's our expert on that subject. Ric, would you like to tell this lady and gentleman about the city's entertainment?*
Mr. Austen	*Is there anything you could recommend to two U.S. visitors and their 16-year-old daughter?*
Ricardo	*Well, there's the performing arts center, where you will find plenty to entertain you if you like classical music or theater.*
Mr. Austen	*We like classical music, but we must exclude theater if it's in Spanish.*
Mrs. Austen	*We don't mind films with subtitles.*
Ricardo	*The cinema in the nearby plaza often has films with subtitles.*
Mr. Austen	*What else is nearby?*
Ricardo	*There are two concert halls; then there is another place, which is for recitals.*
Mrs. Austen	*All three for classical music?*
Ricardo	*Not always, it depends. Let's have a look at the newspaper. The National Ballet are doing Swan Lake at the Festival Hall; there's a 1930's jazz concert at the Music Hall; and there's traditional folk music at the Folkloric Center.*
Mr. Austen	*What else is there?*
Ricardo	*There's the theater, but that's in Spanish. Then there's the contemporary art museum. They've got two exhibitions there at the moment, one of the painter and sculptor Gerardo Rueda.*
Mrs. Austen	*Let's go to the plaza, John.*

SIGHTSEEING

Which are the best museums for modern art?	**¿Cuáles son los mejores museos de arte moderno?** *kwa*les son los me*hor*es mooseyos deh *ar*teh mo*der*no?
What style was this built in?	**¿En qué estilo fue construído este edificio?** en keh es*tee*lo fweh konstrooy*ee*do esteh edee*fee*seeyo?
Who was the architect?	**¿Quién fue el arquitecto?** kee*yen* fweh el arkee*tek*to?
Is there a guided tour?	**¿Hay visitas con guía?** ay vee*see*tas kon *ghee*ya?
Do you have a commentary in English?	**¿Tienen la explicación (cinta) en inglés?** teeyenen la ekspleekasee*yon* (*seen*ta) en een*gles*?

Historic buildings

battlements	**las almenas** las al*men*as
castle	**el castillo** el kas*teel*-yo
drawbridge	**el puente levadizo** el *pwen*teh leva*dee*so
dungeons	**las mazmorras** las mas*morr*as
fountains	**las fuentes** las *fwen*tes
minaret	**el minarete** el meena*ret*eh
moat	**el foso** el *fo*so
monument	**el monumento** el monoo*men*to
mosque	**la mezquita** la mes*kee*ta
palace	**el palacio** el pa*las*eeyo
pyramid	**la pirámide** la peera*meed*eh
ruin	**la ruina** la roo*ee*na

site	**sitio arqueológico** *see*teeyo arkeyo*lo*heeko
square	**la plaza** la *pla*sa
street	**la calle** la *ka*l-yeh
walls	**los muros** los *moo*ros

Churches

aisle	**la nave lateral (el pasillo)** la *na*veh late*ra*l (el pa*see*l-yo)
altar	**el altar** el al*tar*
arches	**los arcos** los *ar*kos
bell tower	**el campanario** el kampa*na*reeyo
cathedral	**la catedral** la kate*dra*l
chancel	**el presbiterio** el presbee*te*reeyo
chapel	**la capilla** la ka*pee*l-ya
choir stalls	**las sillas del coro** las *see*l-yas del *ko*ro
church	**la iglesia** la ee*gle*seeya
churchyard	**el cementerio** el semen*te*reeyo
cloister	**el claustro** el *kla*wstro
crypt	**la cripta** la *kree*pta
dome	**la cúpula** la *koo*poola
font	**la pila bautismal** la *pee*la baootees*ma*l
nave	**la nave** la *na*veh
organ	**el órgano** el *o*rgano
pews	**los bancos** los *ban*kos
portico	**el pórtico** el *po*rteeko
pulpit	**el púlpito** el *poo*lpeeto
spire	**la aguja** la a*goo*ha
steeple	**el campanario** el kampa*na*reeyo
tombs	**los sepulcros** los se*poo*lkros
transept	**el crucero** el kroo*se*ro

Buildings

ceiling	**el techo**	el *te*cho
courtyard	**el patio**	el *pa*teeyo
doors	**las puertas**	las *pwer*tas
façade	**la fachada**	la fa*cha*da
fireplace	**la chimenea**	la cheeme*ne*ya
floor	**el suelo**	el *swe*lo
gates	**las rejas (verjas)**	las *re*has (*ber*has)
passage	**el pasillo**	el pa*seel*-yo
roof	**el tejado**	el te*ha*do
rooms	**las salas/las habitaciones**	las *sa*las/las abeetasee*yo*nes
windows	**las ventanas**	las ven*ta*nas

Art galleries

ceramics	**la cerámica**	la se*ra*meeka
drawing	**el dibujo**	el dee*boo*ho
engraving	**el grabado**	el gra*ba*do
miniature	**la miniatura**	la meeneeya*too*ra
mosaic	**el mosaico**	el mosa*ye*eko
mural	**el mural**	el moo*ral*
oil painting	**el óleo**	el *o*leyo
paintings	**las pinturas**	las peen*too*ras
landscape	**el paisaje**	el payee*sa*heh
portrait	**el retrato**	el re*tra*to
seascape	**la marina**	la ma*ree*na
still life	**el bodegón**	el bode*gon*
pottery	**la cerámica**	la se*ra*meeka
sculpture	**la escultura**	la eskool*too*ra
bust	**el busto**	el *boos*to

Period

art nouveau	**modernista** moder*nee*sta
Aztec	**azteca** as*te*ka
colonial	**colonial** kolonee*yal*
contemporary	**contemporáneo** kontempo*ra*neyo
Gothic	**gótico** *go*teeko
impressionist	**impresionista** eempreseeyo*nee*sta
Inca	**incaico (inca)** een*ka*yeeko (*een*ka)
Mayan	**maya** *ma*ya
mission	**misión** meesee*yon*
Mozarabic	**mozárabe** mo*sa*rabeh
neoclassical	**neoclásico** neyo*kla*seeko
pre-Columbian	**precolombino** prekolom*bee*no
renaissance	**renacentista** renasen*tee*sta
Roman	**romano** ro*ma*no
romanesque	**románico** ro*ma*neeko

Museum

art exhibitions	**exposiciones de arte** eksposeesee*ye*ones deh *ar*teh
audio visual material	**el material audio-visual** el materee*yal* aoo*dee*yo-veesoo*al*
collection	**la colección** la koleksee*yon*
exhibit	**el objeto expuesto/la exhibición** el ob*he*to eks*pwes*to/la ekseebeesee*yon*
guided tour	**la visita con guía** la vee*see*ta kon *ghee*ya
lecture	**la conferencia** la konfe*ren*seeya
library	**la biblioteca** la beebleeyo*te*ka
modern art	**el arte moderno** el *ar*teh mo*der*no
museums	**los museos** los moo*se*yos
painting	**la pintura** la peen*too*ra
sculpture	**la escultura** la eskool*too*ra
tableau	**el cuadro viviente** el *kwa*dro veeveey*en*teh

Dialog: Sightseeing

Sr. Martínez	Si tienen tiempo podrían ir a pasar una mañana o una tarde al río.
Sr. Austen	¿Y qué haríamos tanto tiempo?
Sr. Martínez	Muchas cosas. Si quieren pasar todo el día paseando, les aconsejo que empiecen por el palacio.
Sra. Austen	Siempre he querido visitar el palacio.
Sr. Martínez	Después del palacio, pueden ir al puente que está al lado que es uno de los más famosos del mundo. Luego, al otro lado del río, pueden visitar el buque de guerra.
Sra. Austen	¿Cree que eso le interesará a mi hija?
Sr. Austen	Un barco así resulta interesante para todo el mundo.
Sr. Martínez	Después, pueden coger el ferry y ver un velero del siglo diecinueve.
Sra. Austen	¿Y a dónde vamos desde ahí?
Sr. Austen	Río arriba.
Sr. Martínez	Así es. Si bajan del ferry en el embarcadero pueden echar un vistazo a la Corte Suprema y al Congreso. Luego, crucen la plaza hasta la abadía y, para terminar, sigan hasta la catedral.
Sra. Austen	Es mucho para un sólo día.
Sr. Austen	Creo que es mucho mejor organizar una visita turística de un día que visitar solamente un sitio cada día.
Sr. Martínez	Estoy de acuerdo con usted, incluso si no hacen más visitas turísticas durante su estancia.
Sr. Austen	Depués del recorrido que usted ha sugerido, ¡no creo que tenga fuerzas para más visitas!

Mr. Martínez	*If you have time, you could spend a morning or afternoon on the river.*
Mr. Austen	*But what would we do in all that time?*
Mr. Martínez	*Lots of things. If you want to spend the whole day going round, then I suggest you begin at the palace.*
Mrs. Austen	*I have always wanted to visit the palace.*
Mr. Martínez	*After the palace you can visit the nearby bridge, one of the most famous bridges in the world. After that, on the opposite side of the river, you can visit the warship.*
Mrs. Austen	*Do you think our daughter would be interested?*
Mr. Austen	*A ship like that is interesting for everyone.*
Mr. Martínez	*Then you can take the riverbus and see a nineteenth-century sailing ship.*
Mrs. Austen	*Where do we go from there?*
Mr. Austen	*Up the river.*
Mr. Martínez	*That's right. You get off the riverbus at the pier. Have a look at the supreme court and congress. Then walk across the plaza to the abbey and finally to the cathedral.*
Mrs. Austen	*It's a lot to do in one day.*
Mr. Austen	*I think it is much better to plan an organised day's sightseeing than to visit just one place a day.*
Mr. Martínez	*I quite agree, even if you don't do any more sightseeing for the rest of the holiday.*
Mrs. Austen	*After the itinerary you have suggested for one day, I wouldn't have the strength!*

OUTDOOR EXCURSIONS

I'd like a hike suitable for beginners.

Me gustaría una excursión apropiada para principiantes. meh goostareeya oona ekskoorseeyon apropeeyada para preenseepeeyantes

Stop, please. I need to take a rest.

Pare, por favor. Necesito descansar. pareh, por favor. neseseeto deskansar

What type of animal/bird/plant is that?

¿Qué clase de animal/pájaro/planta es ése/ésa? keh klaseh deh aneemal/paharo/planta es eseh/esa?

How deep is the pool?

¿Qué tan honda es la alberca? (¿Cómo es de profunda la piscina?) keh tan onda es la alberka? (komo es deh profoonda la peestheena?)

Is it safe to swim here?

¿Es seguro nadar aquí? es segooro nadar akee?

How much is it to rent scubagear for an hour?

¿Cuánto cuesta rentar (alquilar) el equipo para buceo por hora? kwanto kwesta rentar (alkeelar) el ekeepo para booseyo por ora?

In the park

park	**los parques** los parkes
bushes	**los arbustos** los arboostos
fish pond	**el estanque** el estankeh
flowerbeds	**las jardineras (los parterres)** las hardeeneras (los partehrres)
gardens	**los jardines** los hardeenes
grass	**el pasto (la hierba)** el pasto (la eeyerba)
lake	**el lago** el lago

paths	**los senderos/los caminos**
	los senderos/los kameenos
refreshments	**los refrescos** los refreskos
seats	**los asientos** los aseeyentos
benches	**los bancos** los bankos
tennis courts	**las canchas (pistas) de tenis**
	las kanchas (peestas) deh tenees
trees	**los árboles** los arboles
water birds	**los pájaros acuáticos**
	los paharos akwateekos
wild flowers	**las flores silvestres**
	las flores seelvestres

At the zoo

zoo	**el parque zoológico**
	el parkeh soh-oloheeko
apes house	**la casa de los changos (monos)**
	la kasa deh los changos (monos)
aquarium	**el acuario** el akwareeyo
aviary	**el aviario** el aveeyareeyo
cages	**las jaulas** las hawlas
insect house	**la casa de los insectos**
	la kasa deh los eensektos
lion and tiger house	**la casa de las fieras**
	la kasa deh las feeyeras
mammals	**los mamíferos** los mameeferos
reptile house	**el serpentario (terrario)**
	el serpentareeyo (terrareeyo)

By the river

river	**el río** el reeyo
barge	**la barca (la barcaza)** la barka (la barkasa)
bridge	**el puente** el pwenteh
docks	**los muelles** los mwel-yes

ferry	**el ferry** el *fe*rree
flood barrier	**el dique contra inundaciones** el *dee*keh *kon*tra eenoondasee*yo*nes
island	**la isla** la *ees*la
motorboat	**el barco (a) motor** el *bar*ko (a) mo*tor*
pier	**el embarcadero** el embarka*de*ro
rapids	**los rápidos** los *ra*peedos
river cruise	**el crucero por el río** el kroo*se*ro por el *ree*yo
riverbank	**la orilla del río** la oree*l*-ya del *ree*yo
riverbus	**el ferry** el *fe*rree
sailing boat	**el barco de vela** el *bar*ko deh *ve*la
sailing club	**el club de vela (club náutico)** el kloob deh *ve*la (kloob na*oo*teeko)
tide	**la marea** la ma*re*ya
high tide	**marea alta** ma*re*ya *al*ta
low tide	**marea baja** ma*re*ya *ba*ha
wharf	**el muelle** el *mw*el-yeh

Resorts

amusement park	**el parque de atracciones** el *par*keh deh atraksee*yo*nes
roller coaster	**la montaña rusa** la mon*ta*nya *rroo*sa
beach	**la playa** la *pla*ya
pier	**el embarcadero** el embarka*de*ro
promenade	**el paseo marítimo** el pa*se*yo ma*ree*teemo
sea	**el mar** el mar
spa	**el balneario** el balne*ya*reeyo
tourist information center	**la oficina de información turística** la ofee*see*na deh eenformasee*yon* too*rees*teeka
town	**el pueblo** el *pwe*blo
village	**la aldea** la al*de*ya

Excursions

countryside	**el paisaje/el campo** el payeesaheh/el kampo
excursions/trips	**las excursiones** las ekskoorseeyones
guide book	**la guía** la gheeya
map	**el mapa (plano)** el mapa (plano)
street plan	**el plano de calles** el plan deh kal-yes
historical tours	**visitas a los lugares históricos** veeseetas a los loogares eestoreekos

Hiking

canyon	**el cañón** el kanyon
cave	**la cueva** la kweva
cliff	**el acantilado** el akanteelado
desert	**el desierto** el deseeyerto
forest	**el bosque** el boskeh
hill	**la colina** la koleena
jungle	**la selva** la selva
lake	**el lago** el lago
meadow	**el prado** el prado
mountain	**la montaña** la montanya
national park	**el parque nacional** el parkeh naseeyonal
picnic	**el picnic** el peekneek
volcano	**el volcán** el volkan

Weather

What's the weather forecast?	**¿Qué dice el boletín meteorológico?** keh deeseh el boleteen meteyoroloheeko?
It's sunny.	**Hace sol.** aseh sol
It's freezing.	**Hace mucho frío.** aseh moocho freeyo
It's pouring.	**Está diluviando.** esta deelooveeyando

cloud	**la nube** la *noo*beh
fog	**la niebla** la nee*y*ebla
lightning	**el relámpago** el re*lam*pago
rain	**la lluvia** la *l-yoo*veeya
thunder	**el trueno** el *trw*eno
thunderstorm	**la tormenta** la tor*men*ta
wind	**el viento** el vee*y*ento

Flora

branch	**la rama** la *rama*
bush	**el arbusto** el ar*boo*sto
cactus	**el cactus** el *kak*toos
flower	**la flor** la flor
leaf	**la hoja** la *oha*
pine tree	**el pino** el *pee*no
plant	**la planta** la *plan*ta
tree	**el árbol** el *ar*bol

Fauna

ant	**la hormiga** la or*mee*ga
bear	**el oso** el *oso*
bee	**la abeja** la a*beh*a
bird	**el pájaro** el *pah*aro
butterfly	**la mariposa** la maree*po*sa
cow	**la vaca** la *vak*a
deer	**el ciervo** el see*y*ervo
ducks	**los patos** los *pa*tos
eagle	**el águila** el a*ghee*la
fox	**el zorro** el *sorro*
frog	**la rana** la *rrana*
goat	**la cabra** la *kab*ra
hen	**la gallina** la ga*l-yee*na
insect	**el insecto** el een*sek*to

lizard	**el lagarto** el la*gar*to
parrot	**el loro** el *lo*ro
rabbit	**el conejo** el ko*ne*ho
sheep	**la oveja** la o*ve*ha
snake	**la serpiente** la serpee*yen*teh
spider	**la araña** la a*ra*nya
stork	**la cigüeña** la see*gwe*nya
swans	**los cisnes** los *sees*nes

Seaside

bathingsuit	**el traje de baño (bañador)** el *tra*heh deh *ba*nyo (banya*dor*)
beach	**la playa** la *pla*ya
coast	**la costa** la *kos*ta
fish	**el pescado (pez)** el pes*ka*do (pes)
to go diving	**ir a bucear** eer a boose*yar*
island	**la isla** la *ees*la
jet ski	**la moto acuática** la *mo*to a*kwa*teeka
ocean	**el océano** el o*se*yano
reef	**el arrecife** el arre*see*feh
sand	**la arena** la a*re*na
sea	**el mar** el mar
shark	**el tiburón** el teeboo*ron*
sun	**el sol** el sol
sunglasses	**los anteojos (las gafas) de sol** los ante*yo*hos (las *ga*fas) deh sol
sunscreen	**el protector contra el sol** el protek*tor kon*tra el sol
surf	**surf, las olas rompientes** soorf, las *o*las rompee*yen*tes
to swim	**nadar** na*dar*
swimming pool	**la alberca (piscina)** la al*ber*ka (pees*thee*na)
wave	**la ola** la *o*la

EMERGENCIES & HEALTH

Where is the restroom?	**¿Dónde están los baños (servicios)?** *dondeh estan los banyos (serveeseeyos)?*
Help!	**¡Socorro!** *sokorro!*
Stop, thief!	**¡Alto, (Al) ladrón!** *alto, (al) ladron!*
Leave me alone!	**¡Déjeme en paz!** *dehemeh en pas!*
Please call the police!	**Llame a la policía, por favor.** *l-yameh a la poleeseeya, por favor*
Fire!	**¡Fuego!** *fwego!*
I feel sick.	**Estoy enfermo(-a).** *estoy enfermo(-a)*
Call an ambulance.	**Llame a una ambulancia.** *l-yameh a oona amboolanseeya*
It's an emergency.	**Es una emergencia.** *es oona emerhenseeya*
May I borrow your mobile phone.	**¿Me presta su celular (móvil)?** *meh presta soo seloolar (mobeel)?*
There's been an accident.	**Ha habido un accidente.** *a abeedo oon akseedenteh*
Someone has been injured.	**Alguien está herido.** *algeeyen esta ereedo*

Police

Where is the nearest police station?	**¿Dónde está la estación de policía más cercana?** *dondeh esta la estaseeyon deh poleeseeya mas serkana?*
I need an English-speaking lawyer.	**Necesito un abogado que hable inglés.** *neseseeto oon abogado keh ableh eengles*

Can you give me the address of the American Embassy, please?	**¿Me puede dar la dirección de la Embajada de los Estados Unidos, por favor?** meh *p*wedeh dar la deerekseey*on* deh la emba*h*ada deh los es*t*ados oo*n*eedos, por fa*v*or?
I need to call...	**Necesito llamar...** neseseeto l-ya*m*ar
I want to report...	**Quiero reportar... (denunciar...)** keey*e*ro repor*t*ar (denoon*th*eey*ar*)
an assault	**un asalto** oon asa*l*to
a rape	**una violación** *oo*na veeyolaseey*on*
a theft	**un robo** oon *rr*obo
My handbag has been stolen.	**Me robaron la bolsa. (Me han robado el bolso.)** meh *rr*obaron la *bol*sa (meh an *rr*obado el *bol*so)
I have lost my credit card.	**Perdí mi tarjeta de crédito.** per*dee* mee tar*h*eta deh *kr*edeeto
Where is the lost and found?	**¿Dónde está la oficina de objetos perdidos?** *don*deh es*t*a la ofeeseena deh ob*h*etos perdeedos?
Can I have a report for my insurance company?	**¿Me puede dar un reporte (informe) para mi compañía de seguros?** meh *p*wedeh dar oon re*p*orteh (een*f*ormeh) *p*ara mee compa*ny*eeya deh segooros?

Lost and stolen

car keys	**las llaves del coche** las *l*-ya*v*es del *k*ocheh
credit card	**la tarjeta de crédito** la tar*h*eta deh *kr*edeeto
driver's license	**la licencia (el permiso) de conducir** la lees*en*seeya (el per*m*eeso) deh kondoos*eer*

handbag	**el bolso** el *bol*so
money	**el dinero** el dee*ne*ro
passport	**el pasaporte** el pasa*por*teh
purse	**el monedero** el mone*de*ro
rental car	**el coche rentado (alquilado)** el *ko*cheh rren*ta*do (alkee*la*do)
suitcase	**la maleta** la ma*le*ta
ticket	**el boleto (billete)** el bo*le*to (bil-*ye*te)
traveler's checks	**los cheques de viajero (viaje)** los *che*kes deh veeya*he*ro (bee*ya*he)
visa	**la visa** la *vee*sa
wallet	**la cartera** la kar*te*ra

Missing

My daughter is missing.	**No encuentro a mi hija.** no en*kwen*tro a mee *ee*ha
She wears glasses.	**Usa anteojos. (Lleva gafas.)** *oo*sa ante*yo*hos (l-*ye*ba *ga*fas)
I last saw my wife 4 hours ago.	**La última vez que vi a mi esposa fue** **hace cuatro horas.** la *ool*teema ves keh vee a mee es*po*sa fweh a*seh *kwa*tro *o*ras
She has black hair.	**Tiene (el) pelo negro.** tee*ye*neh (el) *pe*lo *ne*gro
He is 5'8 tall.	**Mide 1.74 m.** *mee*deh oon *me*tro se*ten*ta ee *kwa*tro

Parts of the body

skin	**la piel** la pee*yel*
hair	**el pelo** el *pe*lo
blonde	**rubio** *roo*beeyo
brown	**moreno** mo*re*no

black	**negro** *ne*gro
gray	**canoso** ka*no*so
curly	**rizado** rees*a*do
straight	**lacio (liso)** *la*seeyo (*lee*so)
balding	**está perdiendo el pelo (calvo)** es*ta* perdee*yen*do el *pe*lo (*kal*bo)
beard	**la barba** la *bar*ba
moustache	**el bigote** el bee*go*teh
chin	**la barbilla** la bar*beel*-ya
head	**la cabeza** la ka*be*sa
face	**la cara** la *ka*ra
nose	**la nariz** la na*rees*
ear	**la oreja** la o*re*ha
hearing aid	**el audifono** el aoodee*fo*no
eyes	**los ojos** los *o*hos
eyebrow	**la ceja** la *se*ha
mouth	**la boca** la *bo*ka
throat	**la garganta** la gar*gan*ta
tongue	**la lengua** la *len*gooa
teeth	**los dientes** los dee*yen*tes
gums	**las encías** las ense*ey*as
body	**el cuerpo** el *kwer*po
neck	**el cuello** el *kwel*-yo
shoulder	**el hombro** el *om*bro
back	**la espalda** la es*pal*da
chest	**el pecho** el *pe*cho
breasts	**los pechos** los *pe*chos
nipples	**los pezones** los pe*so*nes
stomach	**el estómago** el es*to*mago
hip	**la cadera** la ka*de*ra
bottom	**el trasero** el tra*se*ro
arm	**el brazo** el *bra*so

elbow	**el codo** el *kodo*
hand	**la mano** la *mano*
fingers	**los dedos** los *dedos*
leg	**la pierna** la *peeyer*na
knee	**la rodilla** la rrodeel-ya
ankle	**el tobillo** el to*beel*-yo
foot	**el pie** el pee*yeh*
heel	**el talón** el ta*lon*
toe	**el dedo del pie** el *dedo* del pee*yeh*
lungs	**los pulmones** los pool*mones*
heart	**el corazón** el kora*son*
digestive system	**el sistema digestivo** el sees*tema* deehes*teevo*
testicles	**los testículos** los tes*teekoolos*
penis	**el pene** el *peneh*
vagina	**la vagina** la va*heena*
blood	**la sangre** la *sangreh*
vein	**la vena** la *vena*
muscle	**el músculo** el *mooskoolo*
bone	**el hueso** el *weso*

Getting treatment

Can I make an appointment to see...?	**¿Podría darme una cita (hora) para ver a...?** po*dreeya* *darmeh* *oona* *seeta* (*ora*) *para* ver a?
the doctor	**el doctor/la doctora** el dok*tor*/la dok*tora*
the nurse	**la enfermera** la enfer*mera*
the dentist	**el dentista** el den*teesta*
the hospital	**el hospital** el ospee*tal*
health insurance plan	**el plan de seguro médico** el plan deh se*gooro* *medeeko*
insurance card	**la tarjeta del seguro** la tar*heta* del se*gooro*

inoculations	**las vacunas** las va*koo*nas
doctor's office	**el consultorio (la consulta) del doctor** el konsool*to*reeyo (la kon*soo*lta) del dok*tor*
the waiting room	**la sala de espera** la *sa*la deh es*pe*ra
I have an appointment to see...	**Tengo una cita para ver a...** *ten*go *oo*na *see*ta *pa*ra ver a

Filling out forms

Por favor ¿Podría rellenar esta ficha?	Can you fill in this form, please?
Apellido	Surname
Nombre	First Name
Edad	Age
Fecha de nacimiento	Date of Birth
Lugar de nacimiento	Place of Birth
Nacionalidad	Nationality
Dirección	Address
Número de teléfono	Telephone Number
Familiar más cercano	Next of Kin
Historial médico	Medical History
Detalles sobre previas operaciones	Details of previous operations
Enfermedades	Serious illnesses
Alergias	Allergies
¿Ha tenido alguna de estas enfermedades?	Have you ever had any of the following illnesses?

The consultation

Voy a...	I am going to...
tomarle la presión sanguínea	to take your blood pressure
tomarle el pulso	to take your pulse
tomar una muestra de sangre	to take a blood sample
hacerle una prueba de orina	to do a urine test

auscultarle el corazón/el pecho	to listen to your heart/chest
mirarle la garganta	to look down your throat
comprobar los reflejos	to test your reflexes
Podría…	Could you …
subirse las mangas	roll up your sleeves
levantarse la camisa	lift up your shirt
qitarse la ropa	take off your clothes
quitarse todo salvo la ropa interior	take everything off except your underwear (pants)
ponerse esta bata	put this gown on
subirse a la cama	climb on the bed
acostarse	lie down
abrir la boca	open your mouth wide
hacer una muestra de orina/feces	do a urine/stool sample

Doctor's questions and instructions

¿Dónde le duele?	Where does it hurt?
Muéstreme dónde le duele.	Show me where it hurts.
¿Le duele aquí mucho?	Does it hurt much?
¿Puede mover…?	Can you move your…?
Debe guardar cama.	You should stay in bed.
No debe ir al trabajo/al colegio/de viaje.	You should not go to work/school/travel.
Me gustaría hacer más pruebas.	I would like to do further tests.
Necesito tomarle unos rayos X.	You need an X-ray.
Necesita un scan.	You need a scan.
Le voy a arreglar una cita para que vaya al hospital.	I will make an appointment at the hospital for you.
No es nada grave.	It is nothing serious.
Se pondrá bien pronto.	You will be better soon.
¿Tiene alguna alergia a algo?	Are you allergic to anything?

Conditions

allergy	**una alergia** *oo*na a*ler*heeya
arthritis	**la artritis** la ar*tree*tees
asthma	**el asma** el *as*ma
backache	**los dolores de espalda** los do*lo*res deh es*pal*da
bronchitis	**la bronquitis** la bron*kee*tees
bruise	**un moretón (cardenal)** oon more*ton* (karde*nal*)
cancer	**el cáncer** el *kan*ser
constipation	**el estreñimiento** el estrenyeemee*yen*to
cough	**la tos** la tos
cut	**una cortada (un corte)** oona kor*ta*da (oon *kor*teh)
flu	**la gripa (gripe)** la *gree*pa (*gree*peh)
heart mumur	**un murmullo (soplo)en el corazón** oon moor*mool*-yo (*so*plo) en el kora*son*
heartburn	**la acidez** la asee*des*
hemorrhoids	**las hemorroides** las emo*rro*yeedes
hernia	**una hernia** oona *er*neeya
hip replacement	**un reemplazo de la cadera** oon re-em*pla*so deh la ka*de*ra
indigestion	**la indigestión** la eendeehestee*yon*
infection	**la infección** la eenfeksee*yon*
insect bite	**un piquete (una picadura) de insecto** oon pee*ke*teh (oona peeka*doo*ra) deh een*sek*to
kidney stone	**un cálculo renal** oon *kal*koolo rre*nal*
migraine	**una migraña** oona mee*gran*ya
nosebleed	**una hemorragia nasal** oona emo*rra*heeya na*sal*
pacemaker	**un marcapasos** oona marka*pa*sos
rash	**un sarpullido** oon sarpool-*yee*do
rheumatism	**el reumatismo** el reyooma*tee*smo

sciatica	**la ciática** la see*y*ateeka
swelling	**una hinchazón** *oo*na eenchas*on*
sunstroke	**una insolación** *oo*na eensolasee*yon*
tetanus	**el tétano** el *t*etano
tonsillitis	**la amigdalitis** la ameegda*l*eetees
toothache	**el dolor de muelas** el do*lor* deh *m*welas
ulcer	**una úlcera** *oo*na *oo*lsera
vomiting	**vómitos** *v*omeetos
wound	**una herida** *oo*na e*r*eeda

The treatment

una receta	a prescription
la medicina	medicine
los antibióticos	antibiotics
la aspirina	aspirin
una cápsula	a capsule
una crema antihistamínica	antihistamine cream
una crema antiséptica	antiseptic cream
un inhalador	an inhaler
una pastilla	a tablet
la penicilina	penicillin
un supositorio	a suppository
el ungüento	ointment
untar	to rub on
la dosis	the dosage
tragar/tomar	to swallow/take
Agitar la botella antes de usar.	Shake the bottle before use.
tres veces al día	three times a day
antes/después de la comidas	before/after meals
Tómese con las comidas.	Take with food.
Tómese en ayunas.	Take on an empty stomach.
No tome esto en caso de embarazo.	Do not take if pregnant.

GENERAL INFORMATION

Days of the week

on Monday	**el lunes** el *loo*nes
next Tuesday	**el próximo martes** el *prok*seemo *mar*tes
last Wednesday	**el miércoles pasado** el *mee*yerkoles pa*sa*do
the Thursday before last	**el jueves antepasado (hace dos jueves)** el *hwe*ves antepa*sa*do (*athe* dos *hwe*bes)
Friday	**viernes** vee*yer*nes
Saturday	**sábado** *sa*bado
Sunday	**domingo** do*meen*go

Months of the year

In January	**en enero** en e*ne*ro
February	**febrero** fe*bre*ro
March	**marzo** *mar*so
April	**abril** *abril*
May	**mayo** *ma*yo
June	**junio** *hoo*neeyo
July	**julio** *hoo*leeyo
August	**agosto** a*gos*to
September	**septiembre** septee*yem*breh
October	**octubre** ok*too*breh
November	**noviembre** novee*yem*breh
December	**diciembre** deesee*yem*breh

Seasons

Spring	**primavera** preema*ve*ra
Summer	**verano** ve*ra*no
Fall/Autumn	**otoño** o*ton*yo
Winter	**invierno** eenvee*yer*no

Holidays

New Year's Day	**Año Nuevo** *anyo nwevo*
Mardi Gras	**Martes de Carnaval** *martes deh karnaval*
Easter	**Pascua** *paskwa*
May Day/Labor Day	**Día del Trabajo** *deeya del trabajo*
Christmas	**Navidad** *naveedad*
New Year's Eve	**Nochevieja** *nocheveeyeha*

Time expressions

It's one o'clock.	**Es la una.** *es la oona*
It's ten past two.	**Son las dos y diez.** *son las dos ee deeyes*
before three o'clock	**antes de las tres** *antes deh las tres*
around quarter to four	**alrededor del cuarto para las cuatro (de las cuatro menos cuarto)** *alrededor del kwarto para las kwatro (deh las kwatro menos kwarto)*
after five o'clock	**después de las cinco** *despwes deh las seenko*
twenty to six	**veinte para las seis (las seis menos veinte)** *veynteh para las seys (las seys menos veynteh)*
at seven thirty	**a las siete y media** *a las seeyeteh ee medeeya*
between eight to nine	**entre las ocho y las nueve** *entreh las ocho ee las nweveh*
from ten til eleven	**desde las diez hasta las once** *desdeh las deeyes asta las onseh*
midnight	**medianoche** *medeeyanocheh*
noon	**mediodía** *medeeyodeeya*
in the morning	**por la mañana** *por la manyana*
in the afternoon	**por la tarde** *por la tardeh*
this evening	**esta noche** *esta nocheh*
at night	**por la noche** *por la nocheh*

On January 23rd	**El 23 de enero** el veynteh*tres* deh e*ne*ro
From the 6th to the 7th February	**Del 6 al 7 de febrero** del seys al seeye*teh deh fe*brero
March 9th, 2004	**el 9 de marzo del 2004** el *nwe*veh deh *mar*so del dos meel *kwa*tro
In 2003	**en el 2003** en el dos meel tres
In the nineties	**en los años noventa** en los anyos no*ven*ta
today	**hoy** oy
tomorrow	**mañana** ma*nya*na
the day before yesterday	**antier (anteayer)** antee*yer* (anteya*yer*)
next week	**la semana que viene** la se*ma*na keh vee*ye*neh
ten years ago	**hace diez años** aseh dee*yes* anyos
yesterday afternoon	**ayer por la tarde** a*yer* por la *tar*deh
last night	**anoche** a*no*cheh
nowadays	**hoy en día** oy en *dee*ya
day after tomorrow	**pasado mañana** pasado ma*nya*na
every day	**todos los días** *to*dos los *dee*yas
at this moment	**en este momento** en esteh mo*men*to
early	**temprano** tem*pra*no
late	**tarde** *tar*deh
on time	**a tiempo** a tee*yem*po
in 10 minutes	**en (durante) diez minutos** en (doo*ran*teh) dee*yes* mee*noo*tos
for two hours	**por (desde hace) dos horas** por (*des*deh aseh) dos oras
20 minutes ago	**hace veinte minutos** aseh *veyn*teh mee*noo*tos

Numbers

one half	**una mitad** *oo*na mee*tad*
one quarter	**un cuarto** oon *kwar*to
one third	**un tercio** oon *ter*seeyo

0	**cero** *sero*	60	**sesenta** *sesenta*
1	**uno** *oono*	70	**setenta** *setenta*
2	**dos** *dos*	80	**ochenta** *ochenta*
3	**tres** *tres*	90	**noventa** *noventa*
4	**cuatro** *kwatro*	100	**cien/ciento** *seeyen/seeyento*
5	**cinco** *seenko*	101	**ciento uno**
6	**seis** *seys*		*seeyento oono*
7	**siete** *seeyeteh*	200	**doscientos/-as**
8	**ocho** *ocho*		*doseeyentos/-as*
9	**nueve** *nweveh*	300	**trescientos/-as**
10	**diez** *deeyes*		*treseeyentos/-as*
11	**once** *onseh*	400	**cuatrocientos/-as**
12	**doce** *doseh*		*kwatro-seeyentos/-as*
13	**trece** *treseh*	500	**quinientos/-as**
14	**catorce** *katorseh*		*keeneeyentos/-as*
15	**quince** *keenseh*	600	**seiscientos/-as**
16	**dieciséis** *deeyesee-seys*		*seys-seeyentos/-as*
17	**diecisiete** *deeyesee-seeyeteh*	700	**setecientos/-as**
18	**dieciocho** *deeyesee-yocho*		*seteh-seeyentos/-as*
19	**diecinueve**	800	**ochocientos/-as**
	deeyesee-nweveh		*ocho-seeyentos/-as*
20	**veinte** *veynteh*	900	**novecientos/-as**
21	**veintiuno** *veyntee-oono*		*noveh-seeyentos/-as*
22	**veintidós** *veyntee-dos*	1,000	**mil** *meel*
23	**veintitrés** *veyntee-tres*	1st	**1º primero** *preemero*
24	**veinticuatro** *veyntee-kwatro*	2nd	**2ª segundo** *segoondo*
30	**treinta** *treynta*	3rd	**3ª tercero** *tersero*
31	**treinta y uno** *treynta-ee-oono*	4th	**4ª cuarto** *kwarto*
32	**treinta y dos** *treynta-ee-dos*	5th	**5ª quinto** *keento*
40	**cuarenta** *kwarenta*	6th	**6ª sexto** *seksto*
41	**cuarenta y uno**	7th	**7ª séptimo** *septeemo*
	kwarenta-ee-oono	8th	**8ª octavo** *oktavo*
50	**cincuenta** *seenkwenta*	9th	**9ª noveno** *noveno*
		10th	**10ª décimo** *deseemo*

ENGLISH-SPANISH
DICTIONARY

DICCIONARIO
INGLÉS-ESPAÑOL

ABREVIATURAS USADAS
EN ESTE DICCIONARIO

adj., adj.	adjetivo	*def.*	definido;
adv., adv.	adverbio		defectivo
AGR.	agricultura	DEP.	deportes
AJED.	ajedrez	DER.	derecho; forense
ÁLG.	álgebra	desus.	desusado
ANAT.	anatomía	DIB.	dibujo
ant.	antiguamente;	*dim.*	diminutivo
	anticuado		
ARIT.	aritmética	ECLES.	eclesiástico;
ARQ.	arquitectura		iglesia
ARQUEOL.	arqueología	ECON.	economía
art.	artículo	E. U.	Estados Unidos
ARTILL.	artillería	ELECT.	electricidad
ASTR.	astronomía;	ENT.	entomología
	astrología	EQUIT.	equitación
AUTO.	automóvil;	ESC.	escultura
	automovilismo	ESGR.	esgrima
aux.	verbo auxiliar	esp.	especialmente
AVIA.	aviación		
		f.	femenino; nombre
B. ART.	bellas artes		femenino
BIB.	Biblia	fam.	familiar
BIOL.	biología	FARM.	farmacia
BOT.	botánica	FERROC.	ferrocarriles
BOX.	boxeo	fig.	figurado
		FIL.	filosofía
CARN.	carnicería	FÍS.	física
CARP.	carpintería	FISIOL.	fisiología
CERÁM.	cerámica	FORT.	fortificación
CINEM.	cinematografía	FOT.	fotografía
CIR.	cirugía		
COC.	cocina	GEOGR.	geografía
COM.	comercio	GEOL.	geología
compar.	comparativo	GEOM.	geometría
Cond.	Condicional	ger., GER.	gerundio
conj.	conjunción	gralte.	generalmente
CONJUG.	Conjugación	GRAM.	gramática
contr.	contracción		
CRIST.	cristalografía	HIST.	historia

i., i.	verbo intransitivo	PERSP.	perspectiva
ICT.	ictiología	*pl.*	plural
impers.	verbo impersonal	poét.	poético
IMPR.	imprenta	POL.	política
IND.	industria	pop.	popular
indef.	indefinido	*pos.*	posesivo
INDIC.,	indicativo	*p. p.*, p. p.	participio pasivo
indic.		*pref.*	prefijo
inf.	infinitivo	*prep.*	preposición
ING.	ingeniería	Pres., *pres.*	presente
Ingl.	Inglaterra	Pret., *pret.*	pretérito
interj.	interjección	*pron.*	pronombre
irreg.	irregular		
		QUÍM.	química
JOY.	joyería		
		RADIO.	radiotelefonía; radiotelegrafía
LIT.	literatura	*ref.*	verbo reflexivo
LITUR.	liturgia	REL.	religión
LÓG.	lógica		
		S.	sur
m.	masculino; nombre masculino	*s.*	nombre substantivo
MAR.	marina; marítimo		
MAT.	matemáticas	SUBJ.	Subjuntivo
may.	mayúscula	*superl.*	superlativo
MEC.	mecánica		
MED.	medicina	*t.*, t.	verbo transitivo
METAL.	metalurgia	TEAT.	teatro
METEOR.	meteorología	TEJ.	tejeduría
MÉTR.	métrica	TELEF.	telefonía
MIL.	militar; milicia	TELEGR.	telegrafía
MIN.	minería	TELEV.	televisión
min.	minúscula	TEOL.	teología
MINER.	mineralogía	TOP.	topografía
MIT.	mitología	TRIG.	trigonometría
MÚS.	música		
		us.	usado
NAT.	natación		
n. pr.	nombre propio	V.	Véase
		vulg.	vulgarismo
ORN.	ornitología	VET.	veterinaria
PART. PAS.	Participio pasivo	ZOOL.	zoología
pers.	persona(s); personal		

SIGNOS DE LA A.F.I. EMPLEADOS EN LA TRANSCRIPCIÓN FONÉTICA DE LAS PALABRAS INGLESAS

Vocales

[i]   como en español en *vida, tigre*.

[e]   como en español en *guerra, dejar*, pero aún más abierta.

[æ]   sin equivalencia en español. Sonido intermedio entre la *a* en *caso* y la *e* en *perro*.

[ɑ]   como en español en *laurel, ahora*, pero enfatizada y alargada.

[ɔ]   como en español en *roca, manojo*, pero aún más abierta.

[u]   como en español en *uno*, pero con el sonido más prolongado.

[ʌ]   sin equivalencia en español. Sonido intermedio entre la *o* y la *e*.

[ə]   sin equivalencia en español. Parecida a la [ə] francesa en *venir, petit*.

Semiconsonantes

[j]   como en español en *labio, radio*.

[w]   como en español en *luego, huevo*.

Consonantes

[p]   como en español en *puerta, capa*, pero aspirada.

[t]   como en español en *todo, tienda*, pero aspirada.

[k]   como en español en *copa, queso*, pero aspirada.

[b]   como en español en *barco, vela*, pero aspirada.

[d]   como en español en *conde, candado,* pero aspirada.

[ð]   como en español en *adivinar, adorar.*

[g]   como en español en *guerra, gato,* pero aspirada.

[f]   como en español en *fuerza, fuego.*

[θ]   como en español en *hacer, ácido.*

[s]   como en español en *saber, silencio.*

[ʃ]   sin equivalencia en español. Fricativa palato-alveolar sorda. Parecida a la pronunciación de *chico,* si se alarga la consonante y se redondean los labios.

[v]   sin equivalencia en español. Fricativa labiodental. Al pronunciarla los incisivos superiores tocan el labio inferior y hay vibración de las cuerdas vocales. Es la pronunciación del francés en *avec.*

[z]   como en español en *mismo, asno.*

[ʒ]   sin equivalencia en español. Fricativa palato-alveolar sonora. Parecida a la pronunciación argentina de la *ll* pero con proyección de los labios.

[tʃ]   como en español en *chico, chocolate.*

[dʒ]   sin equivalencia exacta en español. Africada palato-alveolar sonora. Sonido semejante al de la *y* española en *conyuge, yugo.*

[l]   como en español en *labio, cola.*

[m]   como en español en *madre, lima.*

[n]   como en español en *nota, notable.*

[ŋ]   como en español en *cuenca, ángulo.*

[r]   sonido fricativo parecido al de la *r* española en *pero.*

[h]   sonido parecido al de la *j* española en *jerga,* pero mucho más suave.

Otros signos

[']   indica el acento tónico primario.

[,]   indica el acento tónico secundario.

[:]   indica un alargamiento de la vocal.

A

a (ei, ə) *art. indef.* un, una.

abash (to) (əˈbæʃ) *t.* avergonzar, confundir.

abate (to) (əˈbeit) *t.* rebajar, reducir. 2 *i.* menguar.

abduct (to) (æbˈdʌkt) *t.* raptar.

abide (to) (əˈbaid) *i.* morar, habitar. 2 quedar, permanecer. 3 sufrir, tolerar. ¶ Pret. y p. p.: *abode* (əˈboud) o *abided* (əˈbaidid).

ability (əˈbiliti) *s.* habilidad, aptitud. 2 talento.

able (ˈeibəl) *a.* que puede: *to be ~ to*, poder. 2 hábil.

aboard (əˈbɔːd) *adv.* a bordo.

abode (əˈboud) V. TO ABIDE. 2 *s.* morada, domicilio.

abolish (to) (əˈbɔliʃ) *t.* abolir, suprimir.

abort (to) (əˈbɔːt) *i.* abortar.

about (əˈbaut) *prep.* cerca de, junto a, alrededor de. 2 por, en. 3 sobre, acerca de. 4 hacia, a eso de. 5 *to be ~ to*, estar a punto de, ir a. 6 *adv.* alrededor, en torno. 7 casi, aproximadamente.

above (əˈbʌv) *prep.* sobre, por encima de. 2 más de o que. 3 *adv.* arriba, en lo alto.

abreast (əˈbrest) *adv.* de frente.

abroad (əˈbrɔːd) *adv.* afuera, en el extranjero.

absent (ˈæbsənt) *a.* ausente.

absorb (to) (əbˈsɔːb) *t.* absorber. 2 *ref.* abstraerse.

absorption (əbˈsɔːpʃən) *s.* absorción. 2 ensimismamiento.

abstain (to) (əbˈstein) *i.* abstenerse.

abstract (ˈæbstrækt) *a.* abstracto. 2 *s.* extracto, resumen.

absurd (əbˈsəːd) *a.* absurdo.

abundant (əˈbʌndənt) *a.* abundante.

abuse (əˈbjuːs) *s.* abuso.

abuse (to) (əˈbjuːz) *t.* abusar de. 2 maltratar, denigrar

abyss (əˈbis) *s.* abismo.

accede (to) (ækˈsiːd) *i.* acceder. 2 ascender, subir.

accent (to) (ækˈsent) *t.* acentuar.

accept (to) (ək'sept) *t.* aceptar. 2 admitir, creer.

acceptation (,æksep'teiʃən) *s.* acepción.

access ('ækses) *s.* acceso. 2 aumento, añadidura.

accessory (æk'sesəri) *a.* accesorio. 2 *s.* accesorio.

accident ('æksidənt) *s.* accidente. 2 casualidad.

accomodate (to) (ə'kɔmədeit) *t.* acomodar, alojar. 2 *i.* acomodarse.

accompany (to) (ə'kʌmpəni)*t.* acompañar.

accomplish (to) (ə'kɔmpliʃ) *t.* efectuar, llevar a cabo.

accord (ə'kɔ:d) *s.* acuerdo, concierto, armonía.

accord (to) (ə'kɔ:d) *t.* conceder, otorgar. 2 *i.* concordar.

according (ə'kɔ:diŋ) *a.* acorde, conforme. 2 ~ *to*, según, conforme a.

accordingly (ə'kɔ:diŋli) *adv.* de conformidad [con]. 2 por consiguiente.

account (ə'kaunt) *s.* cuenta. 2 causa. 3 explicación. 4 relación, informe.

accumulate (to) (ə'kju:mjuleit) *t.* acumular. 2 *i.* acumularse.

accurate ('ækjurit) *a.* exacto, correcto. 2 preciso.

accursed (ə'kə:sid) *a.* maldito.

accuse (to) (ə'kju:z) *t.* acusar.

accustom (to) (ə'kʌstəm) *t.* acostumbrar.

ache (eik) *s.* dolor; achaque.

ache (to) (eik) *i.* doler.

achieve (to) (ə'tʃi:v) *t.* realizar. 2 conseguir

achievement (ə'tʃi:vmənt) *s.* logro. 2 hazaña, proeza.

acid ('æsid) *a.-s.* ácido.

acidity (ə'siditi), **acidness** ('æsidnis) *s.* acidez. 2 acritud.

acknowledge (to) (ək'nɔlidʒ)*t.* reconocer. 2 agradecer.

acorn ('eikɔ:n) *s.* bellota.

acquaint (to) (ə'kweint) *t.* enterar, informar, hacer saber.

acquaintance (ə'kweintəns) *s.* conocimiento.

acquiesce (to) (,ækwi'es) *i.* asentir, consentir, conformarse.

acquiescence (,ækwi'esəns) *s.* aquiescencia, conformidad.

acquire (to) (ə'kwaiəʳ) *t.* adquirir. 2 contraer.

acquit (to) (ə'kwit) *t.* absolver, declarar inocente.

acre ('eikəʳ) *s.* acre [40.47 a.].

across (ə'krɔs) *prep.* a través de; al otro lado de.

act (ækt) *s.* acto, hecho, acción.

act (to) (ækt) *i.* obrar, actuar, conducirse.

action ('ækʃən) *s.* acción.

active ('æktiv) *a.* activo.

actor ('æktəʳ) *s.* actor.

actress ('æktris) *s.* actriz.

actual ('æktjuəl) *a.* real, efectivo, de hecho. 2 actual.

actually ('æktjuəli) *adv.* realmente, efectivamente.

acuity (ə'kju:iti) *s.* agudeza.

acumen (ə'kju:men) *s.* perspicacia.

acute (ə'kju:t) *a.* agudo.

adapt (to) (ə'dæpt) *t.-ref.* adaptar(se).

add (to) (æd) *t.* añadir, agregar. 2 *t.-i.* sumar.

addition (ə'diʃən) *s.* adición, suma.

address (ə'dres) *s.* discurso,

alocución. 2 *form of* ~, tratamiento. 3 dirección, señas.

adequate ('ædikwit) *a.* adecuado, suficiente.

adipose ('ædipous) *a.* adi-
poso.

adjacent (ə'dʒeisənt) *a.* adyacente, contiguo.

adjoin (to) (ə'dʒɔin) *t.* unir.

adjourn (to) (ə'dʒə:n) *t.* aplazar, suspender. 2 *i.* levantar
la sesión. 3 trasladarse.

adjust (to) (ə'dʒʌst) *t.* ajustar.

administer (to) (əd'ministə^r)
t.-i. administrar.

admirable ('ædmərəbl) *a.* admirable.

admiral ('ædmərəl) *s.* almirante.

admiration (,ædmi'reiʃən) *s.*
admiración.

admire (to) (əd'maiə^r) *t.* admirar. 2 *i.* admirarse.

admit (to) (əd'mit) *t.* admitir.

adolescent (,ædou'lesənt)*a.-s.*
adolescente.

adopt (ə'dɔpt) *t.* adoptar.

adore (to) (ə'dɔ:^r) *t.* adorar.

adult ('ædʌlt) *a.-s.* adulto.

advance (əd'va:ns) *s.* avance.

advantage (əd'va:ntidʒ) *s.*
ventaja; provecho: *to take* ~
of, aprovecharse de.

adventure (əd'ventʃə^r) *s.*
aventura.

adversary ('ædvəsəri) *s.* adversario.

advertise o **-tize (to)** ('ædvə-
taiz) *t.* avisar, informar.

advertisement (əd'və:tis-
mənt) *s.* aviso, anuncio.

advice (əd'vais) *s.* consejo.

advise (to) (əd'vaiz) *t.* aconsejar. 2 avisar.

advocate (to) ('ædvəkeit) *t.*
abogar por; defender.

aeroplane ('ɛərəplein) *s.* aeroplano.

afar (ə'fa:^r) *adv.* lejos, a lo
lejos.

affair (ə'fɛə^r) *s.* asunto, negocio.

affect (to) (ə'fekt) *t.* afectar.

affectionate (ə'fekʃnit) *a.*
afectuoso, cariñoso, tierno.

affirm (to) (ə'fə:m) *t.* afirmar.

afford (to) (ə'fɔ:d) *t.* producir, dar. 2 poder, tener medios para; permitirse [un
gasto, etc.]. | Gralte. con
can o *may.*

afraid (ə'freid) *a.* temeroso.

after ('a:ftə^r) *prep.* después
de. 2 según. 3 *adv.* después,
luego. 4 *a.* siguiente.

afternoon ('a:tə'nu:n) *s.*
tarde.

afterwards ('a:ftəwedz) *adv.*
después, luego.

again (ə'gən, ə'gein) *prep.* de
nuevo, otra vez, aún.

against (ə'gənst) *prep.* contra.

age (eidʒ) *s.* edad.

agent ('eidʒənt) *a.-s.* agente.

agglomerate (to) (ə'glɔmə-
reit)*t.* aglomerar. 2 *i.* aglo-
merarse.

ago (ə'gou) *adv.* atrás, hace,
ha.

agonize (to) ('ægənaiz) *i.* ago-
nizar.

agony ('ægəni) *s.* agonía.

agree (to) (ə'gri:) *i.* asentir.

agreeable (ə'griəbl) *a.* agradable. 2 conforme.

agreement (ə'gri:mənt) *s.*
acuerdo, convenio, pacto. 2
armonía, unión.

agriculture ('ægrikʌltʃə^r) *s.*
agricultura.

ahead (ə'hed) *adv.* delante.

aid (eid) *t.* ayuda. auxilio.

aid (to) (eid) *t.* ayudar.

aim (eim) *s.* puntería. 2 blanco [al que se tira].

aim (to) (eim) *t.* apuntar.

air (εə^r) *s.* aire. 2 céfiro, aura. 3 ambiente. 4 aire, semblante, continente, aspecto. 5 afectación, tono: *to put on airs,* darse tono. 6 MÚS. aire, tonada. 7 *a.* de aire, neumático, aéreo.

aircraft ('εəkrɑ:ft) *s.* avión.

airplane ('εə-plein) *s.* aeroplano.

airtight ('εə-tait) *a.* hermético.

aisle (ail) *s.* pasillo [en un teatro, etc.] 2 ARQ. nave lateral.

alarm (ə'lɑ:m) *s.* alarma.

alarm (to) (ə'lɑ:m) *t.* alarmar.

alarm-clock (ə'lɑ:mklɔk) *s.* despertador.

ale (eil) *s.* cerveza.

alert (ə'lə:t) *a.* vigilante. 2 vivo, listo. 3 MIL. alarma.

alien ('eiljən) *a.* ajeno, extraño. 2 *a.-s.* extranjero.

alike (ə'laik) *a.* igual, semejante. 2 *adv.* igualmente.

alive (ə'laiv) *a.* vivo, viviente. 2 vivo, activo.

all (ɔ:l) *a.* todo, -da; todos, -das. 2 *pron.* todo, totalidad: *after ~,* después de todo; *at ~,* absolutamente, del todo; *not at ~,* de ningún modo; no hay de qué; *for ~ that,* con todo. 3 todos, todo el mundo. 4 *adv.* completamente, muy; bueno, competente, satisfactorio; *~ right!* ¡está bien!, ¡conformes!; *~ round,* por todas partes; *~ the better,* tanto mejor; *~*

the same, igualmente, a pesar de todo.

allege (to) (ə'ledʒ) *t.* alegar, afirmar.

allegiance (ə'li:dʒəns) *s.* obediencia, fidelidad [a un soberano].

allied (ə'laid) *a.* aliado. 2 afín.

allow (to) (ə'lau) *t.* conceder.

ally ('ælai) *s.* aliado.

ally (to) (ə'lai) *t.-i.* aliar(se.

almost ('ɔ:lmoust) *adv.* casi.

aloft (ə'lɔft) *adv.* arriba, en alto.

alone (ə'loun) *a.* solo.

along (ə'lɔŋ) *prep.* a lo largo de. 2 *adv.* a lo largo.

aloud (ə'laud) *adv.* en voz alta.

already (ɔ:'redi) *adv.* ya.

also ('ɔ:lsou) *adv.* también.

alter (to) ('ɔ:ltə^r) *t.-i.* alterar(se, modificar(se.

alternate (to) ('ɔ:ltə:neit) *t.-i.* alternar(se.

alternative (ɔ:l'tə:nətiv) *a.* alternativo. 2 GRAM. disyuntivo. 3 *s.* alternativa [opción].

although (ɔ:l'ðou) *conj.* aunque.

altogether (,ɔ:ltə'geðə^r) *adv.* enteramente, del todo.

always ('ɔ:lwəz, -iz, -eiz) *adv.* siempre.

amaze (to) (ə'meiz) *t.* asombrar, pasmar.

ambassador (æm'bæsədə^r) *s.* embajador.

ambition (æm'biʃən) *s.* ambición.

ambitious (æm'biʃəs) *a.* ambicioso.

ambulance ('æmbjuləns) *s.* ambulancia.

ambush (to) ('æmbuʃ) *t*: emboscar. *2 i*. estar emboscado, al acecho.

amend (to) (ə'mend) *t*. enmendar, corregir, mejorar. *2 i*. enmendarse.

amiable ('eimiəbl) *a*. amable.

amid (ə'mid), **amidst** (-st) *prep*. en medio de, entre.

among (st) (ə'mʌŋ,-st) *prep*. entre, en medio de.

amount (ə'maunt) *s*. cantidad, suma. *2* importe.

amount (to) (ə'maunt) *i*. **to ~ to**, ascender a; equivaler a.

ample (æmpl) *a*. amplio. *2* extenso, capaz, holgado.

amuse (to) (ə'mju:z) *t.-ref*. entretener(se, divertir(se.

an (ən, æn) *art. indef*. un, una.

analyse, -ze (to) ('ænəlaiz) *t*. analizar.

ancestor ('ænsistə^r) *s*. progenitor, antepasado.

anchor ('æŋkə^r) *s.* ancla, áncora.

anchor (to) ('æŋkə^r) *t*. sujetar con el ancla. *2 i*. anclar.

ancient ('einʃənt) *a*. antiguo.

and (ænd, ənd) *conjug*. y, e.

angel ('eindʒəl) *s*. ángel.

anger ('æŋgə^r) *s*. cólera, ira.

anger (to) ('æŋgə^r) *t*. encolerizar, enfurecer, enojar.

angry ('æŋgri) *a*. colérico, airado, enojado.

anguish ('æŋgwiʃ) *s*. angustia, congoja, ansia, aflicción.

ankle ('æŋkl) *s*. tobillo.

annex ('ænəks) *s*. anexo.

annex (to) (ə'neks) *t*. añadir.

announce (to) (ə'nauns) *t*. anunciar, hacer saber.

annoy (to) (ə'nɔi) *t*. molestar.

another (ə'nʌðə^r) *a.-pron*. otro.

answer ('ɑ:nsə^r) *s*. respuesta, contestación. *2* solución.

answer (to) ('ɑnsə^r) *t.-i*. responder, contestar.

ant (ænt) *s*. ENT. hormiga.

anticipate (to) (æn'tisipeit) *t*. anticipar [una acción]. *2* anticiparse a. *3* prevenir; prever. *4* gozar de antemano.

anxiety (æŋ'zaiəti) *s*. ansiedad, inquietud. *2* ansia, afán.

anxious (æŋkʃəs) *a.* ansioso.

any ('eni) *a.-adv.-pron*. cualquier, todo, todos los, algún, alguno; [en frases negativas] ningún, ninguno: ~ *place,* cualquier lugar. *2* A veces no se traduce: ~ *more,* más, más tiempo.

anybody ('eni‚bɔdi) *pron*. alguien, alguno; [en frases negativas] ninguno, nadie. *2* cualquiera.

anyhow ('enihau) *adv*. de cualquier modo.

anyone ('eniwʌn) *pron*. ANYBODY.

anything ('eniθiŋ) *pron*. algo, alguna cosa, cualquier cosa, todo cuanto; [con negación] nada.

anyway ('eniwei) *adv*. de todos modos, con todo.

anywhere ('eniweə^r) *adv*. doquiera; adondequiera.

apart (ə'pɑ:t) *adv*. aparte; a un lado. *2* separadamente.

apartment (ə'pɑ:tmənt) *s*. aposento. *2* piso, apartamento.

ape (eip) *s*. mono, mico, simio.

ape (to) (eip) *t*. imitar, remedar.

apostle (ə'pɔsl) *s*. apóstol.

appal(l (to) (ə'pɔ:l) *t.* espantar, aterrar. *2* desanimar.

apparent (ə'pærənt) *a.* evidente. *2* aparente.

appeal (ə'pi:l) *s.* apelación. *2* llamamiento; súplica. *3* atractivo.

appear (to) (ə'piəʳ) *i.* aparecer. *2* parecer.

applause (ə'plɔ:z) *s.* aplauso.

apple ('æpl) *s.* BOT. manzana, poma. *2 ~ of the eye*, pupila.

application (ˌæpli'keiʃən) *s.* aplicación. *2* petición.

appreciate (to) (ə'pri:ʃieit) *t.* apreciar, valuar.

approach (ə'proutʃ) *s.* aproximación. *2* entrada.

appropriate (ə'proupriit) *a.* apropiado. *2* propio, peculiar.

approval (ə'pru:vəl) *s.* aprobación.

approve (to) (ə'pru:v) *t.* aprobar, sancionar; confirmar.

apricot ('eiprikɔt) *s.* BOT. albaricoque.

April ('eipril) *s.* abril.

arch (ɑ:tʃ) *s.* ARQ. arco; bóveda. *2 a.* travieso.

arch (to) (ɑ:tʃ) *t.* arquear. *2* abovedar. *3 i.* arquearse.

archbishop ('ɑ:tʃ'biʃəp) *s.* arzobispo.

argue (to) ('ɑ:gju:) *i.* argüir, argumentar. *2 t.-i.* discutir.

argument ('ɑ:gjumənt) *s.* argumento. *2* discusión.

arid ('ærid) *a.* árido.

arise (to) (ə'raiz) *i.* subir, elevarse. ¶ Pret.: *arose* (ə'rouz); p. p.: *arisen* (ə'rizn).

arm (ɑ:m) *s.* brazo. *2* rama [de árbol]. *3* arma.

arm-chair ('ɑ:m'tʃɛəʳ) *s.* sillón.

armour ('ɑ:məʳ) *s.* armadura.

army ('ɑ:mi) *s.* ejército.

around (ə'raund) *adv.* alrededor. *2* por todas partes.

arouse (to) (ə'rauz) *t.* despertar.

arrange (to) (ə'reindʒ) *t.* arreglar. *2* concertar. *3* acordar.

arrival (ə'raivəl) *s.* llegada.

arrive (to) (ə'raiv) *i.* llegar.

arrow ('ærou) *s.* flecha, saeta.

art (ɑ:t) *s.* arte.

artist ('ɑ:tist) *s.* artista.

artistic ('ɑ:'tistik) *a.* artístico.

as (æz, əz) *adv.* como. *2* (en comparativos) ~ *big* ~, tan grande como. *3* ~ *far* ~, hasta [donde]: ~ *for*, ~ *to*, en cuanto a; ~ *much* ~, tanto como; ~ *well* ~, así como; ~ *yet*, hasta ahora. *4 conj.* mientras, cuando. *5* ya que. *6* a pesar de. *7 pron.* que.

ascend (to) (ə'send) *i.* ascender, subir. *2 t.* subir.

ascent (ə'sent) *s.* subida.

ascertain (to) (ˌæsə'tein) *t.* averiguar, hallar.

ash (æʃ) *s.* ceniza.

ashamed (ə'ʃeimd) *a.* avergonzado.

ashore (ə'ʃɔ:, ə'ʃɔə) *adv.* en tierra, a tierra.

aside (ə'said) *adv.* al lado, a un lado, aparte.

ask (to) (ɑ:sk) *t.* preguntar. *2* pedir, solicitar, rogar que. *3* requerir, exigir. *4* invitar.

asleep (ə'sli:p) *a.-adv.* dormido: *to fall* ~, dormirse.

asparagus (æs'pærəgəs) *s.* BOT. espárrago.

aspect ('æspekt) *s.* aspecto.

aspirate (to) ('æspəreit) *t.* aspirar.

ass (æs, ɑ:s) *s.* burro, asno.

assail (to) (ə'seil) *t.* asaltar.

assault (ə'sɔ:lt) *s.* asalto.

assault (to) (ə'sɔ:lt) *t.* asaltar.

assay (ə'sei) *s.* ensayo.

assemble (to) (ə'sembl) *t.* congregar, reunir, agrupar.

assembly (ə'sembli) *s.* asamblea, junta. *2* reunión, fiesta. *3* concurrencia.

assent (ə'sent) *s.* asentimiento.

assent (to) (ə'sent) *i.* asentir.

assert (to) (ə'sɔ:t) *t.* aseverar, afirmar. *2* mantener, defender. *3* **to ~ oneself,** hacer valer sus derechos.

assign (to) (ə'sain) *t.* asignar.

associate (ə'souʃiit) *a.* asociado; adjunto.

associate (to) (ə'souʃieit) *t.-i.* asociar(se, juntar(se.

assume (to) (ə'sju:m) *t.* asumir. *2* atribuirse. *3* suponer.

assumption (ə'sʌmpʃən) *s.* postulado. *2* suposición.

assurance (ə'ʃuərəns) *s.* seguridad, certeza.

assure (to) (ə'ʃuəʳ) *t.* asegurar.

astonish (to) (əs'tɔniʃ) *t.* asombrar, pasmar.

astound (to) (əs'taund) *t.* pasmar, sorprender.

at (æt, ət) *prep.* en, a, de, con, cerca de, delante de.

ate (et) *pret.* de TO EAT.

atom ('ætəm) *s.* átomo.

attach (to) (ə'tætʃ) *t.* atar, ligar, unir, sujetar; agregar. *2* granjearse el afecto de. *3* dar, atribuir [importancia, etc.]. *4* DER. embargar.

attack (ə'tæk) *s.* ataque.

attack (to) (ə'tæk) *t.* atacar.

attain (to) (ə'tein) *t.* lograr.

attempt (ə'tempt) *s.* intento. *2* atentado.

attempt (to) (ə'tempt) *t.* intentar. *2* atentar contra.

attend (to) (ə'tend) *t.* atender a, cuidar de. *2* acompañar. *3* servir, escoltar. *4* asistir, concurrir. *5* aguardar.

attentive (ə'tentiv) *a.* atento. *2* cuidadoso.

attire (ə'taiəʳ) *s.* traje, vestidura.

attire (to) (ə'taiəʳ) *t.* vestir.

attorney (ə'tɔ:ni) *s.* apoderado. *2* procurador, abogado. *3* **~ general,** fiscal.

attraction (ə'trækʃən) *s.* atracción. *2* atractivo.

auburn ('ɔ:bən) *a.* castaño.

audience ('ɔ:djəns) *s.* auditorio, público. *2* audiencia [entrevista].

augment (to) (ɔ:g'ment) *t.-i.* aumentar(se.

August ('ɔ:gəst) *s.* agosto.

aunt (ɑ:nt) *s.* tía.

austere (ɔs'tiəʳ) *a.* austero.

author ('ɔ:θəʳ) *s.* autor, escritor.

authority (ɔ:'θɔriti) *s.* autoridad. *2* *pl.* autoridades.

authorize (to) ('ɔ:θəraiz) *t.* autorizar. *2* justificar.

autumn ('ɔ:təm) *s.* otoño.

avail (ə'veil) *s.* provecho.

avail (to) (ə'veil) *i.* servir, ser útil. *2* aprovechar, servir [a uno].

available (ə'veiləbl) *a.* disponible.

avaricious (ˌævəˈriʃəs) *a.* avaro.

avenge (to) (əˈvendʒ) *t.* vengar.

avenue (ˈævənjuː) *s.* avenida. paseo. alameda.

average (ˈævəridʒ) *s.* promedio. término medio.

avoid (to) (əˈvɔid) *t.* evitar. eludir. 2 anular.

avow (to) (əˈvau) *t.* confesar. reconocer.

await (to) (əˈweit) *t.-i.* aguardar. esperar.

awake (əˈweik) *a.* despierto.

awake (to) (əˈweik) *t.* despertar. 2 *i.* despertarse. ⸨ Pret.: *awoke* (əˈwouk); p. p.: *awaked* (əˈweikt) o *awoke*.

award (əˈwɔːd) *s.* sentencia. 2 adjudicación. 3 premio.

award (to) (əˈwɔːd) *t.* DER. adjudicar. 2 dar. conceder.

aware (əˈweəʳ) *a.* sabedor. enterado.

away (əˈwei) *adv.* lejos. fuera. alejándose. 2 Indica libertad o continuidad en la acción: *they fired* ~, fueron disparando.

awful (ˈɔːful) *a.* atroz. horrible. 2 tremendo. espantoso.

awhile (əˈwail) *adv.* un rato.

awkward (ˈɔːkwəd) *a.* torpe. desmañado. desgarbado.

awoke (əˈwouk) V. TO AWAKE.

ax, axe (æks) *s.* hacha.

B

baby ('beibi) *s.* criatura, bebé, nene, niño.

bachelor ('bætʃələ^r) *s.* soltero, -ra. célibe. 2 bachiller, licenciado.

back (bæk) *s.* espalda. 2 espinazo. 3 lomo [de animal, libro, etc.]. 4 *a.-adv.* posterior, dorsal, trasero; atrasado; atrás, hacia atrás; de vuelta, de regreso.

back (to) (bæk) *t.* apoyar, sostener. 2 apostar por.

background ('bækgraund) *s.* fondo, último término.

backward ('bækwəd) *a.* retrógrado. 2 atrasado.

bacon ('beikən) *s.* tocino.

bad (bæd) *a.* malo, mal. 2 enfermo. 3 *adv.* mal.

bade (beid) V. TO BID.

baffle (to) ('bæfl) *t.* confundir, desconcertar. 2 burlar.

bag (bæg) *s.* saco, bolsa. 2 maleta. 3 zurrón.

bag (to) (bæg) *t.* embolsar.

baggage ('bægidʒ) *s.* equipaje.

bait (beit) *s.* cebo, carnada.

bait (to) (beit) *t.* cebar.

bake (to) (beik) *t.* cocer, asar al horno. 2 *i.* cocerse.

baker ('beikə^r) *s.* panadero.

balance ('bæləns) *s.* balanza. 2 equilibrio. 3 COM. saldo.

balance (to) ('bæləns) *t.* pesar, comparar. 2 equilibrar. 3 COM. saldar. 5 *i.* equilibrarse.

bald (bɔːld) *a.* calvo.

ball (bɔːl) *s.* bola, globo, esfera. 2 pelota. 3 baile [fiesta].

balloon (bə'luːn) *s.* globo.

ballot ('bælət) *s.* balota 2 votación.

ban (bæn) *s.* proscripción.

ban (to) (bæn) *t.* proscribir.

banana (bə'nɑːnə) *s.* plátano.

band (bænd) *s.* faja, tira. 2 MÚS. banda. 3 pandilla.

band (to) (bænd) *t.* atar, fajar, vendar. 2 acuadrillar.

bandage ('bændidʒ) *s.* venda, vendaje.

bang (bæŋ) *s.* golpe, porrazo.

bang (to) (bæŋ) *t.* golpear [con ruido].

banish (to) ('bæniʃ) *t.* desterrar.

bank (bæŋk) *s.* ribazo, talud.

2 margen, orilla. 3 banco [de arena]. 4 COM. banco.

bank (to) (bæŋk) t. amontonar. 2 represar. 3 depositar en un banco.

banker ('bæŋkə^r) s. banquero.

bankrupt ('bæŋkrəpt) a. quebrado: *to go* ~, quebrar.

banner ('bænə^r) s. bandera.

banter ('bæntə^r) s. burla.

baptize (to) (bæp'taiz) t. bautizar.

bar (bɑ:^r) s. barra. 2 tranca [de puerta]. 3 obstáculo. 4 bar; mostrador de bar. 5 raya.

bar (to) (bɑ:^r) t. atrancar [una puerta]. 2 listar, rayar. 3 obstruir; obstar, impedir.

barbarian (bɑ:'bɛəriən) a.-s. bárbaro.

barber ('bɑ:bə^r) s. barbero.

bard (bɑ:d) s. bardo. 2 barda.

bare (bɛə^r) a. desnudo.

bare (to) (bɛə^r) t. desnudar, despojar, descubrir.

barefoot(ed ('bɛəfut, 'bɛə'futid) a. descalzo.

barely ('bɛəli) adv. apenas.

bargain ('bɑ:gin) s. trato.

bark (bɑ:k) s. corteza [de árbol]. 2 ladrido. 3 barca.

bark (to) (bɑ:k) t. descortezar. 2 i. ladrar.

barley ('bɑ:li) s. BOT. cebada.

barn (bɑ:n) s. granero, pajar.

barn-yard ('bɑ:n-'jɑ:d) s. patio [de granja].

baron ('bærən) s. barón.

barracks ('bærəks) s. pl. cuartel.

barrel ('bærəl) s. barril, tonel. 2 cañón [de un arma].

barren ('bærən) a. estéril.

barrier ('bæriə^r) s. barrera.

barrow ('bærou) s. carretilla.

barter ('bɑ:tə^r) s. trueque, cambio, cambalache.

barter (to) ('bɑ:tə^r) t.-i. trocar, cambiar.

base (beis) a. bajo, ruin, vil. 2 s. base. 3 basa.

base (to) (beis) t. basar, fundar. 2 i. basarse.

baseball ('beisbɔ:l) s. béisbol.

basement ('beismənt) s. sótano.

bashful ('bæʃful) a. vergonzoso, tímido, modesto.

basic ('beisik) a. básico.

basin ('beisn) s. jofaina.

basis ('beisis) s. base, fundamento.

bask (to) (bɑ:sk) i. calentarse.

basket ('bɑ:skit) s. cesto, canasta.

basket-ball ('bɑ:skitbɔ:l) s. baloncesto.

bastard ('bæstəd) a.-s. bastardo.

bat (bæt) s. ZOOL. murciélago. 2 DEP. palo, bote.

bat (to) (bæt) t. golpear.

batch (bætʃ) s. hornada.

bath (bɑ:θ) s. baño. 2 bañera.

bathe (to) (beið) t.-i. bañar(se.

bath-room ('bɑ:θrum) s. cuarto de baño.

battalion (bə'tæljən) s. batallón.

batter ('bætə^r) s. COC. batido.

batter (to) ('bætə^r) t. batir.

battery ('bætəri) s. batería. 2 pila eléctrica.

battle ('bætl) s. batalla, combate.

battle (to) ('bætl) i. combatir.

bay (bei) a.-s. bayo [caballo]. 2 s. bahía. 3 ladrido. 4 laurel.

bayonet ('beiənit) *s.* bayoneta.

baza(a)r (bə'za:ᵣ) *s.* bazar.

be (to) (bi:) *i.* ser; estar. 2 hallarse. 3 existir. 4 tener: *he is ten,* tiene diez años. 5 *impers.* haber [precedido de *there*]. 6 hacer: *it's cold,* hace frío. 7 *aux.* Forma la pasiva: *he is loved,* es amado; la conjug. progresiva: *he is coming,* va a venir; la conjug. de obligación: *I'm to go out,* he de salir. ¶ CONJUG: INDIC. Pres.: *I am* (æm, əm, m), *you are* (a:ᵣ, aᵣ, əᵣ) [*art*], *he is* (iz, z, s), *we are,* etc. | Pret.: *I, he was* (wɔz, wəz), *you, we, they were* (wə:ᵣ, wəᵣ). ‖ SUBJ. PRES.: *be.* | PRET.: *were.* ‖ PART. PAS.: *been* (bi:n, bin). ‖ GER.: *being* ('bi:iŋ).

beach (bi:tʃ) *s.* playa, orilla.

beach (to) (bi:tʃ) *i.-t.* varar.

beak (bi:k) *s.* pico [de ave, etc.].

beam (bi:m) *s.* viga, madero. 2 rayo [de luz, calor, etc.].

beam (to) (bi:m) *t.* emitir [luz, etc.]. 2 *i.* brillar.

bean (bi:n) *s.* haba, judía.

bear (beəᵣ) *s.* ZOOL. oso, osa.

bear (to) (beəᵣ) *t.* llévar, cargar. 2 soportar. 3 dar a luz; *he was born in London,* nació en Londres ¶ Pret.: *bore* (bɔːᵣ); p. p.: *borne* o *born* (bɔːn).

beard (biəd) *s.* barba.

beard (to) (biəd) *t.* desafiar.

beast (bi:st) *s.* bestia, animal.

beat (bi:t) *s.* golpe; latido.

beat (to) (bi:t) *t.* pegar; golpear. ¶ Pret.: *beat* (bi:t); p. p.: *beaten* (bi:tn).

beautiful ('bju:tiful) *a.* hermoso, bello. 2 lindo.

became (bi'keim) V. TO BECOME.

because (bi'kɔz) *conj.* porque. 2 ~ *of,* a causa de.

beckon (to) ('bekən) *t.* llamar por señas. 2 *i.* hacer señas.

become (to) (bi'kʌm) *t.* convenir, sentar, caer o ir bien. 2 *i.* volverse, hacerse, convertirse en; ponerse. ¶ Pret.: *became* (bi'keim); p. p.: *become* (bi'kʌm).

bed (bed) *s.* cama, lecho.

bedroom ('bedrum) *s.* dormitorio.

bee (bi:) *s.* abeja.

beer (biəᵣ) *s.* cerveza.

beet (bi:t) *s.* remolacha.

beetle ('bi:tl) *s.* ENT. escarabajo.

before (bi'fɔːᵣ, -fɔəᵣ) *adv.* antes. 2 delante. 3 *prep.* antes de o que. 4 delante de.

beforehand (bi'fɔ:hænd)*adv.* de antemano.

beg (to) (beg) *t.* pedir, solicitar; rogar. 2 *i.* mendigar.

began (bi'gæn) V. TO BEGIN.

beggar ('begəᵣ) *s.* mendigo, -ga.

beggar (to) ('begəᵣ) *t.* empobrecer, arruinar.

begin (to) (bi'gin) *t.-i.* empezar, comenzar, principiar. ¶ Pret.: *began* (bi'gæn); p. p.: *begun* (bi'gʌn); ger.: *beginning.*

beginning (bi'giniŋ) *s.* principio.

beguile (to) (bi'gail) *t.* engañar, seducir.

behalf (bi'ha:f) *s.* cuenta, interés; *on ~ of,* en nombre de.

behave (to) (bi'heiv) *i.-ref.* obrar, proceder.

behavio(u)r (bi'heivjə^r) *s.* conducta, comportamiento.

behead (to) (bi'hed) *t.* decapitar.

behind (bi'haind) *adv.* detrás. 2 *prep.* detrás de; después de.

behold (to) (bi'hould) *t.* ver, contemplar, observar. ¶ Pret. y p. p.: *beheld* (bi'held).

being ('bi:iŋ) *ger.* de TO BE. 2 *s.* ser, existencia. 3 persona. 4 *for the time* ~, por ahora.

belief (bi'li:f) *s.* creencia. 2 opinión. 3 fe, confianza.

believe (to) (bi'li:v) *t.-i.* creer. 2 pensar, opinar.

believer (bi'li:və^r) *s.* creyente.

bell (bel) *s.* campana.

bellow ('belou) *s.* bramido, mugido, rugido.

belly ('beli) *s.* vientre, panza.

belly (to) ('beli) *t.* combar, abultar. 2 *i.* pandear.

belong (to) (bi'lɔŋ) *-i.* pertenecer. 2 ser habitante de.

belongings (bi'lɔŋiŋz) *s. pl.* bienes.

beloved (bi'lʌvd) *a.* querido, amado, dilecto.

below (bi'lou) *adv.* abajo, debajo. 2 *prep.* bajo, debajo de; por debajo de.

belt (belt) *s.* cinturón, faja.

bench (bentʃ) *s.* banco. 2 tribunal.

bend (bend) *s.* inclinación.

bend (to) (bend) *t.* encorvar, doblar, torcer. 2 inclinar. 3 *i.* inclinarse. ¶ Pret. y p. p.: *bent* (bert).

beneath (bi'ni:θ) *adv.* abajo, debajo. 2 *prep.* bajo, debajo de.

benefit ('benifit) *s.* beneficio, favor. 2 beneficio, bien.

bent (bent) *pret.* y *p. p.* de TO BEND. 2 *a.* torcido, doblado. 3 ~ *on*, empeñado en. 4 *s.* curvatura. 5 inclinación.

bequeath (to) (bi'kwi:ð) *t.* legar, dejar.

bequest (bi'kwest) *s.* legado.

berry ('beri) *s.* baya; grano.

berth (bə:θ) *s.* MAR. amarradero. 2 camarote, litera.

beseech (to) (bi'si:tʃ) *t.* implorar; suplicar. ¶ Pret. y p. p.: *besought* (bi'sɔ:t) o *beseeched* (bi'si:tʃt).

beset (to) (bi'set) *t.* asediar, acosar. ¶ Pret. y p. p.: *beset;* ger.: *besetting.*

beside (bi'said) *adv.* cerca, al lado. 2 *prep.* al lado de, cerca de.

besides (bi'saidz) *adv.* además, por otra parte. 2 *prep.* además de. 3 excepto.

besiege (to) (bi'si:dʒ) *t.* sitiar. 2 asediar, acosar.

besought (bi'sɔ:t) V. TO BESEECH.

best (best) *a. superl.* de GOOD; mejor, óptimo, superior. 2 *adv. superl.* de WELL: mejor; mucho; más.

bestow (to) (bi'stou) *t.* otorgar. 2 emplear, dedicar.

bet (bet) *s.* apuesta.

bet (to) (bet) *t.-i.* apostar.

betray (to) (bi'trei) *t.* traicionar. 2 revelar, descubrir.

betroth (to) (bi'trouð) *t.-i.* desposar, prometer.

better ('betə^r) *a.-adv.* mejor. 2 *s.* lo mejor; *so much the* ~, tanto mejor. 3 *pl.* superiores.

better (to) ('betə^r) *t.* mejorar. 2 *i.* mejorarse.

between (bi'twi:n) *adv.* en medio. 2 *prep.* entre [dos].

beverage ('bevəridʒ) *s.* bebida.

beware (to) (bi'wεə^r) *i.* guardarse de, precaverse.

bewilder (to) (bi'wildə^r) *t.* desconcertar, aturdir.

bewitch (to) (bi'witʃ) *t.* embrujar, hechizar, encantar.

beyond (bi'jɔnd) *adv.* más allá, más lejos. 2 *prep.* más allá de. 3 *s.* la otra vida.

bias ('baiəs) *s.* sesgo, oblicuidad. 2 parcialidad, prejuicio.

bib (bib) *s.* babero.

Bible ('baibl) *s.* Biblia.

bicycle ('baisikl) *s.* bicicleta.

bid (bid) *s.* licitación, puja.

bid (to) (bid) *t.* decir. 2 ofrecer [un precio], pujar. 3 ordenar, mandar. 4 invitar. ¶ Pret.: *bade* (beid); p. p.: *bidden* ('bidn).

big (big) *a.* grande, importante. 2 corpulento.

bigot ('bigət) *s.* fanático.

bigotry ('bigetri) *s.* fanatismo, intolerancia.

bill (bil) *s.* pico [de ave]. 2 pica, alabarda. 3 cuenta, nota, factura, lista: ~ *of fare,* minuta, lista de platos. 4 letra, pagaré. 5 patente, certificado. 6 cartel, programa [de teatro], prospecto. 7 proyecto de ley; ley.

bill (to) (bil) *t.* cargar en cuenta. 2 anunciar por carteles.

billion ('biljən) *s.* (Ingl.)billón. 2 (E.U.) mil millones.

billow ('bilou) *s.* oleada. 2 ola.

billow (to) ('bilou) *i.* ondular.

bin (bin) *s.* caja, recipiente.

birch (bə:tʃ) *s.* vara [de abedul].

birch (to) (bə:tʃ) *t.* azotar.

bird (bə:d) *s.* ave, pájaro.

birth (bə:θ) *s.* nacimiento. 2 cuna, origen. 3 linaje.

birthday ('bə:θdei) *s.* cumpleaños.

biscuit ('biskit) *s.* galleta, bizcocho. 2 CERÁM. bizcocho.

bishop ('biʃəp) *s.* ECLES. obispo. 2 AJED. alfil.

bit (bit) *s.* trozo, pedacito.

bit (bit) *pret.* de TO BITE.

bite (bait) *s.* mordedura. 2 mordisco. 3 bocado, tentempié.

bite (to) (bait) *t.-i.* morder. ¶ Pret.: *bit* (bit); p. p.: *bit* o *bitten* ('bitn).

biting ('baitiŋ) *a.* mordaz; picante.

bitten ('bitn) V. TO BITE.

bitter ('bitə^r) *a.* amargo.

black (blæk) *a.* negro. 2 puro [café]. 3 *s.* negro.

black (to) (blæk) *t.* ennegrecer. 2 *i.* ennegrecerse.

blackberry ('blækbəri) *s.* BOT. zarza. 2 zarzamora.

blackboard ('blækbɔ:d) *s.* pizarra.

blackish ('blækiʃ) *a.* negruzco.

blackmail ('blækmeil) *s.* chantaje.

blackmail (to) ('blækmeil) *t.* hacer un chantaje a.

blackness ('blæknis) *s.* negrura, oscuridad.

blacksmith ('blæksmiθ) *s.* herrero.

blade (bleid) s. hoja, cuchilla [de arma, etc.]. 2 pala [de remo, etc.]. 3 hoja [de hierba].

blame (bleim) s. censura, culpa.

blank (blæŋk) a. en blanco. 2 vacío; sin interés. 3 desconcertado, confuso. 4 s. blanco, espacio, laguna. 5 diana [de un blanco].

blanket ('blæŋkit) s. manta.

blast (bla:st) s. ráfaga [de viento]. 2 soplo [de un fuelle]; chorro [de aire, vapor, etc.]. 3 sonido. 4 explosión, voladura. 5 ~ **furnace,** alto horno.

blast (to) (bla:st) t. agostar, marchitar. 2 maldecir.

blaze (bleiz) s. llama. 2 hoguera.

blaze (to) (bleiz) i. arder, llamear. 2 brillar, resplandecer. 3 t. encender, inflamar.

bleak (bli:k) a. desierto, frío.

bleed (to) (bli:d) t.-i. sangrar. ¶ Pret. y p. p.: **bled** (bled).

blemish ('blemiʃ) s. tacha, defecto. 2 mancha, borrón.

blend (blend) s. mezcla.

blend (to) (blend) t.-i. mezclar(se, combinar(se. 2 t. matizar, armonizar. ¶ Pret. y p. p.: **blended** ('blendid) o **blent** (blent).

blew (blu:) V. TO BLOW.

blind (blaind) a. ciego. 2 oscuro, tenebroso. 3 ~ **alley,** callejón sin salida. 4 s. pantalla, persiana. 5 engaño.

blind (to) (blaind) t. cegar.

blindness ('blaindnis) s. ceguera.

blink (bliŋk) s. pestañeo, guiño. 2 destello, reflejo.

blink (to) (bliŋk) i. parpadear, pestañear. 2 oscilar.

bliss (blis) s. bienaventuranza.

blissful ('blisful) a. bienaventurado, dichoso.

blister ('blistə') s. vejiga, ampolla. 2 vejigatorio.

blithe (blaið), **blithesome** (-səm) a. alegre, gozoso.

block (blɔk) s. bloque. 2 trozo grande. 3 manzana, *cuadra [de casas]. 4 bloc [de papel]. 5 obstáculo.

block (to) (blɔk) t. obstruir, bloquear, atascar.

blockade (blɔ'keid) s. MIL. bloqueo, asedio.

blockade (to) (blɔ'keid) s. MIL. bloquear.

blood (blʌd) s. sangre.

bloodshed ('blʌdʃəd) s. matanza.

bloody ('blʌdi) a. sangriento.

bloom (blu:m) s. flor. 2 floración. 3 frescor, lozanía.

bloom (to) (blu:m) i. florecer.

blossom ('blɔsəm) s. flor.

blossom (to) ('blɔsəm) i. florecer.

blouse (blauz) s. blusa.

blow (blou) s. golpe, porrazo. 2 desgracia. 3 soplo [de aire].

blow (to) (blou) t. soplar. 2 to ~ **one's nose,** sonarse las narices. 3 to ~ **out,** apagar; ELECT. fundir. 4 impers. hacer viento. ¶ Pret.: **blew** (blu:); p. p.: **blown** (bloun).

blue (blu:) a. azul. 2 pl. **the blues,** tristeza, melancolía.

bluff (blʌf) a. escarpado. 2 rudo, francote. 3 s. escarpa, risco. 4 farol, envite falso.

bluff (to) (blʌf) i. hacer un farol; fanfarronear.

bluish ('blu(:)iʃ) a. azulado.

blunder ('blʌndə^r) s. disparate, yerro, plancha.

blunder (to) ('blʌndə^r) i. equivocarse.

blunt (blʌnt) a. embotado.

blur (blə^r) s. borrón.

blur (to) (blə:^r) t. manchar.

blush (blʌʃ) s. rubor, sonrojo.

blush (to) (blʌʃ) i. ruborizarse, sonrojarse.

bluster (to) ('blʌstə^r) i. enfurecerse. 2 fanfarronear.

boar (bɔ:^r) s. verraco. 2 *wild* ~, jabalí.

board (bɔ:d) s. tabla, tablero [de madera].

board (to) (bɔ:d) t. entarimar, enmaderar. 2 tomar o poner a pupilaje. 3 abordar.

boast (boust) s. jactancia.

boast (to) (boust) i. jactarse. 2 ostentar.

boastful ('boustful) a. jactancioso.

boat (bout) s. bote, barca.

bodily ('bɔdili) a. corporal. 2 adv. en persona. 3 en peso.

body ('bɔdi) s. cuerpo. 2 persona, individuo.

bog (bɔg) s. pantano, cenagal.

boil (bɔil) s. ebullición.

boil (to) (bɔil) i. hervir. 2 t. cocer.

boiler ('bɔilə^r) s. olla, caldero.

boisterous ('bɔistərəs) a. estrepitoso, ruidoso.

bold (bould) a. intrépido, valiente. 2 atrevido.

bolster ('boulstə^r) s. cabezal, travesaño [de cama].

bolster (to) ('boulstə^r) t. apoyar. 2 apuntalar.

bolt (boult) s. saeta, virote. 2 rayo, centella. 3 salto; fuga. 4 cerrojo, pestillo.

bolt (to) (boult) t. echar el cerrojo a. 2 engullir. 3 i. salir, entrar, etc., de repente; huir.

bomb (bɔm) s. bomba.

bomb (to) (bɔm) t.-i. bombardear.

bombardment (bɔm'bɑ:dmənt) s. bombardeo.

bond (bɔnd) s. atadura. 2 vínculo. 3 trabazón. 4 pacto. 5 fiador [pers.]. 6 COM. bono. 7 *pl.* cautiverio.

bondage ('bɔndidʒ) s. esclavitud, servidumbre.

bone (boun) s. hueso. 2 espina [de pescado].

bone (to) (boun) t. deshuesar.

bonfire ('bɔn,faiə^r) s. fogata.

bonnet ('bɔnit) s. gorro; gorra. 2 AUTO. capó.

bonus ('bounəs) s. prima, gratificación.

bony ('bouni) a. huesudo.

book (buk) s. libro. 2 cuaderno, libreta. 3 libreto.

book (to) (buk) t. anotar, inscribir.

bookcase ('bukkeis) s. armario o estante para libros.

booklet ('buklit) s. folleto.

bookshop ('bukʃɔp), **bookstore** (-stɔ:^r) s. librería [tienda].

boom (bu:m) s. estampido. 2 fig. auge repentino.

boom (to) (bu:m) i. retumbar. 2 prosperar. 3 popularizarse.

boor (buə^r) s. patán.

boot (bu:t) s. bota.

border ('bɔ:də^r) s. borde, orilla, margen. 2 frontera.

bore (bɔ:^r) V. TO BEAR.

bore (bɔ:^r) s. taladro, barreno [agujero].

bore (to) (bɔ:^r) t. horadar, taladrar.

born, borne (bɔːn) V. TO
BEAR.

borough ('bʌrə) s. villa;
burgo.

borrow (to) ('bɔrou) t. tomar o
pedir prestado.

bosom ('buzəm) s. pecho,
seno, corazón.

boss (bɔs) s. protuberancia,
giba. 2 fam. amo, jefe.

boss (to) (bɔs) t.-i. mandar.

bossy ('bɔsi) a. mandón.

both (bouθ) a.-pron. ambos,
entrambos, los dos.

bother ('bɔðər) s. preocupación. 2 fastidio, molestia.

bother (to) ('bɔðər) t.-i. preo-
cupar(se, molestar(se.

bottle ('bɔtl) s. botella, frasco.

bottle (to) ('bɔtl) t. embote-
llar.

bottom ('bɔtəm) s. fondo. 2
base, fundamento. 3 fam.
trasero. 4 hondonada. 5 a.
fundamental. 6 del fondo,
más bajo.

bough (bau) s. rama [de ár-
bol].

bought (bɔːt) V. TO BUY.

boulder ('bouldər) s. canto rodado.

bounce (bauns) s. salto, bote.
2 fanfarronada.

bound (baund) V. TO BIND. 2
a. obligado. 3 encuader-
nado. 4 destinado a. 5 s.
límite, confín. 6 salto,
brinco.

bound (to) (baund) t. limitar.
2 i. lindar. 3 saltar, brincar.

boundary ('baundəri) s.
límite, confín, frontera.

bounty ('baunti) s. liberali-
dad, generosidad. 2 subvención.

bow (bau) s. inclinación, re-

verencia, saludo. 2 MAR.
proa.

bow (bou) s. arco [arma,
violín]. 2 curva.

bow (to) (bau) i. inclinarse,
saludar. 2 doblarse; ceder.
3 t. doblar, inclinar, agobiar.

bow (to) (bou) t.-i. arquear-
(se.

bower ('bauər) s. glorieta.

bowl (boul) s. cuenco, escu-
dilla, bol; copa. 2 bola, bo-
cha.

bowl (to) (boul) t. hacer rodar. 2 i. jugar a bochas o a
los bolos.

bowman ('boumən) s. ar-
quero.

box (bɔks) s. caja, arca,
baúl. 2 TEAT. palco.

box (to) (bɔks) t. encajonar.
2 abofetear. 3 i. boxear.

boxer ('bɔksər) s. boxeador.

boxing ('bɔksiŋ) s. boxeo.

boxwood ('bɔkswud) s. boj.

boy (bɔi) s. chico, muchacho.

brace (breis) s. abrazadera. 2
pl. tirantes [del pantalón].

bracelet ('breislit) s. brazalete.

bracket ('brækit) s. ménsula,
repisa. 2 anaquel, rinco-
nera. 3 IMPR. corchete;
paréntesis.

brain (brein) s. ANAT. cerebro, seso. 2 pl. inteligencia.

brake (to) (breik) t. frenar.

bramble ('bræmbl) s. zarza.

bran (bræn) s. salvado.

branch (brɑːntʃ) s. rama;
ramo; ramal. 2 COM. sucursal.

branch (to) (brɑːntʃ) i. echar
ramas. 2 bifurcarse.

brand (brænd) s. tizón, tea. 2 hierro [para marcar]. 3 marca de fábrica.

brand (to) (brænd) t. marcar [con hierro]. 2 estigmatizar.

brandish (to) ('brændiʃ) t. blandir.

brandy ('brændi) s. coñac.

brass (brɑ:s) s. latón, metal: ~ *band*, charanga. 2 descaro.

brave (breiv) a. bravo, valiente.

brave (to) (breiv) t. desafiar.

brawl (brɔ:l) s. reyerta, riña.

brawl (to) (brɔ:l) i. alborotar.

bray (brei) s. rebuzno.

brazen ('breizn) a. de latón. 2 desvergonzado.

breach (bri:tʃ) s. brecha, abertura. 2 fractura. 3 hernia.

breach (to) (bri:tʃ) t. hacer brecha en.

bread (bred) s. pan.

breadth (bredθ) s. anchura.

break (breik) s. break [coche]. 2 rotura, ruptura. 3 comienzo. 4 interrupción, pausa.

break (to) (breik) t. romper, quebrar. 2 interrumpir. 3 *to* ~ *down*, demoler. 4 *to* ~ *ground*, comenzar una empresa. 5 *to* ~ *up*, desmenuzar, romper. 6 i. romperse, partirse. 7 debilitarse. 8 irrumpir. 9 aparecer, salir, nacer, botar; apuntar [el alba]. 10 *to* ~ *away*, soltarse; escapar. 11 *to* ~ *down*, parar por avería. 12 *to* ~ *out*, estallar, desatarse. ¶ Pret.: *broke* (brouk); p. p.: *broken* ('broukən).

breakfast ('brekfəst) s. desayuno.

breakfast (to) ('brekfəst) i. desayunarse, almorzar.

breast (brest) s. pecho, seno.

breath (breθ) s. aliento, respiración. 2 soplo.

breathe (to) (bri:ð) i. respirar. 2 exhalar. 3 soplar.

bred (bred) V. TO BREED.

breed (bri:d) s. casta, raza.

breed (to) (bri:d) t. engendrar. 2 criar [animales]. ¶ Pret. y p. p.: *bred* (bred).

breeding ('bri:diŋ) s. cría, producción. 2 crianza, educación.

breeze (bri:z) s. brisa, airecillo.

brew (bru:) s. infusión [bebida].

brew (to) (bru:) t. hacer [cerveza]. 2 preparar [el té, un ponche, etc.]. 3 urdir, tramar.

bribe (braib) s. soborno.

bribe (to) (braib) t. sobornar.

brick (brik) s. ladrillo.

brick (to) (brick) enladrillar.

bridal ('braidl) a. nupcial. 2 s. boda.

bride (braid) s. novia, desposada.

bridge (bridʒ) s. puente.

bridge (to) (bridʒ) t. pontear.

brief (bri:f) a. breve, conciso. 2 fugaz. 3 s. resumen.

brier ('braiəʳ) s. zarza; brezo.

brigantine ('brigəntain) s. bergantín, goleta.

bright (brait) a. brillante.

brightness ('braitnis) s. brillo.

brilliant ('briljənt) a. brillante. 2 s. brillante [piedra].

brim (brim) s. borde [de un

vaso, etc.]. 2 ala [de sombrero].

brim (to) (brim) *t.* llenar hasta el borde. 2 *i.* rebosar.

bring (to) (briŋ) *t.* traer, llevar. 2 acarrear, causar. 3 inducir [persuadir]. 4 aportar, aducir. 5 poner [en un estado, condición, etc.] ¶ Pret. y p. p.: *brought* (brɔ:t).

brink (briŋk) *s.* borde, orilla, extremidad.

brisk (brisk) *a.* vivo, activo.

bristle ('brisl) *s.* cerda, porcipelo.

bristle (to) ('brisl) *t.-i.* erizar(se.

brittle ('britl) *a.* quebradizo.

broad (brɔ:d) *a.* ancho. 2 amplio, extenso, lato.

broadcast ('brɔ:dkɑ:st) *s.* emisión de radio.

broadcast (to) ('brɔ:dkɑ:st) *t.* esparcir, difundir. 2 radiar.

broaden (to) ('brɔ:dn) *t.-i.* ensanchar(se.

broil (brɔil) *s.* asado a la parrilla. 2 riña, tumulto.

broken ('broukən) V. TO BREAK.

broker ('broukə^r) *s.* COM. corredor, agente. 2 bolsista.

bronze (brɔnz) *s.* bronce.

bronze (to) (brɔnz) *t.-i.* broncear(se.

brooch (broutʃ) *s.* broche.

brood (bru:d) *s.* cría, pollada, nidada. 2 progenie. 3 casta.

brook (bruk) *s.* arroyo, riachuelo.

brook (to) (bruk) *t.* sufrir, aguantar, tolerar.

broom (bru(:)m) *s.* escoba.

brother ('brʌðə^r) *s.* hermano.

brother-in-law ('brʌðərinlɔ:) *s.* cuñado, hermano político.

brotherly ('brʌðəli) *a.* fraternal.

brought (brɔ:t) V. TO BRING.

brow (brau) *s.* ANAT. ceja. 2 frente, entrecejo. 3 cresta, cumbre.

brown (braun) *a.* pardo, moreno, castaño.

brown (to) (braun) *t.* tostar.

browse (to) (brauz) *t.* rozar.

bruise (bru:z) *s.* magulladura.

bruise (to) (bru:z) *t.* magullar. 2 machucar, abollar. 3 majar.

brush (brʌʃ) *s.* cepillo.

brush (to) (brʌʃ) *t.* cepillar.

bubble ('bʌbl) *s.* burbuja.

buck (bʌk) *s.* gamo. 2 macho.

bucket ('bʌkit) *s.* cubo, balde.

buckle ('bʌkl) *s.* hebilla.

buckle (to) ('bʌkl) *t.* abrochar.

bud (bʌd) *s.* yema, capullo.

bud (to) (bʌd) *i.* brotar, abotonar, pimpollecer.

budget ('bʌdʒit) *s.* presupuesto.

budget (to) ('bʌdʒit) *t.-i.* presuponer, presupuestar.

buff (bʌf) *a.* de ante. 2 *s.* ante.

buffet ('bʌfit) *s.* bofetada, puñada. 2 ('bufei) aparador [mueble]. 3 bar [de estación].

bug (bʌg) *s.* insecto; chinche.

build (bild) *s.* estructura. 2 forma, figura, talle.

build (to) (bild) *t.* construir, edificar. 2 fundar, cimentar. ¶ Pret. y p. p.: *built* (bilt).

building ('bildiŋ) *s.* construcción, edificación. 2 edificio, casa.

built (bilt) V. TO BUILD.

bulb (bʌlb) *s.* BOT., ZOOL. bulbo. 2 ELECT. bombilla.

bulk (bʌlk) *s.* bulto, volumen, tamaño. 2 mole. 3 la mayor parte. 4 COM. *in* ~, a granel.

bulk (to) (bʌlk) *i.* abultar.

bull (bul) *s.* ZOOL. toro: ~ *ring,* plaza de toros. 2 bula [pontificia]. 3 COM. alcista.

bullfight ('bulfait) *s.* corrida de toros.

bullfighter ('bulfaitə^r) *s.* torero.

bully ('buli) *s.* matón, valentón.

bully (to) ('buli) *t.* intimidar con amenazas; maltratar.

bulwark ('bulwək) *s.* baluarte.

bump (bʌmp) *s.* choque, porrazo, batacazo. 2 chichón.

bump (to) (bʌmp) *t.-i.* golpear; chocar [con].

bun (bʌn) *s.* bollo [panecillo]. 2 moño, castaña.

bunch (bʌntʃ) *s.* manojo, ristra. 2 racimo. 3 grupo, hato.

bunch (to) (bʌntʃ) *t.-i.* juntar(se, arracimar(se.

bundle ('bʌndl) *s.* atado, manojo, haz. 2 bulto, paquete.

bundle (to) ('bʌndl) *t.* liar, atar.

bungalow ('bʌngəlou) *s.* casita.

buoy (bɔi) *s.* boya, baliza.

buoy (to) (bɔi) *t.* mantener a flote. 2 sostener, animar.

burden ('bə:dn) *s.* carga, peso; gravamen.

burden (to) ('bə:dn) *t.* cargar, agobiar.

burglar ('bə:glə^r) *s.* ladrón.

burial ('beriəl) *s.* entierro.

burn (to) (bə:n) *t.* quemar, abrasar. 2 *i.* arder, quemarse, abrasarse. ¶ Pret. y p. p.: *burned* (bə:nd) o *burnt* (bə:nt).

burner ('bə:nə^r) *s.* mechero.

burnt (bə:nt) V. TO BURN.

burrow ('bʌrou) *s.* madriguera.

burrow (to) ('bʌrou) *t.-i.* minar [como los conejos].

burst (bə:st) *s.* explosión, estallido, reventón.

burst (to) (bə:st) *i.* reventar; romperse. 2 prorrumpir. 3 *t.* reventar, hacer estallar. ¶ Pret. y p. p.: *burst.*

bury (to) ('beri) *t.* enterrar.

bus (bʌs) *s.* autobús.

bush (buʃ) *s.* arbusto.

business ('biznis) *s.* oficio, ocupación, trabajo, asunto. 2 negocio, comercio, tráfico. 3 negocio, empresa, establecimiento.

bust (bʌst) *s.* busto.

bustle ('bʌsl) *s.* movimiento, agitación.

bustle (to) ('bʌsl) *t.-i.* bullir, menearse, no parar.

busy ('bizi) *a.* ocupado, atareado. 2 activo, diligente.

busy (to) ('bizi) *t.-ref.* ocupar(se, atarear(se.

but (bʌt, bət) *conj.* mas, pero; sino; sin que, que no; [con *cannot, could not* + inf.] no puedo [evitar] menos de, sino. 2 *adv.* sólo. 3 *prep., conj.* excepto, salvo; menos.

butcher (to) ('butʃə^r) *t.* matar, sacrificar [reses].

butler ('bʌtləʳ) *s.* mayordomo.
butter ('bʌteʳ) *s.* mantequilla.
butterfly ('bʌtəflai) *s.* ENT. mariposa.
button ('bʌtn) *s.* botón.
button (to) ('bʌtn) *t.-i.* abrochar(se.
buy (to) (bai) *t.-i.* comprar: *to ~ up,* acaparar. ¶ Pret. y p. p.: *bought* (bɔ:t).

buzz (bʌz) *s.* zumbido.
buzz (to) (bʌz) *i.* zumbar, susurrar.
by (bai) *prep.* junto a, cerca de, al lado de, cabe. 2 a, con, de, en, por, etc. 3 ~ *the way,* de paso, a propósito. 4 *a.* lateral, apartado. 5 *adv.* cerca, al lado, por el lado. 6 aparte.

C

cab (kæb) s. cabriolé. 2 coche de punto; taxi. 3 cabina.

cabbage ('kæbidʒ) s. col.

cabin ('kæbin) s. cabaña, choza. 2 MAR. camarote: ~ *boy,* grumete. 3 cabina.

cabinet ('kæbinit) s. gabinete; escritorio. 2 vitrina.

cable ('keibl) s. cable.

cable (to) ('keibl) t. cablegrafiar.

cackle ('kækl) s. cacareo.

cackle (to) ('kækl) i. cacarear.

café ('kæfei) s. café [local].

cage (keidʒ) s. jaula.

cage (to) (keidʒ) t. enjaular.

cajole (to) (kə'dʒoul) t. engatusar, lisonjear.

cake (keik) s. pastel, bollo. 2 pastilla, pan [de jabón, etc.].

calculate (to) ('kælkjuleit) t. calcular. 2 i. hacer cálculos.

calendar ('kælindəʳ) s. calendario, almanaque.

calf (kɑːf) pl. **calves** (kɑːvz)s. ZOOL. terñero, -ra. 2 pantorrilla.

call (kɔːl) s. grito, llamada. 2 toque de señal. 3 reclamo [de caza]. 4 exigencia. 5 derecho, motivo. 6 visita corta.

call (to) (kɔːl) t. llamar. 2 convocar, citar. 3 invocar. 4 considerar. 5 pregonar. 6 to ~ *at,* detenerse en; to ~ *attention to,* llamar la atención sobre; to ~ *back,* hacer volver; anular; to ~ *for,* ir a buscar; exigir, pedir; to ~ *forth,* ser la causa de; hacer salir; to ~ *names,* insultar; to ~ *off,* suspender; to ~ *on,* visitar; exhortar; to ~ *the roll,* pasar lista; to ~ *up,* llamar por teléfono; poner a debate; to ~ *upon,* exhortar. 7 i. gritar. 8 hacer una visita a. 9 [de un barco] hacer escala; [del tren] parar.

caller ('kɔːləʳ) s. visitante.

calm (kɑːm) s. calma, sosiego. 2 serenidad. 3 a. sosegado, tranquilo.

calm (to) (kɑːm) t. calmar, sosegar. 2 i. to ~ *down,* calmarse.

came (keim) V. TO COME.

camera ('kæmərə) *s.* ANAT., FÍS. cámara. 2 máquina fotográfica.

camp (kæmp) *s.* campamento.

camp (to) (kæmp) *t.-i.* acampar.

campaign (kæm'pein) *s.* campaña.

camping ('kæmpiŋ) *s.* campamento.

can (kæn) *s.* jarro [de metal], bote, lata.

can (kæn, kən) *aux.* poder o saber [hacer una cosa]. ¶ Pret. y cond.: **could** (kud, kəd).

can (to) (kæn) *t.* enlatar, conservar en lata.

canal (kə'næl) *s.* canal.

cancel (to) ('kænsəl) *t.* cancelar. 2 anular. 3 tachar.

cancer ('kænsə^r) *s.* MED. cáncer.

candidate ('kændidit) *s.* candidato. 2 aspirante.

candle ('kændl) *s.* vela.

candy (kændi) *s.* confite.

cane (kein) *s.* BOT. caña; caña de azúcar. 2 bastón.

canker ('kæŋkə^r) *s.* úlcera maligna. 2 fig. cáncer.

canker (to) ('kæŋkə^r) *t.* gangrenar, cancerar. 2 *i.* cancerarse.

cannot ('kænɔt) forma compuesta de *can* y *not*.

canoe (kə'nu:) *s.* canoa.

canopy ('kænəpi) *s.* dosel.

canvas ('kænvəs) *s.* lona.

canyon ('kænjən) *s.* hondonada.

cap (kæp) *s.* gorro, gorra; cofia, bonete, capelo. 2 cima.

cap (to) (kæp) *t.* cubrir [la cabeza]. 2 coronar, acabar.

capable ('keipəbl) *a.* capaz.

capacity (kə'pæsiti) *s.* capacidad. 2 calidad. 3 condición.

cape (keip) *s.* GEOGR. cabo. 2 capa corta, esclavina.

caper ('keipə^r) *s.* cabriola; travesura. 2 BOT. alcaparra.

caper (to) ('keipə^r) *i.* cabriolar.

capital ('kæpitl) *a.* capital. 2 *a.-s.* mayúscula. 3 *s.* COM. capital. 4 capital [población]. 5 ARQ. capitel.

capitalist ('kæpitəlist) *a.-s.* capitalista.

captain ('kæptin) *s.* capitán.

captivity (kæp'tiviti) *s.* cautividad, cautiverio.

capture ('kæptʃə^r) *s.* captura.

capture (to) ('kæptʃə^r) *t.* capturar, prender. 2 apresar.

car (kɑ:^r) *s.* coche, automóvil.

card (kɑ:d) *s.* carta, naipe. 2 tarjeta, cédula, ficha. 3 carda.

card (to) ((kɑ:d) *t.* cardar.

cardboard ('kɑ:dbɔ:d) *s.* cartón.

care (kɛə^r) *s.* preocupación, inquietud. 2 cuidado.

care (to) (kɛə^r) *i.* preocuparse: cuidar [de]; hacer caso; importarle a uno.

careful ('kɛəful) *a.* cuidadoso. 2 solícito.

careless ('kɛəlis) *a.* descuidado, negligente.

caress (kə'res) *s.* caricia, halago.

cargo ('kɑ:gou) *s.* MAR. carga, cargamento.

carol ('kærəl) *s.* villancico.

carpenter ('kɑ:pintə^r) *s.* carpintero.

carpet ('kɑ:pit) *s.* alfombra.

carpet (to) ('kɑ:pit) *t.* alfombrar.

carrier ('kæriəʳ) s. portador. 2 porteador, transportista. 3 portaviones.

carrot ('kærət) s. zanahoria.

carry (to) ('kæri) t. llevar; traer, conducir, transportar; acarrear. 2 to ~ away, llevarse; to ~ forward, sumar y seguir; to ~ off, llevarse, ganar; lograr; to ~ on, continuar, seguir; to ~ out, llevar a cabo, ejecutar; to ~ through, completar.

cart (kɑːt) s. carro, carreta.

cart (to) (kɑːt) t. acarrear.

cartoon (kɑːˈtuːn) s. caricatura. 2 dibujos animados.

cartridge ('kɑːtridʒ) s. cartucho: ~-belt, canana.

case (keis) s. caso. 2 DER. pleito, causa. 3 caja, estuche, maleta.

case (to) (keis) t. embalar, encajonar, enfundar.

cash (kæʃ) s. efectivo, dinero contante.

cash (to) (kæʃ) t. cobrar, pagar.

cashier (kəˈʃiəʳ) s. cajero.

cashier (to) (kəˈʃiəʳ) t. destituir. 2 MIL. degradar.

cask (kɑːsk) s. tonel, barril.

cast (kɑːst) s. tiro, lanzamiento. 2 fundición. 3 molde, mascarilla. 4 disposición, tendencia. 5 matiz. 6 TEAT. reparto; actores. 7 a. ~ iron, hierro colado. 8 V. TO CAST.

cast (to) (kɑːst) t. echar, tirar, arrojar. 2 verter, derramar. 3 despedir, desechar. 4 proyectar [sombra]. 5 formar, arreglar. 6 fundir, moldear. 7 hacer [cuentas]. 8 TEAT. repartir [los papeles]. 9 dar [un voto]. 10 to ~ away, desechar. 11 to ~ lots, echar suertes. ¶ Pret. y p. p.: cast.

castle ('kɑːsl) s. castillo. 2 AJED. torre.

casual ('kæʒjuəl) a. casual. 2 distraído, superficial.

casually ('kæʒjuəli) adv. casualmente.

casualty ('kæʒjuəlty) s. accidente, desgracia. 2 MIL. baja.

cat (kæt) s. ZOOL. gato, gata.

catalogue ('kætələg) s. catálogo.

catalogue (to) ('kætələg) t. catalogar.

catapult ('kætəpʌlt) s. catapulta. 3 tirador [juguete].

catch (kætʃ) s. cogedura. 2 pesca, redada. 3 engaño, trampa. 4 pestillo.

catch (to) (kætʃ) t. coger, agarrar, retener, sujetar. 2 coger, pillar [una enfermedad]. 3 coger, sorprender. 4 i. enredarse, engancharse. ¶ Pret. y p. p.: caught (kɔːt).

category ('kætigəri) s. categoría.

cater (to) ('keitəʳ) i. abastecer.

cathedral (kəˈθiːdrəl) s. catedral. 2 a. catedralicio.

catholicism (kəˈθɔlisizəm) s. catolicismo.

cattle ('kætl) s. ganado.

caught (kɔːt) V. TO CATCH.

cause (kɔːz) s. causa; razón.

cause (to) (kɔːz) t. causar.

caution ('kɔːʃən) s. cautela, precaución. 2 aviso.

caution (to) ('kɔːʃən) t. cautelar, advertir, avisar.

cautious ('kɔːʃəs) a. cauto, prudente.

cavalry ('kævəlri) *s.* caballería.

cave (keiv) *s.* cueva, caverna.

cave (to) (keiv) *i.* **to ~ in,** hundirse [el suelo, etc].

cavity ('kæviti) *s.* cavidad.

cease (to) (si:s) *i.-t.* cesar, dejar de.

cede (to) (si:d) *t.* ceder.

ceiling ('si:liŋ) *s.* techo.

celebrate (to) ('selibreit) *t.-i.* celebrar.

celebrity (si'lebriti) *s.* celebridad.

celibacy ('selibəsi) *s.* celibato.

cell (sel) *s.* celda. 2 célula.

cellar ('seləʳ) *s.* sótano.

cement (si'ment) *s.* cemento.

cement (to) (si'ment) *t.* unir con cemento.

cemetery ('semitri) *s.* cementerio.

censure ('senʃəʳ) *s.* censura, crítica, reprobación.

censure (to) ('senʃəʳ) *t.* censurar, criticar, reprobar.

census ('sensəs) *s.* censo, padrón.

cent (sent) *s.* centavo [moneda]. 2 ciento.

centre ('sentəʳ) *s.* centro.

centre (to) ('sentəʳ) *t.* centrar. 2 concentrar [en].

century ('sentʃəri) *s.* siglo.

cereal ('siəriəl) *a.-s.* cereal.

ceremony ('seriməni) *s.* ceremonia. 2 cumplido.

certain ('sə:tn,-tin) *a.* cierto, seguro. 2 fijo, determinado.

certificate (sə'tifikit) *s.* certificado, partida.

chafe (to) (tʃeif) *t.* frotar. 2 *t.-i.* rozar(se. 3 irritar(se.

chain (tʃein) *s.* cadena.

chair (tʃεəʳ) *s.* silla, sillón.

chairman ('tʃeəmən) *s.* presidente [de una reunión].

chalk (tʃɔ:k) *s.* creta; marga. 2 tiza, yeso.

chalk (to) (tʃɔ:k) *t.* enyesar.

challenge ('tʃælindʒ) *s.* reto, desafío. 2 MIL. quién vive.

challenge (to) ('tʃælindʒ) *t.* retar, desafiar. 2 recusar.

champion ('tʃæmpjən) *s.* campeón, paladín.

chance (tʃɑ:ns) *s.* ventura, suerte; azar, casualidad. 2 oportunidad. 3 probabilidad.

chancellor ('tʃɑ:nsələʳ) *s.* canciller.

change (tʃeindʒ) *s.* cambio.

change (to) (tʃeindʒ) *t.* cambiar, alterar, variar, mudar, convertir, trocar.

channel ('tʃænl) *s.* canal.

chaos ('keiɔs) *s.* caos.

chapel ('tʃæpəl) *s.* capilla.

chapter ('tʃæptəʳ) *s.* capítulo [de un libro].

character ('kæriktəʳ) *s.* carácter [en todos sus sentidos]. 2 calidad. 3 fama. 4 HIST., LIT. personaje. 5 sujeto, tipo.

charge (tʃɑ:dʒ) *s.* carga [de un arma, etc.]. 2 cargo, obligación, 3 orden, encargo. 4 carga, gravamen. 5 precio, costa. 6 cargo, acusación.

charge (to) (tʃɑ:dʒ) *t.* cargar [un arma, etc.], 2 confiar, encargar. 3 mandar, exhortar. 4 cargar, gravar. 5 pedir [un precio]. 6 COM. adeudar, cargar. 7 *t.-i.* atacar.

charm (tʃɑ:m) *s.* encanto, embeleso. 2 amuleto.

charm (to) (tʃɑ:m) *t.* encantar, hechizar. 2 embelesar.

chart (tʃɑ:t) *s.* carta de marear. 2 mapa, plano.

chart (to) (tʃɑ:t) *t.* trazar [un mapa, etc.].

charter ('tʃɑ:təʳ) *t.* fuero, privilegio. 2 escritura.

charter (to) ('tʃɑ:təʳ) *t.* fletar. 2 alquilar.

chase (tʃeis) *s.* caza, persecución.

chase (to) (tʃeis) *t.* dar caza a.

chat (tʃæt) *s.* charla, plática.

chat (to) (tʃæt) *i.* charlar.

chatter ('tʃætəʳ) *s.* charla, parloteo.

chatter (to) ('tʃætəʳ) *i.* charlar.

cheap (tʃi:p) *a.-adv.* barato.

cheat (tʃi:t) *s.* timo, estafa, trampa. 2 timador.

cheat (to) (tʃi:t) *t.* engañar, timar. 2 *i.* hacer trampas.

check (tʃek) *s.* restricción, represión, obstáculo. 2 comprobación, repaso. 3 COM. cheque, 4 AJED. jaque.

check (to) (tʃɔk) *t.* detener. 2 comprobar, 3 marcar [con señal]. 4 dar jaque.

cheek (tʃi:k) *s.* mejilla; carrillo. 2 fig. descaro.

cheer (tʃiəʳ) *s.* alegría, ánimo. 2 viandas, comida. 3 viva, vítor.

cheer (to) (tʃiəʳ) *t.-i.* alegrar(se, animar(se: ~ *up!*, ¡ánimo! 2 *t.* vitorear;aplaudir.

cheese (tʃi:z) *s.* queso.

chemistry ('kemistri) *s.* química.

cherish (to) ('tʃeriʃ) *t.* acariciar. 2 apreciar. 3 abrigar.

chest (tʃest) *s.* cofre, arca. 2 pecho.

chew (to) (tʃu:) *t.* mascar, masticar. 2 *t.-i.* rumiar, meditar.

chick (tʃik), **chicken** ('tʃikin) *s.* pollo, polluelo.

chide (to) ('tʃaid) *t.* regañar. ¶ Pret.: *chid* (tʃid) o *chided* ('ʃaidid); p. p.: *chidden* ('tʃidn).

chief (tʃi:f) *a.* principal. 2 *s.* jefe, cabeza, caudillo.

child (tʃaild) *pl.* **children** ('tʃildrən) *s.* niño, niña, criatura. 2 hijo, hija.

childish ('tʃaildiʃ) *a.* pueril.

chill (tʃil) *s.* frío [sensación]. 2 escalofrío. 3 frialdad.

chill (to) (tʃil) *t.* enfriar, helar. 2 desalentar.

chimney ('tʃimni) *s.* chimenea: ~*-top*, chimenea.

chin (tʃin) *s.* barbilla, mentón.

chirp (tʃə:p) *s.* chirrido.

chirp (to) (tʃə:p) *i.* chirriar, piar, gorjear.

choice (tʃɔis) *s.* preferencia. 2 opción. 3 cosa escogida. 4 *a.* escogido, selecto.

choir ('kwaiəʳ) *s.* coro.

choke (to) (tʃouk) *t.-i.* ahogar(se, sofocar(se. 2 *t.* to ~ *up*, obstruir.

choose (to) (tʃu:z) *t.* escoger, elegir. ¶ Pret.: *chose* (tʃouz); p. p.: *chosen* ('tʃouzn).

chop (tʃɔp) *s.* corte. 2 chuleta.

chop (to) (tʃɔp) *t.* cortar, tajar; picar [carne, etc.].

chosen ('tʃouzn) V. TO CHOOSE.

Christian ('kristjən) *a.-s.* cristiano: ~ *name*, nombre de pila.

Christmas ('krisməs) *s.* Navidad: ~ *carol*, villancico.

chronicle ('krɔnikl) *s.* crónica.

chronicle (to) ('krɔnikl) *t.* narrar, historiar.

chuck (to) (tʃʌk) *t.* dar un golpecito [debajo de la barba]. 2 echar, tirar, arrojar.

church (tʃəːtʃ) *s.* iglesia.

churchyard ('tʃəːtʃ'jɑːd) *s.* cementerio.

churn (tʃəːn) *s.* mantequera.

churn (to) (tʃəːn) *t.* batir.

cigar (si'gaːᵣ) *s.* cigarro puro.

cigarette (ˌsigə'ret) *s.*, cigarrillo, pitillo: ~-*case*, pitillera.

cinema ('sinimə) *s.* cine.

cipher ('saifəᵣ) *s.* cero. 2 cifra.

cipher (to) ('saifəᵣ) *t.* cifrar. 2 calcular.

circle ('səːkl) *s.* círculo.

circle (to) ('səːkl) *s.* circuir, rodear. 2 *i.* girar.

circumference (sə'kʌmfərəns) *s.* circunferencia.

circus ('səːkəs) *s.* circo.

cite (to) (sait) *t.* citar, llamar.

citizen ('sitizn) *s.* ciudadano, vecino.

citizenship ('sitiznʃip) *s.* ciudadanía.

civic ('sivik) *a.* cívico.

civil ('siv(i)l) *a.* civil: ~ *servant*, funcionario público.

claim (kleim) *s.* demanda, reclamación.

claim (to) (kleim) *t.* reclamar, exigir. 2 reivindicar.

clamber (to) ('klæmbəᵣ) *i.* trepar.

clamp (klæmp) *s.* tornillo de sujeción, abrazadera.

clamp (to) (klæmp) *t.* sujetar.

clang (to) (klæŋ), **clank** (to)(klæŋk) *i.* resonar. 2 *t.* hacer sonar.

clap (klæp) *s.* ruido o golpe seco: trueno. 2 aplauso.

clap (to) (klæp) *t.* batir, golpear, aplaudir.

clash (klæʃ) *s.* estruendo. 2 choque. 3 conflicto.

clash (to) (klæʃ) *i.* sonar [al chocar]. 2 chocar. 3 oponerse; discordar.

clasp (klɑːsp) *s.* broche, cierre, manecilla. 2 abrazo.

clasp (to) (klɑːsp) *t.* abrochar, cerrar. 2 asir.

class (klɑːs) *s.* clase.

class (to) (klɑːs) *t.* clasificar.

clatter ('klætəᵣ) *s.* martilleo, golpeteo, trápala. 2 alboroto.

claw (klɔː) *s.* garra. 2 garfio.

claw (to) (klɔː) *t.-i.* arañar, rasgar, desgarrar.

clay (klei) *s.* arcilla, barro.

clean (to) (kliːn) *t.* limpiar. 2 asear. 3 mondar. 4 purificar.

cleanly ('klenli) *a.* limpio, aseado. 2 ('kliːnli) *adv.* limpiamente.

cleanse (to) (klenz) *t.* limpiar, lavar. 2 purificar, depurar.

clear (kliəᵣ) *a.* claro. 2 limpio. 3 *s.* claro, espacio.

clear (to) (kliəᵣ) *t.* aclarar, disipar. 2 limpiar; librar [de estorbos, etc.]. 3 *t.-i.* ~ *away*, quitar; disiparse. 4 *i.* ~ *up*, despejarse, aclarar. 5 ~ *off*, *out*, largarse.

clearing ('kliəriŋ) *s.* aclaramiento. 2 claro [en un bosque]. 3 com. liquidación, compensación.

1) **cleave (to)** (kliːv) *t.-i.* pegarse, adherirse. ¶ Pret. y p. p.: *cleaved* (kliːvd).

2) **cleave (to)** (kli:v) *t.-i.* hender(se, rajar(se, partir(se. ¶ Pret.: *cleft* (kleft), *cleaved* (kli:vd) o *clove* (klouv); p. p.: *cleft, cleaved* o *cloven* (klouvn).

clench (to) (klentʃ) *t.* apretar [los puños, etc.]. 2 agarrar.

clerk (klɑːk) *s.* empleado, dependiente, pasante.

clever ('klevəʳ) *a.* diestro, hábil. 2 listo, avisado.

click (klik) *s.* golpecito seco.

click (to) (klik) *i.* sonar.

cliff (klif) *s.* risco, acantilado.

climate ('klaimit) *s.* clima.

climb (klaim) *s.* subida.

climb (to) (klaim) *t.* trepar, subir, escalar. 2 *i.* subir, encaramarse.

clinch (klintʃ) *s.* remache. 2 agarro.

clinch (to) (klintʃ) *t.* TO CLENCH. 2 *i.* agarrarse.

cling (to) (kliŋ) *i.* asirse, aferrarse. 2 persistir. ¶ Pret. y p. p.: *clung* (klʌŋ).

clinic ('klinik) *s.* clínica.

clip (klip) *s.* grapa, sujetapapeles. 2 tijeretazo, corte.

clip (to) (klip) *t.* abrazar, sujetar. 2 cortar, recortar.

cloak (klouk) *s.* capa.

cloak (to) (klouk) *t.* encapar, cubrir.

clock (klɔk) reloj [de pared].

cloister ('klɔistəʳ) *s.* claustro.

1) **close** (klouz) *s.* fin, conclusión. 2 (klous) cierre, clausura.

2) **close** (klous) *a.* cerrado. 2 cercado, acotado. 3 apretado, ajustado. 4 secreto. 5 pesado, sofocante [tiempo]. 6 espeso, tupido. 7 estrecho, riguroso. 8 *adv.* de cerca. 9

~ *by,* muy cerca.

close (to) (klouz) *t.* cerrar. 2 tapar, obstruir. 3 apretar, tupir. 4 cercar, rodear. 5 concluir, ultimar. 6 clausurar. 7 *i.* cerrarse. 8 acercarse. 9 luchar, agarrarse. 10 terminarse.

closet (klɔzit) *s.* gabinete, camarín. 2 retrete.

cloth (klɔθ) *s.* paño, tela.

clothe (to) (klouð) *t.* vestir. ¶ Pret. y p. p.: *clothed* (klouðd) o *clad* (klæd).

clothes (klouðz) *s. pl.* vestido, ropa.

cloud (klaud) *s.* nube.

cloudy ('klaudi) *a.* nuboso, nublado. 2 turbio.

clown (klaun) *s.* payaso.

club (klʌb) *s.* clava, porra. 2 DEP. bate; palo [de golf]. 3 trébol o bastos [de la baraja]. 4 club, círculo.

club (to) (klʌb) *t.* apalear. 2 *i.* unirse, escotar [para un fin].

clue (klu:) *s.* indicio, pista.

clump (klʌmp) *s.* grupo [de árboles]. 2 masa, terrón..

clump (to) (klʌmp) *t.-i.* agrupar(se.

clumsy ('klʌmzi) *a.* torpe.

cluster ('klʌstəʳ) *s.* racimo, ramo. 2 grupo, hato.

cluster (to) ('klʌstəʳ) *i.* arracimarse, agruparse. 2 *t.* apiñar.

clutch (klʌtʃ) *s.* garra. 2 agarro. 3 MEC. embrague.

clutch (to) (klʌtʃ) *t.-i. to ~,* o *to ~ at,* asir, agarrar.

coach (koutʃ) *s.* coche, carroza, diligencia; autocar. 2 DEP. entrenador.

coal (koul) *s.* carbón, hulla.

coal (to) (koul) *t.-i.* proveer de carbón, carbonear.

coarse (kɔːs) *a.* tosco, grosero.

coast (koust) *s.* costa; litoral.

coast (to) (koust) *i.* navegar cerca de la costa.

coat (kout) *s.* chaqueta; abrigo. 2 capa, mano [de pintura, etc.]. 3 cubierta, revestimiento.

coax (to) (kouks) *t.* engatusar.

cobweb ('kɔbweb) *s.* telaraña.

cock (kɔk) *s.* gallo. 2 macho de un ave. 3 llave, espita.

cock (to) (kɔk) *i.* gallear. 2 *t.* amartillar [un arma]. 3 levantar, inclinar.

coconut ('koukənʌt) *s.* coco.

cod (kɔd) *s.* bacalao.

code (koud) *s.* código. 2 cifra.

coffee ('kɔfi) *s.* café.

coffin ('kɔfin) *s.* ataúd.

coil (kɔil) *s.* rollo [de cuerda, etc.]; rosca.

coil (to) (kɔil) *t.* arrollar, enrollar. 2 *i.* enroscarse.

coin (kɔin) *s.* moneda.

coin (to) (kɔin) *t.* acuñar. 2 forjar.

coincide (to) (ˌkouin'said) *i.* coincidir.

coke (kouk) *s.* cock, coque.

cold (kould) *a.* frío. 2 débil, perdido [pista]. 3 *s.* frío. 4 resfriado.

collapse (kə'læps) *s.* derrumbamiento, desplome. 2 fracaso, ruina. 3 MED. colapso.

collar ('kɔləʳ) *s.* cuello [de una prenda]. 2 collar.

colleague ('kɔliːg) *s.* colega.

collect (to) (kə'lekt) *t.* recoger, coleccionar. 2 colegir, inferir. 3 recaudar, cobrar. 4 *i.* congregarse.

college ('kɔlidʒ) *s.* colegio.

collide (to) (kə'laid) *i.* chocar.

collision (kə'liʒən) *s.* colisión, choque. 2 oposición.

colony ('kɔləni) *s.* colonia.

colour ('kʌləʳ) *s.* color. 2 *pl.* bandera, pabellón.

colour (to) ('kʌləʳ) *t.* colorar, pintar. 2 colorear, paliar. 3 *i.* colorearse. 4 enrojecer.

colourless ('kʌləlis) *a.* descolorido.

column ('kɔləm) *s.* columna.

comb (koum) *s.* peine.

comb (to) (koum) *t.* peinar. 2 cardar, rastrillar.

come (to) (kʌm) *i.* venir. 2 provenir. 3 aparecer. 4 suceder. 5 entrar [en acción, en contacto, etc.]. 6 importar, montar a, ser lo mismo [que]. 7 *to ~ about*, ocurrir. 8 *to ~ back*, volver, retroceder. 9 *to ~ forward*, avanzar, presentarse. 10 *to ~ in*, entrar. 11 *to ~ off*, efectuarse; salir [bien, mal, etc.]; salir, despegarse. 12 *to ~ on*, avanzar; proseguir; entrar. 13 *to ~ out*, salir; ponerse de largo. ¶ Pret.: *came* (keim); p. p.: *come* (kʌm).

comely ('kʌmli) *a.* gentil.

comfort ('kʌmfət) *s.* consuelo. 2 comodidad.

comfort (to) ('kʌmfət) *t.* confortar. 2 aliviar, consolar.

comfortable ('kʌmfətəbl) *a.* confortable, cómodo.

coming ('kʌmiŋ) *a.* próximo, venidero. 2 *s.* llegada.

command (kə'maːnd) *s.* orden, mandato. 2 mando.

command (to) (kə'mɑ:nd)*t.-i.* mandar, comandar, imperar. 2 dominar.

commander (kə'mɑ:ndə^r) *s.* comandante, jefe.

commend (to) (kə'mend) *t.* encomendar. 2 recomendar.

comment ('kɔmən) *s.* comentario.

comment (to) ('kɔment) *i.* comentar.

commit (to) (kə'mit) *t.* cometer, perpetrar. 2 encargar, confiar. 3 comprometer.

committee (kə'miti) *s.* comisión, comité.

common ('kɔmən) *a.* común. 2 vulgar, corriente. 3 regular, usual.

commonwealth ('kɔmənwelθ) *s.* comunidad de naciones.

communist ('kɔmjunist) *a.-s.* comunista.

compact ('kɔmpækt) *s.* pacto, convenio. 2 polvera.

compact (kəm'pækt) *a.* compacto, denso. 2 breve, conciso.

compact (to) (kəm'pækt) *t.* comprimir, condensar.

companion (kəm'pænjən) *s.* compañero; camarada.

company ('kʌmpəni) *s.* compañía.

comparison (kəm'pærisn) *s.* comparación.

compartment (kəm'pɑ:tmənt) *s.* departamento.

compass ('kʌmpəs) *s.* área, ámbito. 2 brújula. 3 MÚS. (a veces en *pl.*) compás [instrumento].

compass (to) ('kʌmpəs) *t.* idear, planear. 2 conseguir. 3 rodear.

compassionate (kəm'pæʃənit) *a.* compasivo.

compel (to) (kəm'pel) *t.* obligar, forzar. 2 imponer.

compensate (to) ('kɔmpenseit)*t.* compensar.

competent ('kɔmpitənt) *a.* competente, capaz.

competition (,kɔmpi'tiʃən) *s.* competición, competencia. 2 certamen, concurso.

competitive (kəm'petitiv) *a.* de concurso.

compile (to) (kəm'pail) *t.* compilar, recopilar.

complain (to) (kəm'plein) *s.* quejarse.

complaint (kəm'pleint) *s.* queja. 2 DER. demanda.

complement ('kɔmplimənt) *s.* complemento.

complete (kəm'pli:t) *a.* completo. 2 concluido.

complete (to) (kəm'pli:t) *t.* completar. 2 llenar.

complexion (kəm'plekʃən) *s.* cutis, tez, color. 2 carácter.

compose (to) (kəm'pouz) *t.* componer. 2 calmar.

compound ('kɔmpaund) *a.-s.* compuesto. 2 *s.* mezcla.

compound (to) (kəm'paund) *t.* componer, mezclar. 2 transigir. 3 *i.* pactar, avenirse.

comprehend (to) (,kɔmpri'hend) *t.* comprender.

comprehensive (,kɔmpri'hensiv) *a.* comprensivo. 2 amplio, extenso.

compress (to) (kəm'pres) *t.* comprimir. 2 apretar.

comprise (to) (kəm'praiz) *t.* comprender, incluir.

compulsory (kəm'pʌlsəri) *a.* obligatorio.

conceal (to) (kən'si:l) *t.* ocultar, encubrir.

conceit (kən'si:t) *s.* vanidad. 2 concepto, conceptismo.

conceited (kən'si:tid) *a.* vano, engreído, presuntuoso.

conceive (to) (kən'si:v) *t.-i.* concebir. 2 *t.* comprender.

concentrate (to) ('kɔnsentreit)*t.-i.* concentrar(se.

concept ('kɔnsept) *s.* concepto.

concern (kən'sə:n) *s.* interés, afecto. 2 preocupación, inquietud. 3 interés, parte. 4 importancia. 5 asunto.

concern (to) (kən'sə:n) *t.* concernir, atañer. 2 importar. 3 preocupar.

concert ('kɔnsə(:)t) *s.* acuerdo. 2 ('kɔnsət) MÚS. concierto.

concert (to) (kən'sə:t) *t.* concertar, planear. 2 *i.* concertarse.

concord ('kɔnkɔ:d) *s.* concordia. 2 acuerdo.

concrete (kən'kri:t) *a.* concreto. 2 *s.* hormigón.

concrete (to) ('kɔnkri:t) *t.-i.* solidificar(se.

condemn (to) (kən'dem) *t.* condenar.

condense (to) (kən'dens) *t.-i.* condensar(se. 2 *t.* abreviar.

condescend (to) (ˌkɔndi'send) *i.* condescender.

conduct ('kɔndəkt) *s.* conducta.

conduct (to) (kən'dʌkt) *t.* conducir. 2 dirigir, mandar.

conductor (kən'dʌktəᵣ) *s.* conductor. 2 MÚS. director. 3 cobrador [de tranvía]; (E. U.) revisor [de tren].

confer (to) (ken'fə:ᵣ) *t.* conferir. 2 *i.* conferenciar.

conference ('kɔnfərəns) *s.* conferencia, entrevista.

confess (to) (kən'fes) *t.* confesar. 2 reconocer.

confide (to) (kən'faid) *t.-i.* confiar.

confident ('kɔnfidənt) *a.* seguro.

confine ('kɔnfain) *s.* límite.

confine (to) (kənˌfain) *i.* confinar. 2 *t.* limitar, restringir.

confirm (to) (kən'fə:m) *t.* confirmar, corroborar.

conflict ('kɔnflikt) *s.* conflicto.

conflict (to) (kən'flict) *i.* chocar, estar en conflicto.

confront (to) (kən'frʌnt) *t.* confrontar. 2 cotejar.

congenial (kən'dʒi:njəl) *a.* simpático, agradable.

congenital (kən'dʒenitl) *a.* congénito.

congest (to) (kən'dʒest) *t.-i.* congestionar(se. 2 aglomerar(se.

congratulate (to) (kən'grætjuleit) *t.* congratular, felicitar.

conjecture (kən'dʒektʃəᵣ) *s.* conjetura, presunción.

conjecture (to) (kən'dʒektʃəᵣ) *t.* conjeturar, presumir.

conjure (to) (kən'dʒuəᵣ) *t.* implorar. 2 ('kʌndʒəᵣ) *to ~ up,* evocar. 3 *i.* hacer juegos de manos.

connect (to) (kə'nekt) *t.* unir, enlazar. 2 conectar. 3 *i.* unirse, enlazarse.

connection, connexion (kə'nekʃən) *s.* conexión, enlace. 2 relación.

conquer (to) ('kɔŋkəᵣ) *t.* conquistar. 2 vencer, dominar.

conscience ('kɔnʃəns) *s.* conciencia.

conscientious (ˌkɔnʃi'enʃəs)*a.* concienzudo. 2 de conciencia.

consent (kən'sent) *s.* consentimiento, asentimiento.

conservative (kən'sə:vətiv) *a.* conservativo. 2 *a.-s.* POL. conservador.

conserve (kən'sə:v) *s.* conserva, confitura.

consider (to) (kən'sidə^r) *t.* considerar, pensar.

considering (kən'sidəriŋ) *prep.* considerando [que].

consign (to) (kən'sain) *t.* consignar, confiar, depositar.

consist (to) (kən'sist) *i.* consistir. 2 constar [de].

consistent (kən'sistənt) *a.* consistente, sólido. 2 compatible. 3 consecuente.

consolation (ˌkɔnsə'leiʃən) *s.* consolación, consuelo.

consolidate (to) (kən'sɔlideit) *t.-i.* consolidar(se.

consort ('kɔnsɔ:t) *s.* consorte.

consort (to) (kən'sɔ:t) *i.* juntarse, acompañarse.

conspiracy (kən'spirəsi) *s.* conspiración.

conspire (to) (kəns'paiə^r) *i.* conspirar, conjurarse. 2 *t.* tramar.

constable ('kʌnstəbl) *s.* condestable. 2 policía [uniformado].

constipate (to) ('kɔnstipeit) *t.* estreñir.

constipation (ˌkɔnsti'peiʃən) *s.* extreñimiento.

constituency (kən'stitjuənsi) *s.* distrito electoral. 2 electores.

constituent (kəns'titjuənt) *a.* constitutivo. 2 POL. constituyente. 3 *s.* componente. 4 elector [de un diputado].

constraint (kən'streint) *s.* coacción. 2 represión.

consume (to) (kən'sju:m) *t.-i.* consumir(se.

consummate (to) ('kɔnsʌmeit)*t.* consumar.

consumption (kən'sʌmpʃən)*s.* consumo. 2 MED. tisis.

contact ('kɔntækt) *s.* contacto.

contact (to) ('kɔntækt) *t.* ponerse o estar en contacto con.

contain (to) (kən'tein) *t.* contener; tener cabida para.

contemplate (to) ('kɔntempleit) *t.* contemplar. 2 proponerse. 3 *i.* meditar.

contemporaneous (kənˌtempə'reinjəs) *a.* **contemporary** (kən'tempərəri) *a.-s.* contemporáneo.

contempt (kən'tempt) *s.* desprecio.

contemptible (kən'temptəbl)*a.* despreciable. 2 desdeñoso.

contend (to) (kən'tend) *i.* contender. 2 competir, oponerse.

content (to) (kən'tent) *t.* contentar, satisfacer.

contention (kən'tenʃən) *s.* contienda, disputa. 2 afirmación.

contentment (kən'tentmənt)*s.* satisfacción, contento.

contest ('kɔntest) *s.* contienda, lucha, lid. 2 disputa, litigio. 3 torneo, concurso.

contest (to) (kən'test) *t.* disputar, luchar por. 2 impugnar.

continual (kən'tinjuəl) *a.* continuo, incesante.

contour ('kɔntuə^r) *s.* contorno.

contract ('kɔntrækt) *s.* contrato.

contract (to) (kən'trækt) *t.-i.* contraer(se, encoger(se. *2 t.* contratar, pactar. *3* contraer [matrimonio, etc.].

contradict (to) (ˌkɔntrə'dikt)*t.* contradecir. *2* desmentir.

contrary ('kɔntrəri) *a.* contrario. *2* adverso. *3* díscolo, terco. *4 s.* lo contrario.

contrivance (kən'traivəns) *s.* inventiva. *2* traza, invención.

contrive (to) (kən'traiv) *t.* idear, inventar. *2* tramar.

control (kən'troul) *s.* mando, autoridad. *2* gobierno, dirección. *3* sujeción, freno. *4* inspección. *5* comprobación. *6* MEC. mando, control.

control (to) (kən'troul) *t.* sujetar, reprimir. *2* gobernar, dirigir. *3* controlar.

convent ('kɔnvənt) *s.* convento.

convention (kən'venʃən) *s.* convocación. *2* asamblea, convención. *3* convenio.

converse ('kɔnvəːs) *a.* opuesto.

converse (to) (kən'vəːs) *i.* conversar.

convert ('kɔnvəːt) *s.* converso.

convert (to) (kən'vəːt) *t.* convertir. *2 i.* convertirse.

convey (to) (kən'vei) *t.* llevar, transportar. *2* transmitir.

conveyance (kən'veiəns) *s.* transporte. *2* transmisión.

convict ('kɔnvikt) *s.* presidiario.

convict (to) (kən'vikt) *t.* DER. declarar culpable. *2* condenar.

convince (to) (kən'vins) *t.* convencer.

convoy ('kɔnvɔi) *s.* convoy.

convoy (to) ('kɔnvɔi) *t.* convoyar, escoltar.

coo (kuː) *s.* arrullo.

coo (to) (kuː) *i.* arrullar(se.

cook (kuk)) *s.* cocinero, -ra.

cook (to) (kuk) *t.-i.* cocer, guisar, cocinar.

cookery ('kukəri) *s.* cocina [arte].

cool (kuːl) *a.* fresco. *2* frío, tibio. *3* sereno, osado.

cool (to) (kuːl) *t.-i.* refrescar(se, enfriar(se.

copy ('kɔpi) *s.* copia, reproducción, imitación. *2* ejemplar [de un libro]; número [de un periódico]. *3* IMPR. original. *4 rough* ~, borrador.

copy (to) ('kɔpi) *t.* copiar. *2* imitar, remedar.

copyright ('kɔpirait) *s.* [derechos de] propiedad literaria.

coral ('kɔrəl) *s.* coral.

cord (kɔːd) *s.* cordel; cuerda.

core (kɔːʳ) *s.* corazón, centro, alma. *2* corazón [de una fruta].

core (to) (kɔː) *t.* despepitar.

cork (kɔːk) *s.* corcho. *2* tapón de corcho. *3* ~ *-oak,* alcornoque.

cork (to) (kɔːk) *t.* tapar [con corcho], encorchar.

corn (kɔːn) *s.* grano, trigo. *2* (E. U.) maíz. *3* mies. *4* callo: *corned beef,* cecina.

corner ('kɔːnəʳ) *s.* ángulo, esquina, recodo. *2* rincón.

corner (to) (kɔːnəʳ) *t.* arrinconar, poner en un aprieto.

corps (kɔ:^r, *pl.* kɔ:z) *s.* cuerpo de ejército.

corpse (kɔ:ps) *s.* cadáver.

correct (kə'rekt) *a.* correcto.

correspond (to) (ˌkɔris'pɔnd)*i.* corresponder, corresponderse [en analogía]. 2 escribirse.

corridor ('kɔridɔ:^r) *s.* corredor, pasillo.

corrugate (to) ('kɔrugeit) *t.* arrugar. 2 plegar, ondular.

corsair ('kɔ:sɛə^r) *s.* corsario.

cosmonaut ('kɔzmə'nɔ:t) *s.* cosmonauta.

cost (kɔst) *s.* coste, precio, expensas. 2 *pl.* costas.

cost (to) (kɔst) *i.* costar, valer. ¶ Pret. y p. p.: *cost* (kɔst).

costly ('kɔstli) *a.* costoso, caro. 2 suntuoso.

costume ('kɔstju:m) *s.* traje, vestido. 2 *pl.* TEAT. vestuario.

cot (kɔt) *s.* choza. 2 camita.

cottage ('kɔtidʒ) *s.* casita de campo.

cotton ('kɔtn) *s.* algodón.

couch (kautʃ) *s.* cama, lecho.

couch (to) (kautʃ) *t.* acostar, tender. 2 *i.* acostarse, tenderse.

cough (kɔ:f) *s.* tos.

cough (to) (kɔ:f) *i.* toser.

could (cuk, kəd) V. CAN.

council ('kaunsil) *s.* concilio. 2 consejo, junta. 3 ayuntamiento.

council(l)or ('kaunsilə^r) *s.* concejal.

counsel (to) ('kaunsəl) *t.* aconsejar, asesorar.

count (to) (kaunt) *t.* contar, computar. 2 considerar, tener por.

countenance ('kauntinəns) *s.* rostro, semblante.

counter (to) ('kauntə^r) *t.* oponerse a.

counteract (to) (ˌkauntə'rækt)*t.* contrarrestar.

counterfeit ('kauntəfit) *a.* falso. 2 fingido. 3 *s.* falsificación.

counterfeit (to) ('kauntəfit) *t.* falsificar, contrahacer. 2 fingir.

countess ('kauntis) *s.* condesa.

country ('kʌntri) *s.* país, nación, región. 2 tierra, patria. 3 campo, campiña.

county ('kaunti) *s.* condado. 2 distrito.

couple ('kʌpl) *s.* par, pareja.

couple (to) ('kʌpl) *t.* aparear, emparejar. 2 acoplar, conectar. 3 *i.* aparearse.

courage ('kʌridʒ) *s.* valor.

courageous (kə'reidʒəs) *a.* valeroso, valiente.

course (kɔ:s) *s.* curso, marcha. 2 camino, trayecto, recorrido. 3 rumbo, derrotero. 4 transcurso [del tiempo]. 5 línea [de conducta]. 6 carrera [en la vida]. 7 curso [de estudios], asignatura. 8 plato, servicio [de una comida]. 9 ALBAÑ. hilada. 10 *adv. of* ~, naturalmente, desde luego, por supuesto.

course (to) (kɔ:s) *t.* correr por. 2 perseguir. 3 *i.* correr.

court (kɔ:t) *s.* patio; atrio; plazuela, cerrada. 2 pista [de tenis]. 3 corte [de un soberano; la que se hace a una pers.]. 4 tribunal. 5 consejo superior.

court (to) (kɔ:t) *t.* cortejar. *2* galantear. *3* solicitar, buscar.

courteous ('kə:tjəs) *a.* cortés.

courtesy ('kə:tisi) *s.* cortesía.

courtier ('kɔ:tjəʳ) *s.* cortesano, palaciego.

courtship ('kɔ:t-ʃip) *s.* cortejo, galanteo. *2* noviazgo.

courtyard ('kɔ:t'jɑ:d) *s.* patio.

cousin ('kʌzn) *s.* primo, -ma.

cove (kouv) *s.* cala, ensenada.

covenant ('kʌvinənt) *s.* convenio, pacto.

cover ('kʌvəʳ) *s.* tapa, tapadera. *2* cubierta, envoltura, funda, forro. *3* ENCUAD. tapa, cubierta. *4* portada [de revista]. *5* tapete, cobertor. *6* abrigo, cubierto, techado. *7* *under ~ of,* so capa de.

cover (to) ('kʌvʳ) *t.* cubrir.

coverlet ('kʌvəlit) *s.* colcha.

covet (to) ('kʌvit) *t.* codiciar.

cow (kau) *s.* ZOOL. vaca.

cow (to) (kau) *t.* acobardar.

coward ('kauəd) *a.-s.* cobarde.

cowardise ('kauədis) *s.* cobardía.

cowardly ('kauədli) *a.* cobarde.

cowboy ('kaubɔi) *s.* vaquero.

crab (kræb) *s.* cangrejo de mar. *2* cascarrabias.

crack (kræk) *s.* crujido, estampido. *2* hendidura, raja. *3* *a.* fam. de primera.

crack (to) (kræk) *i.* crujir, *2* reventar. *4 t.* romper, rajar.

cracker ('krækəʳ) *s.* petardo. *2* galleta.

crackle ('krækl) *s.* crujido.

crackle (to) ('krækl) *i.* crujir, chasquear, crepitar.

cradle ('kreidl) *s.* cuna.

cradle (to) ('kreidl) *t.* acunar.

craft (krɑ:ft) *s.* arte, destreza. *2* oficio; gremio.

craftsman ('krɑ:ftsmən) *s.* artesano.

crafty ('krɑ:fti) *a.* astuto, artero.

crag (kræg) *s.* risco, despeñadero.

cram (to) (kræm) *t.* henchir, atestar.

cramp (kræmp) *s.* calambre.

cramp (to) (kræmp) *t.* dar calambres.

crane (krein) *s.* ORN. grulla. *2* MEC. grúa.

crane (to) (krein) *t.* levantar con grúa.

crash (kræʃ) *s.* estallido, estrépito. *2* caída, choque.

crash (to) (kræʃ) *t.-i.* romper(se, estallar; caer(se.

crater ('kreitəʳ) *s.* cráter.

cravat (krə'væt) *s.* corbata.

crave (to) (kreiv) *t.-i.* pedir.

craving ('kreiviŋ) *s.* deseo, anhelo, ansia.

crawl *s.* reptación, arrastramiento. *2* NAT. crol.

crawl (to) ('krɔ:l) *i.* reptar, arrastrarse; gatear.

crazy ('kreizi) *a.* loco, insensato. *2* extravagante.

creak (to) (kri:k) *i.* crujir.

cream (kri:m) *s.* crema, nata.

crease (kri:s) *s.* pliegue, doblez, arruga.

crease (to) (kri:s) *t.* plegar, doblar, arrugar.

credit ('kredit) *s.* crédito. *2* valimiento. *3* honor.

credit (to) ('kredit) *t.* dar crédito a.

creditor ('kreditəʳ) *s.* acreedor.

creed (kri:d) *s.* credo; creencia.

creek (kri:k) *s.* abra, cala.

creep (to) (kri:p) *i.* arrastrarse, gatear. 2 correr [los insectos]; trepar [las plantas]. 3 insinuarse. ¶ Pret. y p. p.: *crept* (krept).

crept (krept) V. TO CREEP.

crescent ('kresnt) *a.* creciente. 2 *s.* media luna.

crest (krest) *s.* cresta. 2 penacho. 3 cimera.

crevice ('krevis) *s.* raja.

crew (kru:) *s.* MAR., AVIA. tripulación, equipaje. 2 equipo, cuadrilla. 3 *pret.* de TO CROW.

cricket ('krikit) *s.* ENT. grillo. 2 DEP. cricquet.

crime (kraim) *s.* delito. 2 crimen.

crimson ('krimzn) *a.-s.* carmesí.

cringe (krindʒ) *s.* adulación servil.

cringe (to) (krindʒ) *i.* encogerse [ante un peligro, etc.]. 2 arrastrarse [servilmente].

cripple ('kripl) *s.* cojo, lisiado.

cripple (to) ('kripl) *t.* encojar, lisiar. 2 *i.* lisiarse. 3 cojear.

crisp (krisp) *a.* crespo, rizado. 2 crujiente.

crisp (to) (krisp) *t.* encrespar, rizar. 2 tostar bien. 3 hacer crujir. 4 *i.* encresparse, rizarse.

croak (krouk) *s.* graznido [de cuervo]. 2 croar [de rana]

croak (to) (krouk) *i.* graznar. 2 croar. 3 gruñir.

crocodile ('krɔkədail) *s.* cocodrilo.

crook (kruk) *s.* curva, curvatura. 2 gancho, garfio. 3 cayado. 4 trampa. 5 fam. estafador.

crook (to) (kruk) *t.-i.* torcer(se, encorvar(se.

crop (krɔp) *s.* cosecha. 2 cabello corto. 3 buche [de ave]. 4 *pl.* campos, mieses.

cross (krɔs) *s.* cruz. 2 signo de la cruz. 3 cruce [de caminos, etc.].

cross (to) (krɔs) *t.* atravesar [la calle]. 2 cruzar [cheque; razas]. 3 *it crossed my mind,* se me ocurrió.

crouch (to) (krautʃ) *i.* agacharse, agazaparse. 2 arrastrarse [servilmente].

crow (krou) *s.* ORN. cuervo.

crow (to) (krou) *i.* cantar [el gallo]. 2 jactarse, bravear.

crowd (kraud) *s.* multitud, gentío.

crowd (to) (kraud) *t.-i.* agolpar(se, apiñar(se.

crown (kraun) *s.* corona. 2 cima, cumbre.

cruise (kru:z) *s.* crucero, viaje.

cruise (to) (kru:z) *t.* MAR., AVIA. cruzar, navegar.

cruiser ('kru:zəʳ) *s.* crucero.

crumb (krʌm) *s.* miga.

crumb (to) (krʌm) *t.* migar.

crumble (to) ('krʌmbl) *t.* desmenuzar, deshacer.

crusade (kru:'seid) *s.* cruzada.

crush (krʌʃ) *s.* aplastamiento, machacamiento.

crush (to) (krʌʃ) *t.* aplastar, machacar. 2 estrujar.

crust (krʌst) *s.* corteza, [de pan, etc.]. 2 mendrugo.

cry (krai) *s.* grito. 2 lamento, lloro, llanto. 3 pregón.

cry (to) (krai) *i.-t.* gritar. 2 *i.* aullar. 3 llorar, lamentarse.

4 *t*. exclamar. 5 *to ~ down*, rebajar, desacreditar.

cub (kʌb) *s*. cachorro.

cube (kju:b) *s*. GEOM. MAT. cubo.

cuckoo ('kuku:) *s*. ORN. cuclillo.

cucumber ('kju:kəmbə) *s*. BOT. cohombro; pepino.

cuddle (to) ('kʌdl) *t*. abrazar, acariciar. 2 *i*. estar abrazado.

cudgel ('kʌdʒəl) *s*. garrote.

cue (kju:) *s*. señal, indicación.

cuff (kʌf) *s*. puño [de camisa o vestido]: *~ links*, gemelos.

cuff (to) (kʌf) *t*. abofetear.

cull (to) (kʌl) *t*. escoger, elegir. 2 coger [frutos, etc.].

culminate (to) ('kʌlmineit) *t*. culminar.

culprit ('kʌlprit) *s*. culpable, reo.

cult (kʌlt) *s*. culto.

cunning (kʌniŋ) *a*. hábil, ingenioso. 2 *s*. habilidad, ingenio.

cup (kʌp) *s*. taza, copa.

cupboard ('kʌbəd) *s*. aparador, armario; alacena.

curb (kə:b) *s*. barbada [del freno]. 2 sujeción, freno. 3 bordillo. 4 brocal [de pozo].

curb (to) (kə:b) *t*. refrenar.

curd (kə:d) *s*. cuajada.

curdle (to) ('kə:dl) *t.-i*. cuajar(se; coagular(se.

cure (kjuəʳ) *s*. cura, curación.

curfew ('kə:fju:) *s*. toque de queda.

curing ('kjuəriŋ) *s*. curación.

curio ('kjuəriou) *s*. curiosidad, antigüedad [objeto].

curl (kə:l) *s*. rizo, bucle.

curl (to)(kə:l) *t.-i*. rizar(se, ensortijar(se.

currant ('kʌrənt) *s*. pasa de Corinto. 2 grosella.

currency ('kʌrənsi) *s*. curso, circulación. 2 moneda corriente, dinero.

curse (to) (kə:s) *t*. maldecir.

curtail (to) (kə:'teil) *t*. acortar, cercenar. 2 abreviar.

curtain ('kə:tn) *s*. cortina.

curtsy ('kə:tsi) *s*. reverencia.

curtsy (to) ('kə:tsi) *i*. hacer una reverencia.

curve (kə:v) *s*. curva.

curve (to) (kə:v) *t.-i*. encorvar(se, torcer(se.

cushion ('kuʃən) *s*. cojín.

custard ('kʌstəd) *s*. natillas.

custom ('kʌstəm) *s*. costumbre. 2 parroquia, clientela. 3 *pl*. aduana; derechos de aduana.

customary ('kʌstəməri) *a*. acostumbrado, habitual.

customer ('kʌstəməʳ) *s*. parroquiano, cliente.

cut (kʌt) *s*. corte, incisión. 2 labra, tallado. 3 corte, reducción. 4 trozo [de carne], tajada. 5 hechura, corte [de un vestido]. 6 *p. p*. de TO CUT.

cut (to) (kʌt) *t*. cortar, partir, separar. 2 cortar [un vestido; la retirada; los naipes; el gas, el agua, etc.]. 3 segar. 4 abrir, excavar. 5 labrar, tallar. 6 herir. 7 *to ~ down*, cortar, rebajar, reducir. 8 *to ~out*, cortar, quitar; desconectar. 9 *to ~ short*, interrumpir. 10 *i*. cortar. 11

salir [los dientes]. *12* pasar, atajar. *13 to ~ in*, meter baza. ¶ Pret. y p. p.: *cut* (kʌt); ger.: *cutting*.

cute (kju:t) *a.* listo, astuto; mono.

cycle (to) ('saikl) *i.* ir en bicicleta.

cylinder ('silindəʳ) *s.* GEOM., MEC. cilindro.

D

dad (dæd), **daddie, daddy** ('dædi) s. fam. papá, papaíto.

daily ('deili) a. diario, cotidiano. 2 s. periódico diario. 3 adv. diariamente.

dainty ('deinti) a. delicado, exquisito. 2 elegante. 3 s. golosina.

dairy ('dɛəri) s. lechería.

daisy ('deizi) s. BOT. margarita.

dale (deil) s. cañada.

dam (dæm) s. dique, presa.

dam (to) (dæm) t. represar, embalsar. 2 cerrar, obstruir.

damage ('dæmidʒ) s. daño, perjuicio.

damage (to) ('dæmidʒ) t. dañar, perjudicar, deteriorar.

damn (dæm) s. maldición.

damn (to) (dæm) t. TEOL. condenar. 2 maldecir.

damp (dæmp) a. húmedo, mojado. 2 s. humedad.

damp (to) (dæmp) t. humedecer, mojar. 2 apagar, amortiguar. 3 desalentar.

dance (dɑ:ns) s. danza, baile.

dance (to) (dɑ:ns) i.-t. danzar, bailar.

danger ('deindʒə^r) s. peligro, riesgo. 2 trance.

dangerous ('deindʒərəs) a. peligroso.

dare (dɛə^r) s. reto, desafío.

dare (to) (dɛə^r) t. atreverse a, osar. ¶ Pret.: **dared** (dɛəd) o **durst** (də:st); p. p.: **dared**.

dark (dɑ:k) a. oscuro; moreno [pers.]. 2 s. oscuridad, tinieblas.

darken (to) ('dɑ:kən) t.-i. oscurecer(se; nublar(se.

darkness ('dɑ:knis) s. obscuridad. 2 tinieblas.

darling ('dɑ:liŋ) a. amado.

darn (dɑ:n) s. zurcido.

darn (to) (dɑ:n) t. zurcir.

darnel ('dɑ:nl) s. BOT. cizaña.

dart (dɑ:t) s. dardo, flecha.

dart (to) (dɑ:t) t. lanzar, arrojar. 2 i. lanzarse.

dash (dæʃ) s. arremetida. 2 IMPR. guión largo, raya.

dash (to) (dæʃ) t. lanzar, arrojar. 2 i. chocar, estrellarse. 3 lanzarse.

date (deit) s. fecha, data. 2

cita [para verse]. *3* BOT. dátil.

date (to) (deit) *t.* fechar, datar. *2 i.* anticuarse.

daughter ('dɔ:təʳ) *s.* hija.

daughter-in-law ('dɔ:tərinlɔ:) *s.* nuera, hija política.

daunt (to) (dɔ:nt) *t.* intimidar, acobardar, desanimar.

dawn (dɔ:n) *s.* alba, aurora, amanecer.

dawn (to) (dɔ:n) *i.* amanecer, alborear.

day (dei) *s.* día.

day-break ('dei-breik) *s.* amanecer.

daylight ('deilait) *s.* luz del día.

daze (deiz) *s.* deslumbramiento, aturdimiento.

daze (to) (deiz) *t.* deslumbrar, aturdir.

dazzle ('dæzl) *s.* deslumbramiento.

dazzle (to) ('dæzl) *t.* deslumbrar.

deacon ('di:kən) *s.* diácono.

dead (ded) *a.* muerto. *2* difunto.

deadly ('dedli) *a.* mortal. *2 adv.* mortalmente; sumamente.

deaf (def) *a.* sordo.

deafen (to) ('defn) *t.* ensordecer.

deal (di:l) *s.* porción, cantidad.

deal (to) (di:l) *t.* dar, distribuir, dispensar. *2 i. to ~ in, with, at,* comerciar; *to ~ with,* tratar con. ¶ Pret. y p. p.: *dealt* (delt).

dealer ('di:ləʳ) *s.* comerciante, tratante.

dear (diəʳ) *a.* caro, querido.

death (deθ) *s.* muerte.

debate (di'beit) *s.* debate.

debate (to) (di'beit) *t.-i.* debatir, discutir. *2* reflexionar.

debris ('debri:) *s.* ruinas, escombros; deshecho.

debt (det) *s.* deuda, débito.

debtor ('detəʳ) *s.* deudor.

decade ('dekeid) *s.* década.

decay (di'kei) *i.* decaimiento.

decay (to) (di'kei) *i.* decaer.

decease (di'si:s) *s.* defunción.

decease (to) (di'si:s) *i.* morir.

deceit (di'sit) *s.* engaño.'

deceitful (di'si:tful) *s.* engañoso. *2* falso, engañador.

deceive (to) (di'si:v) *t.* engañar. *2* defraudar, burlar.

December (di'sembəʳ) *s.* diciembre.

decide (to) (di'said) *t.-i.* decidir. *2 to ~ to,* decidirse a.

decisive (di'saisiv) *a.* decisivo. *2* decidido, firme.

deck (deck) *s.* MAR. cubierta.

declaration (deklə'reiʃən) *s.* declaración. *2* manifiesto.

declare (to) (di'kleəʳ) *t.-i.* declarar. *2 t.* manifestar.

decline (di'klain) *s.* declinación, decadencia, ocaso.

decline (to) (di'klain) *t.-i.* inclinar(se, bajar. *2 t.* rehusar, negarse a.

declivity (di'kliviti) *s.* declive.

decompose (to) (di:-kəm'pouz) *t.-i.* descomponer(se.

decorate (to) ('dekəreit) *t.* decorar. *2* condecorar.

decoy (di'kɔi) *s.* señuelo, reclamo, cimbel. *2* añagaza.

decoy (to) (di'kɔi) *t.* atraer con señuelo. *2* seducir.

decrease ('di:kri:s) *s.* decrecimiento, disminución.

decrease (to) (di:'kri:s) *i.* decrecer. 2 *t.-i.* menguar.

decree (di'kri:) *s.* decreto, orden.

decry (to) (di'krai) *t.* desacreditar, rebajar, censurar.

deed (di:d) *s.* hecho; acción.

deem (to) (di:m) *t.-i.* juzgar, creer, estimar.

deep (di:p) *a.* hondo, profundo.

deepen (to) ('di:pən) *t.-i.* ahondar(se, intensificar(se.

deer (diə^r) *s.* ciervo, venado.

defame (to) (di'feim) *t.* difamar, infamar, calumniar.

default (di'fɔ:lt) *s.* falta, carencia. 2 negligencia.

default (to) (di'fɔ:lt) *t.-i.* faltar [a un deber, etc.].

defeat (di'fi:t) *s.* derrota.

defeat (to) (di'fi:t) *t.* derrotar.

defective (di'fektiv) *a.* defectivo, defectuoso.

defence (di'fens) *s.* defensa.

defend (to) (di'fand) *t.* defender.

defendant (di'fendənt) *s.* DER. demandado; acusado.

defer (to) (di'fə:^r) *t.* diferir, aplazar, retardar.

defiance (di'faiəns) *s.* desafío, reto, provocación.

defiant (di'faiənt) *a.* desafiador, provocativo.

defile ('di:fail) *s.* desfiladero.

defile (to) (di'fail) *t.* ensuciar. 2 manchar, profanar.

define (to) (di'fain) *t.* definir.

definition (,defi'niʃən) *s.* definición. 2 precisión, claridad.

deflate (to) (di'fleit) *t.-i.* desinflar(se, deshinchar(se.

defy (to) (di'fai) *t.* desafiar.

degenerate (di'dʒenərit) *a.-s.* degenerado.

degrade (to) (di'greid) *t.-i.* degradar(se. 2 *t.* minorar, rebajar.

degree (di'gri:) *s.* grado.

deign (to) (dein) *i.* dignarse.

deject (to) (di'dʒekt) *t.* abatir, desanimar.

delay (di'lei) *s.* dilación, retraso.

delay (to) (di'lei) *t.* diferir, aplazar, retrasar. 2 *i.* tardar.

delegate ('deligit) *a.-s.* delegado.

delegate (to) ('deligeit) *t.* delegar, comisionar.

deliberate (di'libərit) *a.* deliberado, premeditado. 2 cauto.

delicacy ('delikəsi) *s.* delicadeza. 2 finura, sensibilidad.

delicious (di'liʃəs) *a.* delicioso. 2 sabroso.

delight (di'lait) *s.* deleite, delicia, placer, gozo, encanto.

delight (to) (di'lait) *t.* deleitar, encantar, recrear. 2 *i.* deleitarse, gozarse, complacerse.

delightful (di'laitful) *a.* deleitable, delicioso.

delirious (di'liriəs) *a.* delirante.

deliver (to) (di'livə^r) *t.* libertar. 2 librar, salvar. 3 entregar. | Gralte. con *over* o *up*. 4 repartir [géneros, correspondencia]. 5 pronunciar [un discurso]. 6 descargar [un golpe].

deliverance (di'livərəns) *s.* liberación, rescate.

delivery (di'livəri) *s.* liberación, rescate. 2 entrega. 3

pronunciación [de un discurso]. 4 remesa. 5 parto.

deluge ('delju:dʒ) s. diluvio.

deluge (to) ('delju:dʒ) t. inundar.

delusion (di'lu:ʒən) s. engaño.

demand (di'ma:nd) s. demanda, petición.

demand (to) (di'ma:nd) t. demandar, pedir, exigir.

demeano(u)r (di'mi:nəʳ) s. comportamiento.

demolish (to) (di'mɔliʃ) t. demoler. 2 arrasar, derruir.

demon ('di:mən) s. demonio.

demonstrate (to) ('demənstreit) t. demostrar. 2 i. manifestarse.

demoralize (to) (di'mɔrəlaiz)t. desmoralizar.

demur (di'məːʳ) s. irresolución.

demur (to) (di'məːʳ) i. objetar. 2 vacilar.

den (den) s. caverna. 2 guarida.

denial (di'naiəl) s. negación. 2 denegación, negativa.

denote (to) (di'nout) t. denotar. 2 indicar, señalar.

denounce (to) (di'nauns) t. denunciar. 2 anunciar.

dense (dens) a. denso, espeso.

density ('densiti) s. densidad.

dental ('dentl) a. dental.

deny (to) (di'nai) t. negar.

depart (to) (di'pa:t) i. partir.

department (di'pa:tmənt) s. departamento. 2 distrito.

departure (di'pa:tʃəʳ) s. partida, marcha, salida.

depend (to) (di'pend) i. depender.

dependence (di'pəndəns) s. dependencia. 2 confianza.

depict (to) (di'pikt) t. pintar, representar, retratar.

deport (to) (di'pɔ:t) t. deportar, desterrar.

deportment (di'pɔ:tmənt) s. conducta, proceder.

depose (to) (di'pouz) t. deponer, destituir. 2 t.-i. declarar.

deposit (di'pɔzit) s. depósito, sedimento. 2 com. depósito.

deposit (to) (di'pɔzit) t. depositar(se, sedimentar(se.

depot ('depou) s. depósito, almacén.

depreciate (to) (di'pri:ʃieit) t. depreciar. 2 despreciar.

depress (to) (di'pres) t. deprimir. 2 abatir, desanimar.

depression (di'preʃən) s. depresión. 2 abatimiento.

deprive(to) (di'praiv) t. privar.

depth (depθ) s. profundidad, hondura.

deputy (di'pjuti) s. diputado.

deride(to) (di'raid) t. burlarse.

derive(to) (di'raiv) t. derivar.

descend (to) (di'send) i.-t. descender, bajar.

descent (di'sent) s. descenso, bajada. 2 linaje, descendencia. 3 pendiente.

descry (to) (dis'krai) t. descubrir, divisar, columbrar.

1) **desert** (di'zə:t) s. mérito, valía.

2) **desert** ('dezət) a. desierto. 2 s. desierto, yermo.

desert (to) (di'zə:t) t. abandonar, dejar. 2 t.-i. desertar.

deserve (to) (di'zə:v) t.-i. merecer.

design (di'zaïn) s. plan. 2 intención, mira, 3 dibujo, diseño.

design(to) (di'zain) t. destinar. 2 idear, proyectar, tramar. 3

proponerse. 4 trazar, diseñar.

designer (di'zainə^r) s. dibujante. 2 inventor.

desirable (di'zaiərəbl) a. deseable, apetecible.

desire (to) (di'zaiə^r) t. desear, anhelar, ansiar. 2 rogar.

desirous (di'zaiərəs) a. deseoso, ansioso, ganoso.

desk (desk) s. pupitre.

desolate (to) ('desəleit) t. desolar, devastar. 2 afligir.

despair (dis'pɛə^r) s. desesperación; desesperanza.

despatch = DISPATCH.

desperate ('despərit) a. desesperado. 2 arriesgado.

desperation (despə'reiʃən) s. desesperación; furor.

despise (to) (dis'paiz) t. despreciar, menospreciar.

despite (dis'pait) prep. ~ *of*, *in* ~ *of*, a pesar de.

despot ('despɔt) s. déspota.

dessert (di'zə:t) s. postres.

destination (desti'neiʃən) s. destinación, destino.

destitute ('destitju:t) a. desprovisto. 2 desvalido.

destroy (to) (dis'trɔi) t. destruir. 2 demoler. 3 romper.

detach (to) (di'tætʃ) t. separar, desprender.

detail ('di:teil) s. detalle, pormenor.

detail (to) ('di:teil) t. detallar, especificar. 2 MIL. destacar.

detain (to) (di'tein) t. retener, detener. 2 arrestar.

detect (to) (di'tekt) t. descubrir, averiguar.

deter (to) (di'tə:^{r}) t. detener, disuadir, impedir.

detest (to) (di'test) t. detestar.

develop (to) (di'veləp) t. de-

senvolver, desarrollar. 2 fomentar, mejorar.

device (di'vais) s. artificio, invención.

devil ('devl) s. demonio, diablo.

devilish ('devliʃ) a. diabólico. 2 endiablado.

devise (to) (di'vaiz) t. inventar, discurrir.

devoid (di'vɔid) a. falto, exento.

devote (to) (di'vout) t. consagrar, dedicar. 2 destinar.

devout (di'vaut) a. devoto, piadoso.

dew (dju:) s. rocío; relente.

dew (to) (dju:) t.-i. rociar, refrescar.

dexterity (deks'teriti) s. destreza, habilidad, maña.

dial ('daiəl) s. reloj de sol. 2 esfera [de reloj]. 3 disco [de teléfono, etc.].

diameter (dai'æmitə^r) s. diámetro.

diamond ('daiəmənd) s. diamante. 2 GEOM. rombo.

diary ('daiəri) s. diario, dietario.

dice (dais) s. dados.

dictate ('dikteit) s. mandato.

dictate (to) (dik'teit) t. dictar. 2 i. mandar.

dictionary ('dikʃənri) s. diccionario, léxico.

did (did) *pret.* de TO DO.

die (to) (dai) i. morir, fallecer. ¶ Pret. y p. p.: *died* (daid); ger.: *dying* ('daiiŋ).

differ (to) ('difə^r) i. diferir.

difficult ('difikəlt) a. difícil.

diffidence ('difidəns) s. cortedad, timidez, apocamiento.

diffuse (di'fj:s) a. difuso.

diffuse (to) (di'fju:z) *t.-i.* difundirse.

dig (dig) *s.* metido, codazo.

dig (to) (dig) *t.* cavar, ahondar. 2 escarbar. ¶ Pret. y p. p.: *dug* (dʌg).

digest ('daidʒest) *s.* compendio, recopilación.

digest (to) (di'dʒest) *t.-i.* digerir(se. 2 *t.* resumir.

digress (to) (dai'gres) *i.* divagar.

dike (daik) *s.* dique, malecón.

diligence ('dilidʒəns) *s.* diligencia, aplicación.

dilute (to) (dai'lju:t) *t.-i.* diluir(se. 2 *t.* aguar

dim (dim) *a.* obscuro, opaco.

dim (to) (dim) *t.* obscurecer.

dime (daim) *s.* diezmo. 2 (E. U.) diez centavos.

dimension (di'menʃən) *s.* dimensión.

diminish (to) (di'miniʃ) *t.* disminuir. 2 abatir, humillar.

din (din) *s.* fragor, estrépito.

din (to) (din) *t.* golpear con ruido. 2 *i.* hacer resonar.

dine (to) (dain) *i.* comer, cenar.

diner ('dainəʳ) *s.* comensal. 2 vagón restaurante.

dingy ('dindʒi) *a.* obscuro, negruzco, sucio; sórdido.

dining-room ('daininrum) *s.* comedor [pieza].

dinner ('dinəʳ) *s.* comida, cena.

dip (dip) *s.* zambullida.

dip (to) (dip) *t.* sumergir, bañar, mojar.

dire ('daiəʳ) *a.* horrendo, terrible. 2 extremo, sumo.

direct (di-, dai'rekt) *a.* directo, derecho.

direct (to) (di-, dai'rekt) *t.* dirigir. 2 encaminar.

dirge (də:dʒ) *s.* canto fúnebre.

dirt (də:t) *s.* barro, lodo. 2 suciedad, basura. 3 bajeza.

dirty ('də:ti) *a.* manchado, sucio. 2 cochino, indecente. 3 bajo, vil.

dirty (to) ('də:ti) *t.-i.* ensuciar(se.

disable (to) (dis'eibl) *t.* inutilizar, imposibilitar. 2 lisiar.

disadvantage (ˌdisəd'va:ntidʒ) *s.* desventaja.

disagree (to) (ˌdisə'gri:) *i.* discordar, discrepar.

disagreeable (ˌdisə'griəbl) *a.* desagradable, ingrato.

disagreement (ˌdisə'gri:mənt) *s.* discordancia, discrepancia, desacuerdo.

disappear (to) (ˌdisə'piəʳ) *i.* desaparecer.

disappoint (to) (ˌdisə'pɔint) *t.* defraudar, frustrar.

disapproval (ˌdisə'pru:vəl) *s.* desaprobación, censura.

disapprove (to) ('disə'pru:v) *t.* desaprobar.

disarm (to) (dis'a:m) *t.-i.* desarmar(se. 2 calmar.

disc (disk) *s.* DISK.

discard (to) (di'ka:d) *t.-i.* descartarse [de]. 2 *t.* descartar.

discern (to) (di'sə:n) *t.* discernir, distinguir. 2 percibir.

discharge (dis'tʃa:dʒ) *s.* descarga.

discharge (to) (dis'tʃa:dʒ): *t.* descargar.

disclose (to) (dis'klouz) *t.* descubrir, destapar. 2 revelar.

discomfort (dis'kʌmfət) *s.* incomodidad, molestia.

disconcert (to) (,diskən'sə:t) *t.* desconcertar, confundir.

discontent ('diskən'tent) *s.* descontento, disgusto. 2 *a.* descontento.

discontent (to) ('diskən'tent)*t.* descontentar, disgustar.

discontinuous ('diskən'tinjues) *a.* discontinuo.

discord ('disko:d) *s.* discordia.

discord (to) (dis'ko:d) *i.* desconvenir, discordar.

discount ('diskaunt) *s.* descuento; rebaja.

discount (to) ('diskaunt) *t.* descontar, rebajar.

discourage (to) (dis'kʌridʒ) *t.* desalentar. 2 disuadir.

discourse (dis'ko:s) *s.* discurso. 2 plática.

discourse (to) (dis'ko:s) *i.* discurrir, disertar, razonar.

discover (to) (dis'kʌvəʳ) *t.* descubrir, hallar. 2 revelar.

discovery (dis'kʌvəri) *s.* descubrimiento, hallazgo.

discredit (dis'kredit) *s.* descrédito; desprestigio.

discredit (to) (dis'kredit) *t.* desacreditar, desprestigiar.

discreet (dis'kri:t) *a.* discreto.

discretion (dis'kreʃən) *s.* discreción [sensatez, reserva].

discuss (to) (dis'kʌs) *t.-i.* discutir. 2 ventilar, hablar de.

disdain (dis'dein) *s.* desdén, menosprecio.

disease (di'zi:z) *s.* enfermedad, dolencia.

disfigure (to) (dis'figəʳ) *t.* desfigurar, afear.

disgrace (dis'greis) *s.* desgracia, disfavor. 2 deshonra.

disgrace (to) (dis'greis) *t.* deshonrar.

disgraceful (dis'greisful) *a.* deshonroso, vergonzoso.

disguise (dis'gaiz) *s.* disfraz.

disguise (to) (dis'gaiz) *t.* disfrazar. 2 ocultar, disimular.

disgust (dis'gʌst) *s.* aversión.

disgust (to) (dis'gʌst) *t.* hastiar, repugnar, asquear.

dish (diʃ) *s.* plato, fuente.

dish (to) (diʃ) *t.* servir. 2 burlar, frustar.

dishearten (to) (dis'hɑ:tn) *t.* descorazonar, desanimar.

dishevel (to) (di'ʃevəl) *t.* desgreñar, despeinar.

dishonest (dis'ɔniʃt) *a.* ímprobo, falso. 2 poco honrado. 3 **-ly** *adv.* de mala fe.

dishono(u)r (dis'ɔnəʳ) *s.* deshonor, deshonra. 2 afrenta.

dishono(u)r (to) (dis'ɔnəʳ) *t.* deshonrar.

disillusion (,disi'lu:ʒən) *s.* desilusión, desengaño.

disillusion (to) (,disi'lu:ʒən)*t.* desilusionar.

disinterested (dis'intristid) *a.* desinteresado. 2 imparcial.

disjoint (to) (dis'dʒɔint) *t.* desarticular, descoyuntar.

disk (disk) *s.* disco.

dislike (dis'laik) *s.* aversión.

dismal ('dizməl) *a.* triste, sombrío.

dismay (dis'mei) *s.* desmayo.

dismay (to) (dis'mei) *t.* desanimar, espantar, acongojar.

dismiss (to) (dis'mis) *t.* despedir [a uno]. 2 disolver [una junta, etc.]. 3 destituir.

dismount (to) ('dis'maunt) *t.* desmontar. 2 *i.* bajar, apearse.

disobey (to) ('disə'bei) *t.-i.* desobedecer.

disorder (dis'ɔːdə^r) *s.* trastorno, desarreglo.

disorder (to) (dis'ɔːdə^r) *t.* desordenar, desarreglar.

dispatch (dis'pætʃ) *s.* despacho.

dispatch (to) (dis'pætʃ) *t.* despachar.

dispel (to) (dis'pel) *t.-i.* dispersar(se, disipar(se.

dispense (to) (dis'pens) *t.* dispensar, distribuir, conceder. 2 dispensar, eximir.

disperse (to) (dis'pəːs) *t.-i.* dispersar(se.

displace (to) (dis'pleis) *t.* cambiar de sitio, remover.

display (dis'plei) *s.* despliegue, exhibición, manifestación. 2 ostentación, alarde.

display (to) (dis'plei) *t.* desplegar, abrir, extender.

displease (to) (dis'pliːz) *t.* desagradar, disgustar.

displeasure (dis'pleʒə^r) *s.* desagrado, descontento.

disposal (dis'pouzəl) *s.* disposición, arreglo.

dispose (to) (dis'pouz) *t.* disponer [arreglar, ordenar; establecer; disponer el ánimo de].

dispute (dis'pjuːt) *s.* disputa, discusión. 2 litigio, pleito.

dispute (to) (dis'pjuːt) *t.-i.* disputar, discutir. 2 controvertir.

disqualify (to) (dis'kwɔlifai) *t.* inhabilitar.

disquiet (dis'kwaiət) *s.* inquietud, desasosiego.

disregard ('disri'gɑːd) *s.* desatención, descuido.

disregard (to) ('disri'gɑːd) *t.* desatender, descuidar.

disreputable (dis'repjutəbl)*a.* desacreditado. 2 deshonroso.

disrespect ('disris'pekt)*s.* falta de respeto, desacato.

disrespectful (,disris'pekful)*a.* irrespetuoso.

dissatisfaction ('dis,sætis'-fækʃən) *s.* descontento.

dissatisfy (to) ('dis'sætisfai) *t.* descontentar, no satisfacer.

dissect (to) (di'sekt) *t.* disecar, anatomizar.

dissension (di'senʃən) *s.* disensión, discordia.

dissent (di'sent) *s.* disentimiento.

dissent (to) (di'sent) *i.* disentir, diferir. 2 disidir.

dissipate (to) ('disipeit) *t.* dispersar. 2 disipar.

dissolute ('disəluːt) *a.* disoluto, relajado.

dissolve (to) (di'zɔlv) *t.-i.* disolver(se. 2 *i.* deshacerse.

dissuade (di'sweid) *t.* disuadir.

distance ('distəns) *s.* distancia.

distasteful (dis'teistful) *a.* desagradable, repugnante.

distemper (dis'tempə^r) *s.* mal humor. 2 enfermedad.

distil(l (to) (dis'til) *t.* destilar.

distinct (dis'tiŋkt) *a.* distinto, claro. 2 diferente.

distort (to) (dis'tɔːt) *t.* torcer.

distract (to) (dis'trækt) *t.* distraer, apartar. 2 perturbar.

distress (to) (dis'tres) *t.* afligir, angustiar.

distrust (dis'trʌst) *s.* desconfianza, recelo.

disturb (to) (dis'təːb) *t.* turbar, agitar, perturbar.

disturbance (dis'təːbəns) *s.* perturbación, alteración.

ditch (ditʃ) *s.* zanja, foso.

dive (daiv) *s.* zambullida, inmersión. 2 buceo.

dive (to) (daiv) *i.* zambullirse, sumergirse.

diver ('daivə^r) *s.* buzo.

divert (to) (dai'və:t) *t.* desviar, apartar. 2 divertir.

divine (di'vain) *a.* divino; sublime. 2 *s.* sacerdote.

divine (to) (di'vain) *t.-i.* adivinar. 2 conjeturar.

diviner (di'vainə^r) *s.* adivino.

diving ('daiviŋ) *s.* buceo.

divinity (di'viniti) *s.* divinidad. 2 teología.

divorce (di'vɔ:s) *s.* divorcio.

divorce (to) (di'vɔ:s) *t.-i.* divorciar(se. 2 divorciarse de.

dizziness ('dizinis) *s.* vértigo, mareo, vahído.

dizzy ('dizi) *a.* vertiginoso.

do (to) (du:) *t.* [en sentido general] hacer [justicia; un favor, etc.]. 2 concluir, despachar. 3 cumplir con [un deber, etc.]. 4 producir, preparar, arreglar. 5 cocer, guisar. 6 *i.* obrar, portarse; estar: *how ~ you ~?*, ¿cómo está usted? 7 servir, bastar: *that will ~*, esto basta. 8 *do* se usa también: a) como auxiliar en frases negativas [*he did not go*, no fue] e interrog. [*does he go?*, ¿va él?]; b) para dar énfasis: *I do like it*, de verdad me gusta; c) para substituir un verbo que no se quiere repetir: *she plays the piano better now than she did last year*, ella toca el piano mejor ahora que [lo tocaba] el año pasado. ¶ INDIC. Pres.,

3.ª pers.: *does* (dʌ, dəz). | Pret.: *did* (did). | Part. p.: *done* (dʌn).

dock (dɔk) *s.* dique; dársena.

dock (to) (dɔk) *t.* cortar, cercenar.

doctor ('dɔktə^r) *m.* doctor.

doctor (to) ('dɔktə^r) *t.* doctorar. 2 medicinar.

doctrine ('dɔktrin) *s.* doctrina.

dodge (ddʒ) *s.* regate. 2 argucia, artificio.

dodge (to) (dɔdʒ) *i.* regatear; evitar, burlar.

doe (dou) *s.* ZOOL. gama.

doer ('du(:)ə^r) *s.* autor, agente.

does (dʌz, dəz) V. TO DO.

doff (to) (dɔf) *t.* quitarse.

dog (dɔg) *s.* perro, perra can.

dog (to) (dɔg) *t.* perseguir, seguir, espiar.

doing ('du(:)iŋ) *ger.* de TO DO. 2 *s. pl.* hechos, acciones.

doll (dɔl) *s.* muñeca, muñeco.

dollar ('dɔlə^r) *s.* dólar.

dolly ('dɔli) *s.* muñequita.

dolphin ('dɔlfin) *s.* ZOOL. delfín.

domain (də'mein) *s.* heredad, finca. 2 campo, esfera.

dome (doum) *s.* ARQ. cúpula.

don (to) (dɔn) *t.* vestirse.

done (dʌn) *p. p.* de TO DO.

donkey ('dɔŋki) *s.* asno, burro.

doom (du:m) *s.* sentencia, condena. 2 destino, suerte.

doom (to) (du:m) *t.* condenar.

door (dɔ:^{r}, dɔə^r) *s.* puerta.

door-keeper ('dɔ:ˌki:pə^r) *s.* portero.

doorway ('dɔ:wei) *s.* puerta, entrada, portal.

dope (doup) *s.* droga, narcótico. 2 información.

dose (dous) *s.* dosis, toma.

dose (to) (dous) *t.* medicinar, dar una toma a. 2 dosificar.

dot (dɔt) *s.* punto, señal.

dot (to) (dɔt) *t.* poner punto a [la i]. 2 puntear, salpicar.

double ('dʌbl) *a.* doble, duplo. 2 doble [de dos partes; insincero, ambiguo].

double (to) ('dʌbl) *t.* doblar, duplicar.

doubt (daut) *s.* duda. 2 incertidumbre. 3 objeción, reparo.

doubt (to) (daut) *t.-i.* dudar.

doubtful ('dautful) *a.* dudoso.

doubtless ('dautlis) *a.* indudable.

dough (dou) *s.* masa [del pan].

down (daun) *s.* plumón. 2 bozo, vello. 3 pelusa. 4 duna. 5 loma. 6 *ups and downs*, altibajos. 7 *adv.-prep.* abajo, hacia abajo, por.

down (to) (daun) *t.* derribar.

downright ('daunrait) *a.* claro, categórico.

downstairs ('daun'stεəz) *adv.* abajo [en el piso inferior].

downward ('daunwəd) *a.* descendente. 2 *adv.* DOWNWARDS.

downwards ('daunwədz) *adv.* hacia abajo.

downy ('dauni) *a.* velloso.

dowry ('dauəri) *s.* dote.

doze (douz) *s.* sueño ligero.

doze (to) (douz) *i.* dormitar.

dozen ('dʌzn) *s.* docena.

drab (dræb) *s.* pardusco.

draft, draught (to) (drɑ:ft) *s.* ac-

ción de sacar. 2 corriente [de aire]. 3 tiro [de chimenea]. 4 inhalación, trago; bebida. 5 atracción, tracción, tiro. 6 redada. 7 trazado; boceto. ¶ En las acepciones. 4 y 6 úsase de preferencia *draught*.

draft, draught (to) (drɑ:ft) *t.* hacer el borrador de, redactar. 2 dibujar, bosquejar.

drag (dræg) *s.* rastra, grada.

drag (to) (dræg) *t.* arrastrar.

drain (drein) *s.* drenaje.

drain (to) (drein) *t.* sacar, apurar, escurrir. 2 vaciar, empobrecer, sangrar.

drainage ('dreinidʒ) *s.* desagüe. 2 drenaje.

drake (dreik) *s.* pato [macho].

drank (dræŋk) V. TO DRINK.

drape (to) (dreip) *t.* cubrir con ropajes. 2 entapizar.

drapery ('dreipəri) *s.* pañería. 2 ropaje.

draught (drɑ:ft) *s.* DRAFT.

draught (to) (drɑ:ft) *t.* TO DRAFT.

draw (drɔ:) *s.* arrastre, tracción, tiro. 2 atracción.

draw (to) (drɔ:) *t.* arrastrar, tirar de. 2 dibujar, bosquejar. ¶ Pret.: *drew* (dru:); *p. p.: drawn* (drɔ:n).

drawback ('drɔ:bæk) *s.* inconveniente, desventaja.

drawer (drɔ:ʳ, drɔəʳ) *s.* cajón.

drawl (to) (drɔ:l) *t.-i.* arrastrar las palabras.

drawn (drɔ:n) *p. p.* de TO DRAW. 2 *a.* de aspecto fatigado.

dread (dred) *s.* miedo, temor. 2 *a.* temible, terrible.

dread (to) (dred) *t.-i.* temer [a], tener miedo [de].

dreadful ('dredful) *a.* terrible, espantoso. 2 horrible.

dream (dri:m) *s.* sueño.

dream (to) (dri:m) *t.-i.* soñar ¶ Pret. y *p. p.*: *dreamed* o *dreamt* (dremt).

dreamt (dremt) V. TO DREAM.

dreary ('driəri) *a.* triste.

drench (to) (drentʃ) *t.* mojar.

dress (dres) *s.* vestido, indumentaria. 2 traje; hábito.

dress (to) (dres) *t.* vestir, ataviar, adornar. 2 peinar, arreglar [el cabello]. 3 *i.* vestirse, ataviarse.

dresser ('dresəʳ) *s.* cómoda con espejo.

dressmaker ('dresˌmeikəʳ) *s.* modista, costurera.

drew (dru:) V. TO DRAW.

dried (draid) V. TO DRY.

drift (drift) *s.* lo arrastrado por el mar, el viento, etc. 2 corriente [de agua, de aire]. 3 MAR., AVIA. deriva. 4 rumbo, dirección, giro.

drift (to) (drift) *t.* impeler, llevar, amontonar. 2 *i.* flotar, ir a la deriva.

drill (dril) *s.* taladro. 2 dril [tela]. 3 ejercicio.

drill (to) (dril) *t.* taladrar, perforar. 2 ejercitar. 3 *i.* ejercitarse.

drink (driŋk) *s.* bebida. 2 trago.

drink (to) (driŋk) *t.* beber. 2 *i.* emborracharse.

drinking ('driŋkiŋ) *s.* bebida: ~-*bout*, borrachera.

drip (drip) *s.* goteo. 2 gotera.

drip (to) *i.* gotear, chorrear.

drive (draiv) *s.* paseo en coche.

drive (to) (draiv) *t.* impeler, impulsar, mover, llevar. 2 guiar, conducir. ¶ Pret.: *drove* (drouv); *p. p.*: *driven* ('drivn).

driver ('draivəʳ) *s.* conductor.

driving ('draiviŋ) *s.* conducción. 2 impulso. 3 *a.* motriz.

drone (droun) *s.* ENT. y *fig.* zángano. 2 zumbido.

droop (dru:p) *s.* inclinación, caída.

droop (to) (dru:p) *t.-i.* inclinar(se, bajar(se.

drop (drɔp) *s.* gota [de líquido]. 2 JOY. pendiente.

drop (to) (drɔp) *t.* dejar caer, soltar, echar, verter. 6 *i.* gotear, chorrear.

drought (draut) *s.* sequía.

drove (drouv) V. TO DRIVE. 2 *s.* manada, rebaño.

drown (to) (draun) *t.-i.* ahogar(se, anegar(se. 2 *t.* inundar.

drowsy ('drauzi) *a.* soñoliento.

drudgery ('drʌdʒəri) *s.* reventadero, trabajo penoso.

drug (drʌg) *s.* droga; medicamento.

drug (to) (drʌg) *t.* narcotizar; medicinar. 2 tomar drogas.

druggist ('drʌgist) *s.* (Ingl.) droguero, farmacéutico.

drug-store ('drʌgstɔːʳ) *s.* (E. U.) tienda a la vez farmacia, perfumería, colmado, comedor, etc.

drum (drʌm) *s.* tambor.

drum (to) (drʌm) *i.* tocar el tambor. 2 tabalear.

drunk (drʌŋk) *p. p.* de TO

DRINK. *2 a.* borracho, embriagado.

drunkard ('drʌŋkəd) *s.* borrachín.

drunken ('drʌŋkən) *a.* borracho, embriagado.

dry (drai) *a.* seco; árido.

dry (to) (drai) *t.-i.* secar(se, enjugar(se.

duchess ('dʌtʃis) *s.* duquesa.

duchy ('dʌtʃi) *s.* ducado [territorio].

duck (dʌk) *s.* ORN. ánade, pato. *2* agachada rápida, zambullida.

duck (to) (dʌk) *t.-i.* zambullir(se. *2* agachar(se rápidamente.

due (dju:) *a.* debido: ~ *to*, debido a.

duel ('dju(:)əl) *s.* duelo, desafío.

dug (dʌg) V. TO DIG. teta, ubre.

duke (dju:k) *s.* duque.

dull (dʌl) *a.* embotado, obtuso, romo. *2* torpe, lerdo.

dull (to) (dʌl) *t.* embotar.

dullness ('dʌlnis) *s.* embotamiento. *2* torpeza, estupidez. *3* pesadez.

duly ('dju:li) *adv.* debidamente. *2* puntualmente.

dumb (dʌm) *a.* mudo, callado, sin habla.

dump (dʌmp) *s.* vertedero; depósito. *2 pl.* murria.

dunce (dʌns) *s.* zote, ignorante.

dung (to) (dʌŋ) *t.* estercolar.

dungeon ('dʌndʒən) *s.* calabozo, mazmorra.

duplicate ('dju:plikit) *a.-s.* duplicado.

durable ('djuərəbl) *a.* durable, duradero.

during ('djuəriŋ) *prep.* durante.

dusk (dʌsk) *s.* crepúsculo, anochecida. *2* sombra.

dusky ('dʌski) *a.* obscuro, negruzco. *2* sombrío.

dust (dʌst) *s.* polvo. *2* restos mortales. *3* polvareda. *4* basura.

dust (to) (dʌst) *t.* desempolvar, quitar el polvo a.

dusty ('dʌsti) *a.* polvoriento.

duty ('dju:ti) *s.* deber, obligación. *2* obediencia, respeto.

dwarf (dwɔ:f) *a.-s.* enano, -na.

dwarf (to) (dwɔ:f) *t.* impedir el crecimiento de. *2* empequeñecer, achicar.

dwell (to) (dweel) *i.* habitar, morar, residir, vivir. *2* permanecer. ¶ Pret., y *p. p.*: *dwelt* (dwelt).

dweller ('dwelə^r) *s.* habitante.

dwindle (to) ('dwindl) *i.* menguar, disminuirse.

dye (dai) *s.* tintura, tinte, color.

dye (to) (dai) *t.-i.* teñir(se.

E

each (i:tʃ) *a.-pr.* cada, todo; cada uno: ~ *other*, uno a otro, los unos a los otros.

eager ('i:gə^r) *a.* ávido, ansioso, anheloso.

eagerness ('i:gənis) *s.* avidez, ansia, afán, ardor.

eagle ('i:gl) *s.* águila.

ear (iə^r) *s.* oreja. 2 oído, oídos. 3 BOT. espiga, mazorca [de cereal].

earl (ə:l) *s.* conde [título].

early ('ə:li) *a.* primitivo, antiguo, remoto. 2 próximo [en el futuro]. 3 precoz. 4 *adv.* temprano, pronto.

earn (to) (e:n) *t.* ganar, merecer, lograr. 2 devengar.

earnest ('ə:nist) *a.* serio, formal. 2 sincero, ardiente.

earnestness ('ə:nistnis) *s.* seriedad, buena fe. 2 ahínco.

earnings ('ə:niŋz) *s. pl.* ganancias; sueldo, salario.

ear-ring ('iəriŋ) *s.* pendiente, arete.

earshot ('iə-ʃɔt) *s.* alcance del oído.

earth (ə:θ) *s.* tierra, barro. 2

tierra [mundo; país; suelo]. 3 madriguera.

earthen ('ə:θen) *a.* de barro.

earthenware ('ə:θən-wεə^r) *s.* ollería, vasijas de barro.

earthly ('ə:θli) *a.* terrestre. 2 terrenal. 3 mundano, carnal.

earthquake ('ə:θkweik) *s.* terremoto.

earthworm ('ə:θ-wə:m) *s.* lombriz de tierra.

ease (i:z) *s.* alivio, descanso. 2 tranquilidad. 3 comodidad.

ease (to) (i:z) *t.* aliviar, moderar.

easily ('i:zili) *adv.* fácilmente.

east (i:st) *s.* este, oriente, levante. 2 *a.* oriental, del este.

Easter ('i:stə^r) *s.* Pascua de Resurrección.

eastern ('i:stən) *a.* oriental.

easy ('i:zi) *a.* fácil. 2 sencillo, natural. 3 cómodo.

eat (to) (i:t) *t.-i.* comer. 2 consumir, gastar. ¶ Pret.: *ate* (et, eit); *p. p.: eaten* (i:tn).

eaves (i:vz) *s. pl.* alero.

ebb (eb) *s.* MAR. menguante, reflujo.

ebb (to) (eb) *i.* menguar [la marea]. 2 decaer.

ebony ('ebəni) *s.* BOT. ébano.

ecclesiastic (i,kli:zi'æstik) *a.-s.* eclesiástico.

echo ('ekou) *s.* eco.

echo (to) ('ekou) *t.* hacer eco a. 2 *i.* repercutir, resonar.

economics (,i:kə'nɔmiks) *s.* economía [ciencia].

ecstasy ('ekstəsi) *s.* éxtasis.

eddy ('edi) *s.* remolino.

eddy (to) ('edi) *i.* arremolinarse.

edge (edʒ) *s.* filo, corte. 2 canto, borde, esquina.

edge (to) (edʒ) *t.* afilar, aguzar. 2 ribetear; orlar.

edict ('i:dikt) *s.* edicto, decreto.

edifice ('edifis) *s.* edificio.

edit (to) ('edit) *t.* revisar, preparar para la publicación. 2 redactar, dirigir [un periódico].

edition (i'diʃən) *s.* edición.

editor ('editə^r) *s.* director, redactor [de una publicación].

editorial (,edi'tɔ:riəl) *a.* de dirección o redacción: ~ *staff*, redacción [de un periódico]. 2 *s.* editorial, artículo de fondo.

educate (to) ('edjukeit) *t.* educar, enseñar, instruir.

education (,edju:'keiʃən) *s.* educación. | No tiene el sentido de urbanidad. 2 enseñanza.

eel (i:l) *s.* ICT. anguila.

effect (to) (i'fekt) *t.* efectuar, realizar.

effective (i'fektiv) *a.* efectivo.

effort ('efət) *s.* esfuerzo. 2 obra, trabajo.

egg (eg) *s.* huevo.

egg (to) (eg) *t.* cubrir con huevo. 2 *to* ~ *on*, incitar, instigar.

egress ('i:gres) *s.* salida.

eight (eit) *a.-s.* ocho.

either ('aiðə^r, 'i:ðə^r) *a.-pr.* [el] uno o [el] otro; [el] uno y [el] otro. 2 *adv.* también; [con negación] tampoco. 3 *conj.* ~ ... *or*, o ... o.

elaborate (to) (i'læbəreit) *t.* elaborar. 2 *i.* extenderse.

elbow ('elbou) *s.* codo. 2 recodo. 3 brazo [de sillón].

elder ('eldə^r) *a.* mayor [en edad]. 2 *s.* persona mayor. 3 saúco.

elderly ('eldəli) *a.* mayor, anciano.

eldest ('eldist) *a. superl.* mayor [en edad]. 2 primogénito.

elect (i'lekt) *a.* elegido, escogido. 2 electo.

elect (to) (i'lekt) *t.* elegir.

election (i'lekʃən) *s.* elección.

electricity (ilek'trisiti) *s.* electricidad.

elegance ('eligəns) *s.* elegancia.

elegant ('eligənt) *a.* elegante.

element ('elimənt) *s.* elemento. 2 *pl.* elementos [rudimentos; fuerzas naturales].

elementary (,eli'mentəri) *a.* elemental.

elephant ('elifənt) *s.* ZOOL. elefante.

elevate (to) ('eliveit) *t.* elevar, levantar, alzar.

elevation (,eli'veiʃən) *s.* elevación. 2 exaltación. 3 altura. 4 GEOGR. altitud.

elevator ('eliveitə^r) *s.* elevador. 2 montacargas. 3 (E. U.) ascensor. 4 (Ingl.) escalera mecánica. 5 almacén de granos.

eleven (i'levn) *a.-s.* once.

eleventh (i'levnθ) *a.* undécimo.

elf (elf) *s.* duende. 2 diablillo.

elicit (to) (i'lisit) *t.* sacar, arrancar, sonsacar.

elm (elm) *s.* BOT. olmo.

eloquent ('eləkwənt) *a.* elocuente.

else (els) *a.* más, otro: *nobody* ~, nadie más. 2 *adv.* de otro modo. 3 *conj.* si no.

elsewhere ('els'weə^r) *adv.* en [cualquier] otra parte.

elucidate (to) (i'lu:sideit) *t.* elucidar, dilucidar.

elude (to) (i'lu:d) *t.* eludir.

elusive (i'lu:siv) *a.* huidizo, esquivo.

embankment (im'bæŋkmənt)*s.* terraplén, dique, presa.

embark (to) (im'ba:k) *t.-i.* embarcar(se.

embarkation (͵emba:'keiʃən)*s.* embarco, embarque.

embarrass (to) (im'bærəs) *t.* turbar, desconcertar. 2 embarazar, estorbar. 3 poner en apuros.

embassy ('embəsi) *s.* embajada.

embitter (to) (im'bitə^r) *t.* amargar. 2 enconar.

emblem ('embləm) *s.* emblema. 2 símbolo, signo.

embody (to) (im'bɔdi) *t.* encarnar, personificar. 2 incorporar, incluir, englobar.

embrace (im'breis) *s.* abrazo.

embrace (to) (im'breis) *t.-i.* abrazar(se. 2 *t.* abarcar.

embroider (to) (im'brɔidə^r) *t.* bordar, recamar. 2 adornar.

embroidery (im'brɔidəri) *s.* bordado, recamado.

embroil (to) (im'brɔil) *t.* embrollar, enredar.

emerald ('emərəld) *s.* esmeralda.

emerge (to) (i'mə:dʒ) *i.* emerger. 2 salir, aparecer, surgir.

emergence (i'mə:dʒəns) *s.* emergencia; salida, aparición.

emergency (i'mə:dʒənsi) *s.* emergencia, apuro.

emigrant ('emigrənt) *s.* emigrante, emigrado.

emigrate (to) ('emigreit) *i.* emigrar.

emit (to) (i'mit) *t.* emitir.

emotional (i'mouʃənl) *a.* emotivo.

emperor ('empərə^r) *s.* emperador.

emphasis ('emfəsis) *s.* énfasis. 2 insistencia, intensidad.

emphasize (to) ('emfəsaiz) *t.* dar énfasis a. 2 recalcar, acentuar, insistir en.

emphatic(al (im'fætik, -əl) *a.* enfático. 2 enérgico, fuerte.

empire ('empaiə^r) *s.* imperio.

employ (im'plɔi) *s.* empleo, servicio, ocupación.

employ (to) (im'plɔi) *t.* emplear. 2 colocar, ocupar.

employee (͵emplɔi'i:) *s.* empleado, dependiente.

employer (im'plɔiə^r) *s.* patrón, amo, jefe.

employment (im'plɔimənt) *s.*

empleo. 2 trabajo, colocación.

empower (to) (im'pauə^r) *t.* autorizar, facultar.

empty ('empti) *a.* vacío. 2 vacante. 3 vacuo, vano.

empty (to) ('empti) *t.* vaciar, evacuar. 2 descargar, verter. 3 *i.* vaciarse.

enable (to) (i'neibl) *t.* habilitar, facultar. 2 facilitar.

enact (to) (i'nækt) *t.* aprobar y sancionar [una ley]. 2 TEAT. representar [una escena]; desempeñar [un papel].

enactment (i'næktmənt) *s.* ley, estatuto. 2 ejecución.

enchant (to) (in'tʃɑːnt) *t.* encantar, hechizar. 2 deleitar.

enchantment (in'tʃɑːntmənt) *s.* encantamiento, hechicería. 2 encanto, hechizo, embeleso.

enclose (to) (in'klouz) *t.* cercar, rodear. 2 incluir.

enclosure (in'klouzə^r) *s.* cercamiento. 2 cerca, vallado, reja. 3 cercado, coto.

encounter (in'kauntə^r) *s.* encuentro. 2 choque, combate.

encourage (to) (in'kʌridz) *t.* alentar, animar. 2 incitar.

end (end) *s.* fin, cabo, extremo: *on ~,* derecho; de punta, erizado; seguido, consecutivo. 2 cabo, colilla. 3 conclusión, muerte. 4 fin, objeto. 5 resultado. 6 FÚTBOL extremo.

end (to) (end) *t.* acabar, terminar. 2 *i.* acabar, finalizar.

endear (to) (in'diə^r) *t.* hacer amar, hacer querido o amado.

endearment (in'diəmənt) *s.* expresión cariñosa, terneza.

endeavo(u)r (in'devə^r) *s.* esfuerzo, empeño, tentativa.

endeavo(u)r (to) (in'devə^r) *i.* esforzarse, empeñarse.

ending ('endiŋ) *s.* fin, final, conclusión. 2 GRAM. terminación.

endorsement (in'dɔːsmənt) *s.* endoso.

endow (to) (in'dau) *t.* dotar [una fundación; de cualidades].

endure (to) (in'djuə^r) *t.* soportar, sufrir, resistir. 2 *i.* durar.

enemy ('enimi) *s.* enemigo.

energy ('enədʒi) *s.* energía.

enforce (to) (in'fɔːs) *t.* hacer cumplir [una ley, etc.]. 2 imponer [obediencia, etc.].

engage (to) (in'geidʒ) *t.* comprometer, empeñar. 2 tomar, contratar. 3 ocupar, absorber. 4 trabar [batalla, conversación]. 5 *i.* comprometerse, obligarse: *engaged couple,* novios. 6 ocuparse.

engagement (in'geidʒmənt) *s.* compromiso, cita. 2 palabra de casamiento; noviazgo. 3 ajuste, contrato. 4 MIL. encuentro, combate.

engine ('endʒin) *s.* máquina, motor; locomotora.

engineer (,endʒi'niə^r) *t.* ingeniero. 2 (E. U.) maquinista.

engineer (to) (,endʒi'niə^r) *t.* proyectar. 2 arreglar.

enhance (to) (in'hɑːns) *t.* acrecentar, realzar.

enjoy (to) (in'dʒɔi) *t.* gozar o disfrutar de.

enlarge (to) (in'lɑːdʒ) *t.-i.* agrandar(se; aumentar. 2 ampliar(se.

enlighten (to) (in'laitn) *t.* iluminar, alumbrar. 2 ilustrar.

enlist (to) (in'list) *t.* alistar. 2 *i.* alistarse, sentar plaza.

enmity ('enmiti) *s.* enemistad.

ennoble (to) (i'noubl) *t.* ennoblecer.

enormous (i'nɔːməs) *a.* enorme. 2 **-ly** *adv.* enormemente.

enough (i'nʌf) *a.* bastante, suficiente. 2 *adv.* bastante.

enquire (to) = TO INQUIRE.

enrage (to) (in'reidʒ) *t.* enfurecer, encolerizar, exasperar.

enrich (to) (in'ritʃ) *t.* enriquecer. 2 AGR. fertilizar.

enrol(l (to) (in'roul) *t.* alistar, matricular. 2 *i.* alistarse.

ensign ('ensain: in the navy, ensn) *s.* bandera, pabellón, enseña. 2 insignia. 3 (E. U.)alférez [de marina]. 4 *ensign-bearer*, abanderado.

ensue (to) (in'sju:) *i.* seguir, suceder. 2 seguirse, resultar.

entail (in'teil) *s.* vinculación.

entail (to) (in'teil) *t.* vincular [bienes]. 2 ocasionar.

entangle (to) (in'tæŋgl) *t.* enredar, enmarañar.

enter (to) ('entəʳ) *t.* entrar en o por. 2 inscribirse para.

enterprise ('entəpraiz) *s.* empresa. 2 energía, resolución.

entertain (to) (,entə'tein) *t.* entretener, divertir. 2 hospedar, agasajar. 3 tomar en consideración. 4 tener, abrigar [ideas, sentimientos]. 5 *i.* recibir huéspedes, dar comidas o fiestas.

entertainment (,entə'teinmənt) *s.* acogida, hospitalidad; fiesta. 2 entretenimiento, diversión; función, espectáculo.

enthusiasm (in'θjuːziæezəm) *s.* entusiasmo.

entice (to) (in'tais) *t.* atraer, tentar, incitar.

entire (in'taiəʳ) *a.* entero, completo, íntegro.

entitle (to) (in'taitl) *t.* titular. 2 dar derecho a, autorizar.

entrance ('entrəns) *s.* entrada, acceso, ingreso: *no* ~, se prohíbe la entrada.

entreat (to) (in'tri:t) *t.-i.* suplicar, rogar, implorar.

entrust (to) (in'trʌst) *t.* confiar, dejar al cuidado de.

entry ('entri) *s.* entrada, ingreso. 2 puerta, vestíbulo, zaguán. 3 asiento, anotación.

enunciate (to) (i'nʌnsieit) *t.* enunciar. 2 pronunciar.

envelop (to) (in'veləp) *t.* envolver, cubrir, forrar.

envelope ('enviloup) *s.* sobre [de carta]. 2 envoltura, cubierta.

enviable ('enviəbl) *a.* envidiable.

envious ('enviəs) *a.* envidioso.

environment (in'vaiərənmənt) *s.* ambiente, medio ambiente. 2 alrededores.

envoy ('envɔi) *s.* mensajero.

envy ('envi) *s.* envidia.

envy (to) ('envi) *t.* envidiar.

epic ('epik) *a.* épico. 2 *s.* epopeya; poema épico.

epidemic (,epi'demik) *a.* epidémico. 2 *s.* epidemia.

episcopal (i'piskəpəl) *a.* episcopal.

episode ('episoud) *s.* episodio.

epitaph ('epitɑːf) *s.* epitafio.

epoch ('iːpɔk) *s.* época, edad.

equal ('iːkwəl) *a.* igual. 2 justo, imparcial.

equal (to) ('iːkwəl) *t.* igualar.

equality (iːˈkwɔliti) *s.* igualdad.

equation (iˈkweiʃən) *s.* ecuación.

equator (iˈkweitəʳ) *s.* ecuador.

equilibrium (ˌiːkwiˈlibriəm) *s.* equilibrio.

equip (to) (iˈkwip) *t.* equipar.

equipage ('ekwipidʒ) *s.* equipo, avíos.

equipment (iˈkwipmənt) *s.* equipo, equipaje. 2 pertrechos.

equivalence (iˈkwivələns) *s.* equivalencia.

era ('iərə) *s.* era [de tiempo].

erase (to) (iˈreiz) *t.* borrar. 2 tachar, rayar, raspar.

erode (to) (iˈroud) *t.* corroer.

err (to) (əːʳ) *i.* errar, equivocarse, pecar. 2 vagar.

errand ('erənd) *s.* encargo, recado, mandado.

erroneous (iˈrounjəs) *a.* erróneo, falso.

error ('erəʳ) *s.* error. 2 yerro.

eructate (to) (iˈrʌkteit) *i.* eructar.

escalade (ˌeskəˈleid) *s.* MIL. escalada.

escalade (to) (ˌeskəˈleid) *t.* escalar [una pared, etc.].

escalator ('eskəleitəʳ) *s.* escalera mecánica.

escape (isˈkeip) *s.* escape, fuga. 2 escape [de gas, etc.].

escape (to) (isˈkeip) *i.* escapar(se; huir. 2 *t.* evitar, rehuir.

escort (isˈkɔːt) *s.* escolta, convoy; acompañante.

especial (isˈpeʃəl) *a.* especial, peculiar, particular.

espy (to) (isˈpai) *t.* divisar, columbrar.

esquire (isˈkwaiəʳ) *s.* título pospuesto al apellido en cartas [Esq.]. Equivale a Señor Don. 2 *ant.* escudero.

essay (to) (eˈsei) *t.* ensayar, examinar. 2 intentar.

essence ('esns) *s.* esencia.

essential (iˈsenʃəl) *a.* esencial. 2 capital, vital, indispensable.

establishment (isˈtæbliʃmənt) *s.* establecimiento. 2 fundación.

estate (isˈteit) *s.* estado [orden, clase, de pers.]. 2 bienes. 3 heredad, finca. 4 herencia [bienes].

esteem (to) (isˈtiːm) *t.* estimar, apreciar.

estimate (to) ('estimeit) *t.* estimar, evaluar, juzgar.

eternity (iˈtəːniti) *s.* eternidad.

etiquette (ˌetiˈket) *s.* etiqueta.

evade (to) (iˈveid) *t.* evadir.

eve (iːv) *s.* víspera, vigilia.

even ('iːvən) *a.* llano, liso. 2 uniforme, regular. 3 ecuánime. 4 igualado, equilibrado. 5 igual. 6 par [número]. 7 en paz, desquitado. 8 *adv.* aun, hasta, también, incluso; ~ *if*, aunque, aun cuando; ~ *so*, aun así. 9 siquiera: *not* ~, ni siquiera.

even (to) ('iːvən) *t.* igualar, allanar, nivelar.

evening ('i:vniŋ) *s.* tarde, anochecer.

event (i'vent) *s.* caso, hecho, suceso, acontecimiento.

eventual (i'ventjuəl) *a.* eventual, contingente. 2 final, consiguiente. 3 **-ly** *adv.* eventualmente; finalmente.

ever ('evə^r) *adv.* siempre. 2 alguna vez. 3 [después de negativa] nunca: *hardly* ~, casi nunca.

evergreen ('evəgri:n) *s.* siempreviva.

evermore ('evə'mɔ:^r) *adv.* eternamente, siempre.

every ('evri) *a.* cada, todo, todos.

everybody ('evribɔdi) *pron.* todos, todo el mundo; cada uno.

everyday ('evridei) *a.* diario, cotidiano, ordinario.

everyone ('evriwʌn) *pron.* EVERYBODY.

everything ('evriθiŋ) *pron.* todo, cada cosa.

everywhere ('evriweə^r) *adv.* por todas partes; a todas partes.

evidence ('evidəns) *s.* evidencia. 2 prueba.

evil ('i:vil) *a.* malo. 2 maligno. 3 *s.* mal; desastre. 4 *adv.* mal, malignamente.

evince (i'vins) *t.* mostrar, revelar, indicar.

ewe (ju:) *s.* oveja.

exact (ig'zækt) *a.* exacto. 2 preciso, riguroso.

exact (to) (ig'zækt) *t.* exigir, imponer.

exacting (ig'zæktiŋ) *a.* exigente.

examination (ig‚zæmi'neiʃən) *s.* examen. 2 DER. interrogatorio.

examine (to) (ig'zæmin) *t.* examinar. 2 DER. interrogar.

example (ig'zɑ:mpl) *s.* ejemplo.

excavate (to) ('ekskəveit) *t.* excavar. 2 extraer cavando.

exceed (to) (ik'si:d) *t.* exceder, sobrepujar, aventajar.

exceeding (ik'si:diŋ) *a.* grande, extremo.

excel (to) (ik'sel) *t.* aventajar, sobrepujar, superar. 2 *i.* distinguirse, sobresalir.

excellence ('eksələns) *s.* excelencia.

except (ik'sept) *prep.* excepto, salvo, a excepción de. 2 *conj.* a menos que.

except (to) (ik'sept) *t.* exceptuar.

excerpt ('eksə:pt) *s.* cita, pasaje, fragmento.

exchange (iks'tʃəindʒ) *s.* cambio, trueque.

exchange (to) (iks'tʃeindʒ) *t.* cambiar, canjear.

exchequer (iks'tʃekə^r) *s.* (Ingl.) hacienda pública: *Chancellor of the* ~, Ministro de Hacienda. 2 bolsa, fondos.

excite (to) (ik'sait) *t.* excitar.

exciting (ik'saitiŋ) *a.* excitante. 2 emocionante.

exclaim (to) (iks'kleim) *t.-i.* exclamar.

exclude (to) (iks'klu:d) *t.* excluir.

excursion (iks'kə:ʃən) *s.* excursión.

excuse (iks'kju:s) *s.* excusa.

excuse (to) (iks'kju:z) *t.* excusar. 2 perdonar, dispensar.

execrable ('eksikrəbl) *a.* execrable, abominable.

execute (to) ('eksikju:t) *t.* ejecutar, cumplir, llevar a
cabo. 2 TEAT. desempeñar. 3
ejecutar, ajusticiar.

executive (ig'zekjutiv) *a.* ejecutivo. 2 *s.* poder ejecutivo.
3 director, gerente.

exempt (ig'zempt) *a.* exento.

exempt (to) (ig'zempt) *t.* eximir, exceptuar, dispensar.

exercise ('eksəsaiz) *s.* ejercicio. 2 práctica.

exercise (to) ('eksəsaiz) *t.*
ejercer, practicar. 2 em-
plear. 3 *t.-i.-ref.* ejerci-
tar(se.

exert (to) (ig'zə:t) *t.* ejercer,
poner en acción. 2 *t.-pr.* es-
forzar(se.

exertion (ig'zə:ʃən) *s.* esfuerzo.

exhale (to) (eks'heil) *t.-i.* ex-
halar(se.

exhaust (ig'zɔ:st) *s.* MEC. escape, descarga [de gases,
vapor, etc.]. 2 tubo de escape.

exhaust (to) (ig'zɔ:st) *t.* agotar. 2 MEC. dar salida o escape a.

exhaustion (ig'zɔ:stʃən) *s.*
agotamiento. 2 MEC. vacia-
miento.

exhibit (ig'zibit) *s.* objeto expuesto.

exhibit (to) (ig'zibit) *t.* exhibir. 2 exponer [a la vista].

exhibition (,eksi'biʃən) *s.* exhibición. 2 exposición [de
productos, cuadros, etc.].

exile ('eksail) *s.* destierro,
exilio. 2 desterrado, exi-
liado.

exile (to) ('eksail) *t.* desterrar.

exist (to) (ig'zist) *i.* existir.

exit ('eksit) *s.* salida.

expand (to) (iks'pænd) *t.-i.*
extender(se; dilatar(se. 2
abrir(se; desplegar(se. 3 de-
sarrollar(se. 4 *i.* expansio-
narse.

expanse (iks'pæns) *s.* extensión.

expansion (iks'pænʃən) *s.* expansión. 2 dilatación.

expect (to) (iks'pekt) *t.* esperar [contar con]. 2 suponer.

expectant (iks'pektənt) *a.* en-
cinta.

expectation (,ekspek'teiʃən)*s.*
espera, expectación. 2 perspectiva, esperanza.

expel (to) (iks'pel) *t.* expeler.

expenditure (iks'penditʃər) *s.*
gasto, desembolso.

expense (iks'pens) *s.* gasto,
desembolso. 2 expensas.

expensive (iks'pensiv) *a.* costoso.

experience (iks'piəriəns) *s.*
experiencia. 2 experimento.
3 aventura, lo que sucede a
uno.

experience (to) (iks'piəriəns)
t. experimentar. 2
probar, sentir.

experiment (iks'perimənt) *s.*
experimento, prueba.

experiment (to) (iks'perimənt)*t.-i.* experimentar [en-
sayar, probar].

expert ('ekspə:t) *a.* experto,
diestro. 2 *s.* experto, perito.

expire (to) (iks'paiər) *i.* expirar, morir. 2 expirar [un
plazo]. 3 *t.-i.* FISIOL. espi-
rar.

explain (to) (iks'plein) *t.* explicar, exponer, aclarar.

explanation (,eksplə'neiʃən)
s. explicación.

exploit ('eksplɔit) *s.* hazaña.

exploit (to) (iks'plɔit) *t.* explotar.

export ('ekspɔ:t) *s.* exportación.

export (to) (eks'pɔ:t) *t.* exportar.

expose (to) (iks'pouz) *t.* exponer [a la vista, a un riesgo]; poner en peligro, comprometer. 2 FOT. exponer.

exposition (,ekspə'ziʃən) *s.* exposición.

exposure (iks'pouʒəʳ) *s.* exposición [a la intemperie, al peligro, etc.]; falta de protección. 2 FOT. exposición. 3 orientación. 4 desenmascaramiento.

express (iks'pres) *a.* expreso, claro, explícito.

express (to) (iks'pres) *t.* expresar(se. 2 prensar.

exquisite ('ekskwizit) *a.* exquisito. 2 primoroso.

extend (to) (iks'tend) *t.-i.* extender(se, prolongar(se, alargar(se. 2 *t.* dar, ofrecer.

extension (iks'tenʃən) *s.* extensión. 2 prolongación.

extensive (iks'tensiv) *a.* extensivo. 2 extenso, ancho.

extent (iks'tent) *s.* extensión; amplitud, magnitud.

exterior (eks'tiəriəʳ) *a.* exterior, externo. 2 *s.* exterior.

external (eks'tə:nl) *a.* externo, exterior.

extinct (iks'tiŋkt) *a.* extinto.

extinguish (to) (iks'tiŋgwiʃ) *t.* extinguir. 2 apagar.

extol (to) (iks'tɔl) *t.* exaltar.

extract ('ekstrækt) *s.* QUÍM., FARM. extracto. 2 cita.

extract (to) (iks'trækt) *t.* extraer. 2 seleccionar, citar.

extreme (iks'tri:m) *a.* extremo. 2 extremado, riguroso. 3 *s.* extremo, extremidad.

extricate (to) ('ekstrikeit) *t.* desembarazar, desenredar.

exultation (,egzʌl'teiʃən) *s.* alborozo, alegría.

eye (ai) *s.* ojo [órgano de la visión; atención, vigilancia], vista, mirada: *to catch the ~ of*, llamar la atención; *to see ~ to ~*, estar completamente de acuerdo. 2 ojo [de una aguja, del pan, del queso]. 3 COST. corcheta, presilla.

eye (to) (ai) *t.* mirar, clavar la mirada en.

F

fable ('feibl) *s.* fábula; ficción.

fabric ('fæbrik) *s.* tejido, tela. 2 textura. 3 fábrica, edificio.

fabulous ('fæbjuləs) *a.* fabuloso.

face (feis) *s.* cara, rostro, semblante; *in the ~ of,* ante, en presencia de. 2 osadía, descaro. 3 mueca, gesto. 4 aspecto, apariencia: *on the ~ of it,* según las apariencias. 5 superficie; frente, fachada. 6 esfera [de reloj].

fact (fækt) *s.* hecho; verdad, realidad.

factious ('fækʃəs) *a.* faccioso.

factory ('fæktəri) *s.* fábrica, manufactura.

fade (to) (feid) *t.-i.* marchitar(se, debilitar(se, desteñir(se.

fail (feil) *s.* *without ~,* sin falta.

fail (to) (feil) *i.* faltar. 2 decaer, acabarse. 3 fallar, inutilizarse. 4 fracasar. 5 fallar, frustrarse. 6 errar. 7 *to ~ to,* dejar de.

failure ('feiljə^r) *s.* fracaso, fiasco, malogro.

faint (feint) *a.* débil. 2 desfallecido. 3 *s.* desmayo.

faint (to) (feint) *i.* desmayarse. 2 desfallecer.

fair (fɛə^r) *a.* hermoso, bello. 2 bueno [regular; favorable; bonancible]. 3 justo, honrado. 4 razonable. 5 blanca [tez]; rubio [cabello]. 6 *adv.* favorablemente. 7 *s.* feria, mercado. 8 **-ly** *adv.* completamente.

fairness ('fɛənis) *s.* limpieza, pureza. 2 imparcialidad. 3 hermosura. 4 blancura [de la tez]. 5 color rubio.

fairy ('fɛəri) *s.* hada, duende.

faith (feiθ) *s.* fe.

faithful ('feiθful) *a.* fiel. 2 leal.

fall (fɔ:l) *s.* caída. 2 decadencia, ruina. 3 declive, pendiente. 4 cascada, catarata. 5 (E. U.) otoño.

fall (to) (fɔ:l) *i.* caer. 2 caerse. 3 venirse abajo. 4 bajar, descender. 5 disminuir. 6 decaer. 7 ponerse: *to ~ to*

work, ponerse a trabajar. *8* tocar, corresponder [a uno una cosa]. *9 to ~ away,* enflaquecer; desvanecerse; rebelarse; apostatar. *10 to ~ in love,* enamorarse. *11 to ~ in with,* estar de acuerdo con; coincidir; armonizar con. *12 to ~ out,* reñir, desavenirse; acontecer. *13 to ~ through,* fracasar. *14 to ~ upon,* atacar, embestir. ¶ Pret.: *fell* (fel); p. p.: *fallen* ('fɔlən).

fallen ('fɔ:lən) *p. p.* de TO FALL.

false (fɔ:ls) *a.* falso.

fame (feim) *s.* fama.

familiarity (fə,mili'æriti) *s.* familiaridad. *2* intimidad.

famine ('fæmin) *s.* hambre.

famous ('feiməs) *a.* famoso.

fan (fæn) *s.* abanico. *2* ventilador. *3* hincha, aficionado.

fan (to) (fæn) *t.* abanicar. *2* aventar. *3* ventilar.

fancy ('fænsi) *s.* fantasía, imaginación. *2* capricho, antojo. *3* afición. *4 a.* caprichoso, de fantasía.

far (fa:ʳ) *adv.* lejos, a lo lejos: *~ and wide,* por todas partes; *as ~ as,* tan lejos como; hasta; en cuanto; *as ~ as I know,* que yo sepa; *in so ~ as,* en cuanto, en lo que; *so ~,* hasta ahora; *~-fetched,* rebuscado. *2* muy, mucho: *~ away,* muy lejos; *~ off,* lejano; a lo lejos. *3 a.* lejano, distante.

fare (to) (fɛəʳ) *i.* pasarlo [bien o mal]. *2* pasar, ocurrir.

farewell ('fɛə'wel) *interj.* ¡adiós! *2 s.* despedida, adiós.

farm (fa:m) *s.* granja, cortijo.

farm (to) (fa:m) *t.* cultivar, labrar; explotar [la tierra].

farmer ('fa:məʳ) *s.* granjero, labrador, hacendado.

farmhouse (fa:mhaus) *s..* granja, alquería.

farmyard ('fa:m-ja:d) *s.* corral.

farther ('fa:ðəʳ) *adv.* más lejos, más allá. *2* además.

farthest ('fa:ðist) *a. superl.* [el más lejano]. *2 adv.* más lejos.

fashion ('fæʃən) *s.* forma. *2* modo, manera. *3* moda, costumbre, uso. *4* elegancia, buen tono.

fashionable ('fæʃnəbl) *a.* a la moda. *2* elegante.

fast (fa:st) *a.* firme, seguro; fiel; sólido, duradero. *2* atado, fijo; íntimo. *3* rápido, veloz. *4* adelantado [reloj]. *5* profundo [sueño]. *6 adv.* firmemente. *7* estrechamente. *8* aprisa. *9 s.* ayuno, abstinencia. *10* amarra, cable.

fasten (to) ('fa:sn) *t.* fijar, atar, sujetar. *2* unir, pegar. *3 i.* fijarse, pegarse.

fat (fæt) *a.* gordo, obeso; grueso. *2* graso, pingüe. *3* fértil. *4* rico, opulento. *5 s.* gordura; grasa; manteca.

fate (feit) *s.* hado, destino. *2* sino, suerte.

father ('fa:ðəʳ) *s.* padre. *2* Dios Padre.

father (to) ('fa:ðəʳ)*t.* engendrar. *2* adoptar.

father-in-law ('fa:ðərinlɔ:) *s.* padre político, suegro.

fathom ('fæðəm) *s.* braza [medida].

fathom (to) ('fæðəm) *t.* MAR. sondar. 2 penetrar.

fatigue (fə'ti:g) *s.* fatiga.

fatigue (to) (fə'ti:g) *t.* fatigar, cansar.

fatten (to) ('fætn) *t.* engordar, cebar. 2 fertilizar.

fault ('fɔ:lt) *s.* falta, defecto, tacha; error, equivocación; culpa, desliz.

faultless ('fɔ:ltlis) *a.* impecable, perfecto, irreprochable.

favo(u)r ('feivəᵣ) *s.* favor.

favo(u)r (to) ('feivəᵣ) *t.* favorecer. 2 apoyar.

favo(u)rable ('feivərəbl) *a.* favorable, propicio.

fawn (fɔ:n) *s.* ZOOL. cervato.

fawn (to) (fɔ:n) *i. to ~ on* o *upon,* adular, halagar.

fear (fiəᵣ) *s.* miedo, temor.

fear (to) (fiəᵣ) *t.-i.* temer.

feasible ('fi:zəbl) *a.* factible, hacedero, posible, viable.

feast (fi:st) *s.* fiesta. 2 festejo.

feast (to) (fi:st) *t.* festejar.

feat (fi:t) *s.* proeza, hazaña.

feather ('feðəᵣ) *s.* pluma [de ave]. 2 clase, calaña.

feather (to) (feðəᵣ) *t.* emplumar. 2 cubrir con plumas.

feature ('fi:tʃəᵣ) *s.* rasgo, facción [del rostro].

febrile ('fi:brail) *a.* febril.

February ('februəri) *s.* febrero.

fed (fed) *pret.* y p. p. de TO FEED.

federal ('fedərəl) *a.* federal.

fee (fi:) *s.* honorarios, derechos; cuota. 2 propina.

fee (to) (fi:) *t.* retribuir, pagar.

feeble ('fi:bl) *a.* débil. 2 flaco.

feed (fi:d) *s.* alimento, comida [esp. de los animales].

feed (to) (fi:d) *t.-i.* alimentar(se, nutrir(se. 2 *i.* pacer. ¶ Pret. y p. p.: *fed* (fed).

feel (fi:l) *s.* tacto. 2 sensación.

feel (to) (fi:l) *t.* tocar, tentar. 2 tomar [el pulso]. 3 examinar. 4 sentir, experimentar. 5 creer, pensar. 6 *i.* sentirse, estar, tener: *to ~ bad,* sentirse mal; *to ~ cold,* tener frío. 7 ser sensible, sentir. 8 *to ~ like,* tener ganas de. ¶ Pret. y p. p.: *felt* (felt).

feeling ('fi:liŋ) *s.* tacto [sentido]. 2 sensación, percepción. 3 sentimiento. 4 *a.* sensible, tierno.

feet (fi:t) *s. pl.* de FOOT, pies.

feign (to) (fein) *t.* fingir.

fell (fel) *pret.* de TO FALL. 2 *a.* cruel. 3 *s.* tala [de árboles].

fell (to) (fel) *t.* derribar, tumbar. 2 cortar [árboles].

fellow ('felou) *s.* compañero. 2 individuo, muchacho. 3 igual, pareja. 4 *a.* indica igualdad o asociación: *citizen,* conciudadano.

female ('fi:meil) *s.* hembra. 2 *a.* femenino, hembra.

feminine ('feminin) *a.* femenino.

fence, (fens) *s.* empalizada, valla, cerca. 2 esgrima.

fence (to) (fens) *t.* vallar. 2 proteger. 3 *i.* esgrimir.

ferment ('fə:mənt) *s.* fermento. 2 fermentación, agitación.

fern (fə:n) *s.* BOT. helecho.

ferocious (fə'rouʃəs) *a.* fiero, feroz, terrible.

ferry ('feri) *s.* balsadero. 2 barca, balsa, transbordador. 3 *~-boat,* barca de pasaje.

ferry (to) ('feri) *t.-i.* cruzar [un río] en barca.

fertilize (to) ('fə:tilaiz) *t.* fertilizar. 2 fecundar. 3 abonar.

fertilizer ('fə:tilaizə^r) *s.* fertilizante, abono.

fervour ('fə:və^r) *s.* fervor, ardor.

festoon (fes'tu:n) *s.* festón.

fetch (to) (fetʃ) *t.* ir por, ir a buscar. 2 venderse a o por.

fetter ('fetə^r) *s.* grillete, prisión.

fetter (to) ('fetə^r) *t.* encadenar.

feud (fju:d) *s.* rencilla.

fever ('fi:və^r) *s.* MED. fiebre.

feverish ('fi:vəriʃ) *a.* febril.

few (fju:) *a.-pron.* pocos: *a ~*, unos cuantos, algunos.

fiancé (fi'a:nsei) *s.* novio, prometido.

fiancée (fi'a:nsei) *s.* novia, prometida.

fiber, fibre ('faibə^r) *s.* fibra.

fickle ('fikl) *a.* mudable, inconstante, voluble.

fiddle ('fidl) *s.* MÚS. fam. violín.

fidget (to) ('fidʒit) *i.* estar inquieto, agitarse.

field (fi:ld) *s.* campo.

fiend (fi:nd) *s.* demonio, diablo.

fierce (fiəs) *a.* fiero, feroz.

fiery ('faiəri) *a.* ígneo. 2 ardiente, encendido.

fife (faif) *s.* pífano.

fifth (fifθ) *a.-s.* quinto.

fiftieth ('fiftiiθ) *a.-s.* quincuagésimo.

fifty ('fifti) *a.-s.* cincuenta.

fight (fait) *s.* lucha, combate.

fight (to) (fait) *i.* luchar, pelear, contender. 2 *t.* luchar con o contra. 3 lidiar [un toro]. 4 librar [una batalla]. ¶ Pret. y p. p.: *fought* (fɔ:t).

figure ('figə^r) *s.* figura. 2 tipo, cuerpo, talle. 3 ARIT. cifra, número. 4 precio, valor. 5 dibujo; estatua.

figure (to) ('figə^r) *t.* adornar con [dibujos, etc.]. 2 figurarse, imaginar.

file (fail) *s.* lima, escofina. 2 carpeta, archivador. 3 legajo, expediente. 4 fila.

file (to) (fail) *t.* limar. 2 archivar, registrar. 3 *i.* desfilar.

fill (fil) *s.* hartazgo. 2 colmo.

fill (to) (fil) *t.-i.* llenar(se. 2 *t.* henchir, completar. 3 llevar a cabo.

film (film) *s.* película, filme.

filter ('filtə^r) *s.* filtro.

filter (to) ('filtə^r) *t.-i.* filtrar(se.

filth (filθ) *s.* suciedad.

filthy ('filθi) *a.* sucio.

final ('fainl) *a.* final.

finance (fai'næns, fi-) *s.* ciencia financiera. 2 *pl.* hacienda, fondos.

find (to) (faind) *t.* encontrar, hallar; descubrir; adivinar: *to ~ fault with,* hallar defectos, censurar; *to ~ out,* averiguar. ¶ Pret. y p. p.: *found* (faund).

fine (fain) *s.* multa. 2 *a.* fino. 3 de ley. 4 hermoso, bello. 5 bueno, excelente. 6 primoroso. 7 guapo, elegante.

fine (to) (fain) *t.* multar.

finger ('fiŋgə^r) *s.* dedo.

finger (to) ('fiŋgə^r) *t.* tocar, manosear. 2 hurtar. 3 teclear.

finish ('finiʃ) *s.* fin, final, término, remate.

finish (to) ('finiʃ) *t.* acabar, terminar, concluir.

fir (fə:^{r}) *s.* BOT. abeto.

fire ('faiə^r) s. fuego, lumbre. 2 fuego, incendio. 3 fuego [disparos]. 4 ardor, pasión; inspiración.

fire (to) ('faiə^r) t. encender. 2 disparar [un arma de fuego]. 3 inflamar, enardecer. 4 i. encenderse. 5 enardecerse.

fireman ('faiəmən) s. bombero. 2 fogonero.

fire-place ('faiə-pleis) s. hogar, chimenea.

firm (fə:m) a. firme. 2 s. firma, casa, razón social.

first (fə:st) a. primero. 2 prístino, primitivo. 3 anterior, original. 4 temprano. 5 adv. primero. 6 antes, al principio. 7 s. primero. 8 principio.

first-rate ('fə:st'reit) a. excelente, de primera.

fish (fiʃ) s. ICT. pez. 2 pescado: ~ *market*, pescadería.

fish (to) (fiʃ) t.-i. pescar.

fisherman ('fiʃəmən) s. pescador.

fishmonger ('fiʃ‚mʌŋgə^r) s. pescadero.

fist (fist) s. puño.

fit (fit) s. ataque, acceso, paroxismo. 2 arranque, arrebato. 3 capricho, antojo. 4 ajuste, encaje. 5 a. apto, capaz, apropiado. 6 bien de salud. 7 listo, preparado.

fit (to) (fit) t.-i. adaptarse, ajustarse [a]; encajar [en]; convenir [con]; corresponder [a]; ser propio o adecuado [de o para]. 2 caer, venir [bien o mal]. 3 t. ajustar, encajar. 4 disponer, preparar.

fitting ('fitiŋ) a. propio, adecuado, conveniente. 2 s. ajuste, encaje.

five (faiv) a.-s. cinco.

fix (fiks) s. apuro, aprieto.

fix (to) (fiks) t. fijar. 2 señalar; poner, establecer. 3 arreglar, reparar. 4 i. fijarse, solidificarse.

fixture ('fikstʃə^r) s. cosa, mueble, etc., fijos en un lugar. 2 pl. instalación [de gas, etc.].

flabby ('flæbi) a. fláccido, flojo.

flag (flæg) s. bandera, estandarte, banderola.

flag (to) (flæg) i. desanimarse. 2 aflojar, flaquear.

flake (fleik) s. copo [de nieve]. 2 escama, pedacito.

flame (fleim) s. llama; fuego.

flame (to) (fleim) i. llamear, flamear, encenderse.

flank (flæŋk) s. ijada. 2 costado, lado. 3 MIL. flanco.

flank (to) (flæŋk) t. flanquear.

flannel ('flænl) s. TEJ. franela.

flap (flæp) s. SAST. cartera, pata; haldeta. 2 golpe, aletazo.

flap (to) (flæp) t. batir, agitar [las alas]. 2 i. batir, aletear.

flare (fleə^r) s. llamarada.

flare (to) (fleə^r) i. llamear, fulgurar.

flash (flæʃ) s. llamarada, destello; ráfaga de luz.

flash (to) (flæʃ) t. encender. 2 despedir [luz, destellos]. 3 i. relampaguear.

flask (flɑ:sk) s. frasco, redoma.

flat (flæt) a. plano, llano,

liso, raso. 2 MÚS. bemol. 3 s. llanura, planicie, plano. 4 palma [de la mano].

flatter (to) ('flætə^r) *t.* adular.

flattery ('flætəri) *s.* adulación.

flavo(u)r (to) ('fleivə^r) *t.* sazonar, condimentar.

flaw (flɔ:) *s.* grieta, raja. 2 falta, defecto, imperfección.

flax (flæks) *s.* lino.

flea (fli:) *s.* pulga.

fled (fled) V. TO FLEE.

flee (to) (fli:) *i.* huir. 2 *t.* huir de, evitar. ¶ Pret. y p. p.: *fled* (fled).

fleece (fli:s) *s.* vellón, lana.

fleece (to) (fli:s) *t.* esquilar.

fleet (fli:t) *s.* armada. 2 flota, escuadra. 3 *a.* veloz, ligero.

flesh (fleʃ) *s.* carne: *to put on ~*, engordar.

flew (flu:) *Pret.* de TO FLY.

flexible ('fleksəbl) *a.* flexible.

flick (flik) *s.* golpecito.

flicker ('flikə^r) *s.* luz trémula.

flicker (to) ('flikə^r) *i.* vacilar.

flight (flait) *s.* vuelo. 2 trayectoria [de un proyectil]. 3 bandada [de pájaros]; escuadrilla [de aviones]. 4 fuga, huida. 5 tramo [de escalera].

flinch (to) (flintʃ) *i.* vacilar.

fling (fliŋ) *s.* tiro, echada. 2 prueba, tentativa. 3 brinco.

fling (to) (fliŋ) *t.* echar, arrojar, tirar, lanzar. 2 *i.* arrojarse, lanzarse. ¶ Pret. y p. p.: *flung* (flʌŋ).

flint (flint) *s.* pedernal.

flip (to) (flip) *t.* arrojar, lanzar [con el pulgar y otro dedo].

flirt (flə:t) *s.* galanteador. 2 coqueta.

flirt (to) (flə:t) *i.* flirtear, coquetear. 2 juguetear.

flit (to) (flit) *i.* volar, revolotear.

float (flout) *s.* corcho, flotador. 2 boya. 3 balsa.

float (to) (flout) *i.* flotar. 2 *t.* hacer flotar. 3 COM. emitir.

flock (flɔk) *s.* rebaño; manada; bandada [de aves].

flock (to) (flɔk) *i.* reunirse, congregarse, juntarse.

flog (to) (flɔg) *t.* azotar.

flood (flʌd) *s.* riada, crecida. 2 inundación. 3 torrente.

flood (to) (flʌd) *t.* inundar.

floor (flɔ:^r, flɔə^r) *s.* suelo, piso. 2 piso [de una casa].

flounder ('flaundə^r) *s.* ICT. platija. 2 esfuerzo torpe.

flounder (to) (flaundə^r) *i.* esforzarse torpemente. 2 vacilar; equivocarse.

flour ('flauə^r) *s.* harina.

flourish ('flʌriʃ) *s.* molinete ostentoso con el sable, etc. 2 rasgo caprichoso. 3 toque de trompetas. 4 prosperidad.

flourish (to) ('flʌriʃ) *i.* prosperar. 2 rasguear [con la pluma; la guitarra]. 3 *t.* adornar. 4 blandir [la espada, etc.].

flow (flou) *s.* flujo, corriente.

flow (to) (flou) *i.* fluir, manar.

flower ('flauə^r) *s.* BOT. flor.

flower (to) ('flauə^r) *i.* florecer.

flown (floun) *p. p. de* TO FLY.

flu (flu:) *s.* MED. fam. gripe.

flung (flʌŋ) V. TO FLING.

flurry ('flʌri) *s.* agitación, excitación. 2 barullo. 3 ráfaga.

flurry (to) ('flʌri) *t.* agitar.

flush (flʌʃ) *a.* lleno, rico, abundante. 2 rojo, encendido. 3 parejo, raso, nivelado. *4 s.* flujo rápido. *5* rubor, sonrojo.

flush (to) (flʌʃ) *i.* afluir [la sangre]. *2* encenderse; ruborizarse. *3* salir, brotar. *4 t.* encender, ruborizar.

flutter ('flʌtəʳ) *s.* vibración, aleteo, palpitación.

flutter (to) ('flʌtəʳ) *i.* temblar, aletear, palpitar.

fly (flai) *s.* ENT. mosca. *2* braqueta. *3 pl.* TEAT. bambalinas.

fly (to) (flai) *i.* volar. *2* huir. ¶ Pret.: *flew* (flu:); p. p.: *flown* (floun).

foam (foum) *s.* espuma.

foam (to) (foum) *i.* echar espuma.

focus ('foukəs) *s.* foco; enfoque.

focus (to) ('foukəs) *t.* enfocar.

fodder ('fɔdəʳ) *s.* forraje, pienso.

foe (fou) *s.* enemigo.

fog (fɔg) *s.* niebla, bruma.

foggy ('fɔgi) *a.* neblinoso.

foist (to) (fɔist) *t.* endosar [una mercancía, etc.] con engaño.

fold (fould) *s.* pliegue, doblez. *2* redil, aprisco. *3* grey.

fold (to) (fould) *t.-i.* doblar(se, plegarse.

folk (fouk) *s.* gente, pueblo.

folk-lore ('fouk-lɔːʳ) *s.* folklore.

follow (to) ('fɔlou) *t.* seguir.

follower ('fɔlouəʳ) *s.* seguidor. *2* imitador, discípulo.

following ('fɔlouiŋ) *a.* siguiente.

folly ('fɔli) *s.* tontería.

fond (fɔnd) *a.* cariñoso. *2 to be ~ of,* ser amigo de; querer; ser aficionado a.

fondle (to) ('fɔndl) *t.* tratar con amor; mimar; acariciar.

food (fu:d) *s.* alimento, comida.

fool (fu:l) *s.* tonto, bobo.

foolish ('fu:liʃ) *a.* tonto, necio. *2* absurdo, ridículo.

fool (to) (fu:l) *t.* engañar. *2* embromar. *3 i.* bromear.

foolishness ('fu:liʃnis) *s.* tontería, simpleza, necedad.

foot (fut), *pl.* **feet** (fi:t) *s.* pie [de pers.]: *on ~,* a pie. *2* pata, pie [de animal, mueble, objeto].

football ('futbɔ:l) *s.* DEP. fútbol.

for (fɔːʳ, fəʳ) *prep.* para; por; a causa de. *2* durante. *3 as ~ me,* por mi parte. *4 conj.* (fɔːʳ) ya que, pues.

forage ('fɔridʒ) *s.* forraje.

forage (to) ('fɔridʒ) *t.* forrajear. *2* saquear, pillar.

foray ('fɔrei) *s.* correría.

forbade (fə'beid) V. TO FORBID.

forbear (to) ('fɔːbɛəʳ) *t.* dejar de, abstenerse de. *2* sufrir con paciencia. ¶ Pret.: *forbore* (fɔː'bɔːʳ); p. p.: *forborne* (fɔː'bɔːn).

forbid (to) (fə'bid) *t.* prohibir, vedar, negar. ¶ Pret.: *forbade* (fə'beid) o *forbad* (fə'bæd); p. p.: *forbidden* (fə'bidn).

force (fɔːs) *s.* fuerza. *2* virtud, eficacia. *3 in ~,* en vigor.

force (to) (fɔːs) *t.* forzar. *2* obligar. *3* imponer.

forcible ('fɔːsəbl) *a.* fuerte.

ford (fɔːd) *s.* vado.

ford (to) (fɔːd) *t.* vadear.

fore (fɔː, fɔəʳ) *a.* delantero. *2*

s. parte delantera; proa. *3 adv.* a proa.

forecast ('fɔkɑ:st) *s.* pronóstico, previsión.

forecast (to) ('fɔ:kɑ:st) *t.* pronosticar, predecir. ¶ Pret. y p. p.: *forecast* o *-ted* (-tid).

forefather ('fɔ:,fɑ:ðəʳ) *s.* antepasado.

forefinger ('fɔ:,fiŋgəʳ) *s.* dedo índice.

foregoing (fɔ:'gouiŋ) *s.* anterior, precedente.

forehead ('fɔrid) *s.* ANAT. frente.

foreign ('fɔrin) *a.* extranjero, exterior. *2* forastero.

foreigner ('fɔrinəʳ) *s.* extranjero [pers.].

foresee (to) (fɔ:'si:) *t.* prever. ¶ Pret.: *foresaw* (fɔ:'sɔ:); p. p.: *foreseen* (fɔ:'si:n).

foresight ('fɔ:sait) *s.* previsión, perspicacia.

forest ('fɔrist) *s.* bosque, selva.

forestall (to) (fɔ:'stɔ:l) *t.* anticiparse a; prevenir, impedir.

foretell (to) (fɔ:'tel) *t.* predecir. ¶ Pret. y p. p.: *foretold* (fɔ:'tould).

forever (fə'revəʳ) *adv.* siempre, para siempre.

forfeit ('fɔ:fit) *s.* pena, multa. *2* prenda [en los juegos].

forfeit (to) ('fɔ:fit) *t.* perder [algo] como pena o castigo.

forge (fɔ:dʒ) *s.* fragua; herrería.

forge (to) (fɔ:dʒ) *t.* forjar, fraguar [metal]. *2* forjar [mentiras]. *3* falsificar.

forgery ('fɔ:dʒəri) *s.* falsificación.

forget (to) (fə'get) *t.-i.* olvidar. ¶ Pret.: *forgot* (fə'gɔt); p. p.: *forgotten* (fə'gɔtn).

forgetful (fə'getful) *a.* olvidadizo.

forgive (to) fə'giv) *t.* perdonar, dispensar. ¶ Pret.: *forgave* (fə'geiv); p. p.: *forgiven* (fə'givn).

fork (fɔ:k) *s.* tenedor. *2* horca, horquilla. *3* bifurcación.

fork (to) (fɔ:k) *i.* bifurcarse.

forlorn (fə'lɔ:n) *a.* abandonado. *2* triste. *3* desesperado.

former ('fɔ:məʳ) *a.* anterior, precedente; antiguo. *2 pron.* el primero [de dos]; *the ~ ..., the latter...,* éste ..., aquél...

formerly ('fɔ:məli) *adv.* antes.

forsake (to) (fə'seik) *t.* abandonar, desamparar. ¶ Pret.: *forsook* (fə'suk); p. p.: *forsaken* (fə'seikən).

forswear (to) (fɔ:'sweəʳ) *t.* abjurar, renunciar. ¶ Pret.: *forswore* ('fɔ:swɔ:ʳ); p. p.: *forsworn* (fɔ:'swɔ:n).

forth (fɔ:θt) *adv.* delante, adelante. *2* en adelante.

forthcoming (fɔ:θ'kʌmiŋ) *a.* venidero, próximo.

fortnight ('fɔ:tnait) *s.* quincena.

fortress ('fɔ:tris) *s.* fortaleza.

fortune ('fɔ:tʃən) *s.* fortuna.

forty ('fɔ:ti) *a.-s.* cuarenta.

forward ('fɔ:wəd) *a.* delantero. *2* precoz, adelantado. *3 s.* DEP. delantero.

forward (to) ('fɔ:wəd) *t.* enviar, remitir, expedir; reexpedir. *2* promover.

foster ('fɔstəʳ) *a.* de leche; adoptivo.

foster (to) ('fɔstəʳ) *t.* criar, nutrir. *2* alentar, fomentar.

fought (fɔ:t) V. TO FIGHT.

foul (faul) *a.* sucio, asqueroso.

foul (to) (faul) *t.-i.* ensuciar(se. 2 enredar(se.

found (faund) TO FIND.

found (to) (faund) *t.* fundar. 2 METAL. fundir.

founder ('faundə^r) *s.* fundador. 2 fundidor.

founder (to) ('faundə^r) *t.* MAR. hundir, echar a pique. 2 *i.* MAR. irse a pique.

foundry ('faundri) *s.* fundición.

fountain ('fauntin) *s.* fuente; surtidor. 2 ~*-pen,* pluma estilográfica.

four (fɔ:^{r}, fɔə^r) *a.-s.* cuarto.

fourteen ('fɔ:'ti:n) *a.-s.* catorce.

fourteenth ('fɔ:'ti:nθ) *a.* decimocuarto.

fourth (fɔ:θ) *a.-s.* cuarto.

fowl (faul) *s.* ave de corral.

fox (fɔks) *s.* zorro, raposa.

frail (freil) *a.* frágil. 2 débil.

frame (freim) *s.* armazón, armadura, esqueleto. 2 cuerpo [del hombre, etc.]. 3 bastidor, marco.

frame (to) (frem) *t.* formar, construir. 2 encuadrar, enmarcar. 3 idear. 4 expresar.

framework ('freimwə:k) *s.* armazón, esqueleto.

franchise ('fræntʃaiz) *s.* privilegio. 2 derecho político.

frank (fræŋk) *a.* franco [sincero, claro]. 2 *s.* franquicia postal.

frankfurter ('fræŋkˌfɔ:tə^r) *s.* salchicha de Francfort.

frankness ('fræŋknis) *s.* franqueza, sinceridad.

frantic ('fræntik) *a.* frenético, furioso, desesperado.

fraud (frɔ:d) *s.* fraude, dolo, engaño. 2 farsante.

freak (fri:k) *s.* capricho, antojo, rareza. 2 monstruosidad.

freckle ('frekl) *s.* peca.

free (fri:) *a.* libre. 2 franco, exento. 3 gratuito. 4 espontáneo. 5 liberal, generoso. 6 desocupado, vacante. 7 *adv.* libremente.

freedom ('fri:dəm) *s.* libertad. 2 facilidad, soltura.

freeze (to) (fri:z) *t.-i.* helar(se, congelar(se. ¶ Pret.: *froze* (frouz); p. p.: *frozen* (frouzn).

freight (freit) *s.* carga, flete.

French (frentʃ) *a.-s.* francés.

frenzy ('frenzi) *s.* frenesí.

frequency ('fri:kwənsi) *s.* frecuencia.

frequent ('fri:kwənt) *a.* frecuente. 2 habitual, regular.

frequent (to) (fri'kwent) *t.* frecuentar.

fresh (freʃ) *a.* fresco, nuevo, reciente. 2 tierno [pan]. 3 puro [aire]. 4 ~ *water,* agua dulce.

freshness ('freʃnis) *s.* frescor.

fret (fret) *s.* roce. 2 raedura.

fret (to) (fret) *t.-i.* rozar(se, raer(se, desgastar(se.

fretful ('fretful) *a.* irritable, enojadizo; nervioso, impaciente.

friction ('frikʃən) *s.* fricción, rozamiento, roce, frote.

Friday ('fraidi) *s.* viernes.

friend (frend) *s.* amigo, amiga: *boy* ~, novio; *girl* ~, novia.

friendly ('frendli) *a.* amistoso, amigable. 2 benévolo.

friendship ('frendʃip) s. amistad.

fright (frait) s. miedo, terror.

frighten (to) ('fraitn) t. asustar, espantar.

frightful ('fraitful) a. espantoso, terrible. 2 horroroso.

fringe (frindʒ) s. franja, fleco, orla. 2 flequillo.

fringe (to) (frindʒ) t. orlar, adornar con flecos o franjas.

frisk (to) i. retozar, triscar.

frisky ('friski) a. juguetón.

fro (frou) adv. to and ~, de un lado a otro.

frock (frɔk) s. hábito [monacal]. 2 vestido [de mujer]. 3 ~ coat, levita.

frog (frɔg) s. rana. 2 alamar.

frolic ('frɔlik) s. juego, retozo. 2 holgorio, diversión.

frolic (to) ('frɔlik) i. juguetear, retozar, divertirse.

from (frɔm, frəm) prep. de, desde. 2 a partir de. 3 de parte de. 4 según. 5 por, a causa de.

front (frʌnt) s. frente, fachada. 2 MIL. frente. 3 delantera. 4 in ~ of, delante de, frente a. 5 a. delantero.

front (to) (frʌnt) t. hacer frente a. 2 mirar a, dar a.

frontier ('frʌntjəʳ) s. frontera. 2 a. fronterizo.

frost (frɔst) s. escarcha, helada.

froth (frɔθ) s. espuma.

froth (to) (frɔθ) t. espumar.

frothy ('frɔθi) a. espumoso.

frown (fraun) s. ceño, entrecejo.

frown (to) (fraun) i. fruncir el entrecejo.

fruit (fru:t) s. fruto. 2 fruta.

fruit (to) (fru:t) i. fructificar.

fruitful ('fru:tful) a. fructífero, fructuoso. 2 fértil.

fry (to) (frai) t.-i. freír(se.

fuel (fjuəl) s. combustible.

fulfil(l (to) (ful'fil) t. cumplir, realizar, verificar, efectuar.

fulfilment (ful'filmənt) s. ejecución, realización. 2 colmo.

full (ful) a. lleno, colmado, repleto, atestado. 2 pleno, entero, completo. 3 plenario. 4 copioso, abundante. 5 extenso, detallado. 6 ~ stop, punto [final].

fullness ('fulnis) s. llenura, plenitud, colmo. 2 abundancia. 3 hartura.

fully ('fuli) adv. plenamente.

fumble (to) ('fʌmbl) i. buscar a tientas, revolver [buscando].

fumbler ('fʌmbləʳ) s. chapucero.

fume (fju:m) s. humo.

fun (fʌn) s. broma, diversión: in [for] ~, de broma: to be ~, ser divertido. 2 chanza.

function ('fʌŋkʃən) s. función. 2 fiesta, reunión, acto.

function (to) ('fʌŋkʃən) i. funcionar.

fund (fʌnd) s. fondo, capital.

funeral ('fju:nərəl) s. entierro. 2 exequias. 3 a. fúnebre.

fungus ('fʌŋgəs) s. BOT. hongo.

funnel ('fʌnl) s. embudo. 2 chimenea [de vapor].

funny ('fʌni) a. cómico, gracioso, divertido. 2 raro.

fur (fəːʳ) s. piel: ~ coat, abrigo de pieles. 2 sarro.

furious ('fjuəriəs) a. furioso.

furnace ('fəːnis) s. horno.

furnish (to) ('fə:niʃ) *t.* surtir, proveer. 2 equipar, amueblar. 3 suministrar.

furniture ('fə:nitʃəʳ) *s.* mobiliario, muebles: *piece of ~*, mueble.

furrow ('fʌrou) *s.* surco. 2 arruga.

furrow (to) ('fʌrou) *t.* surcar.

further ('fə:ðəʳ) *a.* adicional, ulterior, nuevo, otro. 2 más lejano. 3 *adv.* más allá. 4 además, aún.

further (to) ('fə:ðəʳ) *t.* adelantar, fomentar, apoyar.

furthermore ('fə:ðə'mɔ:ʳ)*adv.* además.

fury ('fjuəri) *s.* furia. 2 entusiasmo, frenesí.

fuse (fju:z) *s.* espoleta, cebo, mecha. 2 ELECT. fusible.

fuss (fʌs) *s.* alboroto, alharaca.

fuss (to) (fʌs) *i.* bullir, ajetrearse, alborotarse.

fussy ('fʌsi) *a.* bullidor, inquieto. 2 minucioso, exigente.

futile ('fju:tail) *a.* fútil. 2 frívolo. 3 vano, inútil.

future ('fju:tʃəʳ) *a.* futuro, venidero. 2 *s.* futuro, porvenir.

G

gabble ('gæbl) s. charla.

gabble (to) ('gæbl) t. charlar.

gad (to) (gæd) i. callejear.

gag (gæg) s. mordaza. 2 TEAT. morcilla.

gag (to) (gæg) t. amordazar. 2 TEAT. meter morcilla.

gaiety ('geiəti) s. alegría.

gain (gein) s. ganancia. 2 ventaja.

gain (to) (gein) t. ganar. 2 i. ganar, progresar.

gainful ('geinful) a. provechoso.

gait (geit) s. paso, marcha.

gale (geil) s. vendaval.

gall (gɔ:l) s. bilis, hiel. 2 descaro.

gall (to) (gɔ:l) t. rozar. 2 irritar. 3 hostigar.

gallant ('gælənt) a. galano. 2 gallardo, valiente. 3 galante. 4 s. galán.

gallon ('gælən) s. galón [medida].

gallop ('gæləp) s. galope.

gallop (to) ('gæləp) i. galopar.

gallows ('gælouz) s. horca, patíbulo: ~-*bird*, reo de muerte.

gamble (to) ('gæmbl) i. jugar [dinero].

game (geim) s. juego, diversión. 2 partida [de juego]. 3 DEP. partido. 4 caza [animales]. 5 a. valiente.

gander ('gændəʳ) s. ZOOL. ganso.

gang (gæŋ) s. cuadrilla.

gangster ('gæŋstəʳ) s. gangster.

gaol (dʒeil) s. cárcel.

gap (gæp) s. boquete, brecha. 2 hueco, claro, vacío.

gape (geip) s. bostezo.

gape (to) (geip) i. bostezar.

garage ('gæra:ʒ, -ridʒ) s. garaje.

garbage ('ga:bidʒ) s. basura.

garden ('ga:dn) s. jardín.

gardener ('ga:dnəʳ) s. jardinero.

gardening ('ga:dniŋ) s. jardinería, horticultura.

garland ('ga:lənd) s. guirnalda.

garlic ('ga:lik) s. BOT. ajo.

garment ('ga:mənt) s. vestido, prenda.

garner ('ga:nəʳ) s. granero.

garnish ('gɑːniʃ) *s.* adorno, guarnición. 2 COC. aderezo.

garret ('gærət) *s.* desván.

garrison ('gærisn) *s.* guarnición.

garrison (to) (gærisn) *t.* MIL. guarnecer.

gas (gæs) *s.* gas: ~ *range*, cocina de gas; ~ *works*, fábrica de gas. 2 (E. U.)gasolina.

gaslight ('gæslait) *s.* luz de gas.

gasp (gɑːsp) *s.* boqueada.

gasp (to) (gɑːsp) *i.* boquear. 2 *t.* decir de manera entrecortada.

gate (geit) *s.* puerta [de ciudad, muro, etc.]; verja; barrera. 2 compuerta.

gateway ('geit-wei) *s.* puerta.

gather (to) ('gæðəʳ) *t.* recoger, juntar. 2 cosechar. 3 deducir, inferir. 4 *i.* reunirse.

gaudy ('gɔːdi) *a.* chillón, llamativo, ostentoso.

gauge (geidʒ) *s.* medida, calibre. 2 regla de medir, etc.

gauge (to) (geidʒ) *t.* medir.

gaunt (gɔːnt) *a.* flaco, desvaído.

gauze (gɔːz) *s.* gasa, cendal.

gave (geiv) *pret.* de TO GIVE.

gay (gei) *a.* alegre. 2 vistoso.

gaze (geiz) *s.* mirada fija.

gaze (to) (geiz) *i.* mirar fijamente. 2 contemplar.

gear (giəʳ) *s.* vestidos, atavíos. 2 guarniciones [del caballo]. 3 herramientas. 4 MEC. engranaje.

gear (to) (giəʳ) *t.* ataviar. 2 enjaezar. 3 engranar.

geese (giːs) *s. pl.* de GOOSE.

gem (dʒem) *s.* gema.

gender ('dʒendəʳ) *s.* género.

general ('dʒenərəl) *a.* general. 2 *m.* MIL., ECLES. general. 3 el público.

generate (to) ('dʒenəreit) *t.* producir.

generous ('dʒenərəs) *a.* generoso. 2 noble. 3 amplio.

genius ('dʒiːnjəs) *pl.* **geniuses** ('dʒiːniəsiz) genio [fuerza creadora]. 2 carácter particular [de una nación, etc.].

genteel (dʒen'tiːl) *a.* [hoy, irónico] cursi; [antes] cortés, bien criado.

gentle ('dʒentl) *a.* de buena posición social. 2 dócil. 3 afable, benigno.

gentleman ('dʒentlmən) *s.* caballero, señor.

gentleness (dʒentlnis) *s.* mansedumbre. 2 afabilidad.

gently ('dʒentli) *adv.* suavemente. 2 despacio, quedito.

gentry ('dʒentri) *s.* señorío [no noble]. 2 irón. gente.

genuine ('dʒenjuin) *a.* genuino, auténtico, legítimo. 2 sincero.

geographer (dʒi'ɔgrəfəʳ) *s.* geógrafo.

geranium (dʒi'reinjəm) *s.* BOT. geranio.

germ (dʒəːm) *s.* germen. 2 BOT. yema. 3 microbio.

germinate (to) ('dʒəːmineit) *i.* germinar. 2 *t.* hacer germinar.

gesture ('dʒestʃəʳ) *s.* ademán.

get (to) (get) *t.* obtener, conseguir. 2 hallar. 3 coger, atrapar. 4 vencer. 5 mandar; hacer que. 6 poner [en un estado, etc.]: *to ~ ready*, preparar(se. 7 procurar, proporcionar. 8 comprender. 9 *to ~ down*, descolgar;

tragar. *10 to* ~ *into,* meterse en. *11 to* ~ *the better of,* llevar ventaja a. *12 i.* ganar dinero. *13* estar, hallarse. *14* ir, llegar, meterse, introducirse, pasar. *15* hacerse, volverse, ponerse *16 to* ~ *back,* volver. *17 to* ~ *down,* bajar, descender. *18 to* ~ *up,* levantarse. ‖ Pret. y p. p.: *got* (gɔt).

ghastly ('gɑːstil) *a.* horrible. *2* fantasmal.

ghost (goust) *s.* espíritu, alma. *2* espectro, fantasma.

giant ('dʒaiənt) *a.-s.* gigante.

giddy ('gidi) *a.* vertiginoso. *2* mareado, que sufre vértigo.

gift (gift) *s.* donación. *2* donativo, regalo. *3* dote, prenda.

gifted (giftid) *a.* dotado.

giggle ('gigl) *s.* risita nerviosa.

giggle (to) ('gigl) *i.* reír nerviosa y tontamente.

gild (to) (gild) *t.* dorar.

gill (gil) *s.* agalla [de pez].

gingerly ('dʒindʒəli) *adv.* cautelosamente.

gipsy ('dʒipsi) *s.* GYPSY.

gird (to) (gəːd) *t.* ceñir, cercar. ‖ Pret. y p. p.: *girded* (gəːdid) o *girt* (gəːt).

girl (gəːl) *f.* niña, muchacha, joven. *2* doncella, criada.

give (to) (giv) *t.* dar; donar; regalar; entregar. *2* empeñar [one's word]. *3* ofrecer, presentar. *4 to* ~ *back,* devolver; *to* ~ *up,* renunciar a; entregar. *5 i.* dar de sí, ceder. *6* [ventana] dar a. *7 to* ~ *out,* agotarse, ceder. ‖ Pret.: *gave* (geiv); p. p.: *given* ('givn).

glad (glæd) *a.* alegre, contento.

gladness ('glædnis) *s.* alegría.

glamo(u)r ('glæməʳ) *s.* encanto, hechizo.

glance (glɑːns) *s.* mirada, vistazo. *2* vislumbre.

glance (to) (glɑːns) *i.-t.* dar una mirada; echar una ojeada.

gland (glænd) *s.* glándula.

glare (glɛəʳ) *s.* fulgor, resplandor. *2* mirada feroz.

glare (to) (glɛəʳ) *i.* brillar, deslumbrar.

glass (glɑːs) *s.* vidrio, cristal. *2* vaso, copa. *3* cristalería [de mesa]. *4* espejo. *5* ÓPT. lente; anteojo.

glaze (to) (gleiz) *t.* vidriar, barnizar. *2* velar [los ojos]. *3* poner cristales a.

gleam (gliːm) *s.* destello.

gleam (to) (gliːm) *i.* destellar, brillar, centellear.

glean (to) (gliːn) *t.* espigar.

glee (gliː) *s.* alegría, gozo.

glen (glen) *s.* cañada.

glide (to) (glaid) *s.* deslizamiento.

glimmer ('gliməʳ) *s.* vislumbre, resplandor, luz débil.

glimmer (to) ('gliməʳ) *i.* brillar; rielar; vislumbrarse.

glimpse (glimps) *s.* resplandor fugaz; visión rápida.

glimpse (to) (glimps) *i.* echar una ojeada. *2* brillar con luz trémula. *3 t.* vislumbrar.

glisten (to) ('glisn) *i.* brillar.

glitter ('glitəʳ) *s.* resplandor.

glitter (to) ('glitəʳ) *i.* brillar.

globe (gloub) *s.* globo, bola.

gloom (gluːm) *s.* oscuridad.

gloomy ('gluːmi) *a.* oscuro, lóbrego. *2* sombrío, triste.

glorify (to) ('glɔ:rifai) *t.* glorificar. 2 ensalzar.

glorious ('blɔ:riəs) *a.* glorioso. 2 espléndido.

gloss (glɔs) *s.* lustre, brillo.

glossy ('glɔsi) *a.* brillante.

glove (glʌv) *s.* guante.

glow (glou) *s.* luz, resplandor. 2 viveza de color.

glow (to) (glou) *i.* dar luz o calor vivos; arder; brillar.

glue (to) (glu:) *t.* encolar, pegar.

gluey ('glu:i) *a.* pegajoso.

gnarl (nɑ:l) *s.* nudo [en madera].

gnash (to) (næʃ) *i.* hacer rechinar los dientes.

gnat (næt) *s.* ENT. mosquito.

gnaw (to) (nɔ:) *t.* roer.

go (gou) *s.* ida. 2 marcha, curso. 3 empuje. 4 tentativa. 5 moda: *it is all the ~*, hace furor.

go (to) (gou) *i.* ir. 2 irse, marchar, partir. 3 andar, funcionar. 4 [el traje] caer bien. 5 morir; decaer. 6 tener éxito. 7 resultar. 8 *to ~ after*, seguir; *to ~ ahead*, avanzar; *to ~ along*, continuar; *to ~ away*, irse; *to ~ back*, volver; *to ~ in, o into*, entrar; *to ~ on*, cóntinuar; *to ~ out*, salir; divulgarse; *to ~ through*, atravesar; sufrir; *to ~ up*, subir; *to ~ wrong*, salir mal; *to let ~*, dejar ir; soltar. 9 *t.* seguir: *to ~ one's way*, seguir su camino. 10 soportar. ¶ Pres. 3.ª pers.: *goes* (gouz); pret.: *went* (went); p. p.: *gone* (gɔn).

goad (to) (goud) *s.* pincho, aguijón.

goad (to) (goud) *t.* aguijar, aguijonear, picar.

goal (goul) *s.* DEP. meta, portería; gol. 2 fin, objeto.

goat (gout) *s.* cabra; cabrón.

gobble (to) ('gɔbl) *t.* engullir.

God (gɔd) *n. pr.* Dios. 2 *m.* dios.

goddess ('gɔdis) *s.* diosa, diva.

godly ('gɔdli) *a.* piadoso, devoto.

gold (gould) *s.* oro.

golden ('gouldən) *a.* de oro, áureo, dorado.

goldsmith ('gouldsmiθ) *s.* orfebre.

golf (fɔlf) *s.* DEP. golf.

gone (gɔn) *p. p.* de TO GO.

good (gud) *a.* bueno. 2 valiente. 3 solvente. 4 *interj.* ¡bien! 5 *'s.* bien; provecho: *what is the ~ of it?*, ¿para qué sirve?, *for ~*, para siempre.

good-by, good-bye ('gud'bai)*s.* adiós; *to say ~ to*, despedirse de. 2 *interj.* ¡adiós!

goodness ('gudnis) *s.* bondad. 2 virtud.

goods (gudz) *s. pl.* géneros, mercancías.

goose (gu:s) *s. pl.* **geese** (gi:s)*s.* ORN. ganso, oca.

gore (gɔ:ʳ) *s.* sangre.

gorge (gɔ:dʒ) *s.* garganta.

gorgeous ('gɔ:dʒəs) *a.* brillante, suntuoso.

gospel ('gɔspəl) *s.* evangelio.

gossip ('gɔsip) *s.* chismografía, comadreo. 2 habladuría. 3 chismoso.

gossip (to) ('gɔsip) *i.* chismear, murmurar, charlar.

got (gɔt) V. TO GET.

govern (to) ('gʌvən) *t.* gobernar, regir. 2 GRAM. regir.

governess ('gʌvənis) s. aya; institutriz.

government ('gʌvnmənt, -'gʌvə-) s. gobierno, dirección; mando, autoridad. 2 gobierno [ministerio].

governor ('gʌvənəʳ) s. gobernador. 2 director.

gown (gaun) s. vestido de mujer. 2 bata; túnica; toga.

grab (to) (græb) t. agarrar.

grace (greis) s. gracia [física; espiritual]. 2 amabilidad.

grace (to) (greis) t. adornar.

gracious ('geiʃəs) a. gracioso, atractivo. 2 afable, cortés.

grade (greid) s. grado. 2 clase, calidad.

grade (to) (greid) s. grado. 2 clase, calidad.

grade (to) (greid) t. graduar. 2 matizar [un color, etc.].

graduate ('grædjuit) a. graduado [en universidad].

graduate (to) ('grædjueit) t.-i. graduar(se.

grain (grein) s. grano [de trigo, uva, etc.]. 2 cereales. 3 átomo, pizca. 4 fibra.

grammar ('græməʳ) s. gramática: ~-school, instituto de segunda enseñanza; (E. U.)escuela primaria.

grand (grænd) a. grande, gran. 2 grandioso, espléndido.

grandfather ('grænd'fɑ:ðəʳ) s. abuelo.

grandmother ('græn'mʌðəʳ)s. abuela.

grandson ('grænsʌn) s. nieto.

granny, -nie ('græni) s. abuela.

grant (grɑ:nt) s. concesión. 2 don, subvención.

grant (to) (grɑ:nt) t. conceder, otorgar, dar.

grape (greip) s. BOT. uva.

grasp (grɑ:sp) s. asimiento. 2 apretón de manos. 3 dominio, poder. 4 comprensión.

grasp (to) (grɑ:sp) t. asir, empuñar. 2 abrazar, abarcar. 3 comprender, entender.

grass (grɑ:s) s. hierba, césped, pasto.

grate (greit) s. reja, verja.

grate (to) (greit) t. rallar. 2 raspar. 3 molestar.

grateful ('greitful) a. agradecido. 2 grato, agradable.

gratify (to) ('grætifai) t. satisfacer, contentar. 2 gratificar.

grave (greiv) a. grave [importante]; serio, digno]. 2 GRAM. (grɑ:v) grave. 3 s. ('greiv) tumba, sepulcro.

gravel ('grævəl) s. arena gruesa, guijo.

gravity ('græviti) s. gravedad.

gravy ('greivi) s. COC. salsa, jugo.

graze (greiz) s. roce. 2 pasto.

graze (to) (greiz) t. rozar; arañar; raspar. 2 i. pacer.

grease (gri:s) s. grasa. 2 sebo.

great (greit) a. grande, gran.

greatness ('greitnis) s. grandeza. 2 amplitud.

green (gri:n) a. verde. 2 pl. verduras.

greengrocer ('gri:n,grousəʳ)s. verdulero.

greenhouse ('gri:nhaus) s. invernáculo.

greet (to) (gri:t) t. saludar.

greeting ('gri:tiŋ) s. saludo.

grew (gru:) pret. DE TO GROW.

grey (grei) a. gris, pardo.

greyhound ('greihaund) s. galgo.

grief (gri:f) s. dolor, pena.
grieve (to) (gri:v) t. afligir. 2 i. afligirse, dolerse.
grim (grim) a. torvo, ceñudo. 2 feo. 3 horrible.
grime (graim) s. tizne, mugre.
grime (to) (graim) t. ensuciar.
grimy ('graimi) a. sucio.
grin (grin) s. mueca de dolor o cólera. 2 sonrisa.
grin (to) (grin) i. hacer muecas. 2 sonreírse.
grind (to) (graind) t. moler. 2 afilar. 3 i. pulirse. ¶ Pret. y p. p.: *ground* (graund).
grip (grip) s. agarro, presa. 2 poder. 3 puño, mango. 4 maletín.
groan (to) (groun) t. gemir.
grocer ('grousəʳ) s. tendero [de comestibles], abacero.
grocery ('grousəri) s. tienda de comestibles. 2 pl. comestibles.
groom (grum) s. mozo de cuadra. 2 lacayo. 3 novio.
groom (to) (grum) t. cuidar [caballos].
groove (gru:v) s. ranura, surco.
groove (to) (gru:v) t. acanalar.
grope (to) (group) t.-i. tentar; andar a tientas.
gross (grous) a. grueso. 2 denso. 3 grosero, tosco.
ground (graund) s. tierra, suelo, piso. 2 terreno. 3 heces, sedimento. 4 pret. y p. p. de TO GRIND.
ground (to) (graund) t. fundamentar, apoyar.
group (gru:p) s. grupo, conjunto.
group (to) (gru:p) t.-i. agrupar(se).
grove (grouv) s. bosquecillo.

grow (to) (grou) i. crecer, desarrollarse. 2 nacer, salir [el pelo, etc.]. 3 ponerse, volverse: *to ~ old,* envejecer. 4 cultivar, criar. ¶ Pret.: *grew* (gru:); p. p.: *grown* (groun).
grudge (grʌdʒ) s. resentimiento, rencor, inquina.
grudge (to) (grʌdʒ) t. regatear, escatimar. 2 envidiar.
gruesome ('gru:səm) a. horrible, 2 repugnante.
grumble ('grʌmbl) s. refunfuño, queja. 2 ruido sordo.
grumble (to) ('grʌmbl) i. refunfuñar. 2 producir ruido sordo.
grunt (grʌnt) s. gruñido.
grunt (to) (grʌnt) i. gruñir.
guarantee (,gærən'ti:) s. garantía, fianza. 2 fiador.
guarantee (to) (,gærən'ti:) t. garantizar, salir fiador.
guard (gɑ:d) s. guardia. 2 vigilancia, protección.
guess (to) (ges) t. conjeturar.
guest (gest) s. huésped, invitado. 2 pensionista.
guidance ('gaidəns) s. guía, gobierno, dirección.
guide (gaid) s. guía [persona, libro].
guide (to) (gaid) t. guiar.
guild (gild) s. gremio, cofradía.
guile (gail) s. astucia, dolo.
guilt (gilt) s. culpa, delito.
guilty ('gilti) a. culpable, reo.
guise (gaiz) s. guisa, modo.
guitar (gi'tɑ:ʳ) s. MÚS. guitarra.
gulf (gʌlf) s. GEOGR. golfo 2 sima, abismo.
gull (gʌl) s. ORN. gaviota.

gull(to) (gʌl) *t.* estafar, engañar.
gullet ('gʌlit) *s.* gaznate.
gulp (gʌlp) *s.* trago, engullida.
gum (gʌm) *s.* encía. *2* goma: *chewing* ~, chiclé.
gum (to) (gʌm) *t.* engomar.
gun (gʌn) *s.* ARTILL. cañón, fusil, escopeta. *3* (E. U.)pistola revólver.
gunner ('gʌnəʳ) *s.* artillero.

gunpowder ('gʌn,paudəʳ) *s.* pólvora.
gush (gʌʃ) *s.* chorro, borbotón. *2* efusión, extremo.
gush (to) (gʌʃ) *i.* brotar, manar a borbotones. *2* ser efusivo.
gust (gʌst) *s.* ráfaga, racha.
gutter ('gʌtəʳ) *s.* arroyo [de la calle]. *2* canal, canalón.
gypsy ('dʒipsi) *a.-s.* gitano.

H

hack (hæk) *s.* caballo de alquiler; rocín. 2 tajo.

hack (to) (hæk) *t.* tajar, cortar.

haggard ('hægəd) *a.* macilento, ojeroso; fatigado.

hail (heil) *s.* granizo, pedrisco. 2 saludo, llamada. 3 *interj.* ¡ave!, ¡salud!

hail (to) (heil) *i.-t.* granizar, pedriscar. 2 saludar, llamar.

hair (hɛə^r) *s.* cabello, pelo.

hairdresser ('hɛə‚dresə^r) *s.* peluquero, -ra. 2 peluquería.

half (hɑ:f), *pl.* **halves** (hɑ:vs)*s.* mitad. 2 *a.-adv.* medio; semi, casi.

hallow (to) ('hælou) *t.* santificar; reverenciar.

halt (hɔ:lt) *s.* alto, parada. 2 cojera. 3 *a.* cojo.

halt (to) (hɔ:lt) *i.* detenerse, hacer alto. 2 cojear. 3 vacilar; tartamudear. 4 *t.* parar.

halter ('hɔ:ltə^r) *s.* cabestro.

ham (hæm) *s.* pernil, jamón.

hammer ('hæmə) *s.* martillo.

hammer (to) ('hæmə^r) *t.* martillar, golpear.

hammock ('hæmək) *s.* hamaca.

hamper ('hæmpə^r) *s.* cesta, canasta. 2 traba, estorbo.

hamper (to) ('hæmpə^r) *t.* estorbar, embarazar.

hand (hænd) *s.* mano. 2 operario; mano de obra. 3 manecilla [del reloj]. 4 letra. ~ *book*, manual; ~-*made*, hecho a mano; ~-*maid*, doncella; ~-*shake*, apretón de manos; *hands up!*, ¡manos arriba!; *in the one* ~ ... *in the other* ~, por una parte ... por otra.

hand (to) (hænd) *t.* dar; entregar, pasar. 2 conducir, guiar.

handicap ('hændikæp) *s.* obstáculo, desventaja.

handicap (to) ('hændikæp) *t.* DEP. poner obstáculos.

handicraft ('hændikrɑ:ft) *s.* oficio mecánico. 2 ocupación o habilidad manual.

handkerchief ('hæŋkətʃif) *s.* pañuelo.

handle ('hændl) *s.* asa, asidero; astil, mango; puño.

handle (to) ('hændl) *t.* tocar, manosear. 2 manejar, tratar. 3 dirigir.

handsome ('hænsəm) *a.* hermoso. 2 guapo. 3 liberal.

hang (hæŋ) *s.* caída [de un vestido, etc.]. 2 sentido, intención.

hang (to) (hæŋ) *t.* colgar, suspender. 2 ahorcar. 3 *i.* colgar, pender. 4 ser ahorcado. 5 depender, descansar. ¶ Pret. y p. p.: *hung* (hʌŋ).

happen (to) ('hæpən) *i.* acontecer, ocurrir. 2 acertar a [ser, estar, etc.]. 3 *to ~ on,* encontrar, dar con.

happening ('hæpəniŋ) *s.* acontecimiento, suceso.

happiness ('hæpinis) *s.* felicidad.

happy ('hæpi) *a.* feliz. 2 contento, alegre.

harass (to) ('hærəs) *t.* atormentar. 2 acosar, hostigar.

harbour (to) ('ha:bəʳ) *t.* resguardar, amparar. 2 acoger. 3 *i.* refugiarse.

hard (ha:d) *a.* duro [en todas sus acepciones]. 2 *adv.* duramente, recio, de firme. 3 difícilmente. 4 *s.* suelo o piso duro.

hardness ('ha:dnis) *s.* dureza. 2 solidez. 3 penalidad.

hardship ('ha:dʃip) *s.* penalidad, privación. 2 injusticia.

hardware ('ha:d-wɛəʳ) *s.* quincalla, ferretería.

hardy ('ha:di) *a.* fuerte, robusto, resistente. 2 valiente.

hare (hɛəʳ) *s.* liebre.

harehound ('hɛə'haund) *s.* lebrel.

harm (ha:m) *s.* mal, daño.

harm (to) (ha:m) *t.* dañar, perjudicar.

harmful ('ha:mful) *a.* dañoso, nocivo, perjudicial.

harmless ('ha:mlis) *a.* inofensivo.

harmonious (ha:'mounjəs) *a.* armonioso.

harness ('ha:nis) *s.* arneses.

harness (to) ('ha:nis) *t.* enjaezar.

harp (ha:p) *s.* MÚS. arpa.

harp (to) (ha:p) *i.* tocar el arpa. 2 *to ~ on,* repetir.

harrow ('hærou) *s.* AGR. grada. 2 instrumento de tortura.

harrow (to) ('hærou) *t.* AGR. gradar. 2 desgarrar, atormentar.

harsh (ha:ʃ) *a.* áspero. 2 discordante. 3 duro, cruel.

hart (ha:t) *s.* ciervo, venado.

harvest ('ha:vist) *s.* cosecha.

harvest (to) ('ha:vist) *t.-i.* cosechar; segar.

has (hæz, həz) *3.ª pers. pres. ind.* de TO HAVE.

haste (heist) *s.* prisa; presteza; precipitación.

haste (to) (heist) *i.* TO HASTEN.

hasten (to) (heisn) *t.* apresurar. 2 *i.* darse prisa.

hat (hæt) *s.* sombrero.

hatchet ('hætʃit) *s.* hacha.

hate (heit) *s.* odio, aversión.

hate (to) (heit) *t.* odiar, aborrecer, detestar.

hateful ('heitful) *a.* odioso.

hatred ('heitrid) *s.* odio.

haughty ('hɔ:ti) *a.* altivo, orgulloso.

haunt (hɔ:nt) *s.* guarida. 2 morada.

haunt (to) (hɔ:nt) *t.* rondar, frecuentar.

have (to) (hæv o həv) *aux.* haber. *2 I had rather*, más quisiera; *we had rather*, vale más que. *3 t.* haber, tener, poseer. *4* tener [cuidado, dolor, un niño, etc.]. *5* saber: *he has no latin*, no sabe latín. *6* tomar, comer, beber. *7* permitir, consentir. *8* mandar hacer; hacer que. *9 to ~ a mind to*, estar tentado de. *10 to ~ to*, tener que, haber de. ¶ *3.ª* pers. pres ind.: *has* (hæz, həz); pret. y p. p.: *had* (hæd, həd).

haven ('heivn) *s.* puerto, abra. *2* asilo, abrigo.

havoc ('hævək) *s.* estrago, destrucción.

hay (hei) *s.* heno, forraje.

hazard ('hæzəd) *s.* azar, acaso. *2* albur, riesgo.

hazard (to) ('hæzəd) *t.* arriesgar. *2 i.* arriesgarse.

haze (heiz) *s.* niebla, calina.

hazy ('heizi) *a.* brumoso.

he (hi:, hi) *pron. pers.* él. *2 pron. indef.* el, aquel: *~ who*, el o aquel que, quien. *3 a.* macho, varón: *~-bear*, oso [macho].

head (hed) *s.* cabeza. *2* cabecera. *3* cima. *4* puño [de bastón]. *5* título, encabezamiento. *6* espuma [de un líquido]. *8* MAR. proa. *9* jefe, principal.

head (to) (hed) *t.* encabezar. *2 i.* ir, dirigirse.

headache ('hedeik) *s.* dolor de cabeza.

headland ('hedlənd) *s.* GEOGR. cabo.

headline ('hedlain) *s.* titulares [de periódico]. *2* título.

headmaster ('hed'mɑ:ster),

headmistress (-'mistris) *s.* director, -ra [de un colegio].

headquarters ('hed'kwɔ:təz)*s.* MIL. cuartel general. *2* jefatura de policía. *3* sede.

heal (to) (hi:l) *t.-i.* curar(se, sanar(se. *2 t.* remediar.

health (helθ) *s.* salud, sanidad.

healthful ('helθful) *a.* sano, saludable.

heap (hi:p) *s.* montón, pila.

heap (to) (hi:p) *t.* amontonar.

hear (to) (hiəʳ) *t.-i.* oír. *2* escuchar: *~ of*, oír hablar de. ¶ Pret. y p. p.: *heard* (hə:d).

heart (hɑ:t) *s.* corazón: *to take to ~*, tomar en serio, a pecho; *by ~*, de memoria.

heartache ('hɑ:t-eik) *s.* aflicción.

hearty ('hɑ:ti) *a.* cordial, sincero. *2* vigoroso. *3* robusto.

heat (hi:t) *s.* calor. *2* acaloramiento. *3* ardor, fogosidad.

heat (to) (hi:t) *t.* calentar. *2* acalorar, excitar.

heating ('hi:tiŋ) *s.* calefacción.

heave (hi:v) *s.* esfuerzo para levantar o levantarse. *2* movimiento de lo que se levanta. *3* jadeo.

heave (to) (hi:v) *t.* levantar, solevar; mover con esfuerzo. *2* exhalar [un suspiro, etc.]. *3* hinchar [el pecho]. *4 i.* levantarse y bajar alternativamente; jadear. ¶ Pret. y p. p.: *heaved* (hi:vd) o *hove* (houv).

heaven ('hevn) *s.* cielo.

heavily ('hevili) *adv.* pesadamente. *2* fuertemente.

heavy ('hevi) *a.* pesado. *2 adv.* pesadamente.

hedge (hedʒ) *s.* seto vivo; cerca, vallado.

hedge (to) (hedʒ) *t.* cercar, vallar; rodear.

heed (hi:d) *s.* atención; caso.

heed (to) (hi:d) *t.* prestar atención a, hacer caso de.

heel (hi:l) *s.* talón; tacón.

height (hait) *s.* altura, altitud. 2 estatura, alzada. 3 cerro.

heighten (to) ('haitn) *t.* levantar. 2 *i.* elevarse.

heir (eəʳ) *s.* heredero.

held (held) V. TO HOLD.

he'll (hi:l) contract. de HE SHALL y de HE WILL.

hell (hel) *s.* infierno.

hello ('he'lou) *interj.* ¡hola! 2 ¡diga! [en el teléfono].

helm (helm) *s.* timón.

helmet ('helmit) *s.* yelmo, casco.

help (help) *s.* ayuda, auxilio. 2 remedio, recurso.

help (to) (help) *t.* ayudar, contribuir a. 2 remediar.

helpful ('helpful) *a.* que ayuda, útil. 2 saludable.

helpless ('helplis) *a.* desvalido. 2 impotente.

hem (hem) *s.* COST. dobladillo, bastilla. 2 borde, orla.

hem (to) (hem) *t.* COST. dobladillar. 2 cercar, rodear.

hen (hen) *f.* ORN. gallina.

hence (hens) *adv.* desde aquí o ahora. 2 de aquí a, dentro de. 3 por tanto, luego.

her (həːʳ, əːʳ, həʳ, əʳ) *pron. f.* (ac. o dat.) la, le. 2 [con prep.] ella. 3 *a. pos. f.* su, sus [de ella].

herald ('herəld) *s.* heraldo.

herald (to) ('herəld) *t.* anunciar.

herb (həːb) *s.* hierba.

herd (həːd) *s.* rebaño.

herd (to) (həːd) *t.-i.* juntar o juntarse en rebaño.

here (hiəʳ) *adv.* aquí, ahí, acá: ~ *it is,* helo aquí.

hereabouts ('hiərə͵bauts)*adv.* por aquí cerca.

hereafter (hiərˈɑːftəʳ) *adv.* en lo futuro.

heritage ('heritidʒ) *s.* herencia.

hermit ('həːmit) *s.* ermitaño.

hero ('hiərou) *s.* héroe.

herring ('heriŋ) *s.* ICT. arenque.

hers (həːz) *s. pron. f.* [el] suyo, [la]suya; [los] suyos, [las] suyas [de ella].

herself (həːˈself) *pron. pers. f.* ella misma, se, sí misma.

he's (hi:z) contrac. de HE IS y de HE HAS.

hesitate (to) ('heziteit) *i.* vacilar, dudar. 2 tartamudear.

hew (to) (hju:) *t.* cortar, picar; labrar. ¶ Pret.: *hewed* (hju:d); p. p.: *hewn* (hju:n).

hidden ('hidn) *a.* escondido. 2 oculto, secreto, latente. 3 *p. p.* de TO HIDE.

hide (haid) *s.* piel, cuero.

hide (to) (haid)) *t.* esconder, ocultar. 2 *i.* esconderse, ocultarse. ¶ Pret.: *hid* (hid); p. p.: *hidden* ('hidn) o *hid.*

hideous ('hidiəs) *a.* horrible. 2 odioso.

high (hai) *a.* alto. | Hablando de una pers. se dice *tall.* 2 subido, caro [precio]. 3 mayor [calle, altar, misa]. 4 ~ *spirits,* buen humor, animación. 5 *adv.* caro. 6 *s.* lo alto.

highland ('hailənd) *s.* montaña, región montañosa.

highway ('haiwei) *s.* carretera.

hiker ('haikəʳ) *s.* excursionista.

hill (hil) *s.* colina, collado.

hilt (hilt) *s.* puño, empuñadura.

him (him, im) *pron. m.* [ac. o dat.] lo, le. 2 [con prep.] él: *to* ~, a él.

himself (him'self) *pron, pers. m.* él, él mismo, se, sí, sí mismo.

hind (haind) *a.* trasero, posterior. 2 *s.* cierva.

hinder (to) ('haində^r) *t.-i.* impedir, estorbar.

hinge (hindʒ) *s.* gozne, bisagra.

hinge (to) (hindʒ) *t.* engoznar.

hint (hint) *s.* indicación, insinuación, indirecta, alusión.

hint (to) (hint) *t.-i.* indicar, insinuar, sugerir, aludir.

hip (hip) *s.* cadera.

hire ('haiə^r) *s.* alquiler.

hire (to) ('haiə^r) *t.* alquilar, arrendar. 2 *i.* alquilarse.

his (hiz, iz) *a.-pron. m.* [el] suyo, [la] suya; [los] suyos, [las] suyas [de él].

historic(al (his'tərik, -əl) *a.* histórico.

hit (hit) *s.* golpe. 2 éxito.

hit (to) (hit) *t.* pegar, golpear, herir, dar con. ¶ Pret. y p. p.: *hit* (hit).

hitch (hitʃ) *s.* tropiezo.

hitch (to) (hitʃ) *t.* mover [a tirones]. 2 enganchar, atar.

hither ('hiðə^r) *adv.* acá, hacia acá. 2 *a.* de este lado.

hitherto ('hiðə'tu:) *adv.* hasta aquí, hasta ahora.

hoard (hɔ:d) *s.* depósito.

hoard (to) (hɔ:d) *t.* acumular, guardar, atesorar.

hoarse (hɔ:s) *a.* ronco, áspero.

hoary ('hɔ:ri) *a.* cano, canoso.

hobble ('hɔbl) *s.* cojera.

hobble (to) ('hɔbl) *i.* cojear. 2 *t.* poner trabas, trabar.

hobby ('hɔbi) *s.* afición.

hog (hɔg) *s.* cerdo, cochino.

hold (hould) *s.* presa, agarro. 2 asidero, sostén. 3 fortaleza, refugio. 4 receptáculo. 5 MAR. bodega. 6 AVIA. cabina de carga. 7 dominio.

hold (to) (hould) *t.* tener, poseer. 2 sujetar, tener asido. 3 aguantar, sostener. 5 sostener, defender. 6 detener. 7 ocupar, absorber. 8 tener cabida para. 9 celebrar [una reunión]; sostener [una conversación]. 10 hacer [compañía]. 11 considerar, tener por. 12 *i.* agarrarse, asirse. 13 mantenerse, sostenerse. 14 valer, estar o seguir en vigor. 15 durar, continuar. ¶ Pret. y p. p.: *held* (held).

holder ('houldə^r) *s.* tenedor, poseedor. 2 mango, agarrador, boquilla. 3 FOT. chasis.

hole (houl) *s.* agujero, boquete. 2 hoyo, hueco.

hole (to) (houl) *t.* agujerear, horadar.

holiday ('hɔlədi, -lid-, -dei) *s.* fiesta, festividad. 2 *pl.* vacaciones. 4 *a.* festivo.

hollow ('hɔlou) *a.* hueco. 2 hundido [ojos, mejillas]. 3 falso, insincero. 4 *s.* hueco.

holy ('houli) *a.* santo; sagrado.

homage ('hɔmidʒ) *s.* homenaje.

home (houm) *s.* hogar, casa, morada. 2 asilo, hospicio. 3 patria, país natal. 4 *a.*

doméstico, hogareño. 5 *adv.* en o a cassa.

homeless ('houmlis) *a.* sin casa.

homely ('houmli) *a.* llano, sencillo, casero. 2 feo, vulgar. 3 rústico, inculto.

homicide ('homisaid) *s.* homicidio. 2 homicida.

honest ('onist) *a.* honrado, probo. 2 justo, recto.

honesty ('onisti) *s.* honradez.

honey ('hʌni) *s.* miel.

hood (hud) *s.* capucha, caperuza, capirote. 2 capota.

hoof (hu:f) *s.* casco, pezuña.

hook (huk) *s.* gancho, garfio.

hook (to) (huk) *t.* encorvar.

hoop (hu:p) *s.* aro, cerco, fleje. 2 anillo, anilla.

hoot (hu:t) *s.* grito; grita. 2 pitido [de locomotora]; bocinazo.

hoot (to) (hu:t) *i.-t.* gritar, dar gritos. 2 *i.* dar pitidos o bocinazos.

hooter ('hu:təʳ) *s.* sirena; bocina.

hop (hɔp) *s.* salto, brinco.

hop (to) (hɔp) *i.* brincar, saltar.

hope (houp) *s.* esperanza.

hope (to) (houp) *t.-i.* esperar [tener esperanza], confiar.

hopeful ('houpful) *a.* esperanzado. 2 risueño, prometedor.

hopeless ('houplis) *a.* desesperado, irremediable.

horizon (hə'raizn) *s.* horizonte.

horn (hɔ:n) *s.* asta, cuerno. 2 bocina.

horrid ('hɔrid) *a.* horroroso.

horse (hɔ:s) *s.* ZOOL. caballo.

horseman ('hɔ:smən) *s.* jinete.

hose (houz) *s.* calza(s, media(s. 2 manga, manguera.

hospitable ('hɔspitəbl) *a.* hospitalario, acogedor.

hospital ('hɔspitl) *s.* hospital.

host (houst) *s.* hospedero, mesonero. 2 huésped, anfitrión.

hostage ('hɔstidʒ) *s.* rehén.

hostess ('houstis) *s.* mesonera. 2 anfitriona. 3 AVIA. azafata.

hot (hɔt) *a.* caliente; ~ *dog,* salchicha caliente. 2 acalorado, ardoroso.

hound (haund) *s.* perro de caza.

hour ('auəʳ) *s.* hora.

house (haus, *pl.* 'hauziz) *s.* casa [habitación, hogar; edificio; familia, linaje].

household ('haushould) *s.* casa, familia [los que viven juntos]. 2 *a.* doméstico.

housekeeper ('haus,ki:pəʳ) *s.* ama de llaves o de gobierno.

housewife ('haus-waif) *s.* ama de casa.

hove (houv) V. TO HEAVE.

how (hau) adv. cómo, de qué manera; por qué: ~ *do you do?,* ¿cómo está usted? 2 qué, cuán [admirativos].

however (hau'evəʳ) *adv.* como quiera que, por muy ... que, por mucho que. 2 *conj.* sin embargo, no obstante.

howl (haul) *s.* aullido. 2 grito.

howl (to) (haul) *i.* aullar; gritar.

huddle ('hʌdl) *s.* montón, tropel, confusión.

huddle (to) ('hʌdl) *t.-i.* amontonar(se; apiñar(se.

hue (hju:) *s.* color, matiz.

hug (hʌg) *s.* abrazo estrecho.
hug (to) (hʌg) *t.* abrazar.
huge (hju:dʒ) *a.* enorme.
hulk (hʌlk) *s.* buque viejo.
hull (hʌl) *s.* cáscara, corteza.
hull (to) (hʌl) *t.* mondar.
hum (hʌm) *s.* zumbido.
hum (to) (hʌm) *i.* zumbar.
humble (ˈhʌmbl) *a.* humilde.
humble (to) (ˈhʌmbl) *t.-ref.* humillar(se.
humiliate (to) (hju(:)ˈmilieit) *t.* humillar.
humility (hju(:)ˈmiliti) *s.* humildad, sumisión.
humour (ˈhju:məʳ) *s.* humorismo. 2 humor, genio.
humour (to) (ˈhju:məʳ) *t.* complacer. 2 adaptarse.
humo(u)rous (ˈhju:mərəs) *a.* humorístico, gracioso.
hump (hʌmp) *s.* jiba, joroba.
hunch (hʌntʃ) *s.* joroba, jiba.
hunch (to) (hʌntʃ) *t.-i.* encorvar [la espalda].
hundred (ˈhʌndrəd) *a.* cien, ciento. 2 *s.* ciento, centena.
hung (hʌŋ) V. TO HANG.
hunger (ˈhʌŋgəʳ) *s.* hambre.
hunger (to) (ˈhʌŋgəʳ) *i.* tener hambre: *to ~ for,* ansiar.
hungry (ˈhʌŋgri) *a.* hambriento.
hunk (hʌŋk) *s.* fam. trozo.
hunt (hʌnt) *s.* caza [acción]; montería. 2 cacería.
hunt (to) (hʌnt) *t.-i.* cazar; perseguir.
hunter (ˈhʌntəʳ) *s.* cazador.
hurl (həːl) *s.* tiro, lanzamiento.
hurl (to) (həːl) *t.* lanzar, tirar, arrojar.
hurricane (ˈhʌrikən) *s.* huracán.
hurry (ˈhʌri) *s.* prisa, premura, precipitación.
hurry (to) (ˈhʌri) *t.* dar prisa, apresurar. 2 *i.* apresurarse, darse prisa.
hurt (həːt) *s.* herida, lesión. 2 daño, dolor. 3 *a.* herido.
hurt (to) (həːt) *t.* herir, lastimar. 2 apenar. 3 *i.* doler. ¶ Pret. y p. p.: *hurt* (həːt).
husband (ˈhʌzbənd) *s.* marido, esposo.
husband (to) (hʌzbənd) *t.* administrar, economizar.
husbandman (ˈhʌzbəndmən) *s.* agricultor.
husbandry (ˈhʌzbənri) *s.* agricultura, labranza. 2 economía.
hush (hʌʃ) *s.* quietud, silencio.
hush (to) (hʌʃ) *t.-i.* callar.
hustle (ˈhʌsl) *s.* actividad.
hustle (to) (ˈhʌsl) *t.* apresurar. 2 *i.* apresurarse, bullir.
hut (hʌt) *s.* choza, cabaña.
hydraulic (haiˈdrɔːlik) *a.* hidráulico.
hypocrisy (hiˈpɔkrəsi) *s.* hipocresía.
hypocrite (ˈhipəkrit) *s.* hipócrita.
hypothesis (haiˈpɔθisis) *s.* hipótesis.
hysterical (hisˈterikəl) *a.* histérico.

I

I (ai) *pron. pers.* yo.

ice (ais) *s.* hielo: ~ *cream,* helado de crema.

ice (to) (ais) *t.* helar, congelar.

icy ('aisi) *a.* helado, frío.

idea (ai'diǝ) *s.* idea.

identify (to) (ai'dentifai) *t.* identificar.

idiom ('idiǝm) *s.* idioma, lengua. 2 locución, idiotismo.

idiot ('idiǝt) *s.* idiota.

idle ('aidl) *a.* ocioso; inactivo.

if ((if)) *s. conj.* si. 2 aunque, aun cuando.

ignoble (ig'noubl) *a.* innoble.

ignorance ('ignǝrǝns) *s.* ignorancia.

I'll (ali) *contr.* de I SHALL y I WILL.

ill (il) *a.* enfermo. 2 *s.* mal, desgracia. 3 *adv.* mal.

illicit (i'lisit) *a.* ilícito.

illiterate (i'litǝrit) *a.* iletrado, analfabeto.

illness ('ilnis) *s.* enfermedad.

I'm (aim) *contr.* de I AM.

image ('imidʒ) *s.* imagen.

immigrant ('imigrǝnt) *a.-s.* inmigrante.

immigration (ˌimi'greiʃǝn) *s.* inmigración.

imminent ('iminǝnt) *a.* inminente.

immortal (i'mɔ:tl) *a.-s.* inmortal.

immovable (i'mu:vǝbl) *a.* inamovible, inmóvil, fijo.

immunize (to) ('imju(:)naiz)*t.* inmunizar.

impact ('impækt) *s.* golpe, choque, impacto.

impair (to) (im'pɛǝ^r) *t.* dañar.

impartial (im'pɑ:ʃǝl) *a.* imparcial.

impatient (im'peiʃǝnt) *a.* impaciente.

impede (to) (im'pi:d) *t.* impedir, estorbar.

impediment (im'pedimǝnt) *s.* impedimento, estorbo.

impel (to) (im'pel) *t.* impeler, impulsar. 2 mover, obligar.

impending (im'pendiŋ) *a.* inminente, amenazador.

imperious (im'piǝries) *a.* imperioso.

impious ('impiǝs) *a.* impío.

implement ('implimǝnt) *s.* instrumento. 2 *pl.* enseres.

implicate (to) ('implikeit) *t.* implicar. 2 entrelazar.

implore (to) (im'plɔ:ʳ) *t.* implorar.

imply (to) (im'plai) *t.* implicar.

import ('impɔ:t) *s.* importancia. 2 significado. 3 importación.

import (to) (im'pɔ:t) *t.-i.* importar. 2 *t.* significar.

importance (im'pɔ:təns) *s.* importancia. 2 cuantía.

impose (to) (im'pouz) *t.* imponer.

impoverish (to) (im'pɔvəriʃ) *t.* empobrecer.

impress ('impres) *s.* impresión, huella.

impress (to) (im'pres) *t.* imprimir, grabar. 2 inculcar.

impressive (im'presiv) *a.* impresionante, emocionante.

imprint ('imprint) *s.* impresión, huella.

imprint (to) (im'print) *t.* imprimir, estampar. 2 grabar.

imprison (to) (im'prizn) *t.* encarcelar.

improbable (im'prɔbəbl) *s.* improbable. 2 inverosímil.

improper (im'prɔpəʳ) *a.* impropio. 2 indecoroso.

improve (to) (im'pru:v) *t.* mejorar, desarrollar.

impute (to) (im'pju:t) *t.* imputar, atribuir, achocar.

in (in) *prep.* en, con, de, dentro de, durante, entre, por. 2 *adj.* interior, de dentro. 3 *adv.* dentro, adentro; en casa; en el poder.

inability (ˌinə'biliti) *s.* incapacidad, impotencia.

inaccessible (ˌinæk'sesəbl) *a.* ináccesible.

inadequate (in'ædikwit) *a.* inadecuado. 2 insuficiente.

incapable (in'keipəbl) *a.* incapaz.

incessant (in'sesnt) *a.* incesante. 2 **-ly** *adv.* sin cesar.

inch (intʃ) *s.* pulgada [2.54 cm].

income ('inkəm) *s.* ingresos.

incomprehensible (inˌkɔmpri'hensəbl) *a.* incomprensible.

inconceivable (ˌinkən'si:vəbl) *a.* inconcebible. 2 increíble.

inconsistent (ˌinkən'sistənt) *a.* incompatible, contradictorio. 2 inconsecuente.

inconvenience (to) (ˌinkən'vi:njəns) incomodar.

increase ('inkri:s) *s.* aumento. 2 ganancia.

increase (to) (in'kri:s) *t.* aumentar, acrecentar. 2 agrandar. 3 *i.* aumentarse, crecer.

incumbent (to) ('inkʌmbənt) *a.* obligatorio: *to be ~ on.* incumbir. 2 *s.* beneficiado.

incur (to) (in'kə:ʳ) *t.* incurrir en, atraerse. 2 contraer.

incurable (in'kjuərəbl) *a.* incurable.

indebted (in'detid) *a.* endeudado.

indeed (in'di:d) *adv.* realmente, de veras.

indefatigable (ˌindi'fætigəbl) *a.* infatigable.

indemnity (in'demniti) *s.* indemnidad. 2 indemnización.

indent (to) (in'dent) *t.* mellar, dentar.

independence (ˌindi'pendəns) *s.* independencia.

indescribable (ˌindis'kraibəbl) *a.* indescriptible.

index ('indeks) *s.* índice.
Indian ('indjən) *a.-s.* indio.
indict (to) (in'dait) *t.* acusar.
indignant (in'dignənt) *a.* indignado.
indite (to) (in'dait) *t.* redactar.
individual (‚indi'vidjuəl) *a.* individual. 2 *s.* individuo.
indomitable (in'dɔmitəbl) *a.* indomable.
indoors ('indɔːz) *adv.* dentro de casa; en local cerrado.
indorse (to), indorsee, etc., ENDORSE (TO), ENDORSEE, etc.
induce (to) (in'djuːs) *t.* inducir, instigar. 2 causar.
inducement (in'djuːsmənt) *s.* móvil, incentivo, aliciente.
indulge (to) (in'dʌldʒ) *t.* satisfacer [pasiones, etc.]. 2 complacer; consentir.
industrial (in'dʌstriəl) *a.* industrial.
industrious (in'dʌstriəs) *a.* industrioso, laborioso.
industry ('indəstri) *s.* industria. 2 diligencia, laboriosidad.
ineffectual (‚ini'fektjuəl) *a.* ineficaz. 2 inútil, vano.
inept (i'nept) *a.* inepto.
inequality (‚ini(ː)'kɔliti) *s.* desigualdad. 2 desproporción.
inexpensive (‚iniks'pensiv) *a.* barato, poco costoso.
inexperience (‚iniks'piəriəns) *s.* inexperiencia, impericia.
infamous ('infəməs) *a.* infame.
infantry ('infəntri) *s.* MIL. infantería.
infect (to) (in'fekt) *t.* infectar.
infer (to) (in'fəːʳ) *t.* inferir.
infest (to) (in'fest) *t.* infestar.

infirmity (in'fəːmiti) *s.* enfermedad. 2 flaqueza.
inflate (to) (in'fleit) *t.* inflar.
inflict (to) (in'flikt) *t.* infligir.
informant (in'fɔːmənt) *s.* informador.
infuriate (to) (in'fjuərieit) *t.* enfurecer.
ingenious (in'dʒiːnjəs) *a.* ingenioso, hábil, sutil.
inhabit (to) (in'hæbit) *t.* habitar, morar en.
inhabitant (in'hæbitant) *s.* habitante.
inhale (to) (in'heil) *t.* inhalar.
inherit (to) (in'herit) *t.* heredar.
inheritance (in'heritəns) *s.* herencia.
inject (to) (in'dʒekt) *t.* inyectar.
injunction (in'dʒʌŋkʃən) *s.* orden, mandato.
injure (to) ('indʒəːʳ) *t.* dañar, perjudicar. 2 herir, lastimar.
injury ('indʒəri) *s.* daño, perjuicio. 2 herida. 3 injuria.
ink (iŋk) *s.* tinta.
inkling ('iŋkliŋ) *s.* insinuación. 2 atisbo, vislumbre.
inland (in'lənd) *a.* de tierra adentro. 2 *adv.* (in'lænd) tierra adentro.
inlay (to) (in'lei) *t.* incrustar, embutir. 2 taracear. ¶ Pret. y p. p.: *inlaid* ('n'leid).
inlet ('inlet) *s.* abra, caleta; ría. 2 acceso, entrada.
inmate ('inmeit) *s.* recluido en, una casa, asilo, cárcel etc.; asilado, preso.
inn (in) *s.* posada, fonda.
inner ('inəʳ) *a.* interior, íntimo.
inordinate (i'nɔːdinit) *a.* inmoderado, excesivo.

inquest ('inkwest) *s.* información judicial.

inquire (to) (in'kwaiə^r) *t.* averiguar, investigar.

inquiry (in'kwaiəri) *s.* indagación, investigación; pregunta.

inroad ('inroud) *s.* incursión.

insane (in'sein) *a.* loco, demente.

insect ('insekt) *s.* ZOOL. insecto.

insert (to) (in'sə:t) *t.* insertar, introducir.

inside (in'said) *s.* interior. *2 adv.* dentro; adentro. *3 prep.* dentro de.

insight ('insait) *s.* perspicacia, penetración.

insist (to) (in'sist) *i.* insistir.

install (to) (ins'tɔ:l) *t.* instalar.

instance ('instəns) *s.* ejemplo, caso. *2* vez, ocasión. *3* instancia.

instant ('instənt) *s.* instante, momento. *2 a.* instante, insistente. *3* corriente, actual: *the 10th ~,* el diez del corriente.

instead (ins'ted) *adv.* en cambio, en lugar. *2 ~ of,* en lugar de, en vez de.

instinct ('instiŋkt) *s.* instinto.

insulate (to) ('insjuleit) *t.* aislar.

insurance (in'ʃuərəns) *s.* COM. seguro. *2* garantía.

insure (to) (in'ʃuə^r) *t.* COM. asegurar. *2* garantizar.

insurgent (in'sə:dʒənt) *a.-s.* insurgente, insurrecto.

insurmountable (,insə(:)'mauntəbl) *a.* insuperable.

insurrection (,insə'rekʃən) *s.* insurrección.

intemperate (in'tempərit) *a.* excesivo, extremado. *2* intemperante. *3* bebedor.

intend (to) (in'tend) *t.* proponerse. *2* querer decir.

intensify (to) (in'tensifai) *f.* intensificar. *2* FOT. reforzar.

intent (in'tent) *a.* fijo [pensamiento, mirada]. *2 s.* intento, intención.

inter (to) (in'tə:^{r}) *t.* enterrar, sepultar.

interchange ('intə'tʃeindʒ) *s.* intercambio. *2* comercio.

intercourse ('intəkɔ:s) *s.* trato, comunicación. *2* comercio.

interest ('intrist) *s.* interés. *2* participación.

interest (to) ('intrist, 'intərest) *t.* interesar.

interesting ('intristiŋ) *a.* interesante.

intervene (to) (,intə'vi:n) *i.* intervenir. *2* interponerse.

interview ('intəvju:) *s.* entrevista.

interweave (to) (,intə'wi:v) *t.* entretejer.

intestine (in'testin) *a.* intestino, interno.

intimidate (to) (in'timideit) *t.* intimidar.

into ('intu) *prep.* en, dentro [indicando movimiento, transformación, penetración, inclusión].

intoxicate (to) (in'tɔksikeit) *t.* embriagar. *2* MED. intoxicar.

intrigue (in'tri:g) *s.* intriga.

introduce (to) (,intrə'dju:s) *t.* introducir.

intrude (to) (in'tru:d) *t.* imponer.

invade (to) (in'veid) *t.* invadir.

invaluable (in'væljuəbl) *a.* inestimable, precioso.

invasion (in'veiʒən) *s.* invasión. 2 usurpación.

invent (to) (in'vent) *t.* inventar.

invert (to) (in'və:t) *t.* invertir [alterar el orden].

invest (to) (in'vest) *t.* invertir [dinero]. 2 MIL. sitiar.

investigate (to) (in'vestigeit) *t.* investigar. 2 indagar.

investment (in'vestmənt) *s.* investidura. 2 inversión [de dinero]. 3 MIL. cerco, sitio.

invite (to) (in'vait) *t.* invitar.

invoke (to) (in'vouk) *t.* invocar. 2 evocar [los espíritus].

involve (to) (in'vɔlv) *t.* envolver, enrollar. 2 enredar.

inward ('inwəd) *a.* interior.

inwards ('inwədz) *adv.* hacia dentro.

Irish ('aiərʃ) *a.* irlandés.

iron ('aiən) *s.* hierro. 2 *pl.* cadenas. 3 *a.* de hierro.

iron (to) ('aiən) *t.* planchar.

irony ('aiərəni) *s.* ironía.

irrigate (to) ('irigeit) *t.* regár.

irritable ('iritəbl) *a.* irritable.

island ('ailənd) *s.* isla, ínsula.

isle (ail) *s.* isla. 2 isleta.

isolate (to) ('aisəleit) *t.* aislar.

issue ('isju:, 'iʃju:) *s.* salida, regreso. 2 fuente, principio. 3 solución, decisión; resultado. 4 beneficios, rentas. 5 edición, tirada.

issue (to) ('isju:, 'iʃju:) *t.* arrojar, verter. 2 dar, expedir. 3 emitir. 4 publicar. 5 *i.* salir, nacer.

it (it) *pr. neutro* él, ella, ello, eso, lo, la, le.

italic (i'tælik) *a.* itálico. 2 *s. pl.* IMPR. bastardilla, cursiva.

itch (to) (itʃ) *i.* sentir picazón.

item ('aitəm) *adv.* item. 2 *s.* partida [de una cuenta]. 3 punto, detalle. 4 noticia.

its (its) *a.-pron. neutro* su, sus, suyo, suyos [de él, ella, etc.].

itself (it'self) *pron. neutro* él mismo, ella misma, ello mismo, sí, sí mismo.

ivory ('aivəri) *s.* marfil.

ivy ('aivi) *s.* BOT. hiedra.

J

jab (dʒæb) *s.* pinchazo, hurgonazo, codazo.

jab (to) (dʒæb) *t.* pinchar, hurgonear; dar un codazo.

jack (dʒæk) *s.* hombre, mozo; marinero.

jacket ('dʒækit) *s.* chaqueta, americana; cazadora.

jade (dʒeid) *s.* MINER. jade. 2 rocín, jamelgo.

jail (dʒeil) *s.* cárcel, prisión.

jail (to) (dʒeil) *t.* encarcelar.

jam (dʒæm) *s.* confitura. 2 atasco; embotellamiento [del tráfico]. 3 aprieto, lío.

jam (to) (dʒæm) *t.* apretar, apiñar. 2 obstruir.

January (d'ʒænjuəri) *s.* enero.

Japanese (ˌdʒæpə'ni:z) *a.-s.* japonés.

jar (dʒɑ:ʳ) *s.* jarra, tarro. 2 sonido áspero, chirrido. 3 desavenencia.

jar (to) (dʒɑ:ʳ) *t.-i.* [hacer] sonar, vibrar con sonido áspero. 2 *i.* producir un efecto desagradable. 3 disputar.

jaunty ('dʒɔ:nti) *a.* vivo, garboso, airoso.

jaw (dʒɔ:) *s.* ZOOL. mandíbula, quijada. 2 MEC. mordaza.

jazz (dʒæz) *s.* jazz.

jealous ('dʒeləs) *a.* celoso.

jean (dʒein) *s.* TEJ. dril. 2 *pl.* (dʒi:nz) pantalones tejanos.

jeer (dʒiəʳ) *s.* burla, mofa.

jeer (to) (dʒiəʳ) *t.-i.* burlarse, mofarse [de].

jelly ('dʒeli) *s.* jalea. 2 gelatina.

jeopardize (to) ('dʒepədaiz) *t.* arriesgar, exponer.

jerk (dʒə:k) *s.* tirón, sacudida. 2 salto, repullo.

jest (dʒest) *s.* broma, burla.

jest (to) (dʒest) *i.* bromear.

jet (dʒet) *s.* MINER. azabache. 2 surtidor, chorro; ~ *plane,* avión de reacción.

Jew (dʒu:) *a.-s.* judío, israelita.

jewel ('dʒu:əl) *s.* joya, alhaja. 2 piedra preciosa.

jewellery, jewelry ('dʒu:əlri) *s.* joyas, pedrería.

Jewess ('dʒu(:)is) *s.* judía, israelita.

jib (dʒib) *s.* MAR. foque.

jingle ('dʒiŋgl) *s.* tintineo.

jingle (to) ('dʒiŋgl) *i.* tintinear. 2 rimar.

job (dʒɔb) *s.* obra, trabajo, tarea. 2 empleo, ocupación. 3 asunto, negocio.

jocund ('dʒɔkənd) *a.* jocundo.

jog (dʒɔg) *s.* empujoncito.

join (to) (dʒɔin) *t.* unir, juntar, acoplar. 2 *i.* unirse, juntarse.

joining ('dʒɔiniŋ) *s.* unión, juntura.

joke (dʒouk) *s.* chiste; chanza, broma.

joke (to) (dʒouk) *i.* bromear.

jolly ('dʒɔli) *a.* alegre, divertido. 2 *adv.* muy.

jolt (dʒoult) *s.* traqueteo, sacudida.

jolt (to) (dʒoult) *i.* dar tumbos. 2 *t.* traquetear, sacudir.

jostle (to) ('dʒɔsl) *t.* empujar. 2 *i.* empujarse.

journal ('dʒə:nl) *s.* diario, periódico.

journey ('dʒə:ni) *s.* viaje.

journey (to) ('dʒə:ni) *i.* viajar. 2 *t.* viajar por.

joust (dʒaust) *s.* justa.

joust (to) (dʒaust) *i.* justar.

jovial ('dʒouvjəl) *a.* jovial.

joy (dʒɔi) *s.* gozo, júbilo.

joyful ('dʒɔiful) *a.* jubiloso, alegre, gozoso.

judge (dʒʌdʒ) *s.* juez, magistrado.

judge (to) (dʒʌdʒ) *t.-i.* juzgar. 2 creer, suponer.

judg(e)ment ('dʒʌdʒment) *s.* decisión, fallo. 2 juicio.

juice (dʒu:s) *s.* zumo, jugo.

juicy ('dʒu:si) *a.* jugoso.

July (dʒu(:)'lai) *s.* julio [mes].

jump (dʒʌmp) *s.* salto, brinco.

jump (to) (dʒʌmp) *i.* saltar, brincar. 2 *t.* saltar, salvar.

jumpy ('dʒʌmpi) *a.* saltón.

junction ('dʒʌŋkʃən) *s.* unión; confluencia.

June (dʒu:n) *s.* junio [mes].

jungle ('dʒʌŋgl) *s.* selva virgen, manigua. 2 matorral.

junior ('dʒu:njəʳ) *a.* menor, más joven, hijo. 2 *s.* joven.

jurisdiction (ˌdʒuəris'dikʃən) *s.* jurisdicción.

jury ('dʒuəri) *s.* DER. jurado.

just (dʒʌst) *a.* justo, recto. 2 merecido. 3 fiel, exacto. 4 verdadero, bien fundado. 5 *adv.* justamente, precisamente. 6 hace poco: ~ **now,** ahora mismo. 7 ~ **as,** al tiempo que, cuando; lo mismo que; semejante a.

justice ('dʒʌstis) *s.* justicia.

jut (to) (dʒʌt) *i.* [a veces con *out*] salir, sobresalir.

jute (dʒu:t) *s.* yute.

K

keel (ki:l) *s.* quilla.
keen (ki:n) *a.* agudo, afilado. *2* agudo, intenso. *3* muy interesado [por].
keep (ki:p) *s.* mantenimiento, subsistencia.
keep (to) (ki:p) *t.* guardar, tener guardado. *2* tener, mantener. *3* cuidar, custodiar, guardar. *4* dirigir, tener [un establecimiento]. *5* mantener, sustentar. *6* detener, impedir. *7* retener. *8* callar, ocultar. *9* observar, cumplir, guardar [silencio]. *10* atenerse a, seguir. *11 to ~ away,* tener alejado. *12 to ~ out,* no dejar entrar. *13 i.* mantenerse, conservarse. *14* seguir, continuar, permanecer, quedarse. ¶ Pret. y p. p.: *kept* (kept).
keeper ('ki:pə') *s.* guardián. *2* custodio, velador, defensor.
keg (keg) *s.* cuñete, barril.
kennel ('kenl) *s.* perrera. *2* jauría.
kept (kept) V. TO KEEP.
kerb (kə:b) *s.* encintado [de la acera].

kerchief ('kə:tʃif) *s.* pañuelo.
kernel ('kə:nl) *s.* grano [de trigo, etc.]. *2* almendra, núcleo [del fruto].
kettle ('ketl) *s.* caldero, olla.
key (ki:) *s.* llave. *2* clave.
kick (kik) *s.* puntapié, patada.
kick (to) (kik) *t.* dar puntapiés a, acocear. *2 i.* patear.
kid (kid) *s.* cabrito. *2* fam. niño, -ña; chico, -ca.
kidnap (to) ('kidnæp) *t.* secuestrar, raptar.
kill (to) (kil) *t.* matar.
kin (kin) *s.* parientes, parentela, familia. *2 a.* pariente.
kind (kaind) *a.* bueno, bondadoso, benévolo. *2 s.* género, especie, clase.
kindle (to) ('kindl) *t.-i.* encender(se. *2* inflamar(se.
kindly ('kaindli) *a.* bondadoso, amable. *2* benigno. *3 adv.* bondadosamente.
king (kiŋ) *s.* rey, monarca.
kingdom ('kiŋdəm) *s.* reino.
kiss (kis) *s.* beso.
kiss (to) (kis) *t.-i.* besar(se.
kitchen ('kitʃin) *s.* cocina.

kite (kait) *s.* cometa [juguete].

kitty (kiti) *s.* gatito, minino.

knave (neiv) *s.* bribón, pícaro.

knead (to) (ni:d) *t.* amasar.

knee (ni:) *s.* ANAT. rodilla.

kneel (to) (ni:l) *i.* arrodillarse. *2* estar de rodillas. ¶ Pret. y p. p.: **knelt** (nelt) o **kneeled** ('ni:ld).

knew (nju:) *pret.* de TO KNOW.

knife, *pl.* **knives** (naif, naivz)*s.* cuchillo; cuchilla; navaja.

knight (nait) *s.* caballero [de una orden].

knight (to) (nait) *t.* armar caballero.

knit (to) (nit) *t.* tejer [a punto de aguja o malla]. ¶ Pret. y p. p.: **knit** (nit) o **knited** ('nitid).

knob (nɔb) *s.* bulto, protuberancia. *2* botón, tirador [de puerta, etc.]. *3* terrón.

knock (nɔk) *s.* golpe, porrazo. *2* aldabonazo.

knock (to) (nɔk) *t.-i.* golpear.

knoll (noul) *s.* loma, otero.

knot (nɔt) *s.* nudo, lazo.

knot (to) (nɔt) *t.* anudar.

know (to) (nou) *t.* conocer. *2* saber. *3* ver, comprender. *4* distinguir, discernir. *5 i.* saber: *to ~ best,* saber mejor lo que conviene. ¶ Pret.: *knew* (nju:); p. p.: *known* (noun).

knowing ('nouiŋ) *a.* inteligente; astuto; entendido; enterado. *2* de inteligencia.

knowledge ('nɔlidʒ) *s.* conocimiento.

known (noun) *p. p.* de TO KNOW.

knuckle ('nʌkl) *s.* ANAT. nudillo.

knuckle (to) ('nʌkl) *t.* golpear o apretar con los nudillos. *2 i. to ~ down* o *under,* someterse, ceder.

L

label ('leibl) *s.* rótulo, etiqueta.

label (to) ('leibl) *t.* rotular.

laboratory (lə'bɔrətəri) *s.* laboratorio.

labo(u)r ('leibə^r) *s.* trabajo, labor; pena, fatiga. *2 Labour Party,* partido laborista.

labo(u)rer ('leibərə^r) *s.* trabajador, obrero, jornalero.

lace (leis) *s.* cordón, cinta.

lace (to) (leis) *t.* atar [los zapatos, el corsé, etc.].

lack (læk) *s.* falta, carencia.

lack (to) (læk) *s.* faltar [no existir]. *2 i.-t.* carecer de, faltarle, necesitar.

lad (læd) *s.* muchacho, mozo.

ladder ('lædə^r) *s.* escalera de mano, escala.

lade (to) (leid) *t.* cargar *2* sacar o servir con cucharón. ¶ P. p.: *laded* ('leidid) o *laden* ('leidn).

lady ('leidi) *s.* señora, dama. *2* (Ingl.) título de las señoras de la nobleza.

lag (læg) *s.* retardo, retraso.

lag (to) (læg) *i.* moverse lentamente, rezagarse.

lain (lein) *p. p.* de TO LIE *2.*

lake (leik) *s.* lago, laguna. *2* laca, carmín [color].

lamb (læm) *s.* cordero.

lame (leim) *a.* cojo, lisiado.

lame (to) (leim) *t.* encojar, lisiar.

lamp (læmp) *s.* lámpara, candil, farol.

land (lænd) *s.* tierra. *2* tierra, país, nación, región.

land (to) (lænd) *t.* desembarcar. *2* arrear [un golpe]. *3* coger, sacar [un pez]; conseguir, obtener. *4 i.* desembarcar. *5* apearse. *6* aterrizar. *7* ir a parar, caer.

landlady ('læn,leidi) *s.* propietaria; casera. *2* patrona, posadera, mesonera.

landlord ('lænlɔ:d) *s.* propietario [de tierras]; casero. *2* patrón, mesonero.

landowner ('lænd,ounə^r) *s.* hacendado, terrateniente.

landscape ('lænskeip) *s.* paisaje, vista. *2* paisaje.

lane (lein) *s.* senda, vereda.

language (læŋgwidʒ) *s.* lenguaje. 2 lengua, idioma.
languish (to) ('læŋgwiʃ) *i.* languidecer. 2 consumirse.
lap (læp) *s.* falda, regazo.
lap (to) (læp) *t.* sobreponer, encaballar.
lapse (læps) *s.* lapso, error, caída. 4 lapso, transcurso.
lapse (to) (læps) *i.* pasar, transcurrir. 2 decaer, pasar. 3 caer, recaer en.
lard (lɑːd) *s.* tocino gordo. 2 manteca de cerdo.
large (lɑːdʒ) *a.* grande, grueso, cuantioso, copioso. 2 amplio. 3 extenso, lato.
lass (læs) *f.* chica, moza.
last (lɑːst) *a.* último, final: ~ *but one*, penúltimo. 2 pasado; ~ *night*, anoche. 3 *s.* fin, final, término; lo último: *at* ~, al fin, por fin.
last (to) (lɑːst) *i.* durar, permanecer.
late (leit) *a.* que llega, ocurre, o se hace tarde; retrasado, tardío. 2 anterior, último. 3 difunto. 4 reciente. 5 *adv.* tarde.
lately ('leitli) *adv.* últimamente, recientemente.
later ('leitə^r) *a.-adv. comp.* de LATE: ~ *on*, más adelante.
lather ('lɑːðə^r) *s.* espuma.
latter ('lætə^r) *a.* más reciente, moderno. 2 último. 3 *the* ~, éste, este último.
laugh (lɑːf) *s.* risa.
laugh (to) (lɑːf) *i.* reír, reírse; *to* ~ *at*, reírse de.
laughter ('lɑːftə^r) *s.* risa.
launch (lɔːntʃ) *s.* MAR. lanzamiento, botadura. 2 MAR. lancha, chalupa.

launch (to) (lɔːntʃ) *t.* lanzar. 2 MAR. botar. 3 *i.* arrojarse.
laundry ('lɔːndri) *s.* lavadero [cuarto]. 2 lavandería. 3 ropa lavada.
lavender ('lævində^r) *s.* espliego.
lavish ('læviʃ) *a.* pródigo, dadivoso. 2 abundante.
lavish (to) ('læviʃ) *t.* prodigar.
law (lɔː) *s.* ley, regla, precepto. 2 derecho, jurisprudencia. 3 derecho, código, legislación.
lawful ('lɔːful) *a.* legal, legítimo; lícito.
lawless ('lɔːlis) *a.* sin ley. 2 ilegal, ilícito. 3 revoltoso.
lawn (lɔːn) *s.* césped, prado.
lawsuit ('lɔːsjuːt) *s.* acción, pleito.
lawyer ('lɔːjə^r) *s.* letrado, abogado.
lax (læks) *a.* laxo. 2 impreciso.
1) lay (lei) *pret.* de TO LIE 2).
2) lay (lei) *a.* laico, seglar. 2 lego, no profesional. 3 *s.* situación. 4 LIT. lay, balada.
lay (to) (lei) *t.* tumbar, acostar, tender. 2 poner, dejar; colocar. 3 enterrar. 4 tender [un cable, etc.]. 5 extender, aplicar [sobre]; cubrir, tapizar. 6 disponer, preparar, urdir. 7 imponer [cargas]. 8 poner [huevos; la mesa]. 9 calmar, sosegar. 10 echar [la culpa]. 11 presentar, exponer. 12 apostar [dinero]. ¶ Pret. y p. p.: *laid* (leid).
lazy ('leizi) *a.* perezoso, holgazán. 2 lento, pesado.
1) lead (led) *s.* plomo.
2) lead (liːd) *s.* primacía, primer lugar. 2 dirección,

mando, guía. 3 TEAT. primer papel.

1) **lead (to)** (led) *t.* emplomar.

2) **lead (to)** (li:d) *t.* conducir, guiar; dirigir; impulsar, inducir. 2 ser el primero. ¶ Pret. y p. p.: *led* (led).

leader (li:dəʳ) *s.* conductor, guía. 2 jefe, caudillo. 3 director [de orquesta]; primer violín. 4 editorial.

leadership ('li:dəʃip) *s.* dirección, jefatura.

leaf (li:f) *pl.* **leaves** (li:vz) BOT. hoja; pétalo. 2 hoja [de libro, puerta, etc.].

league (li:g) *s.* liga, unión.

league (to) (li:g) *t.* ligar, confederar. 2 *i.* unirse, aliarse.

leak (li:k) *s.* escape [de un fluido]. 2 *fig.* filtración [de dinero, etc.]. 3 grieta.

leak (to) (li:k) *i.* tener escapes o pérdidas [un recipiente]. 2 filtrarse, escaparse [un fluido; dinero, noticias]. 3 gotear [un techo].

lean (li:n) *a.* delgado, flaco.

lean (to) (li:n) *t.-i.* apoyar(se; reclinar(se; recostar(se. 2 *i.* inclinarse. ¶ Pret. y p. p.: *leant* (lent) o *leaned* (li:nd).

leap (li:p) *s.* salto, brinco.

leap (to) (li:p) *i.* saltar, brincar. 2 latir fuertemente. 3 *t.* saltar; hacer saltar. ¶ Pret. y p. p.: *leapt* o *leaped* (lept).

learn (to) (lə:n) *t.-i.* aprender. 2 *t.* enterarse de. ¶ Pret. y p. p.: *learned* (lə:nd)o *learnt* (lə:nt).

learned ('lə:nid) *a.* ilustrado, docto, sabio; versado [en].

learning ('lə:niŋ) *s.* instrucción, ilustración, saber.

learnt (lə:nt) V. TO LEARN.

lease (to) (li:s) *t.* arrendar.

least (li:st) *a. superl.* de LITTLE. 2 mínimo, menor.

leather ('leðəʳ) *s.* cuero.

leave (li:v) *s.* permiso, licencia. 2 despedida.

leave (to) (li:v) *t.* dejar [en varios sentidos]: *to ~ behind,* dejar atrás; dejar olvidado; *to ~ off,* dejar de [hacer una cosa]; dejar [el trabajo, un hábito, un vestido]. 4 *i.* partir, salir, irse. ¶ Pret. y p. p.: *left* (left).

lecture ('lektʃəʳ) *s.* conferencia, disertación.

lecture (to) ('lektʃəʳ) *i.* dar una conferencia.

lecturer ('lektʃərəʳ) *s.* conferenciante. 2 lector, catedrático.

led (led) V. TO LEAD.

ledge (ledʒ) *s.* repisa.

lees (li:z) *s. pl.* heces, poso.

left (left) *pret.* y *p. p.* de TO LEAVE: *to be ~ over,* quedar, sobrar. 2 *a.* izquierdo. 3 *s.* izquierda.

leg (leg) *s.* pierna [de persona, de media, de compás]. 2 pata [de animal, de mueble].

legal ('li:gəl) *s.* legal.

legend ('ledʒənd) *s.* leyenda.

legislation (ˌledʒis'leiʃən) *s.* legislación.

legitimate (li'dʒitimit) *a.* legítimo.

legitimate (to) (li'dʒitimeit) *t.* legitimar.

leisure ('leʒə^r) *s.* ocio, desocupación, tiempo libre.

lemon ('lemən) *s.* BOT. limón.

lemonade (‚lemə'neid) *s.* limonada.

lend (to) (lend) *t.* prestar. ¶ Pret. y p. p.: *lent* (lent).

length (leŋθ) *s.* longitud; extensión; duración.

lengthen (to) ('leŋθən) *t.-i.* alargar(se; prolongar(se.

lent (lent) V. TO LEND.

less (les) *a.-adv.-prep.* menos. 2 menor.

lessen (to) ('lesn) *t.* disminuir. 2 *i.* disminuirse.

lesser ('lesə^r) *a. comp.* de LITTLE. menor.

lesson ('lesn) *s.* lección.

lest (lest) *conj.* para que no, por miedo de que, no sea que.

let (let) *s.* estorbo, obstáculo.

let (to) (let) *t.* arrendar, alquilar. 2 dejar, permitir. 3 dejar o hacer entrar, salir, etc. 4 *i.* alquilarse. 5 AUX. ~ *us run,* corramos; ~ *him come,* que venga. ¶ Pret. y p. p.: *let* (let).

letter ('letə^r) *s.* letra [del alfabeto; signo]. 2 letra [sentido literal]. 3 carta; documento.

lettuce ('letis) *s.* BOT. lechuga.

level ('levl) *a.* liso, llano, horizontal. 2 igual. 3 equilibrado; imparcial. 4 juicioso. 5 *s.* nivel. 6 llano, llanura.

level (to) ('levl) *t.* nivelar. 2 allanar. 3 apuntar [un arma].

lever ('li:və^r) *s.* palanca.

levy ('levi) *s.* leva, recluta. 2 recaudación [de tributos].

levy (to) ('levi) *t.* reclutar. 2 recaudar [tributos].

lewd (lu:d) *a.* lujurioso.

liability (‚laiə'biliti) *s.* riesgo, tendencia. 2 responsabilidad [pecuniaria].

liable ('laiəbl) *a.* expuesto, sujeto, propenso. 2 responsable [pecuniariamente].

liar ('laiə^r) *s.* embustero.

liberal ('libərəl) *a.* liberal. 2 abundante. 3 *s.* POL. liberal.

liberate (to) ('libəreit) *t.* libertar. liberar.

librarian (lai'brɛəriən) *s.* bibliotecario.

library ('laibrəri) *s.* biblioteca.

license, licence ('laisəns) *s.* licencia, libertinaje. 2 licencia [poética]. 3 licencia, permiso. 4 autorización, matrícula, patente.

license, licence (to) ('laisəns) *t.* autorizar, dar permiso.

lick (lik) *s.* lamedura.

lick (to) (lik) *t.* lamer.

lid (lid) *s.* tapa, tapadera. 2 párpado.

lie (lai) *s.* mentira, embuste. 2 disposición, situación.

1) **lie (to)** (lai) *i.* mentir. ¶ Pret. y p. p.: *lied* (laid); ger.: *lying* ('laiiŋ).

2) **lie (to)** (lai) *i.* tenderse, apoyarse. 2 estar tendido o acostado, yacer. 3 estar, permanecer. 4 consistir. 5 hallarse, extenderse. ¶ Pret.: *lay* (lei); p. p.: *lain* (lein); ger.: *lying* ('laiiŋ).

lieutenant (lef'tenənt) *s.* lugarteniente. 2 MIL. teniente.

life (laif), *pl.* **lives** (laivz) *s.* vida. 2 animación.

lift (lift) *s.* elevación, alzamiento. 2 alza, aumento. 3 (Ingl.) ascensor.

lift (to) (lift) *t.* alzar, levantar. 2 *i.* levantarse.

light (lait) *s.* luz. 2 fuego, cerilla [para encender]. 3 lumbrera [pers.]. 4 aspecto, punto de vista. 5 *a.* de luz. 6 blondo, rubio; blanca [tez]. 7 claro [color]. 8 ligero. 9 leve. 10 *adv.* ligeramente; fácilmente.

light (to) (lait) *t.-i.* encender(se. 2 iluminar(se. 3 *i.* posarse, descender. 4 topar [con]. ‖ Pret. y p. p.: *lighted* ('laitid) o *lit* (lit).

lighten (to) (laitn) *t.-i.* iluminar(se. 2 aclarar(se, avivar(se [un color]. 3 alegrar(se. 4 aligerar(se. 5 *t.* alumbrar. 6 *i.* relampaguear.

lighter ('laitə^r) *s.* encendedor [pers.; mechero].

lighthouse ('laithaus) *s.* MAR. faro, farola.

lighting ('laitiŋ) *s.* iluminación. 2 alumbrado. 3 encendido.

lightning ('laitniŋ) *s.* relámpago; rayo.

like (laik) *a.* igual, semejante, parecido, tal, como. 2 probable. 3 *adv.* como: ~ *this,* así. 4 *s.* igual [pers. o cosa]. 5 *pl.* gustos.

like (to) (laik) *t.* querer, tener simpatía a; gustar de, gustarle a uno; desear.

likely ('laikli) *a.* probable. 2 *adv.* probablemente.

liken (to) ('laikən) *t.* asemejar, comparar.

liking ('laikiŋ) *s.* inclinación, afición. 2 preferencia.

limb (limb) *s.* miembro [del hombre o del animal].

lime (laim) *s.* cal.

limestone ('laimstoun) *s.* piedra caliza.

limp (to) (limp) *i.* cojear.

linden ('lindən) *s.* BOT. tilo.

line (lain) *s.* cuerda, cabo, cordel, sedal. 2 línea [raya, trazo; renglón; fila, hilera, etc.]. 3 conducción, tubería. 4 verso [línea]. 5 arruga [en la cara]. 6 ramo de negocios, especialidad. 7 TEAT. papel.

line (to) (lain) *t.* linear, rayar. 2 arrugar [el rostro]. 3 alinearse a lo largo de. 4 forrar, revestir. 5 *i. to ~ up,* ponerse en fila.

lineage ('liniidȝ) *s.* linaje.

linen ('linin) *s.* lienzo, lino.

liner ('lainə^r) *s.* vapor o avión de línea.

linger (to) ('liŋgə^r) *i.* demorar.

lining ('lainiŋ) *s.* forro.

link (liŋk) *s.* eslabón. 2 vínculo, enlace. 3 *pl.* campo de golf.

link (to) (liŋk) *t.-i.* eslabonar(se, enlazar(se.

linoléum (li'nouljəm) *s.* linóleo.

lion ('laiən) *s.* león.

lioness ('laiənis) *s.* leona.

lip (lip) *s.* labio. 2 pico.

lip-stick ('lip-stik) *s.* lápiz para labios.

liquid ('likwid) *a.-s.* líquido. 2 *a.* claro, cristalino.

lisp (to) (lisp) *i.* cecear.

list (list) *s.* lista, catálogo, rol, matrícula. 2 orillo.

list (to) (list) *t.* poner en lista; registrar. 2 alisar. 3 COM. cotizar, facturar. 4 listar, orillar. 5 *i.* alistarse.

listen (to) ('lisn) *i.* escuchar, oír, atender. | Gralte. con *to*.

listener ('lisnə^r) *s.* oyente.

lit (lit) *pret.* y *p. p.* de TO LIGHT.

lithe (laiδ), **lithesome** (-səm)*a.* flexible, cimbreño, ágil.

litter ('litə^r) *s.* litera [vehículo]. 2 camilla, parihuelas. 3 tendalera; basura.

litter (to) ('litə^r) *t.* esparcir cosas por; poner o dejar en desorden.

little ('litl) *a.* pequeño, chico, menudo. 2 *adv.-s.* poco; un poco de; algo.

live (laiv) *a.* vivo [que vive]; enérgico, activo]. 2 ardiente, encendido.

live (to) (liv) *i.-t.* vivir. 2 *t.* llevar, pasar [tal o cual vida].

lively (laivli) *a.* vivo, vivaz, vivaracho. 2 animado. 3 vivo [brioso, airoso, rápido; alegre, brillante; intenso: pronto]. 4 *adv.* vivamente.

liver ('livə^r) *s.* hígado.

livery ('livəri) *s.* librea.

livestock ('laivstɔk) *s.* ganado, animales que se crían.

lizard ('lizəd) *s.* ZOOL. lagarto.

load (loud) *s.* carga. 2 peso.

load (to) (loud) *t.* cargar [un buque, un arma, etc.]. 2 oprimir. 3 cubrir. 4 *i.* cargar, tomar carga.

loaf (louf) *s.* pan, hogaza.

loan (loun) *s.* préstamo.

loan (to) (loun) *t.-i.* prestar [dinero].

loath (louθ) *a.* renuente, poco dispuesto.

loathe (to) (louδ) *t.* aborrecer, detestar.

loathsome ('louδsəm) *a.* aborrecible, odioso.

lobster ('lɔbstə^r) *s.* ZOOL. langosta; bogavante.

lock (lɔk) *s.* rizo, bucle. 2 mechón. 3 cerradura. 4 llave [de arma de fuego].

lock (to) (lɔk) *t.* cerrar [con llave]; encerrar. 2 apretar, abrazar. 3 sujetar, trabar.

lockout ('lɔkaut) *s.* lockout [cierre de fábrica por los patronos].

locomotive ('loukə‚moutiv) *a. s.* locomotora.

lodge (lɔdʒ) *s.* casita, pabellón. 2 logia [masónica].

lodge (to) (lɔdʒ) *t.* alojar, hospedar. 2 depositar. 3 presentar [una denuncia, etc.]. 4 *i.* alojarse.

lodging ('lɔdʒiŋ) *s.* alojamiento, posada. 2 morada.

loft (lɔft) *s.* desván.

log (lɔg) *s.* leño, tronco.

logic ('lɔdʒik) *s.* lógica.

logical ('lɔdʒikəl) *a.* lógico.

loiter (to) ('lɔitə^r) *i.* rezagarse; pasear, holgazanear.

lone (loun) *a.* solo.

loneliness ('lounlinis) *s.* soledad.

lonely ('lounli) *a.* solo, solitario. 2 que siente la soledad.

long (lɔŋ) *a.* largo. 2 extenso, prolongado. 3 que tarda. 4 *adv.* durante [un tiempo]; mucho tiempo 5 *s.* longitud, largo.

long (to) (lɔŋ) *i.* [con *for, after* o *to]* ansiar, anhelar; añorar.

longing ('lɔŋiŋ) *s.* ansia, anhelo. 2 *a.* ansioso.

look (luk) *s.* mirada, ojeada. 2 semblante, cara. 3 aspecto, apariencia, cariz.

look (to) (luk) *i.* mirar; considerar. | Gralte. con *at.* 2 mirar, dar a, caer; estar situado. 3 parecer. 4 aparecer, manifestarse. 5 sentar, caer [bien o mal]. 6 *to ~ after,* cuidar de. 7 *to ~ for,* buscar. 8 *to ~ out,* asomarse; tener cuidado: ~ *out!,* ¡cuidado! 9 *t.* mirar.

looking-glass ('lukiŋglɑ:s) *s.* espejo.

lookout ('luk'aut) *s.* vigía, atalaya. 2 atalaya, miradero. 3 *pl.* perspectivas.

loom (lu:m) *s.* TEJ. telar.

loom (to) (lu:m) *t.-i.* aparecer, asomar [de una manera confusa o impresionante]. 2 vislumbrarse, amenazar.

loop (lu:p) *s.* curva, vuelta muy pronunciada. 2 lazo; presilla; asa. 3 AVIA. rizo.

loop (to) (lu:p) *t.* doblar en forma de gaza. 2 asegurar con presilla. 3 AVIA. *to ~ the loop,* rizar el rizo.

loose (lu:s) *a.* suelto, flojo. 2 suelto, en libertad, no sujeto. 3 vago, indeterminado; libre [traducción]. 4 *s.* libertad, soltura.

loose (to) (lu:s) *t.* soltar, desatar, aflojar. 2 dejar en libertad. 3 lanzar [flechas, etc.].

loosen (to) ('lu:sn) *t.* soltar, desatar. 2 aflojar, desceñir. 3 *i.* aflojarse, desatarse.

lord (lɔ:d) *s.* señor, dueño, amo. 2 lord [título].

lordship ('lɔ:dʃip) *s.* señoría, dominio.

lorry ('lɔri) *s.* camión.

lose (to) (lu:z) *t.* perder. 2 *i.* perder, tener una pérdida. 3 *i.* perderse; extraviarse; engolfarse, ensimismarse. ¶ Pret. y p. p.: *lost* (lɔst).

loss (lɔs, lɔ:s) *s.* pérdida.

lost (lɔst) V. TO LOSE. 2 *a.* perdido. 3 arruinado. 4 olvidado. 5 desorientado, perplejo.

lot (lɔt) *s.* lote, parte. 2 solar. 3 suerte [para decidir]. 4 suerte, sino. 5 hato, colección. 6 *a ~ of, lots of,* la mar de. 7 *adv. a ~,* mucho.

loud (laud) *a.* fuerte [sonido]. 2 alta [voz]. 3 chillón, llamativo. 5 vulgar, ordinario.

loud-speaker ('laud'spi:kəʳ) *s.* RADIO altavoz.

lounge (laundʒ) *s.* salón de descanso o tertulia.

lounge (to) (laundʒ) *i.* pasear, pasar el rato.

louse (laus), *pl.* **lice** (lais) *s.* ENT. piojo.

love (lʌv) *s.* amor, cariño, afecto, afición. 2 amor [persona amada]. 3 *fam.* preciosidad.

love (to) (lʌv) *t.* amar, querer. 2 gustar de, tener afición a.

lovely ('lʌvli) *a.* amable, adorable, encantador, hermoso.

lover ('lʌvəʳ) *s.* enamorado. 2 amante. 3 aficionado [a].

low (lou) *a.* bajo. 2 pobre. 3 escaso, insuficiente. 4 débil, enfermo; abatido. 5 *adv.* bajo. 6 bajamente. 7 sumisamente. 8 barato. 9 *t.* mugido, berrido.

1) **lower (to)** ('louəʳ) *t.* bajar. 2 arriar. 3 agachar. 4 rebajar, reducir. 5 abatir, humi-

llar. 6 *i.* bajar, reducirse, disminuir.

2) **lower (to)** ('laueʳ) *i.* mirar ceñudo. 2 encapotarse [el cielo].

loyal (lɔiəl) *a.* leal, fiel.

luck (lʌk) *s.* suerte, fortuna.

luckless ('lʌklis) *a.* desafortunado. 2 desdichado.

lucky ('lʌki) *a.* afortunado.

luggage ('lʌgidʒ) *s.* equipaje [de viajero].

lull (lʌl) *s.* momento de calma o silencio.

lull (to) (lʌl) *t.* adormecer, arrullar. 2 calmar. 3 *i.* amainar, calmarse.

lumber ('lʌmbəʳ) *s.* madera [aserrada], madera de construcción.

lump (lʌmp) *s.* pedazo, terrón, pella, burujo. 2 bulto, chichón. 3 nudo [en la garganta].

lunch (lʌntʃ), **luncheon** (-ən)*s.* almuerzo, comida del mediodía.

lunch (to) (lʌntʃ) *i.* almorzar, tomar la comida del medio día.

lung (lʌŋ) *s.* pulmón.

lure (ljuəʳ) *s.* señuelo, reclamo. 2 cebo, tentación.

lurk (to) (ləːk) *i.* acechar, estar escondido.

lush (lʌʃ) *a.* lujuriante.

lust (lʌst) *s.* avidez. 2 lujuria.

lust (to) (lʌst) *i.* codiciar. 2 desear [con lujuria].

lustre ('lʌstəʳ) *s.* lustre, brillo. 2 reflejo. 3 esplendor.

lustrous ('lʌstrəs) *a.* lustroso, brillante.

lusty ('lʌsti) *a.* lozano, fuerte, robusto. 2 vigoroso.

luxuriant (lʌg'zjuəriənt) *a.* lujuriante, exuberante.

lying ('laiiŋ) *ger.* de TO LIE. 2 *a.* mentiroso. 3 tendido, echado. 4 situado.

M

machine (mə'ʃiːn) *s.* máquina. 2 bicicleta, automóvil, etc.

machinery (mə'ʃiːnəri) *s.* maquinaria.

mad (mæd) *a.* loco. 2 insensato. 3 furioso.

madam ('mædəm, mæ'dɑːm) *s.* señora [tratamiento de respeto].

madden (to) ('mædn) *t.* enloquecer. 2 *i.* enloquecer, volverse loco.

made (meid) *pret.* y *p. p.* de TO MAKE. 2 *a.* hecho, compuesto, confeccionado.

magazine (,mægə'ziːn) *s.* almacén, depósito. 2 polvorín. 3 revista [periódico].

magic ('mædʒik) *s.* magia. 2 *a.* mágico.

magistrate ('mædʒistrit) *s.* magistrado. 2 juez de paz.

maid (meid) *s.* doncella, soltera, [virgen]. 2 doncella, criada.

maiden ('meidn) *s.* doncella, joven soltera.

mail (meil) *s.* malla, cota de malla. 2 correo, correspondencia.

mail (to) (meil) *t.* echar al correo, enviar por correo.

main (mein) *a.* primero; principal, mayor, maestro. 2 *s.* lo principal, lo esencial. 3 tubería, conducto principal.

maintain (to) (me(i)n'tein) *t.* mantener.

maize (meiz) *s.* BOT. maíz.

majestic (mə'dʒestik) *a.* majestuoso.

majesty ('mædʒisti) *s.* majestad; majestuosidad.

major ('meidʒəʳ) *a.* mayor, principal. 2 *s.* DER. mayor de edad. 3 MIL. comandante.

majority (mə'dʒɔriti) *s.* mayoría. 2 mayor de edad.

make (meik) *s.* hechura, forma; constitución. 2 hechura, obra, fabricación.

make (to) (meik) *t.* hacer [crear, elaborar, fabricar; formar; causar, producir, preparar; efectuar, etc.]: *to make fun*, burlarse; *to ~ a mistake*, equivocarse. 2 hacer [que uno haga una cosa]. 3 poner en cierto estado, dar una cualidad: *to ~ an-*

gry, enfadar. *to ~ good*, cumplir, llevar a cabo; mantener; justificar [con el resultado]. *4 to ~ haste*, apresurarse. *5 to ~ over*, rehacer; ceder, entregar. *6 to ~ up one's mind*, decidirse. *7 i.* dirigirse, encaminarse a. *8* contribuir a. *9 to ~ away*, largarse. *10 to ~ off*, largarse. *11 |to| ~ up*, hacer las paces; pintarse, maquillarse. **ℂ** Pret. y p. p.: **made** (meid).

male (meil) *a.* macho. *2* masculino. *3 s.* varón.

malice ('mælis) *s.* mala voluntad. *2* malicia, malignidad.

man (mæn) *pl.* **men** (men) hombre. *2* [sin artículo] el género humano.

manacles ('mænəklz) *s. pl.* manillas, esposas.

manage (to) ('mænidʒ) *t.* manejar. *2* dirigir, regir. *3 t.-i.* ingeniarse, componérselas; lograr.

management ('mænidʒmənt) *s.* manejo, gobierno, administración; cuidado. *2* gerencia. *3* habilidad.

manager ('mænidʒəʳ) *s.* director, administrador.

mane (mein) *s.* crin [de caballo]; melena [de león, de pers.].

manger ('meindʒəʳ) *s.* pesebre, comedero.

mangle (to) ('mæŋgl) *t.* planchar con máquina. *2* magullar, destrozar, mutilar.

manhood ('mænhud) *s.* virilidad, valor. *2* los hombres.

manifest ('mænifest) *a.* manifiesto, patente.

manifest (to) ('mænifest) *t.*

manifestar; demostrar. *2 i.* manifestarse.

mankind (mæn'kaind) *s.* género humano. *2* los hombres.

manly ('mænli) *a.* varonil, viril, valeroso, noble.

manner ('mænəʳ) *s.* manera, modo. *2* hábito, costumbre. *3 pl.* maneras, modales.

manufacture (,mænju'fæktʃəʳ) *s.* manufactura.

manufacture (to) (,mænju'fæktʃəʳ) *t.* manufacturar.

manufacturer (,mænju'fæktʃərəʳ) *s.* fabricante.

many ('meni) *a.* muchos, -chas. *2 pron.* muchos.

map (mæp) *s.* mapa, carta.

mar (to) (ma:ʳ) *t.* estropear, echar a perder, frustrar.

marble ('ma:bl) *s.* mármol.

March (ma:tʃ) *s.* marzo [mes].

march (ma:tʃ) *s.* marcha.

march (to) (ma:tʃ) *i.* marchar, andar. *2* marchar, progresar. *3 t.* hacer ir.

margin ('ma:dʒin) *s.* margen.

mark (ma:k) *s.* marca, señal. *2* mancha. *3* huella. *4* signo, indicio. *5* rótulo. *6* importancia, distinción. *7* punto, nota, calificación. *8* blanco, hito, fin, propósito. *9* marco [moneda].

mark (to) (ma:k) *t.* marcar, señalar. *2* indicar. *3* delimitar. *4* notar, observar, advertir. *5* puntuar, calificar.

marquis, -quess ('ma:kwis) *s.* marqués.

marriage ('mæridʒ) *s.* matrimonio. *2* boda.

married ('mærid) *a.* casado.

marry (to) ('mæri) *t.* casar. 2 casarse con. 3 *i.* casarse.

marshy ('mɑ:ʃi) *a.* pantanoso. 2 palustre.

marvel ('mɑ:vəl) *s.* maravilla.

marvel (to) ('mɑ:vəl) *i.* maravillarse, admirarse.

marvellous ('mɑ:viləs) *a.* maravilloso, prodigioso.

mask (to) (mɑ:sk) *t.* enmascarar. 2 *i.* ponerse careta. 3 disfrazarse.

mason ('meisn) *s.* albañil. 2 masón.

mass (mæs) *s.* masa, bulto, mole. 2 montón.

Mass o **mass** (mæs, mɑ:s) *s.* LITURG. misa.

massive ('mæsiv) *a.* macizo. 2 voluminoso.

mast (mɑ:st) *s.* MAR. mástil, palo. 2 asta.

master ('mɑ:stə'ʳ) *s.* amo, patrón, dueño. 2 señor, señorito [dicho por un criado]. 3 MAR. patrón, capitán. 4 maestro: **school** ~, maestro; profesor [de instituto].

master (to) ('mɑ:stə'ʳ) *t.* dominar, vencer, subyugar.

masterful ('mɑ:stəful) *a.* dominante, autoritario. 2 hábil, diestro; de maestro.

masterly ('mɑ:stəli) *a.* magistral, hábil. 2 *adv.* magistralmente.

masterpiece ('mɑ:təpi:s) *s.* obra maestra.

mastery ('mɑ:stəri) *s.* dominio [poder; conocimiento].

match (mætʃ) *s.* fósforo, cerilla. 2 pareja, igual. 3 contrincante temible. 4 juego [de dos cosas]. 5 DEP. lucha, partida, partido. 6 casa-

miento, partido: **good** ~, buen partido.

match (to) (mætʃ) *t.* casar, hermanar, aparear. 2 oponer, equiparar. 3 igualar a. 4 proporcionar, adaptar. 5 *i.-t.* hacer juego [con]. 6 *i.* casarse.

mate (meit) *s.* compañero, -ra. 2 consorte, cónyuge.

mate (to) (meit) *t.* casar, desposar. 2 aparear, hermanar. 4 *i.* aparearse.

material (mə'tiəriəl) *a.* material. 2 físico, corpóreo. 3 importante, esencial. 4 *s.* material, materia. 5 tela, género.

mathematics (ˌmæθi'mætiks) *s.* matemáticas.

matter ('mætə'ʳ) *s.* materia: ~ **of course**, cosa lógica, natural, de cajón. 2 motivo, ocasión. 3 cosa: **a** ~ **of ten years**, cosa de diez años. 4 importancia: **no** ~, no importa. 5 **what is the** ~?, ¿qué ocurre?.

matter (to) ('mætə'ʳ) *i.* importar.

mattress ('mætris) *s.* colchón.

mature (mə'tjuə'ʳ) *a.* maduro.

mature (to) (mə'tjuə'ʳ) *t.-i.* madurar.

May (mei) *s.* mayo [mes].

may (mei) *v. aux.* poder [tener facultad, libertad, oportunidad o permiso; ser posible o contingente]. 2 a veces expresa deseo: ~ **it be so**, ojalá sea así. ¶ Pret.: **might** (mait). . Sólo tiene pres. y pret.

maybe ('meibi:) *adv.* acaso, tal vez.

mayor (mɛə'ʳ) *s.* alcalde.

me (mi:, mi) *pron. pers.*, me, mi: *with me,* conmigo.

meadow ('medou) *s.* prado.

meal (mi:l) *s.* comida.

mean (mi:n) *s.* bajo, humilde. 2 ruin, bajo, vil. 3 mezquino, tacaño. 4 (E. U.)avergonzado, indispuesto. 5 medio, mediano, intermedio. 6 *s.* medio [término medio]; media [proporcional]. 7 justo medio. 8 *pl.* medio, medios [de hacer, obtener, etc.]: *by all means,* a toda costa; no faltaba más. 9 *pl.* medios, recursos, bienes de fortuna.

mean (to) (mi:n) *t.* significar, querer decir. 2 pensar, proponerse, tener intención de. 3 destinar. 4 *i.* tener intención [buena o mala]. ¶ Pret. y p. p.: *meant* (ment).

meaning ('mi:niŋ) *s.* significación, sentido, acepción. 2 intención.

meantime ('mi:n'taim), **meanwhile** (-'wail) *adv.* entretanto. 2 *m.* interín.

measure ('meʒəʳ) *s.* medida. 2 cantidad, grado, extensión. 3 ritmo.

measure (to) ('meʒəʳ) *t.-i.* medir. 2 ajustar, proporcionar.

meat (mi:t) *s.* carne [como alimento]. 2 vianda, comida.

mechanics (mi'kæniks) *s.* mecánica [ciencia].

mechanism ('mekənizəm) *s.* mecanismo. 2 mecanicismo.

medal ('medl) *s.* medalla.

meddle (to) ('medl) *i.* entrometerse, meterse [en].

medicine ('medsin) *s.* medicina [medicamento; ciencia].

meet (to) (mi:t) *t.* encontrar, hallar, topar con; enfrentarse con. 2 conocer, ser presentado a. 3 reunirse, entrevistarse con. 4 hacer frente a [gastos, etc.]. 5 satisfacer, llenar, cumplir [necesidades, requisitos, etc.]. 6 refutar, responder. 7 *i.* reunirse, encontrarse. 8 oponerse; pelear. 9 confluir. ¶ Pret. y p. p.: *met* (met).

meeting ('mi:tiŋ) *s.* reunión, junta, sesión. 2 asamblea, mitin. 3 conferencia.

mellow ('melou) *a.* maduro, sazonado [fruto]. 2 tierno, blando, pastoso, meloso. 3 suave [vino]. 4 lleno, puro, suave [voz, sonido, color, luz]. 5 calamocano.

mellow (to) ('melou) *t.-i.* madurar. 2 suavizar(se.

melody ('melədi) *s.* melodía, aire.

melt (to) (melt) *t.-i.* fundir(se, derretir(se.

member ('membəʳ) *s.* miembro. 2 socio, individuo.

memorial (mi'mɔ:riəl) *a.* conmemorativo. 2 *s.* monumento conmemorativo. 3 memorial, petición. 4 nota, apunte.

men (men) *s. pl.* de MAN.

menace ('menəs) *s.* amenaza.

mend (to) (mend) *t.* componer, reparar, remendar. 2 corregir, enmendar. 3 *i.* corregirse, enmendarse.

merchandise ('mə:tʃəndaiz) *s.* mercancía, géneros.

mercy ('mə:si) *s.* misericor-

dia. clemencia, compasión.
2 merced, gracia.

mere (miə^r) *a.* mero, solo.

merge (to) (mə:dʒ) *t.* unir, combinar, fusionar. 2 *i.* fundirse, unirse, fusionarse.

meringue (mə'ræŋ) *s.* merengue.

merit ('merit) *s.* mérito.

merit (to) ('merit) *t.* merecer.

merriment ('merimənt) *s.* alegría, regocijo. 2 fiesta.

merry ('meri) *a.* alegre.

mesh (meʃ) *s.* malla [de red].

mess (mes) *s.* enredo, lío; asco, suciedad.

mess (to) (mes) *t.* desarreglar, enredar, ensuciar.

message ('mesidʒ) *s.* mensaje. 2 recado, mandado.

messenger ('mesindʒə^r) *s.* mensajero. 2 mandadero.

met (met) V. TO MEET.

method ('meθəd) *s.* método.

metre, (E. U.) **meter** ('mi:tə^r) *s.* metro.

mice (mais) *s. pl.* de MOUSE.

mid (mid) *a.* medio.

middle ('midl) *a.* medio, de en medio, mediano, intermedio. 2 *s.* medio, mediados, mitad, centro. 3 promedio.

midnight ('midnait) *s.* medianoche.

midst (midst) *s.* centro, medio.

midsummer ('mid,sʌmə^r) *s.* canícula.

might (mait) *pret.* de MAY. 2 *s.* poderío, fuerza.

mighty ('maiti) *a.* poderoso. 2 vigoroso, potente. 3 importante, grande.

mild (maild) *a.* apacible, blando. 2 manso, dócil. 3 leve, moderado, templado. 4 dúctil.

mile (mail) *s.* milla.

milk (milk) *s.* leche.

mill (mil) *s.* molino. 2 fábrica, taller.

mill (to) (mil) *t.* moler, triturar. 2 aserrar.

mind (maind) *s.* mente, espíritu, entendimiento, juicio; ánimo. 2 mentalidad. 3 intención, propósito, deseo. 4 pensamiento, mientes, memoria, recuerdo. 5 opinión, parecer.

mind (to) (maind) *t.* tener en cuenta; hacer caso de. 2 tener inconveniente en; molestarle a uno [una cosa]. 3 cuidar de, atender, ocuparse de. 4 tener cuidado con. 5 recordar, acordarse de. 6 *i. never* ~, no importa, no se preocupe.

1) **mine** (main) *pron. pos.* mío, -a; míos, -as: *a friend of* ~, un amigo mío.

2) **mine** (main) *s.* MIN., FORT., MIL. mina.

mine (to) (main) *t.* minar. 2 extraer [mineral]; beneficiar [un filón].

miner ('mainə^r) *s.* minero.

mineral ('minərəl) *a.-s.* mineral.

mingle (to) ('miŋgl) *t.* mezclar; entremezclar. 2 *i.* mezclarse; juntarse.

minister ('ministə^r) *s.* ministro.

minister (to) ('ministə^r) *t.* dar, suministrar. 2 *i.* oficiar. 3 asistir, auxiliar.

ministry ('ministri) *s.* ministerio. 2 clero.

minor ('mainə^r) *a.-s.* menor.

mint (mint) *s.* casa de moneda. 2 BOT. menta.

mint (to) (mint) *t.* acuñar [moneda].

1) **minute** (mai'nju:t) *a.* menudo, diminuto. 2 minucioso.

2) **minute** ('minit) *s.* minuto. 2 momento, instante. 3 minuta, nota. 4 acta [de una junta, etc.].

miracle ('mirəkl) *s.* milagro.

miraculous (mi'rækjuləs) *a.* milagroso. 2 maravilloso.

mirror ('mirə^r) *s.* espejo.

mirror (to) ('mirə^r) *t.* reflejar. 2 *i.* reflejarse.

mirth (mə:θ) *s.* alegría.

mischief ('mis-tʃif) *s.* mal, daño, perjuicio.

mischievous ('mis-tʃivəs) *a.* malo, dañino. 2 enredador.

miser ('maizə^r) *a.-s.* mísero.

miserable ('mizərəbl) *a.* miserable.

miserly ('maizəli) *a.* avaro, tacaño, roñoso.

misery ('mizəri) *s.* miseria. 2 desdicha, infelicidad.

misfortune (mis'fɔ:tʃən) *s.* infortunio, desdicha.

Miss (mis) *s.* señorita [antepuesto al nombre].

miss (mis) *s.* errada; fracaso. 2 falta, pérdida.

miss (to) (mis) *t.* errar. 2 perder [un tren, la ocasión, etc.]. 3 echar de menos. 4 *i.* errar el blanco.

missing ('misiŋ) *a.* extraviado, perdido, que falta.

mission ('miʃən) *s.* misión.

mist (mist) *s.* niebla, vapor.

mistake (mis'teik) *s.* equivocación, error, confusión.

mistake (to) (mis'teik) *t.* equivocar; confundir. ¶ Pret.: *mistook;* p. p.: ~ **taken.**

mistaken (mis'teikən) *p. p.* de TO MISTAKE. 2 *a.* equivocado.

mistress ('mistris) *s.* ama, dueña, señora. 2 maestra [de escuela]. 3 querida, manceba.

misty ('misti) *a.* brumoso.

misunderstand (to) ('misʌndə'stænd) *t.* entender mal.

mitten ('mitn) *s.* guante sin división para los dedos, excepto para el pulgar.

mix (miks) *s.* mezcla.

mix (to) (miks) *t.* mezclar. 2 *i.* mezclarse.

mixture ('mikstʃə^r) *s.* mezcla.

moan (moun) *s.* gemido, quejido, lamento.

moan (to) (moun) *i.* gemir, quejarse.

moat (mout) *s.* FORT. foso.

mob (mɔb) *s.* populacho.

mob (to) (mɔb) *t.* atacar en tumulto. 2 *i.* tumultuarse.

mock (mɔk) *a.* ficticio, falso. 2 fingido, burlesco. 3 *s.* burla.

mock (to) (mɔk) *t.* mofarse de, burlarse de; engañar.

model ('mɔdl) *s.* modelo. 2 diseño, muestra. 3 figurín.

model (to) ('mɔdl) *t.* modelar, formar, moldear.

moderate ('mɔdərit) *a.* moderado; templado. 2 mesurado.

moderate (to) ('mɔdəreit) *t.* moderar; templar; reprimir. 2 *i.* moderarse.

modern ('mɔdən) *a.* moderno.

modest ('mɔdist) *a.* modesto.

modify (to) ('mɔdifai) *t.* modificar. 2 moderar, templar.

moist (mɔist) *a.* húmedo.

moisten (to) ('mɔisn) *t.* humedecer, mojar. 2 *i.* humedecerse.

mole (moul) *s.* lunar. 2 rompeolas; muelle.

moment ('moumənt) *s.* momento, instante, coyuntura. 2 momento, importancia.

momentum (mou'mentəm) *s.* ímpetu, impulso.

monarch ('mɔnək) *s.* monarca.

Monday ('mʌndi, -dei) *s.* lunes.

money ('mʌni) *s.* moneda, dinero.

mongrel ('mʌŋgrəl) *a.-s.* mestizo, cruzado.

monk (mʌŋk) *s.* monje, fraile.

monkey ('mʌŋki) *s.* ZOOL. mono, mico, simio.

monkish ('mʌŋkiʃ) *a.* monacal; frailesco.

monotony (mə'nɔtəni) *s.* monotonía.

monster ('mɔnstəʳ) *s.* monstruo. 2 *a.* enorme.

month (mʌnθ) *s.* mes.

monument ('mɔnjumənt) *s.* monumento.

mood (mu:d) *s.* genio, talante. 2 humor, disposición.

moon (mu:n) *s.* ASTR. luna.

Moor (muəʳ) *s.* moro, sarraceno.

mop (mɔp) *s.* bayeta. 2 greña, cabello revuelto.

mop (to) (mɔp) *t.* fregar el suelo.

moral ('mɔrəl) *a.* moral. 2 virtuoso. 3 *s.* moraleja, enseñanza. 4 *pl.* moral, ética.

more (mɔ:ʳ, mɔəʳ) *a.-adv.* más; [not] *any* ~, ya no; ~ *or less*, [poco] más o menos;

once ~, otra vez: *the* ~ *the* *merrier*, cuantos más, mejor.

moreover (mɔ:'rouvəʳ) *adv.* además, por otra parte.

morning ('mɔ:niŋ) *s.* [la] mañana. 2 *a.* matinal, matutino.

morrow ('mɔrou) *s.* mañana, día siguiente.

morsel ('mɔ:səl) *s.* bocado.

mortar ('mɔ:təʳ) *s.* mortero.

mortgage ('mɔ:gidʒ) *s.* hipoteca.

moss (mɔs) *s.* BOT. musgo, moho.

most (moust) *adj. superl.* de MORE, MUCH y MANY. 2 muchos, los más, la mayoría de. 3 *for the* ~ *part*, en su mayor parte. 4 *adv.* sumamente, muy; más. 5 *s.* lo más, lo sumo.

moth (mɔθ) *s.* ENT. polilla.

mother ('mʌðəʳ) *s.* madre. 2 *a.* madre; materno; natal.

motion ('mouʃən) *s.* movimiento, moción. 2 seña, ademán. 3 moción, proposición.

motionless ('mouʃənlis) *a.* inmóvil.

motive ('moutiv) *s.* motivo. 2 *a.* motor, motriz.

motor ('moutəʳ) *s.* motor [lo que mueve]. 2 *a.* motor, motriz.

mound (maund) *s.* montículo, túmulo. 2 terraplén.

mount (maunt) *s.* monte, montaña. 2 montura, cabalgadura.

mount (to) (maunt) *t.* subir [una cuesta, etc.]; elevarse por. 2 subir, levantar. 3 montar(se en o sobre. 4

TEAT. poner en escena. 5 *i.* subir, elevarse, remontarse. 6 ascender [una cuenta].

mountain ('mauntin) *s.* montaña.

mountainous ('mauntinəs) *a.* montañoso, montuoso.

mourn (to) (mɔ:n) *t.* deplorar, lamentar, llorar. 2 *i.* lamentarse, dolerse.

mouse (maus) *s.* pl. **mice** (mais) *s.* ZOOL. ratón.

mouth (mauθ) *s.* ANAT. boca. 2 boca [entrada, orificio]. 3 bocas, desembocadura [de un río].

move (mu:v) *s.* movimiento. 2 jugada. 3 cambio de sitio.

move (to) (mu:v) *t.* mover. 2 inducir, persuadir. 3 menear. 4 remover, trasladar, mudar. 5 conmover, enternecer. 6 excitar [un sentimiento]. 7 proponer [en una asamblea]. 8 jugar [una pieza, un peón]. 9 *i.* moverse, andar. 10 irse. 11 trasladarse, mudarse.

movie ('mu:vi) *s.* película [de cine]. 2 *pl.* **the movies**, el cine.

much (mʌtʃ) *a.* mucho, -cha. 2 *adv.* muy, mucho: **as ~ as**, tanto como; **how ~?**, ¿cuánto?; **so ~ the better**, tanto mejor. 3 *s.* mucho, gran cosa.

mud (mʌd) *s.* barro, lodo.

muddy ('mʌdi) *a.* barroso, fangoso, lodoso. 2 turbio.

muffle (to) ('mʌfl) *t.* envolver, embozar, cubrir, tapar. 2 apagar [un sonido].

mule (mju:l) *s.* ZOOL. mulo.

multiply (to) ('mʌltiplai) *t.-i.* multiplicar(se.

multitude ('mʌltitju:d) *s.* multitud, muchedumbre.

munch (to) (mʌntʃ) *t.* mascar.

murder ('mə:dəʳ) *s.* asesinato, homicidio.

murder (to) ('mə:dəʳ) *t.* asesinar, matar.

murderer ('mə:dərəʳ) *s.* asesino, matador, homicida.

murderous ('mə:dərəs) *a.* asesino, homicida. 2 sanguinario, cruel.

murmur ('mə:məʳ) *s.* murmullo.

murmur (to) ('mə:məʳ) *i.-t.* murmurar, susurrar. 2 *i.* quejarse, refunfuñar.

muscle ('mʌsl) *s.* ANAT. músculo.

muse (to) (mju:z) *i.* meditar, reflexionar.

museum (mju(:)'ziəm) *s.* museo.

mushroom ('mʌʃrum) *s.* BOT. seta, hongo.

music ('mju:zik) *s.* música.

musician (mju(:)'ziʃən) *s.* músico.

1) **must** (mʌst, məst) *s.* mosto. 2 moho, ranciedad.

2) **must** (mʌst, məst) *aux. defect.* [usado sólo en el presente] deber, haber de, tener que. 2 deber de. 3 ser necesario.

mutiny ('mju:tini) *s.* motín.

mutiny (to) ('mju:tini) *i.* amotinarse, rebelarse.

mutter ('mʌtəʳ) *s.* murmullo.

mutter (to) ('mʌtəʳ) *t.-i.* murmurar, musitar, refunfuñar.

mutton ('mʌtn) *s.* carnero, carne de carnero.

mutual ('mju:tjuəl) *a.* mutual, mutuo; recíproco.

my (mai) *a. pos.* mi, mis. 2 *interj.* **oh, my!**, ¡caramba!

myself (mai'self) *pron.* yo, yo mismo; a mí, a mí mismo, me.

N

nail (neil) *s.* ANAT., ZOOL. uña: ~ *clippers*, cortauñas. 2 clavo; punta; tachón.

nail (to) (neil) *t.* clavar; fijar, sujetar. 2 clavetear.

naked ('neikid) *a.* desnudo.

name (neim) *s.* nombre. 2 fama, reputación. 3 *nick* ~, apodo, mote.

name (to) (neim) *t.* llamar, denominar, apellidar. 2 nombrar, hacer mención de.

nameless ('neimlis) *a.* anónimo. 2 innominado. 3 humilde.

namely ('neimli) *adv.* a saber, esto es.

nap (næp) *s.* siesta, sueñecito. 2 pelo [de un tejido].

napkin ('næpkin) *s.* servilleta. 2 toalleta.

narrative ('nærətiv) *a.* narrativo. 2 *s.* narración, relato.

narrow ('nærou) *a.* estrecho, angosto. 2 escaso, reducido. 3 mezquino, tacaño. 4 liberal. 5 *s. pl.* parte estrecha.

narrow (to) ('nærou) *t.-i.* estrechar(se, angostar(se. 2 reducir(se, encoger(se.

nation ('neiʃən) *s.* nación.

native ('neitiv) *a.* nativo [metal]. 2 natal, nativo, patrio. 3 *s.* natural; indígena.

nature ('neitʃə) *s.* naturaleza, natura. 2 carácter, especie. 3 natural, índole, genio.

naught (nɔ:t) *s.* cero. 2 nada.

naughty ('nɔ:ti) *a.* malo, desobediente, travieso.

naval ('neivəl) *a.* naval.

navigation (ˌnævi'geiʃən) *s.* navegación.

navy ('neivi) *s.* armada, flota.

near (niə^r) *a.* cercano, próximo, inmediato. 2 íntimo, estrecho. 3 *adv.* cerca: *to come* ~, acercarse. 4 casi, a punto de. 5 *prep.* cerca de.

near (to) (niə^r) *t.-i.* acercar(se.

nearby ('niəbai) *a.* cercano. 2 *adv.* cerca.

nearly ('niəli) *adv.* cerca, aproximadamente. 2 casi.

neat (ni:t) *a.* pulcro, ordenado. 2 puro; neto.

necessary ('nesisəri) *a.* necesario.

necessity (ni'sesiti) *s.* necesidad, precisión.

neck (nek) *s.* cuello, pescuezo,

garganta. 2 cuello [de una prenda, una vasija, etc.].

need (ni:d) *s.* necesidad.

need (to) (ni:d) *t.* necesitar. 2 *i.* estar necesitado. 3 *impers.* ser menester.

needful (ni:dful) *a.* necesario. 2 necesitado.

needless ('ni:dlis) *a.* innecesario, inútil.

neglect (ni'glekt) *s.* abandono.

neglect (to) (ni'glekt) *t.* abandonar, descuidar, omitir.

Negro ('ni:grou) *a.-s.* negro [pers.].

neighbo(u)r ('neibə^r) *s.* vecino. 2 amigo. 3 prójimo.

neighbo(u)rhood ('neibəhud)*s.* vecindad. 2 cercanías.

neighbo(u)ring ('neibəriŋ) *a.* vecino, adyacente.

neither ('naiðə^r, 'ni:ðə^r) *a.* ninguno [de los dos], ningún, na. 2 *conj.* ni. 3 *adv.* tampoco, ni siquiera. 4 *pron.* ninguno, ni el uno ni el otro.

nephew ('nevju(:) *s.* sobrino.

nerve (nə:v) *s.* ANAT., BOT. nervio. 2 nervio, vigor. 3 sangre fría; valor; descaro.

nervous ('nə:vəs) *a.* nervioso. 2 vigoroso, enérgico. 3 tímido.

nest (nest) *s.* nido.

nest (to) (nest) *i.* anidar. 2 buscar nidos.

net (net) *s.* red. 2 malla, redecilla [tejido]. 3 *a.* COM. neto; líquido.

never ('nevə^r) *adv.* nunca, jamás: ~ *again*, nunca más. 2 de ningún modo, no: ~ *mind*, no importa.

nevertheless (ˌnevəðə'les)*adv. conj.* no obstante, sin embargo.

new (nju:) *a.* nuevo. 2 tierno [pan]. 3 moderno. 4 reciente.

news (nju:z) *s.* noticia, noticias. 2 prensa, periódicos.

newspaper ('nju:sˌpeipə^r) *s.* diario, periódico.

next (nekst) *a.* próximo, inmediato, contiguo; siguiente, sucesivo; futuro, venidero. 2 *adv.* luego, después, a continuación. 3 *prep.* al lado de. 4 después de.

nice (nais) *s.* bueno, agradable; delicioso, exquisito, primoroso. 2 lindo. 3 elegante, refinado.' 4 amable, simpático. 5 fino, sutil; exacto, preciso. 6 concienzudo, escrupuloso.

nickel ('nikl) *s.* QUÍM. níquel. 2 *fam.* (E. U.)moneda de cinco centavos.

nickname ('nikneim) *s.* apodo, nombre familiar.

niece (ni:s) *s. f.* sobrina.

night (nait) *s.* noche. 2 *a.* de noche, nocturno.

nightingale ('naitiŋgeil) *s.* ORN. ruiseñor.

nine (nain) *a.-s.* nueve.

nineteen ('nain'ti:n) *a.-s.* diecinueve.

nineteenth ('nain'ti:nθ) *a.-s.* decimonono.

ninetieth ('naintiiθ) *a.-s.* nonagésimo.

ninety ('nainti) *a.-s.* noventa.

ninth (nainθ) *a.* nono, noveno.

nit (nit) *s.* liendre.

no (nou) *adv.* no. 2 *a.* ningún, ninguno: ~ *one*, ninguno, nadie.

nobility (nou'biliti) *s.* nobleza.

noble ('noubl) *a.-s.* noble.

nobody ('noubədi) *pron.* nadie, ninguno. *2 s.* nadie [pers. insignificante].

nod (nɔd) *s.* inclinación de cabeza [en señal de asentimiento, etc.]. *2* cabezada [el que duerme sentado].

nod (to) (nɔd) *i.-t.* inclinar la cabeza [en señal de asentimiento, saludo, etc.]. *2 i.* dar cabezadas, dormitar.

noise (nɔiz) *s.* ruido, sonido. *2* barullo. *3* rumor.

noise (to) (nɔiz) *t.* esparcir, divulgar, rumorear.

noisome ('nɔisəm) *a.* nocivo, pernicioso. *2* fétido, ofensivo, repugnante.

noisy ('nɔizi) *a.* ruidoso, clamoroso, bullicioso.

nominate (to) ('nɔmineit) *t.* nombrar. *2* proponer.

none (nʌn) *pron.* ninguno; nada. *2* nadie. *3 adv.* no, en ningún modo.

nonsense ('nɔnsəns) *s.* absurdidad, tontería, desatino. *2* tonterías, pamplinas.

noon (nu:n) *s.* mediodía.

nor (nɔ:ʳ) *conj.* ni. *2* tampoco: ~ *I*, yo tampoco.

north (nɔ:θ) *s.* norte. *2 a.* del norte, septentrional.

northern ('nɔ:ðən) *a.* del norte, septentrional.

nose (nouz) *s.* ANAT. ZOOL. nariz, narices. *2* nariz, olfato. *3* morro, hocico.

nostril ('nɔstril) *s.* ventana de la nariz. *2* ollar.

not (nɔt) *adv.* no: ~ *at all*, nada, de ningún modo; de nada.

notable ('noutəbl) *a.* notable. *2* memorable. *3 s.* notable, pers. de nota.

notch (nɔtʃ) *s.* muesca.

notch (to) (nɔtʃ) *t.* hacer muescas en. *2* mellar, dentar.

note (nout) *s.* nota, señal. *2* nota, apunte. *3* billete, esquela. *4* MÚS. nota.

note (to) (nout) *t.* notar, observar. *2* hacer notar. *3* anotar, asentar, registrar.

nothing ('nʌθiŋ) *s.* nada: *for* ~, de balde; inútilmente. *2* ARIT. cero. *3 adv.* nada, de ningún modo, no.

notice ('noutis) *s.* informe, aviso, advertencia. *2* conocimiento, observación, caso; mención. *3* atención, cortesía. *4* despido: *to give* ~, dar uno su despido.

notice (to) 'noutis) *t.* notar, observar, advertir. *2* hacer mención de; reseñar [un libro].

noticeable ('noutisəbl) *a.* notable.

notion ('nouʃən) *s.* noción. *2* idea, concepto. *3* intención; capricho. *4 pl.* (E. U.)mercería.

notorious (nou'tɔ:riəs) *a.* notorio, conocido, famoso. | Ús. gralte. en sentido peyorativo.

notwithstanding (‚nɔtwiθ'stændiŋ) *adv.* no obstante. *2 prep.* a pesar de. *3 conj.* aunque, por más que.

nought (nɔːt) *s.* NAUGHT.

noun (naun) *s.* GRAM. nombre.

nourish (to) ('nʌriʃ) *t.* nutrir, alimentar, sustentar.

novelty ('nɔvəlti) *s.* novedad.

November [nəu'vembəʳ] *s.* noviembre.

now (nau) *adv.* ahora; hoy día; actualmente: *from* ~ *on*, de ahora en adelante; ~ *and then*, de vez en cuando. *2* entonces. *3* ahora, ahora bien. *4* mas, pero.

nowadays ('nauədeiz) *adv.* hoy día, hoy en día.

nowhere ('nou(h)wɛəʳ) *adv.* en ninguna parte.

nucleus (xnju:kliəs) *s.* núcleo.

nuisance ('nju:sns) *s.* daño, molestia, fastidio. *2* pers. o cosa molesta, fastidiosa.

number ('nʌmbəʳ) *s.* número [en todas sus acepciones].

numerous ('nju:mərəs) *a.* nu-meroso. *2* muchos.

nurse (nə:s) *s.* ama [de cría], nodriza, niñera. *2* enfermera.

nurse (to) (nə:s) *t.* criar, ama-mantar. *2* alimentar; abrigar; fomentar. *3* cuidar [de un niño, a un enfermo].

nursery ('nə:sri) *s.* cuarto de los niños: ~ *rhymes,* cuen-tos en verso. *2* criadero, vi-vero.

nut (nʌt) *s.* вот. nuez.

nymph (nimf) *s.* ninfa.

O

oak (ouk) *s.* roble.

oar (ɔːʳ, ɔəʳ) *s.* remo.

oat (out) *s.* BOT. avena.

oath (ouθ) *s.* juramento, jura. 2 juramento, reniego.

obedience (ə'biːdjəns) *s.* obediencia.

obey (to) (ə'bei) *t.-i.* obedecer.

object (ɔbdʒikt) *s.* objeto.

object (to) (əb'dʒekt) *t.* objetar. 2 reprochar.' 3 *i.* oponerse, poner objeción.

objection (əb'dʒekʃən) *s.* objeción, reparo, inconveniente.

obligation (ˌɔbli'geiʃən) *s.* obligación, deber. 2 deuda de agradecimiento.

oblige (to) (ə'blaidʒ) *t.* obligar. 2 complacer, servir, poner en deuda [por un favor].

obscure (əbs'kjuəʳ) *a.* obscuro. 2 vago, indistinto.

obscure (to) (əbs'kjuəʳ) *t.* obscurecer. 2 ocultar.

observation (ˌɔbzə(ː)'veiʃən) *s.* observación.

observe (to) (əb'zəːv) *t.* observar. 2 guardar [una fiesta]. 3 decir, hacer notar.

obsolete ('ɔbsəliːt) *a.* anticuado, desusado.

obtain (to) (əb'tein) *t.* obtener, alcanzar, lograr. 2 *i.* ser general, estar en boga.

obvious ('ɔbviəs) *a.* obvio, evidente, palmario. 2 sencillo, fácil de descubrir.

occasion (ə'keiʒən) *s.* ocasión, oportunidad, caso, circunstancia. 2 causa, motivo, origen; pie.

occasion (to) (ə'keiʒən) *t.* ocasionar, causar, motivar.

occasional (ə'keiʒənl) *a.* ocasional, casual.

occupy (to) ('ɔkjupai) *t.* ocuparse. 2 emplear, invertir.

occur (to) (ə'kəːʳ) *i.* hallarse. 2 ocurrir, suceder. 3 ocurrirse [a uno].

ocean ('ouʃən) *s.* océano.

October (ɔk'toubəʳ) *s.* octubre.

odd (ɔd) *a.* impar, non. 2 suelto, solo. 3 ocasional. 4 y tantos; y pico. 5 raro, curioso, extraño.

odo(u)r ('oudəʳ) *s.* olor.

oft (ɔːf, ɔf) *adv.* lejos, fuera;

enteramente, del todo; indica alejamiento, ausencia, separación, disminución, privación, cesación. 2 *prep.* lejos de, fuera de; de o desde. 3 *a.* alejado, ausente. 4 libre; de asueto. 5 suspendido, interrumpido. 6 cerrado, cortado [gas, agua, etc]. 7 FÚTBOL ~ *side*, fuera de juego.

offence (ə'fens) *s.* ofensa, agravio.

offer ('ɔfəʳ) *s.* oferta, ofrecimiento. 2 propuesta.

offer (to) ('ɔfəʳ) *t.-i.* ofrecer(se. 2 *t.* brindar. 3 hacer, inferir.

office ('ɔfis) *s.* oficio, función, ministerio. 2 cargo, empleo [esp. público o de autoridad]. 3 oficina, despacho, agencia, negociado.

officer ('ɔfisəʳ) *s.* MIL., MAR. oficial. 2 funcionario.

official (ə'fiʃəl) *a.* oficial. 2 *s.* el que tiene un cargo público o de gobierno. 3 funcionario.

oft (ɔ(:)ft), **often** ('ɔ(:)fn)*adv.* a menudo, frecuentemente.

oil (ɔil) *s.* aceite; óleo. 2 petróleo.

old (ould) *a.* viejo; anciano; añoso; añejo; antiguo.

old-fashioned ('ould'fæʃən) *a.* anticuado; pasado de moda.

olive ('ɔliv) *s.* BOT. olivo: ~ *grave*, olivar; 2 aceituna, oliva.

omelet, omelette ('ɔmlit) *s.* tortilla de huevos.

omit (to) (o(u)'mit) *t.* omitir.

on (ɔn, ən) *prep.* en, sobre, a, de, con; por; bajo: ~ *the table*, sobre la mesa; ~ *board*,

a bordo; ~ *foot*, a pie; ~*credit*, al fiado; ~ *arriving*, al llegar; ~ *duty*, de servicio. 2 ~ *Monday*, el lunes. 3 *adv.* puesto: *to have one's hat* ~, llevar puesto el sombrero. 4 adelante, continuando. 5 *a.* que funciona; abierto, encendido.

once (wʌns) *adv.-s.* vez, una vez; ~ *and again*, una y otra vez; ~ *for all*, de una vez para siempre; *at* ~, a la vez, de una vez; en seguida. 2 alguna vez. 3 en otro tiempo. 4 *conj.* una vez que.

one (wʌn) *a.* uno, una: ~ *hundred*, ciento. 2 un solo, único. 3 unido, idéntico, lo mismo: *it is all* ~ *to me*, me da lo mismo. 4 un cierto, un tal. 5 *pron.* uno, una: *no* ~, nadie. 6 *s.* uno. 7 *the* ~ *who*, el que, aquel que; *this* ~, éste.

onion ('ʌnjən) *s.* BOT. cebolla.

only (ounli) *a.* solo, único. 2 *adv.* sólo, solamente, únicamente. 3 *if* ~, ojalá, si, si al menos. 4 *conj.* sólo que, pero.

onto ('ɔntu, -te) *prep.* hacia, sobre.

onward(s ('ɔnwəd(z) *adv.* hacia adelante.

open ('oupən) *a.* abierto: *in the open air*, al aire libre. 2 raso, descubierto. 3 descubierto [coche, etc.]. 4 expuesto [a].

open (to) ('oupən) *t.* abrir. 2 ofrecer a la vista. 3 iniciar, empezar: *to* ~ *up*, descubrir, abrir, hacer accesible. 4 *i.* abrir, abrirse. 5 confiarse, abrir su corazón a.

opening ('oupəniŋ) *s.* apertura. 2 abertura, entrada, brecha, boquete. 3 TEAT. estreno.

operate (to) ('ɔpəreit) *t.* hacer funcionar, mover, manejar, dirigir. 2 efectuar. 3 *i.* obrar, producir efecto. 4 COM., MIL., CIR. operar.

opinion (ə'pinjən) *s.* opinión. 2 buen concepto.

oppose (to) (ə'pouz) *t.* oponer. 2 oponerse a, resistir.

opposite ('ɔpəzit) *a.* opuesto. 2 frontero. 3 contrario, adverso. 4 *prep.* enfrente de. 5 *adv.* enfrente.

oppress (to) (ə'pres) *t.* oprimir. 2 tiranizar. 3 agobiar.

oppression (ə'preʃən) *s.* opresión, tiranía.

optimistic (ˌɔpti'mistik) *a.* optimista.

or (ɔ:ʳ) *conj.* o, u. 2 si no, de otro modo.

oral ('ɔ:rəl) *a.* oral.

orange ('ɔrindʒ) *s.* BOT. naranja: ~ *blossom,* azahar.

orb (ɔ:b) *s.* orbe, esfera.

orbit ('ɔ:bit) *s.* ASTR. órbita.

orchard ('ɔ:tʃəd) *s.* huerto.

orchestra ('ɔ:kistrə) *s.* orquesta. 2 TEAT. platea.

ordain (to) (ɔ:'dein) *t.* ordenar.

order ('ɔ:dəʳ) *s.* orden [disposición o sucesión regular]: *in* ~, en orden; *out of* ~, desordenado; descompuesto. 2 orden [religiosa, militar, etc.]. 3 condecoración. 4 orden, mandato, precepto. 5 orden [sacramento]. 6 orden, clase, grado. 7 COM. pedido, encargo. 8 *in* ~ *to,* para, a fin de.

order (to) ('ɔ:dəʳ) *t.* ordenar [poner un orden; disponer, mandar]. 2 COM. pedir; encargar. 3 ECCL. ordenar.

orderly ('ɔ:dəli) *a.* ordenado.

ordinary ('ɔ:din(ə)ri) *a.-s.* ordinario. 2 *in* ~, en ejercicio.

ore (ɔ:ʳ,ɔəʳ) *s.* MIN. mineral, ganga, mena.

organ ('ɔ:gən) *s.* órgano.

organization (ˌɔ:gənai'zeiʃən)*s.* organización.

organize (to) ('ɔ:gənaiz)*t.-i.* organizar(se.

origin ('ɔridʒin) *s.* origen.

original (ə'ridʒənl) *a.* original. 2 primitivo. 3 *s.* original.

ornament ('ɔ:nəmənt) *s.* ornamento, adorno.

ornament (to) ('ɔ:nəment) *t.* ornamentar, adornar.

orphan (ˌɔ:fən) *a.-s.* huérfano.

other ('ʌðəʳ) *a.* otro, otra, otras, otras. 2 *pron.* (*pl.* **others**) otro, etc. 3 *adv.* [other than], más que; otra cosa que.

otherwise ('ʌðə-waiz) *adv.* de otra manera. 2 en otro caso, fuera de eso. 3 *conj.* si no, de lo contrario.

otter ('ɔtəʳ) *s.* ZOOL. nutria.

1) **ought** (ɔ:t) *pron.-adv.* AUGHT.

2) **ought** (ɔ:t) *def.* y *aux.* [seguido de infinitivo con *to*] deber [en presente o mejor condicional]: *I ~ to write,* debo o debería escribir.

ounce (auns) *s.* onza [28.35 gr.].

our ('auəʳ) *a.* nuestro, nuestra, etc.

ours ('auəz) *pron. pos.* [el] nuestro, [la] nuestra, [los] nuestros, [las] nuestras.

ourselves (‚auə'selvz) *pron.* nosotros mismos. 2 nos, a nosotros mismos.

out (aut) *adv.* fuera, afuera, hacia fuera. 2 claro, sin rodeos: *speak* ~, hable claro. 3 completamente, hasta el fin. 4 por, movido por: ~ *of pity*, por compasión. 5 de, con: ~ *of a bottle*, de una botella. 6 *a.* ausente. 7 cerrado, apagado; expirado. 8 publicado, que ha salido. 9 ~ *and away*, con mucho.

outbreak ('autbreik) *s.* erupción. 2 arrebato, estallido.

outdoor ('aut'dɔ:) . el aire libre, el campo, la calle. 2 **-s** (-z) *adv.* fuera de casa, al aire libre.

outer ('autəʳ) *a.* exterior.

outfit ('autfit) *s.* equipo.

outfit (to) ('autfit) *t.* equipar.

outlet ('aut-let) *s.* salida.

outline ('aut-lain) *s.* contorno, perfil. 2 bosquejo, esbozo.

output ('autput) *s.* producción, rendimiento.

outrage ('aut-reidʒ) *s.* ultraje, desafuero, atropello.

outrage (to) ('aut-reidʒ) *t.* ultrajar, atropellar. 2 violar.

outrageous (aut'reidʒəs) *a.* ultrajante, 2 violento. 3 desaforado, enorme, atroz.

outside ('aut'said) *s.* exterior, parte externa; superficie. 2 apariencia. 3 lo más, lo sumo. 4 *a.* exterior. 5 superficial. 6 extraño. 7 neutral. 8 *adv.* fuera, afuera, por fuera. 9 *prep.* fuera de, más allá de; excepto.

outstanding (aut'stændiŋ) *a.* saledizo, saliente. 2 destacado, notable.

outstretch (to) (aut'stretʃ) *t.* extender, alargar.

outward ('autwed) *a.* exterior. 2 aparente. 3 que va hacia fuera; que sale, de ida. 4 **-s** (-z) *adv.* hacia fuera.

oval ('ouvəl) *a.* oval, ovalado. 2 *s.* óvalo.

oven ('ʌvn) *s.* horno, hornillo.

over ('ouvəʳ) *adv.* arriba, por encima. 2 enfrente. 3 al revés, trastornado. 4 completamente. 5 más, de más. 6 *to run* ~, salirse, derramarse. 7 ~ *again*, de nuevo. 8 ~ *and above*, además de. 9 *prep.* sobre, encima de, por encima de. 10 al otro lado de. 11 más de. 12 durante. 13 por todo [un espacio, camino, etc.]. 14 de, a propósito de. 15 *a.* superior, más alto. 16 acabado.

overcoat ('ouvəkout) *s.* sobretodo, gabán, abrigo.

overcome (to) (‚ouvə'kʌm) *t.* vencer, triunfar de. 2 vencer, superar, allanar [obstáculos, etc.]. 3 sobreponerse a.

overflow ('ouvə-flou) *s.* inundación, 2 desbordamiento.

overflow (to) (‚ouvə'flou) *t.-i.* inundar, desbordar(se.

overhead ('ouvə'hed) *a.-adv.* [situado] arriba, en lo alto.

overloock (to) (‚ouvə'luk) *t.* mirar desde lo alto. 2 dominar [estar más elevado]. 3 tener vista a. 4 inspeccionar, vigilar. 5 repasar, revisar. 6 pasar por alto, no ver.

overrun (to) (‚ouvə'rʌn) *t.* cubrir enteramente, invadir. 2

recorrer. *3* pasar por encima.

oversea ('ouvə'si:) *a.* de ultramar. *2* **-s** (-z) *adv.* ultramar, allende los mares.

overtake (to) (,ouvə'teik) *t.* alcanzar, atrapar.

overthrow (to) (,ouvə'θrou)*t.* volcar, tumbar, derribar.

overwhelm (to) (,ouvə'welm) *t.* inundar. *2* abrumar. *3* confundir, anonadar.

owe (to) (ou) *t.* deber, adeudar.

owl (aul) *s.* ORN. búho.

own (oun) *a.* propio, mismo, de uno: *his* ~ *mother*, su propia madre. *2 s.* *one's* ~, lo suyo, lo de uno.

owner ('ounəʳ) *s.* dueño.

ox (ɔks), *pl.* **oxen** ('ɔksən) *s.* buey: *ox-eye*, ojo de buey.

oxygen (,ɔksidʒən) *s.* oxígeno.

oyster ('ɔistəʳ) *s.* ostra.

P

pace (peis) s. paso.

pacific (pə'sifik) a. pacífico.

pack (pæk) s. lío, fardo, bala; paquete; carga.

pack (to) (pæk) t.-i. empacar, empaquetar; envasar. 2 i. reunirse, juntarse.

package ('pækidʒ) s. fardo.

pad (pæd) s. cojincillo, almohadilla; postizo, relleno.

pad (to) (pæd) t. rellenar, acolchar.

page (peidʒ) s. paje. 2 botones; criado joven. 3 página.

pageant ('pædʒənt) s. cabalgata, desfile.

paid (peid) V. TO PAY.

pail (peil) s. herrada, cubo. 2 MAR. balde.

pain (pein) s. dolor, pena; aflicción. 2 pena [castigo]. 3 trabajo, molestia.

pain (to) (pein) t. doler, punzar. 2 causar dolor, afligir.

painful ('peinful) a. doloroso. 2 penoso, aflictivo, angustioso. 3 arduo.

paint (peint) s. pintura, color. 2 afeite, colorete.

paint (to) (peint) t.-i. pintar.

painter ('peintəʳ) s. pintor.

painting ('peintiŋ) s. pintura [acción, arte; color]. 2 pintura, cuadro.

pair (pɛəʳ) s. par, pareja.

pair (to) (pɛəʳ) t. aparear, casar, acoplar. 2 parear. 3 i. aparearse.

palace ('pælis) s. palacio.

pale (peil) a. pálido. 2 descolorido. 3 s. estaca, palizada.

palm (pɑ:m) s. BOT. palma. 2 fig. palma, victoria. 3 palma [de la mano].

palm (to) (pɑ:m) t. manosear. 2 escamotear.

pan (pæn) s. cacerola, cazuela, cazo.

pane (pein) s. cristal, vidrio [de ventana, etc.].

pang (pæŋ) s. punzada.

panic ('pænik) a.-s. pánico.

pant (pænt) s. jadeo, resuello.

pant (to) (pænt) i. jadear, resollar. 2 palpitar.

pantry ('pæntri) s. despensa.

papa (pə'pɑ:) s. fam. papá.

paper ('peipəʳ) s. papel. 2 papel, periódico, diario.

paper (to) ('peipə^r) *t.* empapelar.

parade (pə'reid) *s.* ostentación; alarde, gala. 2 MIL. parada, revista. 3 desfile.

paradise ('pærədais) *s.* paraíso.

paragraph ('pærəgrɑ:f) *s.* párrafo. 2 suelto, artículo corto.

parallel ('pærəlel) *a.* paralelo. 2 *s.* paralelismo, semejanza. 3 par, igual.

parallel (to) ('pærəlel) *t.* igualar, parangonar.

parcel ('pɑ:sl) *s.* paquete, bulto. 2 hatajo. 3 parcela.

parcel (to) ('pɑ:sl) *t.* parcelar, dividir. 2 empaquetar.

pardon ('pɑ:dn) *s.* perdón.

pardon (to) ('p:dn) *t.* perdonar. 2 indultar. 3 excusar.

parent ('pɛərənt) *s.* padre o madre. 2 *pl.* padres.

parish ('pæriʃ) *s.* parroquia.

park (pɑ:k) *s.* parque.

park (to) (pɑ:k) *t.-i.* aparcar.

parliament ('pɑ:ləmənt) *s.* parlamento, cortes.

parlo(u)r ('pɑ:lə^r) *s.* sala de estar o recibimiento. 2 (E. U.)salón [dé belleza]; sala [de billares]. 3 locutorio.

parson ('pɑ:sn) *s.* párroco, cura, sacerdote.

part (pɑ:t) *s.* parte. 2 cuidado, deber. 3 TEAT. papel. 4 MÚS. parte. 5 MEC. pieza. 6 (E. U.)raya [del cabello]. 7 *pl.* lugares, países. 8 talento, dotes. 9 *a.-adv.* parcial, parcialmente.

part (to) (pɑ:t) *t.* dividir, *partir.* 2 repartir. 3 *to ~ the hair,* hacer la raya. 4 *i.* separarse, desprenderse. 5 irse, despedirse.

particle ('pɑ:tikl) *s.* partícula. 2 pizca.

particular (pə'tikjulə^r) *a.* particular. 2 minucioso, detallado. 3 *s.* pormenor, detalle.

partition (pɑ:'tiʃən) *s.* partición. 2 división. 3 tabique.

partner ('pɑ:tnə^r) *s.* socio [en un negocio]. 2 compañero [en el juego]. 3 pareja [de baile]. 4 cónyuge.

partridge ('pɑ:tridʒ) *s.* ORN. perdiz.

party ('pɑ:ti) *s.* partido [político], bando. 2 partido, causa. 3 reunión, fiesta. 4 parte [en un contrato, una contienda, etc.]. 5 individuo, sujeto.

pass (pɑ:s) *s.* paso, pasaje. 2 paso [acción o permiso de pasar]; pase; salvoconducto. 3 aprobación [en exámenes].

pass (to) (pɑ:s) *i.* pasar [en todas sus acepciones]. 2 *t.* pasar [atravesar; cruzar; dejar atrás]. 3 cruzarse con. 4 pasar de, exceder. 5 pasar, sufrir; tolerar. 6 tomar [un acuerdo]; aprobar [a un examinando, un proyecto de ley]. 7 pasar, hacer pasar, dar. 8 omitir. ¶ Pret. p.: *passed* o *past.*

passage ('pæsidʒ) *s.* paso, pasaje, tránsito. 2 paso, entrada, pasadizo. 3 pasaje [de un buque].

passenger ('pæsindʒə^r) *s.* viajero, pasajero.

passionate ('pæʃənit) *a.* apasionado.

past (pɑ:st) *a.* pasado, pretérito; último, ex, que fue. 2 consumado. 3 GRAM. pasivo [participio]; pretérito [tiempo]. 4 *s.* pasado. 5 *prep.* pasado, después de; fuera de; sin.

paste (peist) *s.* pasta, masa. 2 engrudo.

paste (to) peist) *t.* pegar con engrudo.

pastor ('pɑ:stə^r) *s.* pastor (esp. espiritual).

pastry ('peistri) *s.* pastelería, pasteles, repostería.

pasture ('pɑ:stʃə^r) *s.* pasto.

pasture (to) ('pɑ:stʃə^r) *t.-i.* pacer, apacentarse.

pat (pæt) *a.* exacto, conveniente, oportuno. 2 *adv.* oportunamente. 3 *s.* golpecito, palmadita.

pat (to) (pæt) *t.* dar palmaditas o golpecitos.

path (pɑ:θ) *s.* camino, senda.

patience ('peiʃənt) *s.* paciencia. 2 solitario [juego].

patient ('peʃənt) *a.* paciente. 2 susceptible [de].

patron ('peitrən) *a.* patrón, tutelar. 2 *s.* patrón [santo]. 3 patrono, protector.

pattern ('pætən) *s.* modelo, muestra, dechado; ejemplar, tipo. 2 patrón, plantilla.

pause (pɔ:z) *s.* pausa.

pause (to) (pɔ:z) *i.* pausar.

pave (to) (peiv) *t.* pavimentar.

pavement ('peivmənt) *s.* pavimiento. 2 acera; andén.

pawn (pɔ:n) *s.* peón [de ajedrez]. 2 empeño, garantía.

pawn (to) (pɔ:n) *t.* empeñar [un objeto].

pay (pei) *s.* paga, sueldo.

pay (to) (pei) *t.-i.* pagar. 2 *t.* costear, sufragar. 3 hacer [una visita; la corte]; rendir [homenaje]; prestar [atención]; dirigir [cumplidos]. 4 *i.* compensar, ser provechoso. ¶ Pret. y p. p.: **paid** (peid).

payment ('peimənt) *s.* pago.

pea (pi:) *s.* BOT. guisante.

peace (pi:s) *s.* paz. 2 orden público. 3 quietud.

peaceful ('pi:sful) *a.* pacífico.

peach (pi:tʃ) *s.* BOT. melocotón.

peacock ('pi:kɔk) *s.* ORN. pavo real.

peak (pi:k) *s.* pico, cumbre.

pear (pɛə^r) *s.* BOT. pera.

pearl (pə:l) *s.* perla, margarita.

pearl (to) (pə:l) *t.* perlar. 2 *i.* pescar perlas.

peasant ('pezənt) *s.* labriego.

pebble ('pebl) *s.* guija, guijarro, china.

peck (pek) *s.* picotazo.

peck (to) (pek) *t.* picar.

peculiar (pi'kju:liə^r) *a.* peculiar. 2 particular, especial.

peel (pi:l) *s.* piel, corteza.

peel (to) (pi:l) *t.* pelar, mondar, descascarar. 2 *i.* pelarse, descascararse.

peep (pi:p) *s.* atisbo, ojeada. 2 asomo. 3 pío [de ave].

peep (to) (pi:p) *i.* atisbar, fisgar. 2 asomarse. 3 piar.

peer (piə^r) *s.* par, igual, compañero. 2 par [noble].

peer (to) (piə^r) *i.* mirar [atentamente]. 2 asomar, salir.

peg (peg) *s.* clavija, estaquilla, taco. 2 percha, colgador. 3 estaca, jalón.

pelt (pelt) *s.* pellejo, cuero. 2 golpeo.

pelt (to) (pelt) *t.* apedrear; tirar, hacer llover [algo] sobre. 2 *i.* caer con fuerza [la lluvia]. 3 apresurarse.

pen (pen) *s.* pluma [para escribir].

pen (to) (pen) *t.* escribir. ¶ Pret. y p. p.: *penned* o *pent*.

penalty ('penəlti) *s.* pena. castigo.

pencil ('pensl) *s.* lápiz, lapicero. 2 pincel fino.

penetrate (to) ('penitreit) *t.-i.* penetrar. 2 *i.* atravesar.

penny ('peni), *pl.* **pennies** ('peniz) o [en comp.] **pence** (pens) *s.* penique.

pension ('penʃən) *s.* pensión, retiro, jubilación. 2 ('pɑ:ŋsiɔ:ŋ) pensión, casa de huéspedes.

pension (to) ('penʃən) *t.* pensionar, retirar, jubilar.

people ('pi:pl) *s.* pueblo, raza, nación. 2 pueblo [de un país, etc.]. 3 gente, personas.

people (to) ('pi:pl) *t.* poblar.

pepper ('pepəʳ) *s.* pimienta.

pepper (to) ('pepəʳ) *t.* sazonar con pimienta.

perceive (to) (pə'si:v) *t.* percibir, ver, distinguir.

percentage (pə'sentidz) *s.* porcentaje.

perception (pə'sepʃən) *s.* percepción.

perch (pə:tʃ) *s.* ICT. perca. 2 pértica [medida]. 3 percha, alcándara. 4 pértiga, palo.

perch (to) (pə:tʃ) *t.-i.* encaramar(se. 2 *i.* posarse [en una percha, rama, etc.].

perfect ('pə:fikt) *a.* perfecto. 2 acabado, consumado.

perfection (pə'fekʃən) *s.* perfección.

perform (to) (pə'fɔ:m) *t.* hacer, ejecutar, realizar. 2 *i.* actuar. 3 desempeñar un papel, tocar un instrumento, etc. 4 funcionar.

performance (pə'fɔ:məns) *s.* ejecución, cumplimiento, desempeño. 2 acción, hazaña. 3 función, representación, concierto; actuación de un artista, etc.

perfume ('pə:fju:m) *s.* perfume.

perfume (to) (pə'fju:m) *t.* perfumar, embalsamar.

perhaps (pə'hæps, præps) *adv.* quizá, tal vez.

peril ('peril) *s.* peligro, riesgo.

perilous ('periləs) *a.* peligroso, expuesto.

period ('piəriəd) *s.* período.

perish (to) ('periʃ) *i.* perecer.

perjury ('pə:dʒəri) *s.* perjurio.

permanent (pə:mənənt) *a.* permanente, estable, duradero.

permission (pə'miʃən) *s.* permiso, licencia, venia.

permit ('pə:mit) *s.* permiso, licencia, pase, guía.

perpetual (pə'petjuəl, -tʃuəl) *a.* perpetuo. 2 continuo, incesante.

perplex (to) (pə'pleks) *t.* dejar perplejo; confundir.

persevere (to) (ˌpə:si'viəʳ) *i.* perseverar.

persist (to) (pə'sist) *i.* persistir. 2 insistir, porfiar.

person ('pə:sn) *s.* persona.

personable ('pə:sənəbl) *a.* bien parecido.

personal ('pə:sənl) *a.* personal. 2 *s.* nota de sociedad.

personality (,pə:sə'næliti) *s.* personalidad.

personnel (,pə:sə'nel) *s.* personal, dependencia.

persuade (to) (pə'sweid) *t.* persuadir, inducir.

pertain (to) (pə:'tein) *i.* pertenecer; corresponder.

pertinent ('pə:tinənt) *a.* pertinente, oportuno, atinado.

perturb (to) (pə'tə:b) *t.* perturbar, agitar.

pet (pet) *a.* querido, mimado, favorito. 2 *s.* animal favorito.

pet (to) (pet) *t.* mimar, acariciar.

petition (pi'tiʃən) *s.* petición, solicitud. 2 ruego, súplica.

petition (to) (pi'tiʃən) *t.* solicitar. 2 dirigir una petición a.

petty ('peti) *a.* pequeño, insignificante, mezquino. 2 inferior, subalterno.

phase (feiz) *s.* fase.

philosopher (fi'lɔsəfəʳ) *s.* filósofo.

philosophy (fi'lɔsəfi) *s.* filosofía.

phone (foun) *s.* fam. teléfono.

phone (to) (foun) *t.-i.* telefonear.

photograph ('foutəgrɑ:f) *s.* fotografía.

photograph (to) ('foutəgrɑ:f) *t.-i.* fotografiar.

phrase (freiz) *s.* frase, locución.

physical ('fizikəl) *a.* físico.

physician (fi'ziʃən) *s.* médico.

piano ('pjænou, 'pjɑ:nou) *s.* piano.

pick (pik) *s.* pico [herramienta]. 2 MÚS. púa, plectro. 3 cosecha. 4 selección.

pick (to) (pik) *t.* picar, agujerear. 2 coger [flores, frutos, etc.]. 3 escoger. 4 limpiar, pelar, mondar. 5 forzar [una cerradura]. 6 picotear. 7 comer a bocaditos.

picket ('pikit) *s.* estaca, piquete. 2 MIL. piquete.

pickle ('pikl) *s.* salmuera, escabeche, adobo.

pickle (to) ('pikl) *t.* escabechar, adobar.

picnic (to) ('piknik) *i.* comer o merendar en el campo.

picture ('piktʃəʳ) *s.* pintura, cuadro. 2 imagen, retrato; lámina, grabado. 3 escena, cuadro. 4 descripción. 5 OPT. imagen. 6 *the pictures,* el cine.

picture (to) ('piktʃəʳ) *t.* pintar, retratar. 2 describir. 3 *i.* imaginarse, representarse.

pie (pai) *s.* pastel, empanada.

piece (pi:s) *s.* pieza, trozo, pedazo. 2 pieza [de tela, de un juego]; ejemplo, caso, acto: ~ *of furniture,* mueble. 3 MÚS., LIT., TEAT. pieza, obra.

piece (to) (pi:s) *t.* apedazar, remendar. 2 reunir.

pier (piəʳ) *s.* pilar, estribo. 2 muelle, embarcadero.

pierce (to) (piəs) *t.* atravesar.

pile (pail) *s.* pelo, pelusa, lana. 2 pila, montón. 3 ELECT. pila, batería. 4 pira. 5 estaca, pilote.

pile (to) (pail) *t.* amontonar,

apilar. 2 sostener con pilotes. 3 i. acumularse.

pilgrim ('pilgrim) *s.* peregrino, romero.

pillar ('pilər) *s.* pilar, columna; sostén.

pillow (pilou) *s.* almohada.

pilot ('pailət) *m.* MAR. piloto, práctico. 2 AVIA. piloto.

pilot (to) ('pailət) *t.* pilotar.

pin (pin) *s.* alfiler. 2 prendedor, broche. 3 clavillo, clavija, chaveta. 4 MEC. gorrón; muñón. 5 bolo [para jugar].

pin (to) (pin) *t.* prender [con alfileres]; clavar, sujetar.

pinch (pintʃ) *s.* aprieto, apuro. 2 punzada, dolor. 3 pellizco. 4 pulgarada.

pinch (to) (pintʃ) *t.* pellizcar. 2 apretar [el zapato]. 3 hurtar. 4 reducir, escatimar. 5 coger, prender. 6 i. economizar.

pine (pain) *s.* BOT. pino: ~ *cone*, piña; ~ *nut*, piñón.

pine (to) (pain) *i.* desfallecer, languidecer. | Gralte. con *away*. 2 afligirse.

pineapple ('pain,æpl) *s.* BOT. ananá, piña de América.

pink (piŋk) *s.* BOT. clavel; clavellina. 2 color de rosa. 3 estado perfecto. 4 *a.* rosado.

pint (paint) *s.* pinta, cuartillo [medida].

pioneer (,paiə'niər) *s.* MIL. zapador, gastador. 2 pionero.

pious ('paiəs) *a.* pío, piadoso, devoto.

pipe (paip) *s.* tubo, cañería. 2 flauta, caramillo. 3 pitido, silbido. 4 pipa [para fumar]. 7 MÚS. gaita.

pipe (to) (paip) *t.-i.* tocar [en] el caramillo. 2 chiflar, pitar.

piper ('paipər) *s.* gaitero.

pique (pi:k) *s.* pique, resentimiento.

pique (to) (pi:k) *t.* picar, irritar.

pirate ('paiərit) *s.* pirata.

pirate (to) (p'aiərit) *t.-i.* piratear.

pistol ('pistl) *s.* pistola.

pit (pit) *s.* hoyo; foso, pozo. 2 boca [del estómago]. 3 hueso [de fruta].

pitch (pitʃ) *s.* pez, brea, alquitrán. 2 echada, tiro [en ciertos juegos]. 3 inclinación, pendiente. 4 MÚS., FONÉT. tono.

pitch ((to) (pitʃ) *t.* empecinar, embrear. 2 tirar, arrojar. 3 clavar, fijar en tierra; poner, colocar. 4 i. echarse o caer de cabeza.

pitcher ('pitʃər) *s.* jarro, cántaro. 2 lanzador.

pitiful ('pitiful) *a.* PITIABLE. 2 compasivo.

pity ('piti) *s.* piedad, compasión. *what a* ~ *!*, ¡qué lástima!

pity (to) ('piti) *t.* compadecer, apiadarse de.

pivot ('pivət) *s.* eje, pivote.

place (pleis) *s.* lugar, sitio; parte; local. 2 puesto; rango, dignidad. 3 empleo, cargo. 4 plazuela.

place (to) (pleis) *t.* colocar, poner, situar, acomodar.

plague (pleig) *s.* plaga. 2 peste. 3 calamidad.

plague (to) (pleig) *t.* plagar, infestar. 2 molestar.

plain (plein) *a.* llano, liso. *2* claro, evidente. *3* franco, sincero. *4* simple, corriente. *5* feo, sin atractivo. *6* puro, sin mezcla. *7 adv.* claramente. *8 s.* llanura.

plan (plæn) *s.* plano, diseño, esquema. *2* PERSP., ESC. plano. *3* plan, proyecto.

plan (to) (plæn) *t.* planear, proyectar; planificar.

plane (plein) *a.* plano. *2 s.* plano [superficie]. *3* nivel. *4* aeroplano, avión. *5* cepillo, garlopa. *6* BOT. ~ *tree*, plátano [árbol].

plane (to) (plein) *i.* AVIA. volar; planear.

planet ('plænit) *s.* ASTR. planeta.

plank (plæŋk) *s.* tablón, tabla.

plant (pla:nt) *s.* BOT. planta. *2* mata, esqueje. *3* equipo, instalación. *4* fábrica, taller.

plant (to) (pla:nt) *t.* plantar, sembrar. *2* implantar.

plantation (plæn'teiʃən) *s.* plantación. *2* plantío.

plaster ('pla:stəʳ) *s.* yeso. *2* FARM. parche.

plaster (to) ('pla:stəʳ) *t.* enyesar, enlucir. *2* emplastar.

plate (pleit) *s.* placa. *2* grabado, lámina. *3* plato, fuente. *4* vajilla [de plata, etc.].

plate (to) (pleit) *t.* planchear. *2* dorar, platear, niquelar, chapear. *3* IMPR. clisar.

platform ('plætfɔ:m) *s.* plataforma. *2* FERROC. andén.

play (pleid) *s.* juego [diversión, deporte], broma. *2* MEC. juego. *3* juego, funcionamiento, acción. *4* juego [de luces, colores, etc.]. *5* TEAT. representación. *6* TEAT. comedia, drama, etc.

play (to) (plei) *t.* jugar [una partida, un naipe, etc.]. *2* poner en acción, hacer, causar. *3* fingir. *4* TEAT. representar [una obra]; hacer [un papel]. *5* MÚS. tocar, tañer. *6 i.* divertirse, jugar; bromear.

player ('pleiəʳ) *t.* jugador. *2* TEAT. actor. *3* ejecutante.

playground ('plei-graund) *s.* patio de recreo. *2* campo de juego.

plea (pli:) *s.* argumentación. *2* defensa. *3* disculpa, excusa, pretexto. *4* súplica.

plead (to) (pli:d) *t.* alegar [en defensa, etc.]. *2 i.* pleitear, abogar.

pleasant (pleznt) *a.* agradable.

please (to) (pli:z) *t.-i.* agradar, gustar, placer; complacer. *2 i.* gustar, tener a bien, dignarse.

pleasing ('pli:ziŋ) *a.* agradable.

pleasure ('pleʒəʳ) *s.* placer, deleite, goce, gusto.

pleat (pli:t) *s.* pliegue, doblez.

pledge (pledʒ) *s.* prenda [garantía], rehén, fianza, empeño. *2* brindis.

pledge (to) (pledʒ) *t.* dar en prenda, empeñar. *2* comprometerse. *3* brindar por.

plentiful ('plentiful) *a.* abundante, copioso. *2* fértil.

plenty ('plenti) *s.* abundancia: ~ *of*, mucho, de sobra.

plight (plait) *s.* condición, estado. *2* apuro, aprieto.

plod (to) (plɔd) *i.* afanarse.

plot (plɔt) *s.* porción de terreno, solar, parcela. 2 conspiración, complot, maquinación. 3 LIT. trama.

plot (to) (plɔt) *t.* tramar, urdir. 2 *i.* conspirar.

plough, (E. U.) **plow** (plau)*s.* arado.

plough (to) ((E. U.), **plow (to)** (plau) *t.-i.* arar, labrar.

ploughman, (E. U.) **plowman** ('plaumən) *s.* arador, labrador.

pluck (plʌk) *s.* valor, resolución. 2 tirón, estirón.

pluck (to) (plʌk) *t.* coger, arrancar. 2 desplumar. 3 dar un tirón. 4 MÚS. puntear.

plug (plʌg) *s.* tapón, espita, taco. 2 ELECT. clavija.

plug (to) (plʌg) *t.* ataruga, tapar. 2 enchufar.

plum (plʌm) *s.* BOT. ciruela.

plume (plu:m) *s.* pluma [de ave]. 2 plumaje. 3 penacho.

plump (plʌmp) *a.* regordete.

plunder ('plʌndəʳ) *s.* pillaje.

plunder (to) (plʌndəʳ) *s.* pillar, saquear, robar.

plunge (plʌndʒ) *s.* zambullida; salto, caída.

plus (plʌs) *prep.* más.

ply (plai) *s.* pliegue, doblez.

ply (to) (plai) *t.* usar, manejar. 2 trabajar con ahínco en.

pocket ('pɔkit) *s.* bolsillo, faltriquera.

pocket-book ('pɔkitbuk) *s.* libro de bolsillo. 2 billetero, cartera.

poem ('pouim) *s.* poema.

poet ('pouit) *s.* poeta, vate.

poetry ('po(u)itri) *s.* poesía. No tiene el sentido de verso, poema. 2 poética.

point (pɔint) *s.* punta [extremo, esp. agudo]. 2 punzón, buril, puñal, etc. 3 GEOGR. punta; pico, picacho. 4 punto [en varios sentidos]: ~ *of view*, punto de vista; *to come to the* ~, ir al grano, venir al caso; *beside the* ~, fuera de propósito; *in the* ~ *of*, a punto de. 5 tanto [en el juego]. 6 signo [de puntuación]. 7 fin, propósito.

point (to) (pɔint) *t.* aguzar, sacar punta a. 2 apuntar, asestar, encarar. 3 señalar, indicar, hacer notar. 4 GRAM. puntuar.

poise (pɔiz) *s.* equilibrio.

poise (to) (pɔiz) *t.* equilibrar.

poison ('pɔizn) *s.* veneno.

poison (to) ('pɔizn) *t.* envenenar.

poke (pouk) *s.* empujón, codazo. 2 hurgonazo.

poke (to) (pouk) *t.* picar, aguijonear, atizar, hurgar. 2 meter. 3 *i.* husmear, meterse [en].

pole (poul) *s.* polo. 2 pértiga. 3 (con may.) polaco, ca.

police (pə'li:s) *s.* policía.

policeman (pə'li:smən) *s.* policía; guardia de seguridad, urbano.

policy ('pɔlisi) *s.* política, línea de conducta; maña. 2 póliza [de seguro].

polish ('pɔliʃ) *s.* pulimento. 2 lustre, brillo. 3 betún.

polish (to) ('pɔliʃ) *t.* pulir, bruñir, lustrar. 2 perfeccionar; educar. 3 *i.* pulirse.

polite (pə'lait) *a.* cortés.

political (pə'litikəl) *a.* político [de la política].

politician (͵poli'tiʃən) *s.* político.

politics ('politiks) *s. pl.* política.

poll (poul) *s.* cabeza [pers.] 2 votación; su resultado. 3 lista electoral. 4 *pl.* colegio electoral. 5 urnas electorales.

poll (to) (poul) *t.* recibir y escrutar [los votos]. 2 dar [voto]. 3 trasquilar.

pollution (po'lu:ʃən. -'lju:-) *s.* contaminación.

pomp (pomp) *s.* pompa, fausto.

pond (pond) *s.* estanque, charca.

ponder (to) ('pondər) *t.* ponderar, pesar.

pony ('pouni) *s.* jaquita.

pool (pu:l) *s.* charco, balsa. 2 estanque.

poop (pu:p) *s.* MAR. popa.

poor (puər) *a.* pobre. 2 malo, de mala calidad. 3 débil; enfermo.

pop (pop) *s.* estallido, tapanazo.

pop (to) (pop) *t.* hacer estallar. 2 sacar, asomar.

Pope (poup) *s.* papa, pontífice. 2 pope.

popular ('popjulər) *a.* popular. 2 corriente, general.

popularity (͵popju'læriti) *s.* popularidad.

population (͵popju'leiʃən) *s.* población [habitantes].

porch (po:tʃ) *s.* porche, atrio, pórtico. 2 vestíbulo.

pork (po:k) *s.* cerdo.

port (po:t) *s.* puerto.

portable ('po:təbl) *a.* portátil.

porter ('po:tər) *s.* portero. 2 mozo [de estación, hotel, etc.].

portion ('po:ʃən) *s.* porción, porte. 2 herencia, dote. 3 sino, suerte.

portrait ('po:trit) *s.* retrato.

pose (pouz) *s.* actitud. 2 actitud afectada.

position (pə'ziʃən) *s.* posición. 2 postura, actitud.

positive ('pozitiv) *a.* positivo. 2 categórico. 3 indudable.

possess (to) (pə'zes) *t.* poseer.

possibility (͵posi'biliti) *s.* posibilidad.

possible ('posibl) *a.* posible.

possibly ('posibli) *adv.* posiblemente, tal vez.

post (poust) *s.* poste, pilar. 2 puesto, empleo, cargo. 3 factoría [comercial]. 4 posta [para viajar]. 5 correo, estafeta; correos.

post (to) (poust) *t.* anunciar [con carteles]; fijar [carteles]. 2 apostar, situar. 3 enviar por correo. 4 enterar. 5 *i.* viajar por la posta.

postage ('poustidʒ) *s.* franqueo: ~ *stamp*, sello de correos.

postal ('poustəl) *a.* postal: ~ *order*, giro postal.

pot (pot) *s.* olla, puchero, pote. 2 maceta, tiesto.

potato (pə'teitou) *s.* BOT. patata: *sweet* ~, batata, boniato.

poultry ('poultri) *s.* pollería.

pound (paund) *s.* libra.

pound (to) (paund) *t.* moler, majar, machacar.

pour (to) (po:ʳ,poəʳ) *t.* verter. 2 *i.* fluir, correr.

poverty ('povəti) *s.* pobreza.

powder ('paudəʳ) *s.* polvo; polvillo. 2 polvos [de tocador]. 3 pólvora.

powder (to) ('paudə^r) *t.* polvo-rear. 2 *t.-i.* pulverizar(se. 3 empolvar(se.

power ('pauə^r) *s.* poder, facul-tad. 2 potencia.

powerful ('pauəful) *a.* pode-roso. 2 fuerte. 3 intenso.

practical ('præktikəl) *a.* prác-tico. 2 virtual, de hecho. 3 ~ **joke**, broma, chasco.

practically ('præktikəli) *adv.* prácticamente.

practice ('præktis) *s.* práctica.

practise (to) ('præktis) *t.-i.* practicar. 2 *t.* ejercitar. adiestrar.

prairie ('prɛəri) *s.* pradera.

praise (preiz) *s.* alabanza, elo-gio. 2 fama.

praise (to) (preiz) *t.* alabar, ensalzar.

pray (to) (prei) *t.-i.* rogar, su-plicar. 2 *i.* orar, rezar.

prayer (preeə^r) *s.* ruego, sú-plica. 2 rezo, oración.

preach (to) (pri:t∫) *t.-i.* predi-car, sermonear.

preacher ('pri:t∫ə^r) *s.* predica-dor.

precarious (pri'kɛəriəs) *a.* precario. 2 incierto, inse-guro.

precaution (pri'kɔ:∫ən) *s.* pre-caución.

precede (to) (pri(:)'si:d) *t.-i.* preceder.

precious ('pre∫əs) *a.* precioso.

precipitate (pri'sipitit) *a.* pre-cipitado. 2 súbito. 3 *s.* QUÍM. precipitado.

predict (to) (pri'dikt) *t.* prede-cir, vaticinar.

predominate (to) (pri'dɔmi-neit) *i.* predominar, prevale-cer.

preface ('prefis) *s.* prefacio.

prefer (to) (pri'fə:^{r}) *t.* prefe-rir, anteponer. 2 elevar, exaltar.

preference ('prefərəns) *s.* preferencia. 2 predilección.

preferential (,prefə'ren∫əl) *a.* preferente.

pregnant ('pregnənt) *a.* pre-ñada. 2 importante.

prejudice ('predʒudis) *s.* pre-juicio, prevención. 2 daño, perjuicio.

preliminary (pri'liminəri) *a.-s.* preliminar.

premier ('premjə^r) *a.* pri-mero, principal. 2 *s.* primer ministro.

premise ('premis) *s.* premisa. 2 *pl.* local, casa, finca.

premise (to) (pri'maiz) *t.* su-poner, dar por sentado.

preparative (pri'pærətiv),

preparatory (pri'pærətəri)*a.* preparatorio.

prepare (to) (pri'pɛə^r) *t.* pre-parar. 2 prevenir, disponer.

prescribe (to) (pris'kraib) *t.* prescribir [ordenar; rece-tar].

presence ('prezns) *s.* presen-cia. 2 aire, porte.

present ('preznt) *a.* presente. 2 actual. 3 GRAM. presente [tiempo]; pasivo [partici-pio]. 4 *s.* presente, la actua-lidad.

present (to) (pri'zent) *t.* pre-sentar.

presentation (,prezen'tei∫ən) *s.* presentación. 2 regalo, obsequio.

preserve (pri'zə:v) *s.* con-serva, confitura. 2 vedado.

preserve (to) (pri'zə:v) *t.* pre-servar, proteger. 2 conser-var, mantener.

preside (to) (pri'zaid) *t.-i.*, presidir; dirigir.

president ('prezidənt) *s.* presidente.

press (pres) *s.* muchedumbre. 2 apretura. 3 empuje, presión. 4 prisa, apremio. 5 prensa [máquina, periódicos]. 6 imprenta.

press (to) (pres) *t.* apretar. 2 prensar. 3 abrumar. 4 apremiar. 5 *i.* ejercer presión. 6 avanzar; agolparse; apiñarse. 7 urgir.

pressure ('preʃəʳ) *s.* presión. 2 impulso, empuje. 3 peso, opresión. 4 urgencia, apremio. 5 ELECT. tensión.

prestige (pres'ti:ʒ) *s.* prestigio.

presume (to) (pri'zju:m) *t.* presumir, suponer. 2 *i.* atreverse.

pretence (pri'tens) *s.* pretensión. 2 fingimiento, apariencia, pretexto.

pretend (to) (pri'tend) *t.* aparentar, fingir, simular. 2 *t.-i.* pretender, aspirar [a].

pretext ('pri:tekst) *s.* pretexto.

pretty ('priti) *a.* lindo, bonito; gracioso. 2 bueno, regular; considerable. 3 *adv.* bastante.

prevail (to) (pri'veil) *i.* prevalecer. 2 predominar.

prevalent ('prevələnt) *a.* reinante, corriente, general.

prevent (to) (pri'vent) *t.* prevenir, evitar, impedir.

previous ('pri:vjəs) *a.* previo.

prey (prei) *s.* presa, rapiña. 2 presa, botín; víctima.

prey (to) (prei) *i. to ~ on,* *upon* o *at,* hacer presa; pillar; remorder, preocupar.

price (prais) *s.* precio; coste.

price (to) (prais) *t.* apreciar, estimar, tasar.

prick (prik) *s.* pinchazo, picadura, resquemor. 2 aguijón.

prick (to) (prik) *t.* pinchar, punzar, picar. 2 espolear.

pride (praid) *s.* orgullo.

pride (to) (praid) *t. to ~ oneself on,* enorgullecerse de.

priest (pri:st) *m.* sacerdote.

primary ('praiməri) *a.* primario. 2 prístino.

prime (praim) *a.* primero, principal. 2 albor, amanecer. 3 lo mejor.

primitive ('primitiv) *a.* primitivo. 2 prístino.

prince (prins) *s.* príncipe.

princess (prin'ses) *f.* princesa.

principle ('prinsəpl) *s.* principio [origen; verdad fundamental, regla, ley].

print (print) *s.* impresión.

print (to) (print) *t.-i.* imprimir, estampar.

printing ('printiŋ) *s.* impresión, estampado. 2 imprenta, tipografía [arte]. 3 impreso, estampa.

prior ('praiəʳ) *a.* anterior, previo. 2 *s.* prior.

prison ('prizn) *s.* prisión, cárcel.

prisoner ('priznəʳ) *s.* preso.

private ('praivit) *a.* privado, personal, particular.

privilege ('privilidʒ) *s.* privilegio. 2 prerrogativa.

privy ('privi) *a.* privado, oculto, secreto.

prize (praiz) *s.* premio, recompensa. 2 presa, captura.

prize (to) (praiz) *t.* apreciar, estimar; valuar.

probability (͵prɔbə'biliti) *s.* probabilidad. 2 verosimilitud.

probable ('prɔbəbl) *a.* probable. 2 verosímil.

procedure (prə'si:dʒəʳ) *s.* proceder. 2 procedimiento.

proceed (to) (prə'si:d) *i.* proseguir, seguir adelante. 2 proceder, provenir. 3 proceder, obrar; pasar a [hacer algo].

proceeding (prə'si:diŋ, prou-) *s.* proceder, procedimiento. 2 marcha, proceso.

process ('prouses) *s.* proceso, progreso, marcha. 2 procedimiento, sistema.

proclaim (to) (prə'kleim) *t.* proclamar. 2 promulgar.

proclamation (͵prɔklə'meiʃən) *s.* proclamación. 2 proclama, banda, edicto.

procure (to) (prə'kjuəʳ) *t.* lograr, obtener, procurar.

produce ('prɔdju:s) *s.* producto, producción.

produce (to) (prə'dju:s) *t.* presentar, exhibir. 2 producir. 3 procriar.

producer (prə'dju:səʳ) *s.* productor. 2 TEAT. director.

production (prə'dʌkʃən) *s.* producción. 2 TEAT. dirección escénica, representación.

productive (prə'dʌktiv) *a.* productivo. 2 producente.

profess (to) (prə'fes) *t.* profesar. 2 declarar, confesar. 3 *i.* profesar [en una orden].

professor (prə'fəsəʳ) *s.* profesor, catedrático.

profit ('prɔfit) *s.* provecho, ventaja, utilidad. 2 ganancia, beneficio.

profit (to) ('prɔfit) *t.* aprovechar, ser útil a. 2 *i.* aprovecharse; adelantar, mejorar.

profitable ('prɔfitəbl) *a.* provechoso, beneficioso, útil.

profound (prə'faund) *a.* profundo. 2 hondo. 3 abstruso.

program(me ('prougræm) *s.* programa. 2 plan.

progress ('prougres) *s.* progreso. 2 marcha, curso.

progress (to) (prə'gres) *i.* progresar. 2 avanzar.

progressive (prə'gresiv) *a.* progresivo.

prohibit (to) (prə'hibit) *t.* prohibir. 2 impedir.

prohibition (͵proui'biʃən) *s.* prohibición.

project ('prɔdʒekt) *s.* proyecto, plan.

project (to) (prə'dʒekt) *t.* proyectar.

prolong (to) (prə'lɔŋ) *t.* prolongar. 2 *i.* dilatarse.

prominent ('prɔminənt) *a.* prominente, saliente. 2 notable. 3 distinguido.

promise ('prɔmis) *s.* promesa.

promontory ('prɔməntri) *s.* promontorio.

promote (to) (prə'mout) *t.* promover, ascender.

promotion (prə'mouʃən) *s.* promoción.

prompt (prɔmpt) *a.* pronto, presto, listo, puntual.

prompt (to) (prɔmpt) *t.* incitar, inducir.

prong (prɔŋ) *s.* gajo, púa.

pronounce (to) (prə'nauns) *t.* pronunciar [palabras, sentencias]. 2 *i.* pronunciarse [en pro, en contra].

proof (pru:f) *s.* prueba. demostración. 2 ensayo.

proper ('prɔpəʳ) *a.* propio, característico. 2 propio, apropiado. 3 correcto [en su uso, etc.].

property ('prɔpəti) *s.* propiedad.

prophecy ('prɔfisi) *s.* profecía.

prophet ('prɔfit) *s.* profeta.

proportion (prə'pɔ:ʃən) *s.* proporción; armonía, correlación.

proportion (to) (prə'pɔ:ʃən) *t.* proporcionar.

proportional (prə'pɔ:ʃənl) **proportionate** (prə'pɔ:ʃənit) *a.* proporcional.

proposal (prə'pouzəl) *s.* propuesta, proposición.

propose (to) (prə'pouz) *t.* proponer. 2 proponerse, tener intención de. 3 brindar por.

proposition (‚prɔpə'ziʃən) *s.* proposición. 2 (E. U.) cosa, asunto, negocio.

proprietor (prə'praiətəʳ) *s.* propietario, dueño.

propriety (prə'praiəti) *s.* propiedad, cualidad de apropiado. 2 corrección, decencia. 3 *pl.* urbanidad, reglas de conducta.

prose (prouz) *s.* prosa.

prosecute (to) ('prɔsikju:t) *t.* proseguir, continuar. 2 DER. procesar, enjuiciar.

prospect ('prɔspekt) *s.* perspectiva, paisaje, panorama.

prospect (to) (prəs'pekt) *t.-i.* explorar [terrenos].

prospective (prəs'pektiv) *a.* probable, posible, en perspectiva.

prosper (to) ('prɔspəʳ) *t.-i.* prosperar.

prosperity (prɔs'periti) *s.* prosperidad.

prosperous ('prɔspərəs) *a.* próspero. 2 favorable.

protect (to) (prə'tekt) *t.* proteger.

protection (prə'tekʃən) *s.* protección.

protective (prə'tektiv) *a.* protector. 2 proteccionista.

protest ('proutest) *s.* protesta. 2 protestación.

protest (to) (prə'test) *t.-i.* protestar.

Protestant ('prɔtistənt) *a.-s.* protestante.

proud (praud) *a.* orgulloso, soberbio, altanero.

prove (to) (pru:v) *t.* probar. 2 experimentar, comprobar. 3 *i.* salir, resultar [bien o mal]; demostrar que se es [apto, etc.]. P. p.: *proved*, o *proven*.

provide (to) (prə'vaid) *t.* proveer.

provided (prə'vaidid) *conj.* ~ *that*, con tal que, siempre que.

providence ('prɔvidəns) *s.* providencia, previsión.

province ('prɔvins) *s.* provincia. 2 región, distrito.

provision (prə'viʒən) *s.* provisión.

provocative (prə'vɔkətiv) *a.* provocativo. 2 irritante.

provoke (to) (prə'vouk) *t.* provocar. 2 irritar.

prowess ('prauis) *s.* valor. 2 proeza. 3 destreza.

prudent ('pru:dənt) *a.* prudente; previsor.

prune (to) (pru:n) *t.* podar.

pry (to) (prai) *i.* espiar, acechar. 2 *t.* apalancar.

psalm (sɑ:m) *s.* salmo.

psychologic(al (ˌsaikəˈlɔdʒik (əl) *a.* psicológico.

pub (pʌb) *s.* pop. [Ingl.] cervecería, taberna.

public (ˈpʌblik) *a.* público. 2 *s.* público.

publication (ˌpʌbliˈkeiʃən) *s.* publicación. 2 edición.

publicity (pʌˈblisiti) *s.* publicidad. 2 notoriedad.

publish (to) (ˈpʌbliʃ) *t.* publicar. 2 editar. 3 difundir.

publisher (ˈpʌbliʃəʳ) *s.* editor.

pucker (ˈpʌkəʳ) *s.* arruga.

pucker (to) (ˈpʌkəʳ) *t.* arrugar, plegar.

pudding (ˈpudiŋ) *s.* budín, pudín. 2 embuchado.

Puerto Rican (ˈpwəːtouˈriːkən) *a.-s.* portorriqueño.

puff (pʌf) *s.* soplo, bufido. 2 bocanada. 3 COC. bollo.

puff (to) (pʌf) *i.* soplar, jadear; aspirar bocanadas.

pugilist (ˈpjuːdʒilist) *s.* púgil.

pull (pul) *s.* tirón, sacudida. 2 tirador [botón, cordón, etc.]. 3 esfuerzo prolongado. 4 atracción. 5 trago. 6 chupada [a un cigarro]. 7 ventaja, superioridad.

pull (to) (pul) *t.* tirar de, halar, estirar, arrastrar. 2 arrancar. 3 desgarrar. 4 torcer, distender [un ligamento, etc.]. 5 beber, chupar. 6 *i.* tirar, dar un tirón; ejercer tracción; trabajar.

pulse (pʌls) *s.* pulso, pulsación, latido.

pump (pʌmp) *s.* MEC. bomba.

pump (to) (pʌmp) *t.* impeler. 2 *i.* dar a la bomba.

pumpkin (ˈpʌmpkin) *s.* BOT. calabaza.

punch (pʌntʃ) *s.* ponche. 2 puñetazo. 3 empuje, energía. 4 punzón.

punctual (ˈpʌŋktjuəl) *a.* puntual, exacto.

punish (to) (ˈpʌniʃ) *t.* castigar.

punishment (ˈpʌniʃmənt) *s.* castigo. 2 vapuleo.

pupil (ˈpjuːpl. -pil) *s.* discípulo, alumno. 2 DER. pupilo. 3 ANAT. pupila.

puppet (ˈpʌpit) *s.* títere, muñeco; maniquí.

purchase (ˈpəːtʃəs) *s.* compra.

pure (ˈpjuəʳ) *a.* puro.

Puritan (ˈpjuəritən) *a.-s.* puritano.

purple (ˈpəːpl) *a.* purpúreo, morado, rojo. 2 imperial, regio. 3 *s.* púrpura.

purport (ˈpəːpət) *s.* significado, sentido, tenor.

purport (to) (ˈpəːpət) *t.* significar, querer decir.

purpose (ˈpəːpəs) *s.* propósito, intención, designio. 2 resolución. 3 efecto, resultado.

purpose (to) (ˈpəːpəs) *t.-i.* proponerse, intentar.

purse (pəːˈs) *s.* bolsa, bolsillo, portamonedas.

purse (to) (pəːs) *t.* arrugar, fruncir [la frente, los labios].

pursue (to) (pəˈsjuː) *t.* seguir, perseguir. 2 *i.* proseguir, continuar.

pursuit (pəˈsjuːt) *s.* seguimiento, caza, busca.

purveyor (pəːˈveiəʳ) *s.* proveedor, abastecedor.

push (puʃ) *s.* empujón. 2 impulso, energía, esfuerzo.

push (to) (pʌʃ) *t.* empujar,

impeler. *2* apretar [un botón]. *3* proseguir. *4* impulsar. *5* apremiar. *6 i.* empujar.

put (to) (put) *t.* poner, colocar. *2* obligar, incitar. *3* hacer [una pregunta]. *4* expresar. *5* atribuir, achacar. *6 to ~ aside,* descartar. *7 to ~ down,* poner [en el suelo]; reprimir; deprimir; humillar; apuntar, anotar; rebajar; hacer callar. *8 to ~ in mind,* recordar. *9 to ~ on,* ponerse [una prenda].; engañar; dar [la luz, etc.]; TEAT. poner en escena. *10 to ~ out,* sacar; echar fuera; alargar; exhibir; invertir [dinero, etc.]; apagar [la luz, fuego]; molestar, irritar; desconcertar. *11 to ~ over,* aplazar. *12 to ~ up,* levantar, erigir; armar, montar; ahorrar; envolver; inventar; alojar; TEAT. poner en escena. *13 i.* ir, dirigirse. ¶ Pret. y p. p.: *put* (put); ger.: *putting* ('putiŋ).

puzzle ('pʌzl) *s.* embarazo, perplejidad. *2* enredo, embrollo. *3* acertijo, rompecabezas.

puzzle (to) ('pʌzl) *t.* confundir, dejar perplejo. *2* embrollar.

Q

quaint (kweint) *a.* curioso, singular; atractivo por su rareza.

qualification (ˌkwɔlifiˈkeiʃən) *s.* calificación. 2 condición, requisito. 3 capacidad, idoneidad.

qualify (to) (ˈkwɔlifai) *t.* calificar, capacitar. 2 *i.* capacitarse, habilitarse.

quality (ˈkwɔliti) *s.* calidad, cualidad.

quantity (ˈkwɔntiti) *s.* cantidad.

quarrel (ˈkwɔrəl) *s.* riña.

quarry (ˈkwɔri) *s.* cantera.

quart (kwɔ:t) *s.* cuarto de galón.

quarter (ˈkwɔ:tər) *s.* cuarto, cuarta parte. 2 cuarto [de hora; de la luna]. 3 moneda de veinticinco centavos. 4 trimestre. 5 parte, dirección. 6 barrio, vecindad. 7 cuartel, clemencia. 8 *pl.* cuartel, oficina; vivienda.

quarter (to) (ˈkwɔtər) *t.* cuartear. 2 acuartelar; alojar.

queen (kwi:n) *s.* reina.

queer (kwiər) *a.* raro, extraño, estrafalario.

quench (to) (kwentʃ) *t.* apagar, extinguir, calmar.

quest (kwest) *s.* busca.

quest (to) (kwest) *t.* buscar.

question (ˈkwestʃən) *s.* pregunta. 2 objeción, duda. 3 cuestión, problema, asunto.

queue (kju:) *s.* cola, hilera. 2 coleta.

queue (to) (kju:) *i.* hacer cola.

quick (kwik) *a.* vivo, rápido, pronto. 2 despierto, agudo. 3 vivo, intenso, ardiente. 4 movediza [arena]. 5 viva [agua]. 6 *s.* carne viva; lo vivo. 7 **-ly** *adv.* vivamente, prontamente, aprisa.

quicken (to) (ˈkwikən) *t.* vivificar, resucitar. 2 avivar. 3 *i.* avivarse. 4 apresurarse.

quiet (ˈkwaiət) *a.* quieto, inmóvil. 2 callado, silencioso. 3 tranquilo. 4 sencillo, modesto. 5 *s.* quietud, silencio.

quiet (to) (kwaiət) *t.* aquietar.

quit (kwit) *a.* absuelto, descargado. 2 libre, exento.

quit (to) (kwit) *t.* dejar, abandonar, irse de; dejarse de; desistir, renunciar a. 2 *i.* irse.

quite (kwait) *adv.* completamente, del todo; realmente, verdaderamente.

quiver (ˈkwivəʳ) *s.* aljaba, carcaj. 2 vibración, temblor.

quiver (to) (ˈkwivəʳ) *t.* vibrar, temblar, estremecerse.

quotation (kwouˈteiʃən) *s.* cita [texto citado].

quote (to) (kwout) *t.* citar [un texto, un autor].

R

rabbit (ræbit) *s.* ZOOL. conejo.

race (reis) *s.* raza; casta, linaje. *2* carrera, regata.

race (to) (reis) *i.* correr [en una carrera, etc.]. *2 t.* hacer correr.

rack (ræk) *s.* estante, etc. *2* aparato de tortura.

rack (to) (ræk) *t.* torturar. *2* atormentar.

racket ('rækit) *s.* raqueta. *2* alboroto. *3* diversión.

radiant ('reidjənt) *a.* radiante.

radio ('reidiou) *s.* ELECT. radio; ~ *set,* aparato de radio.

rag (ræg) *s.* trapo, harapo.

rage (reidʒ) *s.* rabia, ira.

rage (to) (reidʒ) *i.* rabiar, encolerizarse. *2* hacer estragos.

ragged ('rægid) *a.* andrajoso, harapiento. *2* roto.

raid (reid) *s.* incursión, ataque.

raid (to) (reid) *t.* hacer una incursión en.

rail (reil) *s.* barra; pasamano, barandal. *2* barandilla, barrera. *3* raíl; ferrocarril.

rail (to) (reil) *t.* cercar, poner barandilla a.

railroad ('reilroud) (E. U.), **railway** (-wei) (Ingl.) *s.* ferrocarril, vía férrea.

rain (rein) *s.* lluvia: ~ *bow,* arco iris; ~ *coat,* impermeable; ~ *drop,* gota de lluvia. ~ *fall,* aguacero.

rain (to) (rein) *i.-impers.-t.* llover.

rainy ('reini) *a.* lluvioso.

raise (reiz) *s.* aumento, alza.

raise (to) (reiz) *t.* levantar, alzar, elevar. *2* cultivar [plantas], criar [animales]. *3* (E. U.) criar, educar.

raisin ('reizn) *s.* pasa [uva seca].

rake (reik) *s.* libertino. *2* AGR. rastro, rastrillo.

rake (to) (reik) *t.* AGR. rastrillar. *2* rascar, raer. *3* atizar, hurgar [el fuego].

rally ('ræli) *s.* reunión.

rally (to) ('ræli) *t.-i.* reunir(se, concentrar(se. *2* reanimar(se, fortalecer(se.

ran (ræn) *pret.* DE TO RUN.

ranch (rɑːntʃ) *s.* rancho.

random ('rændəm) *s.* azar, acaso: *at* ~, al azar. 2 *a.* ocasional, fortuito.

rang (ræŋ) *pret.* de TO RING.

range (reindʒ) *s.* fila, hilera. 2 esfera [de una actividad]. 3 escala, gama, serie. 4 extensión [de la voz]. 5 alcance [de un arma, etc.]: distancia.

range (to) (reindʒ) *t.* alinear; arreglar, ordenar. 2 recorrer. 3 pasear [la mirada por]. 4 *i.* alinearse. 5 extenderse, variar [dentro de ciertos límites].

rank (ræŋk) *a.* lozano, lujuriante, vicioso. 2 rancio. 3 grosero. 4 insalubre. 5 *s.* línea, hilera, fila. 6 rango, grado.

rank (to) (ræŋk) *t.* alinear. 2 ordenar, arreglar.

ransom ('rænsəm) *s.* rescate.

ransom (to) ('rænsəm) *t.* rescatar, redimir.

rap (ræp) *s.* golpe seco.

rap (to) (ræp) *t.-i.* golpear.

rapacious (rə'peiʃəs) *a.* rapaz.

rapid ('ræpid) *a.* rápido.

rapture ('ræptʃəʳ) *s.* rapto, arrobamiento, éxtasis.

rare (rɛəʳ) *a.* raro [de poca densidad; poco común; escaso]. 2 ralo. 3 raro; peregrino. 4 coc. poco cocido.

rascal (rɑ:skəl) *s.* bribón, pillo.

rat (ræt) *s.* zool. rata.

rate (reit) *s.* razón, proporción, tanto [por ciento]. 2 precio, valor. 3 clase, orden. 4 arbitrio, impuesto. 5 *at any* ~, al menos, de todos modos.

rate (to) (reit) *t.* valuar, tasar, apreciar. 2 estimar, juzgar. 3 reñir, regañar. 4 *i.* ser tenido o considerado.

rather ('rɑ:ðəʳ) *adv.* bastante, algo, un tanto. 2 mejor, antes, más. *I would* ~, me gustaría más.

rattle ('rætl) *s.* tableteo, matraqueo. 2 estertor. 3 cascabel [de serpiente]. 4 sonajero [juguete]. 5 matraca.

rattle (to) ('rætl) *t.* hacer sonar, sacudir. 2 aturdir. 3 *i.* tabletear, matraquear.

raw (rɔ:) *a.* crudo [sin cocer], en bruto, en rama. 2 crudo, húmedo, frío [viento, tiempo]. 3 bisoño, novato.

ray (rei) *s.* rayo [de luz, etc.]. 2 GEOM. radio. 3 ICT. raya.

reach (ri:tʃ) *s.* alcance, poder: *in* ~ *of*, al alcance de.

reach (to) (ri:tʃ) *t.* alargar, extender, tender. 2 tocar, llegar a o hasta, alcanzar. 3 *i.* extenderse, llegar, alcanzar [a o hasta].

reactor (ri(:)'æktəʳ) *s.* reactor.

read (to) (ri:d) *t.* leer. ¶ Pret. y p. p.: *read* (red).

reader ('ri:dəʳ) *s.* lector.

readily ('redili) *adv.* prontamente. 2 de buena gana.

reading ('ri:diŋ) *s.* lectura.

ready ('redi) *a.* preparado, pronto, listo, dispuesto.

real (riəl) *a.* real, verdadero.

reality (ri(:)'æliti) *s.* realidad.

realize (to) ('riəlaiz) *t.* comprender, darse cuenta de. 2 realizar, efectuar.

realm (relm) *s.* reino. 2 campo, dominio, región.

reap (to) (ri:p) *t.* segar, guadañar. 2 recoger, cosechar.

reaper ('ri:pə^r) *s.* segador.

reappear (to) ('ri:ə'piə^r) *i.* reaparecer.

rear (riə^r) *a.* trasero, último, posterior. 2 *s.* trasera, parte de atrás.

rear (to) (riə^r) *t.* levantar, alzar; erigir. 2 criar, cultivar.

reason ('ri:zn) *s.* razón. | No tiene el sentido de razón en MAT. ni el de razón social: *it stands to ~*, es razonable, es justo; *by ~ of*, por causa de.

reason (to) ('ri:zn) *t.-i.* razonar. 2 *i.* persuadir o disuadir con razones.

reasonable ('ri:zənəbl) *a.* racional [ser]. 2 razonable.

reasoning (ri:z(ə)niŋ) *s.* razonamiento.

reassure (to) (,ri:ə'ʃuə^r) *t.* tranquilizar.

rebel ('rebl) *a.-s.* rebelde.

rebel (to) (ri'bel) *i.* rebelarse, sublevarse.

rebelion (ri'beljən) *s.* rebelión, sublevación.

rebuke (ri'bju:k) *s.* reproche, censura.

rebuke (to) (ri'bju:k) *t.* increpar, reprender, censurar.

recall (ri'kɔ:l) *s.* llamada [para hacer volver]. 2 recordación. 3 anulación, revocación.

recall (to) (ri'kɔ:l) *t.* llamar, hacer volver. 2 recordar. 3 anular, revocar.

receipt (ri'si:t) *s.* recepción. 2 cobranza. 3 recibo. 4 receta, fórmula. 5 ingresos.

receive (to) (risi:v) *t.* recibir; tomar, aceptar. 2 acoger.

receiver (ri'si:və^r) *s.* receptor. 2 cobrador, tesorero.

recent ('ri:snt) *a.* reciente.

reception (ri'sepʃən) *s.* recepción. 2 admisión, aceptación.

recess (ri'ses) *s.* hueco, entrada, nicho, alcoba. 2 suspensión, descanso.

recipe ('resipi) *s.* récipe, receta.

recite (to) (ri'sait) *t.-i.* recitar. 2 *t.* narrar.

reckon (to) ('rekən) *t.-i.* contar, calcular. 2 *t.* considerar [como]; contar [entre].

reclaim (to) (ri'kleim) *t.* poner en cultivo; hacer utilizable. 2 regenerar [a una pers.]. 3 DER. reclamar.

recognize (to) ('rekəgnaiz) *t.* reconocer. | No tiene el sentido de examinar o registrar.

recollection (,rekə'lekʃən) *s.* recuerdo, memoria.

recommend (to) (,rekə'mend) *t.* recomendar. 2 alabar.

recommendation (,rekəmen'deiʃən) *s.* recomendación. 2 consejo.

reconcile (to) ('rekənsail) *t.* reconciliar.

reconstruct (to) ('ri:-kəns'trakt) *t.* reconstruir.

record ('rekɔ:d) *s.* inscripción, registro. 2 acta, historia. 3 DER. expediente, autos. 4 disco; grabación [en disco]. 5 DEP. récord, marca.

record (to) (ri'kɔ:d) *t.* asentar, inscribir, registrar. 2 fijar en la memoria. 3 grabar en disco o en cinta magnetofónica.

recover (to) (ri'kʌvəʳ) *t.* recobrar, recuperar. *2 i.* restablecerse; volver en sí.

recovery (ri'kʌvəri) *s.* recobro, recuperación.

recreation (ˌrekri'eiʃən) *s.* recreación, recreo.

recruit (ri'kru:t) *s.* recluta.

recruit (to) (ri'kru:t) *t.* reclutar, alistar.

rector ('rektəʳ) *s.* rector.

recur (to) (ri'kə:ʳ) *i.* volver [a un tema]. *2* volver a ocurrir, repetirse.

red (red) *a.* encarnado, colorado, rojo; enrojecido, encendido.

redeem (to) (ri'di:m) *t.* redimir.

redress (ri'dres) *s.* reparación, desagravio.

redress (to) (ri'dres) *t.* deshacer, reparar [injusticias].

reduce (to) (ri'dju:s) *t.* reducir. *2* rebajar, diluir.

reduction (ri'dʌkʃən) *s.* reducción.

reed (ri:d) *s.* BOT. caña.

reel (ri:l) *s.* devanadera, carrete.

reel (to) (ri:l) *t.* aspar, devanar. *2* hacer dar vueltas a. *3 i.* dar vueltas [la cabeza].

re-enlist (to) ('ri:in'list) *t.-i.* reenganchar(se.

refer (to) (ri'fə:ʳ) *t.* referir. *2 i.* referirse, aludir. *4* remitirse.

reference ('refrəns) *s.* referencia, relación.

refine (to) (ri'fain) *t.* refinar. *2 i.* refinarse, pulirse.

refinement (ri'fainmənt) *s.* refinamiento. *2* sutileza.

reflect (to) (ri'flekt) *t.* reflejar, reflector. *2 i.* reflejarse.

reflection (ri'flekʃən) *s.* reflexión, reverberación. *2* reflejo, imagen.

reform (ri'fɔ:m) *s.* reforma.

reform (to) (ri:'fɔ:m) *t.* reformar, mejorar. *2 i.* reformarse, corregirse.

refrain (ri'frein) *s.* estribillo.

refrain (to) (ri'frein) *t.* refrenar, contener. *2 i.* contenerse; abstenerse.

refresh (to) (ri'freʃ) *t.* refrescar. *2* renovar, restaurar.

refreshment (ri'freʃmənt) *s.* refrescadura. *2* refresco.

refrigerator (ri'fridʒəreitəʳ) *s.* refrigerador. *2* nevera.

refuge ('refju:dʒ) *s.* refugio.

refugee (ˌrefju(:)'dʒi:) *s.* refugiado. *2* asilado.

refusal (ri'fju:zəl) *s.* rechazamiento. *2* negativa, denegación, repulsa. *3* opción.

refuse ('refju:s) *s.* desecho, sobras, basura.

refuse (to) (ri'fju:z) *t.* rehusar, rechazar, desechar.

regain (to) (ri'gein) *t.* recobrar, recuperar.

regal ('ri:gəl) *a.* real, regio.

regard (ri'ga:d) *s.* miramiento, consideración. *2* afecto, respeto. *3* relación, respecto: *with ~ to,* con respecto a. *4* mirada. *5 pl.* recuerdos.

regard (to) (riga:d) *t.* mirar, contemplar. *2* tocar a, concernir, referirse a: *as regards,* en cuanto a.

regarding (ri'ga:diŋ) *prep.* tocante a, respecto de.

region ('ri:dʒən) *s.* región.

register ('redʒistə^r) s. registro: archivo. protocolo.

regret (ri'gret) s. pesar. sentimiento. 2 remordimiento.

regret (to) (ri'gret) i. sentir. lamentar. 2 arrepentirse.

regretful (ri'gretful) a. pesaroso.

regular ('regjulə^r) a. regular. No tiene el sentido de mediano. 2 ordenado. metódico. 3 normal. corriente.

regulate (to) ('regjuleit) t. regular. arreglar. reglamentar.

regulation (,regju'leiʃən) s. regulación. 2 reglamentación. 3 regla. orden.

reign (rein) s. reino. soberanía. 2 reinado.

reign (to) (rein) i. reinar.

rein (rein) s. rienda.

reject (to) (ri'dʒekt) t. rechazar. rehusar. repeler.

rejoice (to) (ri'dʒɔis) t.-i. alegrar(se. regocijar(se.

rejoicing (ri'dʒɔisiŋ) s. alegría. regocijo. 2 fiesta.

relate (to) (ri'leit) t. relatar. referir. 2 relacionar. 3 i. relacionarse. referirse.

relation (ri'leiʃən) s. relación. relato. 2 relación [entre cosas o personas]. 3 parentesco. afinidad. 4 pariente. deudo.

relationship (ri'leiʃənʃip) s. relación [entre cosas o pers.]. 2 parentesco.

relative ('relətiv) a. relativo. 2 s. pariente. deudo. allegado.

relax (to) (ri'læks) t.-i. relajar(se. aflojar(se. ablandar(se. 2 i. remitir. amainar. 4 descansar.

release (ri'li:s) s. libertad. ex-carcelación. 2 descargo. exoneración. quita.

release (to) (ri'li:s) t. libertar. soltar. 2 librar. descargar.

reliable (ri'laiəbl) a. confiable. digno de confianza. seguro.

relic ('relik) s. reliquia. 2 pl. restos. ruinas.

relief (ri'li:f) s. ayuda. auxilio. 2 alivio. 3 relieve. realce. 4 MIL. relevo.

relieve (to) (ri'li:v) t. remediar. auxiliar. socorrer. 2 aliviar. 3 desahogar. 4 realzar. hacer resaltar. 5 MIL. relevar.

religion (ri'lidʒən) s. religión.

religious (ri'lidʒəs) a. religioso. 2 piadoso.

relish ('reliʃ) s. buen sabor.

relish (to) ('reliʃ) t. saborear. paladear. 2 gustarle a uno [una cosa]. 3 i. gustar. agradar.

rely (to) (ri'lai) i. [con *on* o *upon*] confiar o fiar en. contar con. fiarse de.

remain (to) (ri'mein) i. quedar. 2 quedarse. 3 permanecer. continuar.

remainder (ri'meində^r) s. resto. sobrante.

remark (ri'ma:k) s. observación. nota. dicho.

remark (to) (ri'ma:k) t. observar. advertir. notar.

remarkable (ri'ma:kəbl) a. observable. 2 notable.

remedy ('remidi) s. remedio.

remedy (to) ('remidi) t. remediar.

remember (to) (ri'membə^r) t. recordar. acordarse de.

remind (to) (ri'maind) t. *to ~*

of, recordar. hacer presente [una cosa a uno].

remnant ('remnənt) *s.* remanente, resto, residuo.

remote (ri'mout) *a.* remoto.

removal (ri'mu:vəl) *s.* acción de quitar o llevarse; remoción, levantamiento. 2 mudanza. 3 eliminación.

remove (to) (ri'mu:v) *t.* trasladar, mudar. 2 *i.* trasladarse, mudarse.

render (to) ('rendəʳ) *t.* dar, entregar. 2 devolver. 3 volver, hacer, poner.

renew (to) (ri'nju:) *t.-i.* renovar(se. 2 reanudar(se.

renown (ri'naun) *s.* renombre, fama.

rent (rent) *s.* renta, arriendo, alquiler. 2 desgarrón; grieta, raja. 3 cisma, división. *4 p. p.* de TO REND.

rent (to) (rent) *t.-i.* arrendar(se, alquilar(se.

repair (ri'peəʳ) *s.* reparación

repay (to) (ri:'pei) *t.* pagar, corresponder a.

repeal (ri'pi:l) *s.* abrogación.

repeal (to) (ri'pi:l) *t.* abrogar.

repeat (to) (ri'pi:t) *t.* repetir, reiterar. 2 recitar. 3 *i.* repetirse periódicamente.

repent (to) (ri'pent) *i.* arrepentirse. 2 *t.* arrepentirse de.

repetition (ˌrepi'tiʃən) *s.* repetición. 2 repaso.

replace (to) (ri'pleis) *t.* reponer, devolver. 2 reemplazar.

reply (ri'plai) *s.* respuesta.

reply (to) (ri'plai) *t.* responder, contestar.

report (ri'pɔ:t) *s.* voz, rumor.

2 noticia, información. 3 relato. 4 parte, comunicado.

report (to) (ri'pɔ:t) *t.* relatar, contar, dar cuenta o parte de. 2 informar.

reporter (ri'pɔ:təʳ) *s.* reportero. 2 informador.

repose (ri'pouz) *s.* reposo.

repose (to) (ri'pouz) *t.* descansar, reclinar.

represent (to) (ˌrepri'zent) *t.* representar, significar.

representation (ˌreprizen'teiʃən) *s.* representación.

representative (ˌrepri'zentətiv) *a.* representativo. 2 *s.* representante, apoderado; (E. U.) diputado.

reproach (ri'proutʃ) *s.* reproche, censura. 2 tacha.

reproach (to) (ri'proutʃ) *t.* reprochar. 2 reprender.

reproduce (to) (ˌri:prə'dju:s)*t.* reproducir. 2 *i.* reproducirse, propagarse.

republic (ri'pʌblik) *s.* república.

repulse (ri'pʌls) *s.* repulsión, rechazo. 2 repulsa, desaire.

repulse (to) (ri'pʌls) *t.* rechazar, repeler. 2 repulsar.

reputation (ˌrepju(:)'teiʃən) *s.* reputación, fama.

request (ri'kwest) *s.* ruego.

request (to) (ri'kwest) *t.* rogar, pedir, solicitar.

require (to) (ri'kwaiəʳ) *t.-i.* requerir, pedir, demandar.

requirement (ri'kwaiəmənt) *s.* requisito, condición.

requisite ('rekwizit) *a.* requerido, necesario. 2 *s.* requisito, cosa esencial.

rescue ('reskju:) *s.* liberación, rescate, salvamento.

rescue (to) ('reskju:) *t.* libertar, rescatar, salvar.

research (ri'sə:tʃ) *s.* búsqueda, investigación.

research (to) (ri'sə:tʃ) *t.* buscar, indagar, investigar.

resemblance (ri'zembləns) *s.* parecido, semejanza.

resemble (to) (ri'zembl) *t.* parecerse, asemejarse a.

resent (to) (ri'zent) *t.* resentirse u ofenderse de o por.

resentment (ri'zentmənt) *s.* resentimiento, enojo.

reservation (,rezə'veiʃən) *s.* reserva [reservación; condición, salvedad]. 2 terreno reservado.

reserve (ri'zə:v) *s.* reserva, repuesto. 2 reserva [discreción; sigilo; frialdad].

reserve (to) (ri'zə:v) *t.* reservar.

reside (to) (ri'zaid) *i.* residir.

residence ('reizidəns) *s.* residencia; morada, mansión.

resident ('rezidənt) *a.* residente. 2 *s.* residente.

resign (to) (ri'zain) *t.* dimitir.

resignation (,rezig'neiʃən) *s.* dimisión, renuncia. 2 resignación, conformidad.

resin ('rezin) *s.* resina.

resist (to) (ri'zist) *t.-i.* resistir. | No tiene el sentido de tolerar, sufrir. 2 *t.* oponerse a.

resistance (ri'zistəns) *s.* resistencia.

resistant (ri'zistənt) *a.* resistente.

resolution ('rezə'lu:ʃən) *s.* resolución. 2 propósito.

resolve (ri'zɔlv) *s.* resolución.

resolve (to) (ri'zɔlv) *t.* resolver.

resonance ('rezənəns) *s.* resonancia.

resort (ri'zɔ:t) *s.* recurso, medio, refugio. 2 balneario.

resort (to) (ri'zɔ:t) *i.* acudir, frecuentar. 2 recurrir.

resource (ri'sɔ:s) *s.* recurso.

respect (ris'pekt) *s.* respeto.

respectable (ris'pektəbl) *a.* respetable. 2 decente.

respond (to) (ris'pɔnd) *i.* responder, contestar.

response (ris'pɔns) *s.* respuesta, contestación.

responsibility (ris,pɔnsi'biliti) *s.* responsabilidad. 2 cometido.

responsible (ris'pɔnsəbl) *a.* responsable.

rest (rest) *s.* descanso, reposo. 2 apoyo, soporte. 3 resto, restante.

rest (to) (rest) *i.* descansar, reposar; estar quieto. 2 cesar, parar. 3 descansar, apoyarse, basarse [en], cargar [sobre]. 4 quedar, permanecer. 5 *t.* asentar, apoyar, basar.

restaurant ('restərənt) *s.* restaurante.

restless ('restlis) *a.* inquieto.

restoration ('restə'reiʃən) *s.* restauración. 2 restitución.

restore (to) (ris'tɔ:ʳ) *t.* restaurar. 2 restablecer.

restrain (to) (ris'trein) *t.* refrenar, contener, reprimir.

restraint (ris'treint) *s.* refrenamiento, cohibición.

restriction (ris'trikʃən) *s.* restricción, limitación.

result (ri'zʌlt) *s.* resultado.

result (to) (ri'zʌlt) *i.* **to ~**

from, resultar. originarse. inferirse. 2 *to ~ in*, dar por resultado. venir a parar en.

resume (to) (ri'zju:m) *t.* reasumir, volver a tomar. 2 resumir.

resumption (ri'zʌmpʃən) *s.* reasunción. 2 recobro.

retain (to) (ri'tein) *t.* retener.

retire (to) (ri'taiəʳ) *i.* retirarse. 2 *t.* retirar, apartar. sacar. 3 *t.-i.* retirar(se, jubilar(se.

retort (ri'tɔ:t) *s.* réplica mordaz. 2 QUÍM. retorta.

retort (to) (ri'tɔ:t) *t.-i.* replicar, redargüir.

retreat (ri'tri:t) *s.* retirada. 2 retiro. 3 refugio.

retreat (to) (ri'tri:t) *i.* retirarse. 2 refugiarse.

return (ri'tə:n) *s.* vuelta, regreso, retorno. 2 devolución. 3 retorno, pago, cambio.

return (to) (ri'tə:n) *i.* volver, retornar; regresar. 2 *t.* volver, devolver, restituir.

reveal (to) (ri'vi:l) *t.* revelar.

revelation (,revi'leiʃən) *s.* revelación. 2 Apocalipsis.

revenge (ri'vendʒ) *s.* venganza. 2 desquite.

revenue ('revinju:) *s.* renta.

reverence ('revərəns) *s.* reverencia, respeto.

reverence (to) ('revərəns) *t.* reverenciar, acatar.

reverend ('revərənd) *a.* reverendo, venerable.

reverse (ri'və:s) *a.* inverso, contrario. 2 *s.* lo inverso o contrario.

reverse (to) (ri'və:s) *t.* invertir, volver al revés, transformar.

review (ri'vju:) *s.* revista [inspección; periódico; espectáculo]. 2 revisión. 3 reseña [de una obra]. 4 MIL. revista.

review (to) (ri'vju:) *t.* rever. 2 revisar, repasar.

revive (to) (ri'vaiv) *t.* reanimar, reavivar, despertar. 2 restablecer, resucitar. 3 *i.* volver en sí. 4 revivir.

revolt (ri'voult) *s.* revuelta.

revolt (to) (ri'voult) *i.* sublevarse, amotinarse. 2 *t.* sublevar; dar asco.

revolution (,revə'lu:ʃən) *s.* revolución.

reward (ri'wɔ:d) *s.* premio, recompensa, galardón.

reward (to) (ri'wɔ:d) *t.* premiar, recompensar, pagar.

rhyme (raim) *s.* LIT. rima.

rhyme (to) (raim) *t.-i.* rimar. 2 *i.* consonar, armonizar.

rib (rib) *s.* ANAT., BOT., MAR. costilla. 2 ENT. nervio [de ala]. 3 varilla [de paraguas o abanico].

ribbon ('ribən) *s.* cinta, galón, banda, tira.

rice (rais) *s.* arroz.

rich (ritʃ) *a.* rico. 2 suculento. 3 muy dulce. 4 fértil, pingüe. 5 fragante.

riches ('ritʃiz) *s. pl.* riqueza.

rid (to) (rid) *t.* librar, desembarazar: *to get ~ of*, librarse, desembarazarse de. ¶ Pret. y p. p *rid* (rid) o *ridded* ('ridid).

ridden ('ridn) *p. p.* de TO RIDE.

riddle ('ridl) *s.* enigma.

riddle (to) ('ridl) *t.* resolver, descifrar.

ride (raid) *s.* paseo o viaje a

caballo, en bicicleta, en coche.

ride (to) (raid) *i.* ir a caballo, en bicicleta, en coche, etc.; cabalgar, montar. 2 girar, funcionar. 3 andar, marchar [el caballo montado, el vehículo]. 4 *t.* montar [un caballo], etc.]; conducir [un vehículo], ir en él. ¶ Pret.: *rode* (roud); p. p.: *ridden* ('ridn).

ridge (ridʒ) *s.* elevación larga y estrecha. 2 cerro, cresta.

ridiculous (ri'dikjuləs) *a.* ridículo.

rifle ('raifl) *s.* rifle, fusil.

rifle (to) ('raifl) *t.* pillar, saquear. 2 robar, llevarse.

right (rait) *a.* recto, derecho [no torcido]. 2 GEOM. recto. 3 recto, justo, honrado. 4 bueno, verdadero, apropiado; que está bien; sano, cuerdo. 5 que tiene razón. 6 derecho, diestro, de la derecha. 7 *adv.* derechamente. 8 exactamente. 9 bien; justamente; con razón. 10 a la derecha. 11 interj. *all ~!*, ¡está bien!, ¡conformes! 12 *s.* derecho, justicia, razón. 13 derecha, diestra.

right (to) (rait) *t.* hacer justicia a. 2 enderezar, corregir.

rigid ('ridʒid) *a.* rígido. 2 preciso, riguroso.

rim (rim) *s.* borde, margen.

ring (riŋ) *s.* anillo, sortija. 2 ojera [en el ojo]. 3 pista, arena, redondel. 4 BOX. ring, cuadrilátero. 5 corro, círculo. 6 sonido vibrante.

1) **ring (to)** (riŋ) *t.* cercar, circundar. 2 poner anillos a. 3 *i.* formar círculo. ¶ Pret. y p. p.: *ringed* (riŋd).

2) **ring (to)** (riŋ) *t.* hacer sonar; tocar, tañer, repicar [campanas]; tocar [un timbre]; *to ~ up*, llamar por teléfono. 2 *i.* tocar el timbre. 3 sonar, tañer, retiñir. 4 zumbar [los oídos]. ¶ Pret.: *rang* (ræŋ); p. p.: *rung* (rʌŋ).

riot (to) ('raiət) *i.* armar alboroto, amotinarse.

rip (rip) *s.* rasgadura.

rip (to) (rip) *t.* rasgar, abrir.

ripe (raip) *a.* maduro.

ripen (to) ('raipən) *t.-i.* madurar, sazonar(se.

ripple ('ripl) *s.* onda, rizo.

ripple (to) ('ripl) *i.* rizarse, ondear. 2 caer en ondas.

rise (raiz) *s.* levantamiento, ascensión, subida. 2 elevación. 3 salida [de un astro]. 4 pendiente, cuesta, altura. 5 encumbramiento, ascenso. 6 aumento, alza, subida. 7 causa, origen.

rise (to) (raiz) *i.* subir, ascender, elevarse, alzarse, remontarse. 2 salir [un astro]. 3 encumbrarse, ascender. 4 levantarse [de la cama, etc.]; ponerse en pie]. 5 erizarse. 6 alzarse, sublevarse. 7 subir, aumentar, crecer; encarecerse. 8 nacer, salir, originarse. 9 surgir, aparecer, presentarse, ocurrir. ¶ Pret.: *rose* (rouz); p. p.: *risen* ('rizn).

risk (risk) *s.* riesgo, peligro.

risk (to) (risk) *t.* arriesgar, aventurar, exponer. 2 exponerse a.

rite (rait) *s.* rito.

rival ('raivəl) *a.* competidor.
2 *s.* rival.

rival (to) ('raivəl) *t.* competir.

river ('rivə^r) *s.* río, cuenca.

road (roud) *s.* carretera, camino.

roam (to) (roum) *i.* rodar, vagar, errar. 2 *t.* vagar por.

roar (rɔ:^r, rɔə^r) *s.* rugido, bramido. 2 grito; griterío.

roar (to) (rɔ:^r, rɔə^r) *i.* rugir.

roast (roust) *s.* asado.

roast (to) (roust) *t.-i.* asar(se.
2 tostar(se.

rob (to) (rɔb) *t.* robar, hurtar.

robber ('rɔbə^r) *s.* ladrón.

robe (roub) *s.* ropaje, vestidura, túnica; toga [de juez, etc.]. 2 bata. 3 vestido de mujer. 4 fig. manto, capa.

robe (to) (roub) *t.-i.* vestir(se.

robust (rə'bʌst) *a.* robusto.

rock (rɔk) *s.* roca, peña, peñasco; escollo.

rock (to) (rɔk) *t.* acunar. 2
t.-i. mecer(se, balancear(se.

rocket ('rɔkit) *s.* cohete.

rocky ('rɔki) *a.* rocoso, pedregoso.

rod (rɔd) *s.* vara, varilla, barra. 2 caña [de pescar].

rode (roud) *pret.* de TO RIDE.

rogue (roug) *s.* pícaro, bribón. 2 holgazán.

role, rôle (roul) *s.* papel [que se hace o representa].

roll (roul) *s.* rollo [de papel, etc.]. 2 lista, nómina, registro, escalafón. 3 bollo, panecillo. 4 ARQ. voluta. 5 retumbo [del trueno]; redoble [del tambor]. 6 balanceo.

roll (to) (roul) *t.* hacer rodar. 2 mover, llevar, etc., sobre ruedas. 3 arrollar, enrollar. 4 liar [un cigarrillo]. 5 envol-

ver, fajar. 6 *i.* rodar, girar. 7 ir sobre ruedas. 8 revolcarse. 9 arrollarse, hacerse una bola. 10 retumbar, tronar.

roller ('roulə^r) *s.* MEC. rodillo, cilindro, tambor. 2 rueda o ruedecita [de patín, etc.].

Roman ('roumən) *a.-s.* romano. 2 *a.* latina [lengua]. 3 *s.* latín. 4 IMPR. redondo [tipo].

romance (rə'mæns) *s.* romance; novela. 2 idilio amoroso. 3 ficción, invención.

romantic (rou'mæntik, rə-) *a.* romántico.

roof (ru:f) *s.* techo, techado, tejado, cubierta.

roof (to) (ru:f) *t.* cubrir, techar.

room (rum, ru:m) *s.* cuarto, pieza, habitación, sala.

roost (ru:st) *s.* percha; gallinero.

roost (to) (ru:st) *i.* dormir [las aves en la percha].

root (to) (ru:t) *i.t.* hozar. 2 *t.* arraigar, implantar. 3 *i.* arraigar, echar raíces.

rope (roup) *s.* cuerda, soga. 2 sarta, ristra.

rose (rouz) *s.* BOT. rosal. 2 BOT. rosa. 3 rosa [color, adorno]. 4 rallo [de regadera]. 5 rosetón [ventana]. 6 *pret.* de TO RISE.

rosy ('rouzi) *a.* rosado.

rot (rɔt) *s.* putrefacción.

rot (to) (rɔt) *i.* pudrirse, corromperse. 2 *t.* pudrir.

rotary ('routəri) *a.* rotatorio.

rotate (to) (rou'teit) *i.* rodar, girar. 2 turnar, alternar. 3 *t.* hacer girar.

rotten ('rɔtn) *a.* podrido.

rouge (ru:ʒ) *s.* colorete, arrebol.

rough (rʌf) *a.* áspero, tosco, basto. *2* escabroso [terreno]. *3* agitado [mar]. *4* en bruto, de preparación, mal acabado. *5* aproximativo.

rough (to) (rʌf) *t.* hacer o labrar toscamente. *2 to ~ it*, vivir sin comodidades.

roughly ('rʌfli) *adv.* ásperamente. *2* toscamente. *3* aproximadamente.

round (raund) *a.* redondo. *2* rollizo. *3* circular. *4* claro, categórico. *5* fuerte, sonoro. *6* cabal, completo. *7 s.* círculo, esfera; corro. *8* redondez. *9* recorrido, ronda. *10* ronda [de bebidas, etc.]. *11* serie [de sucesos, etc.], rutina. *12* salva [de aplausos]. *13* descarga, salva, disparo. *14* BOX. asalto. *15 adv.* alrededor; por todos lados. *16 prep.* alrededor de.

round (to) (raund) *t.* redondear. *2* rodear, cercar. *3* doblar [un cabo, una espina].

roundabout ('raundəbaut) *a.* indirecto, hecho con rodeos. *2 s.* circunloquio. *8* tiovivo.

rouse (to) (rauz) *t.-i.* despertar. *2 t.* animar, excitar.

route (ru:t) *s.* ruta, camino.

routine (ru:'ti:n) *s.* rutina.

rove (to) (rouv) *i.* vagar, errar, corretear. *2* piratear.

rover ('rouvə^r) *s.* vagabundo. *2* pirata.

1) **row** (rau) *s.* riña, pendencia.

2) **row** (rou) *s.* fila, hilera, línea. *2* paseo en lancha o bote.

1) **row (to)** (rau) *t.* fam. pelearse con. *2 i.* pelearse.

2) **row (to)** (rou) *i.* remar, bogar. *2 t.* mover al remo.

royal ('rɔiəl) *a.* real, regio.

royalty ('rɔiəlti) *s.* realeza. *2* derechos [de autor].

rub (rʌb) *s.* friega, frote.

rub (to) (rʌb) *t.* estregar, restregar, fregar, frotar. *2* irritar. *3 i.* rozar.

rubber ('rʌbə^r) *s.* caucho, goma; goma de borrar.

rubbish ('rʌbiʃ) *s.* basura, desecho, escombros.

ruby ('ru:bi) *s.* MINER. rubí.

rudder ('rʌdə^r) *s.* timón.

ruddy ('rʌdi) *a.* colorado.

rude (ru:d) *a.* rudo. *2* tosco.

ruffle ('rʌfl) *s.* lechuguilla, volante fruncido.

ruffle (to) ('rʌfl) *t.* rizar, alechugar, fruncir. *2* arrugar, descomponer. *3* irritar, incomodar. *4* encrespar, erizar.

rug (rʌg) *s.* alfombra, felpudo. *2* (Ingl.) manta [de viaje, etc.].

rugged ('rʌgid) *a.* rugoso; áspero, escabroso. *2* rudo. *3* desapacible. *4* recio.

ruin (ruin) *s.* ruina. *2* destrucción. *3* perdición, deshonra.

ruin (to) (ruin) *t.* arruinar. *2* destruir. *3* seducir, perder. *4 i.* arruinarse, perderse.

rule (ru:l) *s.* regla, precepto. *2* reglamento, régimen. *3* regla [para trazar líneas; para medir].

rule (to) (ru:l) *t.-i.* gobernar, regir, dirigir. *2 t.* regular, reglar. *3* reglar, rayar, pautar.

ruler ('ru:lə^r) *s.* gobernante,

soberano. *2* regla [instrumento].

rumble ('rʌmbl) *s.* rumor.

rumble (to) ('rʌmbl) *i.* retumbar, hacer un ruido sordo.

rumo(u)r ('ru:məʳ) *s.* rumor.

rumo(u)r (to) ('ru:məʳ) *t.* rumorear, propalar.

run (rʌn) *s.* corrida, carrera. *2* curso, marcha, dirección. *3* serie, racha. *4* funcionamiento, operación, manejo. *5* hilo [del discurso]. *6* clase, tipo, etc., usual. *7* viaje, paseo. *8* carrera [en las medias]. *9 in the long* ~, a la larga, tarde o temprano. *10 p. p.* DE TO RUN.

run (to) (rʌn) *i.* correr. *2* girar, rodar. *3* extenderse [hacia, hasta, por]; llegar, alcanzar [hasta]. *4* pasar [a cierto estado]. *5* fluir, manar, chorrear. *6* derretirse. *7* correrse [colores]. *8* supurar. *9* durar, mantenerse. *10* seguir, estar vigente; estar en boga. *11* funcionar, marchar. *12 to* ~ *about*, correr, ir de un lado a otro. *13 to* ~ *across*, encontrar, dar con. *14 to* ~ *against*, chocar con; oponerse [a]. *15 to* ~ *down*, pararse, habérsele acabado la cuerda, el vapor, etc.; agotarse, debilitarse. *16 to* ~ *on*, seguir, continuar. *17 to* ~ *out*, salir; salirse, derramarse; acabarse; extenderse. *18 to* ~ *over*, rebosar, desbordarse; atropellar, pasar por encima. *19 to* ~ *with*, estar chorreando o empapado de; abundar en. *20 t.* correr; cazar, perseguir. *21* pasar [una cosa por

encima de otra]. *22* hacer [un mandado]. *23* tirar [una línea]. *24* pasar de contrabando. *25* correr [un riesgo]. *26 to* ~ *into*, clavar, hundir. *27 to* ~ *out*, sacar, extender; agotar. *28 to* ~ *through*, atravesar, pasar de parte a parte; hojear. ¶ Pret.: *ran* (ræn); p. p.: *run* (rʌn); ger.: *running*.

runner ('rʌnəʳ) *s.* corredor [el que corre]. *2* mensajero. *3* (E. U.) agente [de un total, etc.]. *4* contrabandista.

running ('rʌniŋ) *s.* carrera, corrida, curso. *2* marcha, funcionamiento. *3* dirección, manejo. *4* flujo. *5 a.* corredor. *6* corriente. *7* corredizo. *8 adv.* seguido.

rural ('ruərəl) *a.* rural, rústico.

rush (rʌʃ) *s.* movimiento o avance impetuoso. *2* torrente, tropel, afluencia. *3* prisa, precipitación. *4* ímpetu.

rush (to) (rʌʃ) *i.* arrojarse, abalanzarse, precipitarse. *2 t.* empujar. *3* activar, apresurar. *4* embestir.

Russian ('rʌʃən) *a.-s.* ruso.

rust (rʌst) *s.* moho, orín.

rust (to) (rʌst) *t.* enmohecer(se.

rustic ('rʌstik) *a.-s.* rústico. *2* campesino. *3 a.* campestre.

rustle ('rʌsl) *s.* susurro, crujido.

rustle (to) ('rʌsl) *i.* susurrar, crujir. *2* hacer susurrar o crujir. *3* robar [ganado].

rusty ('rʌsti) *a.* mohoso, herrumbroso. *2* enmohecido.

rye (rai)*s.* BOT. centeno. *2* BOT. ~ *grass*, ballico, césped inglés.

S

sack (sæk) *s.* saco, costal. *2* saco, saqueo.

sack (to) (sæk) *t.* saquear. *2* ensacar. *3* despedir.

sacred ('seikrid) *a.* sagrado.

sacrifice ('sækrifais) *s.* sacrificio.

sacrifice (to) ('sækrifais) *t.* sacrificar; inmolar.

sacrilege ('sækrilidʒ) *s.* sacrilegio.

sad (sæd) *a.* triste. *2* aciago.

saddle ('sædl) *s.* silla [de montar]. *2* sillín.

saddle (to) ('sædl) *t.* ensillar.

sadness ('sædnis) *s.* tristeza.

safe (seif) *a.* salvo, ileso, incólume. *2* seguro. *3 s.* arca, caja de caudales.

safeguard ('seifgɑːd) *s.* salvaguardia, resguardo.

safety ('seifti) *s.* seguridad. *2* prudencia.

sage (seidʒ) *s.* BOT. salvia. *2* sabio, filósofo, hombre prudente. *3 a.* cuerdo.

said (sed) V. TO SAY.

sail (seil) *s.* MAR. vela. *2* aspa [de molino].

sail (to) (seil) *i.* navegar. *2 t.* navegar por, surcar.

sailor ('seiləʳ) *s.* marinero.

saint (seint, san(t) *s.* santo, santa.

sake (seik) *s.* causa, motivo, amor, consideración.

salad ('sæləd) *s.* ensalada.

salary ('sæləri) *s.* salario.

sale (seil) *s.* venta.

salesman ('seilzmən) *s.* vendedor. *2* viajante de comercio.

salmon ('sæmən) *s.* ICT. salmón.

saloon (səˈluːn) *s.* salón [gran sala]. *2* (E. U.) taberna, bar.

salt (sɔːlt) *s.* QUÍM. sal. *2* sal común. *3* ingenio, agudeza. *4 a.* salado, salino.

salt (to) (sɔːlt) *t.* salar.

salute (səˈluːt) *s.* saludo.

salute (to) (səˈluːt) *t.-i.* saludar. *2 i.* MIL. cuadrarse.

same (seim) *a.-pron.* mismo, misma, etc.

sample ('sɑːmpl) *s.* COM. muestra. *2* muestra, cala.

sanction ('sæŋkʃən) *s.* sanción.

sanction (to) ('sæŋkʃən) *t.* sancionar.

sanctuary ('sæŋktjuəri) *s.* santuario.

sand (sænd) *s.* arena.

sandwich ('sænwidʒ) *s.* emparedado, bocadillo.

sane (sein) *a.* sano. 2 cuerdo.

sang (sæŋ) V. TO SING.

sap (sæp) *s.* savia. 4 vigor

sap (to) (sæp) *t.* zapar, minar.

sash (sæʃ) *s.* faja, ceñidor, banda. 2 parte movible de la ventana de guillotina.

satin ('sætin) *s.* TEJ. raso.

satiric (sə'tirik) *a.* satírico.

satisfaction (,sætis'fækʃən) *s.* satisfacción.

satisfactory (,sætis'fæktəri) *a.* satisfactorio. 2 suficiente.

satisfy (to) ('sætisfai) *t.* satisfacer. 2 contentar. 3 convencer. 4 compensar, pagar.

sausage ('sɔsidʒ) *s.* salsicha.

savage ('sævidʒ) *a.* salvaje.

save (seiv) *prep.* salvo, excepto. 4 *conj.* si no fuera.

save (to) ·(seiv) *t.* salvar, librar. 2 guardar, preservar.

saving ('seiviŋ) *s.* economía, ahorro. 2 *pl.* ahorros. 3 *prep.* salvo, excepto.

saw (sɔ:) *s.* sierra [herramienta]. 2 dicho, refrán, proverbio. 3 *pret.* de TO SEE.

saw (to) (sɔ:) *t.-i.* serrar, aserrar. ¶ Pret.: *sawed* (sɔ:d); *p. p.: sawn* (sɔ:n).

say (sei) *s.* dicho, aserto. 2 turno para hablar.

say (to) (sei) *t.* decir. 2 recitar, rezar. ¶ Pres.: *says* (sɛz)pret. y. p. p.: *said* (sed).

saying ('seiiŋ) *s.* lo que se dice. 2 dicho, sentencia.

scale (skeil) *s.* platillo [de balanza]. 2 balanza, báscula, romana. 3 escala [serie graduada; proporción].

scale (to) (skeil) *t.* pesar.

scalp (skælp) *s.* cuero cabelludo.

scalp (to) (skælp) *t.* arrancar la cabellera.

scandal ('skændl) *s.* escándalo. | No tiene el sentido de alboroto. 2 ignominia. 3 difamación, maledicencia.

scandalous ('skændələs) *a.* escandaloso, vergonzoso.

scanty ('skænti) *a.* escaso, insuficiente, exiguo.

scar (skɑ:ʳ) *s.* cicatriz.

scarce (skɛəs) *a.* escaso, raro.

scare (skɛəʳ) *s.* susto, alarma.

scare (to) (skɛəʳ) *t.* asustar, amedrentar, alarmar.

scarf (skɑ:f) *s.* echarpe.

scarlet ('skɑ:lit) *a.* rojo, de color escarlata.

scatter (to) ('skætəʳ) *t.* dispersar. 2 disipar, desvanecer.

scene (si:n) *s.* escena [en todas sus acepciones]. 2 escenario. 3 TEAT. decorado. 4 cuadro, vista, paisaje.

scenery ('si:nəri) *s.* paisaje. 2 TEAT. decorado.

scent (sent) *s.* olfato. 2 olor; fragancia. 3 rastro, pista.

scent (to) (sent) *t.* oler, olfatear, husmear, ventear. 2 sospechar. 3 perfumar.

schedule ('ʃedju:l, [E. U.] 'skedju:l) *s.* lista, inventario.

scheme (ski:m) *s.* esquema, diseño. 2 plan, proyecto.

schism ('sizəm) *s.* cisma.

scholar ('skɔlə^r) s. licenciado que disfruta de beca. 2 hombre docto, erudito.

scholarship ('skɔləʃip) s. saber, erudición. 2 beca [para estudiar].

school (sku:l) s. escuela. 2 a. escolar, de enseñanza.

schoolmaster ('sku:l,mɑ:stə^r) s. profesor de instituto.

science ('saiens) s. ciencia. 2 ciencias naturales.

scientist ('saiəntist) s. hombre de ciencia.

scold (to) (skould) t. reñir, regañar.

scope (skoup) s. alcance [de un arma]. 2 campo o radio [de acción]. 3 mira, designio.

score (skɔ:^r, skɔə^r) s. muesca, entalladura. 2 cuenta [de lo que se debe]. 3 tantos, tanteo. 4 razón, motivo. 5 veintena. 6 MÚS. partitura.

score (to) (skɔ:^r, skɔə^r) t. esclopear. 2 marcar, ganar [puntos, tantos]. 3 rayar. 4 MÚS. orquestar.

scorn (skɔ:n) s. desdén, desprecio. 2 escarnio.

scorn (to) (skɔ:n) t. desdeñar, despreciar. 2 escarnecer.

Scot (skɔt) s., **Scoth** (skɔtʃ) a.-s. escocés.

scourge (skə:dʒ) s. látigo.

scourge (to) (skə:dʒ) t. azotar, flagelar.

scout (skaut) s. MIL. explorador, escucha.

scout (to) (skaut) t.-i. explorar, reconocer. 2 desdeñar.

scowl (skaul) s. ceño, sobrecejo.

scowl (to) (skaul) i. mirar con ceño.

scramble ('skræmbl) s. lucha, arrebatiña. 2 gateamiento.

scramble (to) ('skræmbl) i. trepar, gatear. 2 andar a la arrebatiña.

scrap (skræp) s. trozo, pedazo. 2 pl. sobras.

scrape (skreip) s. raspadura, rasguño. 2 lío, aprieto.

scrape (to) (skreip) t. raspar, rascar, raer; rayar.

scratch (skrætʃ) s. arañazo.

scratch (to) (skrætʃ) t. arañar, rayar. 2 rascar.

scream (skri:m) s. chillido, grito.

scream (to) (skri:m) t.-i. chillar, gritar.

screen (skri:n) s. pantalla.

screen (to) (skri:n) t. ocultar, tapar. 2 abrigar, proteger.

screw (skru:) s. tornillo, rosca; tuerca. 2 hélice.

screw (to) (skru:) t. atornillar.

Scripture ('skriptʃə^r) s. Sagrada Escritura.

scrub (skrʌb) a. desmirriado. 2 s. fregado, fregoteo.

scrub (to) (skrʌb) t. fregar, estregar.

sculptor ('skʌlptə^r) s. escultor.

sculpture ('skʌlptʃə^r) s. escultura.

sea (si:) s. mar, océano.

seal (si:l) s. ZOOL. foca. 2 sello, sigilo.

seal (to) (si:l) t. sellar, precintar.

seam (si:m) s. costura; sutura.

seam (to) (si:m) t. coser.

seaman ('si:mən) s. marinero, marino.

search (sə:tʃ) s. busca, búsqueda. 2 registro.

search (to) (sə:tʃ) t.-i. buscar. 2 examinar, registrar.

season ('si:zn) s. estación [del año]. 2 tiempo, temporada.

season (to) ('si:zn) t. sazonar. 2 habituar, aclimatar.

seat (si:t) s. asiento [para sentarse]. 2 TEAT. localidad. 3 sitio, sede, residencia. 4 situación.

seat (to) (si:t) t. sentar, asentar. 2 establecer, instalar.

secede (to) (si'si:d) i. separarse [de una comunión].

second ('sekənd) a. segundo. 2 secundario, subordinado. 3 inferior. 4 s. segundo [división del minuto].

second (to) ('sekənd) t. secundar, apoyar, apadrinar.

secondary ('sekəndəri) a. secundar.

secret ('si:krit) a. secreto. 2 recóndito, íntimo. 3 callado, reservado. 4 s. secreto.

secretary ('sekrətri) s. secretario.

section ('sekʃən) s. sección.

secular ('sekjuləʳ) a. secular.
2 s. eclesiástico secular. 3 seglar, lego.

secure (si'kjuəʳ) a. seguro [libre de peligro o riesgo].

secure (to) (si'kjuəʳ) t. asegurar; afianzar; prender.

security (si'kjuəriti) s. seguridad. 2 protección.

see (si:) s. ECLES. sede, silla.

see (to) (si:) t.-i. ver, mirar, observar. 3 considerar, juzgar. 4 to ~ one off, ir a despedir a uno. 5 to ~ after, cuidar; buscar. 6 to ~ into, examinar. ¶ Pret.: saw (sɔ:); seen (si:n).

seed (si:d) s. BOT. semilla.

seed (to) (si:d) t.-i. sembrar.

seek (to) (si:k) t. buscar. ¶ Pret. y p. p.: sought (sɔ:t).

seem (to) (si:m) i. parecer.

seen (si:n) V. TO SEE.

seize (to) (si:z) t. asir, agarrar, coger. 2 apoderarse de.

seldom ('seldəm) adv. raramente, rara vez.

select (si'lekt) a. selecto.

select (to) (si'lekt) t. escoger, elegir, seleccionar.

selection (si'lekʃən) s. selección. 2 trozo escogido.

self (self), pl. **selves** (selvz) a. mismo; idéntico [myself, yourselves, etc.]. 2 self- [en compuestos] auto-, por sí mismo: ~ conscious, tímido; ~ control, dominio de sí mismo; ~ sufficient, presuntuoso.

selfish (selfiʃ) a. interesado, egoísta. 2 -ily adv. interesadamente, egoístamente.

sell (to) (sel) s. fam. engaño, estafa.

sell (to) (sel) t. vender, [enajenar, traicionar]. 2 engañar. 3 i. venderse [un artículo]. ¶ Pret. y p. p.: sold (sould).

seller ('seləʳ) s. vendedor.

senate ('senit) s. senado.

send (to) (send) t. enviar, mandar. 2 lanzar. 3 to ~ away, despedir; to ~ back, devolver. ¶ Pret. y p. p.: sent (sent).

senior ('si:njəʳ) a. mayor, de más edad; más antiguo; decano. 2 (E. U.) del último curso de una facultad. 3 s. anciano.

sense (sens) *s.* sentido [corporal; del humor, etc.]. 2 cordura, buen sentido: *common ~,* sentido común. 3 inteligencia. 4 significado, acepción: *to make ~,* tener sentido. 5 sensación, impresión, conciencia.

sense (to) (sens) *t.* sentir, percibir, darse cuenta.

sensible ('sensibl) *a.* sensible. 2 perceptible. 3 sensato, cuerdo.

sensitive ('sensitiv) *a.* sensitivo. 2 sensible, impresionable.

sent (sent) V. TO SEND.

sentence ('sentəns) *s.* sentencia, fallo; condena. 2 sentencia máxima. 3 GRAM. oración, período.

sentiment ('sentimənt) *s.* sentimiento. 2 sensibilidad. 3 parecer, opinión. 4 concepto, frase.

separate ('seprit) *a.* separado. 2 aparte. 3 distinto.

separate (to) ('sepəreit) *t.* separar. 2 despegar.

separation (,sepə'reiʃən) *s.* separación. 2 porción.

September (səp'tembəʳ) *s.* septiembre.

serene (si'ri:n) *a.* sereno, claro, despejado.

sergeant ('sɑːdʒənt) *s.* MIL. sargento.

series ('siəri:z) *s.* serie.

serious ('siəriəs) *a.* serio.

sermon ('se:mən) *s.* sermón.

serpent ('sə:pənt) *s.* serpiente, sierpe.

servant ('sə:vənt) *s.* sirviente, criado. 2 siervo.

serve (to) (sə:v) *t.-i.* servir. 2 surtir, abastecer.

service ('se:vis) *s.* servicio.

servile ('se:vail) *a.* servil.

session ('seʃən) *s.* sesión.

set (set) *s.* juego, servicio surtido, colección; grupo. 2 aderezo [de diamantes]. 3 equipo, cuadrilla. 4 clase, gente. 5 aparato [de radio, etc.]. 6 dirección; tendencia. 7 colocación; actitud, postura. 8 TEAT., CINEM. decoración. 9 TENIS set. 10 *a.* resuelto, determinado. 11 fijo, inmóvil, firme.

set (to) (set) *t.* poner, colocar, instalar. 2 destinar. Fijar. 3 plantar, erigir. 4 preparar, arreglar. 5 poner [un reloj] en hora. 6 excitar [contra]. 7 dar [el tono]. 8 adornar; sembrar. 9 engastar [una joya]. 10 dar, atribuir [un valor, etc.]. 11 fijar, inmovilizar. 12 IMPR. componer. 13 CIR. encajar [un hueso]. 14 tender [una trampa, etc.]. 15 *to ~ about,* poner a. 16 *to ~ aside,* dejar a un lado. 17 *to ~ fire to,* pegar fuego a. 18 *to ~ free,* libertar. 19 *to ~ going,* poner en marcha. 20 *to ~ off,* adornar; comparar; disparar. 21 *i.* caer bien [una prenda]. 22 ponerse [un astro]. 23 dedicarse a, ponerse a. 24 fijarse [un color]; fraguar, solidificarse. 25 *to ~ off,* salir. ¶ Pret. y p. p.: *set* (set); ger.: *setting* ('setiŋ).

settle ('setl) *s.* escaño, banco.

settle (to) ('setl) *t.* colocar, establecer. 2 fijar, asegurar. 3 colonizar, poblar. 4 ordenar; arreglar. 5 ajustar [cuentas]; zanjar [una disputa]; decidir, resolver. 6 pagar [una deuda]. 7 sosegar. pacificar. 8 *i.* establecerse. instalarse.

settler ('setlə^r) *s.* poblador. colono.

seven ('sevn) *a.-s.* siete.

seventeen ('sevn'ti:n) *a.-s.* diecisiete.

seventeenth ('sevn'ti:nθ) *a.* decimoséptimo.

seventh ('sevnθ) *a.* séptimo.

seventieth ('sevntiəθ, -tiiθ) *a.-s.* septuagésimo.

seventy ('sevnti) *a.-s.* setenta.

several ('sevrəl) *a.* varios.

severe (si'viə^r) *a.* severo.

sew (to) (sou) *t.-i.* coser. ¶ Pret.: *sewed* (soud); p. p.: *sewn* (soun) o *sewed.*

sewing (souiŋ) *s.* costura [acción de coser]: ~*machine*, máquina de coser.

sex (seks) *s.* sexo.

shabby ('ʃæbi) *a.* raído.

shade (ʃeid) *s.* sombra [de un árbol, etc.]. 2 matiz. tinte. 3 pantalla [de lámpara]. 4 visillo. cortina.

shade (to) (ʃeid) *t.* hacer o dar sombra. 2 resguardar de la luz. 3 proteger. esconder.

shadow ('ʃædou) *s.* espacio de sombra definida. oscuridad. 2 sombra [de un objeto: en pintura].

shadow (to) ('ʃædou) *t.* sombrear: oscurecer. 2 espiar.

shaft (ʃa:ft) *s.* astil [de saeta. etc.]. 2 asta [de lanza, bandera]. 3 saeta.

shake (ʃeik) *s.* meneo. sacudida. 2 temblor. estremecimiento. 3 apretón [de manos].

shake (to) (ʃeik) *t.* sacudir. agitar. blandir. 2 hacer temblar. 3 librarse de. ¶ Pret.: *shook* (ʃuk); p. p.: *shaken* ('ʃeikən).

shall (ʃæl. ʃəl) *v. def. aux.* del futuro. En 1.ªs personas denota simple acción futura: en 2.ªs y 3.ªs. voluntad. intención. mandato: *I shall go.* iré; *he shall go.* tiene que ir. 2 *SHOULD* (ʃud, ʃəd) pret. de *shall.* En 1.ªs personas, forma potencial; en 2.ªs y 3.ªs voluntad. intención. mandato: *I should come,* vendría; *you should come,* deberías venir.

shallow ('ʃælou) *a.* bajo. poco profundo. 2 superficial. frívolo. 3 *s.* bajío.

shame (ʃeim) *s.* vergüenza.

shame (to) (ʃeim) *t.* avergonzar. 2 afrentar.

shameful ('ʃeimful) *a.* vergonzoso.

shape (ʃeip) *s.* forma, figura.

shape (to) (ʃeip) *t.* formar. dar forma a; modelar.

share (to) (ʃeə^r) *t.* distribuir. repartir.

sharp (ʃa:p) *a.* agudo. aguzado. afilado. cortante. punzante. 2 puntiagudo.

sharpen (to) ('ʃa:pən) *t.* afilar.

shatter (to) ('ʃætə^r) *t.* romper. hacer astillas.

shave (to) (ʃeiv) *t.-i.* afeitar(se. 2 *t.* pasar rozando.

shaving ('ʃeiviŋ) *s.* afeitado.

shawl (ʃɔ:l) *s.* chal. mantón.

she (ʃi:. ʃi) *pron. pers.* ella. 2 hembra: *she-ass,* borrica.

shear (ʃiə^r) *s.* esquileo. 2 lana esquilada. 3 *pl.* cizalla.

shear (to) (ʃiəʳ) *t.* esquilar, trasquilar. ¶ P. p.: ***shorn*** (ʃɔːn).

shed (ʃed) *s.* cobertizo, alpende. 2 hangar.

shed (to) (ʃed) *t.* verter, derramar. 2 lanzar, esparcir. 3 *i.* mudar [la piel, etc.]. ¶ Pret. y p. p.: ***shed***.

sheep (ʃiːp) *s. sing.* y *pl.* carnero(s, oveja(s.

sheer (ʃiəʳ) *a.* puro, mero.

sheer (to) (ʃiəʳ) *t.-i.* desviar: *to* ~ *off*, apartarse, huir de.

sheet (ʃiːt) *s.* lámina, plancha. 2 sábana [de cama].

shelf (ʃelf), *pl.* **shelves** (ʃelvz)*s.* anaquel, repisa; *pl.* estantería.

shell (ʃel) *s.* ZOOL. concha, caparazón. 2 cáscara [de huevo, nuez, etc.]. 3 vaina [de guisantes, etc.]. 4 casco [de barco]. 5 bala [de cañón], bomba, granada.

shell (to) *t.* descascarar, mondar. 2 bombardear.

shelter (ˈʃeltəʳ) *s.* abrigo, refugio; albergue.

shelter (to) (ˈʃeltəʳ) *t.-i.* guarecer(se, abrigar(se.

shelves (ʃelvz) *s. pl.* de *shelf*.

shepherd (ˈʃepəd) *s.* pastor.

sheriff (ˈʃerif) *s.* alguacil mayor.

shield (ʃiːld) *s.* escudo.

shield (to) (ʃiːld) *t.* proteger, escudar, defender.

shift (ʃift) *s.* recurso, maña. 2 tanda, turno [de obreros; de trabajo]. 3 cambio, desviación.

shift (to) (ʃift) *t.-i.* cambiar, mudar [de posición, etc.]; mover(se, trasladar(se. 2 usar subterfugios.

shilling (ˈʃiliŋ) *s.* chelín.

shine (ʃain) *s.* brillo.

shine (to) (ʃain) *i.* brillar. ¶ Pret. y p. p.: ***shone*** (ʃɔn).

ship (ʃip) *s.* buque, barco.

ship (to) (ʃip) *t.-i.* embarcar(se. 2 *t.* transportar.

shipping (ˈʃipiŋ) *s.* embarque, expedición.

shirk (to) (ʃəːk) *t.* eludir.

shirt (ʃəːt) *s.* camisa.

shiver (ˈʃivəʳ) *s.* temblor.

shiver (to) (ˈʃivəʳ) *i.-t.* temblar, tiritar, estremecerse.

shoal (ʃoul) *s.* bajo, bajío, banco [de arena o de peces].

shock (ʃɔk) *s.* golpe, choque. 2 conmoción; sobresalto, susto. 3 ofensa.

shock (to) (ʃɔk) *t.* chocar; ofender. 2 sobresaltar, causar impresión. 3 sacudir, conmover.

shoe (ʃuː) *s.* zapato: ~ *black*, limpiabotas; ~ *polish*, betún; *shoehorn*, calzador.

shoe (to) (ʃuː) *t.* calzar; herrar [a un caballo]. ¶ Pret. y p. p.: ***shod*** (ʃɔd).

shoemaker (ˈʃuːˌmeikəʳ) *s.* zapatero.

shone (ʃɔn) TO SHINE.

shook (ʃuk) V. TO SHAKE.

shoot (ʃuːt) *s.* BOT. vástago, retoño. 2 conducto inclinado [para carbón, etc.]. 3 cacería.

shoot (to) (ʃuːt) *t.* fusilar. 2 disparar [un tiro, una instantánea]. 3 echar [brotes]. 4 DEP. chutar. 5 *i.* ir de caza. 6 *to* ~ *down*, derribar. 7 *to* ~ *up*, brotar [las plantas, etc.]. ¶ Pret. y p. p.: ***shot*** (ʃɔt).

shop (ʃɔp) *s.* tienda, comercio, almacén.

shop (to) (ʃɔp) *i.* comprar [en tiendas]: *to go shopping*, ir de compras.

shore (ʃɔːʳ) *s.* orilla [del mar, río, etc.], costa, playa.

shorn (ʃɔːn) V. TO SHEAR.

short (ʃɔːt) *a.* corto; breve, escaso, poco. 2 bajo [de estatura]. 3 seco, brusco. 4 ~ **hand**, taquígrafo, taquigrafía; ~ **sighted**, corto de vista. 5 *adv.* brevemente, cortamente; ~ *of*, excepto, si no. 6 *s.* lo corto. 7 CINEM. película corta. 8 *pl.* pantalones cortos [para deporte].

shot (ʃɔt) *a.* tornasolado, matizado. 2 *s.* tiro, disparo. 3 bala; perdigones. 4 tirada [en ciertos juegos]. 5 V. TO SHOOT.

should (ʃud, ʃed) V. TO SHALL.

shoulder (ˈʃouldəʳ) *s.* hombro.

shoulder (to) (ˈʃouldəʳ) *t.* echar o llevar al hombro; cargar con.

shout (ʃaut) *s.* grito, griterío.

shout (to) (ʃaut) *t.-i.* gritar, vocear. 2 vitorear.

shove (ʃʌv) *s.* empujón, empuje. 2 impulso.

shove (to) (ʃʌv) *t.i.* empujar, dar empujones.

shovel (ˈʃʌvl) *s.* pala. 2 palada.

show (ʃou) *s.* presentación, exhibición. 2 exposición [artística, etc.]. 3 espectáculo; función [de teatro, cine]. 4 ostentación, alarde.

show (to) (ʃou) *t.* mostrar, enseñar, exhibir, lucir. 2 sa-

car, asomar. 3 hacer ver, demostrar. 4 revelar, descubrir. 5 indicar; dar [señales]. 6 acompañar. 7 *to ~ how to*, enseñar a [hacer algo]. 8 *to ~ up*, destacar. 9 *i.* mostrarse, aparecer. 10 TEAT. actuar. ¶ Pret.: *showed* (ʃoud); p. p.: *shown* (ʃoun) *showed*.

shower (ˈʃauəʳ) *s.* chubasco, chaparrón. 2 lluvia, abundancia. 3 ~ *bath*, ducha.

shown (ʃoun) V. TO SHOW.

shrew (ʃruː) *s.* ZOOL. musaraña. 2 mujer de mal genio, arpía.

shrewd (ʃruːd) *a.* sagaz, listo.

shriek (ʃriːk) *s.* chillido, alarido.

shriek (to) (ʃriːk) *i.* chillar, gritar.

shrill (ʃril) *a.* agudo, penetrante, chillón.

shrill (to) (ʃril) *t.-i.* chillar.

shrine (ʃrain) *s.* urna, relicario; capilla, santuario.·

shrink (to) (ʃriŋk) *t.-i.* encoger(se, contraerse; disminuir. ¶ Pret.: *shrank* (ʃræŋk) o *shrunk* (ʃrʌŋk); p. p.: *shrunk* o *shrunken* (ˈʃrʌŋkən).

shrub (ʃrʌb) *s.* arbusto.

shrug (to) (ʃrʌg) *t.-i.* encoger(se [de hombros].

shrunk (ʃrʌŋk) V. TO SHRINK.

shudder (ˈʃʌdəʳ) *s.* temblor.

shudder (to) (ˈʃʌdəʳ) *i.* estremecerse. 2 tiritar.

shun (to) (ʃʌn) *t.* rehuir.

shut (to) (ʃʌt) *t.* cerrar [una puerta, etc.]. 3 tapar, obstruir. 3 *to ~ down*, cerrar una fábrica; *to ~ up*, tapar; callarse. ¶ Pret. y p. p.: *shut* (ʃʌt); ger.: *shutting*.

shutter (ˈʃʌtəʳ) *s.* postigo.

shy (ʃai) *a.* tímido, asustadizo. 2 retraído.

shy (to) (ʃai) *i.* esquivar; asustarse.

sick (sik) *a.-s.* enfermo. 2 mareado. *3 to be ~ of*, estar harto de.

sickness ('siknis) *s.* enfermedad. 2 náusea, mareo.

side (said) *s.* lado, costado. 2 orilla, margen. 3 falda [de montaña]. 4 partido, bando. 5 *a.* lateral.

side (to) (said) *t.* ponerse o estar al lado de.

sidewalk ('said-wɔ:k) *s.* (E. U.) acera.

siege (si:dʒ) *s.* sitio, asedio, cerco.

sift (to) (sift) *t.* cerner, tamizar, cribar.

sight (sait) *s.* vista, visión [sentido, órgano; acción de ver]: *at ~, on ~*, a primera vista; *by ~*, de vista. 2 escena, espectáculo. 3 mira [de arma]. 4 **-ly** *a.* vistoso, hermoso. 5 *adv.* vistosamente, bellamente.

sight (to) (sait) *t.-i.* ver, mirar.

sign (sain) *s.* signo, señal, indicio. 2 astro, vestigio.

sign (to) (sain) *t.-i.* firmar, rubricar. 2 contratar.

signal ('signəl) *s.* señal, seña, signo. 2 *a.* señalado, notable.

signature ('signətʃəʳ) *s.* firma, rúbrica.

signify (to) ('signifai) *t.* significar. 2 *i.* importar.

silence ('sailəns) *s.* silencio.

silence (to) ('sailəns) *t.* imponer silencio, hacer callar.

silent ('sailənt) *a.* silencioso.

silhouette (ˌsiluˈet) *s.* silueta.

silk (silk) *s.* seda [materia, hilo, tejido]: *~ worm*, gusano de seda; *~ hat*, sombrero de copa.

silken ('silkən) *a.* de seda.

silliness ('silinis) *s.* tontería.

silly ('sili) *a.* tonto, necio.

silver ('silvəʳ) *s.* plata [metal, moneda; objetos]. 2 *a.* de plata.

similar ('similəʳ) *a.* similar.

simple ('simpl) *a.* simple. 2 tonto, bobo.

simplicity (simˈplisiti) *s.* simplicidad. 2 sencillez.

simply ('simpli) *adv.* simplemente; meramente.

since (sins) *adv.* desde, desde entonces. 2 *prep.* desde, después de. 3 *conj.* desde que, después que. 4 ya que, puesto que.

sing (to) (siŋ) *t.-i.* cantar. ¶ Pret.: *sang* (sæŋ); p. p.: *sung* (sʌŋ).

singer ('siŋəʳ) *s.* cantante, cantor, cantatriz.

single ('siŋgl) *a.* único. 2 célibe: *~ man*, soltero. 3 sencillo, simple. 4 individual.

single (to) ('siŋgl) *t. to ~ out*, singularizar, distinguir.

singular ('siŋgjuləʳ) *a.* singular. 2 raro, estrafalario.

sink (siŋk) *s.* sumidero. 2 fregadero.

sink (to) (siŋk) *t.-i.* hundir(se, sumergir(se, echar a pique; naufragar. *2 to ~ down*, derrumbarse. 3 ponerse [el sol]. ¶ Pret.: *sank* (sæŋk) o *sunk* (sʌŋk); p. p.: *sunk* o *sunken* ('sʌŋkən).

sinner ('sinəʳ) *s.* pecador, pecadora.

sinuosity (ˌsinjuˈɔsiti) *s.* sinuosidad, tortuosidad.

sinuous (ˈsinjuəs) *a.* sinuoso.

sir (səˑ, səʳ) *s.* señor. 2 (Ingl.)tratamiento que se antepone al nombre de un caballero o baronet: *Sir Winston Churchill.*

sire (ˈsaiəʳ) *s.* señor [tratamiento del soberano]. 2 progenitor. 3 animal padre.

sister (ˈsistəʳ) *s.* hermana. 2 sor, monja. 3 enfermera. 4 *sister-in-law.* cuñada.

sit (to) (sit) *t.-i.* sentar(se; posarse [un pájaro]; estar sentado. 2 empollar [las gallinas]. 3 celebrar sesión. 4 sentar bien [un traje]. 5 *to ~ down.* sentarse; establecerse. 6 *to ~ for.* representar [un distrito]; servir de modelo. 7 *to ~ on* o *upon,* deliberar sobre. 8 *to ~ up,* incorporarse [en la cama]. ¶ Pret. y p. p.: *sat* (sæt).

site (sait) *s.* sitio, escenario [de algo]. 2 asiento, situación [de una población, etc.].

situation (ˌsitjuˈeiʃən) *s.* situación; posición. 2 colocación, empleo.

six (siks) *a.-s.* seis.

size (saiz) *s.* medida, tamaño.

skate (skeit) *s.* patín.

skeleton (ˈskelitn) *s.* esqueleto. 2 armazón. 3 esbozo, esquema. 4 ~ *key,* llave maestra.

sketch (sketʃ) *s.* boceto.

sketch (to) (sketʃ) *t.* esbozar.

skilful (ˈskilful) *a.* diestro.

skill (skil) *s.* habilidad.

skilled (skild) *a.* práctico.

skim (to) (skim) *t.* espumar.

skin (skin) *s.* piel. cutis, pellejo. 2 odre. 3 cáscara, hollejo. 4 *skin-deep.* superficial.

skin (to) (skin) *t.* desollar, despellejar. 2 desplumar.

skip (skip) *s.* salto, brinco.

skip (to) (skip) *t.* saltar, brincar. 2 omitir, pasar por alto.

skirt (skəːt) *s.* falda, saya. 2 orilla, margen.

skirt (to) (skəːt)*t.-i.* bordear, rodear, circundar.

skull (skʌl) *s.* cráneo, calavera.

sky (skai) *s.* cielo, firmamento.

slain (slein) V. TO SLAY.

slam (slæm) *s.* golpe, portazo.

slam (to) (slæm) *t.* cerrar de golpe.

slander (ˈslɑːndəʳ) *s.* calumnia, difamación.

slander (to) (ˈslɑːndəʳ) *t.* calumniar, difamar.

slap (slæp) *s.* palmada; bofetón. 2 insulto, desaire.

slate (sleit) *s.* pizarra.

slaughter (ˈslɔːtəʳ) *s.* matanza.

slaughter (to) (ˈslɔːtəʳ) *t.* matar. 2 sacrificar [reses].

slave (sleiv) *s.* esclavo.

slavery (ˈsleivəri) *s.* esclavitud, servidumbre.

slay (to) (slei) *t.* matar. ¶ Pret.: *slew* (sluː); p. p.: *slain* (slein).

sled (sled), **sledge** (sledʒ) *s.* trineo, rastra.

sleep (sliːp) *s.* sueño.

sleep (to) (sliːp) *i.* dormir. ¶ Pret. y p. p.: *slept* (slept).

sleeping (ˈsliːpiŋ) *a.* dormido.

sleepy ('sli:pi) *a.* soñoliento.

sleeve (sli:v) *s.* manga [de vestido].

slender ('slendə^r) *a.* delgado.

slept (slept) V. TO SLEEP.

slew (slu:) V. TO SLAY.

slice (slais) *s.* rebanada, lonja.

slice (to) (slais) *t.* rebanar. 2 tajar, cortar.

slid (slid) V. TO SLIDE.

slide (slaid) *s.* corrimiento de tierra; falla. 2 ÓPT. diapositiva.

slide (to) (slaid) *i.-t.* resbalar. ¶ Pret. y p. p.: *slid* (slid).

slight (slait) *a.* ligero, leve. 2 pequeño, insignificante. 3 delgado, delicado. 4 *s.* desaire, desprecio.

slight (to) (slait) *t.* despreciar.

slim (slim) *a.* delgado, esbelto. 2 pequeño. 3 baladí.

slip (slip) *s.* resbalón. 2 huida, esquinazo. 3 tira [trozo estrecho]. 4 combinación [de mujer].

slip (to) (slip) *t.-i.* resbalar(se.

slipper ('slipə^r) *s.* zapatilla, babucha.

slippery ('slipəri) *a.* resbaladizo. 2 huidizo. 3 astuto.

slope (sloup) *s.* cuesta, pendiente. 2 falda, ladera.

slope (to) (sloup) *i.* inclinarse.

slow (slou) *a.* lento, tardo. 2 torpe. 3 atrasado. 4 *adv.* lentamente, despacio.

slumber ('slʌmbə^r) *s.* sueño.

slumber (to) ('slʌmbə^r) *i.* dormitar. 2 dormirse.

sly (slai) *a.* astuto, socarrón. 2 travieso. 3 furtivo: *on the*

~, a hurtadillas. 4 **-ly** *adv.* astutamente.

small (smɔ:l) *a.* pequeño, chico; insignificante: ~ *change*, dinero suelto. 2 bajo [estatura].

smart (smɑ:t) *a.* elegante: *the* ~ *set*, la gente distinguida. 2 listo, astuto. 3 fuerte, violento. 4 *s.* punzada, escozor. 5 dolor.

smash (smæʃ) *s.* rotura, destrozo. 2 choque [de vehículos, etc.], golpe violento. 3 fracaso, bancarrota.

smash (to) (smæʃ) *t.-i.* romper(se, destrozar(se. 2 quebrar, arruinar(se.

smell (smel) *s.* olfato [sentido]. 2 olor.

smell (to) (smel) *t.* oler [percibir con el olfato]. 2 olfatear, husmear. 3 *i.* oler [exhalar olor]: *to* ~ *of*, oler a. ¶ Pret. y p. p.: *smelt* (smelt)

smile (smail) *s.* sonrisa.

smile (to) (smail) *i.* sonreír(se.

smite (to) (smait) *t.* golpear, herir. 2 asolar. 3 remorder [la conciencia]. ¶ Pret.: *smote* (smout); p. p.: *smiten* ('smitn).

smoke (smouk) *s.* humo.

smoke (to) (smouk) *t.-i.* fumar. 2 ahumar.

smooth (smuð) *a.* liso, terso. 2 llano, igual. 3 fácil. 4 blando, suave. 5 plácido. 6 afable, lisonjero.

smooth (to) (smu:ð) *t.* alisar, allanar. 2 cepillar, pulir. 3 facilitar [las cosas]. 4 suavizar. 5 calmar.

smote (smout) V. TO SMITE.

smother (to) ('smʌðəʳ) *t.-i.* ahogar(se; sofocar(se.

snake (sneik) *s.* culebra, serpiente.

snake (to) (sneik) *i.* serpentear.

snap (snæp) *s.* chasquido. 2 mordisco. 3 energía, vigor. 4 ~ *shot*, foto instantánea.

snap (to) (snæp) *t.-i.* chasquear. 2 arrebatar. 3 tirar un bocado a. 4 hacer una instantánea.

snare (snɛəʳ) *s.* lazo, armadijo. 2 celada, trampa.

snare (to) (snɛəʳ) *t.* atrapar.

snarl (snɑːl) *s.* gruñido.

snarl (to) (snɑːl) *i.* regañar; gruñir.

snatch (snætʃ) *s.* acción de arrebatar. 2 trozo, pedacito. 3 rato: *by snatches*, a ratos.

snatch (to) (snætʃ) *t.* coger, arrebatar, quitar.

sneak (sniːk) *s.* persona ruin.

sneak (to) (sniːk) *t.-i.* andar u obrar furtivamente. 2 hurtar, ratear.

sneer (sniəʳ) *s.* burla, mofa.

sneer (to) (sniəʳ) *i.* reírse con burla o desprecio; burlarse. | Gralte. con *at*.

sniff (snif) *s.* olfato, husmeo.

sniff (to) (snif) *t.* olfatear, husmear.

snob (snɔb) *s.* esnob [persona con pretensiones sociales].

snow (snou) *s.* nieve.

snuffle (to) ('snʌfl) *i.* respirar con la nariz obstruida.

so (sou) *adv.* así; eso, lo mismo: *I hope* ~, así lo esperó. 2 ~ *that*, para que. 3 tan, tanto: ~ *good*, tan

bueno. 4 y así, por tanto. 5 *conj.* con tal que; para que. 6 *and* ~ *forth*, etcétera; ~ *far as*, hasta; ~ *long*, hasta la vista; ~ *much*, tanto; ~ *many*, tantos; *so-so*, regular; *so-and-so*, fulano [de tal]; ~ *far*, hasta ahora, hasta aquí; ~ *to say*, o *to speak*, por decirlo así.

soak (souk) *s.* remojo, remojón. 2 borrachín.

soak (to) (souk) *t.-i.* remojar(se, empapar(se.

soap (soup) *s.* jabón.

soap (to) (soup) *t.* jabonar.

soar (to) (sɔːʳ, sɔəʳ) *i.* elevarse, remontarse.

sob (sɔb) *s.* sollozo; suspiro.

sob (to) (sɔb) *i.* sollozar.

sober ('soubəʳ) *a.* sobrio.

so-called ('sou'kɔːld) *a.* llamado, supuesto; pseudo.

social ('souʃəl) *a.* social.

society (sə'saiəti) *s.* sociedad.

sock (sɔk) *s.* calcetín. 2 golpe.

sod (sɔd) *s.* césped.

soft (sɔft) *a.* blando, maleable, fofo.

soften (to) ('sɔfn) *t.-i.* ablandar(se, suavizar(se.

soil (sɔil) *s.* tierra, terreno.

soil (to) (sɔil) *t.* ensuciar, manchar.

sold (sould) V. TO SELL.

soldier ('souldʒəʳ) *s.* soldado.

sole (soul) *s.* planta [del pie]; palma [del casco del caballo]. 2 suela [del zapato]. 3 suelo, base. 4 ICT. lenguado. 5 *a.* solo, único: ~ *right*, exclusiva.

solemn ('sɔləm) *a.* solemne.

solid ('sɔlid) *a.* sólido.

solitude ('sɔlitjuːd) *s.* soledad.

solution (səˈluːʃən) *s.* solución.

solve (to) (sɔlv) *t.* resolver.

some (sʌm, səm) *a.-pron.* algún, algunos; un, unos; alguna persona. *2* algo de, un poco de.

somebody ('sʌmbəd) *pron.* alguien, alguno.

somehow ('sʌmhau) *adv.* de algún modo.

someone ('sʌmwʌn) *pron.* SOMEBODY.

something ('sʌmθiŋ) *s.* algo, alguna cosa.

sometimes ('sʌmtaimz) *adv.* algunas veces, a veces.

somewhat ('sʌmwɔt) *s.* algo, un poco. *2 adv.* algo, algún tanto; en cierto modo.

somewhere ('sʌmwɛəʳ) *adv.* en alguna parte.

son (sʌn) *s.* hijo; descendiente [varón]. *2 son-in-law*, yerno.

song (sɔŋ) *s.* canto [acción de cantar]. *2* MÚS., LIT. canción, canto, copla, cantar.

soon (suːn) *adv.* pronto, luego; temprano; *as ~ as*, tan pronto como.

soothe (to) (suːð) *t.* aliviar.

sophisticated (səˈfistikietid) *a.* sofisticado. *2* artificial.

sore (sɔːʳ, sɔəʳ) *a.* dolorido. *2 s.* herida, llaga.

sorrow ('sɔrou) *s.* dolor, pesar, sentimiento.

sorrow (to) ('sɔrou) *i.* afligirse.

sorry ('sɔri) *a.* afligido, pesaroso, triste. *2* arrepentido.

sort (sɔːt) *s.* clase, especie. *2* modo, manera: *in a ~*, en cierto modo.

sort (to) (sɔːt) *t.* ordenar, clasificar. *2* escoger, entresacar.

sought (sɔːt) V. TO SEEK.

soul (soul) *s.* alma.

sound (saund) *a.* sano. *2 s.* son, sonido.

sound (to) (saund) *i.* sonar. *2 t.* tocar, tañer [un instrumento].

soup (suːp) *s.* sopa.

sour ('sauəʳ) *a.* ácido, agrio.

sour (to) ('sauəʳ) *t.-i.* agriarse. *2* enranciarse, fermentar.

source (sɔːs) *s.* fuente, manantial.

south (sauθ) *s.* sur, mediodía.

southern ('sʌðən) *a.* del sur.

sovereign ('sɔvrin) *a.* soberano. *2 s.* soberano [monarca; moneda].

soviet ['souviet) *s.* soviet. *2 a.* soviético.

1) **sow** (sau) *s.* cerda, marrana.

2) **sow (to)** (sou) *t.* sembrar. ¶ Pret.: *sowed* (soud); p. p.: *sown* (soun) o *sowed*.

space (speis) *s.* espacio. *2* oportunidad.

space (to) (speis) *t.* espaciar.

spacious ('speiʃəs) *a.* espacioso; vasto. *2* amplio.

spade (speid) *s.* laya, pala.

span (spæn) *s.* palmo, llave de la mano. *2* extensión. *3* luz [de un arco]; ojo [de puente]

Spaniard ('spænjəd) *s.* español.

Spanish ('spæniʃ) *a.* español.

2 s. lengua española o castellana.

spare (speə^r) a. de repuesto. 2 flaco, enjuto. 3 sobrio, frugal.

spare (to) (speə^r) t. ahorrar, economizar. 2 prescindir de, pasar sin.

spark (spɑ:k) s. chispa: centella, chispazo.

spark (to) (spɑ:k) i. chispear, echar chispas.

sparkle (pɑ:kl) s. chispa.

sparrow ('spærou) s. gorrión.

speak (to) (spi:k) i. hablar: *to ~ out*, hablar claro. 2 t. hablar, decir, expresar. 3 hablar [una lengua]. ¶ Pret.: *spoke* (spouk); p. p.: *spoken* ('spoukən).

speaker ('spi:kə^r) s. el que habla. 2 orador. 3 presidente [de una asamblea]. 4 RADIO locutor.

spear (spiə^r) s. lanza, venablo. 2 arpón [para pescar].

spear (to) (spiə^r) t. alancear. 2 atravesar con arpón.

special ('speʃəl) a. especial. 2 particular, peculiar. 3 s. tren, autobús, etc., especial.

species ('spi:ʃi:z) s. especie [imagen; apariencia]. 2 clase, suerte. 3 género humano.

specific(al (spi'sifik, -əl) a. específico. 2 preciso. 3 característico. 4 s. FARM. específico.

specimen ('spesimin) s. espécimen, muestra.

speck (spek) s. manchita; motita. 2 pizca, átomo.

speck (to) (spek) t. manchar.

spectacle ('spektəkl) s. espectáculo. 2 pl. gafas, anteojos.

spectator (spek'teitə^r) s. espectador.

speech (spi:tʃ) s. palabra, lenguaje. 2 idioma. 3 discurso. 4 TEAT. parlamento. 5 conversación.

speed (spi:d) s. rapidez, prisa. 2 marcha, velocidad.

speed (to) (spi:d) t. acelerar, dar prisa a. ¶ Pret. y p. p.: *sped* (sped) o *speeded* ('spi:did).

spell (spel) s. hechizo, encanto. 2 turno, tanda.

spell (to) (spel) t.-i. deletrear. ¶ Pret. y p. p.: *spelled* (speld) o *spelt* (spelt).

spend (to) (spend) t. gastar. 2 pasar [el tiempo]. ¶ Pret. y p. p.: *spent* (spent).

sphere (sfiə^r) s. esfera. 2 globo, orbe.

spice (spais) s. especia.

spice (to) (spais) t. condimentar con especias. 2 sazonar.

spider ('spaidə^r) s. araña.

spill (to) t.-i. derramar(se. ¶ Pret. y p. p.: *spilled* (spild) o *spilt* (spilt).

spin (spin) s. giro, vuelta.

spin (to) (spin) t.-i. hilar. 2 hacer girar. ¶ Pret.: *spun* (spʌn) o *span* (spæn); p. p.: *spun* (spʌn).

spine (spain) s. espinazo.

spire ('spaiə^r) s. cima. 2 ARQ. aguja de torre.

spirit ('spirit) s. espíritu [en todos sus sentidos]. 2 pl. alcohol, bebida espirituosa.

spirit (to) ('spirit) t. alentar, animar. | A veces con *up*.

spiritual ('spiritjuəl) a. espiritual. 2 s. espiritual [canto religioso de los negros].

spit (spit) *s.* asador. *2* esputo.
spit (to) (spit) *i.* escupir, esputar. *2* lloviznar. ¶ Pret. y p. p.: *spat* (spæt).
spite (spait) *s.* despecho, rencor, resentimiento. *2 in ~ of*, a pesar de, a despecho de.
spite (to) (spait) *t.* molestar.
splash (splæʃ) *s.* salpicadura.
splash (to) (splæʃ) *t.* salpicar, rociar. *2 i.* chapotear.
splendid ('splendid) *a.* espléndido. *2* ilustre, glorioso.
splendo(u)r ('splendə^r) *s.* brillo. *2* magnificencia.
splinter ('splintə^r) *s.* astilla.
splinter (to) ('splintə^r) *t.-i.* astillar(se.
split (split) *s.* grieta. *2* división, cisma. *3* astilla, raja.
split (to) (split) *t.-i.* hender(se, rajar(se, partir(se. ¶ Pret. y p. p.: *split* (split).
spoil (spɔil) *s.* despojo, botín.
spoil (to) (spɔil) *t.* saquear, robar: *to ~ of*, privar de. *2* estropear, echar a perder. *3* mimar, malcriar. *4 i.* estropearse. ¶ Pret. y p. p.: *spoiled* (spɔild) o *spoilt* (spɔilt).
spoke (spouk) *pret.* de TO SPEAK. *2 s.* rayo [de rueda].
spoken ('spoukən) V. TO SPEAK.
sponge (spʌndʒ) *s.* esponja.
sponge (to) (spʌndʒ) *t.* lavar con esponja, borrar.
spoon (spu:n) *s.* cuchara.
sport (spɔ:t) *s.* deporte.
sport (to) (spɔ:t) *t.* ostentar, lucir. *2 i.* jugar, retozar.
spot (spɔt) *s.* mancha, borrón. *2* sitio, lugar *3 a.* disponible [dinero].

spot (to) (spɔt) *t.* manchar. *2* localizar.
sprang (spræŋ) V. TO SPRING.
spray (sprei) *s.* líquido pulverizado; rocío [del mar, etc.]. *2* ramita, ramaje.
spray (to) (sprei) *t.* pulverizar.
spread (spred) *pret.* y *p. p.* de TO SPREAD. *2 a.* extendido, etc. *3 s.* despliegue, desarrollo. *4* extensión.
spread (to) (spred) *t.-i.* extender(se, desplegar(se. ¶ Pret. y p. p.: *spread* (spred).
sprig (sprig) *s.* ramita.
spring (spriŋ) *s.* primavera. *2* fuente. *3* origen, principio. *4* salto, brinco. *5* muelle, resorte. *6* elasticidad. *7* vigor.
spring (to) (spriŋ) *i.* saltar, brincar; lanzarse sobre [at]. *2* nacer, brotar. | con *forth, out*, o *up*. *3* arrancar [un arco]. *4* provenir, seguirse. *5* ⚒ hacer saltar o estallar [una mina]. ¶ Pret.: *sprang* (spræŋ); p. p.: *sprung* (sprʌŋ).
sprinkle ('spriŋkl) *s.* rocío.
sprinkle (to) ('spriŋkl) *t.* rociar, regar. *2* lloviznar.
sprint (sprint) *s.* carrera corta y rápida.
spruce (spru:s) *a.* pulcro.
spruce (to) (spru:s) *t.-i.* asear(se.
sprung (sprʌŋ) V. TO SPRING.
spun (spʌn) V. TO SPIN.
spur (spə:^r) *s.* espuela. *2* aguijón, estímulo.
spur (to) (spə:^r) *t.* espolear, picar. *2* estimular.
spy (spai) *s.* espía.
spy (to) (spai) *t.* espiar.
squadron ('skwɔdrən) *s.* MAR.

escuadra. 2 AVIA. escuadrilla. 3 MIL. escuadrón.

square (skwɛə^r) *s.* GEOM. cuadro, cuadrado. 2 MAT. cuadrado. 3 casilla [ajedrez, etc.]. 4 plaza [de ciudad]. 5 escuadra, cartabón. 6 fornido. 7 exacto; justo. 8 recto, honrado. 9 saldado, en paz; empatado. 10 rotundo, categórico. 11 abundante [comida].

square (to) (skwɛə^r) *t.* GEOM., MAT. cuadrar. 2 escuadrar; elevar al cuadrado. 3 saldar [cuentas].

squeak (ski:k) *s.* chillido.

squeak (to) (ski:k) *i.* chillar, chirriar. 2 delatar.

squeeze (skwi:z) *s.* apretón.

squeeze (to) (skwi:z) *t.* apretar, comprimir. 2 estrujar.

squire ('skwaiə^r) *s.* escudero. 2 (Ingl.) hacendado; caballero.

squirrel ('skwirəl) *s.* ardilla.

stable ('steibl) *a.* estable. 2 *s.* establo, cuadra.

stable (to) ('steibl) *t.-i.* poner, tener o estar en un establo.

stack (stæk) *s.* almiar. 2 pila, montón. 3 pabellón [de fusiles]. 4 cañón [de chimenea].

stack (to) (stæk) *t.* apilar, amontonar.

staff (stɑ:f) *s.* palo, bastón. 2 personal [técnico o directivo].

stage (steidʒ) *s.* escenario. 2 campo [de actividades]. 3 parada; jornada. 4 grado, fase.

stage (to) (steidʒ) *t.* poner en escena.

stagger (to) ('stægə^r) *i.* vacilar.

stain (stein) *s.* mancha. 2 tinte.

stain (to) (stein) *t.-i.* manchar(se. 2 teñir.

stair (stɛə^r) *s.* escalón, peldaño.

stake (steik) *s.* estaca; poste.

stake (to) (steik) *t.* estacar. 2 apostar [en el juego].

stale (steil) *a.* pasado; rancio, viejo.

stalk (stɔ:k) *s.* BOT. tallo, caña.

stalk (to) (stɔ:k) *t.* andar majestuosamente. 2 espiar, acechar.

stall (stɔ:l) *s.* establo, cuadra. 2 puesto [de venta].

stall (to) (stɔ:l) *t.-i.* poner o tener en establo o cuadra. 2 atascar(se; ahogar(se [un motor].

stalwart ('stɔ:lwət) *a.-s.* fornido. 2 valiente. 3 leal.

stammer ('stæmə^r) *s.* tartamudeo. 2 balbuceo.

stammer (to) ('stæmə^r) *i.* tartamudear. 2 balbucear.

stamp (stæmp) *s.* estampa, huella, señal. 2 sello. 3 género, suerte.

stamp (to) (stæmp) *t.* estampar, imprimir, marcar. 2 caracterizar. 3 sellar, estampillar. 4 poner sello a.

stand (stænd) *s.* posición, puesto. 2 alto, parada. 3 resistencia. 4 tablado, tribuna. 5 puesto [en el mercado]; quiosco [de venta]. 6 velador, pie, soporte.

stand (to) (stænd) *i.* estar, tenerse o ponerse en pie; levantarse; ~ *up*, ponte en pie. 4 durar. 5 detenerse. 6 mantenerse firme, resistir. 7 *t.* poner derecho. 8 aguantar. 9 *to ~ aside*, apartarse. *10 to ~ by*, apoyar; estar alerta. *11 to ~ for*, representar; estar en lugar de; presentarse para; hacer rumbo a. *12 to ~ off*, apartarse. *13 to ~ out*, sobresalir. ¶ Pret. y p. p.: *stood* (stud).

standard ('stændəd) *s.* norma; nivel. 2 modelo. 3 estandarte. 4 normal, corriente.

standing ('stændiŋ) *a.* derecho, de pie. 2 parado. 3 fijo. 4 vigente [ley]. 5 *s.* posición.

star (stɑ:ʳ) *s.* ASTR. estrella, astro. 2 asterisco.

star (to) (stɑ:ʳ) *t.* tachonar de estrellas. 2 marcar con asterisco.

starch (stɑ:tʃ) *s.* almidón.

starch (to) (stɑ:tʃ) *t.* almidonar.

stare (stɛəʳ) *s.* mirada fija.

stare (to) (stɛəʳ) *t.-i.* mirar fijamente; clavar la vista.

start (stɑ:t) *s.* sobresalto, bote. 2 susto. 3 marcha, partida. 4 delantera, ventaja. 5 *by starts*, a ratos; a empujones.

start (to) (stɑ:t) *i.* sobresaltarse. 2 salir, partir; arrancar [el motor, etc.]. 3 *t.-i.* poner(se en marcha. 4 *t.* empezar, emprender [un negocio, etc.].

startle (to) (stɑ:tl) *t.-i.* asustar(se; sobresaltar(se.

starve (to) (stɑ:v) *i.* morir o padecer hambre. 2 *t.* matar de hambre.

state (steit) *s.* estado, situación.

state (to) (steit) *t.* exponer, declarar, expresar.

stately ('steitli) *a.* majestuoso.

statement ('steitmənt) *s.* declaración, afirmación.

statesman ('steitsmən) *s.* estadista, hombre de estado.

station ('steiʃən) *s.* estación [de tren, meteorológica, etc.]. 2 parada, apeadero. 3 puesto [militar; de servicio]. 4 MAR. apostadero. 5 puesto, situación.

station (to) ('steiʃən) *t.* estacionar, situar.

statistics (stə'tistiks) *s.* estadística.

stay (stei) *s.* MAR. estay, tirante. 2 sostén, apoyo. 3 parada, estancia. 4 aplazamiento. 5 varilla [de corsé]. 6 *pl.* corsé.

stay (to) (stei) *t.* sostener, apoyar. 2 fundar, basar. 3 resistir. 4 detener, frenar. 5 aplazar. 6 aguardar. 7 sosegar. 8 *i.* estar de pie o quieto; pararse. 9 estar o quedarse en casa; *to ~ up*, velar. 10 tardar.

steady ('stedi) *a.* firme.

steak (steik) *s.* tajada [para asar o freír], biftec.

steal (sti:l) *s.* hurto, robo.

steal (to) (sti:l) *t.-i.* hurtar, robar. 2 *to ~ away*, escabullirse, escapar. ¶ Pret.: *stole* (stoul); p. p.: *stolen* ('stoulən).

stealthy ('stelθi) *a.* furtivo.

steam (sti:m) *s.* vapor [esp. de agua].

steam (to) (sti:m) *t.* cocer o

preparar al vapor. 2 *i.* emitir vaho. 3 marchar a vapor.

steamboat ('sti:mbout), **steamer** ('sti:mə^r), **steamship** ('sti:mʃip) *s.* vapor [buque].

steed (sti:d) *s.* corcel.

steel (sti:l) *s.* acero.

steel (to) (sti:l) *t.* acerar.

steep (sti:p) *a.* empinado, pendiente. 2 *s.* cuesta, precipicio.

steep (to) (sti:p) *t.* empapar.

steer (to) (stiə^r) *t.* gobernar [una embarcación]; conducir, guiar [un vehículo].

stem (stem) *s.* bot. tallo, tronco. 2 tronco [de una familia]. 3 raíz [de una palabra]. 4 pie [de copa]. 5 proa.

stem (to) (stem) *t.* estancar, represar. 2 navegar contra [la corriente].

step (step) *s.* paso [del que anda; en el progreso, etc.]. 2 escalón; umbral. 3 estribo [de coche]. 4 huella, pisada.

step (to) (step) *i.* andar, caminar; *to ~ aside*, apartarse; *to ~ back*, retroceder. 2 *t.* sentar [el pie].

stern (stə:n) *a.* duro, riguroso. 2 *s.* popa.

stew (stju:) *s.* estofado, guisado.

stew (to) (stju:) *t.* estofar, guisar.

steward (stjuəd) *s.* mayordomo. 2 camarero.

stick (stik) *s.* palo, garrote.

stick (to) (stik) *t.* clavar, hincar. 2 meter. 3 pegar, adherir. 4 pinchar. 5 sacar, asomar [con *out*]. 6 levantar [con *up*]. ¶ Pret. y p p.: *stuck* (stʌk).

stiff (stif) *a.* tieso [rígido; es-

tirado]. 2 duro, difícil. 3 terco, obstinado. 4 ~ *neck*, torticolis; obstinación; *stiff-necked*, obstinado.

stifle (to) ('staifl) *t.-i.* ahogar(se. 2 *t.* apagar.

still (stil) *a.* quieto, inmóvil. 2 tranquilo, sosegado. 3 silencioso. 4 suave [voz, ruido]. 5 muerto, inanimado: ~ *life*, naturaleza muerta. 6 *adv.* aún, todavía. 7 *conj.* no obstante, a pesar de eso. 8 *s.* silencio, quietud.

still (to) (stil) *t.* acallar. 2 detener, parar. 3 *t.-i.* calmar(se.

stillness ('stilnis) *s.* quietud.

stimulate (to) ('stimjuleit) *t.-i.* estimular.

sting (stiŋ) *s.* picadura, punzada. 2 aguijón, estímulo.

sting (to) (stiŋ) *t.-i.* picar, punzar. 2 escocer, remorder. 3 aguijonear, estimular. ¶ Pret. y p. p.: *stung* (stʌŋ).

stir (stə:^r) *s.* movimiento.

stir (to) (stə:^r) *t.-i.* mover(se, menear(se. 2 *t.* agitar; promover; inspirar.

stitch (stitʃ) *s.* puntada [de costura].

stitch (to) (stitʃ) *t.* coser a puntadas, pespuntar.

stock (stɔk) *s.* tronco [de árbol; del cuerpo; origen]. 2 zoquete. 3 pilar. 4 provisión, existencia. 5 TEAT. repertorio. 6 inventario. 7 ganado. 8 capital de un negocio. 9 COM. título; acción. 10 muebles. 11 mango [de caña de pescar, etc.]; caja [de fusil, etc.]. 12 valores públicos. 13 *pl.* cepo [castigo]. 14 *a.* común, usual.

stock (to) (stɔk) *t.* tener en

existencia. 2 abastecer, proveer.

stocking ('stɔkiŋ) *s.* media, calceta.

stole (stoul), **stolen** ('stoulən) V. TO STEAL.

stolid ('stɔlid) *a.* estólido.

stomach ('stʌmək) *s.* estómago.

stone (stoun) *s.* piedra. 2 hueso [de fruta]. 3 (Ingl.) peso de 14 libras.

stone (to) (stoun) *t.* apedrear.

stony ('stouni) *a.* pedregoso.

stood (stud) V. TO STAND.

stool (stu:l) *s.* taburete, escabel. 2 excremento. 3 retrete.

stoop (stu:p) *s.* inclinación [de espaldas], encorvamiento.

stoop (to) (stu:p) *i.* agacharse, doblar el cuerpo.

stop (stɔp) *s.* alto, parada; fin, pausa. 2 apeadero.

stop (to) (stɔp) *t.-i.* detener(se, parar(se.

storage ('stɔ:ridʒ) *s.* almacenamiento. 2 almacenaje.

store (stɔ:ʳ, stɔəʳ) *s.* abundancia; provisión. 2 tesoro. 3 ~*house*, almacén. 4 (E. U.)tienda, comercio. 5 *pl.* reservas, provisiones.

store (to) (stɔ:ʳ, stɔəʳ) *t.* proveer, abastecer. 2 atesorar.

storey ('stɔ:ri) *s.* ARQ. piso, planta.

storm (stɔ:m) *s.* tempestad.

storm (to) (stɔ:m) *t.* tomar al asalto. 2 *i.* haber tempestad.

stormy ('stɔ:mi) *a.* tempestuoso. 2 violento.

story ('stɔ:ri) *s.* historia, leyenda, cuento. 2 *fam.* chisme, embuste. 3 ARQ. piso [de edificio].

stout (staut) *a.* fuerte, recio.

stove (stouv) *s.* estufa; hornillo. 2 V. TO STAVE.

stow (to) (stou) *t.* apretar.

straight (streit) *a.* recto, derecho; correcto. 2 erguido; lacio [pelo]. 3 sincero; honrado; serio. 4 puro, sin mezcla. 5 *adv.* seguido: *for two hours* ~, dos horas seguidas; ~ *away*, en seguida; ~ *ahead*, enfrente. 6 *s.* recta, plano. 7 escalera [en póker].

straighten (to) ('streitn) *t.-i.* enderezar(se. 2 arreglar.

straightway ('streit-wei) *adv.* inmediatamente, en seguida.

strain (strein) *s.* tensión o esfuerzo excesivo. 2 esguince, torcedura. 3 estirpe. 4 clase, suerte. 5 tono, acento. 6 aire, melodía.

strain (to) (strein) *t.* estirar demasiado. 2 torcer, violentar.

strait (streit) *a.* estrecho, apretado. 2 difícil. 3 *s.* GEOGR. estrecho. 4 aprieto, apuro.

strand (strænd) *s.* playa, ribera.

strand (to) (strænd) *t.-i.* embarrancar.

strange (streindʒ) *a.* extraño, foráneo. 2 ajeno. 3 raro.

stranger ('streindʒəʳ) *s.* extraño, forastero.

strap (stræp) *s.* correa, tira [esp. para atar].

strap (to) (stræp) *t.* atar con correas. 2 precintar.

straw (strɔ:) *s.* paja.

strawberry ('strɔ:bəri) *s.* fresa.

stray (strei) *a.* descarriado.

stray (to) (strei) *i.* desviarse. 2 descarriarse, perderse.

streak ('stri:k) *s.* raya, línea.

streak (to) ('stri:k) *t.* rayar, listar. 2 *i.* ir como un rayo.

stream (stri:m) *s.* corriente.

stream (to) (stri:m) *i.* fluir, manar. 2 salir a torrentes.

street (stri:t) *s.* calle, vía pública; *by-street*, callejuela; *streetcar*, (E. U.) tranvía.

strenght (streŋθ) *s.* fuerza.

strengthen (to) ('streŋθən) *t.-i.* fortalecer(se, reforzar(se.

stress (stres) *s.* fuerza [que obliga], presión, coacción. 2 *to lay ~ on*, dar importancia a. 3 esfuerzo, tensión. 4 MÚS., PROS. acento.

stress (to) (stres) *t.* someter a un esfuerzo. 2 acentuar. 3 recalcar, hacer hincapié en.

stretch (stretʃ) *s.* extensión.

stretch (to) (stretʃ) *t.-i.* extender(se, alargar(se; estirar(se. 2 *t.* forzar; exagerar.

stricken ('strikən) *p. p.* de TO STRIKE. 2 golpeado, herido.

strict (strikt) *a.* estricto.

stridden ('stridn) V. TO STRIDE.

stride (straid) *s.* paso largo, zancada.

stride (to) (straid) *i.* andar a pasos largos. ¶ Pret.: *strode* (stroud); p. p.: *stridden* ('stridn).

strife (straif) *s.* disputa.

strike (straik) *s.* golpe. 2 huelga: *to go on ~*, declararse en huelga; *~ breaker*, esquirol.

strike (to) (straik) *t.* golpear, herir. 2 encender [una cerilla]. 3 producir un efecto súbito. 4 acuñar [moneda]. 5 MÚS. tocar. 6 dar [la hora]. 7 *how does she ~ you?*, ¿qué opina de ella? 8 *i.* marchar, partir. 9 declararse en huelga. ¶ Pret.: *struck* (strʌk); p. p.: *struck* o *stricken* ('strikən).

string (striŋ) *s.* cordón, cordel; hilo. 2 ristra, sarta.

string (to) (striŋ) *t.* atar ¶ Pret. y p. p.: *strung* (strʌŋ).

strip (strip) *s.* tira, lista.

strip (to) (strip) *t.-i.* despojar(se, desnudar(se. ¶ Pret. y p. p.: *stripped* (stript).

stripe (straip) *s.* raya, lista.

stripe (to) (straip) *t.* rayar, listar: *striped*, rayado, listado.

strive (to) (straiv) *i.* esforarse. ¶ Pret.: *strove* (strouv); p. p.: *striven* ('strivn).

strode (stroud) *pret.* de TO STRIDE.

stroke (strouk) *s.* golpe. 2 brazada [del que nada]. 3 MED. ataque [de apoplejía, etc.]. 4 trazo, rasgo, pincelada. 5 caricia.

stroke (to) (strouk) *t.* frotar suavemente; acariciar.

stroll (stroul) *s.* paseo.

stroll (to) (stroul) *i.* pasear.

strong (strɔŋ) *a.* fuerte. 2 *strong-minded*, de creencias arraigadas.

strove (strouv) V. TO STRIVE.

struck (strʌk) V. TO STRIKE.

structure ('strʌktʃəʳ) *s.* estructura. 2 construcción, edificio.

struggle ('strʌgl) *s.* esfuerzo.

struggle (to) ('strʌgl) *i.* esforzarse, luchar, pugnar.

stubborn ('stʌbən) *a.* obstinado, terco; tenaz.

stuck (stʌk) V. TO STICK.

student ('stju:dənt) *s.* estudiante.

study ('stʌdi) *s.* estudio.

stuff (stʌf) *s.* material, materia prima. 2 tonterías.

stuff (to) (stʌf) *t.* llenar, atestar. 2 rellenar; disecar [un animal].

stumble ('stʌmbl) *s.* tropiezo, tropezón. 2 desliz.

stumble (to) ('stʌmbl) *i.* tropezar, dar un traspié. 2 vacilar.

stump (stʌmp) *s.* tocón, cepa. 2 muñón [de miembro ortado]; raigón [de muela, etc.]. 3 colilla [de cigarro]. 4 (E. U.) *to be up a* ~, estar en un brete.

stump (to) (stʌmp) *t.* cortar el tronco [de un árbol]. 2 tropezar. 3 (E. U.) recorrer haciendo discursos electorales.

stung (stʌŋ) *V.* TO STING.

stunk (stʌŋk) *V.* TO STINK.

stupid ('stju:pid) *a.-s.* estúpido, tonto. 2 *a.* atontado.

sturdy ('stə:di) *a.* robusto.

style (stail) *s.* estilo.

subdue (to) (səb'dju:) *t.* sojuzgar, someter. 2 amansar.

subject ('sʌbdʒikt) *a.* sometido, supeditado. 2 expuesto a. 3 *a.-s.* súbdito. 4 *s.* sujeto, asunto, tema; asignatura.

subject (to) (səb'dʒekt) *t.* sujetar, someter. 2 subordinar.

sublime (sə'blaim) *a.* sublime.

submarine (,sʌbmə'ri:n) *a.-s.* submarino.

submerge (to) (səb'mə:dʒ) *t.-i.* sumergir(se. 2 inundar.

submit (to) (səb'mit) *t.-i.* someter(se. 2 presentar.

subsequent ('sʌbsikwənt) *a.* subsiguiente.

substance ('sʌbstəns) *s.* substancia.

substantial (səb'stænʃəl) *a.* substancial. 2 esencial.

substitute ('sʌbstitju:t) *s.* substituto, suplente.

substitute (to) ('sʌbstitju:t) *t.* substituir.

subtle ('sʌtl) *a.* sutil.

suburb ('sʌbə:b) *s.* suburbio.

subway ('sʌbwei) *s.* paso subterráneo. 2 (E. U.) ferrocarril subterráneo.

succeed (to) (sək'si:d) *i.* suceder [a una pers.]. 2 tener buen éxito; salir bien.

success (sək'ses) *s.* éxito.

succesful (sək'sesful) *a.* que tiene éxito; afortunado, próspero.

succession (sək'seʃən) *s.* sucesión.

successive (sək'sesiv) *a.* sucesivo.

successor (sək'səsəʳ) *s.* sucesor, heredero.

such (sʌtʃ) *a.-pron.* tal(es, semejante(s. 2 *pron.* éste, -ta, etc.; *as* ~, como a tal. 3 ~ *as*, el, la, los, las que; tal(es como. 4 *adv.* tan, así, tal: ~ *a good man*, un hombre tan bueno.

suck (to) (sʌk) *t.-i.* chupar.

sudden (sʌdn) *a.* súbito.

suffering ('sʌfəriŋ) *s.* sufrimiento, padecimiento. 2 *a.* doliente, enfermo. 3 sufrido.

suffice (to) (sə'fais) *i.* bastar, ser suficiente.

sufficient (sə'fiʃənt) *a.* suficiente, bastante.

suffrage ('sʌfridʒ) *s.* sufragio, voto.

sugar ('ʃugəʳ) *s.* azúcar.

sugar (to) ('ʃugəʳ) *t.* azucarar.

suggest (to) (sə'dʒest) *t.* sugerir. 2 hacer pensar en.

suggestion (sə'dʒestʃən) *s.* sugestión. 2 indicación. 3 señal.

suicide ('sjuisaid) *s.* suicidio. 2 suicida.

suit (sju:t) *s.* petición. 2 cortejo, galanteo. 3 DER. demanda; pleito. 4 traje. 5 colección, surtido. 6 palo de la baraja.

suit (to) (sju:t) *t.* vestir. 2 *t.-i.* convenir, ir o venir bien.

suitable ('sju:təbl) *a.* propio, conveniente, apropiado.

sullen ('sʌlən) *a.* hosco, huraño. 2 triste.

sulphur ('sʌlfəʳ) *s.* azufre.

sultry ('sʌltri) *a.* bochornoso, sofocante.

sum (sʌm) *s.* MAT. suma. 2 total.

sum (to) (sʌm) (sʌm) *t.-i.* sumar.

summer ('sʌməʳ) *s.* verano.

summer (to) ('sʌməʳ) *i.* veranear, pasar el verano.

summit ('sʌmit) *s.* cúspide, punta, cima.

summon (to) ('sʌmən) *t.* llamar, convocar. 2 DER. citar.

sun (sʌn) *s.* sol.

sun (to) (sʌn) *t.* asolear. 2 *i.* tomar el sol.

sunbeam ('sʌnbi:m) *s.* rayo de sol.

Sunday ('sʌndi, -dei) *s.* domingo.

sunder ('sʌndəʳ) *s.* separación, división.

sunder (to) ('sʌndəʳ) *t.-i.* separar(se, dividir(se.

sung (sʌŋ) V. TO SING.

sunk (sʌŋk) V. TO SINK.

sunlight ('sʌnlait) *s.* sol, luz de sol.

sunny ('sʌni) *a.* soleado.

sunrise ('sʌnraiz) *s.* salida del sol, amanecer.

sunset ('sʌnset) *s.* ocaso.

sunshine ('sʌnʃain) *s.* luz de sol; solana.

sup (to) (sʌp) *t.-i.* cenar. 2 *t.* beber, tomar a sorbos.

superb (sju(:)'pə:b) *a.* soberbio, magnífico.

superintendent (ˌsju:prin'tendənt) *s.* superintendente, inspector. 2 capataz.

superior (sju(:)'piəriəʳ) *a.-s.* superior.

supervision (ˌsju:ə'viʒən) *s.* inspección, vigilancia.

supper ('sʌpəʳ) *s.* cena.

supply (sə'plai) *s.* suministro, provisión. 2 repuesto.

support (sə'pɔ:t) *s.* soporte, apoyo. 2 ayuda. 3 sustento.

support (to) (sə'pɔ:t) *t.* soportar [sostener; tolerar]. 2 apoyar. 3 sustentar, mantener.

suppose (to) (sə'pouz) *t.* suponer. 2 creer, pensar.

supposed (sə'pouzd) *a.* supuesto, presunto. 2 **-ly** *adv.* supuestamente.

suppress (to) (sə'pres) *t.* suprimir. 2 ahogar, sofocar.

supreme (sju(:)'pri:m) *a.* supremo.

sure (ʃuəʳ) *a.* seguro. 2 firme. 3 *to make* ~, asegurar(se de. 4 *adv.* ciertamente.

surface ('sə:fis) *s.* superficie.

surge (sə:dʒ) *s.* ola, oleaje.

surge (to) (sə:dʒ) *i.* hincharse, agitarse.

surgeon ('sə:dʒən) *s.* cirujano. 2 MIL. médico.

surpass (to) (sə'pɑ:s) *t.* sobrepujar, aventajar.

surprise (sə'praiz) *s.* sorpresa.

surprise (to) (sə'praiz) *t.* sorprender.

surrender (sə'rendə^r) *s.* rendición. 2 entrega, renuncia.

surrender (to) (sə'rendə^r) *t.-i.* rendir(se, entregar(se.

surround (to) (sə'raund) *t.* rodear, cercar.

surrounding (sə'raundiŋ) *a.* circundante. 2 *s.* cerco. 3 *pl.* alrededores. 4 ambiente.

survey ('sə:vei) *s.* medición; plano [de un terreno]. 2 inspección, examen. 3 perspectiva, bosquejo [de historia, etc.].

survey (to) (sə'vei) *t.* medir, deslindar [tierras]. 2 levantar el plano de. 3 inspeccionar, examinar. 4 dar una ojeada general a.

surveyor (sə(:)'veiə^r) *s.* agrimensor; topógrafo. 2 inspector. 3 vista [de aduanas].

survive (to) (sə'vaiv) *t.* sobrevivir.

suspect ('sʌspekt) *a.-s.* sospechoso.

suspect (to) (səs'pekt) *t.* sospechar.

suspend (to) (səs'pend) *t.* suspender, colgar. 2 aplazar.

suspicion (səs'piʃən) *s.* sospecha.

suspicious (səs'piʃəs) *a.* sospechoso. 2 suspicaz.

sustain (to) (səs'tein) *t.* sostener. 2 mantener, sustentar.

swallow ('swɔlou) *s.* ORN. golondrina. 2 gaznate. 3 trago. 4 ~ *-tail*, frac.

swallow (to) ('swɔlou) *t.-i.* tragar, engullir.

swam (swæm) V. TO SWIM.

swamp ('swɔmp) *s.* pantano, marisma.

swan (swɔn) *s.* cisne.

swarm (swɔ:m) *s.* enjambre. 2 multitud.

sway (swei) *s.* oscilación, vaivén. 2 desviación. 3 poder, dominio.

sway (to) (swei) *i.* oscilar. 2 tambalear; inclinarse. 3 *t.-i.* dominar, influir en.

swear (to) (swɛə^r) *t.-i.* jurar; renegar, echar maldiciones. ¶ Pret.: *swore* (swɔ:); p. p.: *sworn* (swɔ:n).

sweat (swet) *s.* sudor; trasudor.

sweat (to) (swet) *t.-i.* sudar; trasudar. 2 *t.* hacer sudar; explotar [al que trabaja].

sweep (swi:p) *s.* barrido. 2 barrendero; deshollinador. 3 extensión.

sweep (to) (swi:p) *t.* barrer. 2 deshollinar. 3 arrebatar. ¶ Pret. y p. p.: *swept* (swept).

sweet (swi:t) *a.* dulce, azucarado. 2 amable, benigno. 3 *adv.* dulcemente, etc. 7 *pl.* dulces, golosinas.

sweetheart ('swi:thɑ:t) *s.* novio; amado; novia; amada.

swell (swel) *s.* hinchazón.

swell (to) (swel) *t.-i.* hinchar(se, inflar(se. 2 engreír(se. ¶ Pret.: *swelled* (sweld); p. p.: *swollen* ('swoulən) y *swelled*.

swept (swept) V. TO SWEEP.

swift (swift) *a.* rápido, veloz.

swim (swim) *s.* acción o rato de nadar. 2 ~ *suit*, traje de baño; *swimming-pool*, piscina.

swim (to) (swim) *i.* nadar; flotar. ¶ Pret.: *swam* (swæm); p. p.: *swum* (swʌm).

swing (swiŋ) *s.* oscilación, giro; ritmo. 2 columpio.

swing (to) (swiŋ) *t.-i.* balancear(se, columpiar(se. 2 *t.* hacer oscilar o girar. 3 blandir [un bastón, etc.]. 4 suspender, colgar. 5 *i.* ser ahorcado. Pret. y p. p.: *swung* (swʌŋ).

swirl (swə:l) *s.* remolino.

swirl (to) (swə:l) *t.-i.* girar.

Swiss (swis) *a.-s.* suizo, -za.

switch (switʃ) *s.* vara flexible; látigo. 2 latigazo. 3 añadido [de pelo postizo]. 4 FERROC.

aguja, desvío. 5 ELECT. interruptor, conmutador. 6 cambio.

switch (to) (switʃ) *t.* azotar, fustigar. 2 cambiar, desviar. 3 ELECT. *to ~ on*, conectar [dar la luz]; *to ~ off*, desconectar. 4 *i.* cambiar.

sword (sɔ:d) *s.* espada [arma].

swore (swɔ:ʳ) V. TO SWEAR.

swum (swʌm) V. TO SWIM.

swung (swʌŋ) V. TO SWING.

syllable ('siləbl) *s.* sílaba.

symbol ('simbl) *s.* símbolo.

symmetric(al (si'metrik, -əl) *a.* simétrico.

sympathetic(al (ˌsimpə'θetik, -əl) *a.* simpático. 2 simpatizante. 3 compasivo; comprensivo.

sympathy ('simpəθi) *s.* simpatía. 2 compasión, condolencia. 3 comprensión.

symptom ('simptəm) *s.* síntoma.

system ('sistəm) *s.* sistema.

T

table ('teibl) *s.* mesa: ~ *cloth*, mantel; ~ *ware*, vajilla, servicio de mesa. *2* tabla [de materias, etc.]; lista, catálogo.

table (to) ('teibl) *t.* poner sobre la mesa. *2* poner en forma de índice.

tablet ('tæblit) *s.* tablilla. *2* lápida, placa. *3* FARM. tableta. *4* bloc de papel.

tackle ('tækl) *s.* equipo, aparejos.

tackle (to) ('tækl) *t.* agarrar, forcejear con. *2* abordar [un problema, etc.].

tactless ('tæktlis) *a.* falto de tacto.

tail (teil) *s.* cola, rabo.

tailor ('teiləʳ) *s.* sastre.

take (teik) *s.* toma, tomadura. *2* redada. *3* recaudación [de dinero]. *4 take-off*, remedo, parodia; despegue [del avión].

take (to) (teik) *t.* tomar, coger; agarrar; apoderarse de. *2* asumir. *3* deleitar, cautivar. *4* suponer, entender. *5* llevar, conducir. *6* dar [un golpe, un paseo, un salto, etc.]. *7* hacer [ejercicio, un viaje]. *8 i.* arraigar [una planta]. *9* prender [el fuego; la vacuna]. *10* tener éxito. *11 to ~ a chance*, correr el riesgo. *12 to ~ after*, parecerse a. *13 to ~ amiss*, interpretar mal. *14 to ~ care of*, cuidar de. *15 to ~ cold*, resfriarse. *16 to ~ down*, descolgar; poner por escrito. *17 to ~ in*, meter en; abarcar; recibir; engañar, timar; reducir, achicar [un vestido]. *18 I ~ it that*, supongo que... *19 to ~ leave*, despedirse. *20 to ~ off*, descontar, rebajar; despegar [el avión]; remedar. *21 to ~ place*, ocurrir, tener lugar. ¶ Pret.: *took* (tuk); p. p.: *taken* 'teikən.

tale (teil) *s.* cuento, fábula.

talent ('tælənt) *s.* talento.

talk (tɔːk) *s.* conversación.

talk (to) (tɔːk) *i.* hablar; conversar. *2 to ~ into*, persuadir a. *3 to ~ out of*, disuadir de. *4 to ~ over*, examinar. *5 to ~ up*, alabar; hablar claro.

tall (tɔːl) *a.* alto [pers., árbol]. 2 excesivo, exorbitante.

tame (teim) *a.* manso, dócil.

tan (tæn) *s.* color tostado. 2 *a.* tostado, de color de canela.

tan (to) (tæn) *t.* curtir [las pieles]. 2 tostar, atezar.

tangle (ˈtæŋgl) *s.* enredo.

tangle (to) (ˈtæŋgl) *t.-i.* enredar(se, enmarañar(se.

tank (tæŋk) *s.* tanque, cisterna. 2 MIL. tanque.

tap (tæp) *s.* grifo, espita. 2 golpecito, palmadita.

tap (to) (tæp) *t.* poner espita a; abrir un barril. 2 *t.-i.* dar golpecitos o palmadas [a o en].

taper (ˈteipəʳ) *s.* candela.

taper (to) (ˈteipəʳ) *t.-i.* afilar(se, adelgazar(se.

tariff (ˈtærif) *s.* tarifa.

tarnish (to) (ˈtɑːniʃ) *t.-i.* empañar(se, deslucir(se. 2 *t.* manchar.

task (tɑːsk) *s.* tarea, labor, trabajo.

taste (teist) *s.* gusto [sentido]. 2 sabor. 3 afición. 4 gusto [por lo bello, etc.]. 5 sorbo, bocadito. 6 muestra, prueba.

taste (to) (teist) *t.* gustar, saborear. 2 probar, catar. 3 *i. to ~ of*, saber a.

tavern (ˈtævən) *s.* taberna.

taxation (tækˈseiʃən) *s.* imposición de tributos, impuestos.

taxi (ˈtæksi), **taxicab** (ˈtæksikæb) *s.* taxi [coche].

tea (tiː) *s.* té. ~ *party*, té [reunión]; ~ *pot*, tetera.

teach (to) (tiːtʃ) *t.-i.* enseñar, instruir. ¶ Pret. y p. p.: *taught* (tɔːt).

teacher (ˈtiːtʃəʳ) *s.* maestro, -tra, profesor, -ra.

team (tiːm) *s.* tiro [de animales]. 2 grupo, cuadrilla. 3 DEP. equipo.

team (to) (tiːm) *t.* enganchar, uncir.

1) **tear** (tiəʳ) *s.* lágrima.

2) **tear** (teəʳ) *s.* rotura, desgarro; *wear and ~*, desgaste.

tear (to) (tɛəʳ) *t.* romper, rasgar, desgarrar. ¶ Pret.: *tove* (tɔːʳ, tɔəʳ); p. p.: *torn* (tɔːn).

tease (to) (tiːz) *t.* fastidiar.

teaspoonful (ˈtiːspu(ː)nˌful)*s.* cucharadita.

technical (ˈteknikəl) *a.* técnico.

tedious (ˈtiːdjəs) *a.* tedioso.

teeth (tiːθ) *s. pl.* de TOOTH.

telegram (ˈteligræm) *s.* telegrama.

telegraph (ˈteligrɑːf, -græf)*s.* telégrafo. 2 telegrama.

telephone (ˈtelifoun) *s.* teléfono.

telephone (to) (ˈtelifoun) *t.-i.* telefonear.

telescope (ˈteliskoup) *s.* telescopio.

tell (to) (tel) *t.* contar, numerar. 2 narrar, relatar, decir. 3 mandar, ordenar. 4 distinguir, conocer; adivinar. 5 *there is no telling*, no es posible decir o prever. 6 *it tells*, tiene su efecto. ¶ Pret. y p. p.: *told* (tould).

temper (ˈtempəʳ) *s.* temple [del metal]. 2 genio; humor. 3 cólera, mal genio.

temper (to) (ˈtempəʳ) *t.* templar, moderar. 2 mezclar. 3 templar [el metal].

temperament (ˈtempərəmənt) *s.* temperamento [de una pers.].

temperate (ˈtempərit) *a.* tem-

plado, sobrio, moderado.

temperature ('temprit∫əʳ) *s.* temperatura: *to have a ~*, tener fiebre.

tempest ('tempist) *s.* tempestad.

temple ('templ) *s.* templo. 2 ANAT. sien.

temporary ('tempərəri) *a.* temporal, provisional, interino.

tempt (to) (tempt) *t.* tentar.

temptation (temp'tei∫ən) *s.* tentación. 2 incentivo.

ten (ten) *a.-s.* diez.

tenant ('tenənt) *s.* inquilino.

tend (to) (tend) *t.* cuidar, atender, vigilar. 2 *i.* tender [a un fin]. 3 ir, dirigirse [a].

tendency ('tendənsi) *s.* tendencia; propensión.

tender ('tendəʳ) *a.* tierno. 2 delicado [escrupuloso]. 3 *s.* cuidador, guardador. 4 oferta, propuesta.

tender (to) ('tendəʳ) *t.* ofrecer presentar. 2 *t.-i.* ablandar(se, enternecer (se.

tenderness ('tendənis) *s.* ternura, suavidad. 2 debilidad.

tennis ('tenis) *s.* tenis.

tent (tent) *s.* tienda de campaña: *bell ~*, pabellón.

tent (to) (tent) *i.* acampar en tiendas.

term (tə:m) *s.* plazo, período. 2 período de sesiones [justicia] o de clases [trimestre]. 3 *pl.* condiciones; acuerdo.

term (to) (tə:m) *t.* nombrar.

terrace ('terəs) *s.* terraza.

terrific (te'rifik) *a.* terrífico; terrorífico.

terrify (to) ('terifai) *t.* aterrar.

territory ('teritəri) *s.* territorio.

terror ('terəʳ) *s.* terror, espanto.

test (test) *s.* copela. 2 prueba, ensayo. 3 PSIC. test.

test (to) (test) *t.* examinar, probar, ensayar.

testify (to) ('testifai) *t.* testificar, testimoniar.

testimony ('testiməni) *s.* testimonio, declaración.

text (tekst) *s.* texto.

than (ðæn, ðən) *conj.* que [después de comparativo]. 2 de: *more ~ once*, más de una vez.

thank (to) (θæŋk) *t.* dar gracias. 2 *s. pl.* **thanks,** gracias.

thankful ('θæŋkful) *a.* agradecido.

thanksgiving ('θæŋks,giviŋ) *s.* acción de gracias.

that (ðæt) *a.* ese, esa, aquel, aquella. 2 *pron.* ése, ésa, éso, aquél, aquélla, aquello. 3 *pron. rel.* (ðət, ðæt) que. 4 *conj.* (ðət) que: *so ~*, para que. 5 *adv.* así, tan: *~ far*, tan lejos; *~ long*, de este tamaño.

thaw (θɔ:) *s.* deshielo, derretimiento.

thaw (to) (θɔ:) *t.-i.* deshelar(se, derretir(se.

the (ðə; ante vocal, ði) *art.* el, la, lo; los, las. 2 *adv.* *~ more he has, ~ more he wants,* cuanto más tiene [tanto] más quiere.

theater, theatre ('θiətəʳ) *s.* teatro.

their (ðɛəʳ, ðəʳ) *a. pos.* su, sus [de ellos o de ellas].

theirs (ðɛəz) *pron. pos.* [el] suyo, [la] suya, [los] suyos, [las] suyas [de ellos o de ellas].

them (ðem,ðəm) *pron. pers.* [sin prep.] los, las, les. 2 [con prep.] ellos, ellas.

theme (θi:m) *s.* tema, materia, asunto.

themselves (ðəm'selvz) *pron. pers.* ellos mismos, ellas mismas. 2 se [reflex.], a sí mismos.

then (ðen) *adv.* entonces. 2 luego, después; además. 3 *conj.* por consiguiente. 4 *now ~,* ahora bien; *~ and there,* allí mismo; *now and ~,* de vez en cuando.

thence (ðens) *adv.* desde allí, desde entonces: *~ forth,* desde entonces. 2 por lo tanto, por eso.

theory ('θiəri) *s.* teoría.

there (ðɛəʳ, ðəʳ) *adv.* allí, allá, ahí: *~ is, ~ are,* hay; *~ was, ~ were,* había; *~ he is,* helo ahí. 2 *interj.* ¡eh!, ¡vaya!, ¡ea! 3 *thereabouts,* por allí, aproximadamente. 4 *thereafter,* después de ello; por lo tanto. 5 *thereby,* en relación con esto. 6 *therefore,* por lo tanto. 7 *therein,* en eso; allí dentro. 8 *thereof,* de eso, de ello. 9 *thereon,* encima de ello; en seguida. 10 *thereupon,* por tanto; inmediatamente.

thermometer (θe'mɔmitəʳ) *s.* termómetro.

these (ði:z) *a.* estos, estas. 2 *pron.* éstos, éstas.

they (ðei) *pron. pers.* ellos, ellas.

thick (θik) *a.* espeso, grueso. 2 espeso, poblado [barba], tupido. 3 *s.* grueso, espesor.

thicket ('θikit) *s.* espesura, maleza, matorral.

thickness ('θiknis) *s.* espesor.

thief (θi:f) *s.* ladrón, ratero.

thigh (θai) *s.* ANAT. muslo.

thin (θin) *s.* delgado, fino, tenue. 2 ligero, transparente.

thin (to) (θin) *t.-i.* adelgazar(se. 2 aclarar(se [hacer(se menos espeso].

thine (ðain) *pron. pos.* [el] tuyo, [la] tuya, [los] tuyos, [las]tuyas. 2 *a.* tu, tus. | Úsase sólo en poesía y en la Biblia.

thing (θiŋ) *s.* cosa. *poor ~!,* ¡pobrecito!

think (to) (θiŋk) *t.-i.* pensar, juzgar, creer. ¶ Pret. y p. p.: *thought* (θɔ:t).

third (θə:d) *a.* tercero. 2 *s.* tercio [tercera parte].

thirst (θə:st) *s.* sed. 2 anhelo.

thirst (to) (θə:st) *i.* tener sed. 2 anhelar, ansiar.

thirsty ('θə:sti) *a.* sediento.

thirteen ('θə:'ti:n) *a.-s.* trece.

thirty ('θə:ti) *a.-s.* treinta.

this (ðis) *a.* este, esta. 2 *pron.* éste, ésta, esto.

thither ('ðiðəʳ) *adv.* allá, hacia allá.

thorn (θɔ:n) *s.* espina, púa.

thorough ('θʌrə) *a.* completo, total, acabado. 2 perfecto.

though (ðou) *conj.* aunque, si bien; sin embargo. 2 *as ~,* como si.

thought (θɔ:t) V. TO THINK. 2 *s.* pensamiento, idea, intención.

thoughtful ('θɔ:tful) *a.* pensativo, meditabundo. 2 atento, solícito. 3 previsor.

thoughtfulness ('θɔ:tfulnis) *s.* consideración, atención.

thoughtless ('θɔ:tlis) *a.* irreflexivo, atolondrado, incauto.

throughtlessness ('θɔ:tlisnis) *s.* irreflexión, ligereza.

thousand ('θauzand) *a.* mil.

thousandth ('θauzənθ) *a.-s.* milésimo.

thrash (to) (θræʃ) *t.-i.* trillar.

thrashing ('θræʃiŋ) *s.* THRESHING. 2 zurra, paliza.

thread (θred) *s.* hilo. 2 fibra, hebra.

thread (to) (θred) *t.* enhebrar, ensartar.

threat (θret) *s.* amenaza.

threaten (to) ('θretn) *t.-i.* amenazar.

three (θri:) *a.-s.* tres: ~ *fold*, triple; tres veces más.

thresh (to) (θreʃ) *t.-i.* trillar.

threshing ('θreʃiŋ) *s.* trilla.

threshold ('θreʃ(h)ould) *s.* umbral.

threw (θru:) *pret.* de TO THROW.

thrill (θril) *s.* temblor, estremecimiento, escalofrío, emoción viva.

thrill (to) (θril) *t.* hacer estremecer, dar calofríos, emocionar. 2 *i.* temblar.

thrive (to) (θraiv) *i.* crecer. 2 prosperar, medrar. ¶ Pret.: *throve* (θrouv) o *thrived* (θraivd); p. p.: *thrived* o *thriven* (θrivn).

throat (θrout) *s.* garganta.

throe (θrou) *s.* ángustia.

throne (θroun) *s.* trono.

throng (θrɔŋ) *s.* muchedumbre, gentío, tropel.

throng (to) (θrɔŋ) *i.* apiñarse.

throttle ('θrɔtl) *s.* garganta.

throttle (to) ('θrɔtl) *t.-i.* ahogar(se. 2 *t.* estrangular.

through (θru:) *prep.* por, a través de. 2 por medio de, a causa de. 3 *adv.* de un lado a otro, de parte a parte, hasta el fin; completamente, enteramente: *loyal ~ and ~*, leal a toda prueba; *to be wet ~*, estar calado hasta los huesos; *to carry the plan ~*, llevar a cabo el plan. 4 *a.* directo: ~ *train*, tren directo. 5 de paso. 6 *to be ~ with*, haber acabado con.

throughout (θru:'aut) *prep.* por todo, durante todo, a lo largo de: ~ *the year*, durante todo el año. 2 *adv.* por o en todas partes, desde el principio hasta el fin.

throw (θrou) *s.* lanzamiento, tiro. 2 tirada [de dados].

throw (to) (θrou) *t.* tirar, arrojar, lanzar. 2 empujar, impeler. 3 derribar. 4 *to ~ away*, desperdiciar. 5 *to ~ back*, devolver; replicar; rechazar. 6 *to ~ off*, librarse de; improvisar [versos]. 7 *to ~ out*, echar fuera, proferir. 8 *to ~ over*, abandonar. ¶ Pret.: *threw* (θru:); p. p.: *thrown* (θroun).

thrust (θrʌst) V. TO THRUST. 2 estocada, lanzada.

thrust (to) (θrʌst) *t.* meter, clavar, hincar. 2 empujar. 3 extender [sus ramas]. 4 *i.* meterse, abrirse paso. ¶ Pret. y p. p.: *thrust* (θrʌst).

thumb (θʌm) *s.* pulgar.

thump (θʌmp) *s.* golpe, porrazo.

thump (to) (θʌmp) *t.-i.* golpear, aporrear.

thunder ('θʌndəʳ) *s.* trueno.

thunder (to) ('θʌndə) *i.* tronar.

Thursday ('θə:zdi, -dei) *s.* jueves.

thus (ðʌs) *adv.* así, de este modo. 2 hasta este punto: ~ *far*, hasta aquí; hasta ahora.

thyself (ðai'self) *pron.* tú mismo, ti mismo. | Úsase sólo en poesía y en la Biblia.

ticket ('tikit) *s.* billete, boleto, entrada: *return* ~, billete de ida y vuelta; ~ *office*, taquilla. 2 lista de candidatos. 3 etiqueta.

tide (taid) *s.* marea; corriente. 2 época.

tidings ('taidiŋz) *s.* noticias.

tie (tai) *s.* cinta, cordón, etc. para atar. 2 lazo, nudo. 3 corbata. 4 empate.

tie (to) (tai) *t.* atar. 2 liar, anudar. 3 *t.-i.* empatar.

tiger ('taigəʳ) *s.* tigre.

tight (tait) *a.* bien cerrado, hermético. 2 tieso, tirante. 3 apretado; *it fits* ~, está muy ajustado. 4 duro, severo. 5 tacaño.

tighten (to) ('taitn) *t.-i.* apretar(se; estrechar(se.

tile (tail) *s.* teja. 2 losa.

tile (to) (tail) *t.* tejar. 2 embaldosar.

1) **till** (til) *prep.* hasta. 2 *conj.* hasta que.

2) **till (to)** (til) *t.-i.* labrar.

tilt (tilt) *s.* inclinación, ladeo; declive. 2 justa, torneo. 3 lanzada, golpe. 4 disputa.

tilt (to) (tilt) *t.-i.* inclinar(se, ladear(se. 2 volcar(se. 3 *t.* dar lanzadas, acometer.

timber ('timbəʳ) *s.* madera [de construcción]; viga. 2 bosque, árboles maderables.

time (taim) *s.* tiempo. | No tiene el sentido de estado at-

mosférico. 2 hora; vez; plazo: *at any* ~, a cualquier hora; *behind* ~, retrasado [el tren]; *behind the times*, anticuado; *for the* ~ *being*, de momento, por ahora; *on* ~ puntual; *to have a good* ~, divertirse, pasar un buen rato; *what's the* ~?, *what* ~ *is it?*, ¿qué hora es?

time (to) (taim) *t.* escoger el momento. 2 regular, poner en hora [el reloj]. 3 cronometrar, medir el tiempo.

timid ('timid) *a.* tímido.

tin (tin) *s.* QUÍM. estaño. 2 lata, hojalata. 3 lata, bote.

tin (to) (tin) *t.* estañar, cubrir con estaño. 2 enlatar: *tinned goods*, conservas.

tinge (tindʒ) *s.* tinte, matiz. 2 saborcillo, dejo.

tinge (to) (tindʒ) *t.* teñir, matizar.

tingle ('tiŋgl) *s.* hormigueo.

tingle (to) ('tiŋgl) *i.* hormiguear, picar.

tinkle ('tiŋkl) *s.* tintineo; retintín.

tinkle (to) ('tiŋkl) *i.* retiñir, tintinear.

tint (tint) *s.* tinte, matiz.

tint (to) (tint) *t.* teñir, matizar.

tiny ('taini) *a.* pequeñito.

tip (tip) *s.* extremo, punta. 2 propina. 3 soplo, aviso confidencial.

tip (to) (tip) *t.-i.* inclinar(se, volcar(se. 2 *t.* dar propina a. 3 dar un soplo o aviso confidencial a.

tiptoe ('tiptou) *s.* punta de pie.

tiptoe (to) ('tiptou) *i.* andar de puntillas.

tirade (tai'reid) *s.* andanada, invectiva.

tire ('taiə^r) *s.* llanta, neumático, goma.

tire (to) ('taiə^r) *t.-i.* cansar(se.

tireless ('taiəlis) *a.* incansable, infatigable.

tiresome ('taiəsəm) *a.* cansado, molesto, fastidioso.

tissue ('tisju:, tiʃju:) *s.* tisú, gasa.

tit (tit) *s.* ~ *for tat,* golpe por golpe.

title ('taitl) *s.* título. | No tiene el sentido de título en química.

to (tu:, tu, tə) *prep.* a. hacia, para; hasta: ~ *the right,* a la derecha; *a quarter ~ five,* las cinco menos cuarto: *I have* ~ *go,* tengo que ir. 2 *to* ante verbo es signo de infinitivo y no se traduce. 3 *adv.* **to come** ~, volver en sí; ~ *and fro,* de acá para allá.

toad (toud) *s.* sapo.

toast (toust) *s.* tostada, pan tostado. 2 brindis.

toast (to) (toust) *t.-i.* tostar(se. 2 brindar.

tobacco (tə'bækðu) *s.* tabaco.

today, to-day (tə'dei) *adv.* hoy, hoy en día. 2 *s.* el día de hoy.

toe (tou) *s.* dedo del pie.

together (tə'geðə^r) *adv.* junto; juntos, reunidos, juntamente; de acuerdo; *to call* ~, convocar. 2 al mismo tiempo. 3 sin interrupción.

toil (tɔil) *s.* trabajo, esfuerzo, fatiga. 2 *pl.* red, lazo.

toil (to) (tɔil) *i.* afanarse, esforzarse.

toilet ('tɔilit) *s.* tocador; cuarto de baño; retrete. 2 tocado; peinado; aseo personal.

token ('toukən) *s.* señal, indicio, prueba, recuerdo. 2 moneda, ficha.

told (tould) V. TO TELL.

tomato (tə'mɑ:tou, [E. U.] tə'meitou) *s.* BOT. tomate.

tomb (tu:m) *s.* tumba.

tomorrow (tə'mɔrou) *adv.* mañana. 2 *s.* día de mañana.

ton (tʌn) *s.* tonelada.

tone (toun) *s.* tono; sonido.

tone (to) (toun) *t.* dar tono a: *to* ~ *down,* bajar el tono; *to* ~ *up,* elevar el tono. 2 tomar un tono o color; armonizar [con].

tongue (tʌŋ) *s.* ANAT. lengua. 2 idioma; habla.

tonight (tə'nait, tu-) *s.* esta noche.

too (tu:) *adv.* demasiado [seguido de a. y adv.]. 2 ~ *much,* demasiado; ~ *many,* demasiados [ante subst.]. 3 también, además.

took (tuk) V. TO TAKE.

tool (tu:l) *s.* instrumento, herramienta, utensilio.

tooth (tu:θ) *pl.* **teeth** (ti:θ) *s.* diente; muela; *to have a sweet* ~, ser goloso.

top (tɔp) *s.* parte o superficie superior, cima, cumbre. 2 *a.* superior.

top (to) (tɔp) *t.* desmochar. 2 coronar, rematar. 3 sobresalir.

topic ('tɔpik) *s.* asunto, tema. 2 *pl.* tópicos, lugares comunes.

torch (tɔ:tʃ) *s.* hacha, antorcha. 2 linterna eléctrica.

tore (tɔ:ʳ) V. TO TEAR.

torment ('tɔ:mənt) s. tormento, tortura, pena.

torment (to) (tɔ:'ment) t. atormentar, torturar, molestar.

torn (tɔ:n) V. TO TEAR. 2 a. roto, rasgado.

torrent ('tɔrənt) s. torrente.

torrid ('tɔrid) a. tórrido.

torture ('tɔ:tʃə) s. tortura.

torture (to) ('tɔ:tʃəʳ) t. torturar, martirizar.

toss (tɔs) s. sacudida, meneo. 2 lanzamiento, tiro.

toss (to) (tɔs) t. sacudir, menear, agitar. 2 arrojar, lanzar. 3 i. moverse, agitarse.

total ('toutl) s. total. 2 a. entero, todo.

totter (to) ('tɔtəʳ) i. vacilar.

touch (tʌtʃ) s. toque, tiento. 2 tacto. 3 contacto.

touch (to) (tʌtʃ) t. tocar, tantear, palpar. 2 conmover. 3 alcanzar, llegar a.

tough (tʌf) a. duro, correoso. 2 fuerte, vigoroso. 3 (E. U.)malvado, pendenciero. 4 terco, tenaz. 5 arduo, penoso.

tour (tuəʳ) s. viaje, excursión, vuelta, jira. 2 turno.

tour (to) (tuəʳ) i. viajar por, hacer turismo.

tourist ('tuərist) s. turista.

tournament ('tuənəmənt) s. torneo, justa. 2 certamen.

toward (tə'wɔ:d), **towards** (-z) prep. hacia. 2 cerca de. 3 para. 4 con, para con.

towel ('tauəl) s. toalla.

tower ('tauəʳ) s. torre, torreón. 2 campanario.

tower (to) ('tauəʳ) i. descollar, sobresalir.

town (taun) s. población, ciudad, pueblo; municipio: ~ **council,** ayuntamiento; ~ **hall,** casa del ayuntamiento.

toy (tɔi) s. juguete.

toy (to) (tɔi) i. jugar.

trace (treis) s. huella, pisada.

trace (to) (treis) t. trazar, esbozar. 2 rastrear.

track (træk) s. rastro, pista, huellas; señal, vestigio. 2 vía [de tren, tranvía, etc.].

track (to) (træk) t. rastrear.

tract (trækt) s. área, región.

tractor ('træktəʳ) s. tractor.

trade (treid) s. profesión, ocupación; oficio, arte mecánica: ~ **union,** sindicato obrero. 2 comercio, tráfico: ~ **mark,** marca registrada. 3 parroquia, clientela.

trade (to) (treid) i. comerciar, negociar, tratar.

trader ('treidəʳ) s. comerciante, negociante.

tradition (trə'diʃən) s. tradición.

traduce (to) (trə'dju:s) t. difamar, calumniar.

traffic ('træfik) s. tráfico, comercio. 2 tránsito, tráfico: ~ **lights,** semáforo.

tragedy ('trædʒidi) s. tragedia.

trail (treil) s. cola [de vestido, cometa, etc.]. 2 rastro, huella, pista. 3 senda.

trail (to) (treil) t.-i. arrastrar(se. 2 seguir la pista.

train (trein) s. tren [ferroc.; de máquina; de ondas]. 2 fila, recua; séquito, comitiva. 3 cola [de cometa, vestido, etc.].

train (to) (trein) t.-i. ejercitar(se, adiestrar(se. *2 t.* educar. *3* DEP. entrenar. *4* apuntar [un cañón, etc.].

trainer ('treinə^r) *s.* amaestrador. *2* DEP. preparador.

training ('treiniŋ) *s.* adiestramiento, preparación. *2* DEP. entrenamiento.

traitor ('treitə^r) *a.-s.* traidor.

t r a m (t r æ m), **t r a m c a r** ('træmka:^r) *s.* tranvía.

tramp (træmp) *s.* viandante. *2* vagabundo. *3* caminata.

tramp (to) (træmp) *i.* viajar a pie, vagabundear. *2 t.* pisar; apisonar.

transfer ('trænsfə:^r) *s.* transferencia, traslado, transporte.

transform (to) (træns'fɔ:m) *t.-i.* transformar(se.

translate (to) (træns'leit) *t.* traducir. *2* trasladar.

translation (træns'leiʃən) *s.* traducción. *2* traslado.

transparent (træns'peərənt)*a.* transparente. *2* franco, ingenuo.

transport ('trænspɔ:t) *s.* transporte, acarreo. *2* rapto, éxtasis.

transport (to) (træns'pɔ:t) *t.* transportar, acarrear. *2* transportar, enajenar.

transportation (ˌtrænspɔ:'teiʃən) *s.* transporte, sistemas de transporte. *2* (E. U.)coste del transporte; billete, pasaje. *3* deportación.

trap (træp) *s.* trampa, lazo.

trap (to) (træp) *t.* coger con trampa, atrapar.

travel ('trævl) *i.* viajar. *2 t.* viajar por, recorrer.

travel(l)er ('trævlə^r) *s.* viajero.

traverse ('trævə(:)s) *s.* travesaño.

traverse (to) ('trævə(:)s) *t.* cruzar, atravesar, recorrer.

tray (trei) *s.* bandeja.

treacherous ('tretʃərəs) *a.* traidor, falso, engañoso.

treachery ('tretʃəri) *s.* traición. *2* deslealtad, alevosía.

tread (tred) *s.* paso, pisada. *2* huella, rastro.

tread (to) (tred) *t.* pisar, hollar. *2* pisotear. *3* andar a pie, caminar. ¶ Pret.: *trod* (trɔd); p. p.: *trodden* ('trɔdn)o *trod*.

treason ('tri:zn) *s.* traición.

treasure ('treʒə^r) *s.* tesoro.

treasure (to) ('treʒə^r) *t.* atesorar.

treasurer ('treʒərə^r) *s.* tesorero.

treasury ('treʒəri) *s.* tesorería, erario público.

treat (tri:t) *s.* agasajo, convite. *2* placer, deleite.

treat (to) (tri:t) *t.-i.* tratar. *2 t.* convidar, invitar.

treatment ('tri:tmənt) *s.* trato; tratamiento.

treaty ('tri:ti) *s.* tratado.

tree (tri:) *s.* árbol: *apple ~,* manzano.

tremble ('trembl) *s.* temblor.

tremble (to) ('trembl) *i.* temblar. *2* estremecerse.

tremendous (tri'mendəs) *a.* tremendo.

trench (trentʃ) *s.* foso, zanja. *2* trinchera.

trench (to) (trentʃ) *t.* abrir fosos o zanjas en.

trial ('traiəl) *s.* prueba, ensayo. *2* aflicción, desgracia. *3* juicio, proceso.

tribe (traib) *s.* tribu.

tributary ('tribjutəri) *a.-s.* tributario; afluente [río].

trick (trik) *s.* treta, ardid.

trick (to) (trik) *t.-i.* engañar. estafar, burlar.

trickle (to) ('trikl) *i.* gotear.

tried (traid) V. TO TRY. 2 *a.* probado, fiel.

trifle ('traifl) *s.* fruslería.

trifle (to) ('traifl) *i.* bromear. chancear(se.

trim (trim) *a.* bien arreglado; en buen estado. 2 elegante; pulcro, acicalado. 3 *s.* adorno, aderezo. 4 buen estado.

trim (to) (trim) *t.* arreglar. disponer. 2 cortar [el pelo, etc.]; podar. 3 adornar.

trip (trip) *s.* viaje, excursión.

trip (to) (trip) *i.* saltar, brincar. 2 tropezar.

triumph ('traiəmf) *s.* triunfo.

triumph (to) ('traiəmf) *i.* triunfar, vencer.

troop (tru:p) *s.* tropa, cuadrilla.

tropical ('trɔpikəl) *a.* tropical.

trot (trɔt) *s.* trote: *at a* ~, al trote.

trot (to) (trɔt) *i.* trotar. 2 *t.* hacer trotar.

trouble ('trʌbl) *s.* perturbación, desorden. 2 pena; apuro. 3 avería.

trouble (to) ('trʌbl) *t.* turbar, perturbar. 2 incomodar, molestar. 3 *i.-ref.* preocuparse; molestarse.

trousers ('trauzəz) *s. pl.* pantalón(es.

trout (traut) *s.* trucha.

truant ('tru(:)ənt) *s.* tunante, holgazán. 2 *a.* ocioso; perezoso.

truck (trʌk) *s.* (Ingl.) vagón de plataforma. 2 (E. U.)camión. 3 carretilla de mano. 4 cambio, trueque. 5 *garden* ~. hortalizas frescas.

truculence ('trʌkjuləns) *s.* truculencia, crueldad.

truculent ('trʌkjulənt) *a.* truculento.

true (tru:) *a.* verdadero, cierto, real. 2 fiel, leal.

truism ('tru(:)izəm) *s.* verdad manifiesta; perogrullada.

truly ('tru:li) *adv.* verdaderamente. 2 sinceramente: *yours (very) truly*, su afectísimo.

trumpet ('trʌmpit) *s.* trompeta, clarín.

trunk (trʌŋk) *s.* tronco [de árbol; del cuerpo, etc.]. 2 cofre, baúl. 3 trompa [de elefante]. 4 *pl.* pantalones cortos [para deporte]. 5 ~ *call*, conferencia interurbana.

trust (trʌst) *s.* confianza, fe [en una pers. o cosa]; esperanza. 2 depósito, cargo, custodia. 3 COM. crédito. 4 trust, asociación de empresas.

trust (to) (trʌst) *t.* confiar en.

truth (tru:θ) *s.* verdad.

try (trai) *s.* prueba, ensayo.

try (to) (trai) *t.* probar, intentar, tratar de: *to* ~ *on a suit*, probarse un traje. 2 DER. juzgar; ver [una causa, etc.].

trying ('traiiŋ) *a.* irritante, molesto, fatigoso.

tub (tʌb) *s.* tina, batea. 2 bañera, baño.

tuberculosis (tju͵bə:kju'lousis) *s.* tuberculosis.

tuck (to) (tʌk) *t.* hacer alforzas o pliegues.

Tuesday ('tju:zdi, -dei) *s.* martes.

tug (tʌg) *s.* tirón, estirón.

tug (to) (tʌg) *t.* tirar de, arrastrar. 2 remolcar.

tumble ('tʌmbl) *s.* caída, tumbo, vuelco, voltereta. 2 desorden.

tumble (to) ('tʌmbl) *i.* dar volteretas, voltear. 2 caerse, dejarse caer. 3 *t.* derribar.

tumult ('tju:mʌlt) *s.* tumulto.

tune (tju:n) *s.* melodía; tonada.

tune (to) (tju:n) *t.* templar, afinar. 2 entonar. 3 *i.* armonizar.

tunnel ('tʌnl) *s.* túnel.

Turk (tə:k) *s.* turco.

Turkey ('tə:ki) *n. pr.* GEOGR. Turquía. 2 *minusc.* pavo.

turn (tə:n) *s.* vuelta, giro; revolución. 2 recodo; cambio de rumbo. 3 turno.

turn (to) (tə:n) *t.-i.* volver(se; voltear(se. 2 girar, dar vueltas. 3 tornear, labrar al torno. 4 desviar(se; dirigir(se. 5 trastornar. 6 volverse: *to ~ pale*, ponerse pálido. 7 *to ~ away*, despedir, echar; desviar. 8 *to ~ back*, volver atrás; devolver. 9 *to ~ down*, rechazar [una oferta]; poner boca abajo; bajar [el gas]. 10 *to ~ inside out*, volver al revés. 11 *to ~ off*, cortar [el agua, etc.], apagar [la luz]. 12 *to ~ on*, abrir [la llave del gas, etc.], encender [la luz]. 13 *to ~ out*, expulsar, echar; apagar [la luz]; producir.

turnip ('tə:nip) *s.* nabo.

turtle ('tə:tl) *s.* ZOOL. tortuga.

tutor ('tju:təʳ) *s.* preceptor. 2 tutor.

tutor (to) ('tju:təʳ) *t.* enseñar, instruir.

twelfth (twelfθ) *a.-s.* duodécimo: *~ night*, noche de reyes, epifanía.

twelve (twelv) *a.-s.* doce.

twentieth ('twentiiθ) *a.-s.* vigésimo.

twenty ('twenti) *a.-s.* veinte.

twice (twais) *adv.* dos veces.

twig (twig) *s.* BOT. ramita.

twilight ('twailait) *s.* crepúsculo.

twin (twin) *s.* gemelo, mellizo.

twine (twain) *s.* cordel.

twine (to) (twain) *t.* torcer [hilos, etc.]; tejer.

twinkle ('twiŋkl) *s.* titilación, destello. 2 parpadeo; guiño.

twinkle (to) ('twiŋkl) *i.* titilar, destellar. 2 parpadear; guiñar.

twist (twist) *s.* torsión, torcedura. 2 enroscadura, vuelta.

twist (to) (twist) *t.-i.* torcer(se, retorcer(se. 2 enroscar(se, entrelazar(se.

two (tu:) *a.-s.* dos. 2 *twofold*, doble.

type (taip) *s.* tipo, modelo, ejemplar: *~ writing*, mecanografía; *typist*, mecanógrafa.

typewrite (to) ('taip-rait) *t.* escribir a máquina. 2 *a. typewritten*, escrito a máquina. ¶ Pret.: *typewrote* ('taip-rout); p. p.: *typewriten* ('taip-ˌritn).

typical ('tipikl) *a.* típico.

tyranny ('tirəni) *s.* tiranía.

tyrant ('taiərənt) *s.* tirano.

tyre ('taiəʳ) *s.* TIRE.

U

ugly (´ʌgli) *a.* feo. 2 horroroso. 3 odioso, repugnante. 4 (E. U.) de mal genio.

ultimate (´ʌltimit) *a.* último, final. 2 fundamental.

umbrella (ʌm'brelə) *s.* paraguas. 2 sombrilla.

umpire (´ʌmpaiə') *s.* árbitro.

unable (´ʌn'eibl) *a.* incapaz.

uncle (´ʌŋkl) *s.* tío.

under (´ʌndə') *prep.* bajo, debajo de. 2 menos de; dentro: ~ *an hour,* en menos de una hora. 3 en tiempo de. 4 conforme a, según. 5 *a.* inferior; subordinado.

underbrush (´ʌndə'brʌʃ) *s.* maleza [de un bosque].

undergo (to) (´ʌndə'gou) *t.* sufrir, padecer, aguantar. ¶ Pret.: *underwent* (´ʌndə'went); p. p.: *undergone* (´ʌndə'gɔn).

underground (´ʌndəgraund) *a.* subterráneo. 2 secreto, clandestino. 3 *s.* subterráneo. 4 metro, ferrocarril subterráneo. 7 (´ʌndə'graund) *adv.* bajo tierra. 6 en secreto.

underlying (´ʌndə'laiiŋ) *a.* subyacente. 2 fundamental.

underneath (´ʌndə'ni:θ) *adv.* debajo. 2 *prep.* debajo de.

understand (to) (´ʌndə'stænd) *t.* entender, comprender. ¶ Pret. y p. p.: *understood* (´ʌndə'stud).

understanding (´ʌndə'stændiŋ) *s.* inteligencia, comprensión. 2 *a.* inteligente; comprensivo.

understood (´ʌndə'stud) *pret.* y *p. p.* de TO UNDERSTAND.

undertake (to) (´ʌndə'teik) *t.* emprender, acometer, intentar. 2 comprometerse a. ¶ Pret.: *undertook* (´ʌndə'tuk); p. p.: *undertaken* (´ʌndə'teikən).

undertaking (´ʌndə'teikiŋ) *s.* empresa. 2 contrata. 3 (´ndə'teikiŋ) funeraria.

uneasy (ʌn'i:zi) *a.* intranquilo, inquieto. 2 molesto, incómodo.

unfit (´ʌn'fit) *a.* incapaz, inepto. 2 inadecuado, impropio.

unfold (to) (´ʌn'fould) *t.-i.*

desplegar(se, extender(se. 2
t. descubrir, revelar.

unhappy (ʌn'hæpi) *a.* infeliz,
desgraciado. 2 triste.

union ('juːnjən) *s.* unión: *the
Union*, los Estados Unidos.
2 asociación o sindicato
obrero: *Trade Union*, sindicato obrero.

unique (juː'niːk) *a.* único;
singular, raro.

unit ('juːnit) *s.* unidad.

unite (to) (juː'nait) *t.-i.*
unir(se, juntar(se.

unity ('juːniti) *s.* unidad.

universal (ˌjuːni'vəːsəl) *a.*
universal.

universe ('juːnivəːs) *s.* universo, mundo.

university (ˌjuːni'vəːsiti) *s.*
universidad. 2 a. universitario.

unknown ('ʌn'noun) *a.* desconocido, ignorado, ignoto.

unless (ən'les) *conj.* a menos
que, a no ser que. 2 salvo,
excepto.

unlike ('ʌn'laik) *a.* deseme-
jante, diferente. 2 *adv.* de
diferente modo que. 3 *prep.*
a diferencia de.

unpleasant (ʌn'pleznt) *a.* desagradable, molesto. 2 **-ly**
adv. desagradablemente.

until (ən'til) *prep.* hasta [con
sentido temporal]. 2 *conj.*
hasta que.

unto ('ʌntu) *prep.* poét. y ant.
hacia a, hasta, contra, en.

unwilling ('ʌn'wiliŋ) *a.* rea-
cio, renuente.

up (ʌp) *adv.* hacia arriba. 2
en pie. 3 a la altura de: *well
~ in*, bien enterado. 4 enteramente, completamente: *to
burn ~*, quemar del todo. 5

en contacto o proximidad:
close ~ to, tocando a. 6 en
reserva: *to lay ~*, acumular.
7 hasta: *~ to date*, hasta la
fecha. 8 *prep.* subido a, en
lo alto de: *~ a tree*, subido a
un árbol. 9 hacia arriba: *~
the river*, río arriba. 10 *a.*
ascendente: *~ train*, tren ascendente. 11 derecho; le-
vantado [no acostado]. 12
que está en curso: *what is
~?*, ¿qué ocurre? 13 entendido, enterado. 14 capaz,
dispuesto. 15 acabado: *the
time is ~*, expiró el plazo. 16
s. **ups and downs**, altibajos.
17 *interj.* ¡arriba!, ¡aúpa! 18
~ there!, ¡alto ahí!

uplift ('ʌplift) *s.* levantamiento, elevación.

upon (ə'pɔn) *prep.* sobre, encima. 2 *nothing to live ~*,
nada con qué vivir; *~ pain
of*, bajo pena de; *~ seeing
this*, viendo esto.

upper ('ʌpəʳ) *a. comp.* de UP:
superior, alto, más elevado:
~ classes, la clase alta; *~
House*, cámara alta; *to have
the ~ hand of*, ejercer el
mando. 2 *s.* pala y caña del
zapato; litera alta.

upright ('ʌp'rait) *a.* derecho,
vertical. 2 recto, honrado.

uproar ('ʌpˌrɔː) *s.* gritería,
alboroto, tumulto.

upset ('ʌpset) *a.* volcado,
tumbado. 2 trastornado, de-
sarreglado. 3 *s.* vuelco. 4
trastorno; desorden.

upset (to) (ʌp'set) *t.* volcar. 2
trastornar, desarreglar. 3 alterar, conmover. ¶ Pret. y
p. p.: *upset* (ʌp'set).

upstairs ('ʌp'stɛəz) *adv.*

arriba, al o en el piso de
arriba. *2 a.* de arriba.

urge (ə:dʒ) *s.* impulso. *2* ganas, deseo.

urge (to) (ə:dʒ) *t.* insistir en. *2* recomendar. *3* instar.

us (ʌs, əs, s) *pron. pers.* [caso objetivo] nos. *2* [con prep.] nosotros.

use (juːs) *s.* uso, empleo: *out of* ~, desusado, pasado de moda. *2* utilidad, servicio, provecho: *of no* ~, inútil. *3* práctica, costumbre.

use (to) (juːz) *t.* usar, emplear. *2* practicar, hacer. *3* tratar [bien, mal].

useful (ˈjuːsful) *a.* útil.

useless (ˈjuːslis) *a.* inútil.

usual (ˈjuːʒuəl) *a.* usual, habitual.

usury (ˈjuːʒuri) *s.* usura.

utility (juːˈtiliti) *s.* utilidad, provecho. *2* empresa de servicio público.

utilize (to) (ˈjuːtilaiz) *t.* utilizar, emplear, explotar.

utmost (ˈʌtmoust, -məst) *a.* sumo, extremo. *2 s.* lo más posible.

utter (ˈʌtəʳ) *a.* absoluto, total. *2* terminante.

utter (to) (ˈʌtəʳ) *t.* pronunciar, articular. *2* lanzar [un grito]. *3* decir, expresar.

V

vacation (ve'keiʃən) s. vacación, descanso.

vague (veig) a. vago, indefinido. 2 incierto.

vain (vein) a. vano, fútil.

vale (veil) s. valle, cañada.

valentine ('væləntain) s. tarjeta o regalo el día de san Valentín. 2 novio, novia.

valiant ('væljənt) a. valiente.

valley ('væli) s. valle, cuenca.

valo(u)r ('vælə^r) s. valor.

valuable ('væljuəbl) a. valioso, costoso. 2 s. pl. joyas, objetos de valor.

value ('vælju:) s. valor [de una cosa]; precio, mérito.

value (to) ('vælju:) t. valorar. 2 apreciar, estimar.

van (væn) s. carromato. 2 camión. 3 (Ingl.) furgón de equipajes.

vanish (to) ('væniʃ) i. desaparecer, desvanecerse.

vanity ('væniti) s. vanidad.

vapo(u)r ('veipə^r) s. vapor, vaho. 2 niebla ligera.

variety (və'raiəti) s. variedad.

various ('veəriəs) a. vario [diverso; variable]. 2 varios.

vary (to) ('veəri) t.-i. variar. 2 i. diferenciarse.

vase (va:z) s. jarrón; florero.

vassal ('væsəl) s. vasallo.

vast (va:st) a. vasto. 2 inmenso; enorme, atroz.

vat (væt) s. tina, tanque.

vault (vɔ:lt) s. ARQ. bóveda. 2 sótano; cripta; tumba o panteón subterráneo. 3 salto [con pértiga, etc.].

vault (to) (vɔ:lt) t. abovedar. 2 t.-i. saltar [por encima], saltar con pértiga.

vaunt (to) (vɔ:nt) i. jactarse.

veal (vi:l) s. ternera [carne].

vegetable ('vedʒitəbl) a. vegetal. 2 s. vegetal. 3 legumbre, hortaliza.

veil (veil) s. velo.

veil (to) (veil) t. velar.

vein (vein) s. ANAT. vena. 2 humor, disposición.

velvet ('velvit) s. terciopelo.

vengeance ('ven(d)ʒens) s. venganza.

verdict ('və:dikt) s. veredicto. 2 dictamen.

verse (və:s) s. LIT. verso.

version ('və:ʃən) s. versión.

vertical ('və:tikəl) *a.* vertical.

very ('veri) *a.* mismo, idéntico: *at that ~ moment*, en aquel mismo instante. 2 verdadero, puro, solo: *the ~ truth*, la pura verdad. 3 *adv.* muy, sumamente: *~ much*, mucho, muchísimo.

vessel ('vesl) *s.* vasija, vaso. 2 nave, embarcación.

vest (vest) *s.* chaleco.

vest (to) (vest) *t. to ~ in*, dar, atribuir, conferir a.

vex (to) (veks) *t.* vejar, molestar. 2 disgustar, desazonar. 3 discutir.

vibrate (to) (vai'breit) *t.-i.* vibrar, hacer vibrar.

vice (vais) *s.* vicio. 2 VISE. 3 fam. sustituto, suplente. 4 *pref.* vice-.

vicinity (vi'siniti) *s.* vecindad.

victim ('viktim) *s.* víctima.

victor ('viktə^r) *m.* vencedor.

view (vju:) *s.* vista, visión, consideración; mirada. 2 vista, panorama, escena. 3 opinión, punto de vista, aspecto. 4 propósito.

view (to) (vju:) *t.* ver, mirar. 2 examinar, inspeccionar. 3 considerar.

vigorous ('vigərəs) *a.* vigoroso. 2 fuerte, enérgico.

vigo(u)r ('vigə^r) *s.* vigor.

vile (vail) *a.* vil, ruin.

village ('vilidʒ) *s.* aldea, lugar, pueblo.

villain ('vilən) *s.* bribón, canalla. 2 malo, traidor.

vine (vain) *s.* BOT. vid, parra.

violate (to) ('vaiəleit) *t.* violar, forzar; atropellar.

violence ('vaiələns) *s.* violencia.

violet ('vaiəlit) *s.* violeta. 2 color de violeta.

violin (,vaiə'lin) *s.* violín.

virgin ('və:dʒin) *s.* virgen, doncella. 2 *a.* virgen; virginal.

virtue ('və:tju:) *s.* virtud.

visible (vizibl) *a.* visible.

vision ('viʒən) *s.* vista [sentido]. 2 visión [facultad de ver; cosa vista, aparición].

visit ('vizit) *s.* visita.

visit (to) ('vizit) *t.* visitar. 2 afligir, castigar.

visitor ('vizitə^r) *s.* visita, visitante. 2 visitador.

vivid ('vivid) *a.* vívido. 2 vivo, animado.

voice (vɔis) *s.* voz. 2 habla, palabra. 3 opinión, voto.

voice (to) (vɔis) *t.* expresar, decir, anunciar.

void (vɔid) *a.* vacío; vacante.

volcano (vɔl'keinou) *s.* volcán.

volume ('vɔljum) *s.* volumen, tomo, libro. 2 GEOM., MÚS. volumen. 3 bulto, masa.

volunteer (,vɔlən'tiə^r) *s.* voluntario.

volunteer (to) (,vɔlən'tiə^r) *t.-i.* ofrecer(se voluntariamente.

vote (vout) *s.* voto, votación.

vote (to) (vout) *t.-i.* votar [dar su voto].

voter ('voutə^r) *s.* votante.

vow (vau) *s.* voto, promesa solemne. 2 voto, deseo; súplica.

vow (to) (vau) *t.* hacer voto de; prometer solemnemente.

voyage (vɔidʒ) *s.* viaje por mar o por el aire, travesía.

voyage (to) (vɔidʒ) *i.* viajar, navegar.

vulgar ('vʌlgə^r) *a.* vulgar. 2 común, ordinario, de mal gusto.

W

wade (to) (weid) *i.* andar sobre terreno cubierto de agua, lodo, etc. 2 *t.* vadear.

wag (wæg) *s.* meneo. 2 bromista, guasón.

wag (to) (wæg) *t.* menear [la cabeza, etc.]. 2 *i.* moverse, menearse.

wage (weiʒ) *s.* paga, jornal.

wage (to) (weiʒ) *t.* emprender, sostener; hacer.

wag(g)on ('wægən) *s.* carromato, furgón.

waif (weif) *s.* cosa o animal sin dueño. 2 niño abandonado; golfillo.

wail (weil) *s.* lamento, gemido.

wail (to) (weil) *t.-i.* lamentar(se, deplorar.

waist (weist) *s.* cintura, talle.

wait (weit) *s.* espera. 2 detención, demora.

wait (to) (weit) *i.-t.* esperar, aguardar [con *for*]. 2 *i.* servir: *to ~ at table*, servir a la mesa.

waiter ('weitə^r) *s.* mozo, camarero.

waiting ('weitiŋ) *s.* espera. 2 servicio.

wake (weik) *s.* estela, aguaje. 2 vela, velatorio.

wake (to) (weik) [a veces con *up*] *t.-i.* despertar(se, despabilarse. ¶ Pret.: *waked* (weikt) o *woke* (wouk); p. p.: *waked* o *woken* ('woukən).

waken (to) ('weikən) *t.-i.* despertar.

walk (wɔːk) *s.* paseo, vuelta. 2 paseo, alameda, senda. 3 paso [del caballo, etc.].

walk (to) (wɔːk) *i.* andar, caminar; *to ~ away*, irse; *to ~ out, to ~ out with*, salir con, ser novio de; *to ~ up to*, acercarse a; *to ~ the hospitals*, estudiar medicina. 2 *t.* sacar a paseo. 3 recorrer.

walking ('wɔːkiŋ) *s.* marcha, paseo.

wall (wɔːl) *s.* pared, muro.

walnut ('wɔːlnət) *s.* BOT. nuez.

wand (wɔnd) *s.* vara.

wander (to) ('wɔndə^r) *t.-i.* errar, vagar.

want (wɔnt) s. falta. necesidad. carencia. escasez.

want (to) (wɔnt) t. necesitar. 2 querer. desear.

wanting ('wɔntiŋ) a. falto. defectuoso. 2 necesitado.

war (wɔːʳ) s. guerra.

war (to) (wɔːʳ) i. guerrear. estar en guerra.

ward (wɔːd) s. guarda. custodia. 2 tutela. 3 pupilo.

ward (to) (wɔːd) t. guardar. proteger.

wardrobe ('wɔːdroub) s. armario. guardarropa.

ware (wɛəʳ) s. *sing.* o *pl.* géneros. mercancías.

warehouse ('wɛəhaus) s. almacén. depósito.

warfare ('wɔːfɛəʳ) s. guerra.

warm (wɔːm) a. caliente. cálido. caluroso: *I am* ~, tengo calor: *it is* ~, hace calor.

warm (to) (wɔːm) t.-i. calentar(se. 2 animar(se.

warmth (wɔːmθ) s. calor moderado. 2 afecto. cordialidad.

warn (to) (wɔːn) t. avisar. advertir. prevenir. 2 amonestar.

warning ('wɔːniŋ) s. aviso. advertencia. 2 amonestación. 3 escarmiento.

warp (wɔːp) s. TEJ. urdimbre.

warp (to) (wɔːp) t. urdir.

warrant ('wɔrənt) s. autorización. poder. 2 mandato.

warrant (to) ('wɔrənt) t. autorizar. 2 garantizar.

warrior ('wɔriəʳ) s. guerrero.

wash (wɔʃ) s. lavado. ablución. 2 baño. capa. 3 loción.

wash (to) (wɔʃ) t. lavar. 2 bañar. regar.

washing ('wɔʃiŋ) s. acción de

TO WASH. 2 colada. 3 a. de lavar: ~-*machine*, lavadora.

waste (weist) a. yermo. inculto. 2 s. extensión. inmensidad.

waste (to) (weist) t. devastar. destruir. 2 gastar. mermar.

watch (wɔtʃ) s. reloj de bolsillo. 2 vela. vigilia: ~ *night*, noche vieja. 3 velatorio. 4 vigilancia. observación. cuidado: *on the* ~, alerta. 5 centinela. vigilante.

watch (to) (wɔtʃ) i. velar [estar despierto]. 2 vigilar. estar alerta.

watchful ('wɔtʃful) a. desvelado. 2 vigilante. en guardia.

water ('wɔːtəʳ) s. agua: *in deep* ~, o *waters*, en apuros. 2 a. de agua. acuático.

water (to) ('wɔːtəʳ) t. regar. rociar. mojar. 2 i. chorrear agua o humedad: llorar.

waterfall ('wɔːtəfɔːl) s. cascada. catarata.

wave (weiv) s. ola. 2 onda.

wave (to) (weiv) i. flotar. ondear. ondular.

waver ('weivəʳ) s. oscilación. temblor. 2 titubeo.

waver (to) ('weivəʳ) i. ondear. oscilar. temblar. 2 vacilar.

wax (wæks) s. cera.

wax (to) (wæks) t. encerar. 2 i. crecer. aumentar.

way (wei) s. vía. camino. calle. canal. conducto. 2 viaje. rumbo. curso. dirección. sentido: *the other* ~ *round*, al revés: *this* ~, por aquí. 3 paso. 4 espacio. distancia. trecho. 5 marcha. progreso. 6 modo. manera: *anyway*, de todos modos. 7 lado, aspecto. 8 medio. 9 sistema de vida, costumbre. 10 estado, condición. 11 pl. maneras [de una persona]. 12 by ~ of, pasando por, por vía de. 13 by the ~, a propósito. 14 a. de camino, de tránsito: ~ train, tren, tranvía.

we (wi:, wi) pron. nosotros.

weak (wi:k) a. débil, flojo.

weaken (to) ('wi:kən) t.-i. debilitar(se. 2 i. flaquear.

weakness ('wi:knis) s. debilidad, flaqueza.

wealth (welθ) s. riqueza.

wealthy ('welθi) a. rico.

weapon ('wepən) s. arma.

wear (wɛəʳ) s. uso [de ropa, calzado, etc.]. 2 ropa, vestidos.

wear (to) (wɛəʳ) t. traer puesto, usar, llevar. 2 usar [barba, etc.]. 3 t.-i. gastar(se, deteriorar(se. 4 agotar(se, fatigar(se. 5 to ~ away, gastar(se, consumir(se. ¶ Pret.: wore (wɔ:ʳ, wɔəʳ); p. p.: worn (wɔ:n).

weariness ('wiərinis) s. cansancio, fatiga. 2 aburrimiento.

weary ('wiəri) a. cansado, fatigado. 2 abrumado.

weary (to) ('wiəri) t.-i. cansar(se [fatigar(se, fastidiar(se]. 2 aburrirse.

weather ('weðəʳ) s. tiempo [estado de la atmósfera].

weather (to) ('weðəʳ) t.-i. curar(se, secar(se a la intemperie. 2 t. capear, aguantar.

weave (wi:v) s. tejido, textura.

weave (to) (wi:v) t. tejer. 2 entretejer. 3 urdir, tramar.

¶ Pret.: wove (wouv); p. p.: woven ('wouvən) o wove.

web (web) s. tejido, tela; telaraña.

we'd (wi:d) contrac. de WE HAD, WE SHOULD y WE WOULD.

wedding ('wediŋ) s. casamiento, boda.

wedge (wedʒ) s. cuña, calce.

wedge (to) (wedʒ) t. acuñar, meter cuñas.

Wednesday ('wenzdi, -dei) s. miércoles.

weed (wi:d) s. yerbajo, mala hierba. 2 alga.

weed (to) (wi:d) t. escardar, desyerbar.

week (wi:k) s. semana: -end, fin de semana: a ~ from today, de hoy en ocho días.

weep (to) (wi:p) t.-i. llorar. ¶ Pret. y p.p.: wept (wept).

welcome ('welkəm) a. bien venido. 2 grato, agradable. 3 you are ~, no hay de qué. 4 s. bienvenida, buena acogida.

welcome (to) ('welkəm) t. dar la bienvenida, acoger.

welfare ('welfɛəʳ) s. bienestar.

we'll (wi:l) contrac. de WE SHALL y WE WILL.

1) **well** (wel) s. manantial. 2 pozo. 3 cisterna.

2) **well** (wel) a. bien hecho, satisfactorio, bueno, apto. 2 s. well-being, bienestar. 3 adv. bien, felizmente, del todo: as ~, además; también.

well (to) (wel) t.-i. manar, brotar.

went (went) pret. de TO GO.

wept (wept) V. TO WEEP.

we're (wiəʳ) contrac. de WE ARE.

were (wǝ:ʳ; wǝʳ) V. TO BE.

west (west) *s.* oeste, occidente. 2 *a.* occidental, del oeste.

wet (wet) *a.* mojado. 2 húmedo. 3 *s.* humedad.

wet (to) (wet) *t.* mojar. 2 humedecer. ¶ Pret. y p. p.: *wet* o *wetted*.

wetness ('wetnis) *s.* humedad.

wharf (h)wɔ:f) *s.* muelle.

what (h)wɔt) *a.* y *pron. interr.* qué; cuál: ~ *for?*, ¿para qué? 2 *pron. rel.* lo que. 3 *a. rel.* que: ~ *a man!*, ¡qué hombre! 4 *interj.* ¡eh!, ¡qué!

whatever (wɔt'evǝʳ) *pron.* cualquier cosa que, todo lo que. 2 *a.* cualquiera que.

whatsoever (ˌwɔtsou'evǝʳ) *pron.* y *a.* WHATEVER.

wheat (h)wi:t) *s.* trigo.

wheel (h)wi:l) *s.* rueda. 2 torno. 3 AUTO. volante.

when (h)wen) *adv.-conj.* cuando.

whence (h)wens) *adv.* de donde; por lo cual.

whenever (h)wen'evǝʳ) *adv.* cuando quiera que, siempre que.

where (h)wɛǝʳ) *adv.-conj.* donde, en donde, adonde, por donde.

whereas (wɛǝr'æz) *conj.* considerando que. 2 mientras que.

wherever (wɛǝr'evǝʳ) *adv.* dondequiera que, adondequiera que, por dondequiera que.

whether ('weðǝʳ) *conj.* si. 2 sea, ya sea que, tanto si... (como).

which (h)witʃ) *a.* y *pron. interrog.* [selectivo] ¿qué? ¿cuál?, ¿cuáles?: ~ *book do you prefer?*, ¿qué libro prefiere usted? 2 *pron. rel.* lo que, lo cual. 3 *a. rel.* que [cuando el antecedente es cosa].

whichever (h)witʃ'evǝʳ) *pron.* y *a.* cual(es)quiera [que].

while (h)wail) *s.* rato, tiempo: *for a* ~, por algún tiempo; *to be worth* ~, valer la pena. 2 *conj.* mientras [que].

while (to) (h)wail) *t.* pasar [el rato, etc.]. | Gralte. con *away*.

whine (h)wain) *s.* gemido.

whine (to) (h)wain) *i.* gemir, quejarse.

whip (h)wip) *s.* látigo, azote.

whip (to) (h)wip) *t.* fustigar, azotar, zurrar.

whir (h)wǝ:ʳ) *s.* zumbido.

whir (to) (h)wǝ:ʳ) *i.* zumbar.

whirl (h)wǝ:l) *s.* giro o vuelta rápidos; remolino.

whirl (to) (h)wǝ:l) *i.* girar, dar vueltas rápidamente. 2 *t.* hacer girar.

whisper ('h)wispǝʳ) *s.* susurro, murmullo.

whisper (to) ('h)wispǝʳ) *i.-t.* susurrar, murmurar.

whistle ('h)wisl) *s.* silbato, pito. 2 silbido, pitido.

whistle (to) ('h)wisl) *i.-t.* silbar, pitar.

whit (h)wit) *s.* pizca.

white (h)wait) *a.* blanco: *-hot*, candente. 2 cano. 3 *s.* blanco [del ojo]. 4 clara [de huevo].

whither ('h)wiðǝʳ) *adv.* adonde. 2 ¿adónde?

who (hu:, hu) *pron. rel.* quien, quienes, que, el que, la que, los que, las que. 2 *pron. interr.* ¿quién?, ¿quiénes?

whoever (hu(:)'eva^r) *pron. rel.* quienquiera que, cualquiera que.

whole (houl) *a.* todo, entero. 2 *s.* total, conjunto.

wholesale ('houl-seil) *a.-adv.* al por mayor. 2 *s.* venta al por mayor.

wholesome ('houlsəm) *a.* sano, saludable.

whom (hu:m, hum) *pron.* (caso oblicuo de WHO) a quien, a quienes; que, al que, etc.

whose (hu:z) *pron.* (genitivo de WHO y WHICH) cuyo -a, cuyos -as, del que, de la que, etc.

why (h)wai) *adv. conj.* ¿por qué?, ¿cómo? 2 *interj.* ¡cómo!, ¡toma! 3 *s.* porqué, causa.

wicked ('wikid) *a.* malo, perverso. 2 maligno. 3 travieso.

wide (waid) *a.* ancho. 2 amplio, extenso. 3 *adv.* ampliamente. 4 lejos, a distancia.

widen (to) ('waidn) *t.-i.* ensanchar(se, extender(se.

widow ('widou) *s.* viuda.

width (widθ) *s.* anchura, ancho.

wife (waif), *pl.* *wives* (waivz)*s.* esposa.

wild (waild) *a.* salvaje, montaraz, silvestre.

wilderness ('wildənis) *s.* tierra inculta, desierto.

will (wil) *s.* voluntad.

1) **will (to)** (wil) *t.* querer, ordenar, mandar. 2 dejar en testamento. ¶ Pret. y p. p.: *willed*.

2) **will** (sin to) (wil) *t.* querer, desear. ¶ Pret.: *would* (wud). | No se usa otro tiempo.

3) **will** (sin to) (wil) *v. defect.* y *aux.* pret. y condicional: *would* (wud, wəd). Se usa *will* para formar el fut. y *would* en condicional en 2.ª y 3.ª pers.: *he ~ go*, él irá; en las 1.ªs pers. indica voluntad o determinación: *I ~ not do it*, no quiero hacerlo. En 3.ª pers. indica negativa o costumbre: *he would not help me*, no quería ayudarme; *he would come every day*, acostumbraba a venir todos los días; *would* condicional; *he would come, if he could*, vendría, si pudiera.

willing ('wiliŋ) *a.* deseoso, dispuesto. 2 gustoso.

willow ('wilou) *s.* BOT. sauce.

wilt (to) (wilt) *t.-i.* marchitar(se.

win (to) (win) *t.* ganar. 2 persuadir. 3 *i.* vencer, triunfar. ¶ Pret. y p.p.: *won* (wʌn).

wind (wind) *s.* viento, aire. 2 rumbo, punto cardinal. 3 aliento, respiración.

1) **wind (to)** (wind) *t.-i.* husmear, olfatear. 2 *t.* airear. ¶ Pret. y p. p.: *winded* ('windid).

2) **wind (to)** (waind) *t.* devanar. 2 manejar. 3 dar cuerda a [un reloj]. 4 izar, elevar. ¶ Pret. y p. p. (waund).

3) **wind (to)** (waind) *t.* soplar. 2 hacer sonar [soplando]. ¶ Pret. y p. p.: *winded* ('waindid) o *wound* (waund).

window ('windou) *s.* ventana.

wine (wain) *s.* vino.

wing (wiŋ) *s.* ORN.. POL. ala. 2 vuelo. 3 TEAT. bastidor.

wink (wiŋk) *s.* parpadeo, pestañeo. 2 guiño. 3 destello.

wink (to) (wiŋk) *i.* pestañear, parpadear. 2 hacer guiños. 3 centellear.

winner ('winəʳ) *s.* ganador. 2 vencedor.

winning ('winiŋ) *a.* triunfante, ganador. 2 atractivo, encantador. 3 **-s** *s. pl.* ganancias [en el juego].

winter ('wintəʳ) *s.* invierno.

wipe (to) (waip) *t.* limpiar.

wire ('waiəʳ) *s.* alambre. 2 telegrama; telégrafo.

wireless ('waiəlis) *s.* radio.

wisdom ('wizdəm) *s.* sabiduría, sapiencia.

wise (waiz) *a.* cuerdo, prudente. 2 *s.* manera: *in no ~*, de ningún modo.

wish (wiʃ) *s.* deseo, anhelo.

wish (to) (wiʃ) *t.* desear, anhelar, ansiar.

wit (wit) *s.* agudeza, ingenio.

witch (witʃ) *s.* bruja, hechicera.

with (wið) *prep.* con; para con; a, de, en, entre: *~ all speed*, a toda prisa; *charged ~*, acusado de.

withdraw (to) (wið'drɔ:) *t.* retirar(se. 2 apartar(se, separar(se. ¶ Pret.: *withdrew* (wið'dru:), p. p.: *withdrawn* (wið'drɔ:n).

wither (to) ('wiðəʳ) *t.* marchitar(se, secar(se, ajar(se.

withhold (to) (wið'houl) *t.* detener, contener. 2 suspender [un pago]. 3 negar. ¶

Pret. y p. p.: *withheld* (wið'held).

within (wi'ðin) *prep.* dentro de [los límites de]. en. 2 al alcance de. 3 *adv.* dentro, en o al interior, en la casa.

without (wi'ðaut) *prep.* sin. 2 falto de. 3 fuera de. 4 *adv.* fuera. 5 *conj.* si no, a menos de.

witness ('witnis) *s.* testigo.

witty ('witi) *a.* ingenioso, agudo, chistoso.

wives (waivz) *s. pl.* de WIFE.

woe (wou) *s.* pena, aflicción.

woke (wouk) V. TO WAKE.

wolf (wulf), *pl.* **wolves** (wulvz) *s.* lobo: *~ cub*, lobezno.

woman ('wumən), *pl.* **women** ('wimin) *s.* mujer.

won (wʌn) V. TO WIN.

wonder ('wʌndəʳ) *s.* admiración, asombro: *no ~*, no es de extrañar. 2 incertidumbre, perplejidad. 3 portento, prodigio.

wonder (to) ('wʌndəʳ) *t.* desear, saber, preguntarse.

wonderful ('wʌndəful) *a.* admirable, maravilloso.

wondrous ('wʌndrəs) *a.* sorprendente, asombroso.

wont (wount) *a.* acostumbrado: *to be ~ to*, soler, acos-, tumbrar. 2 *s.* costumbre, hábito.

won't (wount) *contr.* de WILL NOT.

woo (to) (wu:) *t.-i.* cortejar, pretender [a una mujer].

wood (wud) *s.* bosque, selva. 2 madera, leña.

wool (wul) *s.* lana.

word (wə:d) *s.* palabra, vocablo. 2 palabra, promesa. 3 aviso, recado. 4 *pl.* palabras, disputa: *to have words,* disputar.

word (to) (wə:d) *t.* expresar [con palabras]; formular.

wore (wɔːʳ, wɔəʳ) V. TO WEAR.

work (wə:k) *s.* trabajo, labor; ocupación, empleo; operación, funcionamiento. 2 obra. 3 *pl.* fábrica, taller. 4 maquinaria [de un artefacto].

work (to) (wə:k) *i.* trabajar; laborar, 2 surtir efecto, dar resultado. 3 *to ~ out,* resultar [bien o mal]; DEP. entrenarse. 4 *t.* fabricar, producir. 5 *to ~ off,* deshacerse de. 6 *~ up,* inflamar; lograr [con esfuerzo]; elaborar [un plan].

worker (ˈwə:kəʳ) *s.* obrero.

workman (ˈwə:kmən) *s.* obrero, trabajador.

world (wə:ld) *s.* mundo.

worm (wə:m) *s.* gusano.

worm (to) (wə:m) *i.-ref.* introducirse, insinuarse.

worn (wɔ:n) *p. p.* DE TO WEAR. 2 *~ out,* usado, gastado.

worried (ˈwʌrid) *a.* angustiado, preocupado.

worry (ˈwʌri) *s.* cuidado, preocupación; molestia.

worry (to) (ˈwʌri) *t.-i.* inquietar(se, preocupar(se. 2 *to ~ out,* hallar solución.

worse (wə́:s) *a.-adv. comp.* de *bad,* peor. 2 *s.* lo peor.

worship (ˈwə:ʃip) *s.* culto, adoración. 2 veneración.

worship (to) (ˈwə:ʃip) *t.* rendir culto a, adorar.

worst (wə:st) *a. superl.* peor [en sentido absoluto]: *the ~,* el peor. 2 *adv. superl.* peor, pésimamente.

worth (wə:θ) *s.* valor, precio. 2 digno, merecedor de.

worth (wə:θ) *s.* valor, precio. 2 digno, merecedor de.

worthless (ˈwə:θlis) *a.* sin valor, inútil. 2 indigno.

worthy (ˈwə:ði) *a.* estimable, excelente. 2 digno, merecedor. 3 *s.* persona ilustre.

would (wud, wəd) *pret.* de WILL 2; *pret.* y *condicional* de WILL 3.

would-be (ˈwudbi:) *a.* supuesto, seudo. 2 aspirante.

wouldn't (ˈwudənt) *contrac.* de WOULD NOT.

1) **wound** (waund) V. TO WIND.

2) **wound** (wu:nd) *s.* herida.

wound (to) (wu:nd) *t.* herir, lastimar. 2 ofender.

wove (wouv) V. TO WEAVE.

wrap (ræp) *s.* envoltura. 2 manta, abrigo.

wrap (to) (ræp) *t.-i.* cubrir(se, envolver(se, arropar(se.

wrath (rɔ:θ) *s.* cólera, ira.

wreak (to) (ri:k) *t.* infligir.

wreath (ri:θ) *s.* corona, guirnalda.

wreck (rek) *s.* naufragio, ruina, destrucción.

wreck (to) (rek) *t.* hacer naufragar, echar a pique. 2 *t.-i.* arruinar(se, destruir(se, fracasar.

wrench (rentʃ) *s.* tirón.

wrestle (to) (ˈresl) *i.* luchar a brazo partido. 2 esforzarse.

wretch (retʃ) *s.* miserable, desdichado. 2 canalla.

wretched (ˈretʃid) *a.* infeliz. 2 malo, ruin.

wrinkle (ˈriŋkl) *s.* arruga, surco.

wrist (rist) *s.* ANAT. muñeca.

write (to) (rait) *t.-i.* escribir:

to ~ back, contestar por carta; *to ~ down,* anotar; *to ~ out,* redactar; escribir sin abreviar; *to ~ up,* describir extensamente por escrito; poner al día. ¶ Pret.: *wrote* (rout); p. p.: *written* ('ritn).

writer ('raitə^r) *s.* escritor, autor.

writing ('raitiŋ) *s.* escritura, escrito.

wrong (rɔŋ) *a.* malo, injusto. 2 erróneo, equivocado, defectuoso; inconveniente, inoportuno. *2 the ~ side,* el revés [de una tela]. *3 adv.* mal, al revés. *4 s.* agravio, injusticia.

wrought (rɔ:t) *pret.* y *p. p. irreg.* de TO WORK. *2 a.* trabajado, labrado, forjado.

wrung (rʌŋ) V. TO WRING.

Y

yard (jɑ:d) *s.* yarda [medida inglesa de longitud = 0'914 m]. 2 patio, corral, cercado.

yarn (jɑ:n) *s.* hebra, hilo. 2 cuento increíble.

yawn (jɔ:n) *s.* bostezo.

yawn (to) (jɔ:n) *i.* bostezar.

year (jə:ʳ) *s.* año.

yearly ('je:li) *a.* anual.

yearn (to) (je:n) *i.* [con *for* o *after*] anhelar, suspirar por.

yell (jell) *s.* grito, alarido.

yell (to) (jel) *i.* gritar, dar alaridos.

yellow ('jelou) *a.* amarillo.

yeoman ('joumən) *s.* hacendado, labrador rico. 2 ~ *of the guard,* guardián de la Torre de Londres.

yes (jes) *adv.* sí. 2 *s.* sí (respuesta afirmativa].

yesterday ('jestədi, -dei) *s.* y *adv.* ayer.

yet (jet) *adv.* todavía, aún. 2 *conj.* aun así, no obstante, sin embargo.

yield (ji:ld) *s.* producto, rendimiento.

yield (to) (ji:ld) *t.* producir, rendir. 2 entregar, ceder. 3 rendirse.

yoke (youk) *s.* yugo; esclavitud. 2 yunta.

yoke (to) (jouk) *t.* uncir, acoyundar. 2 unir.

yon (jɔn), **yonder** ('jɔndəʳ)*a.* aquel, aquella, etc., aquellos, etc. 2 *adv.* allá; más allá.

you (ju:, ju) *pron.* de 2.ª *pers. sing.* y *pl.* tú, usted, vosotros, ustedes. 2 a ti, te; le, a usted; os, a vosotros; les, a ustedes.

young (jʌŋ) *a.* joven.

youngster ('jʌŋstəʳ) *s.* muchacho, joven.

your (juəʳ, jɔ:ʳ) *a.* tu, tus, vuestro, -a, -os, -as; su, de usted, de ustedes.

yours (juəz, jɔ:z) *pron. pos.* [el] tuyo, -a, -os, -as, [el] vuestro; -a, -os, -as; [el] suyo, -a, -os, -as [de usted o ustedes].

yourself (juə'self, jɔ:-) *pron. pers.* tú, ti, usted mismo; te, se [reflexivos].

yourselves (juə'selvz, jɔ:-)

pron. pl. de YOURSELF.
youth (ju:θ) *s.* juventud, mocedad. 2 joven, mozalbete.

youthful ('ju:θful) *a.* joven, juvenil. 2 fresco, vigoroso.

X

xenophobia (zenə'foubjə) *s.* xenofobia.
Xmas ('krisməs) *s.* abrev. de CHRISTMAS.
X-rays ('eks'reiz) *s. pl.* rayos X.

Z

zeal (zi:l) *s.* celo, fervor, entusiasmo.
zealous (zeləs) *a.* celoso, entusiasta. 2 **-ly** *adv.* celosamente, con ardor.
zero ('ziərou) *s.* cero; *below* ~, bajo cero.
zest (zest) *s.* sabor, gusto. 2 entusiasmo; aliciente.

zigzag ('zigzæg) *s.* zigzag: 2 *a.-adv.* en zigzag.
zigzag (to) ('zigzæg) *i.* zigzaguear.
zinc (ziŋk) *s.* cinc, zinc.
zone (zoun) *s.* zona.
zoological (,zouə'lɔdʒikl) *a.* zoológico.

SPANISH-ENGLISH
DICTIONARY

DICCIONARIO
ESPAÑOL-INGLÉS

ABBREVIATIONS USED IN THIS DICTIONARY

a.	adjective	ECCL.	ecclesiastic
adv.	adverb	EDUC.	education
AER.	aeronautics	ELEC.	electricity
AGR.	agriculture	ENG.	engineering
ALG.	algebra	ENTOM.	entomology
Am.	Spanish America		
ANAT.	anatomy	*f.*	feminine; feminine noun
ARCH.	architecture		
ARCHEOL.	archeology	F. ARTS.	fine arts
Arg.	Argentina	FENC.	fencing
ARITH.	arithmetic	fig.	figuratively
art.	article	FISH.	fishing
ARTILL.	artillery	Fut.	Future
ASTR.	astronomy		
aug.	augmentative	GEOG.	geography
AUTO.	automobile	GEOL.	geology
aux.	auxiliary verb	GEOM.	geometry
		GER.	Gerund
BACT.	bacteriology	GRAM.	grammar
BIB.	Bible; Biblical	GYM.	gymnastics
BILL.	billiards		
BIOL.	biology	HIST.	history
BOOKBIND.	bookbinding		
BOOKKEEP.	bookkeeping	*i.*	intransitive
BOT.	botany	ICHTH.	ichthyology
BULL.	bullfighting	*imper.*	imperative
		IMPERF.	imperfect
CARP.	carpentry	*impers.*	impersonal verb
CHEM.	chemistry	*indef.*	indefinite
coll.	colloquial	INDIC.	Indicative
COM.	commerce	IND.	industry
comp.	comparative	INF.	Infinitive
COND.	Conditional	INSUR.	insurance
conj.	conjunction	*interj.*	interjection
CONJUG.	Conjugation	*interrog.*	interrogative
COOK.	cooking	iron.	ironic
cop.	copulative verb	*irr., irreg.*	irregular
def.	defective; definite		
dim.	diminutive	JEW.	jewelry

LIT.	literature	Pres.	Present
LITURG.	liturgy	*pres. p.*	present participle
LOG.	logic	Pret.	preterit
		PRINT.	printing
m.	masculine;	*pr. n.*	proper noun
	masculine noun	*pron.*	pronoun
MACH.	machinery		
MATH.	mathematics	RADIO.	radio;
MECH.	mechanics		broadcasting
MED.	medicine	*ref.*	reflexive verb
METAL.	metallurgy	*reg.*	regular
Mex.	Mexico	REL.	religion
MIL.	military	RLY.	railway; railroad
MIN.	mining		
MINER.	mineralogy	SUBJ.	Subjunctive
MUS.	music	*superl.*	superlative
MYTH.	mythology	SURG.	surgery
		SURV.	surveying
n.	noun; masculine		
	and feminine	*t.*	transitive verb
	noun	TELEV.	television
NAUT.	nautical	THEAT.	theater
NAV.	naval; navy	THEOL.	theology
neut.	neuter		
not cap.	not capitalized	usu.	usually
obs.	obsolete	V.	Vide; See
OPT.	optics	vul.	vulgar
ORN.	ornithology		
		WEAV.	weaving
PAINT.	painting		
pers., pers.	person; personal	ZOOL.	zoology
PHIL.	philosophy		
PHOT.	photography		
PHYS.	physics		
pl.	plural		
POET.	poetry		
POL.	politics		
poss.	possessive		
p. p.	past participle		
prep.	preposition		

KEY TO PRONUNCIATION IN SPANISH

VOWELS

Letter	Approximate sound
a	Like *a* in English *far, father*, e.g., **casa, mano**.
e	When stressed, like *a* in English *pay*, e.g., **dedo**. When unstressed, it has a shorter sound like in English *bet, net*, e.g., **estado, decidir**.
i	Like *i* in English *machine* or *ee* in *feet*, e.g., **fin**.
o	Like *o* in English *obey*, e.g., **mona, poner**.
u	Like *u* in English *rule* or *oo* in *boot*, e.g., **atún**. It is silent in **gue** and **gui**, e.g., **guerra, guisado**. If it carries a diaeresis (ü), it is pronounced (see Diphthongs), e.g., **bilingüe**. It is also silent in **que** and **qui**, e.g., **querer, quinto**.
y	When used as a vowel, it sounds like the Spanish **i**, e.g., **y, rey**.

DIPHTHONGS

Diph.	Approximate sound
ai, ay	Like *i* in English *light*, e.g., **caigo, hay**.
au	Like *ou* in English *sound*, e.g., **cauto, paular**.
ei, ey	Like *ey* in English *they* or *a* in *ale*, e.g., **reina, ley**.
eu	Like the *a* in English *pay* combined with the sound of *ew* in English *knew*, e.g., **deuda, feudal**.
oi, oy	Like *oy* in English *toy*, e.g., **oiga, soy**.
ia, ya	Like *ya* in English *yarn*, e.g., **rabia, raya**.
ua	Like *wa* in English *wand*, e.g., **cuatro, cual**.
ie, ye	Like *ye* in English *yet*, e.g., **bien, yeso**.
ue	Like *wa* in English *wake*, e.g., **buena, fue**.
io, yo	Like *yo* in English *yoke*, without the following sound of *w* in this word, e.g., **región, yodo**.

Diph.	Approximate sound
uo	Like *uo* in English *quote*, e.g., cuota, oblicuo.
iu, yu	Like *yu* in English *Yule*, e.g., ciudad, triunfo.
ui	Like *wee* in English *week*, e.g., ruido.

TRIPHTHONGS

Triph.	Approximate sound
iai	Like *ya* in English *yard* combined with the *i* in *fight*, e.g., estudiáis.
iei	Like the English word *yea*, e.g., estudiéis.
uai, uay	Like *wi* in English *wide*, e.g., averiguáis, guay.
uei, uey	Like *wei* in English *weigh*, e.g., amortigüéis.

CONSONANTS

Letter	Approximate sound
b	Generally like the English *b* in *boat, bring, obsolete*, when it is at the beginning of a word or preceded by *m*, e.g., baile, bomba. Between two vowels and when followed by *l* or *r*, it has a softer sound, almost like the English *v* but formed by pressing both lips together, e.g., acaba, haber, cable.
c	Before *a, o, u*, or a consonant, it sounds like the English *c* in *coal*, e.g., casa, saco. Before *e* or *i*, it is pronounced like the English *s* in *six* in American Spanish and like the English *th* in *thin* in Castillian Spanish, e.g., cerdo, cine. If a word contains two *cs*, the first is pronounced like *c* in *coal*, and the second like *s* or *th* accordingly, e.g., acción.
ch	Like *ch* in English *cheese* or *such*, e.g., chato.
d	Generally like *d* in English *dog* or *th* in English *this*, e.g., dedo, digo. When ending a syllable, it is pronounced like the English *th*, e.g., usted.
f	Like *f* in English *fine, life*, e.g., final.

VII *Key to Pronunciation*

Letter	Approximate sound
g	Before *a, o,* and *u;* the groups *ue* and *ui;* or a consonant, it sounds like *g* in English *gain,* e.g., **gato, guitar, digno.** Before *e* or *i,* like a strongly aspirated English *h,* e.g., **general.**
h	Always silent, e.g., **hoyo, historia.**
j	Like *h* in English *hat,* e.g., **joven, reja.**
k	Like *c* in English *coal,* e.g., **kilo.** It is found only in words of foreign origin.
l	Like *l* in English *lion,* e.g., **libro, límite.**
ll	In some parts of Spain and Spanish America, like the English *y* in *yet;* generally in Castillian Spanish, like the *lli* in English *million;* e.g., **castillo, silla.**
m	Like *m* in English *map,* e.g., **moneda, tomo.**
n	Like *n* in English *nine,* e.g., **nuevo, canto.**
ñ	Like *ni* in English *onion* or *ny* in English *canyon,* e.g., **cañón, paño.**
p	Like *p* in English *parent,* e.g., **pipa, pollo.**
q	Like *c* in English *coal.* This letter is only used in the combinations *que* and *qui* in which the *u* is silent, e.g., **queso, aquí.**
r	At the beginning of a word and when preceded by *l, n,* or *s,* it is strongly trilled, e.g., **roca.** In all other positions, it is pronounced with a single tap of the tongue, e.g., **era, padre.**
rr	Strongly trilled, e.g., **carro, arriba.**
s	Like *s* in English *so,* e.g., **cosa, das.**
t	Like *t* in English *tip* but generally softer, e.g., **toma.**
v	Like *v* in English *mauve,* but in many parts of Spain and the Americas, like the Spanish **b,** e.g., **variar.**
x	Generally like *x* in English *expand,* e.g., **examen.** Before a consonant, it is sometimes pronounced like *s* in English *so,* e.g., **excepción, extensión.** In the word **México,** and in other place names of that country, it is pronounced like the Spanish **j.**

Letter	Approximate sound
y	When used as a consonant between vowels or at the beginning of a word, like the *y* in English *yet*, e.g., **yate**, **yeso**, **hoyo**.
z	Like Spanish c when it precedes e or i, e.g., **azul**.

A

a *prep.* to [governing the indirect object]. *2* at, by, in, on, to, after, like, etc.

abad *m.* abbot.

abadía *f.* abbey. *2* abbacy.

abajo *adv.* down. *2* below, under. *3* downstairs.

abandonar *t.* to abandon, leave. *2* to give up. *3 ref.* to neglect oneself.

abanicar *t.* to fan. *2 ref.* to fan oneself.

abanico *m.* fan.

abarcar *t.* to clasp, grasp, embrace, comprise, include.

abarrotar *t.* to cram, pack, stow; to overstock.

abastecer *t.* to provision, purvey, supply. ¶ CONJUG. like *agradecer*.

abastecimiento *m.* supply, provision, purveyance.

abatir *t.* to bring down. throw down, overthrow. *2* dishearten. *3* to be disheartened.

abeja *f.* ENT. bee, honeybee: ~ **reina**, queen-bee.

abertura *f.* opening, aperture, hole, slit. gap.

abeto *m.* BOT. fir, silver fir; spruce.

abierto, ta *p. p.* of ABRIR; opened. *2* open. *3* sincere, frank.

abismo *m.* abysm, abyss, gulf.

abnegación *f.* abnegation, self-denial.

abogado *m.* advocate, lawyer, barrister.

abonar *t.* to approve. *2* to guarantee. *3* to improve. *4* to manure. *5* COM. to credit; to discount; to pay. *6 t.-ref.* to subscribe [for].

abono *m.* payment. *2* fertilizer. *3* subscription.

aborrecer *t.* to abhor, hate. ¶ CONJUG. like agradecer.

abrasar *t.* to burn, sear, scorch, parch. *2 ref.* to swelter, feel very hot.

abrazar *t.* to embrace, hug, clasp. *2* to include. *3 ref.* to embrace, hug each other.

abrazo *m.* hug, embrace, clasp.

abrigar *t.* to cover, wrap. *2* to shelter. *3* to entertain, harbour [fears, hopes, etc.]. 4 *ref.* to take shelter.

abrigo *m.* protection against the cold, keeping warm. 2 shelter. 3 protection. 4 overcoat, wrap.

abril *m.* April.

abrir *t.* to open. 2 to unfasten, uncover, unlock, unseal. 3 to split. 4 to head, lead [a procession, etc.]. 5 ~ **paso**, to make way. 6 *t.-ref.* to spread out, unfold. 7 to split, burst open. 8 [of flowers] to b l o s s o m . ¶ P a s t . p.: *abierto*.

absoluto, ta *a.* absolute. 2 *en* ~, absolutely, by no means.

absurdo, da *a.* absurd. 2 *m.* absurdity, nonsense.

abuela *f.* grandmother.

abuelo *m.* grandfather. 2 ancestor. 3 *pl.* grandparents.

abundancia *f.* abundance, plenty.

aburrido, da *a.* bored, weary. 2 boring, tedious, irksome.

aburrir *t.* to annoy, bore. 2 *ref.* to get bored.

abusar *i.* to abuse. 2 ~ **de**, to abuse [misuse, make bad use of]; to take undue advantage of.

abuso *m.* abuse [misuse, bad use].

acá *adv.* here, over here, hither, this way, this side: ~ *y acullá*, here and there.

acabar *t.-i.* to finish, end: ~ *con*, to obtain; to destroy, put an end to; ~ *en*, to end in; ~ *por*, to end by. 2 *t.* to kill. 3 *i.* to die. 4 *ref.* to end, be over. 5 *acaba de llegar*, he has just arrived.

academia *f.* academy.

académico, ca *a.* academic(al. 2 *m.* academic. 3 academician.

acariciar *t.* to caress, fondle. 2 to cherish [hopes, etc.].

acaso *m.* chance, hazard. 2 *adv.* by chance; perhaps.

acceder *i.* to accede, agree, consent.

accidente *m.* accident.

acción *f.* action, act. 2 COM. share, stock. 3 THEAT. plot.

aceite *m.* olive oil.

aceituna *f.* olive [fruit].

acento *m.* accent. 2 stress.

acentuar *t.* to accent, stress. 2 to emphasize.

aceptar *t.* to accept, receive.

acera *f.* pavement, sidewalk.

acerca de *adv.* about, concerning, with regard to.

acercamiento *m.* approach, approximation.

acercar *t.* to bring or place near. 2 *ref.* to come near.

acero *m.* steel.

acertar *t.* to hit [the mark]. 2 to guess. 3 to do well, right; to succeed [in]. 4 *i.* to happen, chance. ¶ CONJUG. INDIC. Pres.: *acierto, aciertas aciertα; aciertan.* | SUBJ. Pres.: *acierte, aciertes, acierte; acierten.* | IMPER: *acierta, acierte; acierten.*

ácido, da *a.* acid, sour, tart. 2 *a.-m.* CHEM. acid.

acierto *m.* good aim, hit. 2 good guess. 3 wisdom, prudence. 4 success.

aclamar *t.* to acclaim, cheer, hail, applaud.

aclarar *t.* to clear, clarify. 2 to rinse. 3 to explain. 4 *i.* to clear up. 5 to dawn. 6 *ref.* to become clear.

acoger *t.* to receive, admit. *2* to shelter. *3 ref.* to take refuge [in]; to resort [to].

acomodar *t.* to accommodate.

acompañar *t.* to accompany, go with. *2* to enclose.

acongojar *t.* to grieve. *2 ref.* to feel anguish.

aconsejar *t.* to advise, counsel. *2 ref.* to take advice.

acontecer *impers.* to happen, occur, befall. ¶ CONJUG. like *agradecer*.

acontecimiento *m.* event, happening, occurrence.

acordar *t.* to decide. *2* MUS. to attune. *3 i.* to agree. *4 ref.* to come to an agreement. *5 acordarse de*, to remember. ¶ CONJUG. like *contar*.

acorde *a.* agreeing. *2* in harmony. *3 m.* MUS. chord.

acostar *t.* to put to bed; to lay down. *2 ref.* to go to bed. ¶ CONJUG. like *contar*.

acostumbrar *tr.* to accustom. *2 i.* to be accustomed, be used [to]. *3 ref.* to get used [to].

acreditado, da *a.* reputable, well-known.

acreditar *t.* to accredit. *2* to prove to be. *3* to bring fame or credit to. *4 ref.* to win credit.

actitud *f.* attitude.

actividad *f.* activity.

activo, va *a.* active. *2 m.* COM. assets.

acto *m.* act, action, deed: *en el ~*, at once. *2* ceremony, meeting, public function. *3* act [of a play].

actor *m.* THEAT. actor.

actriz *f.* actress.

actuación *f.* action [of any agent], performance. *2 pl.* law proceedings.

actual *a.* present, current, of the day.

actualidad *f.* present time. *2* current events. *3 pl.* CINEM. news-reel.

acuático, ca *a.* aquatic, water.

acudir *i.* to go or come [to]. *2* to frequent.

acueducto *m.* aqueduct.

acuerdo *m.* accord, agreement, understanding: *estar de ~*, to agree; *de común ~*, by mutual agreement. *2* resolution [of a meeting].

acusación *f.* accusation, charge, impeachment.

acusado, da *a. m.-f.* accused, defendant.

acusar *t.* to accuse, charge [with]. *2* to acknowledge.

adaptar *t.-ref.* to adapt, fit, suit, accommodate.

adecuado, da *a.* adequate, fit, suitable.

adelantar *t.* to advance. *2 t.-ref.* to be in advance of; to get ahead of. *3 i.* [of a clock] to be fast. *4* to improve.

adelante *adv.* forward, ahead, onward: *en ~*, henceforth. *3 interj.* come in!

adelanto *m.* progress, improvement. *2* advance.

ademán *m.* gesture; attitude. *2 pl.* manners.

además *adv.* moreover, besides. *2 ~ de*, besides.

adentro *adv.* within, inside, indoors.

adiós *interj.* good-bye!

adivinanza *f.* ADIVINACIÓN. *2* ACERTIJO.

adivinar *t.* to divine, guess, foresee. *2* to solve [a riddle].

adjetivo, va *a.-n.* adjective.

administración *f.* administration, management.

administrador, ra *m.-f.* administrator, manager, steward, trustee.

administrar *t.* to administer, manage.

admirable *a.* admirable. *2* -mente *adv.* admirably.

admiración *f.* admiration. *2* wonder, astonishment. *3* exclamation mark (!).

admirar *t.* to admire. *2 ref.* to be astonished.

admitir *t.* to admit. *2* to accept.

adonde *adv.* where.

adoptar *t.* to adopt.

adoración *f.* worship.

adornar *t.* to adorn, decorate, embellish, garnish.

adorno *m.* adornment, ornament, decoration.

adquirir *t.* to acquire. *2* to buy ¶ CONJUG. INDIC. Pres.: *adquiero, adquieres, adquiere; adquieren.* ‖ SUBJ. Pres.: *adquiera, adquieras, adquiera; adquieran.* ‖ IMPER.: *adquiere, adquiera, adquieran.*

aduana *f.* custom-house.

adulto, ta *a.-n.* adult, grown-up.

adverbio *m.* GRAM. adverb.

adversario, ria *m.-f.* adversary, opponent; foe.

advertir *t.* to notice, realize. *2* to advise, to warn. ¶ CONJUG. like *discernir*.

aéreo, a *a.* aerial. *2 correo ~,* air-mail.

aeroplano *m.* aeroplane, airplane.

aeropuerto *m.* airport.

afán *m.* anxiety, eagerness, ardour; desire.

afanar *ref.* to toil, labour, strive.

afectar *t.* to affect *2 ref.* to be affected.

afecto, ta *a.* fond. *2 m.* affection, love.

afición *f.* fondness, liking. *2* hobby.

aficionado, da *m.-f.* amateur. *2* fan, devotee.

aficionar *ref.* to grow fond of, take a liking to.

afilar *t.* to sharpen, grind, whet, point; to taper.

afirmar *t.* to make firm, secure, steady. *2* to affirm, say. *3 ref.* to steady oneself.

aflicción *f.* affliction, grief, sorrow, distress.

afligir *t.* to afflict. *2 ref.* to grieve.

afortunado, da *a.* lucky, fortunate, happy.

afrontar *t.* to confront, face.

afuera *adv.* out, outside. *2 f. pl.* outskirts, environs.

agachar *t.* to lower. *2 ref.* to stoop; to crouch, squat.

agarrar *t.* to seize, take, catch; grasp. *2 ref.* **agarrarse a,** to take hold of.

agencia *f.* agency.

agente *m.* agent. *2 ~ de cambio y bolsa,* stockbroker; *~ de policía,* policeman.

ágil *a.* agile, nimble, quick.

agitación *f.* agitation, flurry, flutter, excitement.

agitar *t.* to agitate; to flurry, excite. *2* to shake, stir. *3 ref.* to be agitated.

agosto *m.* August.

agotar *t.* to exhaust, work out, sell out, tire out. 2 *ref.* run out: to be sold out.

agradable *a.* agreeable, pleasant, enjoyable.

agradar *t.* to please: to suit: *esto me agrada.* I like this.

agradecer *t.* to thank for, be grateful for. ¶ CONJUG. INDIC. Pres.: *agradezco, agradeces, etc.* ‖ SUBJ. Pres.: *agradezca, agradezcas, etc.* ‖ IMPER.: *agradezca, agradezcamos, agradezcan.*

agradecimiento *m.* gratitude, thankfulness.

agrado *m.* affability. 2 pleasure, liking.

agregar *t.* to add, join.

agricultor, ra *m.-f.* farmer.

agricultura *f.* agriculture, farming.

agrio, gria *a.* sour. 2 bitter [orange]. 3 rough. 4 tart.

agrupar *t.* to group.

agua *f.* water: ~ *dulce*, fresh water; ~ *salada*, salt water.

aguantar *t.* to bear, endure, suffer. 2 *ref.* to restrain oneself.

aguardar *t.* to wait [for]; to expect, await.

agudo, da *a.* acute [sharp; keen]. 2 witty. 3 oxytone [word].

águila *f.* eagle.

aguinaldo *m.* Christmas gift.

aguja *f.* needle. 2 hand [of clock]. 3 steeple. 4 *pl.* RLY. switch.

agujero *m.* hole.

ahí *adv.* there.

ahogar *t.* to choke, stifle, smother, suffocate, strangle, quench. 2 to drown. 3 *ref.* to be choked, drowned.

ahora *adv.-conj.* now; at present; *por* ~, for the present.

ahorcar *t.* to hang.

ahorrar *t.* to save, spare.

ahorro *m.* saving, economy, thrift. 2 *pl.* savings.

aire *m.* air *al* ~ *libre*, in the open air. 2 appearance.

aislar *t.* to isolate, insulate. 2 *ref.* to seclude oneself.

¡ajá! *interj.* aha!, good!

ajeno, na *a.* another's, alien, strange. 2 foreign [to].

ajuar *m.* household furniture. 2 trousseau.

ajustar *t.* to adjust, fit. 2 to make [an agreement]. 3 to settle [accounts]. 4 *i.* to fit tight. 6 *ref.* to conform [to].

al *contr.* of. A & EL.

ala *f.* wing. 2 brim [of a hat]. 3 flap [of a table].

alabanza *f.* praise.

alabar *t.* to praise, extol. 2 *ref.* to boast.

alacrán *m.* ZOOL. scorpion.

alambre *m.* wire.

alameda *f.* poplar grove. 2 avenue, mall.

alargar *t.* to lengthen, extend, prolong. 2 to stretch out.

alarma *f.* alarm.

alarmar *t.* to alarm 2 *ref.* to be alarmed.

alba *f.* dawn.

albañil *m.* mason, bricklayer.

albergar *t.* to shelter, lodge. harbour. 2 *ref.* to take shelter; to lodge.

albergue *m.* shelter, lodging, harbour, refuge.

alborotar *t.* to disturb. *2 ref.* to get excited. *3* to riot.

alboroto *m.* uproar, noise. *2* riot.

álbum *m.* album.

alcalde *m.* Mayor, Lord Mayor; head of a town council.

alcaldía *f.* Mayoralty. *2* the Mayor's office.

alcance *m.* overtaking. *2* reach: *al ~ de uno*, within one's reach. *3* range, consequence. *4* understanding.

alcanzar *t.* to overtake, catch up with. *2* to reach. *3* to get, obtain. *4* to understand. *5 i.* to reach [to]. *6* to be sufficient [to or for].

alcoba *f.* alcove, bedroom.

alcohol *m.* alcohol. *2* kohl.

aldaba *f.* door-knocker.

aldea *f.* hamlet, village.

aldeano, na *m.-f.* villager, countryman, countrywoman.

alegar *t.* to allege, plead.

alegrar *t.* to cheer, gladden. *2* to brighten, enliven. *3 ref.* to be glad. *4* to rejoice, cheer.

alegre *a.* glad, joyful. *2* cheerful, merry, jolly. *3* bright, gay. *4* tipsy.

alegría *f.* joy, pleasure. *2* glee, mirth, merriment.

alejar *t.* to remove to a distance, to move away. *2* to separate, estrange. *3 ref.* to go or move away.

aleluya *m.* or *f.* hallelujah. *2 f. pl.* doggerel.

alemán, na *a.-n.* German.

alentar *i.* to breathe. *2 t.* to encourage, cheer, hearten. ¶ CONJUG. like *acertar*.

alerta *adv.* on the watch, on the alert. *2 interj.* look out! *3 m.* sentinel's call.

alfabeto *m.* alphabet.

alfiler *m.* pin.

alfombra *f.* floor carpet, rug.

algo *pron.* something. *2 adv.* somewhat.

algodón *m.* cotton.

alguien *pron.* somebody, someone.

algún *a.* ALGUNO.

alguno, na *a.* some, any: *~ vez*, sometimes. *2 pron.* someone, anyone, somebody, anybody.

aliado, da *a.* allied. *2 m.-f.* ally.

alianza *f.* alliance, league.

aliar *t.-ref.* to ally.

aliento *m.* breath, breathing. *2* spirit, courage.

alimentación *f.* food, feeding, nourishment.

alimentar *t.* to feed, nourish.

alimenticio, cia *a.* nutritious, nourishing.

alimento *m.* aliment, food, nourishment. *2* pabulum.

aliviar *t.* to lighten. *2* to alleviate, allay. *3 ref.* to get better.

alivio *m.* alleviation, allay; relief.

alma *f.* soul. *2* core, heart.

almacén *m.* store, warehouse, shop. *2* depot; magazine.

almacenar *t.* to store, store up, lay up. *2* to hoard.

almanaque *m.* almanac, calendar.

almendra *f.* BOT. almond: *~ garapiñada*, praline.

almidón *m*. starch.

almirante *m*. NAV. admiral.

almohada *f*. pillow, bolster; cushion. 2 pillow-slip.

almorzar *i*. to breakfast; to lunch.

almuerzo *m*. breakfast, lunch.

alojar *t*. to lodge, quarter, billet. 2 *ref*. to put up.

alondra *f*. ORN. lark, skylark.

alquilar *t*. to let, rent; to hire.

alrededor *adv*. ~ *de*, around, about.

alrededores *m. pl*. outskirts, surroundings.

alterar *t*. to alter, change. 2 to excite, unsettle. 3 to disturb, upset. 4 *ref*. to become altered, changed.

altercar *t*. to altercate, dispute, wrangle.

alternar *t.-i*. to alternate. 2 *i*. to mix.

altivo, va *a*. haughty, proud.

alto, ta *a*. high. 2 tall. 3 upper. 4 noble, excellent. 5 loud. 6 *m*. height, hillock. 7 halt, stop. 8 *interj*. halt!, stop!

altura *f*. height, hillock. 2 height, tallness. 3 summit, top. 4 elevation, excellence.

aludir *i*. to allude, refer to, hint at.

alumbrado *m*. lighting, lights: ~ *público*, public lighting.

alumbrar *t*. to light, illuminate, enlighten. 2 *i*. to be delivered, give birth.

alumno, na *m.-f*. pupil.

alzar *t*. to raise, lift, hoist, uplift. 2 to erect, build. 3 *ref*. to rise; to get up, stand up. 4 to rise, rebel.

allá *adv*. there; yonder: *más* ~, farther.

allí *adv*. there; yonder.

amable *a*. kind, nice, amiable, friendly. 2 lovable.

amado, da *m.-f*. love, loved one, beloved.

1) **amanecer** *i*. to dawn. 2 to be or appear at dawn. ¶ CONJUG. like *agradecer*.

2) **amanecer** *m.*, *amanecida* *f*. dawn, daybreak: *al* ~, at dawn.

amante *a*. loving, fond. 2 *m.-f*. lover. 3 paramour; mistress.

amapola *f*. BOT. corn poppy.

amar *t*. to love. 2 to like, be fond of.

amargo, ga *a*. bitter. 2 sour [temper].

amargura *f*. bitterness. 2 sorrow, grief.

amarillento, ta *a*. yellowish. 2 sallow, pale.

amarillo, lla *a.-m*. yellow.

amarrar *t*. to tie, fasten; rope.

ambición *f*. ambition, aspiration.

ambicioso, sa *a*. ambitious, covetous, eager.

ambiente *a.-m*. ambient. 2 *m*. atmosphere, setting.

ambos, bas *a.-pron*. both.

ambulancia *f*. ambulance.

amenaza *f*. threat, menace.

amenazar *t*. to threaten, menace. 2 *i*. to be impending.

americano, na *a.-m*. American.

ametralladora *f*. machinegun.

amigo, ga *a*. friendly. 2 *m.-f*. friend. 4 *m*. lover.

amistad *f*. friendship.

amistoso, sa *a*. friendly, amicable.

amo *m*. master, landlord, proprietor, owner. *2* boss.

amontonar *t*. to heap, pile, hoard. *2 ref*. to heap, be piled; to crowd, throng.

amor *m*. love, affection: ~ *propio*, self-esteem, conceit.

amoroso, sa *a*. loving, affectionate. *2* amorous, of love.

amparar *t*. to protect, shelter.

amparo *m*. protection, shelter, support.

amplio, plia *a*. ample, extensive. *2* roomy, wide. *3* large.

amueblar *t*. AMOBLAR.

análisis *m*. analysis. *2* GRAM. parsing.

anaranjado, da *a.-n.* orange colo(u)r.

anarquía *f*. anarchy.

anciano, na *a*. old, aged. *2 m.-f.* old man or woman; ancient; elder.

ancla *f*. NAUT. anchor.

ancho, cha *a*. broad, wide. *2* lax, elastic [conscience].

andaluz, za *a.-n.* Andalusian.

andante *a*. walking. *2* [knight-] errant. *3* MUS. andante.

1) **andar** *i*. to walk, go, move; to ride. *2* [of a clock] to go; [of a machine] to run, work. ¶ CONJUG. INDIC. Pret.: *anduve, anduviste*, etc. ‖ SUBJ. Imperf.: *anduviera, anduvieras*, etc., or *anduviese, anduvieses*, etc. | Fut.: *anduviere, anduvieres*, etc.

2) **andar** *m*. gait, pace.

andrajoso, sa *a*. ragged, in tatters.

anécdota *f*. anecdote.

angosto, ta *a*. narrow.

ángulo *m*. GEOM. angle.

angustia *f*. anguish, affliction, distress.

angustiar *t*. to afflict, distress, worry.

anhelar *i*. to pant, gasp. *2 t*. to desire, long for.

anhelo *m*. longing, yearning, desire.

anidar *i*. to nest, nestle.

anillo *m*. ring, circlet, finger ring.

ánima *f*. [human] soul.

animación *f*. animation, liveliness, life. *3* bustle, movement, crowd.

animal *a*. animal. *2* stupid. *3 m*. animal. *4* fig. blockhead.

animar *t*. to animate. *2* to cheer up. *3* to encourage, decide. *4* to enliven, brighten. *5 ref*. to take heart.

ánimo *m*. mind, spirit. *2* courage. *3* intention, purpose. *4* interj. *¡ánimo!*, cheer up!

anís *m*. anise. *2* anissette.

aniversario *m*. anniversary.

anoche *adv*. last night.

1) **anochecer** *i*. to grow dark. ¶ CONJUG. like *agradecer*.

2) **anochecer** *m*., **anochecida** *f*. nightfall, dusk, evening.

anotación *f*. annotation. *2* note, entry.

anotar *t*. to write, note down.

ansia *f*. throe, anguish, pang. *2* eagerness, longing.

ansiedad *f*. anxiety, uneasiness, worry.

1) **ante** *m*. ZOOL. elk, moose. *2* muff [leather], buckskin.

2) **ante** *prep.* before, in the presence of. *2 ~ todo*, first of all; above all.

anteayer *adv.* the day before yesterday.

antemano (de) *adv.* beforehand.

anteojo *m.* spyglass. *2 pl.* binocular. *3* spectacles.

antepasado, da *a.* foregone. *2 m.* ancestor, forefather.

anterior *a.* anterior, foregoing, former, previous.

antes *adv.* before, first, previously, formerly. *2* sooner, rather. *3* conj. *antes*, or *~ bien*, rather.

anticipar *t.* to anticipate, advance, hasten. *2 ref. anticiparse a*, to anticipate, forestall.

antigüedad *f.* antiquity. *2* seniority. *3 pl.* antiques.

antiguo, gua *a.* ancient, old; antique.

antipático, ca *a.* disagreeable; uncongenial, unpleasant.

antojarse *ref.* to take a fancy to; to want, desire, long. *2* to think, imagine.

antorcha *f.* torch, flambeau.

anual *a.* annual, yearly. *2* **-mente** *adv.* annually, yearly.

anunciar *t.* to announce. *2* to indicate. *3* to advertise.

anuncio *m.* announcement, notice. *2* advertisement.

anzuelo *m.* fish-hook.

añadir *t.* to add, join.

año *m.* year: *~ bisiesto*, leap-year. *2 pl.* years, age: *tengo 20 años*, I'm 20 years old.

apacible *a.* gentle, mild. *2* placid, pleasant.

apadrinar *t.* to sponsor, act as godfather to; to act as second of [in a duel]. *2* to support.

apagar *t.* to extinguish, put out, turn out. *2* to quench. *3* soften [colours].

aparato *m.* apparatus, appliance, device, set. *2* machine, airplane. *3* exaggeration. *4* pomp, display, show.

aparcar *t.* to park [cars, etc.].

aparecer *i.-ref.* to appear, show up, turn up. ¶ CONJUG. like *agradecer*.

aparejar *t.* to prepare, get ready. *2* to saddle [horses, mules]. *3* NAUT. to rig, rig out.

aparición *f.* apparition, appearance. *2* ghost, vision.

apariencia *f.* appearance, aspect. *2* likelihood. *3* pretence, show. *4 guardar las apariencias*, to keep up appearances.

apartado, da *a.* retired, aloof; distant, out-of-the-way. *2 m.* post-office box. *3* section [of a law, bill, etc.].

apartamento *m.* apartment, flat.

apartar *t.* to separate, set apart. *2* to push, draw or turn aside; to remove, move away. *3 ref.* to move away.

aparte *a.* separate, other. *2 adv.* apart. aside. *3* separately. *4 m.* THEAT. aside. *5* paragraph: *punto y ~*, paragraph.

apasionar *t.* to excite strongly. *2 ref.* to become impassioned. *3* to become passionately fond [of].

apear t. to dismount, help down or out [from horse or carriage]. 2 to survey [land]. 3 ref. to dismount, alight.

apelación f. LAW appeal.

apelar i. LAW to appeal. 2 to have recourse to.

apellido m. surname.

apenado, da a. sorry, troubled.

apenas adv. scarcely, hardly. 2 no sooner than.

apetito m. appetite; hunger.

ápice m. apex, summit. 2 whit.

aplastar t. to flatten. 2 to crush. 3 ref. to become flat.

aplaudir t.-i. to applaud, clap [one's hands]. 2 to approve.

aplicación f. application. 2 sedulouness, studiousness.

aplicado, da a. applied. 2 studious, industrious, diligent.

aplicar t. to apply. 2 ref. to apply. 3 to devote oneself.

apoderar t. to empower, authorize. 2 ref. **apoderarse de**, to seize.

aportar t. to bring, contribute [as one's share].

aposento m. room, apartment.

apóstol m. apostle.

apoyar t. to rest, lean. 2 to support; to found. 3 to prove. 4 to prop. 5 i.-ref. to rest, lean [on]; to be supported [on or by]. 6 ref. to base oneself.

apoyo m. prop, stay, support. 2 protection, help. 3 basis.

apreciar t. to appraise, estimate, value. 2 to esteem, like. 3 to appreciate.

aprender t. to learn.

apresurar t. to hasten, hurry. 2 ref. to hurry up.

apretar t. to press, press down. 2 to tighten. 3 [of garments] to fit tight; [of shoes] to pinch. 4 to spur, urge. 5 ~ **el paso**, to quicken the pace. 6 i. ~ **a correr**, to start running. 7 ref. to crowd. ¶ CONJUG. like **acertar**.

aprisa adv. quickly, hurriedly.

aprobación f. approbation, approval; applause.

aprobar t. to approve. ¶ CONJUG. like **contar**.

apropiado, da a. fit, proper, appropriate.

aprovechar t. to utilize, make use of, benefit from, profit by, improve, spend profitably. 2 to use up [remaining material, etc.]. 3 i. to be useful. 4 ref. to avail oneself of, take advantage of.

aproximar t. to bring near. 2 ref. to approach, come near.

aptitud f. aptitude, fitness, ability, talent.

apuesta f. bet, wager.

apuntar t. to aim, level, point [a gun, etc.]. 2 to point out, indicate, mark. 3 to note, jot down, inscribe. 4 to stitch, pin or tack lightly. 5 THEAT. to prompt. 6 i. to break, dawn.

apuñalar t. to stab, poniard.

apurar t. to drain, use up, exhaust. 2 to hurry, press. 3 to worry, annoy. 4 ref. to get or be worried.

aquel m., **aquella** f. dem. a. sing. that. **aquellos** m., **aquellas** f. pl. those.

aquél m., **aquélla** f. dem. pron. sing. that one; the former.

aquello *neut.* that, that thing. **aquéllos** *m.*, **aquéllas** *f.* those [ones]; the former.

aquí *adv.* here. 2 now: *de ~ en adelante*, from now on. 3 then, at that moment.

arado *m.* AGR. plough, *plow.

araña *f.* ZOOL. spider. 2 chandelier, lustre.

arañar *t.* to scratch. 2 to scrape up.

arar *t.* to plough, plow.

árbitro *m.* arbiter. 2 arbitrator. 3 umpire, referee.

árbol *m.* BOT. tree. 2 MECH. shaft, axle. 3 NAUT. mast.

arboleda *f.* grove, wooded land.

arbusto *m.* BOT. shrub, bush.

arca *f.* coffer, chest, box. 2 strong-box, safe. 3 ark.

arcángel *m.* archangel.

arcilla *f.* clay.

arco *m.* GEOM., ELEC. arc. 2 ARCH., ANAT. arch. 3 METEOR. *~ iris*, rainbow.

arder *t.* to burn, blaze.

ardid *m.* stratagem, trick.

ardiente *a.* ardent, burning, hot. 2 passionate; fiery.

ardor *m.* ardour, heat. 2 eagerness, fervour. 3 courage.

área *f.* area [superficial extent]. 2 are [measure].

arena *f.* sand, grit. 2 arena, circus.

arenque *m.* ICHTH. herring.

argentino, na *m.-f.* Argentine, Argentinean.

argumentación *f.* argumentation, argument.

argumento *m.* argument. 2 plot [of a play, etc.].

árido, da *a.* barren, dry, arid.

aritmética *f.* arithmetic.

arma *f.* weapon, arm.

armada *f.* navy. 2 fleet.

armadura *f.* armo(u)r. 2 framework, truss.

armar *t.* to arm. 2 to fix [a bayonet]. 3 to fit out [a ship]. 4 to assemble, set up, mount. 5 to set [a trap]. 6 to make, stir up.

armario *m.* cupboard, wardrobe.

armonía *f.* harmony.

armonioso, sa *a.* harmonious.

aro *m.* hoop, ring, rim.

aroma *f.* aroma, fragance, scent.

arpa *f.* MUS. harp.

arquitectura *f.* architecture.

arrabal *m.* suburb. 2 *pl.* outskirts.

arrancar *t.* to uproot, pull out. 2 to pluck [feathers, hairs, etc.]. 3 *i.* to start. 6 to come [from].

arrastrar *t.* to drag, trail. 2 to carry away; to wash down. 4 *ref.* to crawl.

arrebatar *t.* to snatch. 2 to carry away. 3 *ref.* to be led away [by emotion].

arreglar *t.-ref.* to settle, arrange. 2 to put in order. 3 to dress, smarten up. 4 to mend, fix up.

arreglo *m.* rule, order. 2 arrangement. 3 settlement, agreement, compromise. 4 mending, fixing up. 5 *con ~ a*, according to.

arrepentimiento *m.* repentance; regret.

arrepentirse *ref.* to repent, regret. ¶ CONJUG. like *hervir*.

arrestar *t.* to arrest, imprison.

arriba *adv.* up, upwards; upstairs; above, on high, at the top, overhead: *cuesta ~*, up the hill; *de ~ abajo*, from top to bottom. 2 *interj.* up!

arribar *i.* to arrive. 2 NAUT. to put into port.

arriesgar *t.* to risk, hazard, venture. 2 *ref.* to expose oneself to danger. 3 to dare.

arrimar *t.* to bring close [to], place [against]. 2 to put away, shelve. 3 *ref. arrimarse a*, to go near; to lean against.

arrodillarse *ref.* to kneel [down].

arrojado, da *a.* bold, intrepid, dashing, rash.

arrojar *t.* to throw, fling. 2 to vomit. 5 to show [a total, a balance]. 6 *ref.* to throw oneself.

arrollar *t.* to roll, roll up. 2 to trample down run over.

arroyo *m.* brook, rivulet, stream. 2 gutter [in a street].

arroz *m.* BOT. rice.

arruga *f.* wrinkle, crease, crumple; line [on the face].

arrugar *t.* to wrinkle; to crease, crumple. 2 SEW. to gather, fold. 3 *~ la frente*, to frown.

arruinar *t.* to ruin. 2 *ref.* to become ruined, go «broke».

arrullo *m.* cooing. 2 lullaby.

arte *m.-f.* art: *bellas artes*, fine arts. 2 craft, skill; cunning.

artificial *a.* artificial.

artificio *m.* artifice, skill. 2 cunning, trick. 3 device.

artista *m.-f.* artist.

artístico, ca *a.* artistic.

as *m.* ace.

asaltar *t.* to assail, assault, storm. 2 to surprise, hold up.

asalto *m.* assault, storm. 3 BOX. round.

asamblea *f.* assembly, meeting.

asar *t.-ref.* to roast.

ascender *i.* to ascend, climb. 2 to accede. 3 to amount [to]. 4 to be promoted. ¶ CONJUG. like *entender*.

aseado, da *a.* clean, neat, tidy.

asegurar *t.* to secure. 2 to fasten. 3 to ensure. 4 to assure. 5 to assert. 6 COM. to insure. 7 *ref.* to make sure.

asentar *t.* to seat. 2 to place, establish. 3 to affirm. 4 to enter. 5 *ref.* to sit down. ¶ CONJUG. like *acertar*.

aseo *m.* cleanliness, tidiness. 2 cleaning, tidying: *cuarto de ~*, toilet-room.

asesinar *t.* to assassinate, murder.

asesinato *m.* assassination, murder.

asesino, na *a.* murderous. 2 *m.-f.* assassin, murderer.

así *adv.* so, thus, in this way. 2 in the same manner, as well. 3 as soon: *~ que*, as soon as. 4 *a.* such. 5 *conj.* would that.

asiento *m.* seat [chair, etc.]. 2 sediment. 3 settlement.

asignación *f.* assignation. 2 allocation [of money], allowance.

asignar *t.* to assign, allot. 2 to assign, fix, appoint.

asignatura *f.* subject of study.

asilo *m.* asylum, shelter.

asimismo *adv.* in like manner, likewise, also.

asistencia *f.* attendance, presence. 2 assistance, aid.

asistir *i.* to attend, be present, go. 2 *t.* to assist, aid, help.

asno *m.* ass, donkey, jackass.

asociación *f.* association.

asociar *t.* to associate. 2 *ref.* to associate, become associated.

asolar *t.* to raze, level with the ground, lay waste, desolate. ¶ CONJUG. like *contar.*

asomar *i.* to begin to appear. 2 *t.* to show, put out [through, behind or over an opening or a wall]. 3 *ref.* to peep out, put one's head out, look out.

asombrar *t.* to frighten. 2 to amaze, astonish. 3 *ref.* to be astonished, amazed.

asombro *m.* fright. 2 amazement, astonishment.

aspecto *m.* aspect, look, appearance.

áspero, ra *a.* rough. 2 harsh. 3 sour, tart. 4 rude, gruff.

aspirar *t.* to inhale, breathe in. 2 to suck, draw in. 3 *i.* ~ *a*, to aspire after or to.

astilla *f.* chip, splinter.

astro *m.* star, heavenly body.

astucia *f.* astuteness, cunning. 2 trick, stratagem.

asumir *t.* to assume, take upon oneself.

asunto *m.* matter subject, theme. 2 affair, business.

asustar *t.* to frighten, scare. 2 *ref.* to be frightened, take fright.

atacar *t.* to attack. 2 to assail. 3 to impugn. 4 to ram, tamp.

ataque *m.* attack. 2 impugnation. 3 fit, access, stroke.

atar *t.* to tie, lace, knot, bind.

1) **atardecer** *impers.* to get or grow dark.

2) **atardecer** *m.* evening, nightfall.

atención *f.* attention. 2 civility, kindness. 3 *pl.* affairs, duties.

atender *i.-t.* to attend, pay attention. 2 to heed. 3 to take care [of]. 4 *t.* to listen to. ¶ CONJUG. like *entender.*

atentado *m.* crime. 2 murder or attempted murder.

atento, ta *a.* attentive. 2 polite, courteous.

aterrizar *t.* AER. to land.

atleta *m.* athlete.

atlético, ca *a.* athletic. 2 robust.

atletismo *m.* athletics.

atmósfera *f.* atmosphere, air.

atómico, ca *a.* atomic.

atormentar *t.* to torment. 2 to torture. 3 *ref.* to torment oneself, worry.

atracción *f.* attraction, appeal.

atractivo, va *a.* attractive. 2 *m.* charm, grace. 3 inducement, attraction.

atraer *t.* to attract, draw. 2 to lure, allure. 3 to charm, captivate. ¶ CONJUG. like *traer.*

atrás *adv.* back, backward(s), behind.

atrasado, da *a.* behindhand. 2 backward. 4 slow.

atravesar *t.* to cross. 2 to pierce. to pass through. ¶ CONJUG. like *acertar.*

atreverse *ref.* to dare, venture, risk.

atrevido, da *a.* daring, bold.

atribuir *t.* to attribute, ascribe. 2 *ref.* to assume. ¶ Conjug. like **huir**.

atrio *m.* courtyard, patio; entrance hall; portico.

atropellar *t.* to run over, trample. 2 to knock down. 3 to outrage. 4 *ref.* to be hasty.

aturdir *t.* to stun, deafen. 2 to make giddy. 3 to rattle, bewilder. 4 to amaze.

audaz, *pl.* **audaces** *a.* audacious, bold, daring.

audición *f.* audition, hearing. 2 concert.

audiencia *f.* audience [formal interview]. 2 Spanish provincial high court.

auditor *m.* judge advocate.

aula *f.* class-room.

aumentar *t.-i.-ref.* to augment, increase, magnify. 2 *i.-ref.* to grow, grow larger.

aumento *m.* enlargement, increase, advance.

aun *adv.* even, still: ~ **cuando,** although.

aún *adv.* yet, as yet, still.

aunque *conj.* though, although.

ausencia *f.* absence. 2 lack.

ausentarse *ref.* to absent oneself; to be absent; to leave.

auto *m.* judicial decree, writ, warrant. 2 col. auto, car. 3 religious or biblical play. 4 *pl.* LAW proceedings.

autobús *m.* bus.

automático, ca *a.* automatic(al.

automóvil *m.* automobile, motor-car.

autor, ra *m.-f.* author, maker. 2. author, authoress [writer]. 3 perpetrator.

autoridad *f.* authority.

autorizar *t.* to authorize. 2 to empower. 3 to permit. 4 to legalize. 5 to approve.

autostop *m.* hitch-hiking: **hacer** ~, to hitch-hike.

1) **auxiliar** *t.* to help, assist.

2) **auxiliar** *a.* auxiliary. 2 *m.* assistant.

auxilio *m.* help, aid, assistance.

avance *m.* advance [going forward; payment beforehand].

avanzar *i.* to advance. 2 to improve, progress.

avariento, ta; avaro, ra *a.* avaricious, miserly, niggard. 2 *m.-f.* miser.

ave *f.* ORN. bird; fowl: ~ **de rapiña,** or **rapaz,** bird of prey.

avemaría *f.* Hail Mary.

avenida *f.* flood, freshet. 2 avenue.

aventura *f.* adventure. 2 hazard, chance, risk.

avergonzar *t.* to shame. 2 *ref.* to be ashamed. 3 to blush. ¶ Conjug. like **contar**.

averiguar *t.* to inquire, investigate, find out.

aviación *f.* aviation; air force.

aviador, ra *m.* aviator, airman, air pilot. 2 *f.* airwoman.

avión *m.* AER. airplane, aircraft.

avisar *t.* to inform. 2 to warn; to advise, admonish.

aviso *m.* notice, information; advice; warning.

avispa *f.* ENT. wasp.

¡ay! *interj.* alas!

ayer *adv.-m.* yesterday; lately; in the past.

ayuda *f.* help, aid, assistance.

ayudante *m.* aid, assistant. *2* MIL. aid, aide; adjutant.

ayudar *t.* to help, aid, assist.

ayuntamiento *m.* town council. *2* town hall.

azada *f.* AGR. hoe.

azar *m.* hazard, chance: *al* ~, at random, haphazard.

azotar *t.* to whip, flog; to flagellate. *2* to spank. *3* [of sea, rain, etc.] to beat, lash.

azote *m.* birch, thong, scourge, whip, etc.

azotea *f.* flat roof.

azúcar *m.-f.* sugar.

azucarar *t.* to sugar, sweeten.

azucena *f.* BOT. white lily.

azul *a.-m.* blue: ~ *celeste*, sky blue; ~ *marino*, navy blue.

B

bacalao *m*. cod-fish.

bacteria *f*. bacterium. 2 *pl*. bacteria.

bachillerato *m*. the Spanish certificate of secondary education.

bahía *f*. [sea] bay.

bailar *i*. to dance. 2 [of a top] to spin.

bailarín, na *a*. dancing. 2 *m.-f.* dancer.

baile *m*. dance; ball.

bajar *i*. to descend, come down, go down. 2 to fall. 3 to alight, get down. 4 *t*. to bring down, get down. 5 to lower, reduce [prices, etc.].

bajo *adv*. softly, in a low voice. 2 *prep*. beneath, under.

bajo, ja *a*. low. 2 short [not tall]. 3 lower: *la clase* ~, the lower classes. 4 *piso* ~, *planta baja*, ground floor. 5 *m*. hollow, deep. 6 shoal, sandbank. 7 bass.

bala *f*. bullet, ball, shot. 2 bale [of goods].

balancear *i.-ref*. to rock, swing, roll. 2 *i*. to hesitate, WAVER. 3 *t*. to balance.

balanza *f*. balance, [pair of] scales.

balar *i*. to bleat.

balcón *m*. balcony [of a house].

balón *m*. [a large, inflated] ball; a football. 2 bag. 3 CHEM. ballon.

baloncesto *m*. basket-ball.

balsa *f*. pool, pond. 2 NAUT. raft.

ballena *f*. whale. 2 whale-bone.

bambú *m*. bamboo.

banca *f*. COM. banking. 2 a card game. 3 bank [in gambling]. 4 bench.

banco *m*. bench, form; pew. 2 bench [work table]. 3 bank, shoal. 4 school [of fish]. 5 COM. bank.

banda *f*. scarf, sash. 2 band, strip. 3 band, gang; flock, herd. 4 side, border. 5 side [of ship]. 6 MUS, RADIO band. 7 CINEM. ~ *de sonido*, sound track.

bandada *f*. flock [of birds].

bandeja *f*. tray, salver.

bandera *f.* flag, banner, colours.

bandido *m.* outlaw. 2 bandit, highwayman.

banquete *m.* banquet, feast.

bañar *t.* to bathe. 2 to coat. 3 *ref.* to bathe, take a bath.

baño *m.* bath; bathing. 2 bathtub. 3 coating. 4 *pl.* bathing place. 5 spa.

bar *m.* bar, tavern.

baraja *f.* pack, deck [of cards].

barato, ta *a.* cheap. 2 *adv.* cheaply. 3 *m.* bargain sale.

barba *f.* chin. 2 beard, whiskers. 3 ~ *de ballena*, whalebone.

bárbaro, ra *a.* barbarian, barbaric, barbarous. 2 rude, cruel, savage. 3 coll. rash. 4 coll. enormous. 5 *m.-f.* barbarian.

barbería *f.* barber's shop.

barbero *m.* barber.

barbudo, da *a.* bearded, long-bearded.

barca *f.* boat, small boat: ~ *de pasaje*, ferry-boat.

barco *m.* boat, vessel, ship.

barómetro *m.* barometer.

barra *f.* bar. 2 MECH. lever, bar; beam, rod. 3 ingot. 4 bar, rail [in law-court]. 5 sand-bar. 6 ~ *de labios*, lipstick.

barraca *f.* cabin, hut, shanty. 2 farmhouse [in Valencia].

barrer *t.* to sweep. 2 NAUT. to rake [with a volley, etc.].

barriada *f.* city ward or district; suburb.

barriga *f.* belly.

barril *m.* barrel, keg.

barrio *m.* town ward, quarter or district: ~ *extremo*, suburb; *barrios bajos*, slums; fig. *el otro* ~, the other world.

barro *m.* mud, clay: ~ *cocido*, terra-cotta. 2 *pl.* pimples [on the face].

basar *t.* to base, found. 2 *ref.* to be based upon.

base *f.* basis, base: *a* ~ *de*, on the basis of.

bastante *a.* enough, sufficient. 2 *adv.* enough, fairly, rather; pretty.

bastar *i.* to suffice, be enough.

bastón *m.* cane, walking-stick.

basura *f.* rubbish, garbage, sweepings, refuse.

bata *f.* dressing-gown. 2 white coat [for doctors, etc.].

batalla *f.* battle. 2 joust, tournament.

batería *f.* battery: ~ *de cocina*, kitchen utensils.

batir *t.* to beat, strike. 2 to batter, beat down. 3 [of water, etc.] to beat, dash against. 4 to flap [wings]. 5 to beat [a metal] into sheets. 6 to coin [money]. 7 to beat, defeat. 8 *ref.* to fight.

baúl *m.* luggage trunk; ~ *mundo*, Saratoga trunk.

bautismo *m.* baptism; christening.

bautizar *t.* to baptize, christen. 2 to name. 3 to water [wine].

beber *t.-ref.* to drink.

bebida *f.* drink; beverage.

becerro *m.* calf, young bull. 2 calfskin. 3 ~ *marino*, seal.

belleza *f.* beauty.

bello, lla *a.* beautiful, fair, fine, handsome, lovely.

bellota *f.* BOT. acorn.

bendecir *t.* to bless.

bendición *f.* benediction, blessing. *2 pl.* wedding ceremony.

bendito, ta *a.* sainted, holy, blessed. *2* happy. *3 m.* simple-minded soul.

beneficiar *t.* to benefit. *2* to cultivate, improve [land]; to exploit, work [a mine]. *3 ref.* to benefit, profit.

beneficio *m.* benefaction. *2* benefit, advantage, profit. *3* cultivation [of land]; exploitation [of mines].

beneficioso, sa *a.* beneficial, profitable, advantageous.

berenjena *f.* egg-plant.

besar *t.* to kiss. *2 ref.* to kiss [one another]. *3* to collide.

beso *m.* kiss. *2* bump [collision].

bestia *f.* beast. *2* boor, idiot.

Biblia *f.* Bible.

bíblico, ca *a.* Biblical.

biblioteca *f.* library.

bicicleta *f.* bicycle.

1) **bien** *adv.* well, properly, right, perfectly, happily. *2* willingly, readily: *yo ~ lo haría, pero...*, I'd willingly do it, but... *3* very much, a good deal, fully, enough. *4* easily: *~ se ve que...*, it is easy to see that... *5 ~... ~*, either... or. *6 ahora ~*, now then. *7 ~ que*, although. *8 más ~*, rather. *9 no ~*, as soon as. *10 si ~*, although. *11 y ~*, well, now then.

2) **bien**, *pl.* **bienes** *m.* good [as opposed to evil]: *hombre de ~*, honest man. *2* good, wel-

fare, benefit: *hacer ~*, to do good; *en ~ de*, for the sake of. *3 fig. mi ~*, my dearest, my love. *4 pl.* property, possessions, estate: *bienes inmuebles* or *raíces*, real estate; *bienes muebles*, movables, personal property.

bienaventurado, da *a.* happy, blessed. *2* simple, guileless.

bienestar *m.* well-being, comfort.

bienhechor, ra *a.* beneficent, beneficial. *2 m.* benefactor. *3 f.* benefactress.

bigote *m.* m(o)ustache. *2* whiskers [of cat].

billar *m.* billiards. *2* billiards-table. *3* billiards-room, hall.

billete *m.* note, short letter. *2* love-letter. *3* ticket [railway, theatre, lottery, etc.]. *4 ~de banco*, bank-note.

bisabuelo, la *m.-f.* great-grandfather; great-grandmother. *2 m. pl.* great-grandparents.

bistec *m.* beefsteak.

bizco, ca *a.* squint-eyed, cross-eyed.

bizcocho *m.* biscut, hardtack. *2* sponge cake.

blanco, ca *a.* white, hoary. *2* white, pale. *3* fair [complexion]. *4* white [race, person, metal]. *5 m.-f.* white person. *6 m.* white colour. *7* target, mark. *8* aim, goal. *9* gap, interval. *10* blank, blank space. *10* white [of eye].

blando, da *a.* soft, bland. *2* gentle, mild. *3* delicate.

blanquear *t.* to whiten. *2* to whitewash. *3 i.* to whiten, turn white.

bloque *m.* block [of stone. etc.].

blusa *f.* blouse.

bobo, ba *a.* silly. foolish. 2 *m.-f.* fool. dunce. booby.

boca *f.* mouth [of man or animals]: *no decir esta ~ es mía*. not to say a word; *oscuro como la ~ del lobo*. pitch-dark: *~ abajo*. face downwards; *~ arriba*. face upwards. 2 mouth. entrance. opening: *~ de un río*. mouth of a river. 3 muzzle [of a gun].

bocado *m.* mouthful [of food]. morsel: *~ de rey*. tit-bit. delicacy. 2 bit [of the bridle].

bocina *f.* MUS. horn. 2 auto-horn. 3 megaphone.

boda *f.* marriage. wedding.

bodega *f.* cellar. wine-cellar. 2 wine shop. 3 pantry. 4 dock warehouse. 5 NAUT. hold [of a ship].

bola *f.* ball.

boletín *m.* bulletin.

boleto *m.* (Am.) ticket.

bolígrafo *m.* ball-point pen.

bolo *m.* skittle. ninepin. 2 dunce. idiot. 3 large pill.

bolsa *f.* bag. pouch. 2 purse. 3 bag. pucker [in cloth. etc.]. 4 stock exchange.

bolsillo *m.* pocket. 2 purse.

bomba *f.* pump: *~ aspirante*. suction pump. 2 bomb: *atómica*. atomic bomb; *noticia ~*. surprising news.

bombero *m.* fireman.

bombilla *f.* ELECT. light bulb.

bondad *f.* goodness. 2 kindness. good nature. 3 kindness. favour.

bondadoso, sa *a.* kind. good.

bonito, ta *a.* pretty. nice. dainty. 2 *m.* ICHTH. bonito.

bono *m.* COM. bond. certificate. debenture. 2 charity food-ticket; *~ del tesoro*. ex-chequer bill.

bordado *m.* embroidering; embroidery.

bordar *t.* to embroider.

borde *m.* border. edge. verge. brink. 2 hem.

borracho, cha *a.* drunk. intoxicated. 2 *m.-f.* drunken person. drunkard.

borrador *m.* draft. rough copy. 2 duster. eraser.

borrico, ca *m.* ass. donkey. 2 *f.* she-ass. 3 CARP saw-horse.

bosque *m.* forest. wood. grove. thicket; woodland.

bosquejar *t.* to sketch. outline.

bosquejo *m.* sketch. outline. rough plan or draft.

bota *f.* small. leather wine bag. 2 cask. 3 boot.

botar *t.* to throw. fling out. 2 to launch [a boat]. 3 *i.* to bound. bounce. 4 to jump.

bote *m.* NAUT. small boat: *~ salvavidas*. life-boat. 2 bound. bounce. 3 jar. pot. canister; tin can. 4 *de ~ en ~*. crowded. crammed with people.

botella *f.* bottle.

botica *f.* chemist's shop; *drug store.

botiquín *m.* medicine case; first-aid kit. 2 (Am.) retail wine store.

botón *m.* button [of garment. electric bell. etc.].

boxeador *m.* SPORT boxer.

boxear *i.* SPORT to box.

boxeo *m.* SPORT boxing.

bravo, va *a.* brave, courageous. *2* fine, excellent. *3* fierce, ferocious [animal]. *4* rough [sea, land]. *5* angry, violent. *6* magnificent.

brazalete *m.* bracelet, armlet.

brazo *m.* arm [of body, chair, lever, etc.]. *2* arm, power, might. *3* branch [of river]. *4* forelegs [of a quadruped]. *5* *pl.* hands, workers.

brea *f.* tar, wood tar. *2* NAUT. pitch.

breve *a.* short, brief. *2 f.* MUS. breve. *3 m.*, apostolic brief. *4 adv.* **en** ~, soon, shortly. *5* **-mente** *adv.* briefly, concisely.

brillante *a.* brilliant, shining, bright. *2* sparkling, glittering; glossy. *3 m.* brilliant [diamond]. *4* **-mente** *adv.* brilliantly.

brillar *i.* to shine. *2* to sparkle, glitter, be glossy. *3* to be outstanding.

brillo *m.* brilliance, brightness, lustre; splendour, shine.

brincar *i.* to spring, skip, leap, jump, hop.

brío *m.* strength, spirit, determination. *2* liveliness, nerve; valour, courage.

brioso, sa *a.* vigorous, spirited, lively.

brisa *f.* northeast wind. *2* breeze.

británico, ca *a.* British, Britannic.

broma *f.* fun, merriment; joke: *gastar una* ~ *a*, to play a joke on: *en* ~, in fun, jokingly; ~ *pesada*, practical joke.

bronce *m.* bronze.

brotar *i.* to germinate, sprout; to bud, burgeon, shoot. *2* [of water, tears, etc.] to spring, gush. *3* [of pimples, etc.] to break out. *4 t.* to put forth [plants, grass, etc.].

bruja *f.* witch, sorceress.

brújula *f.* magnetic needle, compass.

brusco, ca *a.* brusque, rude, gruff. *2* sudden. *3* sharp [curve].

bruto, ta *a.* brute, brutish. *2* stupid, ignorant. *3* rough, unpolished. *4 m.* brute, beast; blockhead.

bueno, na *a.* good. *2* kind. *3* fit, suitable. *4* well [in good health or condition]. *5 a buenas, por la buena,* willingly; *¡buena es ésta!*, that is a good one!; *buenos días*, good morning. *6 adv.* *¡bueno!*, well, very well; all right!

buey *m.* ZOOL. ox, bullock, steer: *carne de* ~, beef.

buharda, buhardilla *f.* dormer window. *2* garret, attic. *3* (Am.) skylight.

bulto *m.* volume, size, bulk *2* shade, form, body. *3* swelling, lump. *4* bundle, pack. *5 a* ~, broadly, roughly.

buque *m.* NAUT. ship, vessel: ~ *de cabotaje*, coaster; ~ *de guerra*, warship; ~ *de vapor*, steamer; ~ *de vela*, sailboat: ~ *cisterna*, tanker; ~ *mercante*, merchant ship. *2* hull [of a ship]. *3* capacity.

burla *f.* mockery, gibe, jeer, scoff: *hacer* ~ *de*, to mock, scoff, make fun of. *2* joke, jest: *de burlas*, in fun. *3* deception, trick.

burlar *t.* to mock. *2* to deceive, seduce. *3* to disappoint, frustrate, evade. *4* *i.-ref.* **burlarse de**, to make fun of, to laugh at: *burla, burlando*, without noticing it; on the quiet.

burro *m.* donkey, ass: *fig.* ~ *de carga*, strong, hardworking man. *2* ignorant, stupid man. *3* saw-horse.

buscar *t.* to look for, search for, seek. *2* to prospect.

butaca *f.* arm-chair. *2* THEAT. orchestra stalls.

C

caballería *f.* riding animal. *2* MIL. horse, cavalry. *3* knighthood: ~ *andante*, knight-errantry.

caballero, ra *a.* riding. *2 m.* ~ *andante*, knight-errant. *3* gentleman. *4* sir [form of address].

caballo *m.* ZOOL. horse. *2* knight [in chess]. *3* CARDS queen. *4* MECH. ~ *de fuerza* or *vapor*, horsepower. *5 a* ~, on horseback.

cabaña *f.* cabin, hut, hovel. *2* large number of sheep or cattle.

cabellera *f.* hair, head of hair. *2* wig. *3* tail [of a comet].

cabello *m.* hair [of the human head]. *2 pl.* hair, head of hair: ~ *de ángel*, sweetmeat.

caber *i.* to fit into, go in or into; to have enough room for; to befall. ¶ CONJUG. INDIC. Pres.: *quepo*, cabes, cabe, etc. | Pret.: *cupe, cupiste*, etc. | Fut.: *cabré, cabrás*, etc. ‖ COND.: *cabría, cabrías*, etc. ‖ SUBJ. Pres.: *quepa, quepas*, etc. | Imperf.: *cupiera, cupieras*, etc. or *cupiese, cupieses*, etc. | Fut.: *cupiere, cupieres*, etc. ‖ IMPER.: cabe, *quepa; quepamos*, cabed, *quepan*.

cabeza *f.* head, mind, understanding. *2* headwaters, source [of a river].

cable *m.* cable; rope, howser.

cabo *m.* end, extremity: *de* ~ *a rabo*, from head to tail. *2* end, termination: *llevar a* ~, to carry out. *3* bit, stump. *4* strand [of rope or thread]. *5* GEOG. cape. *6* MIL. corporal.

cabra *f.* ZOOL. goat.

cabrito *m.* kid.

cacao *m.* cacao [tree, seed]; cocoa [tree, powder, drink].

cacarear *i.* [of fowls] to cackle, crow. *2* coll. to boast, brag.

cacería *f.* hunt, hunting party.

cacerola *f.* casserole, saucepan.

cacique *m.* cacique, Indian chief. *2* political boss.

cacharro *m.* crock, piece of crockery. *2* rickety machine or car.

cachete *m*. slap [on the face]. 2 plump cheek.

cachorro, rra *m*.-*f*. puppy, cub.

cada *a*. each, every: ~ *cual*, ~ *uno*, each one, every one.

cadáver *m*. corpse, cadaver.

cadena *f*. chain: ~ *perpetua*, life imprisonment.

caer *i*.-*ref*. to fall, drop, fall down, come down; to fall off or out. 2 ~ *en la cuenta de*, to realize. 3 to lie, be located. 4 ~ *bien* or *mal*, to suit, fit, or not to suit, fit. ¶ CONJUG. INDIC. Pres.: *caigo, caes,* etc. | Pret.: caí, caíste, *cayó;* caímos, caísteis, *cayeron*. ‖ SUBJ. Pres.: *caiga, caigas,* etc. | Imperf.: *caiga, cayeras,* etc., or *cayese, cayeses,* etc. | Fut.: *cayere, cayeres,* etc. ‖ IMPER.: cae, *caiga; caigamos,* caed, *caigan*. ‖ GER.: *cayendo*.

café *m*. coffee [tree; seeds, beverage]. 2 café [tea-shop].

cafetal *m*. coffee plantation.

cafetera *f*. coffee-pot.

caída *f*. fall, drop; downfall; falling off or out: *a la ~ del sol*, at sunset.

caja *f*. box, chest, case. 2 cashbox, safe; cashier's office. ~ *de ahorros*, savings-bank.

cal *f*. lime [burned limestone].

calamidad *f*. calamity, disaster, misfortune.

calavera *f*. [fleshless] skull. 2 *m*. madcap, reckless fellow.

calcio *m*. calcium.

calcular *t*.-*i*. to calculate. 2 *t*. to conjecture, guess.

cálculo *m*. calculation, estimate. 2 conjecture, guess.

caldero *m*. small kettle or cauldron.

caldo *m*. broth. 2 *pl*. COM. vegetable juices.

calendario *m*. calendar, almanac.

calentar *t*. to warm, warm up, heat up. 2 to beat, spank. 3 *ref*. to become heated, excited or angry.

calentura *f*. MED. fever, temperature.

calidad *f*. quality. 2 character, nature. 3 rank, importance.

cálido, da *a*. warm, hot.

caliente *a*. warm, hot.

calificar *t*. to qualify, rate, class as. 2 to award marks to [in examination].

calma *f*. calm. 2 composure. 4 slowness.

calmar *t*. to calm, quiet. 2 to allay, soothe. 3 *i*.-*ref*. to calm oneself.

calor *m*. heat, warmth: *hace ~*, it is hot; *tengo ~*, I feel warm, hot. 2 enthusiasm, ardour.

calumnia *f*. calumny, slander.

caluroso, sa *a*. hot [weather]. 2 warm, hearty.

calvario *m*. calvary, suffering.

calzado, da *a*. shod. 2 *m*. footwear; boots, shoes.

calzar *t*.-*ref*. to put on [one's shoes, gloves, spurs].

callar *i*.-*ref*. to be, keep or become silent; to shut up, be quiet; to stop, cease [talking].

calle *f*. street, road: ~ *mayor*, high street, main street.

cama *f*. bed, couch; bedstead.

cámara f. chamber, room, hall. 2 granary. 3 ~ *alta,* upper house; ~ *baja,* lower house. 4 inner tube [of tire].

camarada m. comrade, companion, pal, friend.

cambiar t.-i. to change, alter, shift. 2 t. to convert; ~ *en,* to change into; ~ *por,* to exchange for.

cambio m. change [alteration; substitution, etc.]; shift, shifting. 2 exchange, barter. 3 RLY. switch. 4 *libre* ~, free trade; *a* ~ *de,* in exchange for; *en* ~, on the other hand; in exchange; ~ *de marchas,* AUTO. gearshift.

camello m. ZOOL. camel.

caminante m.-f. traveller, walker.

caminar i. to travel, journey. 2 to walk, march, go.

camino m. path, road, way, track, course. 2 way, journey, travel.

camión m. lorry, *truck.

camisa f. shirt: chemise.

camiseta f. vest.

campamento m. camp, camping; encampment.

campana f. bell.

campaña f. level countryside. 2 campaign.

campeón, na m. champion; defender. 2 f. championess.

campeonato m. championship.

campesino, na a. rustic, rural. 2 m.-f. peasant, countryman, countrywoman.

campiña f. stretch of arable land; fields, countryside.

campo m. fields, country, countryside. 2 cultivated land, crops. 3 field, ground. 4 GOLF. links. 5 MIL. camp.

canal m. canal [artificial channel]. 2 GEOG. channel, strait. 3 m.-f. gutter [in a roof]; gutter tile.

canario, ria a.-n. Canarian. 2 m. ORN. canary.

canasta f. basket, hamper.

cancelar t. to cancel, annul.

cáncer m. MED. cancer.

canción f. song.

cancionero m. collection of lyrics. 2 song-book.

cancha f. sports ground; [pelota] court; cockpit.

candado m. padlock.

candela f. candle, taper. 2 candlestick. 3 fire.

candidato, ta m.-f. candidate.

canela f. cinnamon.

canoa f. canoe.

canoso, sa a. gray-haired, hoary.

cansado, da a. tired, weary. 2 worn-out, exhausted.

cansar t.-i. to fatigue, tire. 2 t. to weary, bore, harass. 3 to wear out, exhaust. 4 ref. to get tired, to grow weary; to become exhausted. 5 i. to be tiring or tiresome.

cantante a. singing. 2 m.-f. singer.

1) **cantar** m. song: ~ *de gesta,* epic poem.

2) **cantar** t.-i. to sing. 2 i. coll. to squeak, confess. 3 [of cocks] to crow.

cántaro m. pitcher, jug.

cantera f. quarry, stone pit.

cántico m. canticle, religious song.

cantidad f. quantity, amount.

cantina *f.* canteen, refreshment room.

canto *m.* singing, chant, song. 2 crow [of cock]; chirp, chirr [of insects]. 3 corner, point. 4 edge: *siempre de* ~, this side upside. 5 stone: ~ *rodado*, boulder.

cantor, ra *m.-f.* singer, songster, songstress.

caña *f.* cane [stem]; reed: ~ *de azúcar*, sugar-cane. 2 leg [of boot]. 3 ~ *de pescar*, fishing-rod. 4 glass [of beer].

cañería *f.* pipe.

caño *m.* short tube or pipe.

cañón *m.* tube, pipe. 2 barrel [of gun]. 3 flue [of chimney]. 4 ARTILL. cannon, gun. 5 canyon, ravine. 6 quill.

caoba *f.* MOT. mahogany.

capa *f.* cloak, mantle, cape. 2 coat [of paint, etc.]. 3 stratum.

capacidad *f.* capacity, content. 2 capability, ability.

capataz *m.* foreman, overseer.

capaz *a.* capacious, roomy. 2 capable. 3 able, competent.

capilla *f.* hood, cowl. 2 chapel; oratory.

capital *a.* capital [main, great]: *pena* ~, capital punishment. 2 *m.* property, fortune. 3 ECON. capital. 4 *f.* capital, chief town.

capitán *m.* captain.

capítulo *m.* chapter.

capricho *m.* caprice, whim, fancy. 2 longing.

capturar *t.* to capture, arrest.

capullo *m.* cocoon. 2 flower bud. 3 acorn cup.

cara *f.* face, visage, counte-nance: *echar en* ~, to reproach, throw in one's face; *de* ~ *a*, opposite, facing; ~ *a* ~, face to face. 2 look, mien, aspect. 3 face, front, façade, outside, surface. 4 face, head [of a coin]: ~ *o cruz*, heads or tails.

carabela *f.* NAUT. caravel.

caracol *m.* snail. 2 ARCH. *escalera de* ~, winding [or spiral] staircase.

carácter, *pl.* **caracteres,** *m.* character [type, letter; distintive qualities; moral strength]. 2 nature.

caracterizar *t.* to characterize. 2 to give distinction, honour, etc. 3 *ref.* THEAT. to dress up, make up.

¡caramba! *interj.* good gracious!

caramelo *m.* caramel [burnt sugar], sweetmeat, sweet.

carbón *m.* coal; charcoal. 2 ELEC. carbon, crayon.

cárcel *f.* jail, gaol, prison.

cardenal *m.* ECCL. cardinal. 2 weal, bruise.

carecer de *i.* to lack, be in need of. ¶ CONJUG. like *agradecer*.

careta *f.* mask.

carga *f.* loading, lading; charging. 2 burden. 3 cargo, freight.

cargar *t.* to load. 2 to burden. 3 to charge. 4 to assume responsabilities. 5 to impute. 6 to bother, annoy. 7 *i.* to load up, take on a load: ~ *con*, to shoulder, take the weight of. 8 *ref.* to lean [the body towards].

cargo *m.* loading. 2 burden, weight. 3 employment,

post. 4 duty, charge, responsability. 5 accusation. 6 *hacerse* ~ *de*, to take charge of; to take into consideration, understand.

caricia *f.* caress, endearment.

caridad *f.* charity.

cariño *m.* love, affection, fondness, tenderness; care.

cariñoso, sa *a.* loving, affectionate.

caritativo, va *a.* charitable.

carne *f.* flesh [of man, animal, fruit]. 2 meat [as a food].

carnero *m.* ZOOL. sheep; mutton.

carnicería *f.* butcher's [shop]. 2 carnage, massacre.

carnicero, ra *a.* carnivorous [animal]. 2 bloodthirsty, sanguinary. 3 *m.f.* butcher.

caro, ra *a.* dear, costly; expensive. 2 dear, beloved.

carpeta *f.* writing-table cover. 2 portfolio.

carpintería *f.* carpentry. 2 carpenter's shop.

carpintero *m.* carpenter: *pájaro* ~, woodpecker.

carrera *f.* run, running. 2 road, highway. 3 race. 4 ladder [in a stocking]. 5 career. 6 profession. 7 *pl.* horse-racing.

carreta *f.* long, narrow cart.

carretera *f.* road, high road, highway, main road.

carro *m.* cart. 2 (Am.) car. 3 chariot. 4 MIL. car, tank.

carroza *f.* coach, carriage.

carruaje *m.* carriage, car, vehicle.

carta *f.* letter, missive,

epistle; note: ~ *certificada*, registered letter. 2 chart, map. 3 playing-card.

cartel *m.* poster, placard, bill.

cartera *f.* wallet. 2 portfolio; brief-case. 3 satchel.

cartero *m.* postman.

cartón *m.* cardboard, pasteboard.

casa *f.* house, building: ~ *consistorial* or *de la villa*, town hall; ~ *de socorro*, first-aid hospital; ~ *solariega*, manor. 2 home, family: *en* ~, at home. 3 firm.

casamiento *m.* marriage, wedding.

casar *i.* to marry; to match [colours]; to blend. 2 *ref.* to get married, wed.

cáscara *f.* rind, peel [of orange, etc.]; shell [of egg, etc.]. 2 hull, crust.

casco *m.* helmet. 2 skull. 3 cask, bottle [for liquids]. 4 hull [of ship]. 5 hoof [of horse, etc.]. 6 *pl.* brains.

casero, ra *a.* homely; informal. 2 home-made. 3 home-loving. 4 *m.-f.* landlord, landlady. 5 renter, tenant.

casi *adv.* almost, nearly.

caso *m.* GRAM., MED. case. 2 event: *hacer* or *venir al* ~, to be relevant; *vamos al* ~, let's come to the point; *en* ~ *de que*, in case; *en todo* ~, anyhow, at any rate. 3 notice: *hacer* ~ *omiso*, to take no notice.

casta *f.* caste. 2 race, stock. 3 lineage. 4 kind, quality.

castaña *f.* chestnut [fruit]. 2 knot of hair.

castellano, na *a.-n.* Castilian.

castigar *t.* to punish, chastise. 2 to mortify [the flesh].

castigo *m.* punishment; chastisement; penance, penalty.

castillo *m.* castle.

casualidad *f.* chance, accident; event: *por ~*, by chance.

catálogo *m.* catalogue.

catarata *f.* cataract, waterfall.

catarro *m.* MED. catarrh; head cold.

cátedra *f.* chair [seat of the professor; professorship].

catedral *a.-f.* cathedral [church].

catedrático *m.* professor [holding a chair in Secondary School or University].

categoría *f.* category, rank. 2 class, kind; quality.

católico, ca *a.* catholic. 2 *a.-n.* Roman Catholic.

catorce *a.-n.* fourteen.

catre *m.* cot, light bed.

cauce *m.* river-bed. 2 channel, ditch.

caudal *m.* fortune, wealth; abundance. 2 volume [of water].

caudaloso, sa *a.* full-flowing. 2 rich.

caudillo *m.* chief, leader.

causa *f.* cause, origin, reason, motive.

causar *t.* to cause, do, create, give rise to, bring about.

cautivo, va *a.-n.* captive, prisoner.

cavar *t.-i.* to dig, spade; to excavate.

caverna *f.* cavern, cave.

caza *f.* hunting, chase. 2 game [animals]. 3 *m.* AER. fighter.

cazador, ra *a.* hunting. 2 *m.* hunter. 3 *f.* huntress. 4 hunting jacket.

cazar *t.-i.* to hunt, chase; to track down.

cazuela *f.* earthen cooking pan; large casserole.

cebada *f.* barley.

cebolla *f.* onion.

ceder *t.* to cede, transfer. 2 *i.* to yield, submit, give in, give way.

cedro *m.* cedar.

ceja *f.* brow, eyebrow.

celda *f.* cell [in convent, etc.].

celebración *f.* celebration. 2 holding 3 applause.

celebrar *t.* to celebrate [a birthday, etc]; to make [a festival]; to hold [a meeting]. 2 to praise, honour. 3 to be glad of. 4 to say Mass. 5 *ref.* to take place, be held.

célebre *a.* celebrated, famous.

celeste *a.* celestial, heavenly.

celestial *a.* celestial, heavenly. 2 perfect.

celo *m.* zeal. 2 heat, rut. 3 *pl.* jealousy.

celoso, sa *a.* zealous. 2 jealous. 3 suspicious.

célula *f.* BIOL. ELEC. cell.

cementerio *m.* cemetery, churchyard, graveyard.

cemento *m.* cement. 2 *~ armado*, reinforced concrete.

cena *f.* supper; dinner.

cenar *i.* to sup, have supper; to dine, have dinner.

ceniza *f.* ash, ashes. 2 *pl.* cinders.

censura *f.* censure. 2 censorship.

centenar, centenal m. hundred. 2 rye-field.

centeno m. BOT. rye.

centímetro m. centimetre.

céntimo m. centime, cent.

centinela m.-f. sentinel, sentry.

central a. central. 2 f. main office, headquarters. 3 TELEPH. exchange, *central. 4 ELEC. power-station.

centro m. centre, middle. 2 club. 3 main office.

ceñir t. to gird; to girdle. 2 to fit tight. 3 ~ **espada**, to wear a sword. 4 to be concise. ¶ CONJUG. like **reír**.

cepillo m. brush: ~ **de dientes**, tooth-brush. 2 CARP plane. 3 alms box.

cera f. wax.

1) **cerca** f. enclosure, hedge, fence.

2) **cerca** adv. near, close, nigh. 2 ~ **de**, nearly, about.

cercado, da a. fenced-in, walled-in. 2 m. enclosure.

cercano, na a. near. 2 neighbouring.

cercar t. to fence in, wall in. 2 to surround, hem in. 3 MIL. to invest, lay siege to.

cerco m. circle; hoop, ring, edge. 2 rim [of a wheel]. 3 MIL. siege, blockade.

cerdo m. ZOOL. swine, [domestic] hog, pig. 2 pork [meat].

cereal a.-m. cereal.

cerebro m. ANAT. cerebrum. 2 fig. head, brains.

ceremonia f. ceremony. 2 formality. 3 ceremoniousness.

cereza f. cherry [fruit].

cerilla f. wax match. 2 taper.

cero m. zero, naught, nought.

cerrado, da a. shut; close, closed; fastened; locked.

cerradura f. lock.

cerrar t. to close, shut: ~ **la boca**, to shut up. 2 to fasten, bolt, lock. 3 to clench [the fist]. 4 to block up, bar. 5 to wall, fence. 6 to seal [a letter]. 7 to turn off [the water, etc.]. 8 i. [of a shop, etc.] to shut.

cerro m. neck [of animal]. 2 back, backbone. 3 hill.

certeza, certidumbre f. certainty.

certificado, da a. registered. 2 m. registered letter or package. 3 certificate.

cerveza f. beer, ale.

césped m. lawn, grass.

cesta f. basket, hamper.

ciclón m. cyclone, hurricane.

ciego, ga a. blind. 2 [of a pipe] stopped, blocked. 3 m.-f. blind man or woman.

cielo m. sky. 2 heaven [God]. 3 ~ **raso**, ceiling.

cien a. a or one hundred.

ciencia f. science; knowledge, learning.

científico, ca a. scientific. 2 m.-f. scientist.

cierto, ta a. certain, sure. por ~ **que**, by the way.

cifra f. cipher, figure, number. 2 amount.

cigarrillo m. cigarette.

cigarro m. cigar.

cigüeña m. ORN. stork. 2 MACH. crank, winch.

cilindro m. cylinder. 2 roller.

cima f. summit, top, peak [of mountain]. 2 **dar** ~, to carry out, complete.

cinco *a.* five.

cincuenta *a.-m.* fifty.

cine, cinema *m.* cinema, movies, pictures.

cinta *f.* ribbon, tape. 2 CINEM. film.

cintura *f.* waist.

cinturón *m.* belt.

circo *m.* circus.

circulación *f.* circulation; currency. 2 traffic [of vehicles].

1) **circular** *a.* circular. 2 *f.* circular letter.

2) **circular** *i.* to circulate.

círculo *m.* circle. 2 club.

circunstancia *f.* circumstance.

ciruela *f.* plum: ~ *pasa*, prune.

cirugía *f.* surgery.

cirujano *m.* surgeon.

cisne *m.* ZOOL. swan.

cita *f.* appointment, engagement, date. 2 quotation.

citar *t.* to make an appointment or a date with. 2 to cite, quote. 3 LAW to cite, summon.

ciudad *f.* city, town.

ciudadano, na *a.* civic 2 *m.-f.* citizen.

cívico, ca *a.* civic.

civil *a.* civil. 2 *a.-s.* civilian.

civilización *f.* civilization.

clamar *t.-i.* to clamour [against], cry [out], shout.

claro, ra *a.* bright. 2 clear. 3 obvious. 4 light [colour]. 5 outspoken. 6 adv. clearly. 7 *interj.* ¡claro!, ¡claro está!, of course!, sure! 8 *m.* space, interval. 9 clearing [in woods]. 10 *poner en* ~, to make plain, to clear up.

clase *f.* class, order, profession: ~ *alta, media, baja*, upper, middle, lower classes. 2 kind, sort: toda ~ *de*, all kind of. 3 RLY., EDUC. class. 4 class-room.

clásico, ca *a.* classic(al. 2 *m.* classic [author].

clasificar *t.* to class, classify. 2 to sort, file.

claustro *m.* ARCH., ECCL. cloister.

clavar *t.* to drive, stick, thrust, prick or stab with. 2 to nail. 3 to fix [eyes, etc.].

clave *f.* key [to a riddle, etc.]. 2 code. 3 MUS. clef.

clavel *m.* BOT. pink, carnation.

clavo *m.* nail.

cliente *m.-f.* client. 2 customer.

clima *m.* climate. 2 clime.

clínica *f.* clinic.

club *m.* club, society.

cobarde *a.* cowardly. 2 *m.-f.* coward.

cobijar *t.* to cover, shelter. 2 *ref.* to take shelter.

cobrar *t.* to collect, receive [money]; to cash [cheques]. 2 to recover. 3 to take, gather: ~ *ánimo*, to take courage; ~ *fuerzas*, to gather strength. 4 HUNT. to retrieve.

cobre *m.* copper.

cocer *t.* to cook. 2 to boil. 3 to bake [bread, etc.].

cocido, da *a.* cooked, boiled, baked. 2 *m.* Spanish stew.

cocina *f.* kitchen: ~ *económica*, cooking range.

cocinar *t.* to cook [food]. 2 *i.* to do the cooking.

cocinero, ra *m.-f.* cook.

cocodrilo *m.* ZOOL. crocodile.

coche *m.* coach, carriage, car: ~ *de alquiler, de punto,* cab, taxi. 2 AUTO. car. 3 RLY. car, carriage: ~ *cama,* sleeping-car; ~ *restaurante,* dinning-car.

cochino, na *a.* filthy, dirty; piggish. 2 *m.* ZOOL. pig, hog. 3 *m.-f.* dirty person.

código *m.* code [of laws].

codo *m.* ANAT. elbow. 2 bend [in tube, etc.].

coger *t.* to take, seize, grasp; to take hold of. 2 to pick, gather. 3 [of a bull] to gore.

cojín *m.* cushion.

cojo, ja *a.* lame, crippled.

col *f.* cabbage.

cola *f.* tail; end. 2 train [of gown]. 3 queue, line: *hacer* ~, to queue up. 4 glue.

colaboración *f.* collaboration.

colar *t.* to strain, filter. 2 to bleach with lye. 3 *ref.* to slip or sneak in. ¶ CONJUG. like *contar.*

colcha *f.* counterpane, quilt.

colchón *m.* mattress.

colchoneta *f.* long cushion. 2 thin, narrow mattress.

colección *f.* collection.

colectivo, va *a.* collective.

colegial, la *m.* schoolboy. 2 *f.* schoolgirl.

colegio *m.* school, academy. 2 college, body, association.

cólera *f.* anger, rage, wrath. 2 *m.* MED. cholera.

colgar *t.* to hang, suspend. 2 to impute. 3 *i.* to hang [be suspended], dangle.

colina *f.* hill, hillock.

colmado, da *a.* full, abundant. 2 *m.* grocer's, *foodstore.

colmena *f.* beehive.

colocación *f.* location. 2 placement. 3 employment; job. 4 investment [of capital].

colocar *t.* to place, put; to set, lay. 2 *ref.* to get a job.

colonia *f.* colony. 2 eau-de-Cologne.

colonial *a.* colonial. 2 *m. pl.* colonial products.

colono *m.* colonist, settler. 2 tenant farmer; planter.

color *m.* colo(u)r; colo(u)ring. 2 paint; rouge.

colorado, da *a.* colo(u)red. 2 red; *ponerse* ~, to blush.

columna *f.* column; support.

columpio *m.* swing; seesaw.

collar *m.* necklace. 2 collar.

coma *f.* GRAM. comma. 2 *m.* MED. coma.

comadre *f.* midwife.

comandante *m.* MIL. commander. 2 major.

comarca *f.* district, region, country.

combate *m.* combat, fight, battle. 2 BOX. fight.

combatir *t.-i.* to combat, fight.

combinación *f.* combination.

combustible *a.* combustible. 2 *m.* fuel.

comedia *f.* comedy, play. 2 farce, pretence.

comedor, ra *a.* heavy-eating. 2 *m.* dining-room.

comentar *t.* to comment on.

comentario *m.* commentary. 2 remark; comment.

comenzar *t.-i.* to commence, begin.

comer *t.-ref.* to eat [up]. 2 *i.* to eat, feed. 3 to dine; to have a meal.

comercial *a.* commercial.

comerciante *m.* merchant, trader, tradesman.

comercio *m.* commerce, trade. 2 shop, store.

comestible *a.* eatable, comestible. 2 *m. pl.* food, groceries; victuals, provisions; *tienda de comestibles*, grocer's [shop].

cometer *t.* to entrust, commit. 2 to do, perpetrate.

cómico, ca *a.* comic, dramatic. 2 comical, funny. 3 *m.* actor. 4 *f.* actress.

comida *f.* food; meal. 2 dinner.

comienzo *m.* commencement, beginning, opening.

comisión *f.* commission. 2 committee.

como *adv.* as, like: *tanto* ~, as much as. 2 *conj. así como*, as soon as. 3 if. 4 because, since, as. 5 ~ *quiera que*, since, as, inasmuch. 6 *adv. interr.* how: *¿cómo está usted?*, how do you do? 7 why; what. 8 *interj.* why!, how now!

comodidad *f.* comfort, convenience, ease, leisure.

cómodo, da *a.* comfortable. 2 handy, snug, cosy.

compadecer *t.* to pity, feel sorry for, sympathize with. 2 *ref.* to have pity on.

compañero, ra *m.-f.* companion, fellow, mate, comrade, partner.

compañía *f.* society. 2 COM., MIL., THEAT. company.

comparación *f.* comparison.

comparar *t.* to compare. 2 to confront, collate.

comparecer *i.* LAW to appear [before a judge, etc.].

compartir *t.* to divide in parts. 2 to share.

compás *m.* [a pair of] compasses; dividers. 2 MUS. time, measure.

compasión *f.* compassion, pity.

compatriota *m.-f.* compatriot, fellow-countryman.

compendio *m.* summary, digest.

competencia *f.* competence, ability. 2 rivalry.

competente *a.* competent, suitable. 2 qualified.

competir *i.* to compete, vie. ¶ CONJUG. like *servir*.

complacer *t.* to please. 2 *ref.* to be pleased. ¶ CONJUG. like *agradecer*.

complemento *m.* complement. 2 GRAM. object [of a verb].

completar *t.* to complete, finish.

completo, ta *a.* complete. 2 full up [bus, tram, etc.].

complicado, da *a.* complicate(d.

componer *t.* to compose; compound. 2 to fix. 3 to adorn. 4 to settle [a dispute]. 5 *ref.* to dress up, make up. 6 *componerse de*, to consist. 7 to manage.

comportamiento *m.* behavio(u)r, conduct.

composición *f.* composition. 2 agreement.

compositor, ra *m.-f.* MUS. composer.

comprar *t.* to purchase, buy.

comprender *t.* to comprehend. 2 to understand.

comprensión *f.* comprehension. 2 understanding.

comprobar *t.* to verify, check. 2 to prove.

comprometer *t.* to risk, jeopardize. 2 to become engaged.

compromiso *m.* engagement, obligation. 2 trouble.

comulgar *i.* to communicate. 2 to take Holy Communion.

común *a.* common. 2 ordinary. *3 por lo* ~, generally.

comunicación *f.* communication.

comunicar *t.* to communicate, report. 2 *ref.* to communicate. *3 i.* [of the telephone] to be engaged.

comunidad *f.* community. 2 commonwealth.

comunión *f.* communion.

comunismo *m.* communism.

comunista *a.-s.* communist.

con *prep.* with.

concebir *t.-i.* to conceive. ¶ Conjug. like *servir*.

conceder *t.* to grant, bestow, award. 2 to concede, admit.

concentrar *t.-ref.* to concentrate.

concepto *m.* concept, idea. 2 opinion.

concertar *t.* to arrange; to conclude; to agree upon. 2 *i.-ref.* to agree. ¶ Conjug. like *acertar*.

concesión *f.* concession. 2 grant.

conciencia *f.* conscience. 2 consciousness; awareness.

concierto *m.* agreement. 2 mus. concert.

concluir *t.-i.-ref.* to finish, end. 2 to conclude.

conclusión *f.* conclusion, end.

concretar *t.* to summarize; to fix details. 3 *ref.* to keep close to the point.

concreto, ta *a.* concrete [not abstract]; definite.

concurrencia *f.* concurrence, gathering; audience.

concurso *m.* competition.

concha *f.* zool. shell.

conde *m.* earl, count.

condenar *t.* to condemn, sentence. 2 *ref.* to be damned.

condición *f.* condition [rank; nature; requisite]: *a* ~ *de que*, provided that. 2 *pl.* terms. 3 position.

conducir *t.* to lead. 2 to manage. 3 to drive [a vehicle]. 4 *ref.* to behave, act. ¶ Conjug. Indic. Pres.: *conduzco, conduces,* etc. | Pret.: *conduje, condujiste,* etc. ‖ Subj. Pres.: *conduzca, conduzcas,* etc. | Imperf.: *condujera,* etc., or *condujese,* etc. | Fut.: *condujere,* etc. ‖ Imperat.: *conduce, conduzca; conduzcamos, conducid, conduzcan.*

conducta *f.* conduct, behavio(u)r. 2 management.

conductor, ra *m.-f.* guide, leader. 2 driver [of a vehicle]. 3 phys., rly. conductor.

conectar *t.* to connect; to switch on, turn on.

conejo *a.* zool. rabbit: *conejillo de Indias,* guinea-pig.

conferencia *f.* conference. 2 [public] lecture. 3 teleph. trunk call.

confesar *t.-i.* to confess. 2 to acknowledge.

confesión *f.* confession.

confiado, da *a.* unsuspecting. 2 self-confident.

confianza *f.* confidence, reliance, trust. 2 familiarity.

confiar *i.* to confide, trust, rely on. 2 to entrust.

confirmación *f.* confirmation.

confirmar *t.* to confirm.

conflicto *m.* conflict, struggle. 2 difficulty.

conformar *t.* to adjust. 2 to conform, agree. 3 *ref.* to yield.

conforme *a.* alike; in agreement; resigned; ready to. 2 *adv.* in accordance with.

confundir *t.* to mix up. 2 to confound. 3 *ref.* to get mixed up or lost. 4 to be mistaken; to make a mistake.

confusión *f.* confusion. 2 disorder. 3 bewilderment; shame.

confuso, sa *a.* confused. 2 troubled. 3 obscure.

congregación *f.* congregation.

congresista *m.* congress-man.

congreso *m.* congress, assembly.

conjugación *f.* conjugation.

conjunto, ta *a.* conjunct, united. 2 *m.* whole, total: **en ~,** as a whole; altogether.

conmemoración *f.* commemoration.

conmemorar *t.* to commemorate.

conmigo *pron.* with me, with myself.

conmover *t.* to move, touch, stir. 2 *ref.* to be touched.

conocedor, ra *m.-f.* connoisseur, judge.

conocer *t.* to know. 2 to be acquainted with, meet [a person]. 3 *ref.* to be acquainted with each other.

conocimiento *m.* knowledge; information. 2 intelligence.

conque *conj.* so, so then, and

so; well then.

conquista *f.* conquest.

conquistador, ra *m.-f.* conqueror. 2 *m.* lady-killer.

conquistar *t.* to conquer [by arms]; win, gain.

consagración *f.* consecration.

consagrar *t.* to consecrate, hallow. 2 devote.

consecuencia *f.* consequence.

consecutivo, va *a.* consecutive.

conseguir *t.* to obtain, attain, get, achieve. 2 [with an inf.] to succeed in, manage to.

consejo *m.* advice: piece of advice. 2 council, board.

consentir *t.* to allow, permit. ¶ CONJUG. like *hervir.*

conserje *m.* door-keeper, porter.

conservación *f.* conservation.

conservador, ra *m.* curator. 2 *a.-n.* POL. conservative.

conservar *t.* to conserve, keep, maintain.

considerable *a.* considerable.

consideración *f.* consideration.

considerar *t.* to consider, think over.

consigo *pron.* with him. [her, it, one]; with them; with you.

consiguiente *a.* consequent. 2 *m.* LOG. consequent. 3 *por ~,* therefore.

consistente *a.* consistent, firm, solid.

consistir *i.* to consist [of, in]; to be based on.

consolador, ra *a.* consoling, comforting.

consolar *t.* to console, comfort, cheer, soothe. ¶ CONJUG. like *contar.*

constante a. constant, steady. 2 -mente adv. constantly.

constar i. to be evident or clear; to be on record. 2 to state, record.

constitución f. constitution.

constituir t. to constitue; to establish. 2 ref. to become. ¶ CONJUG. like *huir.*

construcción f. construction, building.

construir t. to construct, build.

consuelo m. consolation, comfort. 2 relief.

consulta f. consultation. 2 opinion.

consultar t.-i. to consult, take advice.

consumidor, ra a. consuming. 2 m.-f. consumer.

consumir t. to consume. 2 to waste away, spend. 3 ref. to burn out.

consumo m. consumption.

contabilidad f. accounting, book-keeping.

contacto m. contact. 2 touch.

contado, da a. counted. 2 rare. 3 m. al ~, cash down.

contador, ra m.-f. computer, counter. 2 book-keeper. 3 counter, meter.

contagioso, sa a. contagious, infectious, catching.

contar t. to count. 2 to tell, narrate, reckon: ~ *con,* to rely on.

contemplar t. to contemplate, look at. 2 to pamper.

contener t. to contain, check. 2 to restrain, refrain. 3 to hold back.

contenido, da a. moderate, temperate. 2 m. contents.

contento, ta a. pleased, glad. 2 m. joy.

contestación f. answer, reply. 2 debate.

contestar t. to answer, reply, write back [a letter].

contigo pron. with you, thee.

contiguo, gua a. contiguous, next, neighbouring.

continente m. continent.

continuación f. continuation.

continuar t. to continue [pursue, carry on]. 2 i. to go on.

continuo, a a. continuous; steady, constant, endless.

contra prep. against. 2 m. con, against: *el pro y el* ~, the pros and cons.

contraer t.-ref. to contract, shrink. 2 to get, catch. ¶ CONJUG. like *traer.*

contrariedad f. contrariety. 2 set-back, disappointment.

contrario, ria a. contrary. 2 harmful. 3 m.-f. opponent, adversary. 4 al ~, on the contrary.

contraste m. opposition. 2 contrast.

contratar t. to contract for. 2 to engage, hire.

contrato m. contract.

contribución f. contribution, tax.

contribuir i. to contribute to.

contrincante m. competitor, rival.

control m. GAL. control, check.

convencer t. to convince.

conveniencia f. utility, advantage. 2 pl. income, property.

conveniente a. convenient. 2 advantageous. 3 -mente adv. conveniently, etc.

convenio m. agreement, pact.

convenir i. to agree. 2 to come

together. 3 to be convenient, advantageous.

convento *m.* convent.

conversación *f.* conversation, talk.

conversar *i.* to converse, talk.

convertir *t.* to convert, transform. 2 *ref.* to be or become converted.

convicción *f.* conviction, belief.

convidar *t.* to invite.

convocar *t.* to convoke, summon, call together.

coñac *m.* cognac, brandy.

cooperación *f.* co-operation.

cooperar *t.* to co-operate.

cooperativa *f.* co-operative.

copa *f.* goblet, wineglass. 2 *tomar una ~* to have a drink. 3 cup. 4 head, top, [of a tree].

copia *f.* copy. 2 imitation.

copiar *t.* to copy. 2 to take down [from dictation].

copla *f.* folk-song, ballad.

coqueta *f.* coquette, flirt. 2 *a.* coquettish.

coraje *m.* courage. 2 anger.

coral *m.* [red] coral.

corazón *m.* ANAT. heart. 2 core [of apple, etc.].

corbata *f.* tie, necktie, cravat.

corcel *m.* steed, charger.

corcho *m.* cork. 2 cork mat.

cordel *m.* string, fine cord.

cordero *m.* lamb.

cordial *a.* friendly, hearty. 2 **-mente** *adv.* heartily.

cordillera *f.* mountain range.

cordón *m.* braid; yarn, cord, string. 2 lace. 3 cordon.

coro *m.* choir. 2 chorus.

corona *f.* crown; wreath.

coronel *m.* MIL. colonel.

corporación *f.* corporation.

corpulento, ta *a.* corpulent, bulky, stout.

corral *m.* yard, farm yard.

correa *f.* leather strap, leash.

correcto, ta *a.* correct, proper, right.

corredor, ra *a.* running, speedy. 2 *m.* SPORT. runner. 3 COM. broker. 4 corridor.

corregir *t.* to correct. 2 to reprimand. ¶ CONJUG. like *servir*.

correo *m.* postman; courier. 2 post-office. 3 mail, correspondence.

correr *i.* to run. 2 to blow. 3 to spread. 4 to pass. 5 to hurry. 6 *t.* to run [a horse; a risk]. 7 to fight. 8 to draw. 9 *~ prisa,* to be urgent, pressing. 10 *ref.* to slide, slip. 11 to be ashamed.

correspondencia *f.* correspondence, letter-writing.

corresponder *i.* to correspond, answer [to, with]. 2 to pertain. 3 *ref.* to love each other.

correspondiente *a.* suitable, appropriate.

corrida *f.* course, race. 2 *~ de toros,* bullfight.

corriente *a.* flowing, running. 2 current. 3 ordinary. 4 *f.* stream. 5 ELEC. current.

cortar *t.* to cut, slash; to cut away, off, out or up; to sever. 2 to carve, chop. 3 to cross. 4 to hew. 5 to cut short. 6 to stop, bar. 7 *ref.* [of milk] to sour, curdle.

1) **corte** *m.* cutting edge. 2 cut 3 art of cutting clothes. 4 lenght. 5 felling [of tress]. 6 ELEC. break.

2) **corte** *f.* court [of sove-

reign]. 2 city [king's residence]. 3 (Am.) court [of justice]. 4 courtship, wooing: *hacer la ~ a*, to court, pay court to.

cortés *a.* courteous, polite.

cortesía *f.* politeness.

corteza *f.* bark [of tree]; crust [of bread, etc.]; rind [of cheese, etc.]; rind, peel [of orange, etc.].

cortina *f.* curtain.

corto, ta *a.* short brief. 2 scant, wanting. 3 bashful, shy. 4 dull, slow-witted. 5 ELEC. *~ circuito*, short circuit. 6 *~ de vista*, short-sighted.

cosa *f.* thing, matter: *como si tal ~*, as if nothing had happened.

cosecha *f.* harvest, crop; vintage. 2 reaping 3 harvest time.

cosechar *t.-i.* to harvest, crop, reap, gather in.

coser *t.* to sew; to seam, stitch. 2 to stab repeatedly.

costa *f.* coast, shore. 2 cost; *a toda ~*, at all costs; *a ~ de*, at the expense of.

costar *i.* to cost. ¶ CONJUG. like *contar*.

coste *m.* cost, price: *~ de vida*, cost of living.

costilla *f.* ANAT. rib. 2 chop, cutlet [to eat]. 3 wife.

costo *m.* cost, price, expense.

costoso, sa *a.* costly, expensive, dear. 2 hard, difficult.

costumbre *f.* custom; habit.

costura *f.* sewing, needlework. 2 seam. 3 stitch(ing.

cotorra *f.* ORN. parrot, small parrot. 2 *fig.* chatterbox.

cráneo *m.* ANAT. skull.

creación *f.* creation.

creador, ra *a.* creative. 2 *m.-f.* creator, maker.

crear *t.* to create. 2 to make.

crecer *i.* to grow, increase. 2 [of a stream] to rise, swell.

crecimiento *m.* growth, increase.

crédito *m.* credit, credence: *dar ~ a*, to believe. 2 good reputation: *a ~*, on credit.

creencia *f.* belief, creed, tenet.

creer *t.-i.-ref.* to believe. 2 to think, suppose.

crema *f.* cream. 2 custard.

crepúsculo *m.* twilight; dawn.

cresta *f.* crest, comb [of a bird]; cock's comb. 2 crest of mountain. 3 tuft.

creyente *a.* believing. 2 *m.-f.* believer, faithful.

cría *f.* nursing, suckling. 2 breeding. 3 brood, young [animals].

criado, da *a.* bred. 2 *m.* manservant. 3 *f.* maid, maidservant.

crianza *f.* nursing. 2 bringing up. 3 manners.

criar *t.* to nurse, suckle. 2 to rear, breed, grow. 3 to put forth. 4 to bring up, educate.

criatura *f.* creature. 2 baby, child.

crimen *m.* serious crime, felony.

criminal *a.-n.* criminal.

crisis *f.* crisis. 2 COM. depression; shortage.

cristal *m.* crystal: *~ de aumento*, magnifying glass. 2 window-pane.

cristalino, na *a.* crystalline. 2 *m.* ANAT. crystalline lens.

cristiano, na *a.-n.* Christian.

Cristo m. pr. n. Christ. 2 m. crucifix.

criterio m. criterion. 2 judgement, discernment.

crítica f. criticism. 2 faultfinding, censure; gossip. 3 the critics.

crítico, ca a. critical. 2 m. critic; fault-finder.

crucificar t. to crucify; to torture.

crudo, da a. raw, uncooked, underdone [food]. 2 raw, bitter [weather]. 3 harsh, rongh. 4 crude, blunt.

cruel a. cruel, ruthless, harsh. 2 **-mente** adv. cruelly.

cruz, pl. **cruces,** m. cross: ~ **Roja,** Red Cross. 2 tails [of coin]: **cara o** ~, heads or tails.

cruzar t. to cross, lie across, intersect. 2 ref. to cross, pass each other.

cuaderno m. note-book, exercise-book.

cuadra f. stable.

cuadrado, da a.-m. square.

cuadrar t. to square. 2 i. to fit, suit. 3 ref. MIL. to stand at attention.

cuadro m. square or rectangle: **a cuadros,** checkered. 2 picture, painting. 3 frame [of door, etc.]. 4 LIT. picture, description. 5 THEAT. tableau. 6 scene, view, spectacle. 7 flower-bed. 8 table, synopsis.

cual, cuales rel. pron. who, which. 2 as, such as. 3 some. 4 adv. as, like.

cuál, cuáles interr. pron. who, which [one, ones], what. 2 adv. how.

cualidad f. quality.

cualquiera, pl. **cualesquiera** pron. anyone, anybody. 2 ~ **que,** whatever, whichever.

cuan adv. **tan... cuan,** as... as. 2 interrog.-exclam. **cuán,** how.

cuando adv. when: **aun** ~, even though; **de** ~ **en** ~, now and then.

1) **cuanto** adv. **en** ~ **a,** with regard to, as for. 2 ~ **antes,** as soon as possible. 3 ~ **más... tanto más,** the more... the more.

2) **cuanto, ta; cuantos, tas** a. all the, every, as much [sing.], as many [pl.]. 2 pron. all [that], everything, as much as [sing.], as many as [pl.], all who. 3 a.-pron. **unos cuantos,** some, a few.

3) **cuánto, ta; cuántos, tas** [with interrog. or exclam.] a.-pron. how much ❬sing.❭, how many [pl.], what.

cuarenta a.-n. forty.

cuartel m. ward [of a town]. 2 MIL. barracks. 3 MIL. quarters.

cuartilla f. sheet of paper.

cuarto, ta a. fourth. 2 m. quarter. 3 room, chamber: ~ **de baño,** bath-room: ~ **de estar,** living-room.

cuatro a. four.

cubo m. bucket, pail, tub. 2 GEOM., MATH. cube. 3 hub [of a wheel].

cubrir t. to cover [up]. 2 to hide, disguise. 3 to roof [a building].

cucaracha f. cockroach.

cuchara f spoon. 2 dipper [of excavator].

cuchilla f. large knife, cleaver. 2 blade.

cuchillo m. knife.

cuenta *f.* account; count, counting; bill, note: *hacer cuentas,* to cast accounts. *2* COM. account: ~ *corriente,* current account; *por* ~ *de,* for account of. *3* report, information: *dar* ~ *de,* to inform of. *4 caer en la* ~, *darse* ~, to realise. *5 tener en* ~, to take into account, bear in mind.

cuento *m.* tale, story, narrative: ~ *de hadas,* fairy tale. *2* gossip. *3* count, number: *sin* ~, numberless.

cuerda *f.* rope, cord, string. *2* MUS. string. *3* spring: *dar* ~ *a un reloj,* to wind up a watch.

cuerdo, da *a.* sane, wise, prudent.

cuerno *m.* horn.

cuero *m.* hide, raw hide. *2* leather. *3* ~ *cabelludo,* scalp; *en cueros,* stark naked.

cuerpo *m.* body; trunk: *hurtar el* ~, to dodge; *luchar* ~ *a* ~, to fight hand to hand. *2* figure, build [of a person]. *3* corpse. *4* company, staff: ~ *de ejército,* army corps.

cuervo *m.* raven, crow.

cuesta *f.* slope, hill.

cuestión *f.* question [problem, matter, point]; affair, business. *2* dispute, quarrel.

cueva *f.* cave. *2* cellar. *3* den.

cuidado *m.* care, carefulness; charge; *al* ~ *de,* in care of; *tener* ~, to be careful; *¡~!,* look out! *2* fear, anxiety.

cuidadoso, sa *a.* careful, painstaking. *2* watchful.

cuidar *t.-i.* to take care of, keep, look after, mind,

nurse. *2 ref.* to take care of oneself.

culebra *f.* snake.

culpa *f.* guilt, fault, blame.

culpable *a.* guilty.

cultivar *t.* to cultivate, labour, farm [land, soil].

cultivo *m.* cultivation, culture, farming.

1) **culto** *m.* cult, worship.

2) **culto, ta** *a.* cultured, educated. *2* civilized. *3* learned.

cultura *f.* CULTIVO. *2* culture.

cumbre *f.* summit, top [of mountain], peak. *2* height.

cumpleaños *m.* birthday.

cumplimiento *m.* fulfilment. *2* observance [of law]. *3* compliment: *por* ~, out of politeness only.

cumplir *t.* to accomplish, perform, fulfil. *2* to keep [a promise]. *3* to do [one's duty]; to observe [a law]. *4* to finish [a term in prison]. *5* reach [of age]. *6 i.* to behove. *7 i.-ref.* [of time] to expire. *8 ref.* to be fulfilled.

cuna *f.* cradle. *2* lineage.

cuneta *f.* ditch, gutter.

cuñada *f.* sister-in-law.

cuñado *m.* brother-in-law.

cuota *f.* membership fee.

cura *m.* parish priest. *2* cure: *primera* ~, first aid.

curar *i.-ref.* to cure, heal, recover, get well. *2* to take care of; to mind. *3 t.* MED. to treat.

curiosidad *f.* curiosity.

curioso, sa *a.* curious, inquisitive, prying. *2* clean, tidy.

cursar *t.* to frequent. *2* to study [law]. *3* to make [a petition].

curso *m.* course, direction. *2*

EDUC. course [of lectures]; school year.

cutis *m.* skin; complexion.

cuyo, ya *pl.* **cuyos, yas** *poss. pron.* whose, of which, of whom.

CH

chancleta *f.* slipper.
chaqueta *f.* jacket, sack coat.
charca *f.* pool, pond.
charco *m.* puddle, pond.
charla *f.* chatter. *2* chat. *3* talk.
charlar *i.* to chatter, prattle. *2* to chat, talk.
charlatán, na *m.-f.* chatterer, chatterbox. *2* charlatan.
cheque *m.* cheque, check; ~ *de viajero*, traveler's check.
chicle *m.* chewing-gum.
chico, ca *a.* small, little. *2 m.* boy, lad. *3 f.* child, girl, lass.
chicharrón *m.* fried piece of fat.
chillar *i.* to shriek, screech, scream. *2 fig.* to shout.
chimenea *f.* chimney. *2* hearth, fireplace. *3* funnel.

China (la) *f. pr. n.* China.
chino, na *a.-n.* Chinese.
chiquillo, lla *a.* small. *2 m.-f.* little boy or girl, child.
chispa *f.* spark, sparkle.
chiste *m.* joke.
chistoso, sa *a.* witty, funny.
chocar *i.* to collide; to clash, bump together. *2* to surprise.
chocolate *m.* chocolate.
chófer *m.* AUT. chauffeur, driver.
choque *m.* collision, clash; shock. *2* MIL. encounter, skirmish. *3* dispute, quarrel.
chorizo *m.* pork sausage.
chorro *m.* jet, spout, gush, flow, stream.
choza *f.* hut, cabin.
chuleta *f.* chop, cutlet.
chupar *t.* to suck, draw.

D

dado, da *a.* given. *2 m* die [*pl.* dice].

dama *f.* lady, dame. *2* king [in draughts]. *3* queen [in chess]

danza *f.* dance; dancing.

danzar *i.* to dance.

dañar *t.* to harm, damage, injure, hurt. *2* to spoil, taint. *3 ref.* to get hurt.

dañino, na *a.* harmful.

daño *m.* harm, damage, loss, injury.

dar *t.* to give, hand, deliver, grant. *2* to produce, bear, yield. *3* ~ *comienzo*, to begin; ~ *un paseo*, to take a walk. *4 dar como* or *por*, to suppose, consider. *5* ~ *a conocer*, to make known; ~ *a luz*, to give birth to; to publish; ~ *que pensar*, to arouse suspicious. *6 i.* ~ *con*, to meet, find. *7* ~ *de sí*, to give, yield, stretch. *8 ref.* to give oneself. *9* to yield, surrender. *10 darse a la bebida*, to take to drink. *11 darse la mano*, to shake hands. ¶ CONJUG. INDIC. Pres.: *doy, das, da; damos, dais, dan.* | Imperf.: *daba, da-bas,* etc. | Pret.: *di, diste, dio; dimos, disteis, dieron.* | Fut.: *daré, darás,* etc. ‖ COND.: *daría, darías,* etc. ‖ SUBJ. Pres.: *dé, des,* etc. | Imperf.: *diera, dieras,* etc., or *diese, dieses,* etc. | Fut.: *diere, dieres,* etc. ‖ IMPER.: *da, dé; demos, dad, den.* ‖ PAST. P.: *dado.* ‖ GER.: *dando.*

dato *m.* datum, fact. *2* document.

de *prep.* of; from, about, for, on, by, at, out of, with: ~ *día*, by day; ~ *noche*, at night. *2* [before inf.] if.

debajo *adv.* underneath, below: ~ *de*, under, beneath.

debate *m.* debate, discussion.

1) **deber** *m.* duty, obligation. *2* homework.

2) **deber** *t.* to owe. *2 aux.* [with an inf.] must, have to; ought to, should.

débil *a.* weak, feeble. *2* slight, faint; sickly.

decano *m.* dean.

decena *f.* ten [ten unities].

decente *a.* decent, proper.

decidir *t.* to decide, settle. *2* to

determine, resolve. *3 ref.* to make up one's mind.

décima *f.* tenth [part]. *2* a stanza of ten octosyllabic lines.

1) **decir** *t.* to say, talk, tell, speak; ~ *para sí*, to say to oneself; *querer* ~, to mean; *es* ~, that is to say. ¶ Conjug. Indic. Pres.: *digo, dices, dice; decimos, decís, dicen.* | Imperf.: *decía, decías, etc.* | Pret.: *dije, dijiste, dijo; dijimos, dijisteis, dijeron.* | Fut.: *diré, dirás,* etc. | Cond.: *diría, dirías,* etc. ‖ Subj. Pres.: *diga, digas,* etc. | Imperf.: *dijera, dijeras,* etc., or *dijese, dijeses,* etc. | Fut.: *dijere, dijeres,* etc. ‖ Imper.: *di, diga; digamos, decid, digan.* ‖ P. P.: *dicho.* ‖ Ger.: *diciendo.*

2) **decir** *m.* saying, maxim.

decisión *f.* decision.

decisivo, va *a.* decisive, final.

declaración *f.* statement.

declarar *t.* to declare. *2* to state, make know, avow. *3* LAW to find [guilty or not guilty]

decorar *t.* to decorate, adorn.

dedal *m.* thimble.

dedicación *f.* dedication.

dedicar *t.* to dedicate [a book, etc.]. *2* to devote. *3 ref.* to devote oneself to.

dedo *m.* ~ *de la mano*, finger; ~ *del pie*, toe.

defecto *m.* defect, fault, blemish; *en* ~ *de*, in default of.

defender *t.-ref.* to defend. *2* assert, maintain. ¶ Conjug. like *entender.*

defensor, ra *m.-f.* defender. *3* advocate, supporter.

deficiencia *f.* deficiency.

definición *f.* definition.

definido, da *a.* definite.

definir *t.* to define; to explain.

definitivo, va *a.* definitive.

defraudar *t.* to defraud, rob, cheat. *2* to frustrate, disappoint. *3* to deceive [hopes]; to ahead.

degollar *t.* to behead; to slash the throat. ¶ Conjug. like *contar.*

dejar *t.* to leave: ~ *en paz*, to let alone. *2* to abandon relinquish, let go. *3* to quit. *4* to allow, let.

delantal *m.* apron; pinafore.

delante *adv.* before, in front of; ahead.

delantero, ra *a.* fore, front, foremost. *2 m.* SPORT. forward.

delegación *f.* delegation. *2* COM. branch.

delicia *f.* delight; pleasure, joy.

delicioso, sa *a.* delicious, delightful.

delincuente *a.-n.* delinquent.

delito *m.* offence, crime, guilt, misdemeano(u)r.

demanda *f.* petition, request. *2* COM. demand. *3* LAW claim, complaint; lawsuit.

demandar *t.* to demand, ask for, beg. *2* to ask, inquire. *3* LAW to sue.

demás *a.* the other, the rest of the. *2 pron.* other, others: *por lo* ~, for the rest.

demasiado, da *a.-pron.* too much [money], too many [books]; excessive.

democracia *f.* democracy.

democrático, ca *a.* democratic.

demonio *m.* demon, devil, fiend.

demostración *f.* demonstration; show; proof.

demostrar *t.* to demonstrate, show; to prove, explain.

denominador *m.* MATH. denominator.

denominar *t.* to denominate, name, call, entitle.

denso, sa *a.* dense, compact, thick.

dentista *m.* dentist.

dentro *adv.* in, inside, within: ~ *de poco*, shortly.

denunciar *t.* to denounce. 2 accuse. 3 to report [a transgression]. 4 to claim [a mine].

departamento *m.* department. 2 compartment.

depender *i.* ~ *de*, to depend on, rely upon.

dependiente *a.* depending, dependent, subordinate. 2 *m.* clerk, assistant.

deporte *m.* sport.

deportista *m.* sportsman. 2 *f.* sportswoman.

deportivo, va *a.* sports, sporting, sportive. 2 sportsman-like.

depositar *t.* to deposit. 2 to place, put.

depósito *m.* trust. 2 sediment. 3 storehouse, warehouse. 4 tank, reservoir.

derecha *f.* right. 2 right hand. 3 POL. right wing. 4 *a la* ~, to the right.

derecho, cha *a.* right, right-hand. 2 straight. 3 standing, upright. 4 *adv.* straight on. 5 *m.* right; justice, equity. 6 law.

derivar *t.* to lead, conduct. 2 *i.-ref.* to derive, come from.

derramar *t.* to pour out, spill. 2 to shed. 3 *ref.* to overflow, run over.

derredor *m.* circuit; contour: *al* ~, *en* ~, around, round about.

derretir *t.-ref.* to melt, thaw.

derribar *t.* to pull down. 2 to fell, knock down, throw down. 3 to overthrow.

derrota *f.* defeat, rout. 2 path, road.

derrotar *t.* to defeat, rout. 2 to dilapidate.

desacato *m.* disrespect, irreverence. 2 disobedience.

desafío *m.* challenge.

desagradable *a.* disagreeable, unpleasant.

desaliento *m.* discouragement, dejection.

desamparar *t.* to abandon, forsake, leave helpless.

desaparecer *i.-ref.* to disappear.

desarrollar *t.* to develop.

desarrollo *m.* development.

desastre *m.* disaster, catastrophe.

desatar *t.* to untie, loose, loosen, unfasten; 2 *ref.* [of a storm] to break out.

desayunar(se *i.-ref.* to breakfast, have breakfast.

desayuno *m.* breakfast.

desbaratar *t.* to destroy, ruin. 2 to frustrate.

desbordar *i.-ref.* to overflow.

descabellado, da *a.* dishevelled. 2 preposterous, absurd.

descalzo, za *a.* barefooted.

descansar *i.* to rest; to lie in sleep or death. 2 to rely on, put trust [in a person].

descanso *m.* rest, repose, relaxation. 2 alleviation. 3 break [half-time]; interval [in theatre]. 4 landing [of stairs].

descarga f. unloading, unburdening, discharge. 2 ARCH., ELEC. discharge. 3 discharge [of firearms], volley.

descargar t. to unload, unburden. 2 to strike [a blow]. 3 to vent [one's fury, etc.]. 4 to fire, discharge [a firearm].

descartar t. to discard.

descendencia f. descent. 2 lineage.

descender i. to descend, go down. 2 [of temperature] to drop. ¶ CONJUG. like *entender*.

descendiente a. descendent. 2 m.-f. descendant, offspring.

descomponer t. to decompose. 2 to put out of order, disarrange, upset. 3 fig. to set at odds. 4 ref. to decompose; to become putrid or tainted. 5 to get out of order. 6 [of the face] to be altered. 7 to lose one's temper. ¶ CONJUG. like *poner*.

desconocer t. not to know, ignore, be unacquainted with. 2 to fail to recognize. 3 to disown. ¶ CONJUG. like *agradecer*.

desconocido, da a. unknown. 2 strange, unfamiliar. 3 unrecognizable. 4 m.-f. stranger.

descontar t. to discount, deduct.

descontento, ta a. displeased. 2 m. discontent, displeasure.

descortés a. impolite, uncivil.

describir t. to describe.

descripción f. description.

descubrimiento m. discovery, find, invention. 2 revealing, disclosure.

descubrir t. to discover, disclose, reveal. 2 to make known. 3 to discover [find out]. 4 ref. to take off one's hat.

descuidado, da a. careless, negligent. 2 slovenly.

descuidar t. to relieve from care. 2 t.-i.-ref. to neglect, fail to attend, be careless.

descuido m. neglect. 2 negligence, carelessness. 3 oversight, inadvertence.

desde prep. from, since. 2 adv. ~ *luego*, of course.

desdén m. disdain, scorn.

desdeñoso, sa a. disdainful, contemptuous, scornful.

desdicha f. misfortune; unhappiness, misery.

desdichado, da a. unfortunate, miserable, unhappy.

desear t. to desire, wish, want.

desechar t. to cast aside, banish, refuse, decline.

desembarcar t. to disembark, land, go ashore.

desembocar i. [of streams] to flow. 2 [of streets, etc.] to end [at], lead into.

desempeñar t. to redeem [what is pledged], take out of pawn. 2 to discharge [a duty]. 3 to act, play [a part].

desengaño m. disillusion, disappointment.

desenvolver t. to unfold. 2 to develop [a theme, etc.]. 3 ref. to develop [be developed]. ¶ CONJUG. like *mover*.

deseo m. desire; wish, longing.

deseoso, sa a. desirous, eager.

desesperación f. despair, desperation. 2 anger, fury.

desesperar t. drive mad. 3 i.-ref. to despair; to be exasperated.

desfilar *t.* to march past [in review, etc.]. 2 to file out.

desfile *m.* defiling; marching past, parade, review.

desgarrar *t.* to tear, rend.

desgracia *f.* misfortune. 2 bad luck, mischance.

desgraciado, da *a.* unfortunate, unhappy, unlucky. 2 *m.-f.* wretch, unfortunate.

deshacer *t.* to undo, unmake. 2 to loosen [a knot]. 3 to destroy. 4 to upset [plans]. 5 to melt. 6 *ref.* to melt, dissolve. 7 *deshacerse de*, to get rid of.

desierto, ta *a.* deserted. 2 *m.* desert, wilderness.

designar *t.* to design, purpose. 2 to designate, appoint.

designio *m.* design, purpose, intention, plan.

desinteresado, da *a.* disinterested. 2 unselfish.

desistir *i.* to desist; to stop, give up.

deslizar *i.-ref.* to slide, glide, slip. 2 *t.* to slip, glide.

deslumbrar *t.* to dazzle, daze.

desmayar *t.* to discourage. 2 *ref.* to faint, swoon.

desnivel *m.* unevenness; slope.

desnudo, da *a.* naked, nude. 2 bare, uncovered.

desobedecer *t.* to disobey. ¶ Conjug. like *agradecer.*

desobediencia *f.* disobedience.

desocupado, da *a.* free, vacant. 2 idle. 3 unemployed.

desocupar *t.* to empty. 2 *ref.* to disengage oneself.

desolar *t.* to desolate, lay waste. ¶ Conjug. like *contar.*

desorden *m.* disorder, confusion. 2 disturbance, riot.

desordenado, da *a.* disorderly. 2 licentious [life].

despacio *adv.* slowly.

despachar *t.* to dispatch [get promptly done; to send off; to kill]. 2 to attend to [correspondence]. 3 to settle business; to sell [goods]. 4 to dismiss, discharge. 5 *i.-ref.* to hasten, be quick.

despacho *m.* dispatch, promptness. 2 sale [of goods]. 3 dismissal. 4 shipment. 5 office.

despedida *f.* farewell, leave, parting. 2 dismissal.

despedir *t.* to throw. 2 to emit, send forth. 3 to dismiss. 4 to say good-bye to. 5 *ref.* to part; to say good bye: *despedirse de*, to take one's leave. 6 to leave [a post]. ¶ Conjug. like *servir.*

despegar *t.* to detach, unglue. 2 *i.* AER. to take off.

despensa *f.* pantry, larder, store-room.

desperdicio *m.* waste. 2 (spec. *pl.*) leavings, refuse.

despertar *t.* to wake, awaken. 2 to excite [appetite]. 3 *i.-ref.* to wake up, awake. ¶ Conjug. like *acertar.*

despierto, ta *a.* awake. 2 lively, smart.

desplegar *t.* to unfold, spread. 2 to display [activity].

desplomarse *ref.* [of a wall] to tumble down. 2 [of a pers.] to collapse.

despojar *t.* to despoil, deprive; to strip. 2 *ref. despojarse de*, to take off [a garment].

despojo *m.* plundering; dispossession. 2 spoils. *3 pl.* leavings. scraps.

desposado, da *a.* newly married. 2 handcuffed.

despreciar *t.* to despise.

desprecio *m.* contempt, scorn.

desprender *t.* to detach, unfasten. *2 ref.* to withdraw from, renounce. 3 to come away from, fall down. 4 to follow.

desprendimiento *m.* detaching. 2 emission [of light, heat, etc.]. 3 generosity, disinterestedness. 4 landslide.

después *adv.* after, afterwards, later; next.

destacar *t.* to detach [troops]. *2 t.-ref.* to stand out.

destapar *t.* to uncover. uncork. 2 to take off the cover or lid of.

destello *m.* sparkle. 2 gleam, flash; beam [of light].

desterrar *t.* to exile, banish. ¶ CONJUG. like *acertar.*

destierro *m.* banishment, exile.

destilería *f.* distillery.

destinar *t.* to destine. 2 to assign, appoint [to a post].

destino *m.* destiny, fate. 2 destination: *con ~ a,* bound for, going to. 3 employment, post.

destituir *t.* to dismiss. 2 to destitute. ¶ CONJUG. like *huir.*

destreza *f.* skill, dexterity.

destrozar *t.* to break in pieces, shatter, rend, destroy.

destrucción *f.* destruction, ruin.

destruir *t.* to destroy. 2 to

bring to ruin. 3 to waste. ¶ CONJUG. like *huir.*

desvalido, da *a.* helpless, unprotected, destitute.

desvanecer *t.* to dissolve. 2 to dispel [clouds, etc.]. 3 to efface [a recollection]. *4 t.-ref.* to swell [with pride]. *5 ref.* to melt, vanish, evaporate. 6 to faint, swoon. 7 RADIO to fade. ¶ CONJUG. like *agradecer.*

desvelar *t.* to keep awake. *2 ref.* to be unable to sleep. 3 to take great pains.

desvelo *m.* sleeplessness, wakefulness. 2 care, solicitude.

desventaja *f.* disadvantage; drawback.

desventura *f.* misfortune.

desviar *t.* to turn aside, swerve. 3 RLY. to switch. *4 ref.* to swerve.

desvío *m.* deviation, deflection. 2 RLY. side-track.

detalle *m.* detail, particular.

detective *m.* detective.

detener *t.* to detain, stop; to check. 2 to arrest, capture. *3 ref.* to stop, halt. 4 to delay. ¶ CONJUG. like *tener.*

determinación *f.* determination. 2 decision. 3 firmness.

determinar *t.* to determine. 2 to resolve, decide.

detrás *adv.* behind, back, in the rear.

deuda *f.* debt; indebtedness.

deudor, ra *m.-f.* debtor.

devoción *f.* piety, devoutness.

devolver *t.* to give back.

devorar *t.* to devour.

devoto, ta *a.* devout, pious.

día *m.* day. ~ *de fiesta,* holiday; ~ *laborable,* workday; *hoy ~,* today, now, nowadays; **¡buenos días!**, good morning! 2 daylight, daytime.

diablo m. devil, demon, fiend; wicked person. 2 bad-tempered, reckless. 3 **pobre ~**, poor devil.

diáfano, na a. transparent, clear.

diálogo m. dialogue.

diamante m. diamond.

diámetro m. diameter.

diantre m. devil. 2 interj. the deuce!

diario, ria a. daily: **a ~**, daily, every day. 2 m. daily newspaper. 3 day-book.

dibujar t. to draw , make a drawing of; to sketch, design. 2 ref. to appear, show.

dibujo m. drawing, sketch, portrayal.

diccionario m. dictionary.

diciembre m. December.

dictadura f. dictatorship.

dictar t. to dictate [a letter, terms, etc.]. 2 to inspire, suggest. 3 to give [laws, etc.].

dicha f. happiness. 2 fortune.

dicho, cha p. p. of DECIR: **~ y hecho**, no sooner said than done. 2 a. said, mentioned. 3 m. saying, proverb.

dichoso, sa a. happy, lucky.

diecinueve a.-m. nineteen. 2 m. nineteenth.

dieciocho a.-m. eighteen. 2 m. eighteenth.

dieciséis a.-m. sixteen. 2 m. sixteenth.

diecisiete a.-m. seventeen. 2 m. seventeenth.

diente m. ANAT., ZOOL. tooth: **hablar entre dientes**, to mutter, mumble; **hincar el ~ en**,

to backbite, slander; to attack [a task, etc.]. 2 fang [of serpent]. 3 tooth [of a comb, saw, etc.]; cog. 4 clove [of garlic].

diestro, tra a. right, right-hand. 2 dexterous, skilful.

dieta f. diet. 2 assembly.

diez a.-m. ten. 2 m. tenth.

diferencia f. difference.

diferenciar t. to differentiate.

diferente a. different.

diferir t. to defer, delay, postpone, put off. 2 i. to differ. ¶ CONJUG. like **hervir**.

difícil a. difficult, hard.

dificultad f. difficulty. 2 objection.

difundir t.-ref. to diffuse, spread out. 2 RADIO to broadcast.

difunto, ta a. deceased, defunt. 2 m.-f. deceased, dead.

digerir t. to digest. ¶ CONJUG. like **hervir**.

digestión f. digestion.

dignarse ref. to deign, condescend.

dignidad f. dignity; rank.

digno, na a. worthy. 2 deserving. 3 suitable.

dilatar t.-ref. to dilate, enlarge, widen, expand.

diligencia f. diligence, activity, dispatch. 2 errand; steps, action. 3 stage-coach.

diligente a. diligent; quick.

dimensión f. dimension, bulk.

diminuto, ta a. little, tiny.

dimisión f. resignation.

dimitir t. to resign, give up.

dinero m. money, currency, wealth.

Dios pr. n. God: ¡adiós!, farewell, good-bye.

diosa f. goddess.

diploma m. diploma. 2 licence.

diplomático, ca a. diplomatic, tactful. 2 m.-f. diplomat.

diputado m. deputy, representative.

dique m. dam mole, dike. 2 NAUT. dry dock.

dirección f. direction: ~ única, one way. 2 direction, management; leadership. 3 postal address.

directivo, va a. directive, managing. 2 m. *executive.

directo, ta a. direct, straight.

director, ra m.-f. director, manager. 2 MUS. conductor.

dirigente a. leading, governing. 2 m.-f. director, *executive.

dirigir t. to direct. 2 to manage, govern; to lead. 3 MUS. to conduct. 4 to address [a letter, etc.]. 5 ref. to address, speak to. 6 to go to. 7 to apply to.

discípulo, la m.-f. disciple. 2 pupil [of a teacher].

disco m. disk. 2 record.

discreción f. discretion: a ~, at will.

discreto, ta a. discreet, prudent. 2 not bad; fairly good.

discurrir i. to go about, roam. 2 [of a river] to flow. 3 [of time] to pass. 4 to reason, meditate; to infer. 5 to invent, contrive.

discurso m. discourse. 2 reasoning. 3 talk, speech.

discusión f. discussion.

discutir t.-i. to discuss, argue.

disfrazar t. to disguise, conceal, mask.

disfrutar t. to enjoy, possess, benefit by.

disgustar f. to displease, annoy; to pain, give sorrow. 2 ref. to be displeased or hurt. 3 to have a difference [with].

disgusto m. displeasure, annoyance, trouble, quarrel: a ~, against one's will.

disipar t. to dissipate, scatter, squander. 2 ref. to vanish.

disminuir t.-i.-ref. to diminish, lessen, decrease. 2 to taper. ¶ CONJUG. like huir.

disolver t.-ref. to dissolve; to melt. ¶ CONJUG. like mover.

disparar t. to discharge, fire, let off: ~ un tiro, to fire a shot. 2 to hurl, throw. 3 ref. to go off.

disparate m. absurdity, nonsense. 2 blunder, mistake.

disparo m. shot, discharge. 2 MACH. release, trip, start.

dispensar t. to grant. 2 to exempt. 3 to excuse.

dispersar t. to disperse, scatter.

disponer t. to dispose, arrange. 2 to prepare, get ready. 3 to order, decree.

disposición f. disposition. 2 disposal. 3 natural aptitude. 4 order.

disputar t. to dispute, contest. 2 i. to argue.

distancia f. distance.

distante a. distant, far.

distinción f. distinction, privilege; rank. 2 clarity.

distinguido, da *a.* distinguished.

distinguir *t.* to distinguish. *2* to discriminate. *3 ref.* to be distinguished; to differ.

distinto, ta *a.* distinct. *2* different.

distraer *t.* to amuse, entertain. *2* to distract [the attention, etc.]. *3 ref.* to amuse oneself. *4* to be inattentive.

distribución *f.* distribution. *2* arrangement.

distribuir *t.* to distribute ¶ CONJUG. like **huir**.

distrito *m.* district; region.

diurno, na *a.* daily, diurnal.

diversión *f.* diversion, amusement, entertainment.

diverso, sa *a.* diverse, different, various. *2 pl.* several, many.

divertido, da *a.* amusing, funny.

divertir *t.* to amuse, entertain. *2* to divert, turn away. ¶ CONJUG. like **hervir**.

dividir *t.* to divide, split, separate.

divino, na *a.* divine, heavenly.

divisar *t.* to descry, sight, perceive, make out.

división *f.* division.

divorcio *m.* divorce, separation.

doblar *t.* to double. *2* to fold. *3* to bend, bow [one's head]. *4* to turn [a page; a corner]. *5 i.* to toll, knell. *6 ref.* to stoop, give in.

doble *a.* double, twofold.

doce *a.-m.* twelve. *2 m.* twelfth.

docena *f.* dozen.

docente *a.* teaching.

doctor, ra *m.-f.* doctor.

doctrina *f.* doctrine. *2* learning, knowledge. *3* catechism.

documento *m.* document.

dólar *m.* dollar [U.S. money].

doler *i.* to ache, hurt, pain. *2 ref.* **dolerse de,** to repent; to feel sorry for. ¶ CONJUG. like **mover.**

dolor *m.* pain, ache, aching: *~ de cabeza,* headache. *2* pain, sorrow, grief.

doloroso, sa *a.* painful, sorrowful; pitiful.

domar *t.* to tame. *2* to break in [horses, etc.].

doméstico, ca *a.* domestic. *2 m.-f.* house servant.

domicilio *m.* domicile, home.

dominar *t.* to dominate. *2* to domineer. *3* to rule over. *4* to control. *5* to master [a subject]. *6* to overlook.

domingo *m.* Sunday.

dominio *m.* dominion. *2* domination, control. *3* mastery [of a subject]. *4* domain.

don *m.* gift, present. *2* talent; knack: *~ de gentes,* charm. *3* Don, Spanish title prefixed to Christian names of men.

doncella *f.* virgin, maiden, maid. *2* maidservant.

donde *adv.-pron.* where, wherein, whither, in which.

dondequiera *adv.* anywhere, wherever.

doña *f.* Spanish title used before the Christian name of a lady.

dorado, da *a.* gilt, golden. *2 m.* gilding.

dorar *t.* to gild. *2* COOK. to brown.

dormir *i.* to sleep, rest. *2 ref.* to go to sleep, fall asleep. ¶

CONJUG. INDIC. Pres.: *duermo, duermes, duerme;* dormimos, dormís, *duermen.* | Pret.: dormí, dormiste, *durmió;* dormimos, dormisteis, *durmieron.* ‖ SUBJ. Pres.: *duerma, duermas, duerma; durmamos, durmáis, duerman.* | Imperf.: *durmiera, durmieras,* etc., or *durmiese, durmieses,* etc. | Fut.: *durmiere, durmieres,* etc. ‖ IMPER.: *duerme, duerma; durmamos,* dormid, *duerman.* | GER.: *durmiendo.*

dormitorio *m.* bedroom.

dos *a.-n.* two.

doscientos, tas *a.-m.* two hundred.

dotar *t.* to endow, dower, bestow.

drama *m.* drama.

dramático, ca *a.* dramatic.

ducha *f.* shower-bath.

duda *f.* doubt.

dudar *i.-t.* to doubt, hesitate.

dudoso, sa *a.* doubtful.

duelo *m.* duel. 2 grief, sorrow. 3 mourning.

duende *m.* goblin, elf; ghost.

dueño *m.* owner, proprietor, master, landlord.

dulce *a.* sweet. 2 saltless, insipid. 3 fresh [water]. 4 *adv.* softly. 5 *m.* sweetmeat, confection.

dulcería *f.* confectionery shop.

duodécimo, ma *a.-m.* twelfth.

duque *m.* duke.

durante *prep.* during, for.

durar *i.* to endure, last, continue.

duro, ra *a.* hard. 2 harsh, severe. 3 obstinate. 4 strong, hardy. 5 stingy. 6 *adv.* hard. 7 *m.* Spanish coin worth 5 pesetas.

E

e *conj.* and.

ébano *m.* BOT. ebony.

ebrio, ebria *a.* drunk, intoxicated.

eclesiástico, ca *a.* ecclesiastic(al. *2 m.* clergyman.

eclipse *m.* eclipse.

eco *m.* echo.

economía *f.* economy. *2* saving, thrift. *3* sparingness.

económico, ca *a.* economic. *2* thrifty, saving.

economizar *t.* to economize; to save, spare.

echar *t.* to throw, cast. *2* to put in, add. *3* to give off [sparks, etc.]. *4* to dismiss. *5* to pour [wine, etc.]. *6 ~ un trago,* to take a drink; *~ a perder,* to spoil; *~ a pique,* to sink; *~ de menos,* to miss. *7 i.-ref. ~ a correr, a reír,* etc., to begin to run. *8 ref.* to lie down. *9* to throw oneself into.

edad *f.* age.

edición *f.* edition. *2* issue. *3* publication.

edificar *t.* to build, construct.

edificio *m.* edifice, building.

editorial *a.* publishing. *2 m.* editorial, leading article. *3 f.* publishing house.

educación *f.* education. *2* breeding, manners; politeness.

educar *t.* to educate; to train, bring up.

efectivo, va *a.* effective, real. *2 m.* cash, specie: *en ~,* in cash.

efecto *m.* effect, result; *en ~,* in fact, indeed. *2* impression.

efectuar *t.* to effect, do, carry out. *2 ref.* to take place.

eficaz *a.* efficient, effective, active, efficacious.

eficiente *a.* efficient.

egoísmo *m.* selfishness.

egoísta *a.* selfish [person].

eje *m.* axis. *2* axle, shaft.

ejecución *f.* execution; carrying out. *2* performance.

ejecutar *t.* to execute, carry out, fulfil, perform.

ejecutivo, va *a.* executive.

ejemplar *a.* exemplary. *2 m.* pattern, model. *3* copy.

ejemplo *m.* example. *2* instance.; *por ~,* for instance.

ejercer t. to exercise. 2 to practise [a profession].

ejercicio m. exercise, training. 2 MIL. drill.

ejercitar t. to practise. 2 t.-ref. to exercise, drill.

ejército m. army.

el def. art. masc. sing. the.

él pers. pron. masc. sing. he; him; it [after prep.].

elaborar t. to elaborate, manufacture, work.

elección f. election. 2 choice.

electricidad f. electricity.

electricista m. electrician; electrical engineer.

eléctrico, ca a. electric(al.

elefante m. elephant.

elegante a. elegant, smart.

elegir t. to elect. 2 to choose, select. ¶ CONJUG. like **servir**.

elemental a. elementary.

elemento m. element.

elevación f. elevation, raising, rise. 2 elevation, height.

elevar t. to elevate, raise. 2 ref. to rise. soar.

eliminación f. elimination, removal.

eliminar t. to eliminate, remove.

elocuente a. eloquent.

elogio m. praise, eulogy.

ella pron. f. sing. she; her, it [after prep.].

ello pron. neuter sing. it.

ellos, ellas pron. m. & f. pl. they; them [after prep.].

embajador m. ambassador.

embarcación f. NAUT. boat, ship, vessel.

embarcar t.-i.-ref. NAUT. to embark.

embargar t. to restrain. 2 [of emotions] to overcome. 3 LAW to attach, seize.

embargo m. LAW attachment, seizure. 2 embargo. 3 sin ~, nevertheless, however.

embarque m. shipment.

embellecer t. to embellish, beautify. ¶ CONJUG. like **agradecer**.

emblema m. emblem, symbol.

emborrachar t. to intoxicate, make drunk. 2 ref. to get drunk.

emboscada f. ambuscade, ambush.

embriagado, da a. intoxicated; drunk.

embrujar t. to bewitch, enchant.

embuste m. lie, falsehood; fraud, trinket.

embustero, ra m.-f. liar.

emergencia f. emergency.

emigración f. emigration.

eminente a. eminent, excellent.

emitir t. to emit. 2 to issue. 3 RADIO to broadcast.

emoción f. emotion, excitement, thrill.

emocionante a. moving, touching, thrilling.

emocionar t. to move, touch, thrill. 2 ref. to be moved.

empalizada f. stockade, palisade.

empapar t. to soak, drench.

empatar t.-i.-ref. to tie, equal, draw.

empate m. tie, draw.

empeñar t. to pledge; to pawn. 2 to engage. 3 ref. to get into debt. 4 **empeñarse en**, to insist on; to engage in.

empeño m. pledge. 2 pawn: **casa de empeños**, pawnbroker. 3 insistence.

emperador *m.* emperor.

empero *conj.* yet, however.

empezar *t.-i.* to begin: ~ *a*, to begin to, to start. ¶ CONJUG. like *acertar*.

empleado, da *m. f.* employee: clerk.

emplear *t.* to employ. 2 to spend, invest [money].

empleo *m.* employment, job; occupation. 2 use. 3 investment [of money].

empolvar *ref.* to powder one's face.

empollar *t.* to brood, hatch [eggs]. 2 coll. to grind, swot up [a subject].

emprender *t.* to undertake; to begin, to start out.

empresa *f.* enterprise. 2 firm. management.

empresario *m.* manager; impresario.

empujar *t.* to push, shove; to impel.

empuñar *t.* to handle. 2 to clutch, grasp, grip.

en *prep.* in, into.

enamorado, da *a.* in love. 2 *m.-f.* lover.

enamorar *t.* to make love to, court, woo. 2 *ref.* to fall in love.

enano, na *a.-m.-f.* dwarf.

encabezamiento *m.* heading, headline. 2 tax roll.

encabezar *t.* to head.

encajar *t.* to thrust in, fit into, insert; to put or force in. 2 to land, take [a blow]. 3 to fit in; to be relevant.

encaje *m.* fitting in. 2 socket, groove. 3 lace.

encallecerse *ref.* to become hardened or callous. ¶ CONJUG. like *agradecer*.

encaminar *t.* to direct. 2 *ref.* to set out for.

encantador, ra *a.* enchanting, charming, delightful.

encantar *t.* to enchant, charm.

encanto *m.* enchantment. 2 charm, delight.

encaramar *t.* to raise, hoist. 2 *ref.* to climb, mount.

encarcelar *t.* to imprison, jail, put in prison.

encargar *t.* to entrust. 2 to order. 3 *ref.* ~ *de*, to take charge of.

encargo *m.* charge. 2 errand. 3 order.

encarnado, da *a.* flesh-coloured. 2 red.

encendedor *m.* lamplighter. 2 cigarette-lighter.

encender *t.* to light, set fire to, kindle. 2 *ref.* to burn. 3 [of war] to break out. ¶ CONJUG. like *entender*.

encendido, da *a.* red, flushed.

encerrar *t.* to shut in, lock up. 2 to enclose, contain. ¶ CONJUG. like *acertar*.

encima *adv.* on, upon, over: ~ *de*, on, upon; *por* ~ *de*, over, above.

encina *f.* BOT. evergreen oak.

encomendar *t.* to commend. ¶ CONJUG. like *acertar*.

encontrar *t.-ref.* to find; to meet. 2 *ref.* to be [in a place]. 3 to feel [ill, well, etc.]. 4 *encontrarse con*, to come across. ¶ CONJUG. like *contar*.

encorvar *t.* to bend, curve. 2 *ref.* to bend over, stoop.

encuentro *m.* meeting, encounter.

enderezar t. to straighten, unbend. 2 to right, set upright.

enemigo, ga a. enemy, hostile. 2 m.-f. enemy, foe.

energía f. energy. 2 MECH. power: ~ *eléctrica*, electric power.

enérgico, ca a. energetic, vigorous, active, lively.

enero m. January.

enfadar t. to displease, annoy, anger. 2 ref. to be displeased, get angry, be cross.

enfermar i. to fall ill.

enfermedad f. illness, disease, sickness.

enfermero, ra m. male nurse. 2 f. [woman] nurse.

enfermo, ma a. sick, ill. 2 m.-f. patient.

enfocar t. to focus. 2 to envisage; to approach.

enfrascar t. to bottle. 2 ref. to become absorbed in.

enfrentar t. to confront, put face to face. 2 t.-ref. to face.

enfrente adv. in front, opposite: ~ *de*, in front of.

enfriar t. to cool. 2 ref. to cool down or off. 3 to get cold.

enganchar t. to hook. 2 to hitch. 3 RLY. to couple. 4 MIL. to recruit.

engañar t. to deceive, beguile, dupe, cheat. 2 ref. to be mistaken.

engaño m. deceit; falsehood; fraud. 2 error, mistake.

engañoso, sa a. deceptive, delusive. 2 deceitful.

engarzar t. JEW. to link. 2 to set, mount.

engendrar t. to engender, beget. 2 to generate, originate.

engordar t. to fatten. 2 i. to grow fat.

engrandecer t. to enlarge. ¶ CONJUG. like *agradecer*.

enjambre m. swarm of bees. 2 crowd.

enjaular t. to cage. 2 coll. to imprison.

enjugar t. to dry; to wipe.

enlace m. tie, bond. 2 link. 3 RLY. junction; connection.

enlatar t. to can [food, etc.].

enlazar t. to lace. 2 to link. 3 ref. to marry. 4 to be connected.

enmarañar t. to entangle. 2 ref. to get tangled.

enmendar t. to correct, amend. 2 repair, make amends for. 3 ref. to reform, mend one's ways. ¶ CONJUG. like *acertar*.

enmienda f. amendment.

enojar t. to anger, make angry, vex, annoy. 2 ref. to become angry, get cross.

enojo m. anger, irritation. 2 annoyance; rage, trouble.

enorme a. enormous, huge.

enredadera f. creeper. 2 bindweed.

enredar t. to tangle, entangle, mat, ravel. 2 to net. 3 to embroil. 4 i. [of children] to be mischievous. 5 ref. to get entangled.

enriquecer t. to enrich. 2 ref. to become wealthy. ¶ CONJUG. like *agradecer*.

ensalada f. salad.

ensanchar t.-ref. to widen, enlarge, expand.

ensayar t. to assay [metals]. 2 to try out, test. 3 to rehearse.

ensayo m. assay. 2 rehearsal.

enseñanza f. teaching, instruction, education.

enseñar t. to teach. 2 to instruct, train. 3 to show.

ensuciar t. to dirty, soil, stain. 2 ref. to get dirty.

ensueño m. day-dream, fantasy; illusion.

1) **entender** m. understanding, opinion.

2) **entender** t. to understand. 2 ref. to get along well together. ¶ CONJUG. IND. Pres.: *entiendo, entiendes, entiende;* entendemos, entendéis, *entienden.* ‖ SUBJ.: Pres.: *entienda, entiendas, entienda;* entendamos, entendáis, *entiendan.* ‖ IMPER.: *entiende, entienda;* entendamos, entended, *entiendan.*

entendimiento m. understanding, comprehension.

enterar t. to inform, acquaint. 2 ref. to learn, be informed of; to know, find out.

entero, ra a. entire, whole. 2 honest, upright.

enterrar t. to bury. 2 ref. to retire, bury oneself. ¶ CONJUG. like *acertar.*

entidad f. entity. 2 association.

entierro m. burial, funeral.

entonar t. to sing in tune. 2 to intone.

entonces adv. then, at that time: *por* ~, at that time.

entrada f. entrance, gate. 2 entry; admission. 3 ticket.

entrambos, bas a. pl. both.

entraña f. the innermost part. 2 pl. entrails. 3 heart.

entrar i. to enter, go in(to, come in(to, get in(to.

entre prep. between, among, amongst. 2 ~ *tanto,* meanwhile.

entregar t. to deliver, hand over. 2 t.-ref. to give up, surrender. 3 ref. to yield, submit. 4 to devote oneself to.

entretanto adv. meanwhile.

entretener t. to delay, detain. 2 to entertain, amuse. 3 ref. to delay. 4 to amuse oneself. ¶ CONJUG. like *tener.*

entrevista f. interview, meeting. 2 date, appointment.

entrevistar t. to interview. 2 ref. to have an interview with.

entristecer t. to sadden. 2 ref. to become sad. ¶ CONJUG. like *agradecer.*

entusiasmar t. to captivate, excite, enrapture. 2 ref. to get excited about.

entusiasmo m. enthusiasm, eagerness, keenness.

entusiasta m.-f. enthusiast, fan, eager fellow.

enumerar t. to enumerate.

envase m. bottling. 2 container.

enviar t. to send, dispatch.

envidia f. envy, jealousy.

envidiar t. to envy, covet.

envidioso, sa a.-n. envious, jealous.

envío m. sending, remittance; shipment; dispatch.

envolver t. to cover, envelop, wrap up. 2 to involve. ¶ CONJUG. like *mover.* | P. P.: *envuelto.*

epidemia f. epidemic.

episodio m. episode; incident.

época f. epoch, age, time.

equilibrio m. equilibrium, balance, poise.

equipaje m. luggage, baggage. 2 equipment, outfit.

equipar t. to equip, fit out.

equipo *m.* equipment. *2* squad. *3* SPORT. team.

equivaler *i.* to be equivalent; to be equal. ¶ CONJUG. like *valer.*

equivocación *f.* mistake, error.

equivocado, da *a.* mistaken. *2* wrong.

equivocar *t.-ref.* to mistake. *2 ref.* to be mistaken; to make a mistake; to be wrong.

erguir *t.* to raise, erect, lift. *2 ref.* to sit up. ¶ CONJUG. INDIC. Pres.: *irgo* or *yergo, irgues* or *yergues, irgue* or *yergue;* erguimos, erguís, *irguen* or *yerguen.* | Pret.: erguí, erguiste, *irguió;* erguimos, erguisteis, *irguieron.* ‖ SUBJ. Pres.: *irga* or *yerga, irgas* or *yergas,* etc. | Imperf.: *irguiera, irguieras,* etc., or *irguiese, irguieses,* etc. | Fut.: *irguiere, irguieres,* etc. ‖ IMPER.: *irgue* or *yergue, irga* or *yerga; irgamos* or *yergamos,* erguid, *irgan* or *yergan.* ‖ P. P.: *erguido.* ‖ GER.: *irguiendo.*

erizar *t.* to set on end; to make bristle. *2 ref.* to stand on end.

erizo *m.* hedgehog, porcupine. *2 ~ de mar,* sea-urchin.

ermita *f.* hermitage.

ermitaño *m.* EREMITA.

errante *a.* errant, wandering, strolling, vagabond.

erróneo, nea *a.* erroneous, wrong.

error *m.* error. *2* mistake, fault.

erudito, ta *a.* erudite, scholarly, learned.

esbelto, ta *a.* slender and graceful.

escabroso, sa *a.* rough, rugged. *2* harsh, rude. *3* scabrous, indecent.

escala *f.* ladder, step-ladder. *2* scale. *3* NAUT. port of call.

escalar *t.* to scale, climb.

escalera *f.* stair, staircase. *2* ladder.

escalón *m.* step of a stair.

escándalo *m.* scandal: *dar un ~,* to make a scene. *2* noise.

escapar *i.-ref.* to escape; to flee, run away. *2 ref.* leak out.

escape *m.* escape, flight. *2* escape, leak.

escarabajo *m.* ENT. beetle.

escarbar *t.* to scratch.

escasear *t.* to be scarce, fall short, be wanting.

escasez *f.* scarcity, lack, shortage; scantiness. *2* poverty.

escaso, sa *a.* scarce, scant. *2* short.

escena *f.* THEAT. stage. *2* scene. *3* THEAT. scenery.

escenario *m.* THEAT. stage.

esclavitud *f.* slavery.

esclavo, va *m.-f.* slave.

escoba *f.* broom.

escoger *t.* to choose, select.

escolar *m.* schoolboy, schoolgirl; student.

esconder *t.* to hide, conceal.

escondite *m.* hiding-place.

escopeta *f.* shot-gun, gun.

escribir *t.-i.* to write. ¶ P. P. irreg.: *escrito.*

escritor, ra *m.-f.* writer, author.

escritorio *m.* writing-desk. *2* office.

escritura *f.* writing. *2* hand-writing. *2* LAW deed.

escuchar *t.* to listen to.

escudero *m.* HIST. squire.

escudo *m.* shield, buckler. 2 coat of arms. 4 gold crown [coin].

escuela *f.* school.

escultura *f.* sculpture.

escupir *i.* to spit.

ese *m.* **esa** *f. sing. dem. a.* that, **esos** *m.* **esas** *f. pl.* those.

ése *m.* **ésa** *f.* **eso** *neut. sing. dem. pron.* that one, **ésos** *m.* **ésas** *f. pl.* those.

esencia *f.* essence. 2 perfume.

esencial *a.* essential.

esfera *f.* GEOM. sphere. 2 social class, rank. 3 dial.

esforzar *t.* to give strength. 2 *ref.* to try hard, strive.

esfuerzo *m.* effort.

eslabón *m.* link.

esmerado, da *a.* careful, conscientious, painstaking.

esmeralda *f.* emerald.

esmero *m.* great care, refinement, nicety.

espacio *m.* space. 2 room. 3 blank. 4 delay, slowness.

espacioso, sa *a.* spacious. roomy.

espada *f.* sword.

espalda *f. sing. & pl.* back; shoulders.

espantar *t.* to frighten, scare. 2 *ref.* to be astonished.

espanto *m.* fright, dread.

espantoso, sa *a.* fearful, frightful, dreadful. 2 astonishing.

español, la *a.* Spanish [person; language]. 2 *m.-f.* Spaniard.

esparcir *t.-ref.* to scatter, spread. 2 to recreate. 3 *ref.* to amuse oneself.

especia *f.* spice [condiment].

especial *a.* especial. 2 special; **en** ~, specially. 3 **-mente** *adv.* especially, specially.

especialidad *f.* speciality.

especialista *a.-n.* specialist.

especie *f.* species. 2 kind, sort.

espectáculo *m.* spectacle; show. 2 scandal: **dar un** ~, to make a scene.

espectador, ra *m.-f.* spectator. 2 *pl.* audience.

espectro *m.* spectre, ghost. 2 PHYS. spectrum.

espejo *m.* mirror, looking-glass.

esperanza *f.* hope. 2 expectation.

esperar *t.* to hope; to expect. 2 to look forward to. 3 *t.-i.* to await, wait [for]. 4 *i.* to hope.

espeso, sa *a.* thick, dense.

espetar *t.* to spit, skewer.

espía *m. f.* spy [person].

espiga *f.* BOT. spike, ear [of wheat]. 2 peg, brad.

espina *f.* thorn.

espiritismo *m.* spiritism, spiritualism.

espiritista *m.-f.* spiritist, spiritualist.

espíritu *m.* spirit; soul. 2 ghost: **Espíritu Santo**, Holy Ghost. 3 vigour; courage.

espiritual *a.* spiritual.

espléndido, da *a.* splendid.

esplendor *m.* splendour.

espolvorear *t.* to powder.

esponja *f.* sponge.

esposa *f.* wife. 2 *pl.* handcuffs.

esposo *m.* husband.

espuela *f.* spur; stimulus.

espuma *f.* foam, froth. *2* lather [of soap]. *3* scum.

esqueleto *m.* skeleton.

esquiar *i.* to ski.

esquimal *a.-n.* Eskimo.

esquina *f.* corner.

estable *a.* stable, steady, firm.

establecer *t.* establish. *2* to decree. *3 ref.* to settle down. ¶ CONJUG. like *agradecer*.

establecimiento *m.* settlement. *2* establishment, shop, store.

establo *m.* stable; cattle barn.

estaca *f.* stake, picket. *2* HORT. cutting. *3* stick, cudgel.

estación *f.* season [of the year]. *2* halt, stop. *3* RLY. station.

estadio *m.* stadium.

estado *m.* state, condition. *2* order, class. *3* POL. state, government. *4* MIL. ~ *mayor*, staff.

estallar *i.* to burst, explode. *2* to break out.

estambre *m.* worsted, woolen yarn. *2* BOT. stamen.

estampa *f.* print, engraving.

estancar *t.* to stem, sta(u)nch, stop the flow of, hold up or back. *2 ref.* to stagnate.

estancia *f.* stay. *2* living-room, *3* (Am.) ranch, farm.

estanco, ca *m.* tobacconist's.

estanque *m.* reservoir, pond.

estante *m.* shelf, bookcase.

estar *i.-ref.* to be; to keep, stay, remain, stand. ¶ CONJUG. INDIC. Pres.: *estoy, estás, está;* estamos, estáis,

están. Pret.: *estuve, estuviste, estuvo,* etc. ‖ SUBJ.: Pres.: *esté, estés, esté;* estemos, estéis, *estén.* | Imperf.: *estuviera, estuvieras,* etc., or *estuviese, estuvieses,* etc. | Fut.: *estuviere, estuvieres,* etc. ‖ IMPER.: *está, esté;* estemos, estad, *estén.* ‖ P. P: *estado.* ‖ GER.: *estando.*

estatua *f.* statue.

estatura *f.* stature, height.

estatuto *m.* statutes, regulations.

1) **este** *m.* east, orient.

2) **este** *m.* **esta** *f. sing. dem. a.* this; **estos** *m.* **estas** *f. pl.* these.

éste *m.* **ésta** *f. sing. dem. pron.* this one; **esto** *neut.* this, this thing; **éstos** *m.* **éstas** *f. pl.* these. *2 éste ... aquél,* the former ... the latter.

estera *f.* mat; matting.

estéril *a.* sterile, barren.

estiércol *m.* dung, manure.

estilo *m.* style. *2* use, custom.

estima *f.* esteem, appreciation.

estimar *t.* to esteem, hold in regard. *2* to judge, think. *3* to estimate, value.

estimular *t.* to stimulate. *2* to incite, to goad.

estímulo *m.* stimulus. *2* incentive. *3* encouragement.

estío *m.* summer.

estirar *t.* to stretch, pull out. *2 ref.* to stretch out.

estómago *m.* ANAT. stomach.

estorbar *t.* to hinder, obstruct. *2* to annoy.

estrechar *t.* to narrow, make less wide. *2* to take in [a garment]. *3* to tighten [bonds, etc.]. *5* ~ *la mano*, to shake hands with.

estrecho, cha *a.* narrow. *2* tight [shoes, etc.]. *3* close. *4 m.* GEOG. straits.

estrella *f.* star.

estrellar *t.-ref.* to smash [against], dash to pieces, shatter.

estremecer *t.-ref.* to shake, shiver, shudder; to thrill; to tremble. ¶ CONJUG. like *agradecer*.

estrenar *t.* to use or wear for the first time; to handsel. *2* to perform [a play] or to show [a film] for the first time.

estrépito *m.* noise, crash, din.

estribar *i.* ~ *en*, to rest on; to be based on; to lie on.

estribo *m.* stirrup.

estricto, ta *a.* strict; severe.

estrofa *f.* strophe, stanza.

estropear *t.* to spoil, ruin, damage. *2* to maim. *3 ref.* to get spoiled, ruined, maimed.

estructura *f.* structure.

estruendo *m.* great noise, clangor, crash. *2* uproar.

estuche *m.* case, sheath.

estudiante *m.* student.

estudiar *t.* to study. *2 i.* to be a student.

estudio *m.* study. *2* studio, library. *3 pl.* learning.

estudioso, sa *a.* studious.

estufa *f.* stove, heater.

estúpido, da *a.-n.* stupid.

etcétera *f.* et cetera, and so on.

eternamente *adv.* eternally.

eternidad *f.* eternity.

eterno, na *a.* eternal, everlasting.

etiqueta *f.* label. *2* formality.

eucalipto *m.* eucalyptus.

europeo, a *a.-n.* European.

evangélico, ca *a.* evangelical.

evangelio *m.* gospel.

evaporar *t.-ref.* to evaporate.

evidencia *f.* evidence.

evidente *a.* evident, obvious.

evitar *t.* to avoid, elude, shun. *2* to prevent.

exactitud *f.* exactness, accuracy.

exacto, ta *a.* exact, accurate. *2 adv.* right.

exaltar *t.* to praise. *2 ref.* to become excited.

examen *m.* examination. *2* inquiry, investigation.

examinar *t.* to examine. *2* to inspect, survey, look into. *3 ref.* to sit for an examination.

exceder *t.* to exceed, surpass, outdo. *2 i.-ref.* to go too far.

excelente *a.* excellent.

excelso, sa *a.* lofty, sublime.

excepción *f.* exception.

excepto *adv.* except, save.

exceptuar *t.* to except, leave out.

excesivo, va *a.* excessive, too much, immoderate.

exceso *m.* excess, surplus. *2* outrage, intemperance.

excitar *t.* to excite, stir up, move. *2 ref.* to get excited.

exclamar *i.* to exclaim, cry out.

excluir *t.* to exclude, debar, shut out. ¶ CONJUG. like *huir*.

exclusivamente *adv.* exclusively.

exclusivo, va *a.* exclusive. *2* sole.

excursión *f.* excursion, trip, tour.

excusa *f.* excuse, apology.

exhibir *t.* to exhibit, show. *2 ref.* to show off.

exigir *t.* to require, demand.

existencia *f.* existence. *2* life. *3 s. & pl.* COM. stocks.

existir *i.* to exist, be.

éxito *m.* issue. *2* success, hit.

expansión *f.* PHYS., ANAT. expansion. *2* emotional effusion. *3* relaxation.

expedición *f.* expedition. *2* dispatch, speed.

experiencia *f.* experience.

experimentar *t.* to experiment, try. *2* to experience, undergo.

experto, ta *a.* expert, skilful. *2 m.* expert.

expiación *f.* expiation.

explicación *f.* explanation.

explicar *t.* to explain.

explorador *m.-f.* explorer. *2 m.* MIL. scout. *3* boy scout.

explorar *t.* to explore.

explosión *f.* explosion [exploding; outburst]. *2* MIN. blast.

explotar *t.* to run, work, exploit.

exponer *t.* to explain, state. *2* to expose, show. *3* to exhibit.

exportación *f.* exportation, export.

exportar *t.* to export.

exposición *f.* exposition. *2* exhibition, show.

expresar *t.-ref.* to express.

expresión *f.* expression.

expresivo, va *a.* expressive. *2* affectionate, kind.

expreso, sa *a.* expressed. *2* express, clear. *3 m.* RLY. express train.

expuesto, ta *a.* exposed. *2* on view, exhibited. *3* dangerous, hazardous. *4* liable.

expulsar *t.* to expel, drive out.

exquisito, ta *a.* exquisite.

extender *t.* to spread out. *2* to stretch out. ¶ CONJUG. like *entender.*

extensión *f.* extension. *2* range. *3* expanse, stretch.

extenso, sa *a.* extensive, vast, spacious.

exterior *a.* exterior, outer. *2* foreign. *3 m.* exterior, outside. *4* appearance. *5* ~ **mente** externally.

exterminar *t.* to exterminate.

extinguir *t.* to extinguish, quench, put out [fire, etc.]. *2 ref.* to die, go out.

extraer *t.* to extract, draw out.

extranjero, ra *a.* foreign. *2 m.-f.* alien, foreigner: *al* or *en el* ~, abroad.

extrañar *t.* to surprise. *2* (Am.) to miss. *4 ref.* to be surprised, wonder.

extraño, ña *a.* strange, foreign. *2* strange, peculiar.

extraordinario, ria *a.* extraordinary, uncommon.

extraviar *t.* to mislay. *2 ref.* to stray, get lost.

extremidad *f.* extremity, end, border. *2 pl.* extremities.

extremo, ma *a.* extreme. farthest. *2* excessive.

F

fábrica f. factory, works, mill. 2 manufacture.

fabricación f. manufacture.

fabricante m. manufacturer.

fabricar t. to make, manufacture. 2 to build.

fábula f. fable.

fácil a. easy, facile, fluent [speech]. 2 probable, likely.

facilidad f. ease, easiness; fluency. 2 pl. facilities.

facilitar t. to make easy, facilitate.

factor m. cause. 3 RLY. luggage clerk. 4 MATH. factor.

factoría f. agency. 2 trading post. 3 agent's office.

facultad f. faculty. 2 power. 3 ability. 4 pl. mental powers.

faena f. work, toil. 2 task, job, *chore.

faja f. scarf. 2 wrapper. 3 stripe, band.

fajar t. to band, bandage, girdle. 2 to swaddle.

falda f. skirt. 2 lap. 3 slope, foothill. 4 hat brim.

falso, sa a. false. 2 untrue. 3 sham. 4 treacherous. 5 counterfeit [money].

falta f. lack, want, shortage: *a ~ de*, for want of. 2 SPORTS fault. 3 LAW misdeed. 4 mistake. 5 *hacer* ~, to be necessary.

faltar i. to be lacking, wanting or missing. 2 to be absent. 3 to offend somebody. 4 to break [one' word].

falto, ta a. wanting, short.

fallar t. to judge, pass sentence. 2 to ruff, trump [at cards]. 3 i. to fail, miss.

fallecer i. to decease, die. ¶ CONJUG. like **agradecer**.

fama f. fame, renown, reputation. 2 report, rumour.

familia f. family. 2 household.

familiar a. [pertaining to the] family. 2 informal. 3 colloquial. 4 m. relative.

famoso, sa a. famous, renowned.

fanático, ca a. fanatic(al. 2 m.-f. fanatic, fan; bigot.

fango m. mud, mire.

fantasía f. fancy, imagination. 2 tale. 3 vanity.

fantasma m. phantom. 2 ghost.

fantástico, ca *a.* fantastic, fanciful. 2 vain, conceited.

fariseo *m.* pharisee, hypocrite.

farmacéutico, ca *a.* pharmaceutic(al. 2 *m.-f.* chemist, *druggist, pharmacist.

farmacia *f.* pharmacy. 2 chemist's shop, *drug-store.

faro *m.* lighthouse, beacon. 2 headlight [of a car].

farol *m.* street lamp, lamp-post. 2 lantern.

fase *f.* phase, aspect, view.

fatal *a.* fatal. 2 bad, deadly.

fatiga *f.* fatigue, weariness. 2 *pl.* hardships.

fatigar *t.* to fatigue, weary, tire. 2 *ref.* to tire, get tired.

favor *m.* help, aid. 2 favo(u)r, kindness.

favorable *a.* favo(u)rable. 2 advantageous. 2 **-mente** *adv.* favo(u)rably.

favorecer *t.* to help, aid, favo(u)r, support. ¶ CONJUG. like **agradecer.**

favorito, ta *a.-n.* favo(u)rite.

faz *f.* face, visage. 2 aspect.

fe *f.* faith: *dar* ~, to believe. 2 ~ *de bautismo*, certificate of baptism.

febrero *m.* February.

fecundo, da *a.* fruitful, fertile.

fecha *f.* date [time]. 2 day.

federal *a.* federal(istic.

felicidad *f.* happiness, bliss. 2 *pl.* congratulations!

felicitación *f.* congratulation.

felicitar *t.* to congratulate.

feliz *a.* happy, lucky. 2 **-mente** *adv.* happily.

femenino, na *a.* femenine.

fenómeno *m.* phenomenon. 2 monster, freak.

feo, a *a.* ugly.

feria *f.* fair, market: ~ *de muestras*, trade exhibition.

feroz *a.* ferocious. 2 *fig.* ravenous, wild, fierce, savage.

ferretería *f.* hardware. 2 ironmonger's shop.

ferrocarril *m.* railway, *railroad.

fértil *a.* fertile.

fertilizar *t.* to fertilize.

ferviente *a.* FERVOROSO.

fervor *m.* fervour, zeal, warmth.

fervoroso, sa *a.* fervent; devout, zealous.

festejar *t.* to feast, celebrate.

festín *m.* feast, banquet.

festivo, va *a.* humourous, witty. 2 merry, joyful. 3 *día* ~, feast day, holiday.

fianza *f.* bail, guaranty, security, bond.

fiar *t.* to answer for, guarantee. 2 *t.-i.* to sell on credit. 3 *ref.* to trust.

fibra *f.* fibre, fiber; staple.

fidelidad *f.* fidelity, faithfulness.

fideos *m. pl.* vermicelli, noodles.

fiebre *f.* MED. fever. 2 excitement, agitation.

fiel *a.* faithful. 2 *m.* faithful. 3 pointer. 4 **-mente** *adv.* faithfully.

fiera *f.* wild beast.

fiero, ra *a.* fierce, cruel, ferocious. 2 wild [beast].

fiesta *f.* feast, entertainment, party; public rejoicing. 2 holiday. 3 endearment.

figura *f.* figure, form, shape.

figurar *t.* to figure, shape. 2 *i.* to be counted [among]. 3 *ref.* to fancy.

fijar *t.* to fix, fasten. 2 to stick.

3 to set [a date, etc.]. *4 ref.* to settle; to pay attention.

fijo, ja *a.* fixed. *2* firm, steady, set. *3* fast [colour].

fila *f.* row, line; file: ~ *india,* single file; *en ~,* in a row.

filosofía *f.* philosophy.

filósofo, fa *a.* philosophic(al. *2 m.-f.* philosopher.

filtro *m.* filter, strainer.

fin *m.* end; *poner ~ a,* to put an end to; *al ~* at the end; finally; *por ~,* at last, lastly. *2* aim, purpose; *a ~ de [que],* in order to.

final *a.* final, last. *2 m.* end. *3* **-mente** *adv.* finally.

finalizar *t.-i.* to end, finish.

finca *f.* property, land, house.

fingir *t.* to feign, simulate, sham, pretend. *2 ref.* to pretend to be.

fino, na *a.* fine [pure]. *2* thin; sheer. *3* polite. *4* sharp.

firma *f.* signature. *2* [act of] signing. *3* COM. firm.

firmamento *m.* firmament, sky.

firmar *t.* to sign, subscribe.

firme *a.* firm [stable, strong, solid, steady].

fiscal *a.* fiscal. *2 m.* LAW public prosecutor; *district attorney.

física *f.* physics.

físico, ca *a.* physical. *2 m.* physicist. *3* looks.

flaco, ca *a.* lean, thin. *2* weak, frail.

flauta *f.* flute.

flecha *f.* arrow, dart. *2* spire.

flexible *a.* flexible, pliant, lithe, supple. *2* soft [hat].

flojo, ja *a.* loose, slack. *2* weak [wine, etc.]. *3* lax.

flor *f.* flower, blossom.

florecer *i.* to flower, bloom, blossom. ¶ CONJUG. like *agradecer.*

florero, ra *m.-f.* florist. *2 m.* flower vase; flowerpot.

florido, da *a.* flowery, a-bloom, florid.

flota *f.* NAUT. fleet.

flotar *i.* to float.

fluido, da *a.* fluid, fluent. *2 m.* fluid.

foco *m.* focus, centre. *2* AUTO., THEAT. headlight, spotlight.

fogón *m.* hearth. *2* cooking-range.

follaje *m.* foliage.

fomentar *t.* to promote.

fomento *m.* fomentation, fostering; encouragement.

fonda *f.* inn, restaurant.

fondo *m.* bottom. *2* depth. *3* farthest end. *4* background. *5* nature. *6 s. pl.* funds.

forma *f.* form, shape.

formación *f.* formation. *2* form, shape.

formal *a.* formal. *2* serious.

formar *t.* to form, shape.

formidable *a.* formidable, fearful. *2* huge.

fórmula *f.* formula. *2* recipe. *3* prescription.

formular *t.* to formulate: ~ *cargos,* to make charges.

foro *m.* forum. *2* bar. *3* THEAT. back-stage.

forrar *t.* to line. *2* to cover [a book, etc.].

forro *m.* lining; book-cover.

fortalecer *t.* to strengthen. *2 ref.* to grow strong. ¶ CONJUG. like *agradecer.*

fortaleza *f.* fortitude. *2* strength, vigour. *3* fortress.

fortuna *f.* fortune, chance, luck. *2* wealth.

fósforo *m*. CHEM. phosphorus. 2 match.

fósil *a.-m*. fossil.

fotografía *f*. photography. 2 photograph.

fotógrafo *m*. photographer.

fracasar *i*. to fail, be unsuccessful.

fracaso *m*. failure, ruin.

fracción *f*. fraction, part.

fragancia *f*. fragrance, aroma.

fragante *a*. fragrant. 2 FLAGRANTE.

frágil *a*. fragile, brittle, breakable. 2 frail, weak.

fragmento *m*. fragment.

fraile *m*. friar, monk.

francés, sa *a*. French. 2 *m*. Frenchman. 3 *f*. Frenchwoman.

franco, ca *a*. frank, open. 2 generous. 3 free. 4 *m*. franc.

franja *f*. band; stripe. 2 strip.

frasco *m*. vial, bottle, flask.

frase *f*. phrase, sentence.

fraternidad *f*. fraternity; brotherhood.

fray *m*. title prefixed to the names of friars.

frecuencia *f*. frequency: *con ~*, frequently.

frecuente *a*. frequent. 2 -**mente** *adv*. frequently, often.

fregadero *m*. kitchen sink.

fregar *t*. to rub, scrub, scour. 2 to mop [the floor]; to wash up [dishes]. ¶ CONJUG. like **acertar**.

freír *t*. to fry. ¶ CONJUG. like **reír**.

freno *m*. bridle. 2 MACH. brake. 3 control, restraint.

frente *f*. forehead; face: *hacer ~ a*, to face, meet. 2 *m*.

front: *~ a*, in front of; *en ~*, opposite.

fresa *f*. BOT. strawberry.

fresco, ca *a*. cool, fresh. 2 bold, cheeky. 3 *m*. coolness, cool air; *hacer ~*, to be cool. 4 PAINT. fresco.

frío, fría *a*. cold. 2 cool, calm. 3 *m*. cold, coldness: *hace ~*, it is cold.

frondoso, sa *a*. leafy, luxuriant.

frontera *f*. frontier, border.

frotar *t*. to rub, scour.

fruta *f*. fruit.

frutal *a*. fruit-bearing. 2 *m*. fruit tree.

frutero, ra *m.-f*. fruiterer. 2 *m*. fruit-dish.

fruto *m*. fruit. 2 consequence.

fuego *m*. fire.

fuente *f*. spring, source; fountain. 2 dish.

fuera *adv*. out [of], outside, without; away, out of town.

fuerte *a*. strong. 2 healthy. 3 loud [voice, etc.]. 4 *m*. fort, fortress. 5 -**mente** *adv*. strongly.

fuerza *f*. strenght, force, power. 2 violence. 3 vigour [of youth]. 4 *sing.-pl*. MIL. force(s.

fuga *f*. flight, escape. 2 elopement. 3 leak.

fugarse *ref*. to flee, escape.

fugaz *a*. fugitive, fleeting, brief.

fulgor *m*. light, brilliancy, glow.

fumar *t.-i*. to smoke.

función *f*. function. 2 show, performance.

funcionamiento *m*. functioning, operation, working.

funcionar *i.* to function, work, run.

funcionario *m.* civil servant, official.

funda *f.* case, sheath, cover.

fundador, ra *m.-f.* founder.

fundamental *a.* fundamental, essential.

fundamento *m.* foundation. *2* ground.

fundar *t.* to found, establish, base, ground.

fundición *f.* founding, melting. *2* foundry.

fundir *t.* to fuse, melt. *2* to found, cast. *3 ref.* to fuse.

furia *f.* fury, rage. *2* speed.

furioso, sa *a.* furious, in a fury.

furor *m.* fury, rage. *2* passion.

fusil *m.* rifle, gun.

fútbol *m.* football.

futuro, ra *a.* future. *2 m.* future [tense; time].

G

gabán *m.* overcoat.

gabinete *m.* lady's private room. *2* library, study. *3* POL. cabinet.

gala *f.* best dress; *de* ~, in full dress. *2* grace in speaking, etc. *3 pl.* dresses, jewels.

galán *a.* gallant, lover. *2* THEAT. leading man.

galardón *m.* recompense, reward.

galería *f.*; gallery; corridor.

galés, sa *a.* Welsh. *2 m.-f.* Welshman, Welshwoman.

galón *m.* galloon, braid. *2* MIL. stripe. *3* gallon [measure].

gallardo, da *a.* elegant, graceful. *2* brave, gallant.

gallego *a.-n.* Galician.

galleta *f.* biscuit, cooky.

gallina *f.* hen. *2* coward.

gallo *m.* cock, rooster.

gana *f.* appetite, desire, will; *tener ganas de*, to wish, feel like; *de buena* ~, willingly; *de mala* ~, reluctantly.

ganadería *f.* cattle raising. *2* livestock. *3* cattle brand.

ganado *m.* cattle, livestock.

ganador, ra *m.-f.* winner.

ganancia *f.* gain, profit.

ganar *t.-ref.* to gain, earn, win. *2* to defeat [in war, etc.]; to beat [in competition]. *3 i.* to improve.

gancho *m.* hook, crook.

gandul, la *a.* idle, loafing. *2 m.-f.* idler, loafer.

ganga *f.* MIN. gangue. *2* windfall, bargain; *snap.

ganso, sa *m.* ORN. goose, gander. *2 m.-f.* slow, lazy person.

garaje *m.* garage.

garantía *f.* guarantee, guaranty. *2* COM. warranty, security.

garantizar *t.* to guarantee. *2* COM. to warrant. *3* to vouch for.

garganta *f.* throat, neck. *2* ravine.

garra *f.* paw, claw [of wild beast]; talon [of bird of prey]. *2 fig.* clutch.

garza *f.* ORN. heron.

gas *m.* gas. *2* gaslight.

gasa *f.* gauze, chiffon.

gaseoso, sa *a.* gaseous. *2 f.* soda water.

gasolina *f.* gasoline, petrol.

gastar *t.* to spend. *2* to use, wear. *3* to waste. *4 ref.* to wear out, become used up.

gasto *m.* expenditure, expense. *2 pl.* expenses, charges, costs.

gato, ta *m.* cat, tom-cat. *2 f.* she-cat: *a gatas*, on all fours. *3* lifting jack. *4* CARP. clamp.

gaveta *f.* drawer, till.

gavilán *m.* ORN. sparrow hawk.

gemelo, la *a.-n.* twin. *2 m. pl.* cuff-links. *3* binoculars.

gemir *i.* to moan, groan, wail, grieve. ¶ CONJUG. like *servir*.

generación *f.* generation.

general *a.* general: *en ~, por lo ~*, in general. *2* common, usual. *3 m.* MIL., ECCL. general.

género *m.* kind, sort. *2* manner, way. *3* race: *~ humano*, mankind. *4* GRAM. gender. *5* BIOL., LOG. genus. *6* F. ARTS., LIT. genre. *7* COM. cloth, goods.

generoso, sa *a.* generous, noble-minded. *2* liberal.

genio *m.* temper, disposition: *de buen ~*, good-tempered; *de mal ~*, evil-tempered. *2* temperament. *3* genius.

gente *f.* people; crowd.

gentil *a.-n.* gentile, heathen, pagan. *2 a.* courteous, graceful.

genuino, na *a.* genuine, true.

geografía *f.* geography.

geográfico, ca *a.* geographic(al.

gerente *m.* manager.

germen *m.* germ. *2* origin.

gestión *f.* negotiation, conduct [of affairs], management; steps.

gestionar *t.* to take steps to; to negotiate, manage; carry out.

gesto *m.* grimace, gesture: *hacer gestos a*, to make faces at.

gigante, ta *a.* giant, gigantic. *2 m.* giant. *3 f.* giantess.

gimnasio *m.* gymnasium.

girar *i.* to gyrate, revolve, turn, whirl, spin. *2* COM. to trade. *3 t.-i.* COM. to draw.

girasol *m.* BOT. sunflower.

giro *m.* gyration, revolution, turn. *2* course, bias; tendency, trend. *3* COM. draft; *~ postal*, money order. *4* COM. trade, bulk of business.

gitano, na *a.* gypsy.

globo *m.* globe, sphere. *2* world, earth. *3* balloon.

gloria *f.* glory. *2* heaven. *3* bliss, delight. *4* boast, pride.

gloriarse *ref.* *~ de*, to boast of; *~ en*, to glory in.

glorificar *t.* to glorify. *2 ref.* GLORIARSE.

glorioso, sa *a.* glorious.

gobernador, ra *a.* governing. *2 m.* governor, ruler.

gobernar *t.-i.* to govern, rule. *2 t.* to lead, direct. *3* to steer [a ship]. ¶ CONJUG. like *acertar*.

gobierno *m.* government, cabinet, administration. *2* direction, control, management.

golondrina *f.* swallow.

golpe *m.* blow, bump, hit, knock, stroke, shock: *~ de Estado*, coup d'état.

golpear *t.-i.* to strike, beat, knock, hit, pound.

goma *f.* gum; rubber. *2* eraser.

gordo, da *a.* fat, plump, stout.

2 bulky. *3* greasy. *4* thick [paper, etc.]. *5* big. *6 dedo ~*, thumb; big toe. *7 hacer la vista ~*, to wink at.

gorra *f.* cap, bonnet. *2 vivir de ~*, to live at another's expense; *~ de visera*, peaked cap.

gorrión *m.* ORN. sparrow.

gorro *m.* cap; baby's bonnet.

gota *f.* drop. *2* MED. gout.

gozar *t.-i.* to enjoy, have, possess. *2 ref.* to rejoice; to take pleasure in.

gozo *m.* joy, delight, pleasure.

gozoso, sa *a.* joyful, delighted.

grabado, da *a.* engraved, stamped [on memory]. *2 m.* engraving, print: *~ en madera*, wood-cut. *3* picture [in a book, etc.]: *~ al agua fuerte*, etching.

gracia *f.* grace(fulness. *2* charm. *3* favo(u)r, kindness. *4* elegance. *5* joke, wittiness. *6* funniness: *hacer ~*, to amuse, please, be funny; *tener ~*, to be funny; *¡qué gracia!*, how funny!; *en ~ a*, for the sake of; *¡gracias!*, thank you; *gracias a*, thanks to, owing to; *dar gracias a*, to thank to; *gracias a Dios*, thank God.

gracioso, sa *a.* graceful, charming. *2* gracious, gratuitous. *3* witty, facetious. *4* funny. *5 m.-f.* THEAT. jester, clown, fool.

grado *m.* step [of stairs]. *2* degree. *3* grade. *4* rank, class. *5 de buen ~*, willingly; *de mal ~*, unwillingly.

graduación *f.* graduation, grading. *2* strength [of spirituous liquors]. *3* MIL. rank, degree

of rank. *4* EDUC. admission to a degree.

graduar *t.* to graduate, give a diploma, degree or rank to. *2* to gauge, measure. *3 ref.* *to graduate, take a degree.

gramo *m.* gram, gramme [weight].

gran *a.* contr. of GRANDE.

granada *f.* BOT. pomegranate [fruit]. *2* MIL. grenade, shell.

grande *a.* large, big; great, grand. *2 m.* grandee, nobleman.

grandeza *f.* bigness, largeness. *2* size. *3* greatness, grandeur. *4* the grandees.

grandioso, sa *a.* grandiose, grand, magnificent.

granero *m.* granary, barn.

granizo *m.* hail; hailstorm.

granja *f.* grange, farm. *2* dairy.

grano *m.* grain. *2* small seed. *3* berry, grape, corn. *4* pimple. *5 ir al ~*, to come to the point.

grasa *f.* grease, fat; suet; filth.

gratis *adv.* gratis, free.

gratitud *f.* gratitude, gratefulness.

grato, ta *a.* agreeable, pleasant.

grave *a.* heavy. *2* grave, weighty, serious; dangerous. *3* difficult. *4* solemn. *5* GRAM. grave [accent]. *6* MUS. deep, low [voice].

gravedad *f.* gravity. *2* importance, seriousness. *3* depth [of sound].

griego, ga *a.-n.* Greek.

grillo *m.* ENT. cricket. *2* sprout [of a potato, et]. *3 pl.* fetters.

gris *a.* grey, gray. *2* cloudy [day].

gritar *i.-t.* to shout, cry out, scream. *2* to hoot.

grito *m.* shout; cry, scream, hoot: *a ~ pelado*, at the top of one's voice.

grosero, ra *a.* coarse. rough. *2* rude. *3 m.-f.* boor, churl.

grúa *f.* MACH. crane, derrick crane.

grueso, sa *a.* thick. *2* bulky, fat, stout. *3* big, heavy. *4 m.* bulk, mass: *en ~*, in bulk. *5* main body. *6* GEOM. thickness.

grupo *m.* group, set, clump.

guante *m.* glove.

guapo, pa *a.* handsome, good-looking. *2* well-dressed, smart. *3 m.* blusterer, bully.

guardar *t.* to keep, watch over, guard. *2* to lay up, store. *3* to observe [laws, etc.]. *4 ref.* to keep from, guard against.

guardia *f.* guard: *~ civil*, Civil Guard: *~ urbano*, policeman. *2* defense, protection.

3 estar de ~, to be on duty.

guardián, na *m.-f.* guardian, keeper, watchman.

guerra *f.* war, warfare: *~ a muerte*, war to death.

guerrear *i.* to make war, wage war against.

guerrero, ra *a.* martial, warlike. *2 m.-f.* warrior, soldier.

gusano *m.* worm; caterpillar. *2* miserable, wretch. *3 ~ de la seda*, silkworm.

gustar *t.* to taste. *2* to experience. *3* to please. *4 me gusta*, I like.

gusto *m.* taste: *de buen, mal ~* in good, bad taste. *2* flavour. *3* pleasure: *con mucho ~*, with pleasure; *dar ~*, to please, delight; *tanto ~*, delighted, pleased to meet you. *4* whim, fancy.

gustoso, sa *a.* tasty, savoury, palatable. *2* agreeable, pleasant. *3* glad, willing, ready.

H

haba *f.* bean, broad bean.

1) **haber**, *pl.* **haberes** *m.* BOOK KEEP. credit side. 2 salary, pay. 3 *sing.-pl.* property, fortune.

2) **haber** *t. aux.* to have. 2 to catch, hold. 3 (with *de*) to have to, to be to, must. 4 *impers.* (3.ª pers. pres. ind. *hay*) to be [with *there* as a subject]: *hay un puente*, there is a bridge. 5 *¿qué hay?*, what's the matter? 6 (with *que*) it is necessary. 7 *cinco días ha*, five days ago. 8 *ref.* **habérselas con**, to deal with, contend with, cope with. ¶ CONJUG. IND. Pres.: *he, has, ha* or *hay; hemos* or *habemos, habéis, han.* | Imperf.: *había, habías*, etc. | Pret.: *hube, hubiste*, etc. | Fut.: *habré, habrás*, etc. ‖ COND.: *habría, habrías*, etc. ‖ SUBJ. Pres.: *haya, hayas*, etc. | Imperf.: *hubiera, hubieras*, etc., or *hubiese, hubieses*, etc. | Fut.: *hubiere, hubieres*, etc. ‖ IMPER.: *he, haya; hayamos, habed, ha-yan.* ‖ PAST. P.: *habido.* ‖ GER.: *habiendo.*

habichuela *f.* BOT. kidney bean, French bean.

hábil *a.* skilful, clever, able. 2 **-mente** *adv.* skilfully.

habilidad *f.* ability, skill, cleverness. 2 talent.

habitación *f.* dwelling, abode. 2 room, chamber.

habitante *m.-f.* inhabitant, resident; citizen.

habitar *t.-i.* to inhabit; to dwell, live, reside in.

hábito *m.* habit, custom. 2 *sing.* or *pl.* habit [of monk].

habitual *a.* habitual, customary. 2 **-mente** *adv.* usually.

hablador, ra *a.* talkative. 2 *m.-f.* chatterer.

hablar *i.* to speak [to], talk [to, with].

Hacedor *m.* Maker, Creator.

hacer *t.* to make [create, build]. 2 to do [perform, carry out]. 3 to deliver [a speech, etc.]. 4 to prepare [a meal]. 5 to pack [luggage]. 6 to compel, cause to act [in a certain way]. 7 to project, cast [shadow]. *8* to lead [a life]. *9* ~ *bien o mal*, to do it rightly, wrongly; ~ *burla de*, to mock; ~ *caso*, to pay attention; ~ *daño*, to hurt; ~ *pedazos*, to break to pieces; ~ *preguntas*, to ask questions. *10 i. no hace al caso*, it is irrelevant; ~ *de*, to act as a [chairman]. *11 ref.* to become, grow, turn to: *me hice limpiar los zapatos*, I had my shoes cleaned. *12 impers. hace frío*, it's cold; *hace tres días*, three days ago; *hace un año que no le veo*, it's a year since. I saw him; *se hace tarde*, it's getting late. ¶ IRREG. CONJUG. INDIC. Pres.: *hago*, haces, etc. | Imperf.: *hacía*, hacías, etc. | Pret.: *hice, hiciste*, etc. | Fut.: *haré, harás*, etc. ‖ CONDIC.: *haría, harías*, etc. ‖ SUB. Pres.: *haga, hagas*, etc. | Imperf.: *hiciera, hicieras*, etc., or *hiciese, hicieses*, etc. | Fut.: *hiciere, hicieres*, etc. ‖ IMPER.: *haz, haga; hagamos*, haced, *hagan*. ‖ PAST. P.: *hecho* ‖ GER.: haciendo.

hacia *prep.* toward(s, to, for: ~ *abajo*, downwards; ~ *arriba*, upwards; ~ *adelante*, forwards; ~ *atrás*, backwards. *2* near, about: ~ *las tres*, toward three o'clock.

hacienda *f.* landed property, farm. *2* (Am.) ranch. *3* property: ~ *pública*, public treasury.

hacha *f.* axe, hatchet. *2* torch.

hada *f.* fairy; *cuento de hadas*, fairy tale.

hallar *t.* to find, come across,

meet with. *2* to find out, discover. *3* to think; to see, observe. *4* to solve [a problem]. *5 ref.* to be [present].

hamaca *f.* hammock.

hambre *f.* hunger; starvation, famine; *tener* ~, to be hungry.

hambriento, ta *a.* hungry [for]; greedy. *2 m.-f.* hungerer.

harina *f.* flour, meal.

hartar *t.* to satiate, glut. *2* to fill up, gorge [with]. *3* to tire, sicken. *4 ref.* to stuff oneself. *5* to tire, become fed up [with].

harto, ta *a.* satiated, glutted. *2* tired, sick [of]; fed up [with]. *3 adv.* enough.

hasta *prep.* till, until; to, as far as; as much as, up to, down to: ~ *ahora*, till now; ~ *aquí*, so far; ~ *luego*, goodbye, see you later.

hazaña *f.* deed, feat, exploit, achievement, prowess.

he *adv.* [used with *aquí* or *allí*] behold, here is: *heme aquí*, here I am.

hebilla *f.* buckle, clasp.

hebra *f.* thread. *2* TEX. fibre, staple. *3* filament.

hectárea *f.* hectare [2.47 acres].

hecho, cha *irr. p. p.* of HACER. made, done. *2* grown, full. *3* ready-made [clothing]. *4* accustomed, used. *5 m.* fact. *6* happening. *7* act, feat.

helada *f.* frost; nip.

helado, da *a.* frozen. *2* frost-bitten. *3* cold, chilly. *4 m.* ice-cream.

helar *t.* to freeze. *2* to frost-bite. ¶ CONJUG. like *acertar*.

hembra *f.* female. 2 nut [of screw].

henchir *t.* to fill. stuff. 2 to swell. *3 ref.* to be filled. ‖ CONJUG. like *servir.*

hender *t.-ref.* to cleave. split. slit. crack. ‖ CONJUG. like *entender.*

heredar *t.* to inherit.

heredero, ra *m.-f.* inheritor. 2 *m.* heir. *3 f.* heiress.

herencia *f.* inheritance. 2 heredity.

herido, da *a.* wounded. injured. hurt. 2 struck. *3 m.-f.* wounded or injured person.

herir *t.* to wound. injure. hurt. 2 to offend. 3 to touch. move. 4 to strike. hit. ‖ CONJUG. like *servir.*

hermana *f.* sister: ~ *política.* sister-in-law.

hermano *m.* brother: ~ *político,* brother-in-law; *primo* ~. *prima* ~. cousin german.

hermoso, sa *a.* beautiful. fair. lovely. 2 handsome. good-looking.

hermosura *a.* beauty. fairness.

héroe *m.* hero.

heroico, ca *a.* heroic; splendid.

heroísmo *m.* heroism.

herramienta *f.* tool. implement.

hervir *i.* to boil. 2 to bubble. 3 to swarm. ¶ IRREG. CONJUG. INDIC. Pres.: *hiervo, hierves, hierve;* hervimos, hervís, *hierven.* ‖ Pret.: herví, herviste, *hirvió;* hervimos, hervisteis, *hirvieron.* ¶ SUBJ.: Pres.: *hierva, hiervas, hierva;* hirvamos, hirváis, *hiervan.* ‖ Imperf.: *hirviera, hirvieras,* etc.. or *hirviese, hirvieses,* etc. ‖ Fut.: *hirviere, hirvieres,* etc. ‖ IMPER.: *hierve, hierva; hirvamos, hervid, hiervan.* ‖ PAST. P.: *hervido.* ‖ GER.: *hirviendo.*

hielo *m.* ice. 2 frost. 3 coldness.

hierba *f.* grass: *mala* ~. weed.

hierro *m.* iron.

higiénico, ca *a.* hygienic. sanitary.

higo *m.* fig.

hija *f.* daughter. child. 2 HIJO.

hijo, hija *m.-f.* child; *m.* son; *f.* daughter: ~ *político.* son-in-law; ~ *política.* daughter-in-law. 2 native.

hilar *t.* to spin [wool. etc.].

hilera *f.* file. line. row.

hilo *m.* thread. 2 yarn. 3 wire. 4 linen [cloth].

himno *m.* hymn: ~ *nacional.* national anthem.

hincar *t.* to drive. thrust in or into: ~ *el diente,* to bite. *2 ref.* ~ *de rodillas,* to kneel down.

hinchar *t.* to swell. inflate. puff up. *2 ref.* to swell.

hipnotizar *t.* to hypnotize.

hipódromo *m.* race track. race course.

hipoteca *f.* mortgage. pledge.

hipotético, ca *a.* hypothetic(al.

hispánico, ca *a.* Spanish.

hispanoamericano, na *a.* Spanish-American.

historia *f.* history.

historiador, ra *m. f.* historian.

histórico, ca *a.* historic(al.

hocico *m.* snout muzzle: *me-*

ter el ~ *en todo*, to poke one's nose into.

hogar *m.* hearth. 2 home.

hoguera *f.* bonfire, fire, blaze.

hoja *f.* leaf [of tree, plant, book, door, etc.]; blade [of grass, sword, knife, etc.]; petal. 2 sheet [of paper]. 3 foil, pane [of metal, wood]; ~ *de afeitar*, razor blade. 4 shutter.

¡hola! *interj.* hello!, hullo!

holandés, sa *a.* Dutch. 2 *m.-f.* Dutchman, Dutchwoman.

hombre *m.* man [male; human being; mankind]. 2 husband. 3 CARDS ombre.

hombro *m.* shoulder: *arrimar el* ~, to help; *encogerse de hombros*, to shrug one's shoulders; *llevar a hombros*, to carry on the shoulder.

homenaje *m.* homage, honour: *rendir* ~, to pay homage to.

hondo, da *a.* deep, profound. 2 *m.* depth, bottom.

honesto, ta *a.* pure, chaste, modest, decent. 2 honest, upright.

honor *m.* honour. 2 honesty. 3 *pl.* honours [civilities]. 4 dignity, rank.

honorable *a.* honourable; worthy.

honra *f.* honour [reputation], dignity. 2 respect. 3 *tener a mucha* ~, to be proud of. 4 *pl.* obsequies.

honrado, da *a.* honest, upright, fair, just.

honrar *t.* to honour. 2 to be a credit to. 3 *ref.* to be proud of; to be honoured.

hora *f.* hour; time: ~ *de co-*

mer, mealtime; ~ *oficial*, standard time; *horas extraordinarias*, overtime; *horas punta*, rush hours; *¿qué* ~ *es?*, what time is it?; *por horas*, by the hour.

horario *m.* hour-hand. 2 time-table, schedule of times.

horizonte *m.* horizon.

hormiga *f.* ant.

horno *m.* oven; furnace; kiln; *alto* ~, blast-furnace.

horrible *a.* horrible, fearful, hideous, heinous.

horror *m.* horror, fright. 2 grimness.

horroroso, sa *a.* horrible, dreadful. 2 frightful.

hortaliza *f.* vegetables, greens.

hospital *m.* hospital.

hostil *a.* hostile, unfriendly.

hotel *m.* hotel. 2 villa.

hoy *adv.* today; now.

hoyo *m.* hole, pit. 2 dent. 3 pock-mark. 4 grave.

hueco, ca *a.* hollow. 2 empty. 3 vain. 4 affected. 5 soft. 6 *m.* hollow, cavity.

huelga *f.* strike.

huelguista *m.-f.* striker.

huella *f.* tread. 2 print; trace, track, footprint, footstep.

huérfano, na *a.-n.* orphan.

huerto *m.* orchard, fruit garden. 2 kitchen garden.

hueso *m.* bone.

huésped, da *m.-f.* guest.

huevo *m.* egg.

huir *i.* to flee, fly, escape, run away [from], slip away. 2 [of the time] to fly, pass rapidly. 3 *t.* to avoid, shun ‖ CONJUG.: INDIC. Pres.: *huyo, huyes, huye;* huimos, huis, *huyen*. | Pret. hui, huiste, *huyó;* huimos, huisteis, *huyeron*. ‖ Subj. Pres.: *huya, huyas,* etc. | Imperf.: *huyera, huyeras,* etc., or *huyese, huyeses,* etc. | Fut.: *huyere, huyeres,* etc. ‖ Imperat.: *huye, huya; huyamos,* huid, *huyan*. ‖ Ger.: *huyendo*.

humanidad *f.* humanity. *2* mankind. *3* benevolence, kindness. *4* corpulence. *5 pl.* humanities.

humanitario, ria *a.* humanitarian.

humano, na *a.* human. *2* humane. *3 m.* human being.

humedad *f.* humidity, moisture, dampness.

húmedo, da *a.* humid, moist, damp, wet.

humildad *f.* humility. *2* humbleness, lowliness, meeckness.

humilde *a.* humble; lowly. *2* meek. *3* **-mente** *adv.* humbly.

humillar *t.* to humiliate. *2* to humble. *3* to shame. *4* to lower [one's head]. *5 ref.* to humble oneself.

humo *m.* smoke. *2* steam, vapour, fume. *3 pl.* conceit, pride.

humor *m.* humour, temper, mood: *buen, mal* ~, good, bad humour. *2* merry disposition. *4* wit.

hundir *t.* to sink, submerge. *2* naut. to founder. *3 ref.* to sink, subside. *4* to collapse.

huracán *m.* hurricane.

I

ida *f.* going, departure: *billete de ~ y vuelta*, return ticket.

idea *f.* idea; notion. *2* intent, purpose. *3* opinion.

ideal *a.-m.* ideal.

idear *t.* to imagine, conceive, think. *2* to plan, design.

identificar *t.* to identify.

idioma *m.* language, tongue.

idiota *a.* silly. *2 m.-f.* idiot.

ídolo *m.* idol.

iglesia *f.* church.

ignorancia *f.* ignorance, illiteracy.

ignorante *a.* ignorant. *2 m.-f.* ignoramus.

ignorar *t.* not to know.

igual *a.* equal [to]. *2* the same. *3* level, even. *4* constant. *5 sin ~*, matchless. *6 adv. al ~*, equally; *~ que*, as well as; *me es ~*, I don't mind.

igualar *t.* to equalize. *2* to even, level. *3* to match.

igualdad *f.* equality. *2* evenness.

ilimitado, da *a.* unlimited.

iluminar *t.* to illuminate, light up. *2* to enlighten.

ilusión *f.* illusion, day-dream.

ilustrado, da *a.* cultured, well-read, educated.

ilustrar *t.* to illustrate. *2* to explain. *3 ref.* to learn.

ilustre *a.* illustrious, celebrated.

imagen *f.* image; symbol; statue.

imaginación *f.* imagination, fancy, fantasy.

imaginar *t.* to imagine, fancy. *2 t.-ref.* suppose.

imán *m.* magnet. *2* loadstone.

imitar *t.* to imitate.

impaciente *a.* impatient, anxious.

imparcial *a.* impartial, fair.

impedir *t.* to impede, hinder, prevent. ¶ CONJUG. like *servir*.

imperativo, va *a.* imperative, commanding. *2 a.-m.* GRAM. imperative.

imperdible *m.* safety-pin.

imperfecto, ta *a.* imperfect.

imperial *a.* imperial.

imperio *m.* empire..

ímpetu *m.* impetus. *2* violence.

impío, a *a.* impious.

implicar t. to implicate, involve. 2 to imply.

implorar t. to implore, entreat, beg.

imponente a. impressible. 2 grandiose, stately.

imponer t. to impose. 2 to inspire. 3 to deposit [money in a bank]. 4 ref. to assert oneself. 5 to be necessary. 6 to impose one's authority on.

importancia f. importance, consequence.

importante a. important. urgent, serious.

importar i. to be important; to matter. 2 t. to amount to. 3 COM. to import.

importe m. COM. amount.

imposible a. impossible. 2 m. impossibility.

imprenta f. printing [art]. 2 press: printing office.

imprescindible a. indispensable.

impresión f. impression, stamp, imprint. 2 mark, footprint.

impresionar t. to impress, affect. 2 to touch. 3 to record sounds. 4 ref. to be moved.

imprimir t. to impress, imprint, print; to stamp.

impropio, pia a. improper, unsuited. 2 unfitting.

impuesto, ta p. p. de IMPONER. 2 a. informed. 3 m. tax, duty.

impulsar t. to impel. 2 to move. 3 MECH. to drive, force.

impulso m. impulse. 2 force, push.

inauguración f. inauguration.

inaugurar t. to inaugurate.

incapaz, pl. **-ces** a. incapable. 2 unable, unfit, inefficient.

incendio m. fire. 2 arson.

incentivo m. incentive, inducement, encouragement.

incesante a. incessant, unceasing.

incidente a. incidental, subsidiary. 2 m. incident, event.

incierto, ta a. not certain, uncertain, doubtful.

inclinación f. slope; liking. 2 bow, nod.

inclinar t.-ref. to slant, bow. 2 t. to dispose. 3 ref. lean, be disposed.

incluir t. to include. 2 to enclose [in an envelope]. ¶ CONJUG. like **huir.**

inclusive adv. including.

incluso, sa a. included. 2 adv. including, even, besides.

incomparable a. incomparable.

inconveniente a. inconvenient. 2 m. drawback.

incorporar t. to incorporate. 2 ref. to sit up. 3 to join.

incrédulo, la a. incredulous; unbelieving. 2 m.-f. unbeliever.

increíble a. incredible.

incurrir, en i. to incur. 2 to fall into.

indefenso, sa a. defenceless.

independencia f. independence.

independiente a. independent, separate, free.

indicación f. indication. 2 hint.

indicar t. to indicate, point out, show. 2 to hint.

índice m. ANAT. index, forefinger. 2 sign.

indicio m. sign, indication, token.

token.

indiferencia *f.* indifference.

indiferente *a.* indifferent.

indígena *a.* indigenous, native. *2 m.-f.* native.

indignar *t.* to irritate, anger. *2 ref.* to become indignant.

indigno, na *a.* unworthy.

indio, dia *a.-n.* Indian. *2* Hindu.

indiscutible *a.* unquestionable, indisputable.

indispensable *a.* indispensable.

individual *a.* individual.

individuo, dua *a.-n.* individual.

inducir *t.* to induce, persuade, instigate. *2* ELEC. LOG. to induce. ¶ CONJUG. like *conducir.*

industria *f.* industry.

industrial *a.* industrial. *2 m.* industrialist, manufacturer.

infame *a.* infamous, vile, hateful.

infancia *f.* infancy, childhood.

infantería *f.* infantry.

infantil *a.* infantile. *2* childish.

infección *f.* infection, contagion.

infeliz *a.* unhappy, wretched.

inferior *a.-n.* inferior. *2 a.* lower, subordinate.

infiel *a.* unfaithful, disloyal. *2* inexact. *3 a.-n.* infidel, pagan.

infierno *m.* hell, inferno.

infinidad *f.* infinity.

infinito, ta *a.* infinite. *2 m.* infinite space.

influencia *f.* influence.

influir *t.* to influence.

información *f.* information. *2* reportage. *3* inquiry.

informar *t.* to inform [tell, notify]. *2 i.* to report. *3 ref.* to inquire, find out.

informe *a.* shapeless. *2 m.* information, report. *3 pl.* references.

ingeniero *m.* engineer.

ingenio *m.* genius; mind, talent. *2* cleverness, wit. *3* engine, machine.

inglés, sa *a.* English. *2 m.* Englishman. *2* Englishwoman.

ingratitud *f.* ingratitude.

ingrato, ta *a.* ungrateful.

ingresar *i.* to enter; to become a member of; to join. *2 t.* to deposit [money].

ingreso *m.* entrance, admittance. *2 pl.* income. *3* COM. profits.

iniciar *t.* to initiate, begin.

iniciativa *f.* initiative.

iniquidad *f.* iniquity, wickedness.

injusticia *f.* injustice.

injusto, ta *a.* unjust, unfair.

inmediato, ta *a.* immediate. *2* close [to], next [to].

inmensidad *f.* immensity. *2* vastness. *3* great number.

inmenso, sa *a.* immense. *2* unbounded, vast, huge.

inmóvil *a.* immobile, motionless, still, fixed. *2* constant.

inmundo, da *a.* dirty, filthy.

innecesario, ria *a.* unnecessary.

innumerable *a.* numberless.

inocente *a.-n.* innocent.

inofensivo, va *a.* inoffensive, harmless.

inolvidable *a.* unforgettable.

inquieto, ta *a.* restless. *2* agitated. *3* worried, anxious.

inquietud *f.* restlessness, anxiety. *2* disturbance, riot.

inscribir t. to inscribe. 2 ref. to register.

inscripción f. inscription. 2 registration.

insecto m. insect.

insensato, ta a. stupid, foolish.

insignificante a. insignificant.

insistir i. to insist [on, that], persist.

inspección f. inspection, survey.

inspector, ra m.-f. inspector, surveyor.

inspiración f. inspiration.

inspirar t. to inspire breathe in. 2 ref. to become inspired.

instalación f. installation. 2 plant.

instalar t. to install. 2 to set up. 3 ref. to settle.

instante m. instant, moment: *al ~*, immediately.

instinto m. instinct.

institución f. institution.

instituir t. to institute, establish, found. 2 LAW appoint [as heir]. ¶ CONJUG. like *huir*.

instrucción f. instruction, teaching. 2 learning. 3 MIL. drill. 4 pl. orders.

instruir t. to instruct, teach. 2 MIL. to drill. 3 ref. to learn. ¶ CONJUG. like *huir*.

instrumento m. instrument, tool.

insultar t. to insult; to call names.

insuperable a. insuperable, unsurpassable.

integrar t. to integrate, form.

integridad f. integrity, wholeness. 2 honesty, uprightness.

intelectual a.-n. intellectual.

inteligencia f. intelligence, understanding.

inteligente a. intelligent.

intención f. intention, purpose, mind, meaning.

intensidad f. intensity.

intenso, sa a. intense, vehement.

intentar t. to try, attempt. 2 to intend.

intento m. intent, purpose: *de ~*, on purpose. 2 attempt.

interés m. interest, profit, concern.

interesante a. interesting.

interesar t. to interest. 2 to concern. 3 MED. to affect [an organ, etc.]. 4 i. to be interesting. 5 to be necessary. 6 ref. to be interested.

interino, na a. temporary.

interior a. interior, inside. 2 m. inland.

intermedio, dia a. intermediate. 2 m. interval.

interminable a. endless.

internacional a. international.

interpretación f. interpretation, explanation.

interpretar t. to interpret, explain. 2 THEAT. to play.

intérprete m.-f. interpreter.

interrogar t. to interrogate, question.

interrumpir t. to interrupt, break off, cut short, stop.

intervención f. intervention. 2 mediation. 3 supervision.

intervenir i. to intervene. 2 to intercede, plead. 3 t. SURG. to operate upon.

intimidad f. intimacy.

íntimo, ma a. intimate. 2 private. 3 close [relation, etc.].

intranquilo, la a. restless, worried, uneasy.

introducción f. introduction.

introducir t. to introduce. 2 ref. to get in(to.

inundación *f.* inundation. flood.

inundar *t.* to inundate. flood.

inútil *a.* useless. 2 **-mente** *adv.* uselessly.

invadir *t.* to invade. overrun.

invasión *f.* invasion.

inventar *t.* to invent. find out.

invento *m.* invention. discovery.

inversión *f.* investment.

invertir *t.* to invert. 2 to spend [time]. 3 com. to invest. ¶ Conjug. like *hervir*.

investigación *f.* investigation. research. enquiry.

investigar *t.* to investigate. inquire into. do research on.

invicto, ta *a.* unconquered.

invierno *m.* winter.

invisible *a.* invisible.

invitación *f.* invitation.

invitado, da *m.-f.* guest.

invitar *t.* to invite.

invocar *t.* to invoke. implore.

inyección *f.* injection.

ir *i.* to go: ~ *a caballo*, to ride on horseback: ~ *a pie*, to go on foot: *¡vamos!*, come on!. let's go! 2 *ref.* to go away. depart. ¶ Irreg. Conjug. Indic. Pres.: *voy, vas, va; vamos, vais, van.* Imperf.: *iba, ibas,* etc. Pret.: *fui, fuiste.* etc. Fut.: *iré, irás,* etc. ‖ Cond.: *iría, irías,* etc. ‖ Subj.: Pres.: *vaya, vayas,* etc. Imperf.: *fuera, fueras.* etc.. or *fuese, fueses,* etc. Fut.: *fuere, fueres.* etc. ‖ Imper.: *ve, vaya; vayamos, id, vayan.* ‖ Past. p.: *ido.* ‖ Ger.: *yendo.*

ira *f.* anger. wrath. rage.

iracundo, da *a.* irritable. angry.

irritar *t.* to irritate. 2 *ref.* to become irritated.

isla *f.* island; isle.

italiano, na *a.-n.* Italian.

itinerario *m.* itinerary. 2 time-table. schedule.

izquierdo, da *a.* left-handed; crooked. 2 *f.* left hand: *a la* ~. to the left. 3 pol. the Left [wing].

J

jabón *m.* soap.

jaguar *m.* ZOOL. jaguar.

jalea *f.* jelly.

jamás *adv.* never.

jamón *m.* ham.

japonés, sa *a.-n.* japanese.

jaqueca *f.* headache.

jardín *m.* [flower] garden.

jardinero *m.* gardener.

jarro *m.* jug, pitcher.

jaula *f.* cage [for birds, etc.].

jefe *m.* chief, head, leader.

jerez *m.* sherry [wine].

jinete *m.* horseman, rider.

jornada *f.* day's journey. 2 working day.

jorobado, da *a.* hunchbacked. 2 bothered.

joven *a.* young. 2 *m.-f.* youth, young man or woman.

joya *f.* jewel; gem.

joyería *f.* jeweller's shop, jewellery.

judío, a *a.* Jewish. 2 *m.* Jew, Hebrew.

juego *m.* play. 2 game. 3 sport. 4 gambling. 5 set, service: ~ **de té**, tea set. 6 ~ **de palabras**, pun; **hacer** ~, to match; ~ **limpio**, fair play.

jueves *m.* Thursday.

juez *m.* judge, justice.

jugada *f.* play, move. 2 mean trick.

jugador, ra *m.-f.* player. 2 gambler.

jugar *t.-i.* to play, sport, frolic, toy, dally. 2 to game, gamble. ¶ IRREG. CONJUG. INDIC. Pres.: *juego, juegas, juega;* jugamos, jugáis, *juegan.* ‖ SUBJ. Pres.: *juegue, juegues, juegue;* juguemos, juguéis, *jueguen.* ‖ IMPER.: *juega, juegue; juguemos,* jugad, *jueguen.*

jugo *m.* juice. 2 substance, pith.

jugoso, sa *a.* juicy, succulent.

juguete *m.* toy, plaything.

juicio *m.* judgement, sense, wisdom. 2 LAW trial.

julio *m.* July.

junio *m.* June.

junta *f.* meeting.

juntar *t.* to assemble. 2 to gather, lay up, store. 3 to join, unite; to connect.

junto, ta *a.* united, together. 2 *adv.* near, close: ~ *a*, near to, close to.

juramento *m.* oath: ~ *falso*, perjury. 2 swear-word, curse.

jurar *t.-i.* to swear, take an oath: ~ *en falso*, to commit perjury. 2 to vow.

justicia *f.* justice: *hacer* ~, to do justice. 2 officers of law-court, judge.

justificar *t.* to justify. 2 to prove. vouch. 3 *ref.* to justify one's conduct.

1) **justo** *adv.* justly, rightly. exactly. 3 tightly, closely.

2) **justo, ta** *a.* just. 2 righteous. 3 exact, correct. 4 tight.

juventud *f.* youth, youthfulness. 2 young people.

juzgar *i.* to judge. 2 to try. 3 to give an opinion; to think.

K

kilo, kilogramo *m.* kilogram, kilogramme, kilo.

kilómetro *m.* kilometre, kilometer.

kiosko *m.* kiosk.

L

1) **la** *def. art. fem. sing.* the. 2 *obj. pron.* her; it; you.

2) **la** *m.* MUS. la, A.

labio *m.* lip. 2 brim [of a cup].

labor *f.* labour, work, task. 2 needlework.

labrador, ra *m.-f.* farmer, peasant.

labrar *t.* to work, carve, cut. 2 to plough, till, cultivate.

labriego, ga *m.-f.* farm labourer, peasant.

ladera *f.* slope, hillside.

lado *m.* side: *dejar a un* ~, to set aside; *al* ~, close by, near by; *al* ~ *de*, beside; *por un* ~ ... *por otro*, on the one hand... on the other hand.

ladrar *i.* to bark.

ladrillo *m.* brick, tile.

ladrón, na *m.-f.* thief, robber.

lágrima *f.* tear, tear-drop.

lamentable *a.* lamentable, deplorable, pitiful, plaintive.

lamentar *t.* to deplore, regret, be sorry for. 2 *ref.* to complain, moan, wail.

lamento *m.* wail, moan, cry.

lamer *t.* to lick; to lap.

lámpara *f.* lamp. 2 RADIO valve.

lana *f.* wool; fleece.

langosta *f.* ENT. locust. 2 ZOOL. lobster.

lanza *f.* lance, spear: ~ *en ristre*, ready for action. 2 shaft.

lanzar *t.* to throw, cast, dart, fling, hurl. 2 to launch. 3 *ref.* to rush.

lápiz, *pl.* **-ces** *m.* pencil.

largar *t.* to let go. 2 to give [a sigh; a slap]. 3 *ref.* to get out, leave.

1) **largo** *adv.* largely, extendedly. 2 *m.* long, length. 3 *pasar de* ~, to pass by.

2) **largo, ga** *a.* long.

larva *f.* ZOOL. larva; grub.

las *def. art. f. pl.* the. 2 *obj. pron. f. pl.* them.

lástima *f.* pity, compassion, grief: *¡qué* ~*!*, what a pity!

lastimar *t.* to hurt, injure, damage; to offend. 2 *ref.* to get hurt. 3 to feel pity for.

látigo *m.* whip.

latir *i.* to beat, throb.

latitud *f.* breadth, width; extent. 2 GEOG. latitude.

latón *m*. brass.

laurel *m*. laurel. 2 *pl*. fig. honours.

lavabo *m*. wash-stand. 2 washroom; lavatory.

lavandería *f*. laundry.

lavar *t.-i*. to wash; to wash up [dishes, etc.]; to clean, 2 to cleanse.

lazo *m*. bow, knot: ~ *corredizo,* slip-knot. 2 tie, bond.

le *pers. pron. m. sing.; direct obj.* him; you [formal]. 2 *indirect obj.* to him, to her, to it; to you [formal].

leal *a*. loyal, faithful [servant]. 2 fair [proceeding].

lección *f*. lesson; reading.

lector, ra *m.-f*. reader. 2 lecturer [in colleges, etc.].

lectura *f*. reading: *libro de ~,* reader.

leche *f*. milk.

lechería *f*. dairy.

lechero, ra *a*. milky. 2 *m*. milkman. 3 *f*. milkmaid.

lecho *m*. bed, couch. 2 river-bed. 3 layer, stratum.

lechuga *f*. lettuce.

leer *t.-i*. to read. 2 to lecture.

legal *a*. legal, lawful.

legión *f*. legion.

legislador, ra *a*. legislative. 2 *m*. legislator.

legislatura *f*. legislature. 2 legislative assembly.

legítimo, ma *a*. legitimate. 2 lawful, 3 genuine, real.

legua *f*. league.

legumbre *f*. legume, pod fruit. 2 *pl*. vegetables.

lejano, na *a*. distant, remote, far.

lejos *adv*. far, far away, far off: *a lo ~,* in the distance.

lengua *f*. tongue. 2 language.

lenguaje *m*. language. 2 tongue, speech.

lentamente *adv*. slowly.

lento, ta *a*. slow, sluggish.

leña *f*. firewood. 2 thrashing.

leñador *m.-f*. woodcutter. 2 *m*. woodman.

león *m*. lion.

leona *f*. lioness.

leopardo *m*. leopard.

les *pers. pron. m.-f. pl*. them, to them; you, to you [formal].

lesionar *t*. to hurt, wound, injure. 2 to damage, harm.

letra *f*. letter. 2 printing type. 3 handwriting. 4 ~ *mayúscula,* capital letter; ~ *minúscula,* small letter. 5 COM. bill of exchange, draft. 6 *pl*. learning.

letrero *m*. label. 2 sign, poster, notice, placard.

levantar *t*. to raise, lift, hoist. 2 to build. 3 to pick up. 4 to stir. 5 ~ *la mesa,* to clear the table. 6 ~ *acta,* to draw up a statement. 7 ~*la sesión,* to adjourn. 8 *ref*. to rise, get up; to rebel.

leve *a*. light. 2 slight, trifling.

ley *f*. law; rule; act, statute.

leyenda *f*. legend, story. 2 reading, inscription.

libertad *f*. liberty, freedom.

libra *f*. pound [weight; coin] ~ *esterlina,* pound sterling.

librar *t*. to free, deliver, save [from danger, etc.]. 2 to pass [sentence]. 3 to draw [a bill, etc.]. 4 to give [battle]. 5 *ref. librarse de,* to get rid of; to escape from.

libre *a*. free: ~ *albedrío,* free will. 2 vacant [seat, etc.]. 3 disengaged, at leisure.

librería *f.* library; bookcase. 2 bookshop, bookstore.

libreta *f.* notebook.

libro *m.* book.

licencia *f.* licence, permission. 2 MIL. leave.

licenciado, da *m.-f.* EDUC. licentiate, bachellor. 2 law-yer. 3 discharged soldier.

licor *m.* liquor; spirits.

líder *m.* leader.

liebre *f.* hare.

lienzo *m.* cotton or linen cloth. 2 canvas; painting.

liga *f.* garter. 2 mixture. 3 league.

ligar *t.* to tie, bind. 2 to join, unite.

1) **ligero, ra** *a.* light, swift. 2 flippant.

2) **ligero** *adv.* fast, rapidly.

lila *f.* lilac.

lima *f.* file [tool]. 2 finish, polishing. 3 sweet lime [fruit].

limitar *t.* to limit. 2 to cut down. 3 *i.* to border on. 4 *ref.* to confine oneself to.

límite *m.* limit. 2 border.

limón *m.* lemon.

limosna *f.* alms, charity.

limpiar *t.* to clean, cleanse. 2 to wipe.

limpieza *f.* cleanness, cleanliness. 2 purity.

limpio, pia *a.* clean. 2 neat, tidy. 3 chaste; honest. 4 clear. net. 5 fair [play].

linaje *m.* lineage, family, race: ~ *humano*, mankind.

línea *f.* line. 2 limit.

lino *m.* linen; flax.

linterna *f.* lantern, lamp: ~ *eléctrica*, flashlight.

liquidar *t.-ref.* to liquefy. 2 *t.* to liquidate. 3 fig. to murder.

líquido, da *a.-n.* liquid.

lira *f.* lira. 2 MUS. lyre.

lírico, ca *a.* lyric(al). 2 *m.-f.* lyric poet. 3 *f.* lyric poetry.

lirio *m.* lily.

liso, sa *a.* smooth, even, flat.

lisonjero, ra *a.* flattering; fawning; promising.

lista *f.* list. catalogue. 2 roll: *pasar* ~, to call the roll.

listo, ta *a.* ready. 2 quick. 3 finished. 4 clever.

literario, ria *a.* literary.

literato, ta *m.-f.* literary person, writer, man-of-letters.

literatura *f.* literature.

litoral *a.* coastal. 2 *m.* coast.

litro *m.* litre, liter.

lo *neut. art.* the. 2 *pers. pron. m. neut.* him; it; you [formal]: *lo que*, what.

lobo, ba *m.* wolf.

local *a.* local. 2 *m.* place, quarters, premises.

localidad *f.* locality. 2 place, town. 3 seat [in a theatre].

localizar *t.* to localize.

loco, ca *a.* mad, crazy. 2 *m.-f.* madman, madwoman. 3 fool.

locomotora *f.* railway engine.

locura *f.* madness, lunacy, insanity, folly.

locutor, ra *m.-f.* radio announcer, radio speaker.

lodo *m.* mud, mire.

lógico, ca *a.* logical. 2 *f.* logic.

lograr *t.* to get, achieve, attain, obtain. 2 to succeed [in + *ger.*] manage to.

logro *m.* success, achievement. 2 gain, profit.

lomo *m.* back 2 loin. 3 sirloin.

longitud *f.* length, longitude.

loro *m.* parrot.

los *def. art. m. pl.* the. 2 ~

que, those, or they who or which. *3 obj. pron. m. pl.* them: ~ *vi,* I saw them.

losa *f.* flagstone, slab. *2* gravestone.

lotería *f.* lottery; raffle.

loza *f.* china, fine earthenware or crockery.

lozano, na *a.* luxuriant. *2* blooming, fresh, vigorous.

lucero *m.* morning star, bright star.

lucir *i.* to shine, glow. *2* to display. *3 ref.* to show off. *4* to shine, be successful. ¶ CONJUG.: INDIC. Pres.: *luzco,* luces, luce, etc. ‖ SUBJ. Pres.: *luzca, luzcas,* etc. ‖ IMPER.: luce, *luzca; luzcamos,* lucid, luzcan.

lucha *f.* fight. *2* strife, struggle. *3* wrestling.

luchar *i.* to fight. *2* to strive, struggle. *3* to wrestle.

luego *adv.* afterwards, next. *2* immediately. *3* later. *4 desde* ~, of course. *5 hasta* ~, so long. *6 conj.* therefore, then.

lugar *m.* place: *en primer* ~, firstly. *2* spot. *3* employment. *4* space. *5 en* ~ *de,* instead of. *6 dar* ~ *a,* to give rise to. *7 tener* ~, to take place, happen.

lujo *m.* luxury: *de* ~, de luxe.

lujoso, sa *a.* luxurious, costly.

luminoso, sa *a.* bright, shining.

luna *f.* moon: ~ *de miel,* honey moon; *estar en la* ~, fig. to be absent-minded. *2* mirror.

lunes *pl.* **-nes** *m.* Monday.

luz *f.* light: ~ *del día,* daylight; *dar a* ~, to give birth to; to publish.

LL

llaga *f.* ulcer, sore; wound.

llagar *t.* to ulcerate, make sore.

llama *f.* flame, blaze. *2* ZOOL. llama.

llamada *f.* call, summons. *2* knock, ring; sign, beckon. *3* TELEPH. call.

llamamiento *m.* call, summons, appeal.

llamar *t.* to call, summon; to name: ~ *por teléfono,* to telephone, call up: ~ *la atención,* to catch the attention; ~ *la atención a,* to warn. *2 i.* to knock [at a door]; to ring the bell. *3 ref.* to be called, or named: *me llamo Juan,* my name is John.

llamarada *f.* flash, sudden blaze or flame. *2* sudden flush, blush.

llamativo, va *a.* showy, flashy, gaudy.

llamear *i.* to blaze, flame.

llaneza *f.* plainness, simplicity. *2* frankness, homeliness.

llano, na *a.* flat, even, level, smooth. *2* open, frank. *3* simple [style]. *4* clear, evident. *5* GRAM. accented on the penultimate syllable. *6 m.* plain.

llanta *f.* steel tyre; hoop.

llanto *m.* crying, weeping.

llanura *f.* evenness, flatness. *2* plain; prairie.

llave *f.* key. *2* cock, faucet. *3* wrench: ~ *inglesa,* monkey-wrench. *4* MUS. clef.

llavero *m.* key-ring.

llavín *m.* latchkey.

llegada *f.* arrival, coming.

llegar *i.* to arrive [at; in]; to get at, reach. *2* to come to [an agreement]. *3* to suffice, amount to. *4* to get to [know]. *5* ~ *a las manos,* to come to blows. *6 ref.* to approach, come near, go to.

llenar *t.* to fill [up]. *2* to stuff. *3* to fulfil, please. *4 ref.* to fill [up]. *5* to get crowded. *6* to overeat.

lleno, na *a.* full [of]; filled [with]; crowded [with]: ~ *hasta el borde,* brimful. *2 m.* fullness, abundance. *3* THEAT. full house. *4 de* ~, fully.

llevadero, ra *a.* bearable, tolerable.

llevar *t.* to carry, convey, take. *2* to wear, have on [a hat]. *3* to lead, guide. *4* to bear, endure. *5* to keep [accounts, books]. *6* to be in charge of, manage. *7* *llevo un mes aquí*, I have been here one month. *8* to be taller, heavier, older than. *9* to lead [a life]: ~ *adelante*, to carry on; ~ *las de perder*, to be at a disadvantage. *10* *ref.* to take off, carry away. *11* to win, carry off [a prize]. *12* ~ *bien*, to get on well with. *13* ~ *un chasco*, to be disappointed.

llorar *i.* to weep, cry.

lloro *m.* weeping, crying, tears.

llorón, na *a.* weeping: *sauce* ~, weeping willow. *2* *m.-f.* cry-baby, weeper, whiner.

lloroso, sa *a.* tearful; weeping.

llover *t.* to rain, shower: ~ *a cántaros*, to rain cats and dogs. ¶ Conjug. like *mover*.

llovizna *f.* drizzle, sprinkle.

lloviznar *impers.* to drizzle, sprinkle.

lluvia *f.* rain: ~ *menuda*, drizzle. *2* shower.

lluvioso, sa *a.* rainy, wet.

M

maceta *f.* flower-pot.

machacar *t.* to pound, crush, mash.

machete *m.* machet, cutlass.

macho *a.* male. 2 *m.* ZOOL. male, jack, buck. 3 he-mule: ~ *cabrío*, he-goat. 4 sledge-hammer.

madera *f.* wood; lumber.

madrastra *f.* stepmother.

madre *f.* mother: ~ *patria,* mother country; ~ *política,* mother-in-law.

madrina *f.* godmother. 2 patroness, protectress.

madrugada *f.* dawn. 2 early morning.

madrugar *i.* to get up early.

madurar *t.* to mature, ripen. 2 to think out [plans, etc.].

maduro, ra *a.* mature, ripe. 2 wise, prudent. 3 middle-aged.

maestro, tra *a.* master, main, principal: *obra maestra,* masterpiece. 2 *m.* master, teacher. 3 *f.* (school)mistress.

mágico, ca *a.* magic(al).

magnético, ca *a.* magnetic.

magnífico, ca *a.* magnificent, splendid.

mago, ga *m.-f.* magician, wizard. 2 *m. pl. los Reyes Magos,* the Magi, the Three Wise Men.

maíz *m.* BOT. maize, Indian corn.

majadero, ra *a.* silly, stupid. 2 *m.-f.* dolt, bore.

majestad *f.* majesty; dignity.

majestuoso, sa *a.* majestic, stately.

1) **mal** *a.* apocopation of MALO. 2 *adv.* badly, wrongly: ~ *que le pese,* in spite of him.

2) **mal,** *pl.* **males** *m.* evil, ill, harm, wrong: *tomar a* ~, to take ill. 2 illness, disease.

malcriado, da *a.* ill-bred, coarse.

maldad *f.* wickedness, badness.

maldecir *t.-i.* to curse, damn. 2 ~ *de,* to speak ill of. ¶ CONJUG. like *decir,* except the Indic. fut.: *maldeciré,* etc.; COND.: *maldeciría,* etc.: PAST. P.: *maldecido* or *maldito.*

maldición f. curse, malediction.

maldito, ta a. accursed, damned. 2 wicked. 3 bad, mean.

malestar m. discomfort, uneasiness, malaise.

maleta f. valise, suit-case: *hacer la ~*, to pack up.

maleza f. weeds. 2 underbrush, brake, thicket.

malgastar t. to waste, squander.

malo, la (before a masc. noun, **mal**) a. bad, evil, wicked, vicious. 2 ill, harmful. 3 naughty, mischievous. 4 ill, sick: *estar malo*, to be ill. 5 unpleasant. 6 *lo malo es que...*, the trouble is that... 7 interj. *¡malo!*, bad!

malta f. malt.

maltratar t. to abuse, illtreat.

malvado, da a. wicked. 2 m.-f. villain.

malla f. mesh [of net]; network. 2 mail.

mama f. ANAT., ZOOL. mamma, breast. 2 mummy [mother].

mamá f. MAMA 2.

mamar t. to suck.

mamífero, ra a. ZOOL. mammal.

manantial m. source, spring.

mancha f. stain, spot, blot.

manchar t. to stain, soil; to defile.

mandamiento m. order, command. 2 LAW. writ. 3 the ten commandments.

mandar t. to command, order, 2 to send. 3 i. to govern.

mandato m. mandate, command, order.

mandíbula f. jaw, jaw-bone.

manejar t. to manage, handle, wield.

manejo m. handling. 2 management. 3 intrigue.

manera f. manner, mode, fashion; style: *de ~ que, so that; de ninguna ~*, by no means; *de todas maneras*, at any rate, anyhow. 2 way, means. 3 pl. manners, behaviour.

manga f. sleeve. 2 hose-pipe.

mango m. handle, haft; penholder. 2 BOT. mango.

manguera f. hose, watering hose.

manía f. mania, frenzy. 2 craze, whim. 3 dislike.

manifestación f. manifestation. 2 statement. 3 POL. public demonstration.

manifestar t. to manifest, show, reveal. 2 to state, declare. 3 ref. to manifest oneself. ¶ CONJUG. like *acertar*.

manjar m. food.

mano f. hand: ~ *de obra*, labour; labourer; *echar una ~*, to lend a hand. *de segunda ~*, second-hand. 2 hand [of clock, etc.]. 3 round [of game].

mansión f. stay, sojourn. 2 abode, dwelling.

manso, sa a. tame. 2 meek, mild. 3 quiet [water].

manta f. blanket. 2 travelling rug.

manteca f. fat: ~ *de vaca*, butter; ~ *de cerdo*, lard.

mantecado m. butter bun. 2 ice-cream.

mantel, pl. **-teles** m. tablecloth. 2 altar cloth.

mantener t. to maintain, support, keep. 2 to sustain,

hold [up]. *3 ref.* to keep, continue.

mantequilla *f.* butter.

manto *m.* mantle, cloak.

manuscrito, ta *a.* written by hand. *2 m.* manuscript.

manzana *f.* BOT. apple. *2* block of houses.

maña *f.* skill, cunning, knack.

mañana *f.* morning, forenoon: *de ~,* early in the morning. *2* morrow. *3 adv.* tomorrow.

mapa *m.* map, chart.

maquillaje *m.* THEAT. make-up.

máquina *f.* machine, engine: *~ de afeitar,* safety-razor; *~ de escribir,* typewriter; *~ de vapor,* steam-engine.

maquinaria *f.* machinery.

mar *m.* or *f.* sea.

maravilla *f.* wonder, marvel.

maravilloso, sa *a.* wonderful, marvellous, wondrous.

marca *f.* mark, brand. *2* SPORT record. *3 de ~,* first-class quality.

marcar *t.* to mark, brand; to stencil. *2* SPORT to score. *3* TELEPH. to dial.

marco *m.* frame, case. *2* mark [German coin].

marcha *f.* march. *2* course, *3* running, working. *4* departure. *5* pace. *6* AUTO. *cambio de marchas,* gearshift.

marchar *i.* to march, walk. *2* to go, proceed. *3* to work, run. *4 i.-ref.* to leave.

marchitar *t.-ref.* to wither, wilt, fade. *2 ref.* to shrivel up.

marea *f.* tide [of sea]: *~ alta,* high tide; *~ baja,* low tide.

marear *t.* to sail [a ship]. *2* to

annoy. *3 ref.* to become nauseated, sick. *4* to get dizzy.

mareo *m.* sickness, seasickness. *2* dizziness. *3* annoyance.

marfil *m.* ivory.

margarita *f.* BOT. daisy, marguerite. *2* pearl; pearl-shell.

margen *m.-f.* margin. *2* border. *3* bank [of river].

marido *m.* husband.

marina *f.* seacoast. *2* PAINT. sea-scape. *3* seamanship. *4* marine [vessels].

marinero, ra *a.* [pertaining to] sea. *2 m.* mariner, sailor.

marino, na *a.* marine, nautical: *azul ~,* navy blue. *2 m.* mariner, sailor, seaman.

mariposa *f.* ENT. butterfly.

marítimo, ma *a.* maritime.

mármol *m.* marble.

marrón *a.* brown, chestnut.

martes *pl.* **-tes** *m.* Tuesday.

martillo *m.* hammer.

mártir *m.-f.* martyr.

martirio *m.* martyrdom. *2* torture, torment.

marzo *m.* March.

mas *conj.* but.

más *adv.* more. *2 ~ grande,* bigger. *3* [with definite article] the most, or -est. *4 ~ bien,* rather; *~ que,* more than; *por ~ que,* however much; *no quiero nada ~,* I don't want anything else. *5 m.* MATH. plus.

masa *f.* dough. *2* MAS. mortar. *3* PHYS. mass. *4* ELEC. ground. *5* volume, lump. *6* crowd of people: *las masas,* the masses; *en ~,* in a body.

mascar *t.* to chew. *2* to mumble.

máscara f. mask. 2 masker, masquerader.

masticar t. to masticate, chew.

mata f. BOT. bush. 2 sprig [of mint, etc.]. 3 head of hair.

matar t. to kill, slay, murder. 2 to butcher. 3 to cancel [stamps]. 4 ref. to commit suicide. 5 to kill one another.

materia f. matter. 2 material, substance, stuff: *primera ~*, raw material. 3 subject.

material a. material. 2 m. ingredient.

matinal a. early, morning.

matiz, pl. **-tices** m. tint, hue, nuance; shade.

matrícula f. register, list, roll; matriculation; registration.

matrimonio m. matrimony, marriage. 2 married couple.

maullar i. to mew, miaow.

máximo, ma a. maximum, greatest, top.

mayo m. May. 2 Maypole.

mayor a. bigger, older. 2 the biggest; the oldest. 3 of age. 4 chief, main. 5 m. head. 6 m. pl. elders, superiors. 7 ancestors.

mayoría f. majority. 2 full age.

mayúsculo, la a. large. 2 coll. awful. 3 f. capital letter.

mazorca f. ear of corn.

me obj. pron. first per. sing. me; to me, for me, myself.

mecánica f. mechanics. 2 machinery, works.

mecánico, ca a. mechanical. 2 m. mechanic, engineer.

mecanismo m. mechanism.

mecer t. to stir [a liquid]. 2 t.-ref. rock, swing.

mecha f. wick.

medalla f. medal.

media f. stocking. 2 MATH. mean proportional.

mediado, da adv. *a mediados de*, about the middle of.

mediano, na a. middling, moderate. 2 mediocre. 3 middlesized; average.

mediante a. intervening: *Dios ~*, God willing. 2 adv. by means of, through.

medicina f. medicine.

médico, ca a. medical. 2 m. doctor, physician.

medida f. measure, measurement. 2 proportion: *a ~ que*, as. 3 step. 4 moderation.

medio, dia a. half. 2 middle, mean, average. 3 medium.

medio adv. half, partially. 2 middle, midst. 3 means, agency: *por ~ de*, by means of. 4 medium, environment.

mediodía m. noon, midday. 2 GEOG. south.

medir t. to measure; to gauge. 2 to scan [verse]. ¶ CONJUG. like *servir*.

meditar t.-i. to meditate, think.

medrar i. to grow, thrive, improve.

médula, medula f. marrow; pith.

mejilla f. cheek.

mejor pl. **mejores** comp. of *bueno*, better; superl. the best. 2 adv. better; rather.

melancolía f. melancholy, sadness, low spirits.

melancólico, ca a. melancholic, melancholy, sad.

melocotón m. BOT. peach [fruit].

melodioso, sa a. melodious.

melón m. BOT. melon.

memoria f. memory: *de ~*, by

heart. 2 recollection: remembrance: **hacer ~**, to remind. 3 memoir, record, statement. 4 *pl.* memoirs.

mención *f.* mention.

mencionar *t.* to mention, cite.

mendigo, ga *m.-f.* beggar.

menear *t.* to shake, stir. 2 *t.-ref.* to wag, waggle, move. 3 *ref.* to hustle. 4 to be loose.

menester *m.* need, want: **ser ~**, to be necessary.

menor *a.* smaller, less, lesser: younger. 2 smallest, least: youngest, junior: **~ de edad**, under age: minor. 3 *m.-f.* minor [person]. 4 *adv.* **al por ~**, by [at] retail.

menos *adv.* less, least: **~ de**, **~ que**, less than: **al ~**, at least: **a ~ que**, unless: **de ~**, less, missing, wanting: **no puede ~ de hacerlo**, he cannot help doing it: **por lo ~**, at least: **venir a ~**, to decline. 2 fewer: **no ~ de**, no fewer than. 3 minus, less. 4 to: **las tres ~ cuarto**, a quarter to three. 5 but, except.

mensaje *m.* message, errand.

mensajero, ra *m.-f.* messenger. 2 carrier [-pigeon].

mensual *a.* monthly. 2 **-mente** *adv.* monthly.

menta *f.* mint, peppermint.

mental *a.* mental. 2 **-mente** *adv.* mentally.

mente *f.* mind, intellect. 2 intention.

mentir *i.* to lie, tell lies, fib. ¶ CONJUG. like **sentir**.

mentira *f.* lie, fib, falsehood.

mentiroso, sa *a.* lying. 2 deceptive. 3 *m-f.* liar.

menudo, da *a.* small, minute, tiny. 2 **a ~**, often.

mercader *m.* merchant, dealer, trader.

mercado *m.* market.

mercancía *f.* commerce, trade. 2 merchandise. 3 *pl.* goods, wares.

merced *f.* gift, favour. 2 mercy, will, power. 3 **a ~ de**, at the mercy of: **vuestra (vuesa, su) Merced**, you, sir: you, madam: **~ a**, thanks to.

mercurio *m.* quicksilver, mercury.

merecer *t.-i.* to deserve. 2 *t.* to be worthy of, be worth. ¶ CONJUG. like **agradecer**.

meridional *a.* meridional, southern.

merienda *f.* afternoon snack: tea. 2 picnic.

mérito *m.* merit, worth: **de ~**, notable.

mero, ra *a.* mere, pure, simple. 2 *m.* ICHTH. grouper.

mes *m.* month.

mesa *f.* table: **~ de noche**, bed-side table.

meseta *f.* table-land, plateau.

metal *m.* metal. 2 MUS. brass.

metálico, ca *a.* metallic. 2 *m.* cash.

meter *t.* to put [in], place, insert, introduce [in], get [in]. 2 to make [a noise: trouble]. 3 *ref.* to get involved in. 4 to interfere. 5 **~ con**, to quarrel with.

método *m.* method. 2 technique.

metro *m.* metre, meter. 2 coll. underground, tube.

mezcla *f.* mixture: blend(ing. 2 MAS. mortar.

mezclar *t.-ref.* to mix, mingle, blend. 2 *ref.* to interfere, meddle.

mezquino, na *a.* neddy, poor. *2* stingy, niggardly. *3* small, short, mean. *4* wretched.

mi, pl. mis *poss. a.* my.

mi *pers. pron.* me, myself.

mico *m.* long-tailed monkey, ape.

microbio *m.* microbe.

micrófono *m.* microphone.

microscopio *m.* microscope.

miedo *m.* fear, dread: *tener* ~, to be afraid.

miedoso, sa *a.* fearful, afraid.

miel *f.* honey: *luna de* ~, honeymoon. *2* molasses.

miembro *m.* member, limb. *2* associate.

mientras *adv.-conj.* while, whilst, when: ~ *tanto,* meanwhile. *2* ~ *que,* while; whereas.

miércoles, pl. **-les** *m.* Wednesday.

miga *f.* bit, small fragment. *2* crumb, soft part of bread. *3* pl. fried crumbs. *4* fig. marrow, pith, substance. *5* *hacer buenas* or *malas migas con,* to get along well or badly with.

mil *a.-m.* thousand.

milagro *m.* miracle, wonder.

milagroso, sa *a.* miraculous.

milicia *f.* art of warfare. *2* military service. *3* militia.

1) militar *a.* military. *2* soldierly. *3 m.* military man, soldier.

2) militar *i.* to serve in the army. *2* to militate.

milla *f.* mile.

millón, pl. **millones** *m.* million.

mimar *t.* to pet, fondle, cuddle. *2* to pamper, spoil: *niño mimado,* spoiled child.

mina *f.* mine [of coal, etc.]. *2* underground passage.

mineral *a.-n.* mineral. *2 m.* ore.

minero, ra *a.* mining. *2 m.* miner. *3* mine owner.

mínimo, ma *a.* minimal, least, smallest. *2 m.* minimum.

ministerio *m.* ministry, cabinet. *2* government, administration: ~ *de Asuntos Exteriores,* Foreign Office; *Department of State; ~ *de Hacienda,* Exchequer; *Department of the Treasury; ~ *de Gobernación,* Home Office; *Department of the Interior.

ministro *m.* minister.

minoría *f.* minority, the few.

minutero *m.* minute hand.

minuto *m.* minute [of an hour].

mío, mía, míos, mías *poss. a.* my, my own, of mine. *2 poss. pron.* mine.

mirada *f.* look, glance, gaze.

mirador *m.* belvedere, open gallery. *2* oriel [bay] window.

mirar *i.* to look at, gaze, behold; to watch, examine, etc. *2* to consider, have in mind. *3* [of a building, etc.] to face. *4 ¡mira!,* look!, behold!

misa *f.* mass.

miserable *a.* miserable, wretched. *2* mean, poor. *3* miserly, stingy. *4* wicked, rascally. *5 m.-f.* miser. *6* wretch, cur, knave.

miseria *f.* misery, wretchedness. *2* poverty, stinginess. *3* bit.

mísero, ra *a.* miserable, wretched, unhappy. *2* miserly, mean.

misión *f.* mission; errand.

1) **mismo** *adv.* right: *ahora* ~, right now; *aquí* ~, right here.

2) **mismo, ma** *a.* same, very, selfsame. *2* [for emphasis] myself, yourself, etc.: *lo haré yo* ~, I'll do it myself.

misterio *m.* mystery: secret.

mitad *f.* half: *a la* ~, or *a* ~ *de*, halfway through. *2* middle: *en* ~ *de*, in the middle of.

mixto, ta *a.* mixed, mingled. *2 m.* match. *3 tren* ~, passenger and goods train.

moda *f.* fashion, mode, style: *estar de* ~, to be in fashion.

modales *m. pl.* manners.

modelar *t.* F. ARTS to model, mould, mold, fashion.

modelo *m.* model, pattern, example. *2 m.-f.* life model.

moderno, na *a.* modern.

modestia *f.* modesty, decency; unaffectedness.

modesto, ta *a.* modest, decent; unpretentious.

módico, ca *a.* moderate, reasonable [price].

modificar *t.-ref.* to modify.

modismo *m.* GRAM. idiom.

modo *m.* mode, manner, way: ~ *de ser*, nature; *de cualquier* ~, anyway; *de ningún* ~, by no means; *de todos modos*, anyhow, at any rate. *2* GRAM. mood. *3 pl.* manners, civility.

mofar *i.-ref.* to mock, jeer, sneer, scoff at, make fun of.

moho *m.* mo(u)ld, mildew. *2* rust [on iron]. *3* rustiness.

mojado, da *a.* wet, damp, moist.

mojar *t.* to wet, moisten, damp. *2* to dip [bread into milk]. *3 ref.* to get wet.

molde *m.* mo(uld), cast; pattern. *2* FOUND. frame.

moler *t.* to grind, crush, pound, mill. *2* to tire out. *3* to destroy. ¶ CONJUG. like *mover*.

molestar *t.* to vex, upset, trouble, annoy, molest. *2 ref.* to bother.

molestia *f.* vexation, annoyance, nuisance, trouble.

molesto, ta *a.* annoying, troublesome. *2* annoyed.

molino *m.* mill.

momento *m.* moment, instant: *al* ~, at once, inmediately.

monarca *m.* monarch, sovereign.

monasterio *m.* monastery; convent.

mondar *t.* to clean out. *2* to prune, trim. *3* to pare, peel.

moneda *f.* coin; money; ~ *corriente*, currency.

monería *f.* grimace; mimicry. *2* prank, playful trick. *3* trifle, gewgaw.

monja *f.* nun, sister.

monje *m.* monk. *2* anchorite.

mono, na *a.* pretty, dainty, *cute. *2 m.* ZOOL. ape, monkey. *3* ~ *de mecánico*, overalls.

monopolio *m.* monopoly.

monótono, na *a.* monotonous.

monstruo *m.* monster; freak.

montaña *f.* mountain. *2* highlands. *3* forested region.

montañoso, sa *a.* mountainous.

montar *i.-ref.* to mount, get on: ~ *a horcajadas*, to

straddle. 2 *i.* to ride [horse-back; on a bicycle]; *silla de ~*, saddle. 3 to be of importance. 4 *~ en cólera,* to fly into a rage. 5 *t.* to mount, put [a person] on a horse, etc. 6 to ride [a horse, a bicycle, etc.]. 7 to amount to. 8 to assemble, set up [machinery]. 9 to set [a gem]. *10* THEAT. to mount [a play].

monte *m.* mount, mountain, hill. 2 woods, wodland; *~ alto,* forest; *~ bajo,* thicket, brushwood. 3 *~ de piedad,* public pawnshop.

montón *m.* heap, pile. 2 lot, crowd, great quantity.

monumento *m.* monument, memorial.

morado, da *a.-n.* dark purple, mulberry-coloured.

moral *a.* moral. 2 *f.* morals, ethics, morality. 3 morale. 4 *m.* BOT. black mulberry-tree.

morar *i.* to live, dwell, stay.

morcilla *f.* blood pudding.

morder *t.* to bite; to nip, gnaw. 2 to nibble at. 3 [of an acid] to eat, corode. 4 to backbite, slander. ¶ CONJUG. like *mover.*

moreno, na *a.* brown, dark.

moribundo, da *m.-f.* moribund, dying person.

morir *i.* to die [of; with]. 2 [of a river, road, etc.] to flow [into]; to end [at]. 3 *ref.* to die, be dying. 4 [of fire, flame, etc.] to die, go out. 5 *~ de hambre,* to starve; fig. to be dying with hunger. 6 *morirse por,* to love dearly; be crazy about. 7 *interj.* ¡*muera...!,* down with...! ¶

CONJUG. like *dormir.* | P. p.: *muerto.*

moro, ra *a.* Moorish. 2 Moslem. 3 unbaptized. 4 dappled, spotted [horse]. 5 *m.* Moor.

morral *m.* nosebag. 2 game-bag. 3 knapsack.

mortal *a.-n.* mortal. 2 *-mente adv.* mortally, deadly.

mortandad *f.* massacre, butchery, slaughter.

mortificar *t.-ref.* to mortify. 2 *t.* to annoy, vex, bother.

mosca *f.* ENT. fly.

mosquito *m.* ENT. mosquito; gnat.

mostrador *m.* counter [shop].

mostrar *t.* to show, exhibit, display. 2 to point out. 3 to demonstrate, prove. 4 *ref.* to show oneself, prove to be. ¶ CONJUG. like *contar.*

motivar *t.* to cause, give rise to. 2 to give a reason for.

motivo *m.* motive, reason; *con ~ de,* owing to; on the occassion of; *por ningún ~,* under no circumstances.

motor, ra *a.* motor, motive. 2 *m.* motor. 3 MACH. engine.

mover *t.* to move; to stir, shake; to drive, propel; to induce, prompt, persuade; to raise, start, excite. 2 *~ a,* to move, stir; to get busy. ¶ IRREG. CONJUG. INDIC. Pres.: *muevo, mueves, mueve; movemos, movéis, mueven.* ‖ SUBJ. Pres.: *mueva, muevas, mueva; movamos, mováis, muevan.* ‖ IMPER.: *mueve, mueva; movamos, moved, muevan.*

móvil *a.* movable, mobile; inconstant. 2 *m.* moving body. 3 motive, inducement.

movimiento *m.* movement, motion; gesture: *en* ~, in motion. 2 stir, agitation.

mozo, za *a.* young. 2 unmarried. 3 *m.* young man, youth, lad. 4 manservant, waiter, porter, errand-boy.

muchacho, cha *a.* young [person]. 2 *m.* boy, lad. 3 *f.* girl, lass. 4 maidservant.

muchedumbre *f.* multitude, crowd.

1) **mucho** *adv.* much, a good or great deal, a lot; *ni* ~ *menos,* not by any means; *por* ~ *que,* however much. 2 often. 3 long, longtime.

2) **mucho, cha** *a.-pron.* much, plenty of, a good or great deal of, a lot of. 2 *pl.* many, a good or great deal of, lots of, a large number of.

mudanza *f.* change. 2 removal. 3 fickleness.

mudar *t.* to change, alter, convert. 2 to remove, move [to another place]. 3 to mo(u)lt, shed. 4 *ref.* to change [in conduct; one's clothes]. 5 to move [change one's residence].

mudo, da *a.* dumb, mute, silent.

mueble *a.* movable, 2 *m.* piece of furniture. 3 *pl.* furniture.

muela *f.* upper millstone. 2 grindstone. 3 ANAT. molar tooth, grinder.

muelle *a.* soft, delicate. 2 voluptuous. 3 *m.* NAUT. wharf, pier, quay, docks. 4 RLY. freight platform. 5 MACH. spring.

muerte *f.* death; murder: *dar* ~, to kill; *de mala* ~, miserable, wretched.

muerto, ta *p. p.* of MORIR and MATAR. 2 *a.* dead; deceased; killed. 3 tired out; dying [with hunger, etc.]. 4 faded, withered. 5 *m.-f.* dead person; corpse.

muestra *f.* signboard; shop-sign. 2 sample. 3 model, pattern. 4 sign, show.

mujer *f.* woman. 2 wife.

mula *f.* ZOOL. she-mule.

mulo *m.* ZOOL. mule; hinny.

multa *f.* fine.

múltiple *a.* multiple, manifold.

multiplicar *t.-ref.* to multiply.

múltiplo *a.-m.* multiple.

multitud *f.* multitude, crowd.

mundanal; mundano, na *a.* mundane, worldly.

mundial *a.* world-wide, world.

mundo *m.* world; earth, globe: *el Nuevo* ~, the New World; *todo el* ~, everybody. 2 trunk [large box].

municipalidad *f.*, **municipio** *m.* municipality, town, council.

muñeca *f.* ANAT. wrist. 2 doll. 3 manikin.

muñeco *m.* puppet. 2 dummy.

muralla *f.* outer wall, rampart.

murciélago *m.* ZOOL. bat.

murmullo *m.* murmur, ripple; whisper; rustle [of leaves, etc.].

murmurar *i.* to murmur, whisper. *2* to mutter, grumble. *3* [of leaves, etc.] to rustle. *4* [of streams] to purl, ripple. *5* to gossip, backbite.

muro *m.* wall. *2* FORT. rampart.

músculo *m.* ANAT. muscle; brawn.

musgo *m.* BOT. moss.

música *f.* music.

músico, ca *a.* musical. *2 m.-f.* musician.

mutuo, tua *a.* mutual, reciprocal.

muy *adv.* very, very much, greatly.

N

nacer *i*. to be born. *2* to grow, sprout. *3* to spring, flow. *4* to start. ¶ CONJUG. INDIC. Pres.: *nazco*, naces. etc. ‖ SUBJ. Pres.: *nazca, nazcas,* etc. ‖ IMPER.: nace. *nazca; nazcamos,* naced. *nazcan.*

nacido, da *a*. born.

naciente *a*. growing. *2* rising [sun].

nacimiento *m*. birth. *2* rising [sun]. *3* source. *4* issue. *5* lineage. *6* crib.

nación *f*. nation.

nacional *a*. national.

nada *f*. naught. *2 indef. pron.* nothing. not anything.

nadar *t*. to swim. *2* to float.

nadie *indef. pron.* nobody. no one. not... anyone.

naranja *f*. BOT. orange.

naranjada *f*. orangeade.

nariz *f*. nose.

narración *f*. narration. account.

narrar *t*. to narrate.

nata *f*. cream.

natal *a*. natal. native. *2 m.* birth. *3* birthday.

nativo, va *a*. native.

natural *a*. natural. *2 a.-n.* native. *3 m.* nature.

naturaleza *f*. nature. *2* temperament. *3* sort. kind. *4* F. ARTS. ~ *muerta,* still life.

naufragar *i*. NAUT. to sink; to be shipwrecked.

náufrago, ga *m.-f.* shipwrecked person. castaway.

navaja *f*. clasp-knife. pocketknife: ~ *de afeitar,* razor.

naval *a*. naval.

nave *f*. ship. vessel. *2* ARCH. nave: ~ *lateral,* aisle.

navegación *f*. navigation. sailing.

navegante *m.-f.* navigator.

navegar *i*. to navigate. sail. steer.

Navidad *f*. Christmas.

navío *m*. vessel. ship: ~ *de guerra,* warship.

neblina *f*. mist. thin fog. haze.

necesario, ria *a*. necessary.

necesidad *f*. necessity; need. want. *2* emergency.

necesitar *t*. to need. want. *2* to have to.

necio, cia *a.-n.* ignorant, foolish, stupid; silly [person].

néctar *m.* nectar.

negar *t.* to deny. 2 to refuse. ¶ CONJUG. like *acertar*.

negativo, va *a.* negative.

negociación *f.* negotiation. 2 business transaction.

negociar *i.* to deal, trade, do business. 2 *t.-i.* to negotiate.

negocio *m.* business, affair. 2 trade; concern. 3 profit, gain.

negro, gra *a.* black; dark. 2 *m.* black. 3 Negro. 4 *f.* Negress.

negruzco, ca *a.* blackish.

nene, na *m.* baby; dear, darling.

nervio *m.* nerve. 2 vigour. 3 sinew.

nervioso, sa *a.* nervous. 2 vigorous. 3 sinewy.

nevada *f.* snowfall, snowstorm.

nevar *impers.* to snow. ¶ CONJUG. like *acertar*.

ni *conj.* neither, nor. 2 ~ *siquiera,* no even.

nido *m.* nest. 2 home, abode.

niebla *f.* fog, mist, haze.

nieto, ta *m.-f.* grandchild. 2 *m.* grandson. 3 *f.* granddaughter.

nieve *f.* snow.

ningun(o, na *a.* no, not... any. 2 *indef. pron. m.-f.* none, no one, nobody; ~ *de los dos,* neither of the two.

niña *f.* female child; little girl. 2 ANAT. ~ *del ojo,* pupil, apple of the eye.

niñez *f.* childhood, infancy.

niño, ña *m.* male child or infant, little boy.

nivel *m.* level: ~ *del mar,* sea level; ~ *de vida,* standard of living; *paso a* ~, level crossing.

no *adv.* no, nay. 2 not; ~ *obstante,* notwithstanding.

noble *a.* noble. 2 *m.-f.* nobleman.

nobleza *f.* nobility, nobleness.

noción *f.* notion, idea. 2 *pl.* rudiments.

noche *f.* night; evening: ~ *buena,* Christmas Eve; ~ *vieja,* New Year's Eve; *buenas noches,* good night; good evening; *de* or *por la* ~, at night, by night.

nombrar *t.* to name, nominate, appoint, commission.

nombre *m.* name: ~ *de pila,* Christian name. 2 GRAM. noun. 3 title. 4 reputation.

norma *f.* norm, pattern, standard.

normal *a.* normal, standard. 2 *f.* training-college.

norte *m.* north. 2 North Pole. 3 guide.

norteamericano, na *a.-n.* North American; American.

nos *pers. pron. pl. m.-f.* [object] us, to us, for us; [recip.] each other; [ref.] ourselves. 2 we, us [used by the king, etc.].

nosotros, tras *pers. pron. m.-f.* we [subject]; us [object]. 2 *nosotros mismos,* ourselves.

nota *f.* note. 2 fame. 3 COM. account, bill. 4 EDUC.. mark, *grade.

notable *a.* notable, remarkable. 2 noticeable. 3 *m.* EDUC. good mark. 4 -mente *adv.* remarkably.

notar *t.* to note, mark. *2* to notice, observe.

noticia *f.* news, news item, notice, piece of news.

notificar *t.* to notify, inform.

notorio, ria *a.* evident, obvious.

novedad *f.* novelty. *2* latest news. *3 pl.* fancy goods.

novela *f.* novel.

noveno, na *a.-m.* ninth.

noviembre *m.* November.

novillo, lla *m.* young bull, bullock. *2 f.* heifer, young cow. *3 hacer novillos*, to play truant.

novio *m.* bridegroom. *2* fiancé, boy-friend.

nube *f.* cloud.

1) **nudo** *m.* knot, noose: ~ *en la garganta*, lump in the throat; ~ *corredizo*, slip knot. *2* bond, tie. *3* tangle,

difficulty. *4* THEAT. plot.

2) **nudo, da** *a.* nude, naked.

nuestro, tra *poss.* a. our, of ours. *2 poss. pron.* ours.

nueva *f.* news, tidings.

nueve *a.-n.* nine.

nuevo, va *a.* new: *¿qué hay de* ~*?*, what's new? *2* fresh, newly arrived. *3* adv. *de* ~, again, once more.

nuez *f.* walnut. *2* nut. *3* adam's apple.

número *m.* ARITH. number. *2* numeral, figure. *3* size.

numeroso, sa *a.* numerous.

nunca *adv.* never: ~ *jamás*, never again.

nutrido, da *a.* nourished. *2* full, abundant.

nutrir *t.* to nourish, feed.

nutritivo, va *a.* nutritious, nourishing.

Ñ

ñapa *f.* (Am.) additional amount; something over or extra: *de* ~, to boot, into the bargain.

O

o *conj.* or: ~ ..., ~ ..., either... or...

obedecer *t.-i.* to obey. 2 to respond, yield [to a force, etc.]. 3 to be due [to]. ¶ CONJUG. like *agradecer*.

obediencia *f.* obedience, compliance.

obediente *a.* obedient, compliant.

obeso, sa *a.* obese, fat, fleshy.

obispo *m.* ECCL. bishop.

objeción *f.* objection, opposition.

objetar *t.* to object, oppose.

objeto *m.* object. 2 thing. 3 subject, matter. 4 end, purpose.

obligar *t.* to obligate, oblige, bind. 2 to compel, force, constrain. 3 *ref.* to blind oneself.

obligatorio, ria *a.* obligatory, compulsory.

obra *f.* work, piece of work. 2 act, deed; ~ *maestra,* masterpiece. 3 THEAT. play, drama. 4 building under construction; repair work. 5 pl., *obras públicas*, public works.

obrar *t.* to work, perform, make, do. 2 to build. 3 *i.* to act, behave. 4 *obra en nuestro poder,* we have received your letter.

obrero, ra *m.-f.* worker, labourer; workman, workwoman.

obsequio *m.* attention, courtesy; treat; present, gift.

observación *f.* observation. 2 remark.

observar *t.* to observe, comply with. 2 to notice. 3 to watch, regard. 4 to remark.

obstáculo *m.* obstacle, hindrance.

obstante (no) *conj.* notwithstanding; nevertheless.

obtener *t.* to attain, obtain, get.

ocasión *f.* occasion, opportunity, chance. 2 motive.

ocasionar *t.* to occasion, cause, bring about, arouse.

occidental *a.* occidental, western.

occidente *m.* occident, west.

océano *m.* ocean.

ocioso, sa *a.* idle; lazy. *2* useless.

octavo, va *a.-m.* eighth.

octubre *m.* October.

ocultar *t.* to conceal, hide.

oculto, ta *a.* hidden, concealed. *2* occult, secret.

ocupar *t.* to occupy. *2* to employ, give work to. *3* to fill [a space]. *4 ref.* ~ **en**, to be employed at; to be busy with.

ocurrencia *f.* occurrence, event. *2* joke, witty remark. *3* bright or funny idea.

ocurrir *i.* to occur, happen. *2 ref.* to occur to one.

ocho *a.-n.* eight.

odiar *t.* to hate, detest, abhor.

odio *m.* hatred, hate, aversion.

odioso, sa *a.* odious, hateful.

ofender *t.* to offend, insult. *2 ref.* to take offence, resent.

oferta *f.* offer. *2* offering, gift. *3* COM. **la** ~ **y la demanda**, supply and demand.

oficial *a.* official. *2 m.* [skilled] workman. *3* MIL. officer. *4* [government] official; magistrate. *5* **-mente** *adv.* officially.

oficina *f.* office.

oficio *m.* occupation, profession; **de** ~, by trade. *2* office [duty, etc.]. *3* official communication. *4* ECCL. service.

oficioso, sa *a.* officious. *2* unofficial. *3* diligent.

ofrecer *t.* to offer, present. *2 ref.* to volunteer. ¶ CONJUG. like *agradecer*.

ofrenda *f.* gift, religious offering.

oído *m.* hearing [sense]; ear [organ of hearing].

oír *t.* to hear; to listen; to understand. ¶ CONJUG. INDIC. Pres.: *oigo, oyes, oye;* oímos, oís, *oyen.* | Pret.: oí, oíste, *oyó;* oímos, oísteis, *oyeron.* ‖ SUBJ. Pres.: *oiga, oigas,* etc. | Imperf.: *oyera, oyeras,* etc., or *oyese, oyeses,* etc. | Fut.: *oyere, oyeres,* etc. ‖ IMPER.: *oye, oiga; oigamos,* oíd, *oigan.* ‖ PAST. P.: *oído.* ‖ GER.: *oyendo.*

¡ojalá! *interj.* would to God!, God grant!, I wish!

ojo *m.* eye: **no pegar el** ~, not to sleep a wink; **a** ~, by guess; **a ojos cerrados**, blindly; **en un abrir y cerrar de ojos;** in the twinkling of an eye; *¡ojo!*, look out!, beware!. *2* eye, hole. *3* span [of a bridge]. *4* well [of stairs]. *5* keyhole.

ola *f.* wave.

oler *t.-i.* to smell.

olfatear *t.* to smell, scent, sniff. *2* to pry into.

olfato *m.* smell.

olímpico, ca *a.* Olympic; Olimpian. *2* fig. haughty.

olivo *m.* BOT. olive-tree.

olor *m.* odour, smell, fragance: **mal** ~, stink.

olvidar *t.-ref.* to forget, leave behind, neglect.

olvido *m.* forgetfulness. *2* omission, neglect. *3* oblivion.

olla *f.* pot, boiler.

omnipotente *a.* omnipotent, allmighty.

once *a.-m.* eleven.

onda *f.* wave [of water, of hair, etc.], ripple.

onza *f.* ounce.

opaco, ca *a.* opaque; dark.

ópera *f.* opera.

operación f. operation, business transaction.

operar t. SURG. to operate upon. 2 i. to take effect, work. 3 to speculate. 4 to manipulate, handle. 5 ref. to occur.

opinar i. to hold an opinion; to think, judge, consider.

opinión f. opinion: *mudar de* ~, to change one's mind.

oponer t. to oppose; to resist, face. ¶ CONJUG. like **poner.**

oportunidad f. opportunity; chance.

oportuno, na a. opportune, suitable, timely. 2 witty.

oposición f. opposition, clash. 2 pl. competitive examination.

oprimir t. to press down, push. 2 to crush, squeeze. 3 to tyranize, oppress.

opuesto, ta a. opposed. 2 opposite. 3 adverse.

opulento, ta a. opulent, wealthy.

oración f. speech, oration. 2 prayer. 3 GRAM. sentence.

orador, ra m.-f. orator, speaker.

orar i. to pray.

orden m. order [arrangement; method]. 2 command: *a sus órdenes,* at your service.

ordenar t. to order, arrange, put in order. 2 to order, command, prescribe. 3 ECCL. to ordain. 4 ref. ECCL. to take orders.

ordinario, ria a. ordinary, usual. 2 common, vulgar.

oreja f. ear. 2 flap [of shoe].

orgánico, ca a. organic.

organizar t. to organize. 2 to set up, start.

órgano m. organ.

orgullo m. pride. 2 haughtiness.

orgulloso, sa a. proud. 2 haughty.

oriental a. oriental, eastern.

orientar t. to orientate; to direct [towards]. 2 NAUT. to trim [a sail]. 3 ref. to find one's bearings.

oriente m. east, orient.

origen m. origin. 2 source, cause. 3 native country.

original a. original. 2 queer, quaint. 3 m. original [of a portrait, etc.]. 4 eccentric, crank. 5 **-mente** adv. originally; eccentrically.

originar t. to originate, give rise to. 2 ref. to arise.

orilla f. border, margin, edge, brink, hem. 2 bank, margin [of river]; shore.

oro m. gold.

orquesta f. MUS., THEAT. orchestra.

oruga f. ENT., MACH. caterpillar.

os pers. pron. pl. m.-f. [object] you, to you, etc.; [recip.] each other; [ref.] yourselves.

osar i. to dare, venture.

oscurecer, oscuridad, etc. = OBSCURECER, OBSCURIDAD.

oso, sa m. bear.

ostentar t. to parade, display, show. 2 to show off; to boast.

otoño m. autumn, fall.

otorgar t. to grant, give. 2 to award [a prize]. 3 to consent.

otro, otra a.-pron. another, other.

oveja f. ewe, female sheep.

oxígeno m. CHEM. oxygen.

oyente m.-f. hearer. 2 listener [to the radio]. 3 pl. audience.

P

pacer *i.-t.* to pasture, graze.
paciente *a.-n.* patient.
pacífico, ca *a.* pacific. 2 calm, peaceful. *3 a.-n.* (cap.) GEOG. Pacific [Ocean].
pacto *m.* pact, agreement, covenant.
padecer *t.-i.* to suffer [from], endure. ¶ CONJUG. like *agradecer*.
padrastro *m.* stepfather.
padre *m.* father: ~ *político*, father-in-law. 2 *pl.* parents; ancestors.
paga *f.* payment. 2 pay, salary.
pagar *t.* to pay [money, etc.] to fee. 2 to pay for.
página *f.* page.
pago *m.* payment.
país *m.* country, nation. 2 region.
paisaje *m.* landscape, scenery.
paja *f.* straw. 2 *fig.* rubbish.
pájaro *m.* bird; ~ *bobo*, penguin; ~ *carpintero*, woodpecker. 2 shrewd fillow.
paje *m.* page [person.]. 2 NAUT. cabin-boy.

pala *f.* shovel. 2 fish-slice. 3 racket, bat. 4 blade [of a shoe, spade, etc.] 5 [baker's] peel.
palabra *f.* word [term; speech, remark].
palacio *m.* palace.
paladar *s.* palate. 2 taste, relish.
palanca *m. f.* lever. 2 crowbar.
palco *m.* THEAT. box.
paleta *f.* PAINT. palette. 2 fire shovel. 3 MAS. trowel.
palidez *f.* paleness, pallor.
pálido, da *a.* pale, ghastly.
palillo *m.* toothpick. 2 drumstick. 3 *pl.* castanets.
paliza *f.* beating, drubbing, thrashing.
palma *f.* BOT. palm, palmtree. 2 palm [of the hand]. 3 *pl.* clapping of hands.
palmada *f.* slap, pat. 2 clapping: *dar palmadas*, to clap.
palmera *f.* palm-tree.
palo *m.* stick. 2 NAUT. mast. 3 suit [at cards]. 4 wood; handle.
paloma *f.* ORN. dove, pigeon.

palomar *m*. pigeon-house, dove-cot.

palpitante *a*. palpitating throbbing: *la cuestión* ~, the burning question.

palpitar *i*. to palpitate, beat, throb.

pan *m*. bread; loaf.

pana *f*. velveteen, corduroy. 2 AUTO. break-down.

panadería *f*. bakery, baker's shop.

panadero, ra *m*. baker.

panal *m*. honeycomb.

panel *m*. panel.

pánico, ca *a.-m*. panic.

panorama *m*. panorama.

pantalón or *pl*. **pantalones** *m*. trousers, breeches, *pants.

pantalla *f*. lamp-shade. 2 fire-screen. 3 CINEM. screen.

pantano *m*. swamp, marsh. 2 small lake or natural pond. 3 a large dam. 4 fig. obstacle.

pantera *f*. ZOOL. panther.

pañal *m*. swaddling-cloth, napkin.

pañuelo *m*. handkerchief. 2 square shawl.

papa *m*. Pope. 2 coll. papa, dad. 3 *f*. fib, lie. 4 potato. 5 *pl*. porridge.

papel *m*. paper: ~ *secante*, blotting-paper. 2 THEAT. part. rôle.

papeleta *f*. slip of paper; card. file card. ticket: ~ *de votación*, ballot

paquete *m*. packet. parcel.

par *a*. like. equal. 2 even [number]. 3 *m*. pair, brace, couple. 4 peer. equal.

para *prep*. for. to. in order to: ~ *que*, in order that. so that: *¿para qué?*, what for? 3

toward. 4 by, on: ~ *entonces*, by then; ~ *Navidad*, on Christmas. 5 *estar* ~, to be on the point of.

parada *f*. stop, halt, standstill. 2 parade [muster of troops].

parador *m*. inn, hostel, motel.

paraguas, *pl*. **-guas** *m*. umbrella.

paraíso *m*. paradise. 2 THEAT. gods, gallery.

paralítico, ca *a.-n*. MED. paralytic, palsied.

paralizar *t*. to paralyze; to stop.

parar *t*. to stop. 2 ~ *mientes en*, to consider. 3 *i.-ref*. to stop. 4 to put up, lodge, 5 *ir a* ~, o *en*. to end in; finally to get to. 6 to desist.

parásito, ta *a*. parasitic. 2 *m*. BIOL. parasite. 3 hanger-on. 4 *pl*. RADIO. strays.

parcela *f*. lot, plot [of land].

pardo, da *a*. brown. reddish grey. 2 dark, cloudy.

1) **parecer** *m*. opinion. mind. 2 looks; *ser de buen* ~, to be good-looking.

2) **parecer** *i*. to appear, show up. 2 to turn up [after lost]. 3 *impers*. to seem. look like: *según parece*, as it seems. 4 *ref*. to resemble [each other]; be alike. ¶ CONJUG. like *agradecer*.

parecido, da *a*. resembling. similar [to]. like. 2 *bien* ~, good-looking; *mal* ~, bad-looking. 3 *m*. resemblance.

pared *f*. wall.

pareja *f*. pair. couple; yoke; team [of horses]. 2 dancing partner. 3 match.

pariente, ta *m.-f.* relation, relative, kinsman.

parir *t.* to give birth to, bring forth; to bear.

paro *m.* MACH. stop, stopping. *2* suspension of work; lock-out, shutdown; ~ *forzoso,* unemployment.

parque *m.* park, garden.

párrafo *m.* paragraph.

parte *f.* part, portion, lot, section: **en** ~, partly. *2* share, interest: *llevar la mejor [peor]* ~, to have the best [the worst] of it. *3* party, side: *estar de* ~ *de,* to support. *4* place, region: *de* ~ *a* ~, through; *en ninguna* ~, nowhere; *por todas partes,* everywhere. *5 de* ~ *de,* in the name of, on behalf of; in favour of; from. *6 por una* ~, ...*por otra,* on the one hand, ...on the other hand. *7* official communication. *8 dar* ~, to report.

participante *a.* participating. *2 m.-f.* participant, sharer.

participar *t.* to notify, inform. *2 i.* to participate, share.

particular *a.* particular, peculiar, private. *2* noteworthy, extraordinary. *3 m.* private, citizen. *4* **-mente** *adv.* particularly; especially.

partida *f.* departure, leave. *2* record [in a register]. *3* [birth, marriage, death] certificate. *4* BOOKKEEP, entry, item. *5* game [at cards, chess]; match [at billiards]; set [at tennis]. *6* squad, gang; band of armed men.

partido, da *p. p.* of PARTIR. *2 m.* party, group. *3* profit, advantage. *4* favour; popularity. *5* SPORT team; game; match; odds. *6* territorial district. *7* match [in marriage].

partir *t.-ref.* to divide, split. *2 i.* to depart, leave. *3* to start from.

parto *m.* childbirth, delivery.

pasado, da *a.* past, gone by. *2* last [week, etc.]. *3* overripe, spoiled [fruit]; tainted [meat]. *4* ~ *de moda,* out of date or fashion. *5* ~ *mañana,* the day after tomorrow. *6 m.* the past.

pasaje *m.* passage, way. *2* passengers in a ship. *3* lane, alley.

1) **pasar (un buen)** *m.* enough to live on.

2) **pasar** *t.* to pass. *2* to carry across. *3* to go [over, in, by, to]. *4* to walk past. *5* to transgress [a limit]. *6* to pierce. *7* to swallow [food]. *8* to go through, suffer. *9* to overlook. *10* to spend [time]. *11 pasarlo bien,* to have a good time. *12 i.* to pass, get through. *13* to come in, or into. *14* ~ *de,* to go beyond. *15 ir pasando,* to get along. *16 impers.* to pass, happen: *¿qué pasa?,* what is the matter? *17 ref.* to get spoiled. *18* to exceed. *19* ~ *sin,* to do without.

pascua *f.* Jewish Passover. *2* ECCL. Easter: ~ *de Resurrección,* Easter Sunday.

pasear *i.-ref.* to walk; to take a walk; to parade: ~ *en auto,* to take a car ride; ~ *a caballo,* to go on horseback riding.

paseo *m.* walk, stroll; ride; drive: *dar un* ~, to go for a walk. *2* promenade.

pasillo *m.* corridor, narrow pasage. *2* aisle.

pasión *f.* passion.

paso *m.* step, pace, footstep: ~ *a* ~, step by step; *de* ~, by the way: ~ *a nivel*, level crossing; *marcar el* ~, to mark time. *2* passage.

pasta *f.* paste. *2* dough. *3* (Am.) cookie.

pastar *t.-i.* to pasture, graze.

pastel *m.* pie, pastry, tart. *2* cake. *3* pastel painting.

pastilla *f.* tablet, lozenge [of medicine]; bar [of chocolate]; cake [of soap].

pastor *m.* shepherd; herdsman. *2* pastor, protestant minister.

pata *f.* foot and leg [of animals]; leg [of table, etc.]; paw; hoof and leg: *a cuatro patas*, on all fours; *a* ~, on foot; *meter la* ~, to make a blunder: *tener mala* ~, to have bad luck.

patada *f.* kick.

patata *f.* potato: *patatas fritas*, chips.

patente *a.* patent, evident. *2 f.* patent.

patilla *f.* side-whiskers.

patio *m.* court, yard, courtyard, patio. *2* THEAT. pit.

pato *m.* duck. *2* drake [male duck].

patria *f.* native country, father-land: ~ *chica*, home town.

patriota *m.-f.* patriot.

patriotismo *m.* patriotism.

patrón *m.* patron. *2* landlord. *3* master, employer, boss. *4* pattern. *5* standard.

pausa *f.* pause. *2* MUS. rest.

pavo *m.* ORN. turkey; turkey cock. *2* ORN. ~ *real*, peacock.

pavor *m.* fear, fright, terror.

paz *f.* peace; quiet, rest.

peca *f.* freckle, spot.

pecado *m.* sin.

pecador, ra *a.* sinful, sinning. *2 m.-f.* sinner.

pecar *i.* to sin.

peculiar *a.* peculiar, characteristic.

pecho *m.* chest, breast, bosom; heart. *2* courage: *tomar a* ~, to take to heart.

pedazo *m.* piece, portion, bit.

pedir *t.* to ask [for], beg, request, demand. *2* COM. to order. *3* ~ *prestado*, to borrow. ¶ CONJUG. like *servir*.

pedrada *f.* blow with a stone. *2* throw of a stone.

pegar *t.-i.* to glue, stick, cement. *2* to tie, fasten. *3* to post [bills]. *4* to set [fire]. *5* to hit, slap. *6* *ref.* to stick; to cling. *7* to come to blows.

peinar *t.* to comb, dress or do the hair: ~ *canas*, to be old.

peine *m.* comb. *2* rack.

pelado, da *a.* bald, bare; hairless. *2* barren; treeless. *3* peeled. *4* fig. penniless.

pelar *t.* to cut, shave the hair of. *2* to pluck [a fowl]. *3* to peel, bark, hull. *4* *ref.* to get one's hair cut.

pelea *f.* fight. *2* wrangle. *3* quarrel. *4* battle; struggle.

pelear *i.-ref.* to fight. *2* to quarrel; to come to blows. *3 i.* to battle.

película *f.* film.

peligro *m.* danger, peril, risk, hazard.

peligroso, sa a. dangerous, perilous, risky.

pelo m. hair. 2 coat, fur [of animals]. 3 down [of birds]. 4 *tomar el* ~, to pull the leg.

pelota f. ball; pelota, ball game: *en pelotas*, naked.

peludo, da a. hairy, shaggy.

peluquería f. haidresser's [shop]; barber's [shop].

pellejo m. skin, hide. 2 wineskin. 3 *salvar el* ~, to save one's skin.

pena f. penalty, punishment, pain: ~ *capital*, capital punishment. 2 grief, sorrow. 3 pity: *dar* ~, to arouse pity. 4 *valer la* ~, to be worth while.

penal a. penal. 2 m. penitentiary.

pendiente a. pending, hanging, dangling. 2 depending on. 3 f. slope, incline. 4 m. ear-ring.

penetrar t.-i. to penetrate, break into. 2 i. to be acute, piercing. 3 to comprehend.

península f. GEOG. peninsula.

penitencia f. penance. 2 penitence.

penoso, sa a. painful. 2 laborious, hard.

pensador, ra a. thinking. 2 m. thinker.

pensamiento m. thought, mind. 2 idea. 3 BOT. pansy.

pensar t. to think [of, out, over, about]; to consider; to imagine; to intend. ¶ CONJUG. like *acertar*.

pensativo, va a. pensive, thoughtful.

pensión f. pension. 2 boarding-house.

peña f. rock, boulder.

peón m. pedestrian. 2 day-labourer; ~ *de albañil*, hodman; ~ *caminero*, roadmender. 3 (Am.) farm hand. 4 pawn [in chess].

peor a.-adv. comp. de MALO worse. 2 *el peor*, the worst.

pepita f. seed [of apple, melon, etc.], pip. 2 MIN. nugget.

pequeño, ña a. little, small. 2 young. 3 low, 4 m.-f. child.

pera f. pear.

percibir t. to perceive, notice. 2 to collect [taxes].

percha f. perch. 2 clothes-rack, hat-rack.

perder t. to lose: ~ *de vista*, to lose sight of. 2 to ruin, spoil, waste. 3 to fade. 4 ref. to go astray, get lost. 5 [of fruits, etc.] to be spoiled. 6 to become ruined. ¶ CONJUG. like *entender*.

pérdida f. loss: *pérdidas y ganancias*, COM. profit and loss. 2 waste [of time].

perdido, da a. lost. 2 mislaid. 3 wasted, useless.

perdón m. pardon, forgiveness, grace; *con* ~, by your leave.

perdonar t. to pardon, forgive. 2 to remit [a debt]. 3 to excuse.

perecer i. to perish, come to an end, die. ¶ CONJUG. like *agradecer*.

peregrino, na a. travelling. 2 migratory [bird]. 3 strange, rare. 4 m.-f. pilgrim.

pereza f. laziness, idleness, sloth.

perezoso, sa a. lazy, slothful, idle. 2 m. ZOOL. sloth.

perfección f. perfection, completion: *a la* ~, perfectly.

perfeccionar *t.* to perfect; to improve; to complete.

perfectamente *adv.* perfectly.

perfecto, ta *a.* perfect, complete.

perfilar *t.* to profile. 2 to outline. 3 *ref.* to show one's profile.

perfumar *t.* to perfume, scent.

perfume *m.* perfume. 2 fragance.

periódico, ca *a.* periodic(al. 2 *m.* journal, newspaper.

periodista *m.-f.* journalist.

período *m.* period. 2 sentence.

perjudicar *t.* to hurt, damage, injure, impair.

perjudicial *a.* harmful, prejudicial.

perjuicio *m.* harm, injury, prejudice, detriment.

perla *f.* pearl: *de perlas*, excellent.

permanecer *i.* to remain, stay. 2 to last, endure. ¶ CONJUG. like *agradecer*.

permanente *a.* permanent, lasting. 2 *f.* permanent wave [in hair]. 3 **-mente** *adv.* permanently.

permiso *m.* permission, leave, license, permit; ~ *de conducir*, AUTO. driving licence; *con su* ~, by your leave.

permitir *t.* to permit, allow, let.

pernil *m.* ham.

pero *advers. conj.* but, yet, except. 2 *m.* objection, fault.

perpetuo, tua *a.* perpetual, everlasting.

perro *m.* dog.

persecución *f.* pursuit, persecution.

perseguir *t.* to pursue, persecute, chase. ¶ CONJUG. like *servir*.

persiana *f.* Venetian blind.

persona *f.* person. 2 excellent man. 3 *pl.* people.

personaje *m.* personage. 2 character [in a play, etc.].

personal *a.* personal. 2 *m.* personnel, staff. 3 **-mente** *adv.* personally, in person.

perspectiva *f.* perspective. 2 prospect, view, outlook. 3 *pl.* prospect(s.

persuadir *i.* to persuade. 2 *ref.* to be persuaded or convinced.

pertenecer *i.* to belong; to pertain, concern. ¶ CONJUG. like *agradecer*.

perteneciente *a.* belonging, pertaining.

perturbado, da *a.* disturbed. 2 insane.

perturbar *t.* to disturb, perturb, upset. 2 to confuse.

perverso, sa *a.* perverse, wicked, depraved.

pervertir *t.* to pervert, lead astray, deprave, corrupt. ¶ CONJUG. like *hervir*.

pesa *f.* weight.

pesadilla *f.* nightmare.

pesado, da *a.* heavy, weighty. 2 tiresome, boring. 3 deep [sleep].

pésame *m.* condolence, expression of simpathy.

1) **pesar** *m.* sorrow, grief, regret. 2 regret. 3 *a* ~ *de*, in spite of.

2) **pesar** *t.* to weigh. 2 to consider. 3 *i.* to have weight. 4 to be sorry, regret.

pesca f. fishing. 2 angling. 3 catch of fish.

pescado m. fish [caught]. 2 salted codfish.

pescador a. fishing. 2 m. fisher. fisherman: ~ **de caña**, angler.

pescar t. to fish. catch [fish]. 2 to angle.

pesebre m. crib. rack. manger. stall; trough.

peseta f. peseta.

peso m. weight: ~ **bruto**, gross weight; ~ **neto**, net weight. 2 load. burden. 3 peso [Spanish-American monetary unit].

pestaña f. eyelash.

peste f. pest. pestilence. plague. 2 epidemic.

pétalo m. BOT. petal.

petición f. petition. request.

petróleo m. petroleum.

pez m. fish. 2 f. pitch. tar.

pezuña f. hoof. cloven hoof.

piadoso, sa a. pious. devout.

piar i. to peep. chirp.

picar t. to prick. pierce. 2 BULLF. to goat. 3 [of insects] to bite. sting. 4 to spur [a horse]. 5 to mince. 6 t.-i. to itch. 7 AER. to dive. 8 ref. [of teeth] to begin to decay. 9 [of the sea] to get choppy. 10 to take offense.

pícaro, ra a. knavish. roguish. 2 mischievous. 3 sly. 4 m.-f. knave. rogue. 5 sly person. 6 m. LIT. pícaro.

pico m. beak. 2 mouth; eloquence. 3 peak [of a mountain]. 4 pick [tool], pickaxe. 6 small surplus: **tres pesetas y** ~, three pesetas odd.

pie m. foot; **a cuatro pies**, on all fours; **a pie**, on foot; **en** ~, standing: **dar** ~, to give occasion for: **al** ~ **de la letra**, literally. 2 bottom. 3 base. stand. 4 trunk. stalk.

piedad f. piety. 2 pity. mercy.

piedra f. stone.

piel f. skin. 2 hide. pelt. 3 leather. 4 fur. 5 m. ~ **roja**, redskin.

pierna f. leg.

pieza f. piece. fragment. 2 game. quarry. 3 THEAT. short play.

pila f. stone trough or basin. 2 baptismal font: **nombre de** ~, Christian name. 3 pile. heap.

píldora f. pill. pellet.

piloto m. pilot.

pillo, lla m.-f. rogue. rascal. 2 sly fellow. urchin.

pimienta f. pepper [spice].

pimiento m. [green. red] pepper.

pincel m. [painter's] brush.

pinchar t. to prick. puncture.

1) pino m. pine. pine-tree.

2) pino, na a. steep.

pintar t. to paint. 2 to describe. 3 ref. to make up one's face.

pintor m. painter; house painter; dauber.

pintoresco, ca a. picturesque.

pintura f. painting.

piña f. BOT. pine cone. 2 ~ **de América**, pineapple. 3 cluster.

pipa f. pipe [of tobacco]. 2 cask. barrel. 3 pip. seed.

pirata m. pirate; corsair.

pisar t. to tread on. step on. 2 to press [grapes. etc.]. 3 to trample under foot.

piscina f. fishpond; swimming-pool.

piso *m*. tread, ·treading. *2* floor; pavement; storey: ~ *bajo,* ground floor. *3* flat, apartment.

pista *f*. trail, trace, track, scent. *2* clue. *3* SPORT racetrack. *4* ring [of a circus]. *5* AER. runway, landing-field.

pistilo *m*. pistil.

pistola *f*. pistol.

pitar *i*. to blow a whistle; to whistle at.

pito *m*. whistle.

pizarra *f*. MINER. slate. *2* blackboard.

placa *f*. plaque [badge of honorary order]. *2* PHOT. plate.

placentero, ra *a*. joyful, pleasant, agreeable.

1) **placer** *m*. pleasure. *2* will. *3* sandbank, shoal. *4* MIN. placer.

2) **placer** *t*. to please, content. ¶ CONJUG. INDIC. Pres.: *plazco,* places, place, etc. | Pret.: plació or *plugo;* placieron or *pluguieron.* ‖ SUBJ. Pres.: *plazca, plazcas,* etc. | Imperf.: placiera or *pluguiera.* | Fut.: placiere or *pluguiere,* etc. ‖ IMPER.: place, *plazca; plazcamos,* placed, *plazcan.*

plaga *f*. plague, pest, calamity, scourge.

plan *m*. plan, project, design, scheme: ~ *de estudios,* EDUC. curriculum. *2* drawing.

plancha *f*. plate, sheet [of metal]. *2* iron [for clothes].

planchar *t*. to iron, press.

planear *t*. to plan, design, outline. *2 i*. AER. to glide.

planeta *m*. planet.

plano, na *a*. plane. *2* flat, even. *3 m*. plane [surface].

planta *f*. BOT. plant. *2* planta-

tion. *3* sole of the foot. *4* plan, design. *5* ~ *baja,* ground floor.

plantar *t*. to plant. *2* to set up, place. *3* to strike [a blow]. *4* to throw [in the street]. *5* to jilt. *6 ref*. to stand firm.

plantel *m*. nursery, nursery garden; nursery school.

plata *f*. silver. *2* money.

plataforma *f*. platform.

platanal *m*. banana plantation.

plátano *m*. BOT. banana [plant and fruit]. *2* BOT. plane-tree.

plateado, da *a*. silver-plated. *2* silvery [in colour].

plato *m*. plate, dish. *2* COOK. dish. *3* course [at meals].

playa *f*. beach, seaside, shore.

plaza *f*. public square. *2* market-place. *3* fortress, stronghold. *4* room, space, seat. *5* job, employment. *6* COM. town, city. *7* ~ *de toros,* bullring.

plazo *m*. term; time-limit; duedate: *a plazos,* by instalments.

pleito *m*. litigation, law-suit. *2* debate, contest.

pleno, na *a*. full, complete.

pliegue *m*. fold, pleat, crease.

plomo *m*. CHEM. lead. *2* plumb bob, sinker. *3* fig. bullet.

pluma *f*. feather, plume [of bird]. *2* [writing] quill; pen, nib.

población *f*. population. *2* city, town.

poblado, da *a*. populated. *2* thick [beard]. *3 m*. town, city.

pobre *a*. poor: ~ *de espíritu,* poor in spirit. *2 m.-f.* poor person; beggar.

pobreza *f.* poverty; need; lack, scarcity; want.

1) **poco** *adv.* little, not much: *a ~*, shortly after; *dentro de ~*, presently; *~ más o menos*, more or less; *por ~*, nearly.

2) **poco, ca** *a.* little, scanty. *2 pl.* few. *3 m.* little, small quantity, time, etc.

podar *t.* to prune, lop off, trim.

1) **poder** *m.* power; authority, control. *2* force, strength, might. *3* POL. *estar en el ~*, to be in the office.

2) **poder** *t.-i.* to be able [to], can, may; *no ~ más*, to be unable to do more. *2 i.* to have power or influence. *3 impers.* to be possible; may: *puede que llueva*, it may rain. ¶ IRREG. CONJUG.: INDIC. Pres.: *puedo, puedes, puede; podemos, podéis, pueden.* | Pret.: *pude, pudiste*, etc. | Fut.: *podré, podrás*, etc. ‖ COND.: *podría, podrías*, etc. ‖ SUB. Pres.: *pueda, puedas, pueda; podamos, podáis, puedan.* | Imperf.: *pudiera, pudieras*, etc. or *pudiese, pudieses*, etc. | Fut.: *pudiere, pudieres*, etc. ‖ IMPER.: *puede, pueda, podamos, poded, puedan.* ‖ GER.: *pudiendo.*

poema *m.* poem.

poesía *f.* poetry. *2* poem.

poeta *m.* poet.

policía *m.* policeman, police officer, detective. *2* police force: *~ secreta*, secret police.

policíaco, ca *a.* [pertaining to the] police. *2 novela policíaca*, detective story.

polilla *f.* moth, clothes-moth.

política *f.* politics. *2* policy. *3* politeness, good manners.

político, ca *a.* politic(al. *2* tactful. *3* -in-law: *padre ~*, father-in-law. *4 m.* politician.

polo *m.* GEOM., ASTR., GEOG., PHYS. pole. *2* SPORTS polo.

polvo *m.* dust. *2* powder.

pólvora *f.* gunpowder.

pollo *m.* chicken. *2* young man.

pompa *f.* pomp: *pompas fúnebres*, funeral. *2* pageant. *3* bubble. *4* NAUT. pump.

poner *t.* to place, put, set: *~ en libertad*, to set free; *~ en práctica*, to carry out. *2* to lay [eggs]. *3* to suppose. *4* to bet [money]. *5* to render [furious]. *6 ~ al día*, to bring up to date; *~ de manifiesto*, to make evident; *~ de relieve*, to emphasize; *~ reparos*, to make objections; *~ en las nubes*, to praise to the skies. *7 ref.* to place or put oneself. *8* to put on [one's hat]. *9* [of the sun, stars, etc.] to set. *10* to become, get, turn. *11 ~ a*, to begin to. *12 ~ al corriente*, to get informed. *13 ~ de acuerdo*, to agree. *14 ponerse en pie*, to stand up. ¶ CONJUG.: INDIC. Pres.: *pongo, pones, pone*, etc. | Pret.: *puse, pusiste, puso*, etc. | Fut.: *pondré, pondrás, etc.* ‖ COND.: *pondría, pondrías*, etc. | SUBJ. Pres.: *ponga, pongas*, etc. | Imperf.: *pusiera, pusieras*, or *pusiese, pusieses*, etc. | Fut.: *pusiere, pusieres*, etc. ‖ IMPER.: *pon, ponga, pongamos*, poned, *pongan.* ‖ PAST. P.: *puesto.*

popular *a.* popular. 2 **-mente** *adv.* popularly.

popularidad *f.* popularity.

por *prep.* by, for, as, along, around, across, through, from, out of, at, in, on, to, etc.: ~ *aquí, around here;* ~ *la noche,* in the night, by night. 2 ~ *ciento,* per cent; ~ *tanto,* therefore; ~ *más que,* however *mucho que,* however much; ¿~ *qué?,* why?; ~ *supuesto,* of course.

porcelana *f.* porcelain, china.

porción *f.* part, share, lot.

pordiosero, ra *n.* beggar.

poro *m.* pore.

porque *conj.* for, because. 2 in order that.

¿por qué? *conj.* why?, wherefore?

porqué m. cause, reason.

porquería *f.* dirt, filth. 2 filthy act or word.

portaaviones *m.* aircraft carrier.

portal *m.* doorway, portal, vestibule. 2 porch, portico, entrance. 3 *pl.* arcades.

portarse *ref.* behave, act.

porte *m.* portage, carriage; freight [act; cost]: ~ *pagado,* portage prepaid, 2 behaviour, bearing; appearance [of a person].

portero, ra *m.* doorkeeper, porter. 2 SPORT. goalkeeper. 3 *f.* portress.

porvenir *m.* future, time to come.

posada *f.* lodging-house, inn.

posar *i.* to·lodge. 2 to rest. 3 F. ARTS to pose. 4 *i.-ref.* [of birds, etc.] to alight, perch, sit. 5 *t.* to lay down [a bur-

den]. 6 *ref.* [of sediment, etc.] to settle.

poseer *t.* to possess, own, hold, have. 2 to master [a subject]. ¶ CONJUG. INDIC. Pret.: poseí, poseíste, *poseyó;* poseímos, poseísteis, *poseyeron.* ‖ SUBJ. Imperf.: *poseyera, poseyeras,* etc., or *poseyese, poseyeses,* etc. ‖ PAST. P.: poseído or *poseso.* ‖ GER.: *poseyendo.*

posesión *f.* possession, tenure, holding.

posibilidad *f.* possibility. 2 *pl.* means, property.

posible *a.* possible: *hacer todo lo* ~, to do one's best. 2 *m. pl.* means, property.

posponer *t.* to postpone, delay, put off.

postal *a.* postal. 2 *f.* postcard.

poste *m.* post, pillar: ~ *indicador,* finger-post, signpost.

postrar *t.* to prostrate, humble. 2 *ref.* to kneel down.

postre *a.* POSTRERO. 2 *m. sing. & pl.* dessert. 3 *adv. a la* ~, at last, finally.

postrero, ra *a.* last. 2 hindermost. 3 *m.-f.* last one.

pote *m.* pot; jug; jar.

potencia *f.* potency. 2 power; faculty, ability; strength. 3 powerful nation.

potente *a.* potent, powerful, mighty. 2 strong, vigorous.

potestad *f.* power, faculty. 2 dominion, authority.

potro, tra *m.-f.* colt, foal. 2 *m.* horse [for torture]. 3 *f.* filly.

pozo *m.* well, pit. 2 MIN. shaft.

práctica *f.* practice: *poner en* ~, to put into practice. 2 skill. 3 *pl.* training.

práctico, ca *a.* practical. 2

skilful, practised. *3 m.* NAUT. pilot.

pradera *f.* prairie. *2* meadowland.

prado *f.* field, meadow, lawn.

precaución *f.* precaution.

precedente *a.* preceding, prior, foregoing. *2 m.* precedent.

preceder *t.-i.* to precede, go ahead of.

precepto *m.* precept, rule; order: *día de ~,* holiday.

precio *m.* price. *2* value, worth.

precioso, sa *a.* precious [costly, valuable, dear]. *2* beautiful.

precipitar *t.* to precipitate [throw headlong; to hurl; to hasten, to hurry]. *2 ref.* to be hasty or rash.

precisamente *adv.* precisely, exactly. *2* just.

preciso, sa *a.* precise, exact, accurate. *2* necessary.

predecir *t.* to predict, foretell, forecast.

predicador, ra *m.-f.* preacher.

predicar *t.-i.* to preach. *2* LOG. to predicate.

predilecto, ta *a.* favourite.

predominar *t.* to prevail. *2* to overlook.

preferencia *f.* preference, choice.

preferible *a.* preferable.

preferir *t.* to prefer, choose: *yo preferiría ir,* I'd rather go.

pregunta *f.* question, inquiry; *hacer una ~,* to ask a question.

preguntar *t.-i.* to ask, inquire; to question. *2 ref.* to wonder.

prejuicio *m.* prejudice, bias.

premiar *i.* to reward.

premio *m.* reward, recompense. *2* prize.

prenda *f.* pledge, security, pawn: token, proof: *en ~ de,* as a proof of. *2* fig. beloved one. *3* garment.

prender *i.* to seize, catch. *2* to attach, pin. *3* to take, arrest [a person]. *4* to set [fire]. *5 i.* [of a plant] to take root. *6* [of fire, etc.] to catch.

prensa *f.* press; printing press. *2* journalism, daily press.

preocupación *f.* preoccupation. *2* care, concern, worry.

preocupar *t.* to preoccupy. *2* to concern, worry. *3 ref.* to worry.

preparación *f.* preparation.

preparar *t.* to prepare, make ready. *2 ref.* to get ready.

preparativo, va *a.* preparatory. *2 m.-pl.* arrangements.

presa *f.* catch, grip, hold. *2* capture. *3* prize, booty. *4* prey. *5* claw. *6* dam.

presencia *f.* presence. *2* figure, bearing.

presenciar *t.* to be present at, witness, see.

presentar *t.* to present. *2* to display, show. *3* to introduce [a person to another]. *4 ref.* to appear.

presente *a.* present; *hacer ~,* to remind of; *tener ~,* to bear in mind. *2* current [month, etc.]. *3 a.-m.* GRAM. present [tense]. *4 m.* present, gift. *5* present [time].

preservar *t.* to preserve, guard, keep safe.

presidencia *f.* presidency. *2* chairmanship.

presidente *m.* president. *2* chairman. *3* speaker.

presidir *t.-i.* to preside over or at.

presión *f.* pressure: ~ *arterial,* blood pressure.

preso, sa *a.* imprisoned. *2 m.-f.* prisoner. *3* convict.

préstamo *m.* loan: *casa de préstamos,* pawnshop.

prestar *t.* to lend, loan. *2* to bestow, give. *3* to do, render [service, etc.]. *4* to give [ear; help, aid]. *5* to pay [attention]. *6* to take [oath]. *7 ref.* to lend oneself. *8 se presta a,* it gives rise to.

prestigio *m.* prestige. *2* spell.

1) **presto** *adv.* quickly. *2* soon.

2) **presto, ta** *a.* prompt, quick. *2* ready.

presumir *t.* to presume, conjecture. *2 i.* to boast [of].

presupuesto, ta *a.* presupposed. *2 m.* presupposition. *3* budget. *4* estimate.

pretender *t.* to pretend to, claim. *2* to try to.

pretensión *f.* pretension, claim.

pretexto *m.* pretext, pretence.

prevalecer *i.* to prevail.

prevención *f.* preparation. *2* supply. *3* foresight. *4* prejudice, dislike. *5* warning. *6* police station.

prevenir *t.* to prepare beforehand. *2* to foresee, forestall. *3* to warn. *4* to prevent. *5 ref.* to get ready.

previo, via *a.* previous.

prieto, ta *a.* tight. *2* closefisted, mean. *3* blackish, dark.

primario, ria *a.* primary, chief.

primavera *f.* spring.

1) **primero** *adv.* first.

2) **primero, ra** *a.* first. *2* foremost. *3* early, former.

primitivo, va *a.* primitive, original.

primo, ma *a.* first. *2* ARITH. prime [number]. *3* raw [material]. *4 m.-f.* cousin. *5* simpleton.

primogénito, ta *a.-n.* firstborn, eldest [son].

primoroso, sa *a.* beautiful, exquisite. *2* skilful, fine.

principal *a.* principal, main, chief. *2 m.* chief, head [of a firm, etc.] *3* first floor. *4* -**mente** *adv:* principally, mainly.

principio *m.* beginning. *2* principle. *3 pl.* principles.

prisa *f.* speed, haste, hurry; *corre ~,* that is urgent; *tener ~,* to be in a hurry.

prisión *f.* prison; imprisonment; jail.

prisionero, ra *m.-f.* prisoner.

privación *f.* privation, want, lack.

privar *t.* to forbid. *2* to impede. *3 ref.* to deprive oneself.

privilegio *m.* privilege, grant, exemption, patent.

pro *m.-f.* profit, advantage: *el ~ y el contra,* the pros and cons.

probabilidad *f.* probability, likelihood.

probable *a.* probable, likely. *2* -**mente** *adv.* probably, likely.

probar *t.* to prove. *2* to test, try out. *3* to taste [wine]. *4* to try on [clothes]. *5 i. ~ a,* to attempt, endeavour to.

problema *m.* problem.

1) **proceder** *m.* behaviour, conduct.

2) **proceder** *i.* to proceed, go on. *2* to come from. *3* to behave. *4* to take action [against]. *5* to be proper or suitable.

procedimiento *m.* procedure; method, way.

procesión *f.* procession.

proceso *m.* process [progress; development]. *2* lapse of time. *3* LAW proceedings. *4* lawsuit.

proclamar *t.* to proclaim.

procurador *m.* attorney, agent. *2* solicitor.

procurar *t.* to try to. *2* to get. *3* to manage.

prodigar *t.* to lavish, squander.

prodigio *m.* prodigy, miracle.

prodigioso, sa *a.* prodigious, marvellous. *2* exquisite.

pródigo, ga *a.-n.* prodigal. *2 a.* extravagant; lavish, wasteful.

producción *f.* production. *2* produce, yield, output.

producir *t.* to produce, yield, bring forth. *2* to cause. *3 ref.* to happen.

productor, ra *a.* productive. *2* *m.-f.* producer.

profecía *f.* prophecy.

profesar *t.-i.* to profess. *2 t.* to show, manifest.

profesión *f.* profession. *2* avowal, declaration.

profesor, ra *m.-f.* professor, teacher.

profeta *m.* prophet.

profundo, da *a.* profound, deep.

progresar *i.* to progress, advance, develop.

progreso *m.* progress, advance.

prohibir *to.* to prohibit, forbid.

prójimo *m.* fellow being, neighbour.

prolongar *t.* to lengthen. *2* to prolong. *3* to protract.

promedio *m.* middle. *2* average.

promesa *f.* promise.

prometer *t.-i.* to promise. *2 ref.* to become engaged, betrothed.

prometido, da *a.* promised. *2* engaged, betrothed. *3 m.* fiancé. *4 f.* fiancée.

prominente *a.* prominent, projecting.

promover *t.* to promote, start. *2* cause, stir up, raise.

pronombre *m.* GRAM. pronoun.

pronto *adv.* soon; *lo más ~ posible,* as soon as possible. *2* promptly, quickly: *de ~,* suddenly; *por lo ~,* for the present. *3 m.* impulse. *4 a.* ready.

pronunciar *t.* to pronunce, utter. *2* to deliver, make [a speech].

propaganda *f.* propaganda. *2* COM. advertising.

propagar *t.* to propagate, spread. *2 ref.* to spread, be diffused.

propicio, cia *a.* propitious, favourable.

propiedad *f.* ownership, property. *2* peculiar quality.

propietario *m.* owner, proprietor, landlord.

propio, pia *a.* one's own. *2* proper, peculiar. *3* suitable. *4* same. *5 amor ~,* pride; *nombre ~,* proper noun.

proponer *t.* to propose, put

forward. *2 ref.* to plan, intend.

proporcionar *t.* to proportion, adapt, adjust. *2* to furnish, supply, give. *3 ref.* to get.

proposición *f.* proposition; proposal, offer. *2* motion.

propósito *m.* purpose, aim, design: *a ~,* apropos, by the way; *de ~,* on purpose; *fuera de ~,* irrelevant.

prosa *f.* prose.

proseguir *t.* to continue, carry on. *2 i.* to go on.

prosperar *i.* to prosper, thrive.

prosperidad *f.* prosperity. *2* success.

próspero, ra *a.* prosperous. *2* successful.

proteger *t.* to protect, defend.

protesta, protestación *f.* protest, protestation.

protestar *t.-i.* to protest [against]; to assure, avow publicly.

provecho *m.* profit, advantage, benefit.

provechoso, sa *a.* profitable, advantageous, useful.

proveedor, ra *m.-f.* supplier, furnisher, purveyor.

proveer *t.* to supply with, furnish, provide, purvey.

proverbio *m.* proverb, saying.

providencia *f.* providence, foresight. *2* Providence [God].

providencial *a.* providential.

provincia *f.* province.

provisional *a.* temporary.

provocar *t.* to provoke, defy, dare, challenge. *2* to rouse.

proximidad *f.* nearness.

próximo, ma *a.* near, neighbouring, close to. *2* next: *el mes ~,* next month.

proyección *f.* projection; jut.

proyectar *t.* to project, throw, cast. *2* to show [a film, etc.]. *3* to plan, intend. *4 ref.* to jut out, stand out. *5* [of a shadow] to fall on.

proyecto *m.* project, design, plan, scheme: *2 ~ de ley,* bill.

prudente *a.* prudent, wise. *2* cautious.

prueba *f.* proof; evidence. *2* sign. *3* test, trial. *4* sample. *5* fitting. *6* ordeal, trial. *7 poner a ~,* to put to test.

psicológico, ca *a.* psychological.

publicación *f.* publication.

publicar *t.* to publish. *2* to issue [a decree]. *3 ref.* to come out.

publicidad *f.* publicity. *2* advertisement.

público, ca *a.* public. *2 m.* public; audience [spectators, etc.].

pueblo *m.* town, village. *2* common people. *3* nation.

puente *m.-f.* bridge. *2* deck.

puerco, ca *a.* dirty, filthy; sluttish. *2 m.* hog, pig. *3 ~ espín,* porcupine. *4 f.* sow.

puerta *f.* door, doorway; gate, gateway; entrance.

puerto *m.* NAUT. port, harbour. *2* fig. refuge. *3* mountain pass.

pues *conj.* because, for, since. *2* then: *así ~,* so then; *~ bien,* well then.

puesta *f.* setting: *~ de sol,* sunset. *2* stake [at cards].

puesto, ta *irreg. p. p.* of PO-

NER. *2* placed, put. *3 m.* place, spot. *4* stall, stand, booth. *5* job. *6* MIL. post, station: ~ *de socorro,* first-aid station. *7* conj. ~ *que,* since, inasmuch as.

púgil *m* boxer, pugilist.

pulga *f.* flea.

pulmón *m.* lung.

pulpo *m.* octopus; cuttle-fish.

pulsera *f.* JEWEL. bracelet. *2* wristlet. *3* watch strap.

punta *f.* point. *2* head. *3* tip, nib. *4* top. *5* horn. *6* tine. *7 está de* ~ *con,* to be on bad terms with.

puntilla *f.* point lace. *2* tracing point. *3* BULLF. short dagger. *4 de puntillas,* softly, on tiptoe.

punto *m.* point; dot; period. stop: ~ *final,* full stop: ~ *y coma,* semicolon; *dos puntos,* colon. *2* SEW. stitch. *3* knitwork: *géneros de* ~, hosiery. *4* place, spot, point: ~ *de partida,* starting-point; ~ *de vista,* point of view.

puntuación *f.* punctuation.

puntual *a.* punctual; exact.

puñado *m.* handful.

puñal *m.* poniard, dagger.

puño *m.* fist. *2* handful. *3* cuff. *4* hilt [of a sword, etc.]. *5* handle [of an umbrella].

pupila *f.* ANAT. pupil.

pupilo *m.* pupil, ward. *2* boarder.

pupitre *m.* [writing] desk.

pureza *f.* purity. *2* virginity.

purificar *t.* to purify, cleanse.

puro, ra *a.* pure, sheer; chaste. *2 m.* cigar.

púrpura *f.* purple.

Q

que *rel. pron.* that; wich; who; whom; *el* ~, who; which; the one who; the one which. *2 conj.* that; to [accusative-infinitive]. *3* than [in comparative sentences]. *4* and [expletive]. *5* let, may. I wish [in command or desiderative sentences]. *6 con tal* ~, provided [that]. *7* for, because, since.

qué *exclam. pron.* how, what [a]; *¡~ bonito!,* how beautiful! *2 interr. pron.* what?, which? *3* how much. *4 ¿a [para]* ~?, what for?; *¿por* ~?, why?; *no hay de* ~, don't mention it!

quebrada *f.* gorge, ravine.

quebradero *m.* ~ *de cabeza,* worry, concern.

quebradizo, za *a.* brittle, fragile.

quebrado, da *a.* broken. *2* bankrupt. *3* rough or rugged [ground]. *4 m.* bankrupt. *5* MATH. fraction.

quebrantar *t.* to break. *2* to pound, crash. *3* to transgress [a law]. *4* to weaken. *5* to vex.

quebranto *m.* breaking. *2* loss. *3* grief, pain. *4* pity.

quebrar *t.* to break, crush; to interrupt. *2* to wither [complexion]. *3* to bend [the body]. *4 i.* to go bankrupt. *5 quebrarse uno la cabeza.* to rack one's brains. ¶ CONJUG. like *acertar.*

queda *f.* curfew.

quedar *i.-ref.* to remain, stay, be left: ~ *atónito,* to be astonished; *nos quedan diez pesetas,* we have ten pesetas left. *2* ~ *en,* to agree; ~ *bien o mal,* to acquit oneself well or badly; *quedarse con,* to take.

quedo, da *a.* quiet, soft, low [voice].

quehacer *m.* job, task, duties.

queja *f.* complaint, moan, groan.

quejarse *ref.* to complain, moan, grumble.

quejido *m.* complaint, moan.

quejoso, sa *a.* complaining, plaintive.

quema *f.* burning; fire.

quemadura *f.* burn, scald.

quemar t. to burn; scald; scorch. 2 i. to burn [be too hot]. 3 ref. to burn, get burnt. 4 to become angry. 5 [of plants] to be scorched, nipped.

quemazón f. burning. 2 itching. 3 great heat.

querella f. complaint. 2 quarrel, controversy.

querellarse ref. to bewail. 2 LAW to complain, bring suit.

1) **querer** m. love affection.

2) **querer** t. to love [be in love with]. 2 to want, will, wish, desire. 3 ~ decir, to mean. 4 no quiso hacerlo, he refused to do it; sin ~, unintentionally. 5 impers. parece que quiere llover, it looks like rain. ¶ CONJUG. INDIC. Pres.: *quiero, quieres, quiere;* queremos, queréis, *quieren.* | Pret.: *quise, quisiste, quiso,* etc. | Fut.: *querré, querrás,* etc. ‖ SUBJ. Pres.: *quiera, quieras, quiera;* queramos, queráis, *quieran.* | Imperf.: *quisiera, quisieras,* etc., or *quisiese, quisieses,* etc. | Fut.: *quisiere, quisieres,* etc. ‖ IMPER.: *quiere, quiera; queramos, quered, quieran.*

querido, da a. dear, beloved. 2 m.-f. lover; paramour. 3 f. mistress.

querubín m. cherub.

queso m. cheese: ~ de bola, Dutch cheese.

quevedos m. pl. pince-nez.

quicio m. hinge [of a door]: *sacar a uno de* ~, to exasperate someone.

quiebra f. break, crack; fissure. 2 ravine. 3 loss. 4 COM. failure, bankrupcy.

quien *(interrog. & exclam.* **quién**), pl. **quienes** pron. who, whom.

quienquiera, pl. **quienesquiera** *pron.* whoever, whomever, whosoever, whomsoever.

quietamente adv. quietly, calmly.

quieto, ta a. quiet, still, motionless; calm.

quietud f. calmness, stillness, quiet, rest.

quijada f. jaw, jawbone.

quijote m. Quixote, quixotic person.

quilate m. carat, karat.

quilo m. KILO.

quilla f. keel.

quimera f. chimera. 2 quarrel. 3 wild fancy.

quimérico, ca a. unreal, fantastic.

química f. chemistry.

químico, ca a. chemical. 2 m.-f. chemist.

quina, quinina f. quinine.

quincalla f. hardware, ironmongery.

quince a.-n. fifteen. 2 fifteenth.

quincena f. fortnight.

quinientos, as a.-n. five hundred.

quinina f. quinine.

quinqué m. oil lamp.

quinta f. country-house, villa 2 MIL. draft, recruitment, call-up.

quinto, ta a. fifth. 2 m. conscript, recruit.

quiosco m. kiosk, pavilion. 2 news-stand. 3 bandstand.

quiquiriquí m. cook-a-doodle-do.

quirúrgico, ca *a.* surgical.

quisquilloso, sa *a.* peevish, touchy.

quisto, ta *a.* **bien** ~, well-liked; welcome; **mal** ~, disliked; unwelcome.

quitamanchas *m.* dry-cleaner, stain remover.

quitanieves *m.* snow-plough.

quitar *t.* to remove, take [away, of, from, out], rub off. *2* to eliminate. *3* to steal, rob of, deprive of. *4* to clear [the table]. *5 ref.* to move away: *quítate de aquí,* get out of here! *6* to take off [one's clothes, etc.]. *7 quitarse de encima,* to get rid of.

quitasol *m.* parasol, sunshade.

quite *m.* hindrance. *2* parry [in fencing]. *3* removal [of a bull, when a fighter is in danger]. *4* dodge.

quizá, quizás *adv.* perhaps, maybe.

R

rabia *f.* MED. rabies. *2* rage, fury.

rabioso, sa *a.* rabid; mad. *2* furious, enraged, angry.

rabo *m.* tail; end: *de cabo a ~,* from beginning to end.

racimo *m.* bunch, cluster.

racional *a.* rational. *2* reasonable.

radiante *a.* radiant; beaming.

radical *a.* radical. *2 m.* root.

radio *m.* GEOM., ANAT. radius. *2* CHEM. radium. *3* spoke [of wheel]. *4* scope. *5* coll. radiogram. *6 f.* coll. radio, broadcasting. *7* coll. radio, wireless set.

raíz *f.* root [of a plant, etc.].

rama *f.* branch, bough.

ramaje *m.* foliage, branches.

ramo *m.* bough, branch. *2* bunch, cluster.

rana *f.* ZOOL. frog.

rancho *m.* MIL. mess. *2* (Am.)cattle ranch.

rapidez *f.* rapidity, quickness.

rápido, da *a.* rapid, fast, swift.

rapto *m.* ravishment. *2* kidnapping. *3* rapture, ecstasy.

raro, ra *a.* rare [gas]. *2* scarce: *raras veces,* seldom. *3* odd, queer, strange.

rascar *t.* to scrape, scratch.

rasgar *t.* to tear, rend, rip.

rasgo *m.* dash, stroke. *2* deed, feat. *3* trait, feature. *4 pl.* features.

raso, sa *a.* flat, level. *2* clear. *3 m.* satin.

raspar *t.* to rasp, scrape, erase.

rastrillo *m.* AGR. rake.

rata *f.* rat. *2* coll. sneak-thief.

rato *m.* time, while: *al poco ~,* shortly after.

ratón *m.* mouse. *2 pl.* mice.

raudal *m.* stream, torrent, flow.

raya *f.* ICHTH. ray, skate. *2* line. *3* score. *4* stripe. *5* crease. *6* parting.

rayar *t.* to draw lines on, line, rule. *2* to scratch [a surface]. *3* to stripe. *4* to cross out. *5 i. ~ con* or *en,* to border on, verge on.

rayo *m.* ray, beam. *2* lightning. *3 rayos X,* X-rays.

raza *f.* race, breed, lineage: *de pura ~,* thoroughbred.

razón f. reason. 2 right: **tener ~**, to be right; **no tener ~**, to be mistaken or wrong. 3 regard, respect: **en ~ a**, with regard to. 5 COM. **~ social**, trade name, firm.

razonable a. reasonable, sensible. 2 fair, moderate.

reacción f. reaction: **avión a ~**, jet [plane].

reaccionar i. to react.

real a. real, actual. 2 royal. 3 grand, magnificent. 4 m. real [Spanish coin].

realidad f. reality, fact. 2 sincerity. 3 **en ~**, really, in fact.

realizar t. to accomplish, carry out, do, fulfill.

reanudar t. to renew, resume.

rebaja f. abatement, reduction. 2 COM. rebate, discount.

rebajar t. to reduce, rebate, discount. 2 to disparage, humiliate. 3 ref. to humble oneself.

rebaño m. herd, flock, drove.

rebelarse ref. to rebel, revolt.

rebelde a. rebellious. 2 m.-f. rebel, insurgent.

rebosar i.-ref. to overflow, run over. 2 i. to abound.

receptor, ra a. receiving. 2 m.-f. receiver.

receta f. MED. prescription. 2 recipe [of a cake, etc.].

recetar t. MED. to prescribe.

recibir t. receive. 2 to admit, let in. 3 to meet.

recibo m. reception; receipt: **acusar ~ de**, to acknowledge receipt of.

reciente a. recent, fresh, late, new. 2 **-mente** adv. recently, lately, newly.

recio, cia a. strong, robust. 2 thick, stout, bulky. 3 hard: **hablar ~**, to speak loudly.

recitar t. to recite.

reclamar t. to claim, demand. 2 to complain.

recobrar t. to recover, regain, retrieve. 2 ref. to get better, recover.

recoger t. to gather, collect, pick up, retake. 2 to fetch, get. 3 to receive, give shelter to. 4 ref. to retire, go home.

recomendación f. recommendation; advice; **carta de ~**, letter of introduction.

recomendar t. to recommend. 2 to request, enjoin. ¶ CONJUG. like **acertar**.

recompensa f. recompense, reward; compensation.

recompensar t. to recompense, reward.

reconocer t. to inspect, examine. 2 MIL. to reconnoitre. 3 to recognize, admit, confess, acknowledge. 4 ref. to avow or own oneself. ¶ CONJUG. like **agradecer**.

reconocimiento m. inspection, examination. 2 MIL. reconnaisance. 3 survey. 4 acknowledgement. 5 gratitude. 6 MED. check-up.

reconstruir t. to rebuild, reconstruct.

récord m. record.

recordar t. to remember, recollect. 2 to remind. ¶ CONJUG. like **contar**.

recorrer t. to go over, travel, walk. 2 to read over.

recorrido m. journey, run, course.

recortar t. to cut away or off, clip, trim. 2 to cut out.

recrear t. to amuse, entertain.

2 to please, delight. 3 *ref.* to amuse oneself, take delight.

recreo *m.* amusement; break [at school]. 2 playground, play-field [at school].

rectángulo *m.* rectangle.

recto, ta *a.* straight; right [angle]. 2 just, honest. 3 literal [sense]. 4 *f.* straight line.

rector, ra *a.* ruling, governing. 2 *m.* principal, head; vice-chancellor [of a University]. 3 ECCL. parish priest.

recuerdo *m.* remembrance, memory. 2 souvenir. 3 *pl.* regards.

recuperar *t.* to recover, retrieve. 2 *ref.* to recover oneself.

recurrir *i.* to appeal, resort.

rechazar *t.* to repel, drive back. 2 to reject; to rebuff.

red *f.* net. 2 network. 3 trap.

redacción *f.* wording. 2 editing. 3 editorial office. 4 editorial staff.

redactar *t.* to draw up, compose, write.

redil *m.* sheep-fold.

redimir *t.* to redeem. 2 to ransom.

redonda *f.* neighbourhood. 2 MUS. whole note. 3 *a la* ~, around, round about.

redondo, da *a.* round.

reducir *t.* to reduce, diminish. 2 to convert [into]. 3 to subdue, suppress. 4 MED. to reset [bones]. 5 *ref.* to economize.

reemplazar *t.* to replace.

referencia *f.* account. 2 reference.

referente *a.* concerning to.

referir *t.* to relate, tell; to report. 2 *ref.* ~ *a,* to refer to, allude. ¶ CONJUG. like *hervir.*

reflector *m.* reflector. 2 searchlight. 3 floodlight.

reflejar *t.* to reflect. 2 to show, reveal. 3 *ref.* to be reflected.

reflejo, ja *a.* reflected. 2 GRAM. reflexive. 3 *m.* PHYSIOL. reflex. 4 reflection [of light, etc.].

reflexión *f.* reflexion. 2 meditation.

reflexionar *t.-i.* to think over, consider.

reforma *f.* reform. 2 improvement. 3 ECCL. Reformation.

reforzar *t.* to strengthen. ¶ CONJUG. like *contar.*

refrán *m.* proverb, saying.

refrescante *a.* cooling; refreshing.

refrescar *t.* to cool, refresh. 2 *i.* to get cool. 3 *i.-ref.* to become cooler. 4 to take air or a drink. 5 to cool down.

refresco *m.* refreshment. 2 cooling drink. 3 *de* ~, new, fresh [troops, etc.].

refugiar *t.* to shelter. 2 *ref.* to take refuge.

refugio *m.* shelter, refuge.

refulgente *a.* shining.

regalar *t.* to present, give; to entertain. 2 to caress, flatter. 3 to delight. 4 *ref.* to treat oneself well.

regalo *m.* gift, present. 2 comfort, luxury.

regañar *i.* to snarl, grumble. 2 to quarrel. 3 *t.* to scold, chide.

regar *t.* to water, to irrigate. ¶ CONJUG. like *acertar.*

régimen, pl. **regímenes** m. regime, system of government. 2 diet, regimen.

regio, gia a. royal.

región f. region; area.

regir t. to govern, rule. 2 to manage. 3 i. to be in force; to prevail. ¶ Conjug. like *servir*.

registro m. search, inspection. 2 register. 3 bookmark.

regla f. rule, norm, precept: *por ~ general*, as a rule. 2 ruler [for drawing lines].

reglamento m. regulations, standing rules, by-law.

regocijar t. to rejoice, gladden. 2 ref. to rejoice, be glad.

regocijo m. rejoicing, joy. 2 pl. festivities.

regresar i. to return, come back, go back.

regreso m. return: *estar de ~*, to be back.

rehabilitación f. rehabilitation.

rehabilitar t. to rehabilitate, restore.

rehusar t. to refuse, decline.

reina f. queen.

reinado m. reign.

reinar i. to reign. 2 to rule, prevail.

reino m. kingdom, reign.

reír i.-ref.: *reírse de*, to laugh at. ¶ Conjug. Indic. Pres.: *río, ríes, ríe; reímos, reís, ríen.* | Pret.: *reí, reíste, rió; reímos, reísteis, rieron.* ‖ Subj. Pres.: *ría, rías,* etc. | Imperf.: *riera, rieras,* etc., or *riese, rieses,* etc. | Fut.: *riere, rieres,* etc. ‖ Imper.: *ríe, ría; riamos,* reíd, *rían.* ‖ Ger.: *riendo.*

relación f. relation, account,

narrative. 2 reference, bearing. 3 list of particulars. 4 pl. intercourse. 5 courtship. 6 connections, friends.

relacionar t. to relate, connect. 2 ref. to be acquainted with or connected with.

relámpago m. lightning, flash of lightning.

relatar t. to relate, tell, state.

relativo, va a.-m. relative.

relato m. story, tale, account.

relevar t. to relieve; to release. 2 to remove [from office, etc.].

relieve m. [high, low] relief. 2 *poner de ~*, to emphasize.

religión f. religion, faith, creed.

religioso, sa a. religious. 2 m. religious, monk. 3 f. nun.

reloj m. clock; watch: *~ de pared*, clock; *~ de pulsera*, wrist; watch; *~ de sol*, sundial; *~ despertador*, alarm-clock.

reluciente a. bright, shining, gleaming; glossy.

relucir i. to be bright; to shine, glisten, gleam.

remediar t. to remedy. 2 to help: *no lo puedo ~*, I can't help that.

remedio m. remedy, cure. 2 help, relief; *sin ~*, hopeless.

remendar t. to mend. 2 to patch; to darn. ¶ Conjug. like *acertar*.

remitir t. to remit, send. 2 to forgive.

remo m. oar, páddle.

remolacha f. beet; beetroot. 2 sugar-beet.

remontar *t.* to rouse, beat [game]. *2* to raise. *3 ref.* to go back to. *4* to soar.

remoto, ta *a.* remote, distant. *2* unlikely.

remover *t.* to remove. *2* to stir.

renacer *i.* to be reborn, revive, grow again.

rencor *m.* rancour, grudge, spite.

rendija *f.* chink, crack, crevice.

rendir *t.* to conquer, subdue. *2* to surrender, give up. *3* MIL. to lower [arms, flags]. *4* to pay. *5* to yield, produce. *6 ref.* to surrender. *7* to become tired out. ¶ CONJUT. like *servir*.

renovar *t.* to renew; to change. ¶ CONJUG. like *contar.*

renta *f.* rent. *2* interest; profit, income. *3* revenue.

rentar *t.* to yield, produce.

renuncia *f.* renouncement, resignation.

renunciar *t.* to renounce, resign, give up. *2* to refuse.

reñido, da *a.* on bad terms, at variance, opposed to.

reñir *i.* to quarrel, wrangle, fight, como to blows. *2 t.* to scold. ¶ CONJUG. like *reír.*

reorganizar *t.* to reorganize.

reparación *f.* repair. *2* reparation, satisfaction.

reparar *t.* to repair, mend. *2* to notice. *3* to restore [one's strenght].

repartir *t.* to distribute, allot, share, deliver.

repasar *t.* to revise, review. *2* to check; to go over [one's lesson, etc.]. *3* to mend [clothes].

repaso *m.* review, revision. *2* checking.

repetir *t.* to repeat. ¶ CONJUG. like *servir.*

replicar *i.* to answer back, reply, retort.

reponer *t.* to put back, replace. *2* THEAT. to revive [a play]. *3* to reply. *4 ref.* to recover.

reposar *i.* to repose, rest; to lie [in the grave].

reposo *m.* rest, repose.

reprender *t.* reprimand, rebuke, scold.

representante *m.-f.* representative.

representar *t.* to represent. *2* THEAT. to perform. *3 ref.* to imagine.

representativo, va *a.* representative. *2* expressive.

reproducción *f.* reproduction.

reproducir *t.-ref.* to reproduce. ¶ CONJUG. like *conducir.*

reptil *m.* reptile.

república *f.* republic.

republicano, na *a.-n.* republican.

repugnante *a.* repugnant, disgusting.

reputación *f.* reputation, renown.

requerir *t.* to intimate. *2* to require; to request. *3* to need. *4* to court. ¶ CONJUG. like *hervir.*

requisito *m.* requisite, requirement.

resbalar *i.-ref.* to slip, slide. *2* to skid.

rescate *m.* ransom, rescue.

reserva f. reserve., reservation. 2 MIL. reserve. 3 reticence, secrecy: *sin ~*, openly.

reservado, da a. reserved, discreet. 2 m. reserved place.

reservar t. to reserve. 2 to keep secret. 3 ref. to spare oneself: *hacer* or *hacerse ~*, to book.

resfriado m. cold; chill.

residencia f. residence.

residente a. resident. 2 m.-f. resident.

residir i. to reside, live. 2 fig. to consist.

resignación f. resignation.

resistencia f. resistance. 2 endurance. 3 reluctance.

resistente a. resistant, tough.

resistir t. to endure, stand. 2 to resist. 3 i. to stand up to. 4 ref. to refuse to.

resolución f. resolution, decision, courage.

resolver t. to resolve, decide [upon]. 2 to solve [a problem]. 3 ref. to resolve, make up one's mind. ¶ CONJUG. like *mover.*

respaldo m. back. 2 endorsement.

respectar i. to concern, relate to.

respectivo, va a. respective.

respecto m. respect, relation: *con ~ a*, or *de*, *~ a* or *de*, with regard to.

respetable a. respectable, worthy.

respetar t. to respect, revere.

respeto m. respect, consideration. 2 reverence. 3 pl. respects.

respetuoso, sa a. respectful.

respirar i. to breathe.

resplandecer i. to shine, glitter, glow. 2 to stand out. ¶ CONJUG. like *agradecer.*

resplandeciente a. bright, shining.

responder t. to answer, reply. 2 to be responsible for. 3 to answer back.

responsabilidad f. responsability.

respuesta f. answer, reply; response.

restablecer t. to re-establish, restore. 2 ref. to recover, get better.

restar t. to subtract; to take away. 2 i. to be left, remain.

restaurante m. restaurant.

restituir t. to restore, return, pay back. 2 ref. to return. ¶ CONJUG. like *huir.*

resto m. remainder, rest. 2 pl. remains.

resucitar t.-i. to revive, return to life.

resultado m. result, effect, outcome.

resultar i. to result. 2 to be, prove to be, turn out to be. 3 to come out [well, badly, etc.].

resumen m. summary: *en ~*, in short, to sum up.

resumir t. to summarize, sum up. 2 ref. to be reduced to.

resurrección f. resurrection, revival.

retener t. to retain, keep back. 2 to detain, arrest.

retirar t.-ref. to retire, withdraw. 2 t. to put back or aside. 3 MIL. to retreat.

retiro m. retirement [of an officer]. 2 withdrawal; retreat; seclusion.

retozar *i.* to frisk. frolic. romp. *2* [of emotions] to tickle. bubble.

retozo *m.* gambol. frolic.

retratar *t.* to portray; to describe. *2* to photograph. *3 ref.* to sit for.a portray or photograph.

retrato *m.* portrait. *2* photograph. *3* description.

retroceder *i.* to turn back. fall or go back.

reunión *f.* reunion. *2* gathering. meeting. party.

reunir *t.* to unite. join together. gather. rally. *2* to raise [funds]. *3 ref.* to meet. gather.

revelar *t.* to reveal. *2* PHOT. to develop.

reventar *i.-ref.* to burst. crack. blow up. *2 i.* [of waves] to break. *3* to weary. annoy. ¶ CONJUG. like *acertar*.

reverencia *f.* reverence. *2* bow. curtsy.

reverendo, da *a.* reverend.

revés *m.* back. wrong-side. *2* slap [with the back of the hand]. *3 al* ~, on the contrary; wrong side out.

revestir *t.* to clothe. cover.

revisar *t.* to revise. review. check.

revista *f.* review. inspection. *2* MIL. review. parade. *3* magazine [journal]. *4* THEAT. revue.

revivir *i.* to revive. come back to life.

revolución *f.* revolution.

revolucionario, ria *a.-n.* revolutionary.

revólver *m.* revolver. pistol.

revolver *t.* to stir. *2* to turn round. *3 ref.* to turn upon. ¶ CONJUG. like *mover*.

rey *m.* king [sovereign; chess. cards]: *día de Reyes*, Twelfth Night; *los Reyes Magos*, the Three Wise Men.

rezar *t.* to say. *2 t.-i.* to say. read. *3 i.* to pray.

rezo *m.* prayer.

riachuelo *m.* rivulet. stream. brook.

ribera *f.* bank [of river]. riverside. *2* shore. strand.

rico, ca *a.* rich. wealthy. *2* tasty. *3 coll.* sweet [baby].

ridículo, la *a.* ridiculous. laughable. *2 m.* ridicule; *poner en* ~, to make a fool of.

riego *m.* irrigation. watering.

riesgo *m.* risk. peril. danger; *correr el* ~, to run the risk.

rifa *f.* raffle. *2* quarrel.

rifle *m.* rifle.

rigoroso, sa; riguroso, sa *a.* rigorous. severe. *2* strict.

rincón *m.* corner. nook.

río *m.* river. stream; *a* ~ *revuelto*, in troubled waters.

riqueza *f.* riches. wealth. *2* richness. *3* fertility.

risa *f.* laugh. laughter. joke; *tomar a* ~, to treat as a joke.

risueño, ña *a.* smiling. cheerful. pleasant. *2* hopeful.

ritmo *m.* rhythm. cadence.

rival *m.-f.* rival. competitor.

rivalidad *f.* rivalry. enmity.

rizar *t.-ref.* to curl [hair]. *2* to ripple [water].

rizo, za *a.* curly. *2 m.* curl. ringlet. *3* ripple [of water].

robar *t.* to rob. steal. thieve.

roble *m.* oak-tree.

robo *m.* theft. robbery. larceny.

robusto, ta *a.* robust. strong.

roca *f.* rock. *2* cliff.

rociar *i*. [of dew] to fall. *2 t*. to sprinkle, spray.

rocío *m*. dew.

rodear *i*. to go round. *2 t*. to surround, encircle.

rodilla *f*. knee.

roer *t*. to gnaw, nibble. *2* to eat away, corrode. *3* to pick [a bone]. ¶ CONJUG.: INDIC. Pres.: roo, *roigo*, or *royo* (1st. person.), roes, roe, etc. | Pret.: roí, roíste, *royó*; roímos, roísteis, *royeron*. ‖ SUBJ. Pres.: roa, *roiga*, or *roya;* roas, *roigas*, or *royas*, etc. | Imperf.: *royera, royeras*, etc., or *royese, royeses*, etc. | Fut.: *royere, royeres*, etc. | IMPER.: roe; roa, *roiga*, or *roya* [for 3rd pers.]; *roigamos*, roed, *roigan*. ‖ PAST. P.: roído. ‖ GER.: *royendo*.

rogar *t*. to ask, beg, pray, beseech, entreat. ¶ CONJUG. like *contar*.

rojo, ja *a*. red. *2* ruddy.

rollo *m*. roll.

romance *a*. Romance, Romanic [languages]. *2 m*. narrative or lyric poem in eight-syllabe meter with even verses rhyming in assonance.

romano, na *a*. Roman.

romántico, ca *a*. romantic. *2 m.-f*. romanticist.

romper *t.-ref*. to break, smash. *2* to wear out.¶ P. P.: *roto*.

ron *m*. rum.

ronco, ca *a*. hoarse, harsh.

ronda *f*. night patrol. *2* rounds, beat [of a patrol]. *3* round [of drinks].

ropa *f*. clothing, clothes: ~ *banca*, linen; ~ *interior*, underwear; *a quema* ~, at point-blank.

rosa *f*. rose.

rosado, da *a*. rosy, pinky.

rosal *m*. rose [bush].

rosario *m*. rosary.

rostro *m*. face, countenance. *2*. beak.

rotación *f*. rotation.

roto, ta *p. p.* of ROMPER. *2 a*. broken, cracked. *3* torn.

rozar *t.-i*. to touch [lightly in passing].

rubí *m*. ruby.

rubio, bia *a*. blond(e, fair-haired.

rudo, da *a*. crude, rough, coarse. *2* dull, stupid.

rueda *f*. wheel.

ruego *m*. entreaty, prayer, request.

rugir *i*. to roar, bellow; to howl [of wind].

ruido *m*. noise. *2* din, report. *3* ado, fuss.

ruin *a*. mean, base, despicable, vile. *2* petty, insignificant. *3* miserly, stingy.

ruina *f*. ruin. *2 pl*. ruins.

ruiseñor *m*. ORN. nightingale.

rumbo *m*. NAUT. bearing, course, direction; *con* ~ *a*, bound for. *2* ostentation.

rumor *m*. murmur; noise. *2* rumour, report.

ruta *f*. way, route. *2* NAUT. course: ~ *aérea*, airline.

S

sábado *m.* Saturday.

sábana *f.* bed sheet.

1) **saber** *m.* knowledge, learning.

2) **saber** *t.* to know; to know how to [write]; to be able to. *2* ~*a*, to taste of, taste like. ¶ Conjug. Indic. Pres.: *sé,* sabes, sabe, etc. | Imperf.: sabía, sabías, etc. | Pret.: *supe, supiste, supo; supimos, supisteis, supieron.* | Fut.: sabré, sabrás, etc. ‖ Cond.: *sabría, sabrías,* etc. | Subj. Pres.: sepa, sepas, etc. | Imperf.: *supiera, supieras,* etc., or *supiese, supieses,* etc. | Fut.: *supiere, supieres,* etc. ‖ Imper.: *sabe, sepa; sepamos, sabed, sepan.* ‖ Past. P: sabido. ‖ Ger.: sabiendo.

sabiduría *f.* knowledge, learning. *2* wisdom.

sabio, bia *a.* learned; wise; *2 m.-f.* learned person, scholar.

sabor *m.* taste, flavour.

sabroso, sa *a.* savoury, tasty. *2* pleasant, delightful.

sacar *t.* to draw [out], pull out, take out. *2* to get, obtain. *3* to solve. *4* to take [a photo]. *5* to make [a copy]. *6* to buy [a ticket]. *7* ~ *a luz,* to publish, print. *8* ~ *a relucir,* to mention.

sacerdote *m.* priest.

saco *m.* bag; sack. *2* bagful, sackful. *3* (Am.) coat.

sacramento *m.* eccl. sacrament.

sacrificar *t.* to sacrifice. *2* to slaughter.

sacrificio *m.* sacrifice.

sacudir *t.* to shake, jerk, jolt. *2* to beat, dust. *3* to deal [a blow]. *4 ref.* to shake off.

sagaz *a.* sagacious, shrewd.

sagrado, da *a.* sacred, holy. *2 m.* asylum, refuge.

sal *f.* salt. *2* wit; charm, grace.

sala *f.* drawing-room. living-room, parlour. *2* hall, room.

salado, da *a.* salty. *2* witty; charming, graceful.

salario *m.* wages, salary, pay.

salchicha *f.* sausage.

salida *f.* start, departure. 2 excursion. 3 rise. 4 exit, outlet; way out.

salir *i.* to go out, come out. 2 to depart, leave, start, set out. 3 to project, stand out. 4 [of a book] to come out. 5 [of the sun] to rise. 6 ~ *bien [mal]*, to turn out well [badly]. 7 ~ *adelante*, to be successful. 8 *ref.* [of a vessel] to leak; to overflow. ¶ IRREG. CONJUG.: INDIC. Pres.: *salgo, sales, sale; salimos, etc.* | *Fut: saldré, saldrás, etc.* ‖ COND.: *saldría, saldrías, etc.* ‖ IMPER.: *sal, salga; salgamos, salid, salgan.* ¶ SUBJ. Pres.: *salga, salgas, etc.*

salmo *m.* psalm.

salmón *m.* salmon.

salpicar *t.* to splash, spatter.

salsa *f.* COOK. gravy, sauce.

saltar *i.* to spring, jump, hop, skip. 2 ~ *a la vista*, to be self-evident. 3 *t.* to leap.

salto *m.* spring, jump, leap, bound, hop, skip: ~ *de agua*, waterfall, falls.

salud *f.* health: 2 welfare.

saludable *a.* salutary, wholesome.

saludar *t.* to greet, salute.

saludo *m.* greeting, salutation, bow. 2 *pl.* compliments, regards.

salvación *f.* salvation.

salvador, ra *a.* saving. 2 *m.-f.* saviour; El Salvador [American country].

salvaje *a.* savage. 2 wild. 3 *m.-f.* savage.

salvar *t.* to save, rescue. 2 to overcome. 3 to go over. 4 *ref.* to be saved. 5 to escape danger.

1) **salvo** *adv.* save, except, but.

2) **salvo, va** *a.* saved, safe: *sano y* ~, safe and sound.

sanatorio *m.* sanatorium.

sangrar *t.* to bleed. 2 to drain.

sangriento, ta *a.* bleeding, bloody. 2 bloodthirsty.

sano, na *a.* healthy, wholesome. 2 sound.

santidad *f.* sanctity, holiness.

santo, ta *a.* holy, blessed, sacred. 2 saintly, godly. 3 *m.-f.* saint. 4 saint's day.

sapo *m.* toad.

sardina *f.* sardine.

sargento *m.* sergeant.

sartén *f.* frying-pan.

sastre *m.* tailor.

satisfacción *f.* satisfaction; pleasure.

satisfacer *t.* to satisfy; to please. 2 to pay.

satisfactorio, ria *a.* satisfactory.

satisfecho, cha *p. p.* of SATISFACER. 2 satisfied, pleased.

savia *f.* sap.

sazonar *t.-ref.* to ripen. 2 *t.* to flavour.

se *ref. pron.* himself; herself; itself; yourself, yourselves [formal]; themselves. 2 *obj. pron.* to him, to her, to it, to you [formal], to them. 3 *reciprocal pron.* each other, one another. 4 passive: *se dice:* it is said.

secar *t.* to dry [up]. 2 *ref.* to get dry.

sección *f.* section; division. 2 department [of a store].

seco, ca *a.* dry; bare, arid. *2* withered, dead. *3* lean, thin.

secretaría *f.* secretary's office.

secretario, ria *m.-f.* secretary.

secreto, ta *a.* secret. *2 m.* secret.

sector *m.* sector.

secular *a.* secular. *2* lay.

secundar *t.* to back up, aid, help.

secundario, ria *a.* secondary.

sed. *f.* thirst: *tener ~,* to be thirsty. *2* craving, desire.

seda *f.* silk.

sediento, ta *a.* thirsty; dry. *2* anxious.

segar *t.* AGR. to harvest, reap, mow. ¶ CONJUG. like *acertar.*

seguir *t.* to follow. *2* to pursue, chase. *3* to go on [doing something]. *4 ref.* to follow as a consequence. ¶ CONJUG. like *servir.*

según *prep.* according to, as. *2 adv.* ~ *y cómo,* that depends.

segundo, da *a.* second. *2 m.* second.

seguridad *f.* security, safety.

seguro, ra *a.* secure, safe. *2* firm, steady. *3* certain. *4 m.* COM. insurance. *5* safety-lock. *6* MECH. click, stop.

seis *a.-m.* six. *2* sixth.

selección *f.* selection, choice.

seleccionar *t.* to select, choose.

selecto, ta *a.* select, choice.

selva *f.* forest; jungle.

sello *m.* seal. *2* stamp.

semana *f.* week.

semblante *m.* face, countenance, look.

sembrar *t.-i.* to sow. *2 t.* to scatter. ¶ CONJUG. like *acertar.*

semejante *a.* resembling, similar, like, such. *2 m.* fellow.

semejanza *f.* resemblance, similarity, likeness.

semestre *m.* semester.

semilla *f.* seed.

senador *m.* senator.

sencillez *f.* simplicity. *2* plainness *3* naturalness.

sencillo, lla *a.* simple. *2* easy. *3* plain, natural.

senda *f.,* **sendero** *m.* path, foot-path, by-way.

sensación *f.* sensation, feeling.

sensacional *a.* sensational.

sensible *a.* perceptible. *2* sensitive. *3* regrettable. *4* -**mente** *adv.* perceptibly.

sentencia *f.* LAW judgement, sentence; veredict: *2* proverb, maxim.

sentenciar *t.* to sentence. *2* to pass judgement, condemn.

sentido, da *a.* felt. *2* touchy. *3 m.* feeling, sense: ~ *común,* common sense. *4* meaning. *5* consciousness: *perder el ~,* to faint. *6* course, direction.

sentimental *a.* sentimental, emotional.

sentimiento *m.* sentiment, feeling. *2* sorrow, regret.

sentir *t.* to feel, perceive; to hear. *2* ~ *frío,* to be cold; *3* to regret, be sorry for. *4 ref.* to feel [well, ill, sad, etc.], suffer pain. ¶ CONJUG. like *hervir.*

seña *f.* sign, token. *2* mark. *3 pl.* address.

señal *f.* sign, mark, token. *2* trace. *3* scar.

señor *m.* mister; sir; gentleman. *2* owner, master; the Lord.

señora *f.* Mrs. madam; lady. *2* landlady, owner, mistress.

señorita *f. dim.* young lady, miss.

separar *t.-ref.* to separate. *2 t.* to dismiss, discharge.

septiembre *m.* September.

séptimo, ma *a.-n.,* seventh.

sepulcro *m.* sepulcher. *2* grave, tomb.

sepultura *f.* sepulture: *dar ~ a,* to bury.

sequía *f.* drought, dry season.

1) ser *m.* being; essence.

2) ser *subst. v.* to be; to live; to exist. *2* to belong to. *3* to be made of. *4* to come from, be native of. ¶ Conjug. Indíc. Pres.: *soy, eres, es; somos, sois, son.* | Imperf.: *era, eras,* etc. | Pret.: *fui, fuiste,* etc. ‖ Fut.: *seré, serás,* etc. ‖ Cond.: *sería, serías,* etc. ‖ Subj. Pres.: *sea, seas,* etc. ‖ Imperf.: *fuera, fueras,* etc., or *fuese, fueses,* etc. | Fut.: *fuere, fueres,* etc. ‖ Imper.: *sé, sea; seamos, sed, sean* ‖ Past. p.: *sido.* ‖ Ger.: *siendo.*

sereno, na *a.* serene. *2* clear, cloudless. *3* calm, cool. *4 m.* night watchman.

serie *f.* series: *producción en ~,* mass production.

serio, ria *a.* serious. *2* grave. *3* reliable. *4 en ~,* seriously.

sermón *m.* sermon.

serpiente *f.* serpent, snake: *~ de cascabel,* rattle-snake.

serrar *t.* to saw. ¶ Conjug. like *acertar.*

serrucho *m.* handsaw.

servicio *m.* service. *2* duty. *3* servants. *4* favour, good [ill] turn. *5* use. *6* service [set of dishes, etc.].

servilleta *f.* napkin, serviette.

servir *i.-t.* to serve, be useful. *2 ~ de,* to act as, be used as; *~ para,* to be good [used] for. *3* to wait upon [a customer]. *4 ref.* to serve or help oneself: *servirse de,* to make use of; *sírvase hacerlo,* please, do it. ¶ Conjug. Indic. Pres.: *sirvo, sirves, sirve;* servimos, servís, *sirven.* | Pret.: serví, serviste, *sirvió;* servimos, servisteis, *sirvieron.* ‖ Subj.: Pres.: *sirva, sirvas,* etc. | Imperf. *sirviera, sirvieras,* etc. or *sirviese; sirvimos; servid,* sirvan. ‖ Ger.: *sirviendo.*

sesenta *a.-m.* sixty. *2* sixtieth.

sesión *f.* session; meeting, conference. *2* show.

setenta *a.-m.* seventy, seventieth.

severo, ra *a.* severe, rigid.

sexo *m.* sex.

sexto, ta *a.-n.* sixth.

si *conj.* if; whether: *~ bien,* although.

sí *adv.* yes; indeed, certainly: *2 ref. pron.* himself, herself, itself, oneself, themselves; yourself, yourselves [formal]: *entre ~,* each other.

siembra *f.* sowing, seeding.

siempre *adv.* always, ever: *para ~,* forever, for good; *~ que,* whenever; provided.

sierra *f.* saw. *2* mountain range.

siervo, va *m.-f.* serf, slave.

siesta *f.* siesta, afternoon nap.

siete *a.-m.* seven. *2* seventh.

siglo *m.* century.

significación *f.*, **significado** *m.*
meaning, sense.

significar *t.* to signify; to
mean; to make known. *2* to
matter, have importance.

signo *m.* sign, mark; symbol.

siguiente *a.* following, next.

silbar *i.* to whistle; to hiss.

silbido, silbo *m.* whistle;
hissing.

silencio *m.* silence.

silla *f.* chair: ~ *de montar*,
saddle.

símbolo *m.* symbol.

simiente *f.* seed. *2* semen.

similar *a.* similar, like.

simpatía *f.* liking, charm,
attractiveness. *2* sympathy.

simpático, ca *a.* pleasant,
nice, charming.

simple *a.* simple. *2* innocent.
3 silly. *4* **-mente** *adv.* simply,
etc.

sin *prep.* without; ~ *embargo*, nevertheless.

sinceridad *f.* sincerity.

sincero, ra *a.* sincere.

sindicato *m.* syndicate. *2*
trade union, labour union.

sinfonía *f.* symphony.

singular *a.* singular; single; *2*
extraordinary. *3* odd.

siniestro, tra *a.* left, left-
hand. *2* sinister. *3* *m.*
disaster, damage or loss. *4* *f.*
left hand.

sino *conj.* but, except: *no
solo... ~ (también)*, not
only... but (also). *2* *m.*
destiny, fate.

sinvergüenza *a.* brazen,
barefaced. *2* *m.-f.* rascal,
scoundrel.

siquier, siquiera *conj.*
although. *2* *adv.* at least. *3*
ni ~, not even

sirvienta *f.* maidservant,
maid.

sistema *m.* system.

sitiar *t.* to besiege, surround.

sitio *m.* place, spot. *2* seat,
room. *3* site. *4* MIL. siege.

situación *f.* situación,
posición; state.

situar *t.* to place, locate. *2* *ref.*
to be placed.

so *prep.* under.

soberanía *f.* sovereignty.

soberano, na *a.-n.* sovereign.

soberbia *f.* arrogance, pride,
haughtiness. *2* magnifi-
cence.

soberbio, bia *a.* arrogant,
proud, haughty. *2* superb.

sobra *f.* excess, surplus: *de* ~,
in excess.

sobrar *i.* to be left over,
exceed, remain. *2* to be
superfluous.

sobre *prep.* on, upon. *2* over;
above: ~ *todo*, above all. *3*
m. envelope.

sobrenatural *a.* supernatu-
ral.

sobrepasar *t.* to exceed; to
excel. *2* *ref.* to go too far.

sobresaliente *a.* outstanding.
2 *m.* distinction [exam.].

sobresalir *t.* to stand out,
project, jut out; to excel.

sobrevivir *i.* to survive. *2* ~ *a*,
to outlive.

sobrina *f.* niece.

sobrino *m.* nephew.

social *a.* social, friendly.

socialista *a.* socialist(ic. *2*
m.-f. socialist.

sociedad *f.* society. *2* company, corporation.

socio, cia *m.-f.* associate;
member, fellow [of a club,
etc.]. *2* COM. partner.

socorrer t. to help, aid, succour.

socorro m. assistance, help, aid.

sofá m. sofa, settee.

sofocar t. to choke, suffocate, smother. 2 to stifle. 3 ref. to blush.

sol m. sun; sunshine: *hace ~,* it is sunny.

soldado m. soldier.

soledad f. solitude, loneliness.

solemne a. solemn.

soler i. translate the present of SOLER by *usually: suele venir el lunes,* he usually comes on Monday. | Imperf.: used to: *solía venir el lunes,* be used to come on Monday. | Only used in INDIC. ¶ CONJUG. like *mover.*

sólido, da a. solid, firm, strong.

solitario, ria a. solitary, lone, lonely. 2 secluded 3 m. solitaire [diamond; game].

solo, la a. alone; by himself, itself, etc. 2 lone, lonely. 3 only, sole. 4 m. MUS. solo.

sólo adv. SOLAMENTE.

soltar t. to unfasten, loosen. 2 to let out, set free, release. 3 to let go, drop. 4 coll. to give [a blow]. 5 to get loose; get free. ¶ CONJUG. like *contar.*

soltero, ra a. single. 2 m. bachelor, single man.

solución f. solution, outcome, break.

sollozar i. to sob.

sollozo m. sob.

sombra f. shade; shadow.

sombrero m. hat: ~ *de copa,* top haft; ~ *hongo,* bowler hat.

sombrío, bría a. gloomy, dark, dismal, somber.

someter t. to submit, subject, subdue. 2 ref. to submit.

sonámbulo, la a.-n. sleep-walker.

sonar t.-i. to sound, ring. 2 i. to strike: ~ *a,* to seem like. 3 ref. to blow one's nose. ¶ CONJUG. like *contar.*

sonido m. sound.

sonoro, ra a. sonorous. 2 talking [of films].

sonreír(se i. to smile.

sonriente a. smiling, pleasant.

sonrisa f. smile.

soñador, ra a. dreaming. 2 m.-f. dreamer.

soñar t.-i. to dream: ~ *con,* ~ *en,* to dream of. ¶ CONJUG. like *contar.*

sopa f. soup.

soplar i. to blow.

soplo m. blowing. 2 breath, puff of wind.

soportar t. to bear, endure, tolerate.

sordo, da a. deaf. 2 dull, low. 3 m.-f. deaf person.

sorprendente a. surprising.

sorprender t. to surprise, astonish. 2 ref. to be surprised.

sorpresa f. surprise.

sortija f. finger ring.

sosegar t. to calm, quiet. 2 ref. to quiet down. ¶ CONJUG. like *acertar.*

soso, sa a. tasteless. 2 dull.

sospecha f. suspicion, mistrust.

sospechar t. to suspect, mistrust.

sospechoso, sa *a.* suspicious. *2 m.-f.* suspect.

sostener *t.* to support, hold up. *2* to maintain, affirm.

sótano *m.* cellar, basement.

soviético, ca *a.* soviet.

su, *pl.* **sus** *poss. a.* his, her, its, their; 2nd pers. [formal] your.

suave *a.* soft, smooth. *2* mild.

súbdito, ta *m.-f.* subject.

subir *i.* to go up, come up, rise, climb. *2 t.* to raise, bring up.

súbito, ta *a.* sudden: *de ~*, suddenly.

sublime *a.* sublime.

submarino, na *a.-m.* submarine.

subsistir *i.* to subsist, exist. *2* to last. *3* to live on.

substancia *f.* substance, essence. *2* extract, juice.

substantivo, va *a.* substantive. *2 m.* GRAM. noun.

substituir *t.* to substitute, replace. ¶ CONJUG. like *huir*.

subterráneo, a *a.* subterranean, underground.

suceder *i.* *~ a*, to succeed. *2* to follow. *3 impers.* to happen, occur.

sucesivo, va *a.* successive, consecutive. *2 en lo ~*, hereafter.

suceso *m.* event, happening. *2* incident; outcome.

sucesor, ra *m.-f.* successor; heir.

sucio, cia *a.* dirty, filthy, foul.

sucursal *a.-f.* branch [office].

sudar *i.* to sweat, perspire.

sudor *m.* sweat, perspiration.

suegra *f.* mother-in-law.

suegro *m.* father-in-law.

suela *f.* sole [of a shoe].

sueldo *m.* salary, pay.

suelo *m.* ground, floor, pavement. *2* soil, land.

sueño *m.* sleep. *2* dream.

suerte *f.* chance, fortune, fate. *2* luck. *3* sort. *4 de ~ que*, so that: *tener ~*, to be lucky.

suficiente *a.* sufficient, enough. *2* able. *3 -mente adv.* sufficiently.

sufrimiento *m.* suffering. *2* endurance.

sufrir *t.* to suffer, endure. *2* to allow, permit. *3* to undergo [an operation, etc.].

sugerir *t.* to suggest, hint. ¶ CONJUG. like *hervir*.

sugestión *f.* suggestion.

suicidarse *ref.* to commit suicide.

suicidio *m.* suicide.

sujetar *t.* to subject, subdue. *2* to hold. *3* to fasten. *4 ref.* to submit, be subjected.

sujeto, ta *a.* subject; liable. *2* fastened. *3 m.* GRAM., LOG. subject. *4* individual. *5* subject, matter.

suma *f.* sum, addition, amount: *en ~*, in short.

sumar *t.* to sum up, add up, amount to. *2 ref. ~ a*, to join.

sumergir *t.-ref.* to submerge, sink.

suministrar *t.* to provide with, supply with.

suministro *m.* provision, supply.

sumiso, sa *a.* submissive, obedient.

sumo, ma *a.* very great: *a lo ~*, at most.

superar *t.* to surpass, exceed. *2* to overcome, surmount.

superficie *f.* surface. *2* area.

superior *a.* superior. *2* upper *3* director, head.

súplica *f.* entreaty. petition. request. prayer.

suplicar *t.* to entreat, pray, beg.

suplir *t.* to supply. make up for. 2 to replace.

suponer *t.* to suppose, assume.

supremo, ma *a.* supreme.

suprimir *t.* to suppress, omit, cut out.

supuesto, ta *a.* supposed, assumed. 2 **dar por** ~, to take for granted; **por** ~, of course. 3 *m.* supposition, assumption.

sur *m.* south. 2 south wind.

surco *m.* furrow. groove. 2 track [of ship].

surgir *i.* to spurt, spring. 2 to come forth. appear.

surtir *t.* to supply, provide. 2 ~ *efecto*, to work.

suscribir, suscripción = SUBSCRIBIR. SUBSCRIPCIÓN.

suspender *t.* to suspend, hang up. 2 to stop; delay. 3 to fail [in an examination].

suspensión *f.* suspension. 2 postponement, delay.

suspirar *i.* to sigh. 2 ~ *por,* to long for.

suspiro *m.* sigh.

sustentar *t.* to sustain, support, feed. 2 to hold up.

sustento *m.* sustenance. 2 food. 3 support.

f3**sustitución, sustituir**, etc. = SUBSTITUCIÓN. SUBSTITUIR. etc.

susto *m.* fright. scare.

sutil *a.* subtle. 2 thin.

suyo, -ya, -yos, -yas *poss. a.* his. her. its. one's. their; your [formal]. 2 *poss. pron.* his. hers. its. one's. theirs; yours [formal].

T

tabaco *m.* tobacco; snuff.

taberna *f.* tavern, public house.

tabla *f.* board. 2 plank. 3 table. 4 *pl.* draw [at chess, etc.]. 5 THEAT. stage.

taburete *m.* stool.

taco *m.* stopper, plug. 2 billiard-cue. 3 swear word, curse.

tacto *m.* tact, finesse. 2 feel, touch.

tachuela *f.* tack, hobnail.

tajo *m.* cut, incision. 2 steep cliff. 3 cutting edge.

tal *a.* such, such a: ~ *vez*, perhaps; *un ~ Pérez*, a certain Pérez; ~ *como*, just as; *con ~ que*, provided that; *¿qué ~?*, how are you?

tala *f.* felling of trees.

talento *m.* talent, intelligence.

talón *m.* heel. 2 voucher.

talla *f.* [wood] carving. 2 size.

taller *m.* workshop, factory.

tallo *m.* stem, stalk. 2 shoot.

tamaño, ña *a.* such a; as big [small] as; so great. 2 *m.* size.

también *adv.* also, too, as well.

tambor *m.* drum. 2 drummer.

tampoco *adv.* neither, not either.

tan *adv.* apoc. of TANTO so, as, such. 2 ~ *sólo*, only.

tanque *m.* water tank. 2 MIL. tank. 3 (Am.) reservoir.

tanto, ta *a.-pron. sing.* so much, as much. 2 *pl.* so many, as many. 3 *m.* certain amount. 4 *tanto por ciento*, percentage; *tanto como*, as well as; as much as; *tanto... como*, both... and; *entre* or *mientras tanto*, meanwhile; *por lo tanto*, therefore.

tapa *f.* lid, cover. 2 snack.

tapar *t.* to cover. 2 to stop up. 3 to conceal. 4 to wrap up.

tapiz *m.* tapestry, hanging.

tapón *m.* stopper, cork.

taquigrafía *f.* shorthand, stenography.

taquígrafo, fa *m.-f.* stenographer.

taquilla *f.* booking-office, box-office.

tardanza *f* delay; slowness.

tardar *i.-ref.* to delay; to be late: *a más ~*, at the latest.

tarde *adv.* late. 2 *f.* afternoon; evening.

tarea *f.* task, job. 2 work.

tarifa *f.* tariff. 2 price list, rate, fare.

tarjeta *f.* card; visiting card: *~ postal*, postcard.

taxi *m.* taxi, taxicab.

taza *f.* cup; bowl. 2 basin.

te *pron.* [to] you, yourself.

té *m.* tea. 2 tea-party.

teatro *m.* theatre, *theater. 2 stage, scene; play-house.

técnico, ca *a.* technical. 2 *m.* technician, technical expert.

teja *f.* tile, slate.

tejado *m.* roof.

tejer *t.* to weave.

tejido, da *a.* woven. 2 *m.* fabric, textile.

tela *f.* cloth, fabric, stuff. 2 PAINT. canvas.

telar *m.* loom.

teléfono *m.* telephone.

telégrafo *m.* telegraph.

telegrama *m.* telegram, wire.

televisión *f.* television.

televisor *m.* television set.

telón *m.* THEAT. curtain.

tema *m.* theme, subject.

temblar *i.* to tremble, quake, shake, shiver, quiver.

temblor *m.* tremble, tremor: *~ de tierra*, earthquake.

temer *t.-i.* to fear, dread; to be afraid of.

temeroso, sa *a.* fearful, timid, suspicious, afraid.

temible *a.* dreadful, frightful, awful.

temor *m.* dread, fear.

temperamento *m.* temperament, nature.

temperatura *f.* temperature.

tempestad *f.* tempest, storm.

tempestuoso, sa *a.* stormy.

templado, da *a.* temperate. 2 lukewarm.

templo *m.* temple, church.

temporada *f.* period of time. 2 season.

temporal *a.* temporary; woldly. 2 *m.* gale, storm. 3 -mente *adv.* temporarily.

temprano, na *a.* early; premature. 2 *adv.* early.

tenaz *a.* tenacious, dogged, stubborn.

tender *t.* to spread [out], stretch out. 2 to hang up [to dry]. 3 to lay [a cable, etc.]; to build [a bridge]. 4 *i.* to have a tendency to. 5 *ref.* to stretch oneself out, lie down. ¶ CONJUG. like *entender*.

tenedor *m.* [table] fork. 2 holder, possessor: *~ de libros*, book-keeper.

tener *t.* to have; possess, own; to hold, keep. 2 *~ hambre*, to be hungry; *~ sed*, to be thirsty; *~ sueño*, to be sleepy; *tengo diez años*, I am ten years old; *~ calor*, to be hot; *~ frío*, to be cold; *tiene usted razón*, you are right; 3 aux. *tengo que estudiar*, I have to study; I must study. ¶ CONJUG. INDIC. Pres.: *tengo, tienes, tiene; tenemos, tenéis, tienen.* | Pret.: *tuve, tuviste, tuvo; tuvimos*, etc. ‖ Fut.: *tendré, tendrás*, etc. ‖ COND.: *tendría, tendrías*, etc. ‖ SUBJ. Pres.: *tenga, tengas*, etc. | Imperf.: *tuviera, tuvieras*, etc., or *tuviese, tuvieses*, etc. ‖ Fut.: *tuviere, tuvieres*, etc. ‖

IMPER.: *ten, tenga; tengamos,* tened, *tengan.*

teniente *m.* MIL. lieutenant.

tenis *m.* tennis.

tenor *m.* MUS. tenor.

tentación *f.* temptation.

tentar *t.* to feel, touch. 2 to try, attempt. 3 to tempt.

tenue *a.* thin, slender.

teñir *t.* to dye, tinge.

teoría *f.* theory.

tercer(o, ra *a. -n.* third.

terciopelo *m.* velvet.

terminar *t.* to end, close, finish. 2 *i.* to be over.

término *m.* end. 2 boundery. 3 aim. 4 word.

termómetro *m.* thermometer.

ternera *f.* female calf, heifer. 2 veal.

ternero *m.* male calf.

ternura *f.* tenderness, softness.

terraza *f.* terrace. 2 flat roof.

terremoto *m.* earthquake, seism.

terreno, na *a.* worldly, earthly. 2 *m.* plot, piece of ground, land.

terrible *a.* terrible, frightful, awful. 2 **-mente** *adv.* terribly.

territorio *m.* territory, region.

terror *m.* terror, fright, dread.

tertulia *f.* gathering, evening party, meeting of friends.

tesorero, ra *m. -f.* treasurer.

tesoro *m.* treasure.

testamento *m.* testament, will.

testificar *t.* to attest, testify, witness, certify.

testigo *m. -f.* witness.

testimonio *m.* testimony.

texto *m.* text. 2 textbook.

tez *f.* complexion [of the face].

ti *pers. pron.* you.

tía *f.* aunt.

tibio, a *a.* tepid, lukewarm. 2 cool, indifferent.

tiburón *m.* shark.

tiempo *m.* time; epoch. 2 weather. 3 GRAM. tense.

tienda *f.* shop, *store. 2 tent.

tierno, na *a.* tender; loving. 2 fresh [bread].

tierra *f.* earth; land; ground. 2 country. 3 AGR. soil. 4 dust.

tieso, sa *a.* stiff, rigid. 2 tight, taut. 3 strong.

tigre, sa *m.* tiger; (Am.) jaguar. 2 *f.* tigress.

tijera *f. sing & pl.* scissors, shears: *silla de* ~, folding chair.

timbre *m.* stamp, seal. 2 bell.

tímido, da *a.* timid, shy.

tina *f.* large jar. 2 vat, tub.

tinaja *f.* large earthen jar.

tiniebla *f.* darkness. 2 *pl.* night; hell.

tinta *f.* ink.

tintero *m.* inkstand, ink-pot.

tío *m.* uncle.

típico, ca *a.* typical.

tipo *m.* type. 2 build [of a person]. 3 guy.

tira *f.* narrow strip; strap.

tiranía *f.* tyranny.

tirano, na *a.* tyrannical. 2 *m. -f.* tyrant.

tirar *t.* to throw, cast, fling. 2 to fire [a shot]. 3 to draw, stretch. 4 to knock down, pull down. 5 waste [time, money]. 6 to attract. 7 to draw. 8 to last, endure. 9 ~ *a,* a) to shoot with; b) to shoot at; c) to turn to [the right, etc.]; d) to aim at. 10 ~ *de,* a) to draw; b) to pull [at; on]. 11 *ref.* to rush, throw oneself. 12 to jump. 13 to lie down.

tiro *m.* throw. 2 shot. 3 throw,

report. *4* team. *5* draft, draught [of a chimney].

titular *a.* titular. *2 m.-f.* holder. *3 m. pl.* headlines.

titular *t.* to title, call, name.

título *m.* title. *2* heading. *3* diplome. *4* qualification.

tiza *f.* chalk.

toalla *f.* towel.

tocador *m.* dressing-table. *2* dressing-room. *3 juego de ~*, perfume and toilet set.

tocar *t.* to touch, feel [with hands]. *2* to play [the piano, etc.]; to ring [a bell]; to beat [a drum]. *3* AUTO. to blow [the horn]. *4* to win [lottery]. *5 ~ a muerto*, to toll. *6* to move, inspire. *7* to find [by experience]. *8 i.* to belong; to be one's turn. *9 ref.* to touch each other. *10.* to cover one's head.

todavía *adv.* still, even, yet. *2* nevertheless.

todo, da *a.* all, every, each: *a ~ prisa*, with all speed. *2 m.-f.* a whole, entirety. *3 adv.* entirely. *4 ante ~*, first of all; *con ~*, however; *sobre ~*, above all.

tomar *t.* to take. *2* to seize, catch; to capture. *3* to have [a meal, a drink, a rest, etc.]. *4 ~ el pelo*, to pull one's leg; *~ a mal*, to take it amiss; *~ las de Villadiego*, to take to one's heels.

tomate *m.* tomato.

tonada *f.* tune, song.

tonelada *f.* ton; *~ métrica*, metric ton.

tono *m.* tone; tune. *2* key, pitch. *3* vigour, strength. *4* accent. *5 darse ~*, to put on airs; *de buen* or *mal ~*, fashionable, or vulgar.

tontada, tontería *f.* silliness, stupidity. *2* nonsense.

tonto, ta *a.* silly, foolish, stupid. *2 m.-f.* fool, dolt.

topo *m.* mole.

toque *m.* touch. *2* blow, tap. *3* sound; ringing [of a bell]; beat [of a drum]. *4* proof, trial. *5 piedra de ~*, touchstone; *~ de queda*, curfew.

torcer *t.* to twist, wrench, bend, crook. *2 i.* to turn to. *3 ref.* to become twisted, bent. *4* to go astray. ¶ CONJUG. like *mover*.

toreo *m.* bullfighting.

torero, ra *a.* bullfighting. *2 m.-f.* bullfighter.

tormenta *f.* storm, tempest.

tormento *m.* torment, pain, anguish. *2* torture.

tormentoso, sa *a.* stormy.

torneo *m.* tournement.

tornillo *m.* screw. *2* clamp. *3* vice.

torpe *a.* awkward, clumsy. *2* heavy. *3 -mente adv.* awkwardly, etc.

torpedo *m.* torpedo.

torre *f.* tower. *2* turret. *3* country-house. *4* CHESS rook, castle.

torrente *m.* torrent; flood.

torta *f.* cake, pie. *2* blow, slap.

tortilla *f.* omelet. *2* (am.) pancake.

tortuga *f.* tortoise; turtle.

tortura *f.* torture, torment; grief.

tos *f.* cough.

tosco, ca *a.* rough, coarse. *2* rude, uncouth.

tostar *t.* to toast: to roast [coffee]. *2* to tan. sunburn.

total *a.* total. *2 m.* total. sum total. *3 adv.* in short.

trabajador, ra *a.* hard-working. *2 m.-f.* worker.

trabajar *i.* to work. labour. to toil. *2* to till the soil.

trabajo *m.* work. labour. toil. *2* task. job.

trabuco *m.* blunderbuss.

tractor *m.* tractor.

tradición *f.* tradition.

tradicional *a.* traditional. *2* -**mente** *adv.* traditionally.

traducir *t.* to translate [into: from]. render.

traer *t.* to bring. *2* to draw. attract. *3* to bring over. *4* to make. keep. ~ *entre manos*, to be busy with. be engaged in. ¶ CONJUG. INDIC. Pres.: *traigo, traes, trae*. etc. Fut.: *traeré, traerás*. etc. ‖ COND.: *traería, traerías*, etc. ‖ SUBJ. Pres.: *traiga, traigas*, etc. ‖ Imperf.: *trajera, trajeras*, etc. or *trajese, trajeses*, etc. Fut.: *trajere, trajeres*, etc. ‖ IMPER.: *trae, traiga; traigamos*, traed. *traigan*. PAST. P.: *traído*. ‖ GER.: *trayendo*.

tráfico *m.* traffic: trade. business.

tragar *t.-ref.* to swallow [up]: to gulp: to engulf: ~ *el anzuelo*, to be taken in.

tragedia *f.* tragedy.

trágico, ca *a.* tragic(al. *2 m.* tragedian.

traición *f.* treason: treachery.

traidor, ra *a.* treacherous. *2 m.* traitor. *3 f.* traitress.

traje *m.* suit [for men]: dress [for women]: clothes [in general]: clothing [collective]: [historical] costume: gown [for women: judges. etc.]: ~ *de baño*, bathing-suit: ~ *de etiqueta*, full dress: ~ *de luces*, bullfighter's costume.

tramo *m.* stretch. section [of a road. etc.]. *2* flight of stairs.

trampa *f.* trap: snare. *2* trapdoor. *3* trick.

tramposo, sa *a.* deceitful. tricky. *2 m.-f.* swindler.

tranquilo, la *a.* calm. quiet. peaceful.

transcurrir *i.* to pass. elapse.

transcurso *m.* course [of time].

transferir *t.* to transfer. ¶ CONJUG. like *hervir*.

transformación *f.* transformation.

transformar *t.* to transform. *2 ref.* to change.

transitar *i.* to pass. go. walk.

tránsito *m.* passage. crossing. *2* traffic.

transmitir *t.* to transmit. *2* RADIO to broadcast.

transparente *a.* transparent. *2* translucent. *3* obvious.

transportar *t.* to transport. carry. convey. *2 ref.* to be enraptured.

transporte *m.* transportation. transport. carriage.

tranvía *m.* tramway. tram: *streetcar.

trapo *m.* rag. *2 pl.* clothes. dresses.

tras *prep.* after. behind.

trasero, ra *a.* back. hind. rear. *2 m.* coll. rump. buttocks.

trasladar *t.* to move. remove.

2 to postpone, adjourn. 3 *ref.* to move from... to.

trastornar *t.* to upset, turn upside down, disturb, overthrow.

trastorno *m.* upset. 2 riot. 3 trouble.

tratamiento *m.* treatment. 2 title, form of address.

tratar *t.* to treat [a pers. well] 2 to deal with [people]. 3 to call [someone a liar]. 4 to address [as *tú*]. 5 *i.* ~ *de* [with infinitive], to try, attempt. 6 ~ *de* to deal with. 7 *ref.* be on terms with. 8 ~ *en*, to deal, trade in. 9 to be on good terms. 10 *se trata de*, it is a question of. 11 *¿de qué se trata?*, what is all about?.

trato *m.* treatment. 2 behaviour. 3 agreement. 4 negotiation.

través *m.* bias. 2 *a* ~ *de*, through, across; *al* or *de* ~, slantwise, crosswise.

travesía *f.* cross-road. 2 distance. 3 passage, crossing [the sea].

travieso, sa *a.* mischievous, naughty [child].

traza *f.* sketch, plan. 2 appearance, aspect.

trazar *i.* to draw, sketch. 2 to lay out, plan out.

trece *a.-m.* thirteen.

trecho *m.* distance, stretch.

tregua *f.* truce, rest, respite.

treinta *a.-m.* thirty; thirtieth.

tremendo, da *a.* dreadful, imposing. 2 huge, tremendous.

tren *m.* train.

trenza *f.* braid, plait. 2 *pl.* tresses.

trepar *i.-t.* to climb, clamber. 2 *t.* to bore, pierce.

tres *a.-m.* three. 2 *a.* third.

triángulo *m.* triangle.

tribu *f.* tribe.

tribulación *f.* tribulation, trouble.

tribuna *f.* tribune, platform. 2 grand-stand.

tribunal *m.* tribunal, court of justice. 2 EDUC. examining board.

tributo *m.* tribute, tax.

trigo *m.* wheat.

trinar *i.* to trill [in singing]; [of birds] to warble, chirp.

trino, na *a.* trine. 2 *m.* trill.

trío *m.* trio.

tripa *f.* gut, intestine, bowels.

triple *a.-m.* triple, treble.

triste *a.* sad. 2 gloomy, dismal. 3 sorrowful. 4 -*mente* *adv.* sadly, etc.

tristeza *f.* sadness, melancholy. 2 sorrow.

triunfar *i.* to triumph, win.

triunfo *m.* triumph; victory success. 2 trump [at cards].

trofeo *m.* trophy; victory.

trompa *f.* MUS. horn. 2 trunk [of elephant].

trompeta *f.* trumpet; bugle. 2 *m.* trumpeter.

trompo *m.* spinning-top.

tronco *m.* trunk; log; stem. 2 team [of horses]. 3 stock.

tronchar *t.* to break off, lop off. 2 *ref.* ~ *de risa,* to burst with laughing.

trono *m.* throne.

tropa *f.* troop, crowd. 2 troops, soldiers; forces, army.

tropezar *i.* to trip, stumble. 2

to meet [a person], come across. 3 to come up against [a difficulty].

tropical *a.* tropical, tropic.

trópico *m.* tropic.

trozo *m.* piece, bit.

truco *m.* trick. 2 *pl.* pool [billiards].

trucha *f.* trout.

trueno *m.* thunder, thunderclap. 2 report [of firearms].

trueque *m.* exchange.

tú *pers. pron.* you; thou.

tú, *pl.* **tus** *poss. a.* your; thy.

tuberculosis *f.* tuberculosis, consumption.

tuberculoso, sa *a.* tuberculous. 2 *a.-n.* consumptive.

tubo *m.* tube, pipe.

tuerto, ta *a.* one-eyed. 2 *m.* wrong, injury.

tulipa *f.* glass lampshade.

tulipán *m.* BOT. tulip.

tumba *f.* tomb, grave.

túnel *m.* tunnel.

túnica *f.* tunic; robe, gown.

turba *f.* crowd, mob. 2 turf.

turbar *t.* to disturb, upset. trouble. 2 *ref.* to get embarrassed.

turismo *m.* tourism. 2 touring car. 3 travel agency.

turista *m.-f.* tourist.

turno *m.* turn. 2 shift.

tuyo, ya *poss. pron.* yours; thine [formal]. 2 *poss. a.* your; thy [formal].

U

u *conj.* [replaces o before a word beginning with o or ho] or.

ufano, na *a.* proud, conceited. 2 cheerful, satisfied.

ultimar *t.* to end, finish, complete.

último, ma *a.* last, final; latest. 2 utmost; finest. 3 *por ~*, lastly, at last.

un, una *indef. art.* a, an. 2 *pl.* some, any. 3 *a.* one.

ungir *t.* to anoint, consecrate.

ungüento *m.* ointment.

unidad *f.* unity. 2 unit.

uniforme *a.-m.* uniform.

unión *f.* union. 2 concord.

unir *t.* to join, unite. 2 to connect, mix.

unísono, na *a.* unison. 2 *al ~*, in unison, together.

universal *a.* universal.

universidad *f.* university.

universitario, ria *a.* university [professor].

universo *m.* universe, world.

uno, una *a.* one. 2 *pl.* a few, some.

uña *f.* nail [of finger, toe]. 2 talon, claw; hoof.

urgente *a.* urgent, pressing.

urgir *i.* to press, be urgent.

usar *t.* to use. 2 to wear. 3 *t.-i.* to be accustomed to. 4 *ref.* to be in use.

uso *m.* use, employment; wear, wear and tear. 2 usage, custom, fashion.

usted, pl. ustedes *pers. pron.* you.

utensilio *m.* implement, tool; utensil.

útil *a.* useful, profitable. 2 MECH. effective, available. 3 *m.-pl.* tools, implements.

utilidad *f.* utility, usefulness. 2 profit, benefit.

utilizar *t.* to utilize, use, make use of.

uva *f.* grape: *~ pasa*, raisin.

V

vaca *f.* cow. 2 beef [meat].

vacación *f. sing.-pl.* vacation, holidays.

vacante *a.* vacant. 2 *f.* vacancy. 3 vacation.

vacilar *i.* to hesitate, shake, flicker. 2 to waver.

vacío, a *a.* empty, void. 2 *m.* void, PHYS. vacuum. 3 blank.

vacuna *f.* vaccine.

vago, ga *a.* roving, errant. 2 vague. 3 *m.* loafer, tramp.

vagón *m.* RLY. carriage, wagon.

vajilla *f.* table service, plate, dishes. 2 crockery.

valer *i.* to be worth, cost, amount to. 2 to deserve; to be equal to; *vale la pena verlo,* it is worth while seeing; ¶ CONJUG. INDIC. Pres.: *valgo,* vales, vale, etc. | Fut.: *valdré, valdrás,* etc. ‖ COND.: *valdría, valdrías,* etc. ‖ SUBJ. Pres.: *valga, valgas,* etc. ‖ IMPER.: *val* or *vale, valga; valgamos,* valed, *valgan.*

valeroso, sa *a.* courageous, brave. 2 valuable.

valiente *a.* valiant, brave. 2 fig. fine. 3 **-mente** *adv.* bravely.

valioso, sa *a.* expensive, valuable, costly. 2 wealthy.

valor *m.* value, worth, price. 2 courage. 3 validity. 4 *pl.* bonds.

vals *m.* waltz.

valle *m.* valley, vale.

vanidad *f.* vanity, conceit.

vanidoso, sa *a.* vain, conceited.

vano, na *a.* vain, useless. 2 *m.* ARCH. opening. 3 *en ~,* in vain.

vapor *m.* vapo(u)r: steam. 2 NAUT. steamship.

vaquero, ra *m.-f.* cow-herd, cowboy.

vara *f.* stick, rod. 2 wand of office.

variedad *f.* variety; diversity.

vario, ria *a.* various, different. 2 *pl.* some, several.

varón *m.* male; man.

vasallo *m.-f.* vassal, liegeman.

vasija *f.* vessel, container, jar.

vaso *m.* glass tumbler. 2 glassful. 3 vessel. 4 vase.

vasto, ta *a.* vast, immense, huge.

vecindad *f.;* **vecindario** *m.* neighbourhood; neighbours: *casa de ~,* tenement house.

vecino, na *a.* nearby, next, neighbouring. *2 m.-f.* neighbour. *3* tenant; inhabitant.

vedar *t.* to prohibit, forbid. *2* to impede, prevent.

vegetación *f.* vegetation.

vegetal *a.* vegetable. *2 m.* plant.

vehículo *m.* vehicle.

veinte *a.-m.* twenty. *2 a.-n.* twentieth.

vejez *f.* old age.

vela *f.* wakefulness. *2* candle. *3* sail; sailing ship: *hacerse a la ~,* to set sail.

velar *i.* to watch, stay awake. *2 ~ por,* to watch over, look after. *3 t.* to veil, hide.

velo *m.* veil.

velocidad *f.* speed, velocity.

veloz, *pl.* **-loces** *a.* fast, speedy, quick, swift.

vena *f.* ANAT. vein. *2* MIN. vein, seam. *3* poetical inspiration.

vencedor, ra *a.* conquering, triumphant. *2 m.-f.* conqueror; victor; winner.

vencer *t.* to defeat, beat. *2* to conquer, subdue. *3 i.* to win. *4* COM. to fall due.

vendedor, ra *a.* selling. *2 m.-f.* retailer. seller.

vender *t.* to sell: *se vende,* for sale. *2* to betray.

veneno *m.* poison, venom.

venerable *a.* venerable.

venerar *t.* to venerate. *2* ECCL. to worship.

venganza *f.* vengeance, revenge.

vengar *t.* to avenge. *2 ref.* to take revenge.

venida *f.* coming, arrival. *2* return. *3* flood, freshet.

venidero, ra *a.* future, forthcoming.

venir *t.* to come. *2 ~ a las manos,* to come to blows; *~ al caso,* to be relevant; *~ a menos,* to decay, decline; *~ bien [mal],* [not] to fit, suit, be becoming; *~ en conocimiento,* to come to know. *4 ref.* to come return; *~ abajo,* to collapse, fall down.* ¶ CONJUG. INDIC. Pres: *vengo, vienes, viene;* venimos, venís, vienen. Pret.: *vine, viniste,* etc. Fut.: *vendré, vendrás,* etc. ‖ SUBJ. Pres.: *venga, vengas.* Imperf.: *viniera, vinieras,* etc., or *viniese, vinieses,* etc. ‖ Fut.: *viniere, vinieres,* etc. ¶ IMPER.: *ven, venga; vengamos,* venid, *vengan.* ‖ PAST. P. venido. ‖ GER.: *viniendo.*

venta *f.* sale: *en ~,* for sale. *2* roadside inn.

ventaja *f.* advantage. *2* gain, profit.

ventana *f.* window.

ventilación *f.* ventilation.

ventilar *t.* to air, ventilate. *2* to discuss.

ventura *f.* happiness. *2* luck, fortune. *3 por ~,* by chance; *a la ~,* at random.

venturoso, sa *a.* happy, lucky, fortunate.

ver *t.* to see. *2* to look [at]. *3 i. ~ de,* to try to. *4 ref.* to be obvious. ¶ CONJUG. INDIC. PRES.: veo, ves, ve, etc. ‖

Imperf.: veía, veías, etc. |
Pret.: *vi, viste*, etc. | Fut.:
veré, verás, etc. ‖ Cond.:
vería, verías, etc. ‖ Subj.
Pres.: vea, veas, etc. or
viese, vieses, etc. ‖ Fut.:
viere, vieres, etc. | Imperf.:
viera, vieras, etc. | Imper.: *ve,
vea*, etc. | Past. p.: *visto*. ‖
Ger.: *viendo*.

veraneo *m.* summer holiday.

verano *m.* summer [season].

verbo *m.* Gram. verb. 2 the
Word.

verdad *f.* truth: *en ~*, in truth,
really.

verdadero, ra *a.* true. 2 real. 3
truthful.

verde *a.* green [colour];
verdant; unripe; young;
obscene: *poner ~*, to abuse;
viejo ~, gay, merry old man.
2 *m.* green colour.

verdugo *m.* hangman, execu-
tioner.

verdura *f.* grenness. 2 ver-
dure. 3 *sing. & pl.* vegetables, greens.

vereda *f.* path, footpath.

vergel *m.* flower and fruit
garden.

vergüenza *f.* shame; bashful-
ness; modesty: *tener* or *sentir
~*, to be ashamed.

verja *f.* grating; iron railing.

versión *f.* version. 2 translation.

verso *m.* verse, poem. 2 line.

verter *t.* to pour. 2 to spill. 3 to
empty, shed. 4 *i.* to run,
flow. 5 *ref.* to spill, flow. ¶
Conjug. like *entender*.

vestido *m.* dress, clothes,
costume, suit; *~ de etiqueta*,
evening dress.

vestidura *f.* clothing. 2 *pl.*
Eccl. vestiments.

vestir *t.* to clothe, dress. 2 to
cover, deck. 3 to cloak. 4 *i.* to
dress. 5 *ref.* to dress, get dres-
sed. ¶ Conjug. like *servir*.

vestuario *m.* clothes. 2
wardrobe; dressing-room.

veterano, na *a.-n.* veteran.

veto *m.* veto.

vez, *pl.* **veces** *f.* turn: *a su ~*,
in turn. 2 time: *a la ~*, at
one time; *alguna ~*,
sometimes; [in questions]
ever; *a veces*, sometimes;
muchas veces, often; *otra ~*,
again; *pocas veces*, seldom;
tal ~, perhaps, maybe; *en ~
de*, instead of.

vía *f.* road, way, street: *~
aérea*, airway; *~ pública*,
thoroughfare. 2 manner.

viajar *i.* to travel, journey.

viaje *m.* travel, journey,
voyage, trip; tour.

viajero, ra *a.* travelling. 2
m.-f. traveller; passenger.

vianda *f. sing & pl.* food,
meal.

vicisitud *f.* vicissitude. 2 *pl.*
ups and downs.

víctima *f.* victim.

victoria *f.* victory, triumph.

victorioso, sa *a.* victorious,
triumphant.

vid *f.* vine, grapevine.

vida *f.* life. 2 liveliness. 3
living, livelihood.

vidrio *m.* glass; glass pane [of
a window].

viejo *a.* old [ancient, antique;
aged]. 2 *m.* old man.

viento *m.* wind.

vientre *m.* belly, abdomen. 2
bowels. 3 womb.

viernes *m.* Friday.

vientre *m.* belly, abdomen. *2* bowels. *3* womb.

viernes *m.* Friday.

vigilancia *f.* vigilance, watchfulness.

vigilar *t.-i.* to watch over, guard.

vigor *m.* vigo(u)r, strenght; validity: *en ~*, in force.

vigoroso, sa *a.* vigorous; forceful.

vil *a.* vile, mean, base.

villa *f.* villa. *2* small town. *3* town council.

villano, na *a.* rustic. *2* mean, base. *3 m.-f.* scoundrel.

vinagre *m.* vinegar.

vino *m.* wine: *~ tinto*, red wine.

viña *f.*, **viñedo** *m.* vineyard.

violar *t.* to violate; to infringe; to ravish.

violencia *f.* violence, fury.

violento, ta *a.* violent. *2* forced, strained.

violeta *f.* violet.

violín *m.* violin. *2 m.-f.* violinist.

virar *t.-i.* NAUT. to tack, veer. *2 i.* AUTO. to turn.

virgen *a.-n.* virgin.

virtud *f.* virtue.

virtuoso, sa *a.* virtuous. *2 m.-f.* virtuoso [in an art].

visible *a.* visible. *2* evident.

visión *f.* vision, sight.

visita *f.* visit, [social] call. *2* visitor. *3* inspection.

visitar *t.* to visit, pay a visit, call upon. *2* to examine.

víspera *f.* eve. *2* ECCL. vespers.

vista *f.* sight, vision; view; eyesight, eye(s): *en ~ de*, in view of; *hasta la ~*, goodbye, so long; *perder de ~*, to

lose sight of. *2* view, scene. *3* aspect. *4* outlook. *5* LAW trial.

vistoso, sa *a.* bright, showy, colourful.

vital *a.* vital. *2* important. *3* lively.

vitamina *f.* vitamin.

vitrina *f.* showcase.

viudo, da *a.* widowed. *2 m.* widower. *3 f.* widow.

vivir *i.* to live. *2 ~ en*, to dwell in; *~ de*, to live on.

vivo, va *a.* live, alive, living. *2* bright, vivid. *3* lively. *4* sharp [pain].

vocablo *m.* word, term.

vocabulario *m.* vocabulary.

vocal *a.* vocal. *2 a.-f.* GRAM. vowel. *3 m.* member [of a council, etc.].

volar *i.* to fly. *2 t.* to blow up. ¶ CONJUG. like *contar*.

volcán *m.* volcano.

volumen *m.* volume. *2* bulk.

voluntad *f.* will. *2* purpose. *3* liking.

volver *t.* to turn [up, over, upside down, inside out]. *2* to make: *~ loco*, to drive crazy. *3 i.* to return, come back, go back. *4* to turn [to right, to left]. *5 ~ a hacer*, to do again. *6 ~ en sí*, to come to. *7 ref.* to go back. *8* to turn around. *9* to become. *10 ~ loco*, to go crazy. ¶ CONJUG. like *mover*. PAST. P.: *vuelto*.

vos *pers. pron.* you, ye.

vosotros, tras *pers. pron.* you, ye.

votar *i.* to vote.

voto *m.* vow [to God]. *2* vote [against, for]. *4* oath.

voz, *pl.* **voces** *f.* voice: *en ~*

vuelo *m.* flight.

vuelta *f.* turn [circuit, revolution]: *dar la ~ a,* to go around. *2* bend, curve. *3* reverse, back. *4* return, coming back: *estar de ~,* to be back. *5* change [of money]. *6* ARCH. vault.

vuestro, tra; vuestros, tras *poss. adj.* your. *2 poss. pron.* yours.

vulgar *a.* vulgar, common, ordinary.

Y

y *conj.* and.

ya *adv.* already. *2* now. *3* at once. *4* ¡~ *lo creo!*, yes, of course! *5* conj. *ya... ya*, now... now; whether... or. *6* ~ *que*, since, as.

yacer *i.* to lie; to lie in the grave.

yanqui *a.-m.* Yankee.

yarda *f.* yard [English measure].

yegua *f.* mare.

yema *f.* BOT. bud. *2* yolk [of an egg]. *3* ~ *del dedo*, tip of the finger.

yerba *f.* HIERBA.

yerno *m.* son-in-law.

yeso *m.* gypsum. *2* plaster. *3* chalk [for writing].

yo *pers. pron.* I.

yodo *m.* iodine.

yugo *m.* yoke.

yunque *m.* anvil.

Z

zafra *f.* olive-oil can. *2* sugar-making season.

zanahoria *f.* BOT. carrot.

zángano *m.* drone. *2* fig. idler, loafer.

zanja *f.* ditch, trench.

zapatería *f.* shoemaking. *2* shoe shop; shoe factory.

zapatero *m.* shoemaker; ~ *remendón,* cobbler.

zapato *m.* shoe.

zarpar *i.* NAUT. to weigh anchor, set sail.

zinc *m.* zinc.

zona *f.* zone, belt, district, area.

zoológico, ca *a.* zoologic(al: *parque* ~, zoo.

zootecnia *f.* zootechny.

zorro, rra *a.* cunning [person]. *2 m.* fox. *3 f.* vixen. *4* coll. harlot.

zozobra *f.* NAUT. foundering. *2* worry, anxiety.

zueco *m.* clog, wooden-soled shoe.

zumbar *i.* to hum, buzz.

zumbido *m.* buzz(ing, hum(ming.

APPENDICES
APÉNDICES

MONETARY UNITS /
UNIDADES MONETARIAS

Country / País	Name / Nombre	Symbol / Símbolo
THE AMERICAS / LAS AMÉRICAS		
Argentina	peso	$
Bahamas	dollar / dólar bahameño	B$
Barbados	dollar / dólar de Barbados	$
Belize / Belice	dollar / dólar	$
Bolivia	peso	$B
Brazil / Brasil	cruzeiro / nuevo cruzeiro	$; Cr$
Canada / Canadá	dollar / dólar canadiense	$
Chile	peso* / peso chileno*	$
Colombia	peso	$; P
Costa Rica	colon / colón	₡; ¢
Cuba	peso	$
Dominican Republic / República Dominicana	peso	RD$
Ecuador	sucre	S/
El Salvador	colon / colón	₡; ¢
Guatemala	quetzal	Q; Q
Guyana	dollar / dólar guayanés	G$
Haiti / Haití	gourde	₲; G; Gde
Honduras	lempira	L
Jamaica	dollar / dólar jamaicano	$
Mexico / México	peso	$

* The Chilean monetary unit, the escudo, was replaced by the peso in 1975.

* El escudo, la unidad monetaria chilena, fue reemplazado por el peso en 1975.

Country / País	Name / Nombre	Symbol / Símbolo
Nicaragua	cordoba / córdoba	C$
Panama / Panamá	balboa	B/
Paraguay	guarani / guaraní	Ǥ; G
Peru / Perú	sol	S/; $
Puerto Rico	dollar / dólar	$
Suriname / Surinam	guilder / gulder de Surinam	g
Trinidad and Tobago / Trinidad y Tabago	dollar / dólar trinitario	TT$
United States / Estados Unidos	dollar / dólar	$
Uruguay	peso	$
Venezuela	bolivar / bolivar	B

WEIGHTS AND MEASURES

Metric System

Unit	Abbreviation	Approximate U.S. Equivalent	
LENGTH			
1 millimeter	mm	0.04	inch
1 centimeter	cm	0.39	inch
1 meter	m	39.37	inches
		1.094	yards
1 kilometer	km	3,281.5	feet
		0.62	mile
AREA			
1 square centimeter	sq cm (cm²)	0.155	square inch
1 square meter	m²	10.764	square feet
		1.196	square yards
1 hectare	ha	2.471	acres
1 square kilometer	sq km (km²)	247.105	acres
		0.386	square mile
VOLUME			
1 cubic centimeter	cu cm (cm³)	0.061	cubic inch
1 stere	s	1.308	cubic yards
1 cubic meter	m³	1.308	cubic yards
CAPACITY (Liquid Measure)			
1 deciliter	dl	0.21	pint
1 liter	l	1.057	quarts
1 dekaliter	dal	2.64	gallons
MASS AND WEIGHT			
1 gram	g, gm	0.035	ounce
1 dekagram	dag	0.353	ounce
1 hectogram	hg	3.527	ounces
1 kilogram	kg	2.2046	pounds
1 quintal	q	220.46	pounds
1 metric ton	MT, t	1.1	tons

PESAS Y MEDIDAS

Sistema métrico

Unidad	Abreviatura	Equivalente aproximado del sistema estadounidense	
LONGITUD			
1 milímetro	mm	0,04	pulgada
1 centímetro	cm	0,39	pulgada
1 metro	m	39,37	pulgadas
		1,094	yardas
1 kilómetro	Km	3.281,5	pies
		0,62	milla
ÁREA			
1 centímetro cuadrado	cm²	0,155	pulgada cuadrada
1 metro cuadrado	m²	10,764	pies cuadrados
		1,196	yardas cuadradas
1 hectárea	ha	2,471	acres
1 kilómetro cuadrado	Km²	247,105	acres
		0,386	milla cuadrada
VOLUMEN			
1 centímetro cúbico	cm³	0,061	pulgadas cúbicas
1 metro cúbico	m³	1,308	yardas cúbicas
CAPACIDAD (Medida líquida)			
1 decilitro	dl	0,21	pinta
1 litro	l	1,057	quarts
1 decalitro	Dl	2,64	galones
MASA Y PESO			
1 gramo	g	0,035	onza
1 decagramo	Dg	0,353	onza
1 hectogramo	Hg	3,527	onzas
1 kilogramo	Kg	2,2046	libras
1 quintal métrico	q	220,46	libras
1 tonelada métrica	t	1,1	toneladas

U.S. Customary Weights and Measures / Unidades de pesas y medidas estadounidenses

Linear measure / Medida de longitud

1 foot / pie	=	12 inches / pulgadas
1 yard / yarda	=	36 inches / pulgadas
	=	3 feet / pies
1 rod	=	5½ yards / yardas
1 mile / milla	=	5,280 feet / 5.280 pies
	=	1,760 yards / 1.760 yardas

Liquid measure / Medida líquida

1 pint / pinta	=	4 gills
1 quart / quart líquido	=	2 pints / pintas
1 gallon / galón	=	4 quarts / quarts líquidos

Area measure / Medida de superficie

1 square foot / pie cuadrado	=	144 square inches / pulgadas cuadradas
1 square yard / yarda cuadrada	=	9 square feet / pies cuadrados
1 square rod / rod cuadrado	=	30¼ square yards / yardas cuadradas
1 acre	=	160 square rods / rods cuadrados
1 square mile / milla cuadrada	=	640 acres

Dry measure / Medida árida

1 quart	=	2 pints / pintas áridas
1 peck	=	8 quarts
1 bushel	=	4 pecks

Some useful measures / Unas medidas útiles

Quantity / Cantidad

1 dozen / docena	=	12 units / unidades
1 gross / gruesa	=	12 dozen / docenas

Electricity / Electricidad

charge / carga	=	coulomb / culombio
power / potencia	=	watt / vatio
		kilowatt / kilovatio
resistance / resistencia	=	ohm / ohmio
strength / fuerza	=	ampere / amperio
voltage / voltaje	=	volt / voltio

NUMBERS / NUMERALES

Cardinal Numbers		Números cardinales	Cardinal Numbers		Números cardinales
zero	0	cero	twenty	20	veinte
one	1	uno	twenty-one	21	veintiuno
two	2	dos	twenty-two	22	veintidós
three	3	tres	twenty-three	23	veintitrés
four	4	cuatro	twenty-four	24	veinticuatro
five	5	cinco	twenty-five	25	veinticinco
six	6	seis	twenty-six	26	veintiséis
seven	7	siete	twenty-seven	27	veintisiete
eight	8	ocho	twenty-eight	28	veintiocho
nine	9	nueve	twenty-nine	29	veintinueve
ten	10	diez	thirty	30	treinta
eleven	11	once	forty	40	cuarenta
twelve	12	doce	fifty	50	cincuenta
thirteen	13	trece	sixty	60	sesenta
fourteen	14	catorce	seventy	70	setenta
fifteen	15	quince	eighty	80	ochenta
sixteen	16	dieciséis	ninety	90	noventa
seventeen	17	diecisiete	one hundred	100	cien, ciento
eighteen	18	dieciocho	five hundred	500	quinientos
nineteen	19	diecinueve	one thousand	1000	mil

Ordinal Numbers		Números ordinales	
1st	first	1.º, 1.ª	primero, -a
2nd	second	2.º, 2.ª	segundo, -a
3rd	third	3.º, 3.ª	tercero, -a
4th	fourth	4.º, 4.ª	cuarto, -a
5th	fifth	5.º, 5.ª	quinto, -a
6th	sixth	6.º, 6.ª	sexto, -a
7th	seventh	7.º, 7.ª	séptimo, -a
8th	eighth	8.º, 8.ª	octavo, -a
9th	ninth	9.º, 9.ª	noveno, -a
10th	tenth	10.º, 10.ª	décimo, -a
11th	eleventh	11.º, 11.ª	undécimo, -a
12th	twelfth	12.º, 12.ª	duodécimo, -a
13th	thirteenth	13.º, 13.ª	decimotercero, -a decimotercio, -a
14th	fourteenth	14.º, 14.ª	decimocuarto, -a
15th	fifteenth	15.º, 15.ª	decimoquinto, -a
16th	sixteenth	16.º, 16.ª	decimosexto, -a
17th	seventeenth	17.º, 17.ª	decimoséptimo, -a
18th	eighteenth	18.º, 18.ª	decimoctavo, -a
19th	nineteenth	19.º, 19.ª	decimonoveno, -a decimonono, -a
20th	twentieth	20.º, 20.ª	vigésimo, -a
21st	twenty-first	21.º, 21.ª	vigésimo (-a) primero (-a)
22nd	twenty-second	22.º, 22.ª	vigésimo (-a) segundo (-a)
30th	thirtieth	30.º, 30.ª	trigésimo, -a
40th	fortieth	40.º, 40.ª	cuadragésimo, -a
50th	fiftieth	50.º, 50.ª	quincuagésimo, -a
60th	sixtieth	60.º, 60.ª	sexagésimo, -a
70th	seventieth	70.º, 70.ª	septuagésimo, -a
80th	eightieth	80.º, 80.ª	octogésimo, -a
90th	ninetieth	90.º, 90.ª	nonagésimo, -a
100th	hundredth	100.º, 100.ª	centésimo, -a

TEMPERATURE /
LA TEMPERATURA

Fahrenheit and Celsius /
Grados Fahrenheit y grados Celsius

To convert Fahrenheit to Celsius, subtract 32 degrees, multiply by 5, and divide by 9.

Para convertir grados Fahrenheit a grados Celsius (centígrados), réstese 32 grados, multiplíquese por 5 y divídase por 9.

$$104°F - 32 = 72 \times 5 = 360 \div 9 = 40°C$$

To convert Celsius to Fahrenheit, multiply by 9, divide by 5, and add 32 degrees.

Para convertir grados Celsius (centígrados) a grados Fahrenheit, multiplíquese por 9, divídase por 5 y agréguese 32 grados.

$$40°C \times 9 = 360 \div 5 = 72 + 32 = 104°F$$

At sea level, water boils at
Al nivel del mar, se hierve el agua a $\Big\}$ 212°F / 100°C

Water freezes at
Se congela el agua en $\Big\}$ 32°F / 0°C

Average human temperature
Temperatura promedia del ser humano $\Big\}$ 98.6°F / 37°C

Some normal temperatures in the Americas / Algunas temperaturas normales en las Américas

	Winter / Invierno	Summer / Verano
North of the equator / Al norte del ecuador		
Churchill, Manitoba	-11°F / -23.9°C	63°F / 17.2°C
Montreal, Quebec	22°F / -5.6°C	79°F / 26.1°C
Anchorage, Alaska	12°F / -11.1°C	58°F / 14.4°C
Chicago, Illinois	24°F / -4.4°C	75°F / 23.9°C
New York, New York	32°F / 0°C	77°F / 25°C
Dallas, Texas	45°F / 7.2°C	86°F / 30°C
Los Angeles, California	57°F / 13.9°C	73°F / 22.8°C
Phoenix, Arizona	51°F / 10.6°C	94°F / 34.4°C
Tegucigalpa, Honduras	50°F / 10°C	90°F / 32°C
South of the equator / Al sur del ecuador		
Tierra del Fuego, Argentina	32°F / 0°C	50°F / 10°C
Sao Paulo, Brazil	57.2°F / 14°C	69.8°F / 21°C
Montevideo, Uruguay	55.4°F / 13°C	71.6°F / 22°C
Buenos Aires, Argentina	52.3°F / 11.3°C	73.8°F / 23.2°C
Lima, Peru	59°F / 15°C	77°F / 25°C

ABBREVIATIONS MOST COMMONLY USED IN SPANISH

A	Aprobado (*in examinations*)
a	área
(a)	alias
AA.	autores
ab.	abad
abr.	abril
A.C., A. de C.	Año de Cristo
admón.	administración
adm.^{or}	administrador
afmo., affmo.	afectísimo
afto.	afecto
ago.	agosto
a la v/	a la vista
a.m.	ante meridiem, antes del mediodía
anac.	anacoreta
ap.	aparte; apóstol
apdo.	apartado
art., art.º	artículo
att.º, atto.	atento
B	beato; Bueno (*in examinations*)
Barna.	Barcelona
B.L.M., b.l.m.	besa la mano; besa las manos
B.L.P., b.l.p.	besa los pies
bto.	bulto; bruto
c.	capítulo
c/	caja; cargo; contra
C.A.	corriente alterna
c.ª	compañía
c/a.	cuenta abierta
cap.	capítulo
C.C.	corriente continua
cénts.	céntimos
cf.	compárese
C.G.S.	cegesimal
Cía., cía.	compañía
C.M.B., c.m.b.	cuya mano beso
comis.º	comisario
comp.ª	compañía
comps.	compañeros
Const.	Constitución
corrte.	corriente
C.P.B., c.p.b.	cuyos pies beso
cps.	compañeros
cs.	cuartos; céntimos
cta.	cuenta
cte.	corriente
c/u	cada uno
C.V.	caballo (*or* caballos) de vapor
D.	Don
D.ª	Doña
descto.	descuento
d/f., d/fha.	días fecha
dha., dho., dhas., dhos.	dicha, dicho, dichas, dichos
dic.	diciembre

dls.	dólares	Hno.,	Hermano,
dna.,	docena, docenas	Hnos.	Hermanos
dnas.		HP., H.P.	caballo (*or*
d/p.	días plazo		caballos) de
Dr., dr.	Doctor		vapor
dra., dro.,	derecha,		
dras.,	derecho,	ib., ibíd.	ibidem (en el
dros.	derechas,		mismo lugar)
	derechos	íd.	ídem
dupdo.	duplicado	i. e.	id est (*that is*)
d/v.	días vista	ít.	ítem
		izq.ª, izq.º	izquierda,
E	este (*east*)		izquierdo
E.M.	Estado Mayor		
E.M.G.	Estado Mayor	J.C.	Jesucristo
	General	jul.	julio
ENE	estenordeste	jun.	junio
ene.	enero		
E.P.D.	en paz descanse	L/	letra
E.P.M.	en propia mano	L.	ley; libro
ESE	estesudeste	Ldo., ldo.	licenciado
etc.	etcétera	lín.	línea
		liq.	liquidación
		liq.º	líquido
f.ª, fact.ª	factura		
f/	fardo(s)	M.	Maestro;
f.a.b.	franco a bordo		Majestad;
F.C., f.c.	ferrocarril		Merced
fcos.	francos	m.	minuto,
feb., febr.	febrero		minutos;
F.E.M.,	fuerza		mañana
f.e.m.	electromotriz	m/	mes; mi, mis;
fha., fho.	fecha, fecho		mío, míos
f.º, fol.	folio	mar.	marzo
fra.	factura	m/cta.	mi cuenta
fund.	fundador	merc.	mercaderías
		m/f.	mi favor
g/	giro	milés.	milésimas
gde.	guarde	m/L.	mi letra
gobno.	gobierno	m/o.	mi orden
gob.ʳ	gobernador	m/p.	mi pagaré
gral.	general	m/r.	mi remesa
gte.	gerente	Mtro.	Maestro

m.a.	muchos años	p. ej.	por ejemplo
M.S.	manuscrito	P.O., p.o.	por orden
		PP.	Padres
N	norte; Notable	P.P., p.p.	porte pagado;
	(*in examina-*		por poder
	tions)	p. pd.º,	próximo pasado
n.	noche	ppdo.	
n/	nuestro, nuestra	pral.	principal
N. B.	nota bene	pralte.	principalmente
n/cta.	nuestra cuenta	prof.	profesor
NE	nordeste	pról.	prólogo
NNE	nornoreste	prov.ª	provincia
NNO	nornoroeste	próx.º	próximo
NO	noroeste	P.S.	Post Scriptum
nov.,	noviembre	ps.	pesos
novbre.		P.S.M.	por su mandato
núm.,	número,	pta., ptas.	peseta, pesetas
núms.	números	pte.	parte; presente
nto.	neto	pza.	pieza
ntra.,	nuestra, nuestro,		
ntro.,	nuestras,	Q.B.S.M.,	que besa su
ntras.,	nuestros	q.b.s.m.	mano
ntros.		Q.B.S.P.,	que besa sus pies
		q.b.s.p.	
O	oeste	Q.D.G.,	que Dios guarde
o/	orden	q.D.g.	
oct.	octubre	q.e.g.e.	que en gloria esté
ONO	oesnoroeste	q.e.p.d.	que en paz
OSO	oessudoeste		descanse
		q.e.s.m.	que estrecha su
P.	Papa; padre;		mano
	pregunta	qq.	quintales
P.A., p.a.	por ausencia;	q.s.g.h.	que santa gloria
	por autori-		haya
	zación		
pág.,	página, páginas	R.	respuesta;
págs.			Reprobado (*in*
paq.	paquete		*examinations*)
Part.	Partida	Rbi.	Recibí
Patr.	Patriarca	R.D.	Real Decreto
pbro.	presbítero	R.I.P.	Requiescat in
p/cta.	por cuenta		pace (descanse
P.D.	posdata		en paz)

Rl., Rls.	real, reales *(royal)*	SSE	sudsudeste
		SSO	sudsudoeste
rl., rls.	real, reales *(coin)*	S.S.S., s.s.s.	su seguro servidor
r.p.m.	revoluciones por minuto	SS. SS.	seguros servidores
S.	San, Santo; sur; Sobresaliente *(in examinations)*	Sta.	Santa; Señorita
		Sto.	Santo
		suplte.	suplente
s/	su, sus; sobre	tit., tít.º	título
S.ª	Señora	tpo.	tiempo
s/c.	su cuenta	trib.	tribunal
S.C., s.c.	su casa		
s/cta.	su cuenta	U., Ud.	usted
S.D.	Se despide	Uds.	ustedes
SE	sudeste		
sep., sept., sepbre.	septiembre	V.	usted; Venerable; Véase
serv.º	servicio	V	versículo
serv.ºr	servidor	vencimto.	vencimiento
s. e. u o.	salvo error u omisión	vers.º	versículo
sigte.	siguiente	vg., v.g., v. gr.	verbigracia
Sn.	San		
SO	sudoeste	Vmd., V.	vuestra merced; usted
S.ʳ, Sr.	Señor		
Sra., Sras.	Señora, Señoras	V.º B.º	Visto bueno
Sres.	Señores	vol.	volumen; voluntad
Sría.	Secretaría		
sria., srio.	secretaria, secretario	vols.	volúmenes
		VV.	ustedes
Srta.	Señorita		
S. S.ª	Su Señoría		

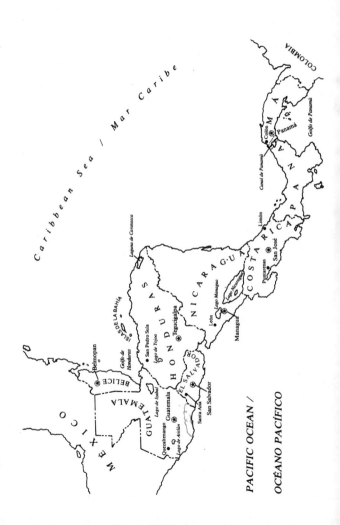

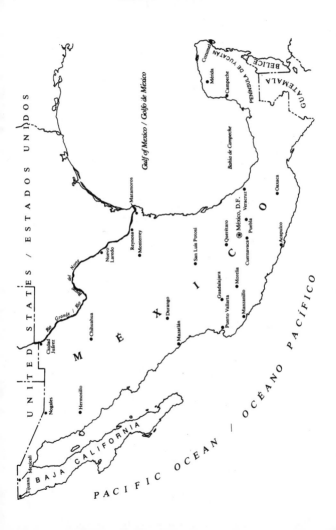

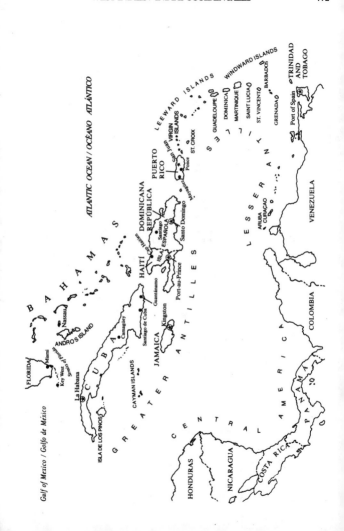

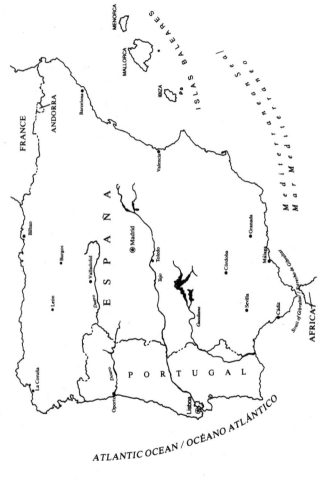

ATLANTIC OCEAN / OCÉANO ATLÁNTICO